# Land Use and
# Landscape Plannin

## SECOND EDITION

# Land Use and Landscape Planning

Edited by Derek Lovejoy

*With a Foreword by*
*HRH The Duke of Edinburgh*

SECOND EDITION

Leonard Hill

Published by
Leonard Hill
a member of the
Blackie Publishing Group
Bishopbriggs, Glasgow, G64 2NZ

First published 1979

ISBN 0 249 44157 8

Printed in Great Britain by Thomson Litho Ltd,
East Kilbride, Scotland.

# FOREWORD TO THE SECOND EDITION BY HRH THE DUKE OF EDINBURGH

 BUCKINGHAM PALACE.

    That a book of this sort has been found to be
necessary at all implies that the people responsible
for development whether industrial, commercial, housing,
transport or power, have failed in one of the most
important aspects of their jobs.  On the other hand that
the demand for this book is such that a second edition
has been called for indicates that this failure has
been recognised.

    The difficulty about land use planning, unlike
technical planning and design, is that it depends to
such a large extent on personal attitudes, taste and
judgement.  If all this book achieves is to encourage
more people in positions of authority to use these faculties
perceptively, it will have been well worthwhile.

1978.

# CONTENTS

# Biographical Notes

Derek Lovejoy is an Architect, Town Planner and Past President of the Landscape Institute. He is also a Past Vice President and Secretary General of the International Federation of Landscape Architects. He is Principal Partner of the firm of Derek Lovejoy and Partners, an international practice covering the total environmental field, and is a member of many environmental committees, including the Department of Transport's Landscape Advisory Committee. His principle commissions include the environmental consultancies of the new capital cities of Pakistan and Tanzania.

John B. Weller has been in private practice since 1960, specialising in agricultural building and rural land-use planning. He is author of *Modern Agriculture and Rural Planning*, and *Farm Wastes Management*. He serves on a number of committees, including the Steering Committee for Land Year 1980, the Professional Institutions Council for Conservation, and Architects in Agriculture. He lectures part-time at the Department of Planning, Chelmer Institute, and is helping to create its Rural Resources Unit for Research.

Clifford R. V. Tandy is a Principal in the firm of Land Use Consultants. He has previously had wide experience in both local and central government, and has specialized in landscape design for industry and industrial dereliction. He is a Past President of the Institute of Landscape Architects (now the Landscape Institute). His publications include *Landscape and Human Life* (Ed.), *Handbook of Urban Landscape* (Ed.) and *Landscape of Industry*. He is currently landscape consultant to the Forestry Commission of Great Britain.

W. J. Cairns is Senior Partner of W. J. Cairns and Partners, Environmental Consultants, Planners, Architects and Landscape Architects, and at present is Visiting Professor of Environmental Design in the University of Manitoba. He is a member of the Scottish Advisory Committee of the Nature Conservancy Council.

Brian D. Clark is Senior Lecturer in Geography, University of Aberdeen, and Director of the Project Appraisal for Development Control (PADC) Unit there. Keith Chapman is Lecturer in Geography and Assistant Director of the PADC unit. Ronald Bisset is Research Fellow in Geography and a further member of the Unit. Peter Wathern, originally a member of the PADC Unit, is now Lecturer in Botany and Microbiology in the University College of Wales, Aberystwyth.

Maurice Keech is Senior Lecturer in Land Resource Planning at the National College of Agricultural Engineering at Silsoe in Bedfordshire. He has specialised in the application of air photo interpretation and satellite imagery to the solution of problems in landscape and natural region evaluation, forestry, and soil conservation and has been involved with development programmes in Africa, Brazil and the United Kingdom.

Charles E. Chulvick is a Research Fellow in the Department of Geography at Edinburgh University. His background is in Government and Town Planning and he has worked as a planner both in the U.K. and the U.S.A. He has participated in research contracts commissioned by the Department of the Environment and the Scottish Development Department, investigating aspects of information system development. Currently he is the Manager of the Planning Data Management Service (PDMS) within the Department of Geography at the University of Edinburgh.

Thomas C. Waugh is a Senior Computing Officer in the Program Library Unit of the University of Edinburgh. He is the designer and implementor of two computer mapping systems: CMS (a line printer system) and GIMMS (a general purpose geographic system using vector graphic output). He has visited, for extended study periods, the Laboratory for Computer Graphics, Harvard University (1969–1970) and Carleton University, Ottawa (1976). Over the last two years, research contracts undertaken by the author have been commissioned by such bodies as the Department of the Environment (London), Census Field of Statistics (Canada), and Institut Géographique Nationale (France).

Arnold E. Weddle is Granada Professor of Landscape Architecture and Dean of the Faculty of Architectural Studies at the University of Sheffield, and Consultant in Planning and Landscape Practice to several bodies, including the Central Electricity Generating Board and Skelmersdale New Town. He is editor of *Techniques of Landscape Architecture* and *Landscape Planning*, is Past President of the Landscape Institute, and has served on Department of the Environment Committees.

Dame Sylvia Crowe is Past President of the Institute of Landscape Architects and a founder member of the International Federation of Landscape Architects. She was landscape consultant to the Forestry Commission for Great Britain and is consultant to several river authorities, and to other bodies on roads, parkways, new towns and power stations throughout Britain. She is author of *Landscape of Power* and *Forestry in the Landscape*.

John Foster is Director of the Countryside Commission for Scotland. After several years in local government he became Director and Planning Officer of the Peak National Park Planning Board, where he remained until taking up his present appointment in Scotland. He has travelled extensively, studying at first hand national parks, recreation development and conservation projects and problems.

Gerhard Olschowy lectures in Landscape Management at the University of Bonn, where he is an Honorary Professor. He is Director of the Federal Institute for Vegetation Science, Nature Conservation and Landscape Management in Bonn-bad Goedesberg, and author of *Landschaft und Technik, Belastete Landschaft—Gefährdete Umwelt*, and *Natur-und Umweltschutz in fünf Kontinenten*. He is also a member of the Environmental Planning Commission of IUCN.

Meto J. Vroom is Professor and Head of the Department of Landscape Architecture at the Agricultural University of Wageningen in the Netherlands. He was previously Landscape Consultant Officer with the Netherlands State Forest Service and has published numerous articles in Dutch on landscape development and research.

Klaas Kerkstra and Peter Vrijlandt are in the Department of Landscape Architecture at the Agricultural University of Wageningen, where they are involved in both teaching and research.

# Preface

The six years since the publication of the first edition of *Land Use and Landscape Planning* have witnessed increasing concern for the environment, not only from the professionals and politicians, but perhaps more especially from the public. That concern is well founded, for land—the most fundamental resource of all—is being developed and exploited ever faster and often without proper assessment either of the need to develop or of the effects that development will have.

But there are hopeful signs: the introduction of environmental impact assessment procedures in many countries following the lead of the United States National Environmental Policy Act of 1969; the increasing emphasis on landscape management techniques; and perhaps even the world economic recession has gone some way to slow the processes of land exploitation.

However there is a need for practical guidance on all aspects of land use and landscape planning. While it is not suggested that this book can give absolute answers to land use planning and management problems, it is hoped to provide a basis for tackling those problems, and to give examples of different approaches used in a wide range of situations.

Before any plan can be formulated, or project affecting the landscape appraised, it is essential to gather all possible information about the area concerned. Therefore, after the introduction, chapter 2 is devoted to applied analysis and evaluation techniques. Arnold Weddle discusses the data used in analysis and the factors to be considered in both territorial and project planning: the techniques of landscape classification; methods for determining intervisibility; and methods of evaluation. He emphasises the need for post-development monitoring and management.

Brian Clark and his colleagues of PADC describe the advances in environmental impact assessment and summarise the different techniques available—from the Leopold matrix to networks and complex models—in each case pointing out the advantages and disadvantages. They also include in their chapter some of the approaches to gathering and organising data for use in environmental impact assessment.

Each of the following five chapters deals with one of the major rural land uses, the problems involved and the means for their solution. John Weller describes the land use needs of modern agriculture and the effects which these will have upon the landscape. This is followed by discussion of the place of afforestation within overall land use patterns. With a variety of examples, Dame Sylvia Crowe outlines the uses and benefits of trees and forests in the landscape and the importance of planting design and good husbandry.

John Foster then treats leisure provision on the basis of landscape type and the compatibility of different activities with different varieties of countryside. In each case he discusses design factors which must be considered in order to minimise adverse impacts, and emphasises the need for good management.

Chapter 7 puts the case for an integrated transportation system. Different transport types and their design and landscape requirements are considered—with emphasis on roads, since it is surely the motorway and road system which have the largest impact on the landscape and therefore require the greatest care in siting, design and implementation.

In the final chapter, Cliff Tandy examines the place of industry in the rural landscape, the immense problems of design when siting a factory or power station in the countryside, and the need for sanctions and inducements to ensure that impact or damage are kept to a minimum. He also gives a full survey of the reclamation of derelict land, particularly in relation to dereliction produced by the extractive industries.

The penultimate part of the book is devoted to four case histories: the first dealing with the assessment of the impacts of alternative limestone quarrying sites in the Netherlands; the second describing the rehabilitation of a flood zone in Ohio and its conversion to a highly successful recreational and agricultural area; the third detailing the rehabilitation of a part of the Rhineland Brown Coal Area; and the fourth describing the environmental impact assessment and planning of the Flotta Oil Handling Terminal in the Shetlands.

Lastly, there are two appendices which will be useful to both practitioners and students: first, the techniques of aerial photography and their use in both landscape assessment and land management; and secondly, the computer techniques available to the land use planner.

D.L

CHAPTER ONE
# THE NEEDS AND OBJECTIVES
# OF LANDSCAPE PLANNING

Derek Lovejoy

The Isle of Skye, looking towards the Cuillin Hills from Portree

(*Photo by courtesy of A. F. Kersting*)

CHAPTER ONE

# THE NEEDS AND OBJECTIVES OF LANDSCAPE PLANNING

## Problems of the Environment

The world is confronted by many complex environmental problems which are exerting an increasing pressure on a deteriorating environment.

Increasing population, perhaps the worst of these problems, is leading to the excessive use of natural resources, and eventually to their exhaustion. Critical examples of over-exploitation are deforestation, over-cultivation and over-grazing—all of which lead to loss of soil fertility, to soil erosion, and eventually to desertification or other forms of environmental dereliction.

If further environmental destruction is to be avoided, the exploitation of natural resources must be controlled. Planning—particularly land use and landscape planning—is now vital for human survival. Environmental damage knows no natural or territorial boundaries; therefore international co-operation is essential if the degradation of land, air, oceans and inland waterways is to be averted. Nature and wildlife can contend with minor environmental damage, but not on a scale now commensurate with the pressures of population and world economic and technical development.

By far the greater part of the Earth's surface is made up of oceans, deserts, mountains and ice, and only a small proportion is habitable and sufficiently fertile for the production of food. Thus land conservation is one of the most fundamental principles of land use planning. Even countries with an abundance of fertile land may eventually see this resource depleted and despoiled, and for those countries already intensively developed conservation of land is of even greater importance. Those who advocate technology as an answer to uncontrolled growth must realise that the resources of the world are finite and that in the next few centuries ultimate limits may be reached. Indeed, it is only by means of planning, prediction, monitoring and the use of controls, either voluntary or statutory, that the destructive processes of exploitation may be halted.

To understand these processes, it is necessary to understand the nature and scale of the environmental problems which arise from them. Therefore the following sections highlight major environmental problems facing the world today.

### Exploitation of Natural Resources

The conservation of the world's non-renewable resources has been giving rise to increasing concern. Unless further resources of essential minerals are found, many may be exhausted by the turn of the century. One of the most satisfactory methods of conservation is the recycling of materials, and there should be a reappraisal of today's policy of built-in obsolescence. Recycling will not only reduce demands on essential resources, but also reduce waste disposal and consequently alleviate many pollution problems. Although the supply of many minerals (mercury, for example) will last another half-century, the rich and consequently economically viable deposits will be exhausted, and future generations must pay dearly for extraction from poor-quality ores. From a land use viewpoint non-renewable mineral deposits should not be sterilised by developments which could prejudice their extraction. Where extraction has taken place, satisfactory restoration and subsequent use as described in Chapter 8, are essential.

In a situation where 5% of the world's population uses 40% of the total resources, there are increasing demands from developing countries for the more affluent nations to reduce their plundering. Clearly these demands are justified.

Figure 1.1    The use of pulverised fuel ash in the construction of the M6 motorway is an excellent example of the after use of a waste material.

(*Photo by courtesy of the Central Electricity Generating Board*)

Figure 1.2    An example of sequential use. 'Before and after' photographs of the rehabilitation of a Derbyshire opencast mining site for agriculture.

(*Photo by courtesy of the University of Reading, Museum of English Rural Life*)

Figure 1.3    Macclesfield Canal, Derbyshire. An example of simultaneous use. Canals may be used for transportation, water supply and recreation.

(*Photo by courtesy of Graham Marsden*)

The industrialised nations must work towards greater conservation of resources, while at the same time seeking appropriate after-uses for the waste materials produced by so many of their technologies.

The most vulnerable of natural resources is good land. It is easily damaged and is difficult to regenerate, so the conservation of arable, pastoral and forest lands should be a priority in land use policies. In order to conserve land, it is essential to secure its maximum potential use, and the aim should be directed towards multiple compatible uses. There are two means of achieving this; one is by simultaneous use, whereby two or three activities can be carried out at the same time, and the other is sequential use, where various functions can follow each other in sequence. Examples of simultaneous use are the use of reservoirs for a wide variety of recreational activities, and the use of low-quality agricultural land, particularly the uplands, for both grazing and recreation. An example of sequential use is land previously mined for minerals being used, after restoration, for agriculture (Figure 1.2), recreation, or urban development, though this last use is not necessarily economic because of the massive cost of land stabilisation.

## Agricultural Degradation and Desertification

Only about 11% of the world's surface is used for food production (see page 92) and much of this land is of limited capacity, in the sense that it can support only a finite amount of crops or stock without breaking down. Even a minor increase in population, leading to demands on the land which it cannot meet, is enough to start the process of degradation and destruction which, once started, is extremely difficult to control, and even more difficult to reverse.

This picture repeats itself in Africa, in Asia and in South America. Many causes—in particular the introduction of prophylactic medicine and the organised relief of famine-stricken areas—have led to an increase in population but,

unfortunately, the ability of the population to feed itself has only increased marginally. The old and well-tried methods which, in the past, maintained a stable relationship between man and land have broken down. The practice of bush fallow, which allowed long periods of rest for the restoration of fertility, is no longer possible; the land is either continuously cropped, or fallowed for an insufficient period. Consequently, not only the biological and chemical, but also the physical, condition of the soil deteriorates. With the onset of the monsoon rains, the heavy storms following a long period of drought beat down on the impoverished earth and the water either runs off, carrying with it the last vestiges of fertility, or penetrates through the degraded soil, leaching out what little nutrient remains.

Figure 1.4   A landslip into the Kishanganga River in Pakistan. Over-grazing and indiscriminate tree felling have produced serious erosion problems.

(*Photo by courtesy of Aerofilms Ltd.*)

Figure 1.5   Dodoma, Tanzania. An example of gully erosion where rainstorms have cut into the denuded earth.

(*Photo: Derek Lovejoy*)

Figure 1.6   Dodoma, Tanzania. Sheet erosion caused by over-grazing and the consequent destruction of soil structure.

(*Photo: Derek Lovejoy*)

Figure 1.7    Drought in the Sahel. Overgrazing destroys soil fertility and by removing all vegetation makes the soil liable to erosion.

(*Photo by courtesy of United Nations/Carl Purcell*)

Figure 1.8    First steps towards desertification. Destitute nomads from Hali came to Christine Wells in Northern Upper Volta in search of pasture, but found a wasteland.

(*Photo by courtesy of United Nations FAO/F. Botts*)

In the semi-arid areas, lack of watering points has also acted as a constraint; large areas of semi-desert could be used by the nomadic pastoralists only when the seasonal rains brought on a flush of grass and filled gullies and depressions with water. When this water dried out, the cattle had to be returned to their permanent pastures, which meanwhile had been rested and restored in the absence of the herds. However, in more recent years, in response to constant demands for more water, dams were built and boreholes sunk, thus bringing water to previously dry areas so that pastures once used seasonally were subject to year-round pressure. The removal of the grass by over-grazing has allowed the inedible woody shrubs to become dominant. So the herds, increasing by the removal of the threat of disease, are faced with poorer and poorer pastures as the years go by. This is the situation, perhaps oversimplified, all along the southern boundary of the Sahara, in the Sahel countries, and extending to the Sudan, Ethiopia and Somalia. Likewise in the arid and semi-arid areas of South Africa, the picture repeats itself in the Kalahari desert, where the sinking of some 2000 boreholes is leading to the devastation of the delicate grasslands which are, in this case, being covered not by sand but by scrub.

Where the farmer both cultivates and herds cattle, the situation is doubly serious. Ideally, the possession of cattle should assist the development of mixed farming systems, which would permit cropping on a sustained yield basis. But after harvest, the cattle graze over the fields, eating the crop residues and exposing the soil to the intense impact of the rain when the rainy season comes. Frequently the manure, which should be returned to the soil, is burnt as fuel as all the woodland and forest in the vicinity has long since disappeared. Thus two opposing spirals widen the hunger gap; the upward spiral of population increase, and the downward spiral of environmental degradation. Unless this process is reversed by natural or technological means, the end result is *desertification.*

Desertification can best be described as a deterioration in vegetation and soil in arid lands, which leads to a reduction in biological productivity. It occurs in two ways: first, by the outward spread of desert conditions known as desert creep, and secondly, the intensification of desert conditions within arid regions. Some desert creep may be linked to climatic changes such as the failure of the monsoons, but it is nearly always the result of man's destruction of the vegetation cover.

Dry areas cover about one-third of the Earth's land surface and are populated by one in eight of the human race, that is 628 million people; of these between 50 and 80 million live in areas that are immediately threatened by desertification (1.1). Desertification is increasing at a rate of 100,000 hectares a year in North Africa alone (1.2), where over the past 50 years the Sahara has invaded one million square kilometres of land suitable for farming; the Thar desert of India and Pakistan has spread at the rate of 1 km² per year over the same period.

Deserts fall into four main categories: *rainless deserts,* (approximately six million square kilometres) which have no rain in most years, and no permanent plant life; *run-off deserts* (approximately two and a half million square kilometres) which have less than 10 cm of rain a year with permanent plant life limited to run-off basins, e.g. wadis; *rainfall deserts* (approximately 21 million square kilometres) which have 10–20 cm of rain a year and are too dry for growing crops; and *man-made deserts* (approximately nine million square kilometres) which have 20–40 cm of rain a year and cover areas of semi-arid steppe which have been transformed into deserts by over-exploitation (1.3).

The provision of water for livestock and irrigation is the first need in regenerating desert lands, but new water sources are few, expensive to tap, and can often be obtained only at the expense of other communities, or by exploiting underground stocks of water.

More than 90% of the world's water is salt, and of the remainder three-quarters is frozen in the great ice caps. Even the small amount of fresh water available is unevenly distributed throughout the world; drought and floods both demonstrate the serious problem of controlling water supply and demand. There is a world shortage of water, not only in quantity for agriculture, but in quality for human and animal consumption, especially in the rural areas of developing countries. There is a technological possibility of transferring water from wet regions to arid areas, but political or economic barriers may make this impracticable, though large-scale construction of massive dams and flood control systems, such as those on the Nile, the Indus, and the great Chinese rivers, can be carried out on an international scale.

In order to understand what life is like in a degenerating environment, an extract from Alan Paton's *Cry the Beloved Country* is appropriate, as he describes the African landscape from the lush green hills to the desolate valleys:

'...Where you stand the grass is rich and matted, you cannot see the soil. But the rich green hills break down. They fall to the valley below, and, falling, change their nature. For they grow red and bare; they cannot hold the rain and mist, and the streams are dry in the kloofs. Too many cattle feed upon the grass, and too many fires have burned it.

Stand shod upon it, for it is coarse and sharp, and the stones cut under the feet. It is not kept, or guarded, or cared for, it no longer keeps men, guards men, cares for men. The titihoya does not cry here any more. The great red hills stand desolate and the earth has torn away like flesh. The lightning flashes over them, the clouds pour down upon them, the dead streams come to life, full of the red blood of the earth. Down in the valleys women scratch the soil that is left, and the maize hardly reaches the height of a man. They are valleys of old men and old women, of mothers and children. The men are away, the young men and the girls are away. The soil cannot keep them any more....' (1.4)

### Salination

There is no easy solution to the problem of salination, which is a legacy from the early days of enthusiastic but unmonitored, massive irrigation, very different in scale from the traditional, carefully controlled techniques of ancient Arabia and Persia.

In Pakistan, British military engineers irrigated thousands of square miles of desert and over a long period this

Figure 1.9    Salt deposits in Pakistan

*(Photo by courtesy of Aerofilms Ltd.)*

raised the water-table to within a metre of the surface. Evaporation during the months of drought drew the salts from the subsoil to the surface, sterilising the soil. Now vast sums are spent annually on the installation of tube wells to lower the water-table by pumping the underground water back into the irrigation canals, and then increasing irrigation in order to leach out the surface salts. Around Lahore there are over 1000 wells operating 24 hours a day to rectify the consequences of the failure to predict the effects of engineering technology on a natural system.

Early irrigation in the USSR's million-hectare Golodnaya Steppe caused severe salination as a result of the low permeability of the soil and lack of experience in irrigation techniques. This has been remedied by the use of closed horizontal and vertical drains allied to a comprehensive agricultural policy. The area now produces 500,000 tonnes of raw cotton annually, as well as much other agricultural produce (1.5), thus demonstrating that salination can be successfully reversed, although the process is both lengthy and expensive.

### Population and Urbanisation

The population of the world reached a thousand million in 1850, and then it took only 80 years for the next doubling as the population increased to two thousand million in 1930. If the population increase continues at this rate, it has been estimated that in 900 years there will be 100 people for each square metre of the Earth's surface. Clearly this is impossible—a finite world can support only a finite population.

Population increase may be checked by modern family planning techniques, but medical advances lower mortality rates and increase life spans; therefore the world will continue to be faced with a population problem.

It is the imbalance in distribution of population which may prove the greatest problem. The continuation of this imbalance is seen in the relative rates at which the population of different countries double: the population of many developing countries has doubled in 20 to 35 years while the period for developed countries is from 50 to 200 years. In most countries the population in rural areas is declining whilst urbanisation is increasing at an alarming rate. Planners must project and monitor population changes and assess the consequences more effectively than has been done in the past.

The land absorbed by increasing and often uncontrolled urbanisation makes severe impacts deep into the rural areas.

It is not so much the quality of urban design that causes alarm, for this can be remedied by replacing sub-standard buildings, but the loss of land urgently needed for grazing, crops, and woodlands, all necessary to man's wellbeing. This loss of food-land places an increased demand on distant food producers and on the transport system serving the conurbation, with the result that in some countries with a poor urban population the large towns are surrounded by zones of denuded countryside from which all firewood, fodder, and edible plants have been stripped.

Figure 1.10    Land take for urbanisation, Cumbernauld, Scotland. The higher space standards required by modern town-dwellers make increasing demands on rural and semi-rural land.

(*Photo by courtesy of Aerofilms Ltd.*)

Figure 1.11    Dharavi, Bombay. Here squatters have invaded the land and built their shacks because no other accommodation within their means is available.

(*Photo by courtesy of Madhu Sarin*)

## Industry and Pollution

Worldwide attention has already been focused on the problems of pollution, and in many countries action has already been taken to rectify the damage done by pollutants. However, there are still many examples of major pollution which are causing concern. Air, land, aquifers, seas and cities are all at risk from pollution, and sometimes the least obvious forms of pollution are most harmful to the environment.

Further, industry's 'pollution' of land may not be merely in terms of effluents and gaseous emission, but also in visual terms as shown by Figure 1.12. Not only must care be taken to control the release of toxic materials but, as discussed in Chapter 8, infinite care is required to avoid 'visual intrusion' (Figure 1.13).

In the air, pollution is chiefly caused by industrial waste gases reaching nuisance proportions, and in most countries the emission of these gases is controlled. In Britain the great fog in the London area in 1952, which killed thousands of people and animals through high concentrations of chemicals from domestic and industrial fires (1.6), led to the Clean Air Act, with the result that 25 years later London enjoys twice as much sunshine penetration. The same problem occurs in Los Angeles, and is liable to arise wherever suitable climatic conditions and airborne pollution problems are present. The other major air pollution problem, particularly in urban areas, is that of vehicle emissions. Lead, hydrocarbons, and other chemicals can be produced by heavy traffic in sufficient quantities to affect plant and animal life along major highways. This problem is discussed more fully in Chapter 7.

The land is subject to many forms of pollution, some more lasting than others. Good land, whether arable, pastoral or forest, can be damaged by the slow accumulation of toxins, as well as by pollution from outside sources.

Figure 1.13 Ferry Bridge Power Station, Staffordshire. The impact of vast buildings on a small scale rural landscape demands infinite care in siting, design and landscape treatment.

Some sources of land pollution which need to be controlled are the excessive application of fertilizers and insecticides, run-off from intensive beef or dairy units, and fallout from radioactive or industrial emissions. Many of these forms of contamination are irreversible, such as the accumulation of DDT or strontium-90 in animals that have fed from polluted pastures, and even when strict precautions are taken to prevent dangerous fallout, accidents such as the Seveso disaster in Italy can occur without warning.

Pollution of water, whether sea, river or lake, is the most obvious and perhaps the most dangerous form of pollution. Water courses can absorb surprisingly large amounts of poisonous material, but in the last 100 years the intensity of pollution has risen to levels which cannot be absorbed. The classic case is that of Lake Erie in the USA, which has been almost completely poisoned by sewage and industrial effluents. Many rivers running through highly developed regions have reached a dangerous state; the Rhine, and many smaller rivers in Europe are affecting inshore fishing by their discharge (1.7), and even rivers running through agricultural or non-industrial regions in China, India, and South America are becoming contaminated by the sheer pressure of population using them as drainage systems.

All these waters end up eventually in the seas and oceans. Already polluted by oil spillage, ships' wastes, radioactive fallout and dumping, the seas are expected to carry the sewage and effluent from every populated region. On the distant shores of the Antarctic, drifts of plastic bottles and other refuse litter the beaches; oil pollution has been found in mid-Pacific and radioactivity has increased in deep

Figure 1.12 This quarry on a Leicestershire hill emphasises the visual impact of industry.

(Photo by courtesy of Aerofilms Ltd.)

Figure 1.14    Pollution of coastal waters. Industrial effluent at South-wick, Sussex. This kind of discharge will be controlled under the European Environmental Programme regulations.

(*Photo by courtesy of Aerofilms Ltd.*)

Figure 1.15    Pollution of the River Avon by industrial effluent.

(*Photo by courtesy of* Warwickshire and Worcestershire Life, *Whitehorn Press Ltd. and the Civic Trust*)

oceans. Unless the levels of pollution are reduced, the food resources of the seas are likely to become seriously reduced or contaminated within the next generation. Already large areas of the Mediterranean are unsafe for fishing or bathing, while the landlocked Caspian Sea is increasing its chemical content at an accelerating rate.

Unseen, and most vital to plant and animal life, are the stores of underground water which supply our springs and wells. All the sources of pollution mentioned above can contaminate the natural reservoirs from which arterial and surface water supplies are taken. Although surface water pollution is controlled in many countries, few have yet undertaken the complete hydrological surveys necessary to conserve and protect this most basic of resources.

# The Public Conscience

Today, almost all nations are showing concern for environmental problems. Such concern ranges from a basic demand that the environment should produce food and shelter to a very sophisticated concern with the preservation of aesthetically attractive landscapes; but all are endeavouring to understand the causes of environmental problems, and to solve them.

The public conscience has at last been awakened by a two-fold attack on the apathy which has nearly brought the world to the point of no return in the exploitation of natural resources. First, the professional ecologists and land use planners have drawn attention to the imminence of environmental destruction; books such as Rachel Carson's *Silent Spring* (1.8) and Ian McHarg's *Design with Nature* (1.9) are typical of the professional's appeal to the public. Secondly, the publicity given to environmental disasters, such as the Sahel drought, the Aberfan tip collapse, the Torrey Canyon and Amoco Cadiz oil spills, and the Seveso chemical accident, has aroused public concern for environmental hazards.

The result of this two-fold stimulation is that worldwide public concern for the quality of the environment has grown enormously in recent years. An increasing number of amenity and conservation groups are taking part in courses, conferences and live projects designed to help adults and children to understand the problems of rural and urban development and dereliction, while government policy on land use and planning shows greater awareness of the need to conserve and regenerate our landscape heritage.

Local authorities, planners and economists are beginning to appreciate that land use planning and landscape architecture have an important part to play in the development of new industries, roads, recreation, etc., since irreversible damage can be done to the environment if ecological safeguards are not built into future development programmes.

## United Nations Conference on the Environment

A step forward was achieved by the United Nations Conference on the Human Environment held in Stockholm in 1972 (1.10). This Conference was attended by over 100 nations and these nations were obliged to consider seriously the environmental problems of their countries in relation to their neighbours, and to discuss methods of solution. There were many political undertones, particularly on population control, but much was achieved and 26 principles directed towards the establishment of permanent international cooperation were agreed.

The statement of the United Nations' belief in the urgent need to control worldwide land use planning is as important today as when it was first put forward at the Stockholm Conference. It is the land's equivalent of the Charter of Human Rights; it is, and must be, the base on which national and international land use planning policies are built.

Since the 26 principles provide a summary of all factors concerned with the conservation and enhancement of the human environment they are quoted here:

1. Man has the fundamental right to freedom, equality and adequate conditions of life, in an environment of a quality which permits a life of dignity and well-being, and bears a solemn responsibility to protect and improve the environment for present and future generations. In this respect, policies promoting or perpetuating *apartheid*, racial segregation, discrimination, colonial and other forms of oppression and foreign domination stand condemned and must be eliminated.

2. The natural resources of the earth including the air, water, land, flora and fauna and especially representative samples of natural ecosystems must be safeguarded for the benefit of present and future generations through careful planning or management as appropriate.

3. The capacity of the earth to produce vital renewable resources must be maintained and wherever practicable restored or improved.

4. Man has a special responsibility to safeguard and wisely manage the heritage of wildlife and its habitat which are now gravely imperilled by a combination of adverse factors. Nature conservation including wildlife must therefore receive importance in planning for economic development.

5. The non-renewable resources of the earth must be employed in such a way as to guard against the danger of their future exhaustion and to ensure that benefits from such employment are shared by all mankind.

6. The discharge of toxic substances or of other substances and the release of heat, in such quantities or concentrations as to exceed the capacity of the environment to render them harmless, must be halted in order to ensure that serious or irreversible damage is not inflicted upon ecosystems. The just struggle of the peoples of all countries against pollution should be supported.

7. States shall take all possible steps to prevent pollution of the seas by substances that are liable to create hazards to human health, to harm living resources and marine life, to damage amenities or to interfere with other legitimate uses of the sea.

8. Economic and social development is essential for ensuring a favourable living and working environment for man and for creating conditions on earth that are necessary for the improvement of the quality of life.

9. Environmental deficiencies generated by the conditions of underdevelopment and natural disasters pose grave problems and can best be remedied by accelerated development through the transfer of substantial quantities of financial and technological assistance as a supplement to the domestic effort of the developing countries and such timely assistance as may be required.

10. For the developing countries, stability of prices and adequate earnings for primary commodities and raw material are essential to environmental management since economic factors as well as ecological processes must be taken into account.

11. The environmental policies of all States should enhance and not adversely affect the present or future development potential of developing countries, nor should they hamper the attainment of better living conditions for all, and appropriate steps should be taken by States and international organisations with a view to reaching agreement on meeting the possible national and international economic consequences resulting from the application of environmental measures.

12. Resources should be made available to preserve and improve the environment, taking into account the circumstances and particular requirements of developing countries and any costs which may emanate from their incorporating environmental safeguards into their development planning and the need for making available to them, upon their request, additional international technical and financial assistance for this purpose.

13. In order to achieve a more rational management of resources and thus to improve the environment, States should adopt an integrated and co-ordinated approach to their development planning so as to ensure that development is compatible with the need to protect and improve the human environment for the benefit of their population.

14. Rational planning constitutes an essential tool for reconciling any conflict between the needs of development and the need to protect and improve the environment.

15. Planning must be applied to human settlements and urbanisation with a view to avoiding adverse effects on the environment and obtaining maximum social, economic and environmental benefits for all. In this respect projects which are designed for colonialist and racist domination must be abandoned.

16. Demographic policies, which are without prejudice to basic human rights and which are deemed appropriate by Governments concerned, should be applied in those regions where the rate of population growth or excessive population concentrations are likely to have adverse effects on the environment or development, or where low population density may prevent improvement of the human environment and impede development.

17. Appropriate national institutions must be entrusted with the task of planning, managing or controlling the environmental resources of States with the view to enhancing environmental quality.

18. Science and technology, as part of their contribution to economic and social development, must be applied to the identification, avoidance and control of en-

vironmental risks and the solution of environmental problems and for the common good of mankind.

19. Education in environmental matters, for the younger generation as well as adults, giving due consideration to the underprivileged, is essential in order to broaden the basis for an enlightened opinion and responsible conduct by individuals, enterprises and communities in protecting and improving the environment in its full human dimension. It is also essential that mass media of communications avoid contributing to the deterioration of the environment, but, on the contrary, disseminate information of an educational nature on the need to protect and improve the environment in order to enable man to develop in every respect.

20. Scientific research and development in the context of environmental problems, both national and multi-national, must be promoted in all countries, especially the developing countries. In this connexion, the free flow of up-to-date scientific information and transfer of experience must be supported and assisted, to facilitate the solution of environmental problems; environmental technologies should be made available to developing countries on terms which would encourage their wide dissemination without constituting an economic burden on the developing countries.

21. States have, in accordance with the Charter of the United Nations and the principles of international law, the sovereign right to exploit their own resources pursuant to their own environmental policies and the responsibility to ensure that activities within their jurisdiction or control do not cause damage to the environment of other States or of areas beyond the limits of national jurisdiction.

22. States shall co-operate to develop further the international law regarding liability and compensation for the victims of pollution and other environmental damage caused by activities within the jurisdiction or control of such States to areas beyond their jurisdiction.

23. Without prejudice to such criteria as may be agreed upon by the international community, or to standards which will have to be determined nationally, it will be essential in all cases to consider the systems of values prevailing in each country, and the extent of the applicability of standards which are valid for the most advanced countries but which may be inappropriate and of unwarranted social cost for the developing countries.

24. International matters concerning the protection and improvement of the environment should be handled in a co-operative spirit by all countries, big or small, on an equal footing. Co-operation through multi-lateral or bilateral arrangements or other appropriate means is essential to effectively control, prevent, reduce and eliminate adverse environmental effects resulting from activities conducted in all spheres, in such a way that due account is taken of the sovereignty and interests of all States.

25. States shall ensure that international organisations play a co-ordinated, efficient and dynamic role for the protection and improvement of the environment.

26. Man and his environment must be spared the effects of nuclear weapons and all other means of mass destruction. States must strive to reach prompt agreement, in the relevant international organs, on the elimination and complete destruction of such weapons.

**International Environmental Programmes**

The United Nations Environment Programme (UNEP) had a target of $100,000,000 for 1973–77, and its role as co-ordinator and catalyst within the UN system is evidence of an increasing international concern for the human habitat. In 1976 the United Nations Conference on Human Settlements gave birth to the United Nations Habitat and Human Settlements Foundation (UNHHSF), based on Nairobi, and although its primary aim is to improve the quality of life in human settlements, it also includes 'An approach to the natural environment which minimises its destruction or disturbance' (1.11). Control of oil spillage, waste recycling, radioactive contamination, water conservation and the control of pesticides are some of the problems studied by UNEP.

The United Nations, aware of the importance of these problems, held two conferences in 1977; one on water and the other on desertification. As a result of the desertification conference, six case studies are being financed by the UN; in southern Tunisia, northern Chile, Niger, north-west India, and in Pakistan and Iraq where water logging and salination of irrigated areas cause agricultural degradation. A Plan of Action (1.12) to combat desertification, whose main objectives are to arrest the process of desertification, to reclaim desertified land, and ultimately to stabilize the productivity of arid and semi-arid areas, was presented at the conference.

One of the most comprehensive environmental programmes in the world is that set up by the Commission of the European Communities in the Action Programme of 1973 (1.13). The rehabilitation and protection of the environment mandated cover all aspects of human, plant, and animal life, but the sections of the programme of interest to land planners are those dealing with water and land pollution, and the conservation of wildlife and the countryside. These are:

The determination of criteria for tolerable levels of pollution;

The fixing of quality objectives for clean air, and water for drinking, farming, industry and bathing;

The monitoring of pollution control networks, linked to the UN Earthwatch system;

The collection, treatment and disposal of domestic, industrial and radioactive wastes;

The protection of the sea against pollution from ships and river outfalls, and from exploitation of the sea bottom;

The cleaning of the Rhine and the Mediterranean Sea;

The protection of wet lands, forest areas, and the support of hill and mountain farming areas, in order to conserve the quality of the countryside;

The protection of wildlife, especially the migratory birds at present subject to mass destruction, in order to preserve the natural ecological balance;

The conservation of scarce natural resources. (1.14)

The great interest in this programme is not so much in its objectives which are, or should be, those of any civilised community, but the fact that any directive on these matters issued by the Commission of the European Communities becomes law in all the member States. This means that action, once agreed upon, is put into force in all countries, usually with a target date for completion. For example, the Commission has stated that the quality of bathing water on the coasts of Europe must reach the specified standard by 1985. This will also result in the improvement of coastal fishing waters, which are of vital economic importance, and the Commission has issued a 'black list' of toxic pollutants which must be controlled; amongst these mercury, cadmium, aldrin, dieldrin, and endrin are listed for priority action (1.15).

One of the most important functions of the Commission is the increase and dissemination of knowledge on the environment and to this end the Ispra Joint Research Council Centre is carrying out studies on pollution effects and monitoring. Research carried out by the Commission is available to all countries, and the European Development Fund can assist in supporting projects concerned with human settlements and the environment.

**British Environmental Programmes**
In Britain, Government organisations and others have helped towards the understanding and conservation of the natural environment. Of 3000 proposed conservation areas of Britain, 2000 have already been designated and the National Trust has acquired 540 km of unspoilt coastline at a cost of £2m. The Scottish Development Department has carried out a complete survey of Scotland's coastline (1.16), much of which is at risk from large-scale North Sea oil development (see Case History 4).

An example of co-operation between local authorities is the Standing Conference on the Green Belt of London, which monitors the threat of encroachment on the green belt areas. The management of national parks is causing some fresh thought to be given to their finance and supervision; in Britain the Sandford Committee (1.17) considered that

control of national parks was inadequate and that further powers would need to be acquired if the parks were to be efficiently developed. The argument here is between the advocates of complete control leading to effective management, and those who believe that the parks should be allowed to develop with the minimum of planning and economic restrictions.

There are between 7 and 8 million people using water recreation amenities in the UK and a Water Space Amenity Commission has been set up to advise the Government on their requirements.

Governments too often adopt negative policies and professional planners can be insular, fallible and sometimes motivated by political doctrine, thus there is no doubt that the existence of powerful environmental pressure groups is of great importance to the planning system. In Britain, for example, the Council for the Protection of Rural England, the National Trust, the Civic Trust and the Tree Council have not only issued major policy statements influencing Government decisions, but have prepared many excellent working reports on specific environmental issues. The composition of these conservation organisations is extremely diverse, comprising men and women with professional expertise and also amateurs, backed up by full time secretariats.

The professional institutions have long felt the need for closer collaboration on environmental matters and in 1973 established the Professional Institutes Council for Conservation which comprises 18 professional institutions and over 50 corresponding organisations.

Many countries in the world have expressed their desire to initiate their own national bodies on the lines of the National Trust, the Civic Trust, and the Professional Institutes Council for Conservation. These countries should have every encouragement to do so, in view of the proved value of these organisations in Britain.

## Planning the Environment

Solutions must be found for all land use and environmental problems. Development plans, supported by legislation, grants, subsidies, sanctions and inducements, are key instruments in these solutions. Without order there is chaos and if order is to prevail, there must be national and regional policies implemented by viable development plans. Most countries have some form of planning; in some it is of a rudimentary nature, whilst in others it is advanced and comprehensive. Britain has perhaps one of the most developed planning legislations and it may be instructive to discuss recent developments in British planning—the successes, failures and reason for change—and to outline the British Government's recent proposals for the complete revision of the form and content of development plans.

**The British Planning Process**

The Town and Country Planning Act of 1947 (1.18) was a landmark in planning legislation in Britain. This Act required local planning authorities (counties and county boroughs) to prepare development plans within a three-year period of the Act coming into force. The Act placed a statutory obligation on local planning authorities to consider the development of their areas on a comprehensive basis, principally to indicate the pattern of land use and communications to be achieved within a 20-year period.

Two types of map were used for this purpose: the town map and the county map. While these provided a reasonable basis for the preparation of detailed plans in urban areas, there was no provision for regional plans or studies to ensure that the proposals were based on sound economic principles. The Government therefore decided to introduce new legislation, under the Town and Country Planning Act, 1968 (1.19), modifying the system of preparing development plan proposals. The fundamental principle of this legislation was a broader basis of physical, economic and social planning, taking proper account of national and regional policies. There is no doubt that the Government's new proposals provide a greater degree of flexibility than the previous arrangements and assist in the closer integration of land use and transportation planning, environmental improvement, resource and social planning.

Linking the central Government and the local authorities are the regional economic councils—a group of consultative bodies whose function is to advise the Government on the problems and proposals for comprehensive planning in each region of Britain. The regional councils deal with such land use matters as highway network proposals, transport in rural areas, depopulation, and port development. Although they have no executive powers, and therefore no direct control over the preparation of development plans, their recommendations are an important factor in the planning decisions made by Government and local authority planning teams.

The development plan (1.20) is divided into two main parts—the *structure plan* and the *local plan*. Structure plans must be prepared and approved by the Secretary of State before local plans become effective. Local plans require the approval of the local authority and not the Secretary of State, unless specifically directed. However, from time to time, it may be necessary to prepare certain detailed plans in order to assist the preparation of structure plans.

STRUCTURE PLANS

Structure plans (see Figure 1.16*a* and *b*) indicate the major problems and strategies of the administrative area and are decision documents. There are two types— the county structure plan and the urban structure plan. The urban plan should be prepared for towns with a population of 50,000 or above or smaller towns of outstanding interest. The main functions of these plans, as outlined in the Government's *Development Plan Manual*, are:

1. Interpreting national and regional policies;
2. Establishing aims, policies and general proposals;
3. Providing a framework for local plans;
4. Indicating action areas;
5. Providing guidance for development control;
6. Providing a basis for co-ordinating decisions;
7. Bringing main planning issues and decisions before the Minister and the public.

The most important aspect of the structure plan is the assessment of the economic resources in order to ensure that the plan is economically viable and can be implemented within the 20 to 30 years suggested programme period. The proposals therefore must be realistic, and full account should be taken of the nation's likely availability of resources and the related competition for such resources— priorities must be established and cost benefits assessed.

The county structure plan must co-ordinate, amongst other things: land use and transportation; changes in agriculture, forestry, minerals, population; impact of motorways on recreation and landscape conservation; journey to work; second homes and urban pressures. Alternative strategies must be examined and fully evaluated.

The landscape planning content of the structure plans will, of course, define the major landscape elements such as national, regional and countryside parks, areas of great landscape value, areas of outstanding natural beauty, green belts, nature reserves, etc. It is, however, in the local plans where the most positive and imaginative proposals may be generated.

LOCAL PLANS

Local plans are the principal instrument for implementing the policies of the structure plan and they fall into three categories—*district, action* and *subject plans*. Their form and presentation must follow similar lines to those of the structure plans, the survey and written statements being essential parts of their presentation. In addition, sketches may be submitted in order to convey the environmental content of the plans so essential for obtaining the public's acceptance and enthusiasm towards these plans.

District plans cover a large area such as part of a large town, small town, rural parts of counties and villages and the functions are:

1. To set out the planning policies of each area, to restate and amplify the long-term planning intentions of the structure plans, to describe specific proposals and to lay down development control criteria;
2. In urban areas, to apply the structure plan policies for environmental planning and management;
3. In rural areas, to apply the structure plan policies for managing the rural environment.

Action plans are intended to bring before the public, in a separate plan, areas of intensive change by redevelopment, or upgrading by local authorities or private development where the changes can be implemented within a ten-year period by the approval of the structure plan.

Subject plans are action plans, but are generally confined to one aspect of planning rather than a multiplicity of functions, for example, reclamation of a derelict site, the landscape treatment of a motorway or a scenic corridor, or the rehabilitation of a derelict canal. These plans are of exceptional importance as far as the detailed implementation of the rural environment is concerned.

LOCAL AUTHORITIES' RESPONSIBILITIES
There is no doubt that the 1968 Act gives the local planning authorities far greater responsibilities than under previous legislation. It is their responsibility (unless specifically directed by the Secretary of State once the structure plan has been approved) to consider the location and desirability of preparing local plans. Stress is laid on the fact that all the proposals must be prepared in a most comprehensive manner, covering the widest aspects of socio-economic and environmental considerations.

Little reference, if any, is made to national policies and here lies a possible weakness in the Government's proposals. It is essential that the local authorities have at their disposal the fullest and most comprehensive information on international and national planning policies in order that these may be incorporated into the structure plans. There does not appear to be any national plan—certainly not a national landscape policy or plan. There is no statement of the information that the Government will supply to the local planning authorities which will have significant influences on strategic and structure planning.

Since the 1968 Act came into force the preparation of structure and local plans has proceeded much more slowly than intended. By early 1978, only 42 out of 69 structure plans had been submitted and the consequent delay in the preparation of local plans has caused 'planning blight' in inner city and small town districts.

There are two major causes of this slow progress. One is the restructuring of local government, which has resulted in the division of control over such planning elements as housing, highways, recreation, and conservation—some of which are the responsibilities of the county or region, while others are the responsibility of the district council—making the co-ordination of planning policies extremely difficult, especially in areas where sub-regional and local interests are at variance.

Secondly, many planners consider that the exercise of detailed planning control over individual dwellings and major developments is occupying professional staff and public money that could be better spent on constructing strategic policies for regional and local land use; and indeed there is considerable pressure on the Government to relax the detailed control of projects where little environmental impact is expected. These projects may amount to as much as 40% of all planning applications, so that their elimination from the planning queue would save much valuable time and professional skill (1.21). At this moment, a select committee is looking into the whole development and

Table 1.1 Possible conflicts which may arise when the need to promote economic development clashes with the desire to conserve and to enhance our landscape heritage

| POLICY UNDER PROMOTION | ACTIONS WHICH MAY BE TAKEN IN CONSEQUENCE (some with grant-aid from the Exchequer) | POLICIES IN POTENTIAL CONFLICT |
|---|---|---|
| Increased food production and productivity | Ploughing, liming and fertilising | Conservation of scene, wildlife, remains; access to open country; pollution control |
| | Drainage work | Wildlife and water conservation |
| | Hedgerow clearance | Conservation of scene and wildlife |
| | Use of fertilisers, pesticides and herbicides | Conservation of wildlife; water quality; pollution control |
| | Farm and storage buildings | Conservation of scene |
| | Woodland clearance | Conservation of scene and wildlife |
| | Fencing | Conservation of scene; access to open country |
| | Bracken removal | Conservation of scene |
| | Straw-burning | Conservation of scene and wildlife; pollution control |
| | Free running bulls | Access (along footpaths) |
| Increased timber production and productivity | Afforestation and fencing | Conservation of scene; access |
| | Block felling | Conservation of scene |

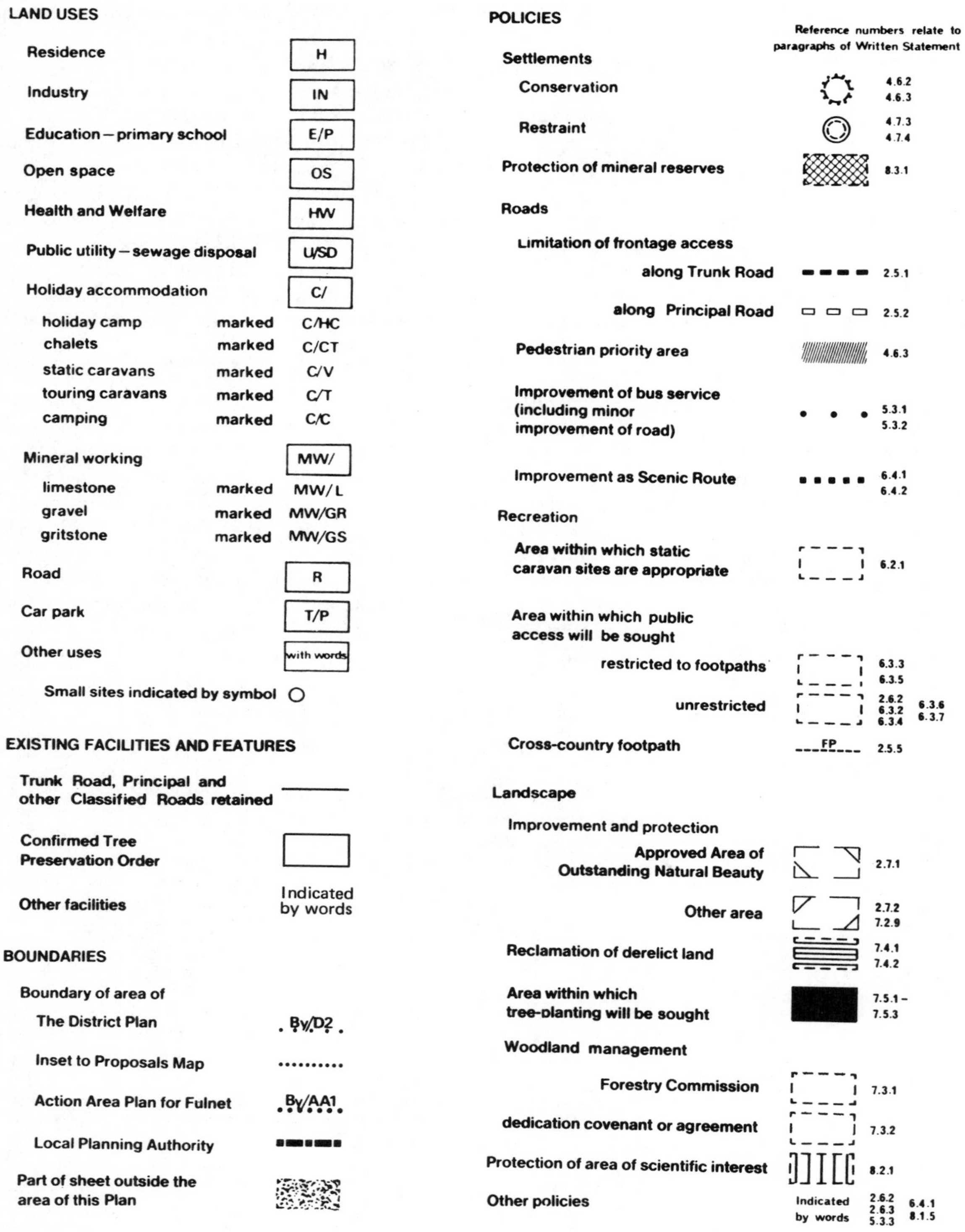
LAND USES
Residence
H
Industry
IN
Education – primary school
E/P
Open space
OS
Health and Welfare
HW
Public utility – sewage disposal
U/SD
Holiday accommodation
C/
holiday camp marked C/HC
chalets marked C/CT
static caravans marked C/V
touring caravans marked C/T
camping marked C/C
Mineral working
MW/
limestone marked MW/L
gravel marked MW/GR
gritstone marked MW/GS
Road
R
Car park
T/P
Other uses
with words
Small sites indicated by symbol
EXISTING FACILITIES AND FEATURES
Trunk Road, Principal and other Classified Roads retained
Confirmed Tree Preservation Order
Other facilities
Indicated by words
BOUNDARIES
Boundary of area of
The District Plan
By/D2
Inset to Proposals Map
Action Area Plan for Fulnet
By/AA1
Local Planning Authority
Part of sheet outside the area of this Plan
POLICIES
Reference numbers relate to paragraphs of Written Statement
Settlements
Conservation
4.6.2
4.6.3
Restraint
4.7.3
4.7.4
Protection of mineral reserves
8.3.1
Roads
Limitation of frontage access
along Trunk Road
2.5.1
along Principal Road
2.5.2
Pedestrian priority area
4.6.3
Improvement of bus service (including minor improvement of road)
5.3.1
5.3.2
Improvement as Scenic Route
6.4.1
6.4.2
Recreation
Area within which static caravan sites are appropriate
6.2.1
Area within which public access will be sought
restricted to footpaths
6.3.3
6.3.5
unrestricted
2.6.2
6.3.2
6.3.4
6.3.6
6.3.7
Cross-country footpath
FP
2.5.5
Landscape
Improvement and protection
Approved Area of Outstanding Natural Beauty
2.7.1
Other area
2.7.2
7.2.9
Reclamation of derelict land
7.4.1
7.4.2
Area within which tree-planting will be sought
7.5.1 –
7.5.3
Woodland management
Forestry Commission
7.3.1
dedication covenant or agreement
7.3.2
Protection of area of scientific interest
8.2.1
Other policies
Indicated by words
2.6.2
2.6.3
5.3.3
6.4.1
8.1.5

Figure 1.16*a* Notation for Country Structure Plans, as given in *Development Plans: A Manual on Form and Content,* enables presentation of the maps to be both attractive and easy to assimilate.

(*Reproduced by courtesy of HMSO*)

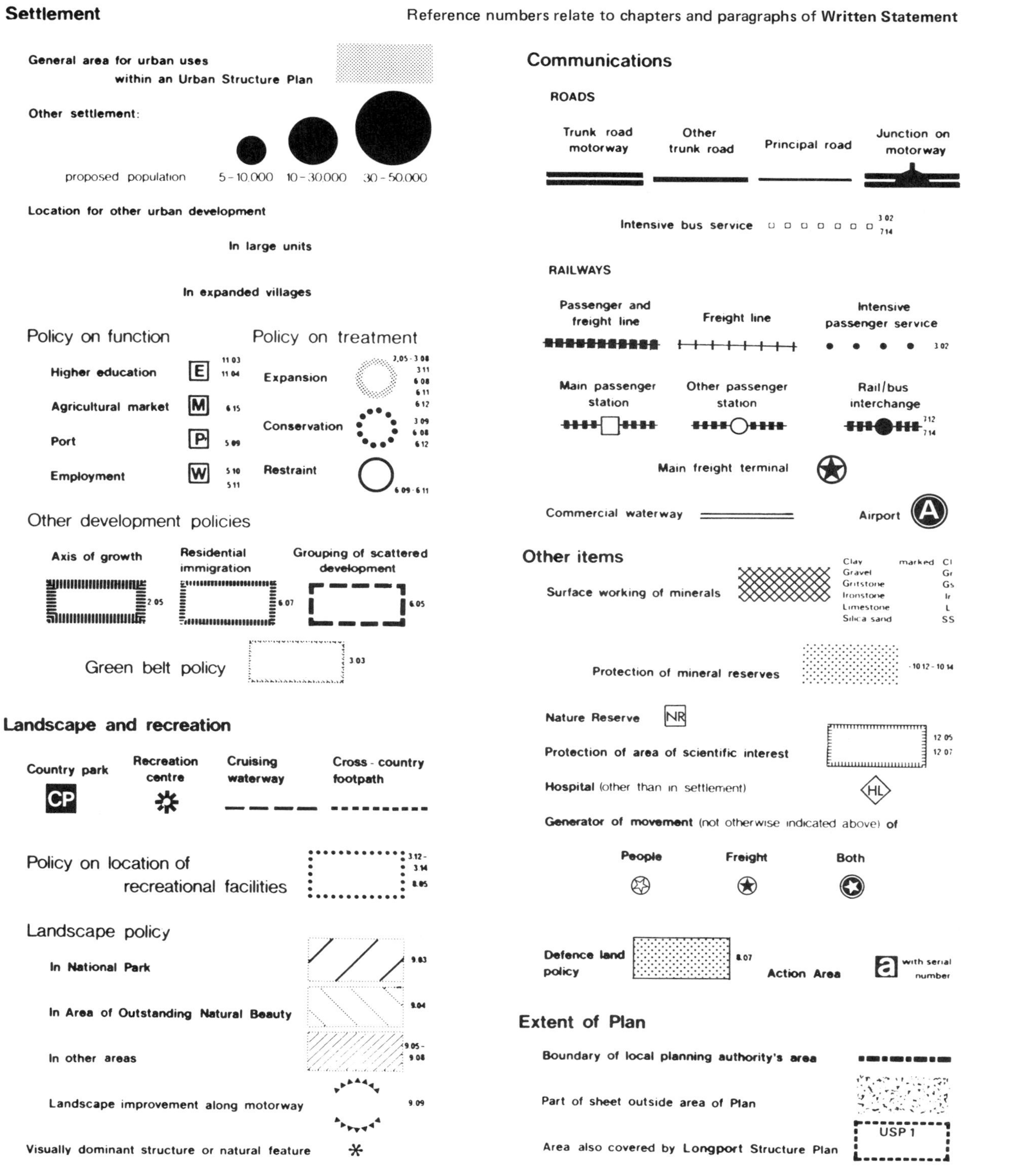

## Settlement

Reference numbers relate to chapters and paragraphs of **Written Statement**

General area for urban uses
within an Urban Structure Plan

Other settlement:

proposed population    5 - 10.000    10 - 30.000    30 - 50.000

Location for other urban development

In large units

In expanded villages

### Policy on function

| | | |
|---|---|---|
| Higher education | E | 11 03 / 11 04 |
| Agricultural market | M | 6 15 |
| Port | P | 5 09 |
| Employment | W | 5 10 / 5 11 |

### Policy on treatment

Expansion    7.05 - 3 08 / 3 11 / 6 08 / 6 11 / 6 12

Conservation    3 09 / 6 08 / 6 12

Restraint    6 09 - 6 11

### Other development policies

| Axis of growth | Residential immigration | Grouping of scattered development |
|---|---|---|
| 2 05 | 6 07 | 6 05 |

Green belt policy    3 03

## Landscape and recreation

| Country park | Recreation centre | Cruising waterway | Cross - country footpath |
|---|---|---|---|
| CP | ✳ | | |

Policy on location of
recreational facilities    3 12 - 3 14 / 8 05

### Landscape policy

In National Park    9 03

In Area of Outstanding Natural Beauty    9 04

In other areas    9 05 - 9 08

Landscape improvement along motorway    9 09

Visually dominant structure or natural feature    ✳

## Communications

### ROADS

| Trunk road motorway | Other trunk road | Principal road | Junction on motorway |
|---|---|---|---|

Intensive bus service    3 02 / 7 14

### RAILWAYS

| Passenger and freight line | Freight line | Intensive passenger service |
|---|---|---|
| | | 3 02 |

| Main passenger station | Other passenger station | Rail/bus interchange |
|---|---|---|
| | | 7 12 / 7 14 |

Main freight terminal    ★

Commercial waterway

Airport    Ⓐ

## Other items

Surface working of minerals

| | marked |
|---|---|
| Clay | Cl |
| Gravel | Gr |
| Gritstone | Gs |
| Ironstone | Ir |
| Limestone | L |
| Silica sand | SS |

Protection of mineral reserves    10 12 - 10 14

Nature Reserve    NR

Protection of area of scientific interest    12 05 / 12 07

Hospital (other than in settlement)    HL

Generator of movement (not otherwise indicated above) of

| People | Freight | Both |
|---|---|---|
| ⊛ | ⊛ | ⊛ |

Defence land policy    8 07

Action Area    a    with serial number

## Extent of Plan

Boundary of local planning authority's area

Part of sheet outside area of Plan

Area also covered by Longport Structure Plan    USP 1

Figure 1.16*b*  Notation for District Plans, which illustrates the presentation of landscape planning in more detail.

(*Reproduced from* Development Plans: A Manual on Form and Content, *by courtesy of HMSO*)

*Table 1.1 continued*

| POLICY UNDER PROMOTION | ACTIONS WHICH MAY BE TAKEN IN CONSEQUENCE (some with grant-aid from the Exchequer) | POLICIES IN POTENTIAL CONFLICT |
|---|---|---|
| Increased piped water supply | Creation of reservoirs | Conservation of scene and productive land |
| Improved water quality | Groundwater schemes and estuarial storage bunds | Conservation of scene and wildlife |
| | Purification works | Conservation of scene |
| Prevention of damage by water | River training and flood protection | Conservation of scene; access |
| Increased mineral production | Excavation and spoil tips | Conservation of productive land; conservation of scene and wildlife; access; water quality; pollution control |
| | Transportation of materials | Conservation of amenity |
| National defence | Maintenance of training grounds | Food, mineral and timber production; conservation of scene; access |
| | Testing equipment and training | Conservation of amenity |
| Promotion of tourism | Erection of catering, accommodation and service facilities | Conservation of scene, amenity and productive land |
| | Holiday traffic (vehicles and people) | Conservation of amenity and wildlife |
| Improved accessibility | New roads; building; widening and straightening of roads | Conservation of scene, wildlife and amenity; production of food |
| Improved housing | Take-up of countryside for new development | Conservation of productive land; conservation of scene, wildlife and amenity |
| Promotion of industrial development | Take-up of countryside for new factories | Conservation of productive land; conservation of scene, wildlife and amenity; pollution control |
| Promotion of the recreational use of the countryside | Improving access to open country, conserving and protecting the footpaths system | Production of food and timber; conservation of wildlife and amenity (of country dwellers) |
| | Providing of more facilities (country parks, picnic sites, etc.) | Production of food and timber; conservation of scene and wildlife |
| Clearing derelict land | Earth moving and creative landscaping | Conservation of wildlife |
| Conserving the amenity of the countryside | Designation of special areas, control of development and noise, dust and other nuisance | Improvement of accessibility: housing and industrial development: tourism, recreation; extraction of minerals |
| Conserving the scene | Designation of special areas, control of development and noise, dust and other nuisance | Hedgerow and woodland clearance; afforestation; development generally |
| Conserving wildlife | Designation of special areas, control of development and noise, dust and other nuisance | Hedgerow and woodland clearance; afforestation; development generally |
| Improved telecommunications | Erection of masts and aerials | Conservation of scene |
| Increasing energy supply | Extraction of oil, gas, coal | Conservation of productive land, scene, wildlife and amenity; pollution control |
| | Generation and transmission of electricity | Conservation of scene |
| Reducing rural depopulation | Promotion of industrial development | Conservation of scene and amenity |

Reproduced by courtesy of the Countryside Review Committee.

planning control machinery, and it is to be hoped that their recommendations will go far towards making British planning the most efficient environmental control system in the world.

As far as landscape planning is concerned, there is still a serious lack of environmental strategies and proposals. For example, agricultural changes may have a serious effect on the tree cover, which in turn will alter the landscape character of a large area—this is not being monitored in the planning process. In Britain, the mass infection of 13 million elm trees in the countryside, together with the vast increase in field sizes, has resulted in a catastrophic tree loss. The conservation and replanting of the tree cover should be incorporated in the planning proposals for the affected areas of countryside.

Throughout the entire field of planning, particularly landscape planning, there are conflicts which must be resolved if a coherent and workable plan is to emerge and, at the same time, a workable plan will assist in resolving such conflicts.

The landscape conflicts in Britain have been tabulated by the Countryside Review Committee (1.22). (Table 1.1) Underlying them all is the basic tension between commitment to economic growth—which is the motivating force for many of the resource use policies—and the aim of conserving the countryside itself which, through the planning and control of urban development, exercises profound constraints on the shape, extent and density of city development.

### The Role of Land Use and Landscape Planning in the Planning Process

As discussed in Chapter 2, land use and landscape planning are descriptions of land-centred design and management processes. They are complementary, as are city planning and architecture, and each requires the co-ordination of many scientific and artistic skills. But, more importantly, both are crucial components of the planning system of any country. Without their effective involvement at all stages of the planning process, the environmental problems discussed earlier in this chapter will lead to the destruction not merely of the countryside but of the human habitat.

# References and Bibliography

1.1 UNITED NATIONS, *CESI Facts*, 3, 1977.
1.2 KOUDA, V. A., *UNESCO Courier*, July 1977.
1.3 EL-KASSAS, M., *UNESCO Courier*, July 1977.
1.4 PATON, A., *Cry the Beloved Country*, Jonathan Cape, London, 1948.
1.5 BABAEV, A. G., *UNESCO Courier*, July 1977.
1.6 *The Times*, April 1953
1.7 Royal Commission on Environmental Pollution, HMSO, London, 1971.
1.8 CARSON, R., *Silent Spring*, Penguin, Harmondsworth, 1965.
1.9 MCHARG, I., *Design with Nature*, Natural History Press, New York, 1969.
1.10 UNITED NATIONS, *Declaration on the Human Environment,* United Nations Conference on the Human Environment, Stockholm, 1972.
1.11 UNHHSF, *Habitat Foundation News*, 1, Nairobi, November 1976.
1.12 UNEP, Draft Plan of Action to Combat Desertification, Nairobi, 1977.
1.13 COMMISSION OF THE EUROPEAN COMMUNITIES, Programme of Action of the European Communities on the Environment, Brussels, November 1973.
1.14 COMMISSION OF THE EUROPEAN COMMUNITIES, *State of the Environment,* 1st Report, Brussels, 1977.
1.15 *ibid.*
1.16 SCOTTISH DEVELOPMENT DEPARTMENT, *The Coast of Scotland*, HMSO, Edinburgh.
1.17 Sandford Committee Report, *National Parks Policy Review*, HMSO, London, 1974.
1.18 The Town and Country Planning Act 1947, HMSO, London.
1.19 The Town and Country Planning Act 1968, HMSO, London.
1.20 *Development Plans: A Manual on Form and Content*, HMSO, London, 1968.
1.21 CHAPMAN, S., 'Parliament probes planning', *Building*, 18 March 1977.
1.22 COUNTRYSIDE REVIEW COMMITTEE, *The Countryside—Problems and Policies*, HMSO, London, 1976.

### Ecology
BENTHAL, J., (ed.), *Ecology, the Shaping Enquiry*, Longman, Harlow, 1972.
DASMANN, R. F., *Ecological Principles for Economic Development*, Wiley, New York, 1973.
EHRLICH, P. R. and A. H., *Human Ecology*, W. H. Freeman, San Francisco, 1973.
MUMFORD, L. (ed.), *The Ecological Basis of Planning,* Martinees Nijhoff, The Hague, 1971.
ODUM, E. P., *Fundamentals of Ecology,* 3rd ed., W. B. Saunders, Philadelphia, 1971.
TANSLEY, A. G., *Britain's Green Mantle*, Allen and Unwin, London, 1956.

### Conservation
BUSH, R., *The National Parks of England and Wales*, J. M. Dent, London, 1973.
DASMANN, R. F., *Environmental Conservation*, 3rd ed., Wiley, New York, 1972.
HARROY, J. P. et al., *National Parks of the World*, Orbis, London, 1974.
HIGHSMITH, R. M. et al., *Conservation in the United States*, Rand McNally, Chicago, 1969.
SHEAIL, J., *Nature in Trust*, Blackie, Glasgow, 1975.
STAMP, D., *Nature Conservation in Britain*, Collins, London, 1969.
WARRE, A. (ed.), *Conservation in Practice,* Wiley, New York, 1974.

## Environment

ALDOUS, T., *Battle for the Environment,* Fontana, London, 1972.

ARVILL, R., *Man and Environment,* Pelican, Harmondsworth, 1967.

BACH, W., *Atmospheric Pollution,* McGraw-Hill, New York, 1972.

GRESSWELL, P., *Environment, an Alphabetical Handbook,* John Murray, London, 1971.

NICHOLSON, M., *The Environmental Revolution,* Pelican, Harmondsworth, 1972.

REEKIE, R. F., *Background to Environmental Planning,* Edward Arnold, London, 1975.

Royal Commission on Environmental Pollution, Fifth Report, HMSO, London, 1976.

## Land Use

BARR, J., *Derelict Britain,* Penguin, Harmondsworth, 1969.

BEST, R. H., *The Changing Use of Land in Britain,* Faber and Faber, London, 1973.

BEST, R. H., *The Major Land Uses of Great Britain,* Faber and Faber, London, 1973.

BEST, R. H. and ROGERS, A. W., *The Urban Countryside,* Faber and Faber, London, 1973.

CLOUT, H. D., *Rural Geography,* Pergamon, Oxford, 1972.

COUNTRYSIDE REVIEW COMMITTEE, *The Countryside—Problems and Policies,* HMSO, London, 1976.

HAINES, G. H., *Whose Countryside?,* J. M. Dent, London, 1974.

HALL, P., *Urban and Regional Planning,* Pelican, Harmondsworth, 1974.

OXENHAM, R. R., *Reclaiming Derelict Land,* Faber and Faber, London, 1966.

PROFESSIONAL INSTITUTIONS COUNCIL FOR CONSERVATION, *Dereliction of Land,* London, 1971.

TANDY, C., *Landscape of Industry,* Leonard Hill, London, 1975.

WALLWORK, K. L., *Derelict Land,* David and Charles, Newton Abbot, 1974.

## Landscape Planning

APPLETON, J., *The Experience of Landscape,* Wiley, New York, 1975.

BLUNDEN, J., *et al., Regional Analysis and Development,* Open University, Milton Keynes, 1973.

BRACEY, H. E., *People in the Countryside,* Routledge and Kegan Paul, London, 1970.

BRETT, L., *Landscape in Distress,* Architectural Press, London, 1965.

COLVIN, B., *Land and Landscape,* John Murray, London, 1970.

CROWE, S., *Tomorrow's Landscape,* Architectural Press, London, 1956.

CROWE, S. and MILLER, Z., (eds.), *Shaping Tomorrow's Landscape,* 2 vols., Djambatan, Amsterdam, 1964.

FAIRBROTHER, N., *The Nature of Landscape Design,* Architectural Press, London, 1974.

FAIRBROTHER, N., *New Lives, New Landscapes,* Architectural Press, London, 1970.

GREGORY, R. G., *The Price of Amenity,* Macmillan, London, 1971.

JELLICOE, G. and S., *The Landscape of Man,* Thames and Hudson, London, 1975.

HACKETT, B., *Landscape Planning: an Introduction to Theory and Practice,* Oriel Press, Newcastle, 1971.

HADFIELD, M., *Landscape with Trees,* Country Life, London, 1967.

HOSKINS, W. G., *The Making of the English Landscape,* Hodder and Stoughton, London, 1965.

LAURIE, M., *An Introduction to Landscape Architecture,* Elsevier, New York, 1975.

McHARG, I., *Design with Nature,* Natural History Press, New York, 1969.

MANLEY, G., *Climate and the British Scene,* Fontana, London, 1970.

MITCHELL, C., *Terrain Evaluation,* Longman, Harlow, 1973.

NEWTON, N. T., *Design on Land: the Development of Landscape Architecture,* Belknap Press of Harvard University, Cambridge, Mass., 1971.

PENNYFATHER, K., *Guide to Countryside Interpretation,* HMSO, London, 1975.

ROBINSON, D. G. *et al., Landscape Evaluation,* University of Manchester, 1976.

SALTER, C., *The Cultural Landscape,* Duxbury Press, London, 1971.

SAWYER, K. E., *Landscape Studies (Geomorphology),* Edward Arnold, London, 1970.

SIMMONDS, J. O., *Landscape Architecture: the Shaping of Man's Natural Environment,* Iliffe, London, 1961.

STAM, P. L. D., *Britain's Structure and Scenery,* Fontana, 1970.

TANDY, C. (ed.), *Handbook of Urban Landscape,* Architectural Press, London, 1972.

TAYLOR, C. *Fields in the English Landscape,* J. M. Dent, London, 1975.

WEDDLE, A., (ed.), *Techniques of Landscape Architecture,* Heinemann, London, 1976.

## Legislation and Control

BIGHAM, D. A., *The Law and Administration relating to Protection of the Environment,* Oyez, London, 1973.

CULLINGWORTH, J. B., *Town and Country Planning in Britain,* 6th ed., Allen and Unwin, London, 1977.

DEPARTMENT OF THE ENVIRONMENT, *Review of Planning Control over Mineral Working,* HMSO, London, 1976.

DEPARTMENT OF THE ENVIRONMENT, *Assessment of Major Industrial Applications,* Research Report 13, HMSO, London, 1976.

HEAP, D., *Outline of Planning Law,* 7th ed., Sweet and Maxwell, London, 1978.

MANNERS, G., *et al., Regional Development in Britain,* Wiley, Chichester, 1972.

CHAPTER TWO

# APPLIED ANALYSIS AND
# EVALUATION TECHNIQUES

A. E. Weddle

Aerial photograph taken during the development of Central Milton Keynes.

(*By courtesy of Milton Keynes Development Corporation*)

CHAPTER TWO
# APPLIED ANALYSIS AND EVALUATION TECHNIQUES

## Introduction

### Description of Terms Used

The process or activity of landscape planning is taken here as one which examines landscape resources, determines and estimates respectively those present and future demands which will have modifying effects on the landscape, and then attempts a resolution of conflicts. The activity has an affinity with other planning endeavours, for example land use planning, natural resources planning, and environmental planning.

The connotation which most strongly attaches to *landscape planning* may be taken as the ecological, the systems approach to an understanding of complex biological forces which need to be understood and respected in caring for landscape which we chose to protect or modify within prescribed limits. *Land use planning* is losing its 'town planning' connotation in most parts of Western Europe and North America. The land managing professions concerned with housing, moving, providing employment and social services for urban populations now have to take account of the land around towns and conurbations as well as the existing development and the plans for redevelopment within the towns themselves. *Resource planning* can be applied to a single resource, for example, water supply, forestry, wildlife, but increasingly it now takes account of the related character of natural resources, the exploitation or protection of any one having chain effects on others. *Environmental planning* began to assume importance as a term and a proposed activity in the structure plans prepared in England and Wales in the early 1960s. With the reorganisation of local government in 1974 many planning authorities set up groups or divisions, separate from structure planning strategies and development control duties, with the specific task

of bringing about improvements by environmental planning. *Conservation* and *resource management*, accepting connotations which closely relate them, are also akin to the activity of landscape planning. Conservation, to be really effective, cannot be preservation and protection alone. It needs positive management of the kind implied by resource management, which involves definite decisions and action to maintain the biophysical environment.

This chapter is concerned with applied techniques, that is the methods of applied analysis and the landscape evaluation attempts made in the process of bringing about action and getting landscape works of protection and development actually carried out. It is important therefore to consider how this can and does or should, relate to existing systems of land planning. Space does not permit a wide ranging review of land planning systems, only to state briefly that these systems do exist and with widely varying powers and degrees of effectiveness in different countries.

In North America there are National Park, Forestry and Agricultural Services of some influence in promoting and controlling land use on a national scale, but generally in fairly closely defined territorial areas. Urban land planning exists, but with limited powers (very limited when compared with what professionals believe to be the magnitude of the problem). Various attempts have also been made at regional planning, again limited in scope and success when seen against the massive movements and growth characteristics of rural to urban, urban to suburban and even regional shifts in North America.

In Great Britain a highly developed system of town and country planning exists. It operates most substantially in the urban areas, however, and is effective in the countryside only in that it restrains urban encroachment on rural areas. Agencies in Britain concerned with extensive use of land tend to be for its single-purpose exploitation. In so far that they have plans, the validity of these is sometimes questioned, for example the economic viability of forestry, and the wisdom of subsidising farming more intensive than the apparent capability of some soils to support. Attention must be drawn to the fact that many British town planners sincerely believe that the activity for which they were trained and in which they now take part does in fact embrace landscape planning. Quite bluntly it does not. The principal extensive users of land, farming and forestry, operate outside their influence. The competition for land for mineral extraction, power production and distribution, and much industry in rural areas, is resolved very largely by the economics of the market, and a highly imperfect market, with purchase power vested in large public or private corporations possessing either overwhelming purchase power or monopoly powers, and ultimately the power of compulsory purchase in some cases. It is true that an umpiring system operates, with planning inquiries to ventilate views and allow a politically expedient control to be operated by the Secretary of State for the Environment. What town planning has managed to achieve in rural areas of Britain in the last 30 years has, however, been a massive holding operation, preventing uncontrolled urban encroachment, reckless minerals extraction, and a host of incursions, many relatively minor in themselves but very significant in aggregate. If all these had not been curbed by county planning policies we would have been left with a very degraded countryside indeed. It is with a view to influencing professionals, the public and politicians, that landscape planning must seek substantive evidence and promote positive plans which can be effective and demonstrably so. The quest for defined landscape evaluation techniques is part of this job.

### The Value of Protest

Until recently, 'planning' outside of towns was generally regarded as a negative activity, which could at least be relied upon to prevent uncontrolled development of land. The developers of roads, electric power generation plants, oil and gas terminals, reservoirs and other major constructions in the landscape are now seen as the 'planners' by a public which includes powerful protest groups. These groups have appeared and consolidated their positions in the United States, Britain, France and Germany. From early beginnings as minor objectors at public inquiries, they have progressed as marchers and protestors able to make powerful representation at planning inquiries and sometimes to disrupt these processes of public examination. In France and Germany the protests have become violent, assuming the character of riots which have been quelled by police forces adopting military containment and dispersal techniques.

The value of protest is limited to the focusing of public attention on an issue. Rather than any permanent change of policy there is a temporary delay which should allow a

further careful scrutiny. The enforced reappraisal may reveal hitherto unnoticed problems or those which have been minimised by specialists concerned with achieving only limited objectives of access, economy, or some special kind of operational efficiency, regardless of environmental considerations. Meanwhile in Britain the farming backcloth of rural landscape has changed under the progress of a second agricultural revolution. How do we value these changing landscapes and what do we do to assess the impact of each force and each change? And what about those cases where we set out deliberately to produce change in landscapes as part of an exercise in a new town development, country park promotion, or in a programme to reclaim new landscapes? Their real-estate values may be low in normal market terms; what social value do we set on them; and what ranking or comparative scale of values can we attach to alternative projects, each calling for relatively high costs either in capital terms or of profits someone must be persuaded to forego?

### Values in Environmental Impact Analysis

US legislation enacted in 1969 and operational from 1970 made mandatory the preparation of an environmental impact statement (EIS) for any proposed Federal development likely to have a significant effect on the human environment. Both the National Environmental Policy Act (NEPA) and the subsequent guidelines for the preparation of EISs are discussed in detail in Chapter 3. While NEPA is limited to Federal projects, some states have introduced their own EIS procedures which, similar to NEPA requirements, make it necessary to define environmental objectives and to determine qualitative and quantitative criteria which the designer must take into account and meet if the project is to have reasonable hope of approval.

The 'critical areas' programme in the USA is also focusing on areas clearly with problems, present or potential, and sharpening identification of those features which make the area critical or vulnerable to development pressures. Values have to be agreed for survey, and values for the goals to be set in attempting planned control or development.

The techniques of environmental impact assessment and the merits of impact assessment statements are described in the next chapter.

### Relationship of Survey, Analysis and Evaluation

There is a long tradition of collection of landscape survey material and the collection processes have been refined, especially with the assistance of specialists able to help with factual information on geology, geomorphology and the like, and the compilation or retrieval of data on climate for example. Classification introduces some sense of order to cataloguing in the inventory. Choice of classification can have an important influence on the usefulness of the survey data. Analytical techniques have moved apace, progressing from simple cartographic analysis to more refined network techniques and the application of computers to both numerical and graphic sorting of complex inter-relationships (see Appendix 2). Again specialists have been able to help, for example, in their ability to interpret climatic relationships and make forecasts of statistically probable means and extremes relevant to the landscape planner. A word of caution must be inserted here, however; the processes of survey, classification, analysis and evaluation are essentially complementary. The stock-taking and inventory stages of landscape survey and classification have little value in themselves; information has to be collected and stored in ways capable of processing at the analysis stage and then interpreted for meaningful evaluation. It is likely that the adoption of impact analysis techniques will sharpen the evidence collection stage, pointing it more selectively to assembly of evidence capable of evaluation upon which decisions can be based. So, for example, a so-called ecological survey will more likely be an analysis, a systematic consideration of interrelated facts of plant distribution, soils, climate and biotic influences.

## Analysis and Synthesis of the Plan

Limited experience to date suggests that environmental assessment techniques need not necessarily be restricted to impact studies of completed development proposals. Environmental assessment can be a formative feature in landscape planning. As a single plan develops or as alternatives are considered, successive examinations can help in the objective selection or rejection of possible options.

## Ecology and Landscape Analysis

The ecological approach to landscape work has provided a useful conceptual framework in which to examine landscape and consider relationships. Some of the writers on this ecological approach have been less than explicit in what they mean by ecology. Many, in common with this writer, lack scientific training in fundamental ecology. They express the virtues of the method as a creed either defying or not needing careful explanation. Before graduating to landscape planning the landscape architect needs to spend some time on maturing his understanding of ecology. This is now possible at several levels. First, the current full-time training of the student on both undergraduate and post-graduate landscape courses now includes a high ecological content. Most courses have progressed from an interim arrangement by which service teaching was obtained from related specialist departments or even outside institutions, to one in which they have their own 'in-house' ecologist as a full-time member of the teaching staff. The ecologists

themselves have had to undergo a kind of professional transformation to acquire some of the understanding and skills of the planner and the landscape architect, and to integrate their teaching in a way useful for professional as well as academic purposes. Secondly, the ecologist has become an acknowledged member of the landscape team. From occasional consultancy involvement in multi-disciplinary teams he has progressed to a full-time specialist, particularly in the environmental teams established by many planning authorities in their staffing reinforcement which accompanied reorganisation of local government in England and Wales in 1974 (in Scotland in 1975). Finally the status of the ecologist has been recognised by the Landscape Institute in Britain by the recent decision on professional expansion to include land scientists as members of equal status to those qualified as designers.

Understanding of the reciprocal relationship of organism and habitat can introduce a proper degree of caution and reduce the likelihood of some planners promoting development in the countryside which could be quite disastrous ecologically. At the present stage of development of both ecology and the landscape profession it is perhaps fair to assert that the greatest value of the ecology approach is to provide an explanatory framework. It is interesting to note that ecological analogies have been employed to help illustrate the complexities of activity and change in urban situations. There has been a jump from that point to systems networks and models, capable of analysis and for use systematically to predict change consequent upon specific investment, transportation, location and density policies for example. Some of these town planning models, however, display a simplification which is startlingly crude when compared with real life, especially that of the biological real world.

## Evaluation and the Plan

In appraising a *territory* the next stage after analysis may seek to determine values; in appraising alternative *projects* the next stage is the comparative one of weighing advantages and disadvantages, and evaluating from a landscape point of view that which indicates the 'best buy' in a given situation.

To be effective the landscape evaluation has to be demonstrated in ways which will permit those concerned with reconciling several evaluations (e.g. accessibility and transportation, employment and industry) and preparing an over-all plan to make proposals. The landscape plan will seldom exist in its own right, but is more likely to arise complementarily to other planning proposals which may be expressed in terms of social goals, budgetary provisions and administrative arrangements, as well as physical land use designs. The evaluation must then be meaningful to fellow professionals and administrators and be such that it is likely to gain support either direct from the general public or by the politician acting in the public interest. It is the quest for evidence that has led to attempts to define criteria and to use as far as possible objective and tangible reasons for supporting landscape planning proposals.

## Applied Landscape Planning

### The Resolution of Conflicts

In most developed and developing countries urban expansion is seen as a threat, an encroachment upon the existing landscape. This is true on the periphery of all towns, and drastically true between towns in conurbations. The extensions of residential development are themselves substantial, but can be checked by relatively simple devices, such as the adoption of comprehensive zoning ordinances which impose 'green belt' restrictions. The green belt planning technique has been very effectively used in England and Wales since 1955 (2.1). Industrial developments are more difficult to control, however, especially those which are related to extractive processes and so are severely limited in location to those places where minerals are found. Planning methods can be used to secure orderly working, screening by planting or other methods, and site reinstatement, as discussed in Chapter 8. Visual intrusion can remain severe, however, and some national park areas contain extensive quarry workings, cement works, chimneys and the like. Electricity authorities have successfully opposed biological and visual objections to power plants being sited on fine coastlines.

The large-scale intrusion of these urban and industrial developments is matched by a host of minor local intrusions which good detailed planning should seek to minimise. For example, playing fields on the edge of residential expansion can act as a buffer to reduce trespass on farmland (see page 111). Careful road alignment should seek to avoid severance of farm holdings in rural areas. In urban areas the newly introduced motorway should avoid severance of residential areas from their community facilities—shops, schools, playing fields and parks. (The problems of severance are considered in detail in Chapter 7, pages 198 and 204.)

Ambitious plans of environmental improvement are needed where land has become degraded and derelict, or is in danger of becoming so. The blighted character of these landscapes is self-evident, but it takes more than enthusiasm to implement land reclamation in such cases. A very careful appreciation of root causes of degradation is needed. Does the dereliction result from misuse, overuse, or abandonment and subsequent neglect? In Britain, a very narrow definition results in only the latter (disused) category being officially recognised as derelict for the purposes of land reclamation financed from central funds. Meanwhile, new dereliction, including the misuse kind, has proceeded at a rate which has outstripped cosmetic and engineering landscape reclamation (page 251). The real problem of misuse of land has not been solved. It will be necessary for planning authorities to secure a bond or payment into trust funds to ensure that extractive industries especially set aside funds for initial, progressive, and reinstatement landscape work. As discussed in Chapter 8, planning consents imposing restoration conditions can become ineffective if developers change their plans, their corporate structure, or go into liquidation. So landscape planning may involve farsighted financial provisions as well as direct design and planting techniques, themselves complex in biologically and visually degraded landscapes, and hopelessly ineffective if not backed by funds in scale with the problem.

Landscape planning also requires a better understanding on the part of the planner of the economic restrictions and the technical limitations on location and methods in many industrial processes. This is especially true of minerals extraction. The knowledge of the planner does need, however, to be matched by a clear understanding on the part of the minerals operator of the role of planning and the need to meet reasonable environmental criteria. The Stevens Committee examined this problem, taking evidence from operators, planners and landscape architects. Its report in 1976 (2.2) was an excellent study but without any drastic or far-ranging solutions.

Only a few planning authorities, mainly in northern counties of England, have applied an imaginative and vigorous approach to landscape improvement. Some of these have engaged landscape consultants at both strategy and project levels. Others have expanded their own professional teams and set up direct labour organisations with the backing of funds from central Government for environmental improvement and in some cases as part of job creation schemes.

Farming communities find themselves under intense competition to catch early markets, produce heavy crops, carry more stock per hectare and generally squeeze all they can from the soil. This pressure, if accepted, can lead to unbalanced specialisation in crops and stocking, intensive methods of fertiliser treatments, cropping and harvesting. Hedgerows are removed and irrigation methods introduced. As described in Chapter 4, the visual changes can be drastic, and some fear that the same may become true biologically. Few agricultural countries appear to have a balanced overview of these rapid changes. In urban areas the system of community land management which we call town planning imposes a measure of control on intensive development of land. This is not yet so in agricultural areas.

The Countryside Commission for England and Wales has given a great deal of thought to the problem of change in agricultural areas. It first considered a countrywide monitoring programme to gauge the rate and significance of change. It then engaged consultants, including a landscape architect, to review and report on changing agricultural landscapes (2.3). More recently it has embarked upon a farms demonstration programme to try to influence the farming community by the example of actual farmers willing to experiment with methods of agricultural husbandry which have due regard for the scenic beauty of the countryside, and with the conservation of natural vegetation and wildlife, whilst at the same time giving proper economic returns (2.4).

Farmlands and the less intensively used rural areas, including those in marginal farming, no longer have the sole right to agricultural use to the exclusion of everything else. In the more spacious countries of North America the extreme is to set land aside as wilderness. Most European and some African countries have large nature reserves for conservation of plants and wildlife. The more densely developed countries have problems of public demand for access to countryside for recreation. Conflicts ensue, as discussed in Chapter 6, and specific landscape planning policies have to be adopted. They may be for exclusive recreation use of countryside or regional parks, or the publicly owned national park on the North American pattern; or forest parks, access arrangements, and the British style of 'national park' which remains in multiple private ownership and use, and may be managed to meet a variety of needs. The input of management is the most important factor in landscape planning here.

The management reports of the United States Forestry Service have been encouraging studies and model guides dealing with the resolution of conflicts in large-scale forests. Methods of visual appreciation have been illustrated, together with techniques for evaluation and the adoption of specific management policies (2.5). Problems of roads (2.6) and range management (2.7) and utilities (2.8) have been examined and management guides published.

The impact of forestry and farming on nature conservation in Britain has been the concern of the Nature Conservancy Council. Much of its experimental work can be carried out on nature reserves, but it has a wider interest in ecological affairs in the countryside as a whole, and has recently published (2.9) a balanced stocktaking account of the present situation in which there is an ever-diminishing area of land not subject to intensive management, draining, farming, fertilising and cultivation. 'Natural' habitats are being replaced by monocultures which are strictly controlled man-made regimes.

## Gauging Land Use Demands on the Landscape

Early post-war planning tended to make use of empirical techniques to forecast land needs for housing, industry and open spaces in towns. This approach characterises the new towns reports (2.10) for example. Then in the early 1960s forecasting of shopping space demand was needed for town centre plans, followed rapidly by interest in the prediction of numbers of vehicles and traffic growth, and car-parking requirements. The next phase of forecasting lay in recreation interests, which shifted emphasis away from the 'acres per thousand population' myths of organised games demand in urban areas to more rational studies of likely demand for rural and coastal recreation.

In the early 1960s the work of the US Outdoor Recreation Resources Review Commission alerted land use planners in many countries. The studies undertaken varied from the emotive and dramatic, implying vast demands as yet unleashed, to the sanguine attitudes of planning ministries, but fortunately backed by careful studies such as those by the National Parks Commission of England and Wales in its coastal survey conferences, which as well as identifying physical problems were able to consider recreation demands and possibilities and to highlight the visual consequences of increasing development pressures.

Landscape architects such as Sylvia Crowe had made early attempts to gauge the visual influence of new electricity generating plants and their overhead distribution networks (2.11). In her book *The Landscape of Power* we see illustrations of power station locations with zones of industrial influence, zones of visual dominance by the power station and zones of 'wirescape' dominance. The descriptions of degree and character are clear and backed by some geometric studies of intervisibility. This kind of measurement of visual intrusion has been progressively developed and is now a fairly standard technique to use (see page 78).

In other fields measures have been devised for different kinds of intrusion, for example noise, and in this case agreed standards have been adopted to relate decibel noise intensities (capable of instrument measurement) to the likely human response in different situations in town and countryside (2.12) (see also page 207). In parallel there have been studies to determine the effects of distance, ground moulding, and tree screening to reduce noise disturbance.

The difficulty with many of the landscape 'intruders' is that their intrusive effect extends far beyond the boundaries of the land they occupy. The dust of quarrying and cement works, and the aerial effluents from brickworks are examples. Instrumentation techniques are now available to confirm what our noses detect in the Peterborough area; and by careful observation of sensitive biological indicators, such as lichens, it is possible to detect changes less dramatic than the occasional scorching of sensitive young tree transplants. This work on the use of biological indicators has been carried out by applied ecologists working in a landscape planning context, and some of their reports have been published in *Landscape Design* and so made readily available to practising landscape architects (2.13, 2.14).

## Evaluating Resource Capacity

Capacity studies are concerned with determining site potential. At the extreme of territorial examination, the level necessary to permit natural regeneration of vegetation, or retention of existing character, may indicate restriction to a very low capacity. In a 'development' situation the study may be concerned with increased potential for timber extraction, water storage, game, recreation, and all without radical change other than more intensive management. In many projects, the planning problem may suggest the creation of an entirely new landscape which is better suited to new needs than the existing 'natural' landscape. In all these cases the landscape designer needs to know the various carrying capacities of the existing site and to have a clear understanding of ways in which a new ecological balance can be attained.

Most effective capacity studies carried out recently have been in the recreation field. Studies are, however, under way to extend our range of understanding of ecological aspects. It is well known that sites suffer degradation during building development; this can be repaired to some extent, but the degradation continues if use is intensified, for example, parkland changed to a university campus (see page 44), or normal rural landscape turned over to informal parks in new towns. Design to reinforce existing character and provide resistance to heavy use is the basis of much of the work of the landscape architect. In many cases this has to be done in environments that are already somewhat hostile to plant growth—reclaimed land, urban areas affected by atmospheric pollution and so on.

In urban areas there is a long history of refinement of design and intensive management techniques for municipal parks. At the national park scale, essentially the existing landscape is taken and protected relatively unchanged under low intensity management. The intermediate scales of countryside, coastal, forest and regional parks may, however, need new techniques of applied design and moderate to low-intensity management to manipulate their effectiveness to absorb increasing numbers of visitors without loss of their essential scenic and recreational qualities.

### Who Does Landscape Planning?

Relatively little landscape planning has yet been carried out, in the full sense of survey, plan, implementation and then monitoring of varying degrees of success. In the Netherlands, parts of Germany, the British Isles, Israel, the United States and Canada and, possibly, a few other countries, a little has been proposed, less started and only fragments completed. Correctly, progress has been coupled with major land reconstruction schemes, for example, land reclamation in the Low Countries and flood protection in river basins. The systematic study of problems and possibilities of landscape planning has started fitfully, building on the skills of many specialists, but has not yet really been drawn together as a mature academic or professional activity. Many landscape architects have appreciated the need intuitively and attempted empirical applications. With their training increasingly strengthened on the natural resources side and less tied to architectural design and urban planning, they have acquired some of the necessary skills themselves and have come into contact with scientists developing parallel skills. Notably the university departments of forestry, which have shifted research and teaching emphasis from crop forestry to forestry and natural resources, have provided the link, together with some of the necessary

expertise in ecology, wildlife conservation and resource management, hydrology and so on. The fusion has been more successful where large-scale regional planning studies have brought all these people together. Nearly all early regional plans include 'landscape' studies of the descriptive kind, with varying degrees of quality in survey information, its analysis and evaluation. Later studies are more thorough in their processing of information. The works of McHarg and Lewis in the United States and Hills in Canada showed this progression from the descriptive, with cartographic and graphic presentation, towards the rigorous analysis and evaluation. As might have been expected, the systems analysis and the computer men have been well placed to explore the problems; hence the later progress by Steinitz at the Department of Landscape Architecture at Harvard University (2.15). This work is characterised by computer analysis (designed for graphic display) (see Appendix 2).

At this stage it is possible to identify two kinds of client for professional landscape planning skills.

1. Those with territories or projects and a budget to enable *implementation* of planning (the customers) such as county planning authorities, national parks, new towns;
2. Agencies which commission or carry out *studies*, for example, regional planning teams, sub-regional planning studies, countryside commissions (e.g. in England and Wales, and in Scotland).

The skills may be in direct salaried employment but are more usually university departments and their research workers, or consultants who bring together *ad hoc* teams to do what is still very often pioneering work. The landscape planners usually have to present their analysis and evaluation in ways which are readily understood by other professional planners, and are capable of providing the basis of information from which political decisions can be taken and substantiated.

# Two Approaches to Landscape Planning

### Introduction

For the purpose of this chapter two approaches to landscape planning will be considered. The approaches are respectively labelled the *territorial* and the *problem solving*. They are categorised because at this stage of development of planning techniques it appears that applied analysis and landscape evaluation are likely to be different, depending upon whether they relate primarily to a territory (which may be large and general, or a smaller and precisely defined territory) or are built up around a specific problem. Size is not the main criterion, but as a generality *problem solving* is more likely to be concerned with relatively limited areas, whilst the territorial approach will usually be applied to very large land areas. A few examples in each category will help to indicate the broad difference between the territorial and the problem solving.

### Examples of Problem-Solving Landscape Planning

The problem can be taken as one professionally, socially and politically acknowledged to exist. The accommodation of industry in the countryside may be quoted. Manufacturing and processing industries and power production all have locational criteria and require sites with special qualities—flat, well drained, capable of taking heavy foundation loads, etc. Locational and site characteristics tend to throw up a limited range of possibilities; or, seen the other way, the less likely sites have been eliminated and the selection technique leaves only a limited range worthy of consideration.

Steelworks, oil refineries and power stations have highlighted this in the last 20 years or so. The modern steelworks may well be on a green field site and near to new deep water berthing facilities. Need to be within range of labour markets will not permit too remote a location, so the resulting site may be one on an estuary which is also valued as a regional recreation area. Oil terminals too need deep-water berths. Power stations, whether thermal or nuclear, have their own locational criteria, especially demanding in the latter case, having hitherto been sited away from well-populated areas in locations highly prized for qualities of scenic beauty and solitude. The discovery and exploitation of petroleum oil and natural gas in the North Sea has had acute consequences, affecting Scottish coastal areas in particular (see Case History 4).

The extractive industries have been particularly difficult as landscape problems. Opencast coal and ironstone workings have been large-area disrupters, but the coal and iron industries have been more systematic in the attempt to reinstate land than some others. Quarrying for the building and construction industries has been a serious intruder, with exploitation problems seldom solved by adequate landscape restoration. Sand, gravel, limestone for aggregates and cement, and clay for bricks, have all left their scars. It may be that newer, late 20th century working for chemicals and the more valuable minerals (potash, fluorspar, tin, lead and gold) will be by deep mining or by opencast strip mining in areas previously worked only on a very small scale. Minerals can, of course, only be extracted where they are found, but whether they should be, to what extent and by what permitted methods, needs to be resolved, especially in national parks.

The selection of routes for new motorways has shown the need to evaluate alternatives in their relative degrees of impact on the existing landscape (see Chapter 7). Early attempts in Britain, the studies for the Durham Motorway for example (2.16) were clearly aimed at problem solving, the objective being a landscape plan to deal with the visual corridor through which the road was routed. Some later studies, and those in North America, have been attempts to evaluate alternatives and discover those less disruptive of visual and other qualities of the landscape.

In the mid-1960s studies for new town development in Britain moved from the master plan for design in an already designated area to studies of a sub-region aimed at defining the land take as well as the design. In landscape terms this shifted the problem from landscape architecture or landscape design, which could shape only the open spaces within the town, to landscape planning, which could make an analysis of urban/rural relationships. The various alternatives of concentrated, clustered or dispersed town developments gave exciting opportunities to be evaluated as alternative town designs, each with differing landscape character and implications. Examples include Leyland-Chorley, Northampton and Peterborough. In the late 1970s we now have a curtailment of the new towns building programme.

These are all examples of problem-solving landscape planning, in which an industry must be accommodated or a road or a new town built in a manner least damaging to the existing landscape.

### The Territorial Approach to Landscape Planning

Development potential rather than existing land use tends to provide the initiative for territorial studies. Thus Canada with its vast areas of land provides a territory which can be examined prior to the establishment of more intensive land uses. In Britain the move from tactical problem solving has come at a time of the introduction of structure planning techniques, in the country areas as well as the towns. For too long the existing land use pattern has been the basis of both protection and projection. Strategic and positive planning has called for wider territorial appreciations to determine what might be permitted, or preferably, promoted. At county and sub-regional scales it has become increasingly obvious that housing, industry and recreational activities can little longer be contained within present urban land allocations. Further, the scale of demand is likely to be too great to curb and reconcile with other interests, especially those of rural communities. In examining land resources the emphasis has shifted to appraisal of potential. County planning authorities, for example South Yorkshire, have examined the countryside and devised techniques of landscape and environmental survey and map presentation aimed to provide positive guidance to development policies.

### Differing Techniques for Territorial and Project Landscape Planning

Territorial techniques allow the landscape planner to look broadly at all aspects of an existing landscape, to discover how it was formed, to find out the natural restraints which inhibit change, and the opportunities which exist for continued development and change. In project planning the field of study can be more closely narrowed to items strictly relevant to the problem. Deliberate comprehensiveness characterises the territorial approach, and empirical selectiveness the problem solving. Size is a contributing factor too, it being more usual to think of square kilometres in up to hundreds and thousands for territorial planning, and to use hectares as the measure for projects. Thus the survey, mapping and processing of information are likely to be of vastly differing detail, and one would not expect there to be standard or universally applicable approaches capable of adoption for the whole range of landscape planning.

## Landscape Management

Conventionally we think of land use plans, landscape planning, landscape design, as being implemented by actual developments within the framework of a master plan for the territory or a design for the project. With landscape work there is a growing appreciation of the way that the territorial plan or the project design must be achieved by a sustained process of management. Landscape architects looking at the project scale have long realised that their planning designs are only the first step in a long process leading to a mature design, and that a good eye and sympathetic maintenance are needed to achieve satisfactory results in the long term. Then designers or planners working at the larger scale are beginning to consider how they might mould the landscape of vast areas by modifying land management regimes. This husbandry of the land approach which requires a blend of aesthetic judgement and ecological understanding (such as helped to create English parklands) can be extended down to the smaller site with its controlled maintenance regime, or up to the national forest policy scale. This management approach is starting fitfully in Britain and has a great potential which has not yet been grasped by those dealing with areas as large as our national parks, for example, in which management techniques are more usually applied to exploitation of the recreation resource and to serving the visitor rather than the landscape itself. In the United States it is interesting to observe the contrast between the national park approach and that of the Forestry Service. The Park Service has expanded the visitor potential with built facilities, and there is some evidence that this has been achieved at the expense of landscape quality. Publications of the Forestry Service now devote considerable attention to visual management to modify and improve vast forest areas, even when they must accommodate roads and such utilities as overhead power lines. The analysis and evaluation techniques needed have required something approaching the forester's time scale. So as well as 'territory' and 'project' we must now try to grasp the implications of a management time scale of planning and design.

# Analysis

## Processing the Survey Information

The analysis follows the survey stage in any landscape planning work. In the survey there is a general collection of information involving map information, field work and specialist knowledge. At this stage it should be possible to identify components which together make up a landscape, and to note attributes of components or inter-related components. What qualities do they possess? Have they recognisable separate values? A mature landscape has a subtle blend of components, qualities and values, but it is possible to look at these analytically one by one and see.

Examination of recent landscape publications shows commonly recurring aspects of study. The practitioner with normal experience can rapidly sketch out a broad classification of *landscape character* and typify different parts of the countryside by their predominantly agricultural, afforested, downland, heathland, etc., characteristics. A more expert attack is needed to assess *landscape quality* which lies very much at the heart of evaluation and to which we must return later. In a developed landscape of land use—that is, one which derives its character and much of its quality from farming, forestry and other extensive land uses—an analysis of farming patterns, farm ownerships, and farmland quality will help towards an understanding of soil, climatic and other determinants which are the 'natural' aspects of a man-made landscape. The study is likely to lead to some assessment of *agricultural* value. The extent to which a landscape provides for *nature conservation* (or could do so with appropriate management) will normally be considered too. A study of existing use for *recreation* will reveal those characteristics which make the countryside attractive for leisure purposes, and provide the basis to estimate future uses and possible problems which may arise from over-use.

We next come to a range of analytical studies prompted by the nature of landscape planning problems. On the assumption that new elements are to be introduced the landscape planner will need to determine their *zones of visual influence*. This may be done arbitrarily for comparative purposes, or on the basis of intervisibility between different parts of the territory. Various aspects of topographic closure may be analysed, together with the modifying effect of vegetation which imparts varying degrees of visual transparency. *Studies of visual complexity* may be included, and some assessment made of the nature and number of *detractors* which reduce the quality of the scene visually (and perhaps aurally and biologically, e.g. roads, water and atmospheric effluents). An objective of some of these studies often appears to be an estimate of the absorption capacity of the landscape to accommodate housing, industry, recreation and so on, with or without design efforts to increase capacity.

For the purpose of this chapter the values which can separately be assigned to each landscape component will be considered under the heading of *analysis*. The attempt to combine values, thus arriving at an over-all landscape assessment, will be covered under *evaluation*.

## Landscape Units

Most published landscape techniques deal with the division of areas into units. These may be called zones, tracts, landscape units, areas of landscape homogeneity, etc. This subdivision or identification of zones may come at an early classification stage and provide the framework for subsequent detailed survey work; it may follow immediately after the survey and thus be a primary stage of analysis within each zone or tract; if the process of analysis is especially sophisticated, the survey material may be processed as a whole and the final zones or tracts then emerge at a late or indeed final stage of analysis.

Landscape tracts normally relate closely to natural features—ridges, watersheds, geological structure, for example, hence the relative ease with which they may be picked out provisionally and confirmed by successive characteristics or landscape components, themselves largely dependent on the same physiographic feature (Figure 2.1a). An interesting variation on the natural division is the kilometre grid square which is superimposed on many North American maps and on most European maps, including those of the Ordnance Survey of Great Britain (Figure 2.1b). This apparently arbitrary method has many advantages. It lends itself to computer storage, processing and display. The tracts are of equal area, so when quantitative methods are used direct comparisons can be made without the need for area adjustments. Much of the landscape planning work at Harvard makes use of information already available on data banks, and referenced on the grid system.

The Coventry-Solihull-Warwickshire sub-regional study makes use of the kilometre square grid. It may be helpful to quote from the section on countryside in that report (2.17).

'Instinctively it seemed that landscape was so closely related to physical features, that its appraisal should begin by defining natural zones such as valleys, steep slopes and ridges. An attempt was made to do this by using ridge lines in order to determine areas of visual containment. Spot heights were assigned to every kilometre grid intersection throughout the sub-region by using the 2½″ OS maps and interpolating to the nearest 10 feet. Working along each grid line it was then possible to identify as a ridge each point where the spot heights on either side were lower. At such points a line was drawn on the map at right angles to the grid line and extending for half a kilometre either side of it. By working along all grid lines in both an east–west and north–south direction it was therefore possible to plot all ridge lines.

The problem was how to measure individual fac-

tors. In certain cases this in itself was not easy, but the difficulties were always magnified when zones of irregular shape and size were used. To alleviate this the idea of using units of uniform shape and size was pursued.

Finally the kilometre square was adopted as the base unit and all measurements made at this level. Primarily this was to conform with the Study's other data which were being collected at this level, but, apart from those advantages of a standard unit which we have already mentioned, the kilometre square proved to have other subsidiary merits, especially when measuring areas, and with the benefit of hindsight has proved a most useful unit. In passing, it is worth mentioning that although a regular cell seemed inappropriate for a landscape evaluation, providing that the mesh is sufficiently fine in relation to the area to be covered, its rigidity will almost disappear.'

Figure 2.1a    Natural boundaries

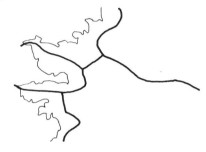

Figure 2.1b    Grid

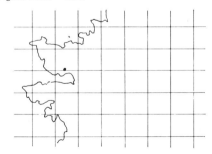

Figure 2.1c    Natural boundaries generalised to grid.

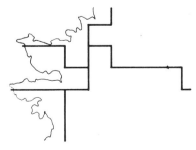

Figure 2.1    Landscape units. Three means of defining boundaries: 1. natural boundaries; 2. grid subdivisions, the grid edges being used; 3. natural boundaries used as the basis of definition, but generalised to the edges of the kilometre grid.

## LANDSCAPE UNITS

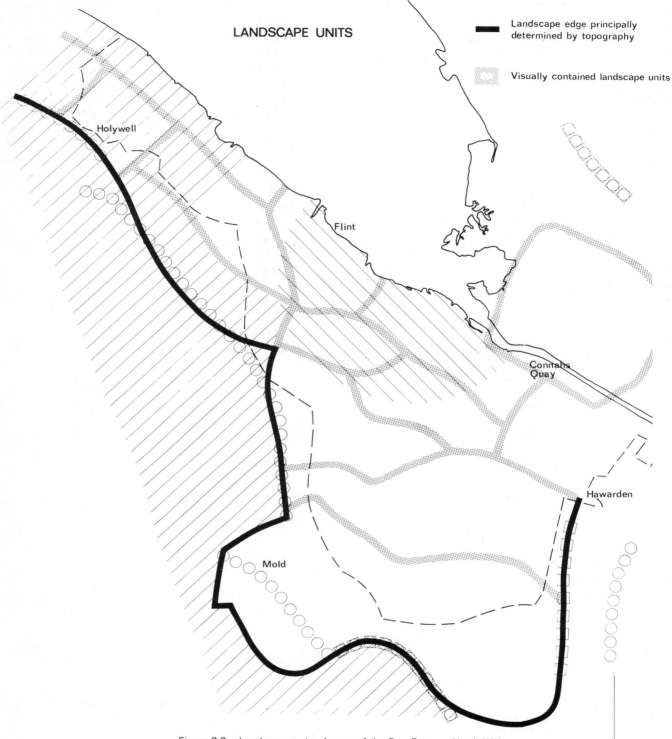

Figure 2.2    Landscape units. A map of the Dee Estuary, North Wales, showing a landscape edge principally determined by topography and visually contained landscape units.

Where there are good reasons for using the 'natural' boundary as the basis for tract definition (Figure 2.2) this can be generalised to the kilometre grid (Figure 2.1c) and the modified tract then used for statistical analysis of data.

### Land Form

Again, most published techniques indicate land form as a key characteristic of landscape and accordingly make some form of analysis. The mere facts of topography, as survey,

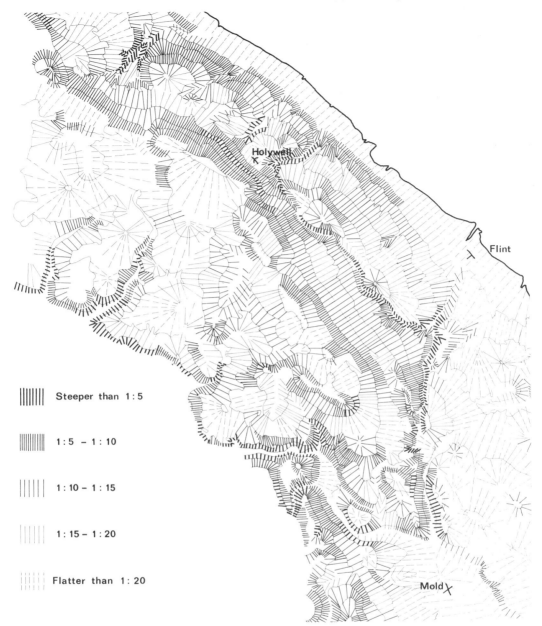

|||||| Steeper than 1 : 5

|||||| 1 : 5 – 1 : 10

|||||| 1 : 10 – 1 : 15

|||||| 1 : 15 – 1 : 20

|||||| Flatter than 1 : 20

Figure 2.3    Land form. A conventional slope analysis map picking out various degrees of slope of land in Flintshire, bordering on the Dee Estuary.

and shown by contour maps, are not enough and usually special analysis maps are prepared. The conventional slope analysis map is the most simple example in which areas between contours are picked out with slopes up to say 1/40 (2½%), 1/20 (5%), 1/10 (10%), 1/5 (20%), and so on (Figure 2.3). This analysis may be extended to cover aspect, picking out south-facing or north-facing slopes, or any other aspects considered significant for a particular territory or problem (Figure 2.4). Alternatively the analysis may use grid squares as the basis of study and representation. For small-scale work to assist site planning for the new Heriot-Watt University campus site at Riccarton near Edinburgh

the 100-metre grid was used, each square having drawn in the direction of slope and its gradient (2.18) (Figure 2.5) (see also page 44). The 1-kilometre grid was used to give an axonometric representation of the slope analysis for the Warwickshire study (2.19). This last example also extended the grid and axonometric technique to examine and illustrate intervisibility between the 1-kilometre grid square landscape units. According to the nature of the problem and the territory, such techniques can be devised to pick out features significant in particular circumstances. The grain, lumpiness, variability, or consistency of slope features can be examined and portrayed.

Figure 2.4   Aspect analysis. This map is an analysis of slopes on the Flintshire coast which are steep and of poor aspect and thus less advantageous for development in this northerly part of Britain.

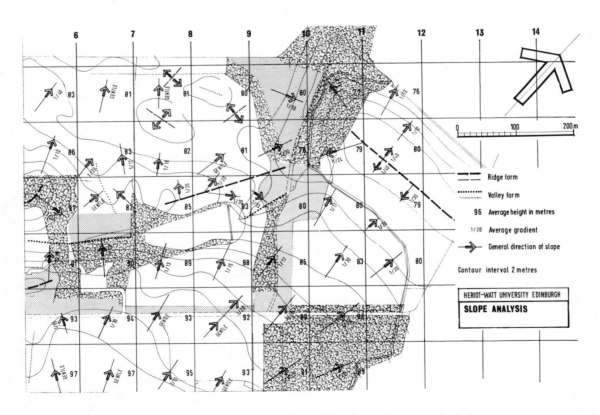

Figure 2.5   A detailed analysis of individual grid squares used for preliminary layout studies for new campus layout for Heriot-Watt University at Riccarton, Edinburgh.

## Intervisibility

Land form studies may lead to capability studies (relationship of slope and development potential), to assessments of micro-climate, or to some form of intervisibility appraisal. In *project* planning this may be done to determine those areas from which proposed developments would be visible or visibility modified by topographic cut-off lines, e.g. studies for the proposed siting of power stations, oil refineries and steel works on the Clyde Estuary (2.20) and a nuclear power station on the Dee Estuary (2.21) (Figure 2.6) In *territorial* planning the intervisibility study may be used to analyse the extent to which areas will be visible from each other (from which later may be evaluated the extent to which they mutually contribute to complexity and diversity of view, reveal more abundantly special scenic qualities, or adversely affect each other by exposing landscape detractors to a multiplicity of view points (2.22)).

The presence (or absence) of conditions of intervisibility can fairly readily be determined by ground survey or by analysis of simple geometric sections set up from maps (Figure 2.7) (see page 44). To measure the amount is more difficult. Quantitative measurement can take into account full views, partial views, and the effects of distance. For a proposed new development in the landscape it may be desirable to adopt a scale of values and define an immediate or dominant *zone of influence* in which size of object, nearness and absence of screening and all other aspects combine to give clear intervisibility and strong visual influence. The next zone, beyond the first, may be accepted as less dominantly influenced. The boundary between these two zones might have to be determined subjectively. If several similar developments are being considered in a particular landscape, an arbitrary distance for selection of the boundary may suffice for the like-with-like comparison of alternatives.

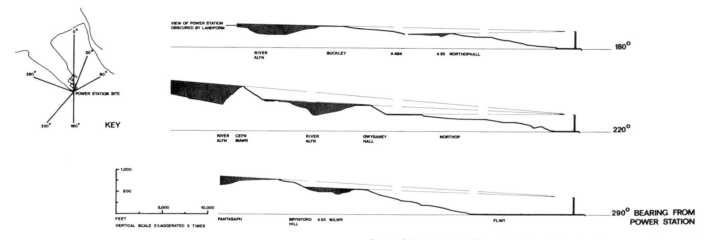

Figure 2.6    Intervisibility. A study to determine those areas from which a proposed nuclear power station would be visible in its proposed setting in the Dee Estuary. Radial sections were drawn at 10° intervals, focussing on the power station. Sections at 180°, 220° and 290° bearings are illustrated here.

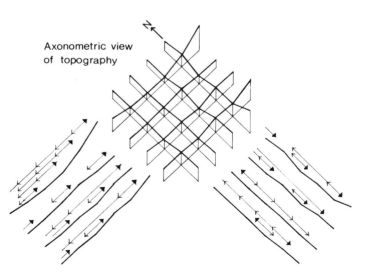

Axonometric view of topography

Figure 2.7    Axonometric representation of land form. Sections drawn along the grid lines indicate intervisibility conditions between areas. This method was developed in the Coventry-Solihull-Warwickshire study. Computer techniques are now being developed at the University of Sheffield to enable rapid application over large areas.

Going a stage further it may be necessary to determine not only the zone of influence of an intrusive object in the landscape but also its degree of visual intrusion. *Visual intrusion* studies have been developed by consultants working on urban motorway problems. They have reached the stage where it is possible to measure fairly accurately the degree of intrusion in the street view, or a householder's view, of a built object such as a road elevated on structure or on an embankment. The solid angle of the object subtended to the view point is measured in steradians, by a protractor overlay of a fish eye camera view taken of the object (2.23). For examination of new proposals, perspective drawings can be set up with the new structure superimposed on the existing urban landscape. Protractor overlays can then be used to assess the degree of visual intrusion by measurement of the solid angle.

The solid angle is a first-stage quantitative measurement only, the basis of fact from which visual intrusion may be assessed in qualitative terms. Account can be taken of the greater intrusiveness of an object nearer to the centre of the picture, within the modified cone of binocular vision and perceptiveness. But what about perception and response? The studies still need to be developed further to discover responses to varying degrees of intrusion, possibly to establish acceptability thresholds.

At the request of the Department of the Environment (now once again Ministry of Transport), the Transport and Road Research Laboratory (TRRL) has been conducting tests on reactions to road proposals. For this photo montages with moving vehicles have been superimposed on to colour ciné film views of actual landscapes. The technique is interesting, but research workers generally are divided on the accuracy of responses gained from photographs of landscape. It has been found, for example, that the response can be influenced by the caption, and in the case of the TRRL films of vehicles on new roads in the landscape a specialist viewing group complained that the background music unfairly influenced the degree of intrusion or acceptability of the proposals.

## Agriculture

In the case of a rural landscape which is under extensive use, for example for agriculture or timber production, the landscape analysis will seek to discern the broad classes and levels of production.

At the most basic level this may involve a resources evaluation which tries to assess farming potential from analysis of soils, climate, drainage, access and so on. This kind of analysis and evaluation is exemplified in the ecological land use planning study published by the Ontario Economic Council (2.24). The study notes that the combination of soils and climate in the area considered produces a high potential for biological production but then goes on to note features such as steepness of slope, erodibility, extreme stoniness or shallowness to bedrock and extreme openness of soil materials which limit potential for cropping. The study gives consideration to both short- and long-term farming potential. The short term takes account only of the limited improvements likely to be made by individual farmers. The strategic value takes account of what could be done with Government aid to assist long-term agricultural development.

Most developed agricultural communities have graded their agricultural lands and attached values to them, that is, separate from the market values of the farmland as real-estate. The grading now being used by the Ministry of Agriculture in England and Wales must be mentioned here.

Quotations from the explanatory notes which accompany the Agricultural Land Classification Map (2.25) are as follows:

'The map classifies land into five grades on a national basis. The major non-agricultural areas are also shown; existing urban areas and land scheduled for urban use are coloured red, and other areas primarily in non-agricultural use, e.g. woodland and large open spaces outside the built-up areas, are coloured orange.

The agricultural land is graded according to the degree to which its physical characteristics impose long-term limitations on agricultural use. The limitations operate in one or more of four principal ways; they may affect the range of crops which can be grown, the level of yield, the consistency of yield, and the cost of obtaining it. Ability to grow a wide range of crops (including grass), whether actual or potential, is given considerable weight but it does not outweigh the ability to produce consistently high yields of a somewhat narrower range of crops.

The main physical factors which have been taken into account are climate (particularly rainfall, transpiration, temperature and exposure), relief (particularly slope) and soil (particularly wetness, depth, texture, structure, stoniness and available water capacity).

*Grade I:* Land with very minor or no physical limitations to agricultural use. The soils are deep well-drained loams, sandy loams, silt loams or peat, lying on level sites or gentle slopes, and are easily cultivated.

*Grade II:* Land with some minor limitations which exclude it from Grade I. Such limitations are frequently connected with the soil; for example, its texture, depth or drainage, though minor climatic or site restrictions, such as exposure or slope may also cause land to be included in this grade.

*Grade III:* Land with moderate limitations due to the soil, relief or climate, or some combination of these factors which restrict the choice of crops, timing of cultivations, or level of yield. Soil defects may be of structure, texture, drainage, depth, stoniness or water-holding capacity. The range of cropping is comparatively restricted on land in this grade. Some of the best-quality permanent grassland may be placed in this grade where the physical characteristics of the land make arable cropping inadvisable.

*Grade IV:* Land with severe limitations due to adverse soil, relief or climate, or a combination of these. Land in this grade is generally only suitable for low-output enterprises. A high proportion of it will be under grass, with occasional fields of oats, barley or forage crops.

*Grade V:* Land with very severe limitations due to adverse soil, relief or climate, or a combination of these. Grade V land is generally under grass or rough grazing, except for occasional pioneer forage crops.'

The explanatory notes go on to point out that care is needed in interpreting the grades, for many reasons, including mapping accuracy, difficulty in determining boundaries between different grades and so on. Care is also needed when considering the agricultural *value* as well as the *grade*. Some of the best dairy farming is carried out on land which is *Grade III* but is not *third class* as far as that profitable form of agriculture is concerned.

Further, there are other matters than land capability studies and farm land grading to be considered in making an analysis of agricultural aspects of a landscape. It may be necessary to look at local farm change in the historical sense, to note long-term sustained change, for example, that made possible by continued improvement of drainage in the Fenlands at little above sea level, and short-term intensification in times of war and periods of low productivity occasioned by trade recession. The analysis may relate farm activity to farmers—how many farm units, what size, what economic strength they possess and what national subsidies they are getting to support present levels of productivity. Are they under severe economic pressure to surrender valley bottom lands which are an integral part of a balanced farmland gradient in which full value from fell farming needs a proportion of more sheltered land; or being bought out by minerals interests for quarrying; or near to growing urban areas and suffering from trespass?

In much project planning the purpose of the analysis will be to discover the likely effects of development. The positive qualities of soils and climate, which have offered potential or facilitated growth of farm patterns, will now be threatened by constraints and limitations which might reduce productive capacity, or profitability, or both. Farm severence, the fragmentation of holdings and increased difficulties of access and working brought about by motorway construction is one example. In Britain efforts are made to avoid severence, and minor adjustments of land ownership and tenancy can overcome some of the difficulties. But perhaps we are approaching the time when it is really an anachronism to fit 20th century communications to an 18th century (or earlier) land subdivision system. Do we need a new system of land enclosure—a new landscape planning—to give us the framework of a rural landscape suited to the 21st century? Certainly the landscape planner needs to develop analytical methods which can indicate the functional needs of the countryside of the future, and an aesthetic appreciation of ways in which this might achieve visual expression.

Only exceptionally will there be found anything like a 'national land use plan' for agriculture. Land use planning and zoning ordinances usually run out of steam at city limits. Although much planning legislation passes as town *and* country legislation, it tends to be restricted to negative control in rural areas and seldom attempts land planning, or redevelopment as in urban areas. Some small European countries such as Denmark appear to be able to indicate farm zones in planning maps (2.26). Studies for land use districts and regulations for the State of Hawaii, USA, did specifically examine and delineate farm land policies (2.27) where there are positive proposals for general rural and specifically agricultural districts, arising out of studies

prompted by knowledge that a stand had to be made before land use pressures cut too deeply into the agricultural economy.

The analyst is left with the scenic qualities of agriculture. Here it is usual for subjective choice to be made, with preferences expressed for certain kinds of cropping and field patterns, field divisions, associated ditches, faces, walls, hedges, trees, copses and shelter belts. The buildings associated with agriculture fall into this preference category, too, with a general ranking from the best hand-crafted barns and windmills, to the less acceptable silos, sheds and other structures using machine-made sheet materials. Clearly most people acquire an emotional attachment to the farm landscapes they know, and analytical techniques can do little more than provide an explanation of how the landscapes got to be that way and why they are changing.

**Woodlands**

In looking at woodlands we must bear in mind that the analysis is for landscape planning, so it is necessary to decide what relationships are important. The ecological approach will serve for natural woodlands; where woods have been eroded or developed by man the historical sequence of events may be helpful. Modern planting and cropping sequences have significant landscape impact, and the time scale of change will be important. Relationships to water, especially water catchment, and to people as recreationists will be significant. Finally the scenic effects of forestry will be relevant.

The ecological approach is exemplified by various analytical studies for the Potomac basin in the areas surrounding Washington DC (2.28). The study covered 1300 km² and was focused on the Washington Metropolitan Region. The aim was to discover areas within the region most suited to urbanisation. Woodlands here were really ecological indicators rather than woodlands examined only for their own resource potential.

In Britain two shifts in attitudes to trees appear to be emerging. First, the now public-spirited work of the Forestry Commission and the increasing maturity of their early forests have been accompanied by a marked decline in objections to the conifer. Secondly, there is an enthusiastic attitude towards new plantings of hardwoods wherever possible. Tree planting campaigns have been relatively successful, and are likely to be followed by even more vigorous efforts now that the results of Dutch Elm Disease are becoming so painfully obvious and we are beginning to note the loss of beech trees as well as a consequence of successive years of drought.

Visual qualities of national forests in the United States have been the subject of systematic study to analyse the changing viewpoints available to the visitor (2.29). In near-to-urban areas, study has concentrated on the relative degrees of visual transparency imparted by different numbers and species of trees (2.30). This kind of analysis might be helpful to assess degrees of absorption of urban development which would result through further planting.

## Conservation

At the largest landscape planning scale, the analysis will be concerned with world relationships in major wildlife problems, consequences of dam construction and accompanying alteration of river regimes, for example, on the African Continent, and so on (2.31, 2.32). Specific planning strategies may be concerned with protection of wilderness areas on a vast scale (2.33), or with attempts to put monetary values on relatively small areas of land set aside as nature reserves (2.34).

Still at the territorial scale, and not yet dealing with *projects* involving conservation interests, it is useful to look at some of the ideas put forward by Helliwell. He puts forward the case for nature reserves (there are a vast number in Britain which have been subject to a nature reserves' review). Next he divides them into categories in each of which there appears to be a specific need and to which a national value could be attached. His list is as follows:

'1   Direct returns—Income from the letting of shooting, etc. or the value of produce sold.

2.   Genetic reserve—Most natural communities possess a wide range of genetic variation. Diverse habitats clearly comprise a greater variety of species and, therefore, of genetical diversity, than uniform habitats.

3.   Ecological balance—The diversity and ubiquity of the community will govern its value, generally, as a buffer against violent fluctuations in the number of pest species in an area.

4.   Educational value—This will depend, to a large extent, on the accessibility of the area to students; on the availability of other suitable areas; and its resistance to trampling and collecting.

5.   Research—Depending on the nature of the research work, scarcity, accessibility, and diversity or uniformity may all be important factors.

6.   Natural history interest—Scarcity and diversity will govern the value of this, coupled to a lesser extent with the presence of 'attractive' species such as orchids or butterflies and with the accessibility of the site.

7.   Local character—Conspicuousness, scarcity and the number of people who see the plant, animal or community will govern its value in this connection.'

Helliwell goes on to suggest ways of computing cash values under each heading, for use in cost benefit studies for example. The method has been as much questioned as accepted (2.35), but it does give a useful start for analytical techniques aimed at deriving values.

It is difficult enough to attempt a scale of conservation values, and the present writer would not recommend attempts to assign monetary values.

## Landscape Character

It is a fairly straightforward notion that most landscapes have a distinguishable character. This character will be imparted by some combination of topography, vegetation, and farming or other use, and by analysis it is possible to detect these characteristics. In a small project area a single landscape character may prevail, and all we need to discover is the significance of special features in relationship to the problem in hand. For example, are there ridges which might lead to 'skylining' of new development or is tree cover so good that the area has a high absorption capacity, or is it undulating, calling for special care in alignment of a new road? In a territorial planning study, areas of like character will need to be detected. Often this can be done by eye and experience; on a country-wide scale, analysis of the survey material will pick out landscape types.

With a fine grain of check list dealing quantitatively with topography, more categories of woodland, fully classified field boundary types (fences, walls, hedges, etc.), agricultural uses defined, and man-made features noted, a more refined sorting system may be needed. This can be done manually, by mapping, by coding systems and orderly grouping of closely matching codes and so on.

Published landscape techniques indicate a wide and sensible variation of criteria used to evaluate landscape character. It is suggested that this variation should continue, it being unreasonable, and even illogical in many instances to set up meaningful criteria suitable for assessing vastly different landscapes.

## Landscape Quality

An interesting scale of landscape values was set up in connection with planning studies for the County of East Sussex Development Plan and has figured largely in the standard literature since then (2.36). For the study, described in more detail in Chapter 3, page 80, a provisional scale of values was tested to eliminate the personal bias in the subjective appreciation of a single landscape assessor. A scale of values was based on the mean value given to the test view by an observer group with design training and experience, and values of characteristic views were assigned on this scale.

Quality can be equated with attractiveness and this can be based on a subjective appraisal. Landscape quality classes are determined after discussions and preliminary surveys involving opinions collected from a variety of observers. Quality grading is not entirely of inherent quality, but can be weighted by scarcity value in some areas. So otherwise comparable areas, at opposite ends of a county, can be differentiated because of the greater value attached to attractive countryside which contrasts most markedly with the large blighted areas nearby. Two important issues are involved here. First, the final value of the landscape is modified from the inherent or intrinsic value to that which it acquires by association, i.e. it is worth more if people prize it more highly for some reason. Secondly, the relationship of adverse landscape features comes into play. A blighting feature within a landscape usually rates as a detractor, and has a negative effect diminishing the total or aggregate value. An area with enough detractors to be considered degraded or blighted may have a positive effect, upgrading an adjoining moderate-quality landscape.

Landscape detractors must be taken into account and this is done systematically in the East Hampshire study discussed further in Chapter 3, page 81. Grading criteria in this example are given as two main types; first, the basic structure of land form and secondly, the surface mantle which is largely affected by use. In this study considerable importance is attached to defining contrasts between vertical and horizontal elements in the landscape. The surface mantle criteria are related closely to tree cover, so for example, agricultural land with a landscape of hedges, hedgrow trees and copses in good order would have a high value. A high landscape value is also given to areas in a natural or semi-natural condition.

A project planning example is that of the Clyde Estuary Project (2.37). A technique was developed for the purpose of assessing landscape values in the Clyde Estuary where it was necessary to make recommendations on the effects of large-scale industrial development in various locations. We can look at this example as an illustration of the approach to more complex evaluations. It was argued that landscape is of value only where it is of some use to the community. The analysis had a two-pronged approach; to discover the nature of the physical beauty of the landscape and, separately at first, the extent to which its attributes were appreciated. The identification of various attributes present in the landscape and the measurement of the extent to which they were present was used to determine an *inherent* or intrinsic quality. The second stage, measuring the extent to which the landscape was appreciated or utilised gave an expressed or acknowledged value, termed an *acquired* value, that is, the additional value which it had acquired as a resource to be exploited. The total measure of landscape value was obtained by combining these two values to give *aggregate value*.

Ordinal methods of ranking for comparing the merits of different planning proposals are discussed in report extracts from work done by the Jack Holmes Planning Group in Scotland (2.38). Criteria are set out in importance classes and various arrangements in comparison matrices are illustrated. This study emphasises the non-arithmetical nature of the method, noting the need to avoid cardinal measurement, and compares aggregate and ordinal methods.

Another Scottish study which dealt with landscape quality was prepared by Land Use Consultants for the Countryside Commission for Scotland (2.39) (see page 82). In the study it is stated that it is considered unrealistic to compare the quality of landscapes of different types. The first stage in the quality classification is to identify primary landscape character types. Field survey is declared to be essential for assessing quality, as it is the total effect of the scene that is important, and this cannot be obtained from

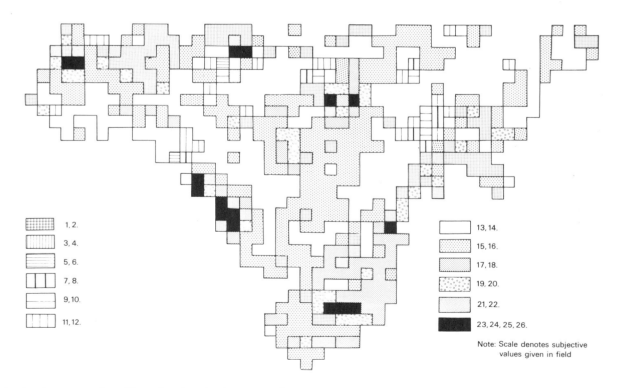

1, 2.
3, 4.
5, 6.
7, 8.
9, 10.
11, 12.

13, 14.
15, 16.
17, 18.
19, 20.
21, 22.
23, 24, 25, 26.

Note: Scale denotes subjective values given in field

Figure 2.8 Landscape quality. Map showing landscape quality assigned to kilometre squares on a scale of subjective values given in the field. (Coventry-Solihull-Warwickshire study).

photographs. The importance of identifying those elements which contribute to or detract from the total quality of the landscape is stressed, these being needed as a guide to planning future change.

The next example in this analysis section is a statistical analysis of quality values first arrived at subjectively. It is taken from the Countryside Report of the Coventry-Solihull-Warwickshire Sub-Regional Planning Study. Subjective scores of visual quality were given to each kilometre square in rank order form (Figure 2.8). Starting from a basic score assigned to typical flat farmland, other scores were added as points for good features and deducted for bad ones (the 'detractors' again) which appeared to be detrimental to the over-all quality. Finally this ranking scale was converted to a scale running from 0 to 26 with the visual quality scores relating to the inherent composition of each square in isolation, with no account taken of its effect on neighbouring squares or any influence they might have on it. The surveyors noted that the subjective appraisal had to be done under uniform weather conditions, as otherwise consistent scoring was clearly upset by the effect of sunlight in revealing shapes and detail which passed unnoticed under duller conditions.

Regression analysis was used to find out to what extent the variations between the surveyed factors (land form, land use and land features) accounted for the variation between the subjective visual quality scores given to those squares. The analysis indicated the weightings appropriate to each factor to reproduce the visual quality scores. Various checks and statistical adjustments were made to give the best fit. Correlation between field scores and the calculated values varied between 0.84 and 0.89, suggesting that subjective field scoring had been very consistent—which was vitally necessary if it could be used as reliable evidence for statistical work. The regression analysis was also claimed to show that 70–80% of the subjective variation between squares could be explained in terms of measured components.

The final stage in this part of the technique was to multiply all the landscape data for each kilometre square by derived weightings and then to sum them all to produce an index of landscape value for each square. This index represented the inherent quality of each kilometre square in isolation. The factors and stages used in this analysis are summarised in Figure 2.9.

This and related techniques used for the Warwickshire job deserve further study and development. They may be open to criticism on some aesthetic and statistical grounds, but they go a long way towards disposing of the erroneous belief that all landscape matters are intangible or not capable of measurement.

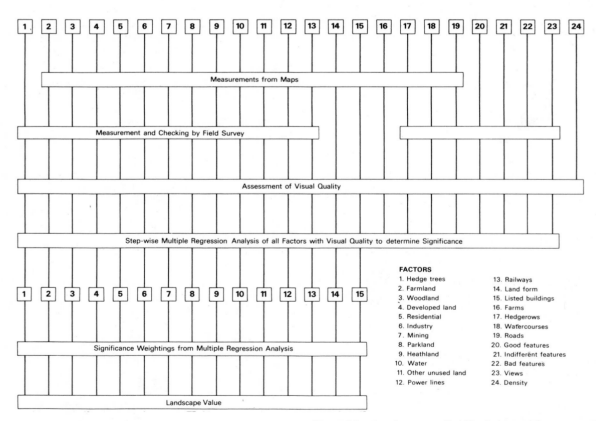

| 1 | 2 | 3 | 4 | 5 | 6 | 7 | 8 | 9 | 10 | 11 | 12 | 13 | 14 | 15 | 16 | 17 | 18 | 19 | 20 | 21 | 22 | 23 | 24 |

Measurements from Maps

Measurement and Checking by Field Survey

Assessment of Visual Quality

Step-wise Multiple Regression Analysis of all Factors with Visual Quality to determine Significance

| 1 | 2 | 3 | 4 | 5 | 6 | 7 | 8 | 9 | 10 | 11 | 12 | 13 | 14 | 15 |

Significance Weightings from Multiple Regression Analysis

Landscape Value

**FACTORS**

1. Hedge trees
2. Farmland
3. Woodland
4. Developed land
5. Residential
6. Industry
7. Mining
8. Parkland
9. Heathland
10. Water
11. Other unused land
12. Power lines
13. Railways
14. Land form
15. Listed buildings
16. Farms
17. Hedgerows
18. Watercourses
19. Roads
20. Good features
21. Indifferent features
22. Bad features
23. Views
24. Density

Figure 2.9    Landscape quality. The factors and stages used in analysis of landscape quality in the Coventry-Solihull-Warwickshire study. Regression analysis showed that 70-80% of the subjective variation between kilometre squares could be explained in terms of measured components.

# Evaluation

### The Aims of Evaluation

The practical straightforward objectives of evaluation were helpfully set out in preliminary papers describing research studies at the University of Manchester, promoted by the Countryside Commission, as follows:

'To assist the formulation of policies for the better protection and enjoyment of the landscape . . . .
To assist decision making by providing generally acceptable, broadly based, spatially defined landscape evaluation which can give rise to the minimum of dispute . . . .
To provide easily understood evaluation based on methods which can be readily applied with limited office resources of staff time and money.' (2.40)

The same papers go on to draw attention to other objectives, some of which it is suggested have received little attention hitherto. Two mentioned are: the need to assess potential for change and so the *design potential* in the landscape; and that this design potential needs a determination of the *absorption capacity* of a landscape. Landscape perception problems are also mentioned.

The report of the study has been published (2.41). It is an interesting compendium of research, but does not break much new ground by way of proposals for applied evaluation techniques.

We have seen that values can be assigned to many of the separate components of landscape in the analysis. However, the gradings or ranked scales of values allow us to compare like with like only. Thus one area has better farmland than another—one nature reserve has great diversity, is unique, has great research value, or in some other ways stands out on a scale of conservation values. Only occasionally is it possible to substitute money values for these rankings to help us trade off one value against another. If separate money prices could be determined for each component it might even be possible to determine a total which represented the total value of any landscape. We would then have to claim that this represented the social value and the price we should be willing to pay (or profits forego) to keep it unspoilt. The lack of a 'market' with the competition of willing buyers and a willing seller would mean that this would reflect its worth in the landscape sense and not as real-estate.

Economists would like to see the development of quantification and (if possible) monetary techniques, but are themselves at present unable to offer any. This is not intended as an unkind comment; the problem is a difficult one and much is still to be learned. It is likely that progress will be in parallel with the development of cost benefit techniques in town and country planning. On the urban side these are fairly well developed already (2.42, 2.43). They are somewhat less well developed in the rural sense to help

resolve conflicts of agricultural versus urban expansion, agriculture versus forest development, and to deal with recreational uses of rural land (2.44, 2.45).

At the analysis stage it may be reasonable to consider 'landscape as landscape', a resource in its own right, and try to fix a scale of values methodically detached from the natural and land use factors which go to make up landscape. This remains a component value and one which in landscape planning goes forward to the summary evaluation which we are dealing with now. The real aim is to produce evidence which, when considered with other planning criteria, will ensure that due weight is given to visual, biological and other landscape factors, and will secure the protection or evolution of a satisfactory landscape. To do this it should be possible to assemble aspects or relationships revealed in the analysis and present them as landscape evidence, if possible as a composite landscape value.

### Casebook Evaluations: Territorial Planning

We can now illustrate some casebook examples to see how various planning and landscape studies have tried to provide composite values to meet the straightforward objectives listed by Laurie.

The first casebook example relates to work done by G. Angus Hills who was the chief research scientist in the Ontario Department of Lands and Forests until 1967. He is a soil scientist, physical geographer and forest ecologist interested in the productivity of land and water, taking into account their biological and ecological potential for forestry, agriculture, wildlife and outdoor recreation. His

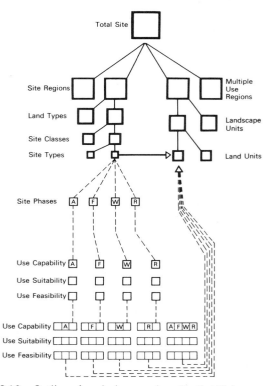

Figure 2.10　Outline of analysis procedure (A. G. Hills)

procedure for total site analysis is to subdivide the territory into smaller physiographic units on a graded scale of climate and landform features as illustrated in Figure 2.10.

The problem of evaluation here is to distinguish between the land's true potential (capability), its existing conditions (suitability) and its present and forecasted socio-economic conditions (feasibility). Hills' solution is the development of three kinds of evaluation—capability, suitability and feasibility. The interested reader should refer to (2.46).

The next casebook illustration relates to work by Philip Lewis, a North American landscape architect and resource analyst, planner and designer, who is interested in the environmental qualities and values of both the natural and man-made landscape. Lewis stresses public awareness of natural and cultural patterns within the landscape. He seeks to 'identify, preserve, protect and enhance the most outstanding intrinsic values and see that introduced man-made values are developed in harmony with these quality resources'. He has a professional interest in preserving outstanding patterns of perceptual quality, and stresses the need to work with other disciplines to identify, preserve and enhance cultural patterns. His work shows the commonly recurring division into intrinsic values and those created by man-made changes which he terms extrinsic values. For his work on recreational resource patterns Lewis makes inventories on the basis of diversified recreational experience. The sequence of analysis is illustrated diagrammatically in Figure 2.11.

The evaluation has to seek to determine priorities among the diverse natural and cultural resources which combine to determine the quality of the environment. Lewis' solution is to assign points for major features,

additional features and groupings, and so provide a numerical system for ranking. Thus he has a way of assigning non-monetary values to these resources.

The third casebook example is of work by Ian McHarg, a Scottish-born landscape architect who went to the United States to study, teach and practice. He is concerned about the ways in which natural processes should be acknowledged as influencing regional planning. He views ecology as the framework of understanding for landscape planning, and sees the landscape architect as bridging the gap between the planning and design professions on the one hand and the natural sciences on the other hand.

The four major values McHarg attributes to natural process are:

1. Inherent qualities.
2. Productivity of the process (agriculture, forestry, recreation).
3. Maintenance of ecological balance.
4. Potential hazards of mis-use of natural processes or resources.

The sequence of analysis through to evaluation is illustrated diagrammatically in Figure 2.12.

McHarg has also developed appraisal techniques for the evaluation of alternative proposals, demonstrating these for major highway projects. The inventory information is mapped, each quality, attribute or constraint being weighted and expressed on the map in tone values. The map overlays are combined, revealing the areas of 'least social cost' in which the land corridor might best be fitted.

The Hills, Lewis and McHarg methods were the subject of a comparative study in the Landscape Architecture Research Office at Harvard University (2.47).

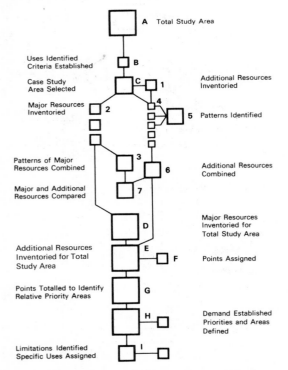

Figure 2.11    Outline of analysis procedure (Philip H. Lewis)

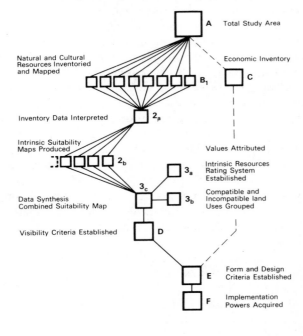

Figure 2.12    Outline of analysis procedure (Ian L. McHarg)

## Casebook Example: Project Planning

The three casebooks so far have been in the territorial planning category. A further casebook will be given, this time at the project planning level. The example is the Clyde Estuary Project (2.48). Within areas evaluated by techniques described above it was necessary to select industrial sites which in the McHarg sense would result in the 'least social cost'. Whilst McHarg's graphic technique was not considered applicable to the problem, the method adopted was fundamentally similar in that an attempt was made to find the development sites which would incur the 'least social cost' to the community. By this was meant all the costs the community is expected to bear as 'part of the price of progress'—pollution, visual intrusion, as well as the cost of upgrading communications systems, for example.

The method involves four stages:

1. Identification and classification of criteria;
2. Evaluating alternative development sites against each criterion;
3. Evaluating alternatives by group ratings;
4. Drawing conclusions from (3).

All the physical factors that might be expected to affect location were considered, as in normal planning procedure. The range of physical planning considerations to be investigated might be broadly similar in any land use problem, but it is obviously necessary to select those of particular significance to the problem in hand. The 'short list' selected in the Clyde study ran as follows:

1. Effect on atmosphere pollution;
2. Effect on water pollution;
3. Loss to farming and forestry;
4. Effect on nature conservation;
5. Loss to green belt;
6. Loss of inherent landscape quality;
7. Effect on acquired landscape value;
8. Cost of land prepared for development;
9. Cost in new housing or journey to work;
10. Cost in provision of suitable communications.

Each of these relevant factors was interpreted as a 'cost'. These factors did not first emerge in this order, but were continuum-listed this way as a sequence in which each item was very closely related to its nearest preceding and following item.

Classification followed readily:

*Environment*     items 1 and 2
*Land*                 items 3, 4, 5 and 6
*Socio-economic*  items 7, 8, 9 and 10

This application of least social cost analysis proved to be a useful working tool in helping to set out and classify criteria, and to provide working tables which, in an orderly way, recorded and ranked conclusions arising from interlinked series of evaluations and rankings. More systematic testing of weightings would be necessary to prove statistical reliability of all scoring methods adopted, but the risk of errors was reduced by adherence to the general principle of like-with-like comparisons. It would not be possible, for example, to use the scoring adopted here to compare with industrial development sites not possessing the general characteristics of those on the Clyde. Nor would it have been possible to compare industrial proposals with other enterprises such as large-scale recreational development, which was later suggested for one of the sites in question. For further applications, various refinements of individual evaluations might be possible, e.g. appraisals (similar to those developed for inherent quality and acquired landscape values) to assess loss to farming and forestry, loss to the green belt, or effect on nature conservation.

This particular evaluation technique was used in a planning study. The survey data had been collected, and planning considerations were being reviewed prior to setting out assessments and so making recommendations. Its principles were easily grasped by clients and co-consultants and the tables formed a basis for systematic discussion. Comparative ease and rapidity of compilation was a quality which made it particularly useful in a planning study that had to be undertaken in a short time.

## Casebook Example: Landscape Management, Territorial Scale

The United States Forest Service has contributed to landscape planning through the development of landscape management techniques. These have been built up by the fruitful collaboration of Forest Service personnel and the academic research of landscape architects such as Burton Litton of Berkeley University. His publication (2.49) is being followed up by a series of handbooks on national forest landscape management. Of these the publication on a visual management system (2.50) is described here. This example is important for a number of reasons including the following.

It is an example of landscape planning suitable for large territorial scales, although it can function at other levels of the land planning process.

The planning is to be achieved through a process of sustained management rather than once-and-for-all design.

It is a visual technique, but one which is to be applied by a systematic method.

The publication is meticulous in its use of landscape terminology, setting out and defining at an early stage some of the more important terms used and finally providing a glossary of more than 50 items. It is well illustrated, with colour photographs, maps and diagrams, and warrants careful study.

VARIETY CLASSES

The first stage is the identification of variety classes, that is by different degrees of variety. This gives a ranked evaluation of those landscapes which are considered to be the most important, and those which are of lesser value from the standpoint of scenic quality. The ranking is based on the premise that all landscapes have some value, but those with the most variety or diversity have the greatest potential for high scenic value. Three variety classes are used to identify the scenic quality of the natural landscape as Class A–distinctive, Class B–common, or Class C–minimal. For any type of landscape, a chart can be prepared to examine separate features which will evaluate the landscape with specific reference to that feature (Table 2.1).

Table 2.1. Variety classes used to identify scenic quality

|  | CLASS A DISTINCTIVE | CLASS B COMMON | CLASS C MINIMAL |
|---|---|---|---|
| Land form |  |  |  |
| Rock form |  |  |  |
| Vegetation |  |  |  |
| Lakes |  |  |  |
| Streams |  |  |  |

Vegetation might read as follows:

CLASS A–distinctive. High degree of pattern in vegetation. Large old-growth timber. Unusual or outstanding diversity in plant species.
CLASS B–common. Continuous vegetative cover with interspersed patterns. Mature but not outstanding old growth. Common diversity in plant species.
CLASS C–minimal. Continuous vegetation cover with little or no pattern. No understorey, overstorey or ground cover.

Map overlays can be prepared to locate classes for each feature and combined to give an overall rating for variety.

SENSITIVITY LEVELS
Sensitivity analysis is an important tool which takes into account both the inherent sensitivity of the landscape and the likely sensitivity of the visitor to its quality or to any intrusive element. In the Forest Service example three levels are used to measure people's concern for the scenic quality of the national forests. Level 1 – highest sensitivity; Level 2 – average sensitivity; Level 3 – lowest sensitivity. Routes, use areas and water bodies can be classified as being of primary or secondary importance. Then the major and minor concern of users for scenic qualities can be identified. People driving for pleasure, walking, camping, using lakes and streams, are likely to have a major concern for aesthetic charms or disruptions, whilst daily travellers, forest workers and commercial users are likely to have not more than minor concern. These evaluations can be combined to give a summary table of sensitivity levels (Table 2.2).

Maps can be prepared using the same base map as that used for determining variety classes. 'Seen areas' having

Table 2.2. Sensitivity levels

|  | SENSITIVITY LEVEL 1 | SENSITIVITY LEVEL 2 | SENSITIVITY LEVEL 3 |
|---|---|---|---|
| Primary travel routes, use areas and water bodies | At least $\frac{1}{4}$ of users have major concern | Less than $\frac{1}{4}$ of users have major concern |  |
| Secondary travel routes, use areas and water bodies | At least $\frac{3}{4}$ of users have major concern | $\frac{1}{4}$ to $\frac{3}{4}$ of users have major concern | Less than $\frac{1}{4}$ of users have major concern |

intervisibility with travel routes, specific use areas and water bodies can be plotted and distance zones identified as foreground, middle ground and background, and given their appropriate sensitivity levels.

QUALITY OBJECTIVES
The evaluation will now have taken account of the diversity of natural features, ranked in variety classes, and the sensitivity in terms of public concern for scenic quality. The management role next comes into play in deciding upon management objectives which might range from the extremes of preservation to maximum modification. Intermediate objectives could be retention, partial retention or modification. These objectives would be related to the values determined in the variety classes and sensitivity levels. Except for preservation, each management objective describes a different degree of acceptable alteration to the natural landscape, based upon its aesthetic value.

**Casebook Example: Landscape Management at the Project Scale**
This management example relates to a university campus on which the first phase of site development took place in the period 1969–77. The Riccarton site for Heriot-Watt University is just outside the city of Edinburgh. When work started its 100 hectares consisted of parkland, farmland, old shelter belt woodlands and some new forestry plantations. The layout of roads and buildings was designed in close collaboration with the landscape consultant, and careful integration of built form and natural features was achieved. This kind of design and integrated development has been possible to varying extents in Britain, York and Stirling each being good examples of a whole new campus designed to provide attractive settings for university buildings.

At Heriot-Watt, as soon as the first buildings and landscape developments were being completed, evaluation studies were set up in order to direct landscape management services on an informed basis. A Site Conservation Committee had already been established to ensure that a whole site approach prevailed in the design and development of the campus landscape. It was appreciated that substantial modifications would be inevitable but an attitude of good husbandry prevailed and had already ensured that layout decisions took as much account of the landscape as did matters of building and engineering layout. As a broad early appreciation it was accepted that there might be a division between intensive use areas and those 'outfield' areas where it would be more appropriate to retain existing natural features, protected if necessary, in relatively unchanged conditions. These two broad categories were drastically refined after ecological evaluations carried out in 1970–72.

ECOLOGICAL SURVEYS
As the basis of ecological evaluation surveys were carried out as follows:

*The Lawn.* An ancient lawn, originally attached to the old country house on the site was surveyed, using eight sample plots. It was believed that the more intensive university use and modern mowing, herbicide and fertiliser regimes might adversely affect the rich species mix.

*The Loch.* The natural watercourses and small artificial lake were important features which should be retained if possible. The loch had been drained and cleaned out, and some watercourses were threatened with culverting.

*Woodlands.* These had been analysed in detail at the beginning of the project and a forestry management plan proposed. With further experience of gale damage, some thinning and clearance, some new planting and observation of progress of young plantations, it was possible to review management policy with more diverse objectives in mind. This led to an assessment of how effective protection could be and a more mature understanding of nature conservation possibilities.

*Other areas.* An avenue of limes, a main footpath routed through woodland, playing field shelter belts, an old walled garden and sites awaiting development were examined.

BIRD AND ANIMAL LIFE
The observations were of particular value because they began to show evidence of typical changes in the bird life associated with increased development and disturbance. Eight breeding species were lost with the addition of only three new species. It was expected that the effects on wildlife would be adverse but that they could be minimised. Three classes of influences were identified; those essentially destructive and resulting in a downgrading of conditions; those which are natural or external to site development; and those where ameliorative action could be taken.

DESTRUCTIVE INFLUENCES
*Habitat destruction.* Clearance for site development had eradicated certain habitats.
*Disturbance.* The loch had lost its duck population, but it was thought possible that some would return on completion of building works on its north bank.

*Habitat alteration.* Loss of over-mature and senile broad-leaved woodland meant loss of tree nesting species. Abundant undergrowth is necessary for successful nesting of several species; rough grass is the favoured habitat of voles upon which certain predatory species feed.

NATURAL AND EXTERNAL INFLUENCES
*External changes.* The site could not be viewed in isolation. With farmland north and west, relatively little change might be expected, but residential areas east and south might encroach on to intervening farmland.
*Natural fluctuations.* Fluctuations might result from drought, severe winters, general population and behavioural changes, and be associated with natural vegetation succession.

AMELIORATIVE ACTION
*Habitat retention.* The deliberate retention of habitats could be of particular value. Potential nesting areas might even permit an increasing density and diversity of wildlife to take advantage of new feeding grounds within the estate.
*Habitat creation.* Extensive new planting should provide new areas of indigenous trees and shrubs which will gradually develop their own wildlife communities. New grassland habitats would provide new food sources for new bird species visiting the area.

DEGREES OF DISTURBANCE
Early landscape planning was based on two simple categories of disturbance as follows:
1. Areas of moderate disturbance, which could be kept in roughly their present condition (or relatively easily reinstated) given appropriate protective measures.
2. Development areas in which considerable change was inevitable, and although some natural features could be retained, substantial reinstatement works would be necessary.

From ecological experience a five-category scale was constructed as follows:
1. Areas with existing landscape features, including water courses and woodlands, which could be excluded from development and encroachment.
2. Existing areas which will serve development needs if managed in accordance with present garden, farmland or forestry standards.
3. Areas with principal natural features retained, but modified to open parkland and intensity of use.
4. Areas substantially modified and with few natural features retained. New planting will be essentially 'artificial', e.g. for playing fields, to provide gardens, or planted courtyards and areas close to buildings, all in areas of moderately intensive use.
5. Areas of heavy encroachment, with most natural features disturbed or destroyed, and where only minor reinstatement planting is possible because of the high density of development and intensity of use.

Table 2.3. Degrees of disturbance of natural conditions due to developmental pressures.

| HERIOT-WATT RANGE | | TOTAL RANGE |
|---|---|---|
| | 0 | Wilderness, either completely untouched or heavily protected |
| | 1 | Natural features intact Vegetation and wildlife remain in balance by natural regenerative capacity exceeding encroachments |
| Existing landscape features including water courses and woodlands which could be excluded from development and protected from encroachment | 2 | National park protection sustaining natural features, forestry, moorland, farming to amenity or nature conservation standards |
| Existing estate areas which will serve development needs if managed to present garden, farmland, forestry standards | 3 | Estate parkland, with farming, forestry and game areas managed to combine productivity and amenity |
| Areas with existing natural features retained, but modified to open parkland standards to suit moderate density of development and intensity of use | 4 | Suburban area parkland Low-intensity farmland |
| Areas substantially modified and a few natural features retained. New planting 'artificial', e.g. gardens or playing fields for intensive use | 5 | Large gardens, playing fields, low-density suburbia Normal farming |
| Heavy encroachment with most natural features disturbed or destroyed. Only minor reinstatement planting possible because of high density of development and intensity of use | 6 | Normal urban and industrial development at moderate densities Intensive farming and horticulture |
| | 7 | Industrial development areas High-density residential development City centres |
| | 8 | Heavy industry Large-scale extensive industry Derelict land Seriously polluted, disturbed, degraded land |
| | 9 | Natural features completely eroded Land entirely built on |

To set the five categories in a nature conservation through to full development context, a theoretical ranking was attempted extending from wilderness areas, parkland, and extending to areas in which all natural features have been completely eroded or entirely built over. This was done on a ten-point scale with the relative position of the Heriot-Watt range of conditions shown alongside (Table 2.3.).

## Limitations

It is suggested that values may be derived not only analytically from examination of systems and so on, but also from time to time be' postulated artistically, philosophically or scientifically. The latter group may be described as the products of human creativity. It is vitally important that evaluation techniques should permit these values by hypothesis to emerge, be created and tested. How would a project by Bridgeman, Brown, Repton or Olmsted have been evaluated by techniques now available? With hindsight we can answer that it would be relatively easy or even unnecessary. But we now need first the creative vision to provide landscape, and obviously on a territorial scale, a level of expertise to deal with present and future problems. Then we need the evaluation techniques to examine alternatives and help us decide which we rate most highly.

In contrast with survey and classification techniques, and to a lesser extent analytical techniques, the stage of landscape planning comprised in *evaluation* studies is underdeveloped and under-used. The means of collecting evidence have been refined, large masses of data can be provided, and analysed. To bring discernment and ranking to a calibrated scale of values appears to have presented greater difficulties. Certainly the policy decisions which are taken, plans proposed or developments carried out subsequent to the survey and analysis seem seldom to take much account of the landscape evidence collected. The weak link would appear to be in relative inability to determine landscape values which can be expressed with sufficient clarity or robustness to provide guidelines for development restraints upon encroachment by competing land uses.

## Subjectivity in Evaluation of Landscape

It is quite fruitless to suggest that in the development of landscape planning a prior aim should be the complete elimination of subjectivity. Landscape evaluation in particular, however systematic the methods of evaluation may be, will rest on subjective assessments at several points.

The wish to undertake landscape planning is a rational but subjective response to evidence which is sufficiently strong to convince some, but not so strong and patently obvious that it carries complete conviction in all levels of society. In any cultural environment only a limited number of people have the acuteness of perception to note with an awareness strong enough for them to respond effectively to change or degradation in their surroundings. Many of those who are able to perceive have a negative or neutral response, regarding the change as 'inevitable', 'natural', 'the normal consequence of economic progress' and so on. The latter can be persuaded, however, in part by rational argument, but more (one suspects) by a climate of opinion, a mood, and developing public attitudes, a cultural and political environment, that perhaps after all there is a human response set of values, to which they too should respond. It might be argued that this response is objective; it is in so far that it is a political response and not as a direct result of personal observation of environment itself. This 'second hand appreciation' may of course have a substantial value in the political awareness sense, in that awareness is likely to be coupled with a clearer understanding that solutions are being demanded to problems which are believed to be capable of resolution. Design, management, planning action, are implicit in the agitation which gives rise to this response. If the problem is recognised it is likely that the need to plan will also be recognised, and possibly accepted.

Having passed the first hurdle of plan or no plan there comes the problem of discovering just how people respond to landscape. What kind of landscape do they want planning to protect or provide? The perception and response field has not been very well studied in this respect, but one survey problem must be underlined; any questionnaire technique which focuses people's attention on an aspect of landscape tends to make them more acutely aware of something hitherto only dimly perceived at a level too low to provoke positive response. The post-question response may thus differ from the pre-question attitude. In the micro-time scale this may be the individual's parallel to the developing public attitudes noted above. He may ask himself 'What is the significance of the question? *Should* I consider the trees they ask about (or wholesome air, or solitude, etc.) as things which I should cherish, safeguard, protect, pay for, etc.?'. The socially motivated designer can accidentally or covertly use his survey techniques to propagate or manipulate landscape values.

We can next consider standards of judgement, taste, and attitudes towards landscape. These standards may be taken as the 'norm' or generally accepted view against which to judge the accuracy or validity of professional and expert thought. An elementary knowledge of the history of landscape appreciation soon reveals that the baseline of 'normal attitudes' is a shifting one, responsive after some lapse of time to the bias of expert views pressed with the greatest enthusiasm. Is the baseline at any time a worthwhile standard? Does it shift from, say, mountain to a gentle rural, to upland scene; even to the landscape of industrial archeology? Which of these do we value most? It is idle to protest that they are not comparable. They are not like-with-like terms to be ranked; but from time to time some of these are extolled and at others 'tamed', 'humanised', 'reclaimed'; cultural appreciation can move on from the romantic to the functional and back again.

Whilst some will be profoundly disturbed by this shifting baseline of values, the confident designer may feel less inhibited. If the appreciation of landscape is seen in human and cultural terms, it could be claimed that the vision and synthesising ability, the creativeness of poet, painter (and dare one say the modern ecologist?) will point in the direction of values to promote. The designer is of course likely to have an eclectic streak. His knowledge of the history of his subject or medium, research into previous successes and failures, his travel or contact with peoples and their landscapes will provide a grounding from which he may choose to extrapolate or to deviate.

## Ecological Values

The quest for values may be on a poetic basis, or aesthetic, or as at present have a somewhat scientific motivation. There seems to be a majority expression of expert opinion that landscape design today should have an ecological basis. Conceptually the idea is attractive, providing a unifying framework to the most complex landscape problem, whether it is at the smallest scale, or dealing with the vastest regional plan. Very strictly it could be argued that the sense of values should be extraneous to the eco-system, but at times one gains the impression that the ecological analyst attaches intrinsic values to the system, either undisturbed or modified only within acceptable capability limits. The study of the system and the ecological balance between its components gives the planner a sense of values to be used as restraints to development and planning.

The work in North America of such men as McHarg has been criticised as focusing on the 'natural' ecology of regions, disregarding or dismissing as irrational the equally natural but erosive behaviour of man, particularly 20th century man, with the vast amount of energy at his disposal. Even the 'energy balance' ecologists have until recently tended to ignore the energy inputs (and energy surpluses wastefully squandered) of industrial and late agricultural man and man the modern traveller. However, a better understanding of the 'natural' ecological balance could lead to improved codes and standards relevant to human exploitation of natural resources.

## Conclusions—Further Developments in Applied Analysis and Evaluation Techniques

The need remains for the further development of landscape evaluation techniques. They are needed in the territorial range to help with landscape planning studies at regional, sub-regional and county scales, to help formulate planning strategies and provide policies which, for example, would permit harmonious resolution of new urban and industrial development problems without visual and ecological disturbance of existing landscapes.

Various rural planning authorities have started to devise survey and analytical techniques for this work. It should be possible to make progress, for example on the lines of the Warwickshire Sub-Regional Study, to grade on a fairly reliable basis, the values of different landscapes in rural areas. In this example most of the landscape scores fell within the average farmland category, but the full range clearly picked out very poor areas in need of landscape improvement at the lower end of the scale. A notional threshold was suggested as the minimum acceptable residential environment, and special areas worthy of conservation and those ranking as 'areas of outstanding natural beauty' came at the top of the scale (Table 2.4).

Table 2.4. Sub-regional scale of landscape values*

| LANDSCAPE VALUE | TYPICAL COUNTRYSIDE |
| --- | --- |
| − 120 | Areas in need of environmental improvement |
| − 100 | Areas in need of environmental improvement |
| − 80 | Areas in need of environmental improvement |
| − 60 | Areas in need of environmental improvement |
| − 40 | Minimum acceptable residential |
| − 20 | Average urban area |
| 0 | |
| + 20 | Average sub-regional countryside |
| + 40 | Landscape worthy of conservation |
| + 60 | |
| + 80 | Landscape comparable to 'areas of outstanding natural beauty' |
| +100 | |
| +120 | |

*Table adapted from *Coventry-Solihull-Warwickshire: A Strategy for the Sub-Region, Supplementary Report No. 5—Countryside*, 1971.

Clearly it would be helpful if local authority development plans could take account of these kinds of carefully derived gradings both in promoting improvement and supporting protective policies. The Warwickshire studies were extended into urban areas, and in addition to giving fairly clear indications of urban landscape quality gave gradings which could be applied in further analysis, to examine likely risk and change which might be brought about by demolition, building development or other activities. It seems very important that new methods of evaluation, whether basically descriptive and on ranked scales, or given more precise numerical values on a calibrated scale, should be

capable of this applied use for correlation with other planning data; and an understanding of landscape potential must be evident as a basis for sensible structure plans.

It may be possible to look at special territories, for example, those with recreational potential, or problem landscapes such as those degraded by derelict land, and decide upon possible courses of action. With the immense land reclamation problems of South Yorkshire, for example, and its legacy of mining and industrial dereliction, it seems prudent to evaluate not only the present landscape quality but also the range of reclamation inputs likely to yield the best over-all results. It is well known that the real-estate values of individual reclamation projects are likely to be low in relation to costs incurred unless sites have very high potential for urban or industrial development. If examined together on a structure plan scale, the sense of values may change; first some sites may need relatively little treatment, others a minor cosmetic improvement, and the rest really serious engineering and landscape work. Evaluation techniques are needed to balance the input mix; then comprehensive evaluation techniques to assess the over-all landscape benefits likely to be achieved.

Structure plans are paralleled or followed by local plans (see page 14). It is here that we can appreciate the distinction made in this chapter between *territorial* and *problem-solving* landscape planning. Local plans are to provide more detail for application within the general approved structure plan. They are to take the form of maps and written statements. They are likely to need the more detailed analytical and evaluation techniques to examine problems and assess alternative solutions. Local plans can be in several categories, as follows (see also page 14):

1. *District plans* which could deal with parts of a rural county. A drawn land use plan is likely to be needed, and in the future it is to be hoped that these will show a greater appreciation of changes in rural economy.
2. *Action area plans*, for example for the design of a country park. A fairly detailed design capable of being carried out is needed here.
3. *Subject plans* such as those needed to deal with minerals or areas of outstanding beauty. Here the proposals which outline policies for development, or deal with systems of management might be more important than features which can be shown on a drawn plan.

Clearly these three kinds of local plan need differing analysis and evaluation techniques. It may be possible to draw on basic survey and landscape classification data, but processing will be geared to solutions appropriate to the problems and projects. Efforts have already been made to do this for urban motorways, taking into account noise, daylight, sunlight and severence as well as visual intrusion. Vibration and pollution by vehicle fumes might also be taken into account, but the weighting to assign to all of these is still difficult to judge. For rural roads the problem is only slightly less difficult, and here the problem of weighting values for landscape character and quality as against farm values and severence of holdings remains largely unresolved.

Also in the local plans and problem-solving category we need more precise methods for evaluation of alternative sites, for mineral workings, power plants, disposal of waste and other intruders in the landscape. The use of impact analysis studies should help by taking account of both local and national farming values, risk of dust and water pollution, local nature conservation interests and those of a research and national value, and visual acceptability. This technique needs to be refined very rapidly, especially in Britain, to help our communities to decide whether the present massive investment on exploration for minerals should be followed by vastly greater sums spent on tearing up some of our most cherished landscapes.

# References

2.1 MINISTRY OF HOUSING AND LOCAL GOVERNMENT, *Green Belts*, Circular No. 42/55, HMSO, London, 1955.

2.2 STEVENS, SIR ROGER (Chairman), *Report of the Committee on Planning Control over Mineral Working*, HMSO, London, 1976.

2.3 WESTMACOTT, R. and WORTHINGTON, T., *New Agricultural Landscapes*, Countryside Commission, CCP 76, HMSO, London, 1974.

2.4 LEONARD, P. L. and COBHAM, R. O., 'The farming landscapes of England and Wales: A changing scene', *Landscape Planning*, **4**, 3, 1977.

2.5 USDA FOREST SERVICE, *National Forest Landscape Management*, Vol. 2, Ch. 1, The visual management system, Agric. Handbook 462, US Government Printing Office, Washington DC, 1974.

2.6 USDA FOREST SERVICE, *National Forest Landscape Management*, Vol. 2, Ch. 4, Roads, Agric. Handbook 483, US Government Printing Office, Washington DC, 1977.

2.7 USDA FOREST SERVICE, *National Forest Landscape Management*, Vol. 2, Ch. 3, Range, Agric. Handbook 484, US Government Printing Office, Washington DC, 1977.

2.8 USDA FOREST SERVICE, *National Forest Landscape Management*, Vol. 2, Ch. 2, Utilities, Agric. Handbook 478, US Government Printing Office, Washington DC, 1975.

2.9 NATURE CONSERVANCY COUNCIL, *Nature Conservation and Agriculture*, 1977.

2.10 NEW TOWNS COMMITTEE, *Interim Report*, Cmnd. 6759, HMSO, London, 1945; *Second Interim Report*, Cmnd. 6794, HMSO, London, 1946; *Final Report*, Cmnd. 6876, HMSO, London, 1946.

2.11 CROWE, DAME SYLVIA, *The Landscape of Power*, Architectural Press, London, 1958.

2.12 WILSON COMMITTEE, *Noise: Final Report of the Committee on the Problem of Noise*, Cmnd. 2056, HMSO, London, 1963.

2.13 GILBERT, O. L., 'An air pollution survey by schoolchildren', *Environmental Pollution*, **6**, 1974.

2.14 GILBERT, O. L. and WEDDLE, A. E., 'Site conservation: A new approach', *Landscape Design*, **107**, August 1974.

2.15 STEINITZ, C. and ROGERS, P., *A Systems Analysis Model of Urbanisation and Change: An Experiment in Interdisciplinary Education*, Graduate School of Design, Harvard University, Cambridge, Mass., 1968.

2.16 ATKINSON, J. R., *Landscape and the Durham Motorway*, County Planning Department, Durham, 1965.

2.17 WARWICKSHIRE COUNTY PLANNING DEPARTMENT, *Coventry, Solihull, Warwickshire: A Strategy for the Sub-region, Supplementary Report 5—Countryside*, County Planning Department, Warwick, 1971.

2.18 WEDDLE, A. E., *Heriot-Watt University*, Site Development Studies, Edinburgh, 1967, unpublished.

2.19 WARWICKSHIRE COUNTY PLANNING DEPARTMENT, *op. cit.*

2.20 WEDDLE, A. E., 'Techniques in landscape planning', *J. Town Planning Institute*, **55**, 9, 1969.

2.21 WEDDLE, A. E., *Deeside Study*, Evidence given at Public Inquiry, Mold, 1971, unpublished.

2.22 WARWICKSHIRE COUNTY PLANNING DEPARTMENT, *op. cit.*

2.23 HOPKINSON, R. G., 'The Quantitative Assessment of Visual Intrusion', *J. Town Planning Institute*, **57**, 10, 1971.

2.24 HILLS, A. G., *Developing a Better Environment*, Ontario Economic Council, Toronto, 1970.

2.25 MINISTRY OF AGRICULTURE, FISHERIES AND FOOD, *Agricultural Land Classification Map of England and Wales, Explanatory Note*, HMSO, London, 1968.

2.26 NIELSON, V. R., *Danish Planning Legislation: A Survey*, Ministry of Housing, Copenhagen, 1963 (reprint 1964).

2.27 ECKBO, DEAN, AUSTIN AND WILLIAMS, *State of Hawaii Land Use Districts and Regulations Revue*, Honolulu, 1969.

2.28 WALLACE, MCHARRIS, ROBERTS AND TODD, *Towards a Comprehensive Landscape Plan for Washington DC*, US Government Printing Office, Washington DC, 1967.

2.29 BURTON LITTON, R., *Forest Landscape Description and Inventories*, USDA Forest Research Paper PSW 49, 1968.

2.30 JACOBS, P. and WAY, D., *Visual Analysis of Landscape Development*, Harvard, 1969.

2.31 FRASER DARLING, F., 'Wilderness and Plenty', Reith Lectures, 1969, BBC, London, 1970.

2.32 NICHOLSON, M., *The Environmental Revolution*, Hodder and Stoughton, London, 1970.

2.33 SIMMONS, I. G., 'Wilderness in the twentieth century USA', *Town Planning Review*, **36**, 4, 1970.

2.34 HELLIWELL, D. R., 'Valuation of wildlife resources', *Regional Studies*, **3**, 1, 1969.

2.35 HOOPER, M. D., 'Critique of D. R. Helliwell: Valuation of wildlife resources', *Regional Studies*, **4**, 1, 1970.

2.36 FINES, K. D., 'Landscape evaluation, A research project in East Sussex, *Regional Studies*, **2**, 1, 1968.

2.37 WEDDLE, A. E., 'Landscape evaluation', *J. Town Planning Institute*, **55**, 9, 1969.

2.38 JACK HOLMES PLANNING GROUP, *Plan Evaluations—an Ordinal Method*, Report extract, December, 1970.

2.39 LAND USE CONSULTANTS, *A Planning Classification of Scottish Land Use Resources*, Countryside Commission for Scotland, Perth, 1971.

2.40 LAURIE, I., *Objectives for Landscape Evaluation Studies,* Landscape Research Group, Paper given at York, 1970.

2.41 UNIVERSITY OF MANCHESTER, *Landscape Evaluation, Landscape Evaluation Research Project 1970–75,* Manchester, 1976.

2.42 LICHFIELD, N., 'Economics of planned development', *Estates Gazette*, London, 1956.

2.43 LICHFIELD, N., 'Cost Benefit Analysis in Plan Evaluation', *Town Planning Review*, **35**, 2, 1964.

2.44 WEDDLE, A. E., 'Rural Land Resources', *Town Planning Review*, **35**, 4, 1965.

2.45 PETERS, G. H., 'Land use studies in Britain: a review of the literature with special reference to application of cost benefit analysis, *Journal of Agricultural Economics*, **21**, 2, 1970.

2.46 HILLS, A. G., *op. cit.* at 2.24.

2.47 BELNAP, R. K., FURTADO, J. G. FORSTER, R. R. and BLOSSOM, H. D., *Three Approaches to Environmantal Resource Analysis*, Harvard University, Cambridge, Mass., 1967.

2.48 PICKARD, P. J., 'Least cost social analysis' *J. Town Planning Institute*, **55**, 9, 1969.

2.49 BURTON LITTON, R., *op. cit.* in 2.29.

2.50 USDA FOREST SERVICE, *National Forest Management,* Vol. 2, Ch. 1, The Visual Management System, Agric. Handbook 462, US Government Printing Office, Washington DC, 1974.

CHAPTER THREE

# ENVIRONMENTAL IMPACT ANALYSIS

Brian D. Clark, Keith Chapman,
Ronald Bisset and Peter Wathern

Without adequate assessment of potential impacts, development in areas of high landscape quality and environmental sensitivity will often produce harmful effects.

The Isle of Skye, looking towards the Cuillin Hills from Portree

(*Photo by courtesy of A. F. Kersting*)

CHAPTER THREE
# ENVIRONMENTAL IMPACT ANALYSIS

## Introduction

Environmental impact analysis is the assessment of the environmental consequences of policies, programmes and development projects. It has evolved from a growing concern that the social, economic and environmental impacts of major developments cannot be assessed ad-equately using conventional planning procedures. The controversies surrounding the decisions to lay the Trans-Alaska Oil Pipeline, to build nuclear power stations in West Germany and to construct oil production platforms in remote areas of west Scotland, have shown that the nature and scale of such development can have profound political, social, economic and environmental consequences. Impact analysis is a means of making a systematic balanced

The views expressed in this chapter are those of the Project Appraisal for Development Control study team and do not necessarily represent the views of the sponsors, the Scottish Development Department, the Department of the Environment and the Welsh Office.

Figure 3.1   Major developments such as power stations can cause significant environmental, social and economic changes in an area.

*(Photo: K. Chapman)*

assessment of impacts, and Environmental Impact Statements (EISs) are a valuable aid for bringing important issues out into the open. Environmental impact analysis complements conventional tools for environmental management such as land use planning and pollution control.

This chapter contains a discussion of environmental impact analysis procedures which have been developed in different countries. Methods for undertaking impact studies are also reviewed. In considering procedures and methods, the experience of the United States is important because the National Environmental Policy Act (NEPA) (3.1) includes a section which requires Federal agencies to prepare EISs detailing the consequences of their proposed actions on the human environment. Subsequently, general guidelines for the preparation of EISs were issued by the Council on Environmental Quality (CEQ) (3.2). This chapter contains not only a critical assessment of the US mandatory system of environmental impact analysis, but also an appraisal of UK experience, where impact analysis has been undertaken within the existing planning framework. In addition, brief descriptions are given of impact analysis procedures in other countries. There follows an evaluation of various methods which can be used for impact analysis. The advantages and disadvantages of a number of methods are analysed, and a method proposed for the assessment of major development projects in the UK is described.

Landscape architects, landscape planners and ecologists involved in impact analysis may be faced with the problem of selecting appropriate techniques for assessing impacts of proposed developments on ecological and landscape resources. A number of techniques, selected because they show the main approaches adopted for impact assessment in the UK, are described. These techniques are concerned with ecological evaluation, determining the extent of visual intrusion and landscape evaluation.

## Current State of Impact Analysis

### Impact Analysis in the United States

Requirements for environmental impact analysis were introduced in the US when NEPA became law in 1970. NEPA outlines a broad environmental policy with the aim of using '... all practicable means ... to create and maintain conditions under which man and nature can co-exist in productive harmony and fulfil the social, economic and other requirements of present and future generations...' (3.3). This is to be achieved in two ways. First, NEPA requires existing Federal policies, regulations and laws to be administered in accordance with these objectives. Secondly, Federal agencies are required to produce EISs for '... major Federal actions significantly affecting the quality of the human environment' (3.4).

The most important section of NEPA is section 102(2)

(C). This contains EIS provisions and specifies the range of factors that must be included in an EIS. Each must contain a discussion of:

1. The environmental impacts of the proposed action;
2. Unavoidable environmental impacts of the proposed action;
3. Alternatives to the proposed action;
4. The effects of the proposed action on the relationships between local short-term use of the environment and the maintenance and enhancement of long-term productivity;
5. The irreversible and irretrievable commitment of resources if the proposal were implemented.

EISs have been produced for a range of Federal actions including development projects, grant allocations, licensing and environmental management programmes. Neither 'major' nor 'significant' is defined adequately in the Act, but development projects for which EISs are produced include power stations, dams, reservoirs, transmission lines and highways. Legislation and regulations for air pollution control and the licensing of off-shore oil and gas exploration also require EISs. In addition, EISs are prepared for proposals by Federal agencies to grant financial aid for projects, such as the construction of subsidised housing financed by the Department of Housing and Urban Development.

NEPA has been likened to an environmental charter, because it '... states a general policy in lofty terms, outlines a fragmentary procedure for implementing that policy, and leaves questions of detail to the good sense of those who must live with and interpret its requirements' (3.5). As the Act is imprecise in many of its crucial sections, two factors have been important in its detailed interpretation. These are guidelines issued by CEQ, an organisation established to administer NEPA, and decisions made by the courts. CEQ guidelines (3.6) outline procedures for EIS preparation. When proposing a project for which an EIS is required, Federal agencies are directed to produce a draft EIS. This is submitted to CEQ, circulated to other agencies and made available to the public. Subsequently, the Federal agency prepares a final EIS which must be responsive to comments made by other agencies and the public. Ninety days and forty-five days respectively must lapse after submission of draft and final EISs before a project can proceed (Figure 3.2). CEQ guidelines also require each Federal agency to prepare detailed guidance notes indicating the administrative procedures to be adopted for implementing NEPA, the proposals for which EISs would be required and the detailed aspects of a proposal which would be considered in an EIS.

The guidelines issued by CEQ and individual Federal agencies have done little to clarify the ambiguous expressions such as 'major', 'significant' and 'human environment' contained in NEPA. This has been the role of the judiciary, as agencies have been challenged in the courts on suspected noncompliance with NEPA. In general,

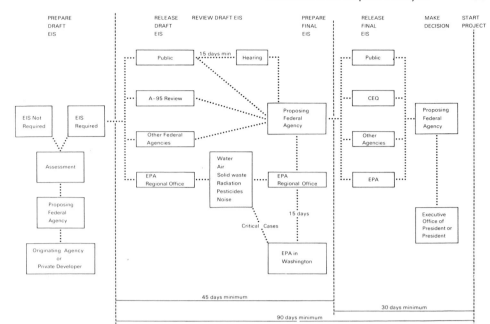

Figure 3.2 Flow diagram for US Federal EISs.

(*By courtesy of the Controller of Her Majesty's Stationery Office*)

these proceedings have focused on two aspects. First, attempts have been made to clarify ambiguous phrases such as 'Federal actions' and 'major'. Secondly, the courts have ruled on whether individual EISs fulfil NEPA requirements.

NEPA applies only to Federal proposals. The courts have resisted attempts to extend interpretation of the Act to include development by state and local administrations and by private developers. The majority of states, however, have introduced EIS procedures. In 1973, 17 states had EIS requirements (3.7). The number had risen to 31 by 1975, when a further 14 states were proposing to introduce similar measures (3.8). Many states require EISs only for public projects. Some state acts are more extensive and cover private developers, although there are considerable differences in the degree to which private developers are affected. California, for example, requires private developers to produce environmental impact reports, while Delaware requires EISs for private development only in pre-defined areas. Certain state legislation requiring impact analysis is very different from NEPA. Some require consideration of aspects excluded from NEPA, such as the requirement that developers describe remedial actions that would be taken to reduce adverse impacts. Other states have based their legislation only on parts of NEPA.

Opinions on the value of NEPA differ widely. Delogu (3.9) describes the Act as '...a device which more effectively than any other to date balances legitimate development and environmental interests'. Voigt (3.10) considers the Act '...an atrocious piece of legislation...it is poorly thought out and ambiguous at all crucial points'. The value of NEPA can be judged only in general terms. If the number of projects stopped after preparation of an EIS were the criterion of success, the Act would have to be judged a failure, as only a few have been discontinued. This generalisation, however, is an oversimplification. It might be more meaningful to ascertain whether project planning since NEPA was implemented has taken greater account of environmental effects. Initially, there was little evidence of proposals being modified as a result of impact analysis, although this situation appears to be changing. Andrews (3.11), in a review of the programmes and policies of the Army Corps of Engineers and the Soil Conservation Service since 1970, concludes that NEPA has been the catalyst for increased environmental awareness during project planning by some Federal agencies.

One of the most serious weaknesses of NEPA arises from the fact that Federal agencies both produce EISs and make decisions on implementing proposals. The failure to separate these responsibilities has led to charges of bias in EISs (3.12). There is some evidence that adverse impacts have been ignored and potentially deleterious projects implemented (3.13). Similarly, EISs have been biased to show developments in the most favourable light (3.14). Many EISs produced by Federal agencies lack balance, with undue emphasis on the physical environment. Although NEPA requires '...the integral use of the natural and social sciences and environmental design and planning in decision making...' (3.15), Albrecht (3.16) notes that most EISs have neglected social impacts until recently. Many criticisms of NEPA also apply to state and local legislation, for much of the legislation has been modelled on NEPA. However, states, which require planning officials or independent consultants to produce EISs, have resolved the problem of potential bias inherent in permitting developers to produce EISs.

The future of impact analysis in the US is uncertain. Despite NEPA and state and local legislation, impact analysis covers only certain developments and policies. Not all public and private developments require EISs. Few EISs have been produced for Federal policies such as the

Figure 3.3   The decision to exempt the Trans-Alaska Pipeline from full compliance with NEPA is regarded as a dangerous precedent for the assessment of proposals of national importance in the US.

(*Photo by courtesy of British Petroleum Ltd.*)

introduction of pollution standards or Federal energy policies. Jellinek (3.17), a senior member of CEQ, argues that the scope of impact analysis will extend as more agencies produce EISs before making major policy decisions. However, the decision of Congress to exempt the Trans-Alaska Pipeline from the requirements of the Act because delays were prejudicing future energy supplies is regarded as an ominous precedent. Major projects may be exempted 'in the national interest' from the requirements of NEPA, if compliance were likely to induce delay. In 1977, CEQ issued draft regulations designed to increase the effectiveness of EISs. Many of the adverse comments on EISs were accommodated in these regulations (3.18).

### Impact Analysis in the United Kingdom

The interest in impact analysis in UK planning partly reflects the influence of events in the US. Growing public concern about the quality of the environment has been reinforced by the effect of certain controversial major development proposals and a realisation that the evaluation of major environmental impacts must be fully considered in the decision-making process. Many planners, and the general public, argue that existing procedures and methods of assessing developments have been inadequate. The immediate impetus, however, for environmental impact analysis in the UK resulted from the discovery of oil and gas in the North Sea. Oil and gas exploitation has led to the need for many related onshore developments, including production platform fabrication yards, and oil and gas terminals. Many of these developments are located in isolated rural areas characterised not only by small communities with distinctive social and cultural attributes, but also by considerable visual and environmental amenity. These factors were instrumental in increasing pressure for the analysis of likely impacts. The demand for impact

analysis came both from environmental and amenity groups, and professional organisations such as the Institution of Civil Engineers. Dobry, in a review of development control in the UK, also advocated impact studies for developments which are 'major, controversial or both' (3.19).

Faced with major North Sea oil and gas developments, both central Government and local authorities commissioned professional consultants to produce environmental impact reports. Consequently, a number of reports have been published which are similar to EISs prepared in the US. These studies were initiated on an *ad hoc* basis and not as a mandatory requirement. They include assessments of proposed production platform fabrication yards on Lochs Broom and Carron (3.20, 3.21), an oil refinery, a natural gas liquids separation plant and an ethylene plant (3.22, 3.23, 3.24) and a report on the Flotta oil terminal prepared for the developer (3.25) (see Case History 4). An assessment of the implications of developing the Beatrice oilfield has also been produced for the developer (3.26).

The early reports were prepared at a time when there was little practical experience of impact analysis in the UK. Consultants were often required to produce reports within a time period which was not conducive to a thorough appraisal. Consequently, some of the early reports have been criticised. Produced at a time when the role of EISs in UK planning had not been defined and little advice had been given on their content, some of the reports lack balance and a coherent structure for appraising impacts. Certain impacts are discussed in great detail, while others are dismissed with inconclusive statements. Two other points can be made about these early reports. First, techniques used in making projections have not been specified. This is an important omission because, not only does it prevent independent verification, but also it prevents discussion of the applica-

Figure 3.4    The exploitation of North Sea oil and gas has required the construction of coastal facilities such as the gas terminal at St. Fergus.

(*Photo: Aberdeen University Geography Department*)

bility of the technique used. Secondly, it must be possible for those reading a report to distinguish between conclusions based on evidence and those based on conjecture. Some reports contain statements which, while they may be correct, are not supported by evidence.

The planning problems posed by oil-related development in Scotland produced a number of responses from the Scottish Development Department (SDD). SDD has issued a considerable amount of literature to guide local planners and has encouraged local authorities to appraise rigorously major oil-related developments (3.27). Although oil-related developments were the major concern, SDD acknowledged that other large-scale and potentially controversial projects may need similar scrutiny and has initiated research on environmental impact analysis. In 1973, a research project entitled Project Appraisal for Development Control (PADC) was commissioned by SDD and the Department of the Environment (DOE). The work was undertaken within the Geography Department of Aberdeen University. The objective of the study was to prepare a method for making a balanced appraisal of the potential impact of major industrial developments on the physical environment, taking economic and social effects into account. The results of the study were published as an interim consultative document in the form of a manual designed to help UK planning authorities assess these impacts in the course of their statutory development control responsibilities (3.28). The method contained in the manual is discussed in the next section.

Another illustration of UK interest in the environmental

aspects of development is provided by a report on the desirability of introducing a system of environmental impact analysis into UK planning (3.29). This study concluded that there was a need for a system of environmental impact analysis for certain types of development in the UK and that the process should be introduced experimentally without amending the Planning Acts, although some legislative changes would be desirable if impact analysis were introduced permanently. The report also recommended that private developers should be involved in the appointment of a steering committee responsible for issuing a brief for the appraisal and for appointing a team to undertake analysis of potential impacts. The decision on whether impact analysis should be initiated would be the responsibility of planning authorities. The cost of impact analysis would be shared between private developers and planning authorities, whereas public sector developers would be responsible for initiating and financing a full appraisal of projects. Analyses of the impacts of public sector developments, however, would be carried out in full co-operation with the planning authority.

Although this study recognised the need for major development proposals to be assessed, some of its detailed recommendations are similar to procedures which have been criticised in the US. In the report the authors, Catlow and Thirlwall, propose a system in which private and public sector developers would be directly involved in preparing EISs. This follows US practice, but many reviewers of the procedures associated with NEPA and similar state legislation have been critical of a system which allows those with a vested interest in a project to influence studies intended to reveal likely adverse and beneficial effects (see page 55. The direct financial involvement of developers in meeting some of the costs of impact analysis, as proposed by Catlow and Thirlwall, might reinforce doubts about the objectivity of the exercise.

As impact assessment can be accommodated within existing procedures, special legislation may not be introduced. Both PADC and Catlow and Thirlwall emphasise the desirability of avoiding rigid procedures for impact assessment. As a result of these studies a flexible approach may be adopted with local planning authorities deciding whether an impact assessment should be prepared for private development proposals. This decision would be based on such factors as the scale of a project, the environmental sensitivity of a proposed site and its surroundings, and whether a project is likely to be controversial. The assessment will be prepared by local planning authorities drawing, when necessary, upon the expertise of statutory bodies such as the Nature Conservancy Council and private consultants.

**Impact Analysis in Other Countries**

Most advanced industrialised nations and several developing countries have been considering the merits of impact

58  Land Use and Landscape Planning

analysis to see if existing practice for assessing development proposals could be improved. Such improvements may involve introducing new procedures or may be achieved by strengthening those already in existence. A number of countries have implemented legislation or procedures for impact analysis, much of it modelled on the US pattern.

## CANADA

There are both national and provincial requirements for environmental impact assessment (3.30). The Environmental Assessment Review Process, which requires an assessment of major projects initiated by or funded by Federal agencies, was introduced by a Cabinet directive in 1973 (3.31). An Environmental Assessment Panel, responsible to the Minister of Fisheries and the Environment was appointed to act as the formal reviewing agency for those Federal projects considered by the initiating departments to have potentially significant environmental impacts. The reviewing process is shown in Figure 3.5. The Panel issues guidelines identifying the factors that should be considered by the agency preparing an assessment. The completed assessment is submitted to the Panel for review. The report is made public and meetings may be held by the Panel to gauge public response to the proposals. The Panel makes recommendations on proposals to the Minister of Fisheries and the Environment based on the adequacy of proposed measures to mitigate or minimise adverse effects. Development cannot proceed until a review has been discussed by the Minister and the proposing agency. When they fail to agree, decisions on whether to implement proposed projects are made by the Cabinet.

Several provinces have introduced impact analysis procedures. Ontario implemented the Environmental Assessment Act in 1976 and Alberta has requirements for impact appraisal under the Land Surface Conservation and Reclamation Act 1973. The Environmental Assessment Act requires an appraisal of all designated public activities. It is anticipated that private development will be incorporated subsequently. The Ontario Ministry of the Environment is responsible both for identifying designated public developments and for reviewing assessments prepared by proposing agencies (3.32). In Alberta, assessments are required for linear disturbances, such as highways and pipelines, extraction proposals, impoundments and intensive land use disturbances, such as residential or industrial development. Planning applications for such development cannot be made until the impacts of the proposals have been reviewed by the provincial government (3.33).

## AUSTRALIA

The Environmental Protection (Impact of Proposals) Act 1974 requires EISs for proposals by or on behalf of the Australian Government that significantly affect the environment. Procedures have been established which require detailed information to be provided so that the Minister may determine whether an EIS should be prepared. EISs are prepared on Ministry guidelines, and a draft is made available to the public. After review a final EIS is prepared which is sent to the Environment Ministry for examination. When decisions are made whether to implement a proposed project, the suggestions and recommendations made by the Environment Minister must be taken into account. State governments also have jurisdiction over developments which may affect the environment. Three states have published administrative procedures for impact appraisal. One state is currently developing procedures, while the remainder have initiated impact appraisal without any procedures or legislation having been established (3.34).

## EUROPE

West Germany, Spain, France and the Republic of Eire have introduced EIS procedures. In addition, several

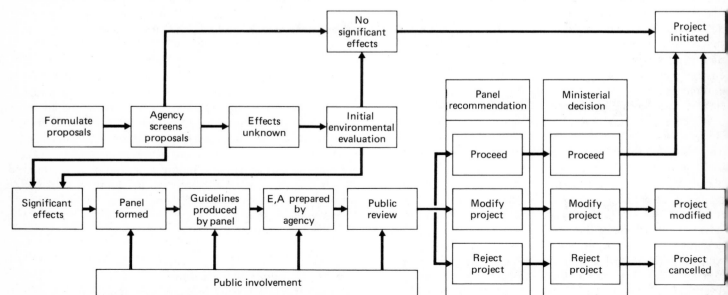

Figure 3.5   Federal environmental impact assessment procedure in Canada.

other countries, including Denmark and the Netherlands, are considering introducing legislation. Sweden has amended an existing law and introduced national guidelines to ensure that environmental factors are considered in the location of major developments (3.35). The Council of the Organisation for Economic Co-operation and Development (OECD) has recommended that member countries, which include most Western European countries, should establish procedures and methods for assessing the 'environmental consequences of significant public and private projects likely to have major impact' (3.36). In October 1975, a declaration by the Commission of the European Economic Community recommended that environmental impact assessment procedures, based on common evaluation criteria, should be introduced in member countries of the European Economic Community (3.37). This could be achieved by a Community Directive. Lee and Wood of Manchester University have been commissioned to examine the potential role of impact analysis within the Community and to recommend a course of action (3.38). Preliminary results from this study indicate that a Community system might cover projects initially. Subsequently, policies and land use plans might be incorporated (3.39).

In 1971, the Government of the Federal Republic of Germany defined a number of objectives which made an 'examination for environmental compatibility an essential step in the formulation of Federal proposals' (3.40). Initially, these proposals were draft laws, regulations and administrative provisions which might affect environmental protection. In 1972, the Minister of the Interior proposed a model procedure to ensure that Federal proposals were examined for compatibility with the environment. The procedure was tested on a small number of agricultural and transport schemes and, as a result, was further refined. It was envisaged that this procedure would be incorporated within legislation covering major actions both by the Federal Government and by individual Länder, but this was found to be impracticable.

Consequently, in 1975 the Cabinet extended the model procedure to all Federal actions. Individual Ministries must amend existing administrative procedures to comply with its requirements. This should ensure that environmental considerations are integrated within Government planning and decision-making processes. However, EISs are not produced as part of the assessment procedure. Although the assessment procedure applies at the Federal level, individual Länder have indicated an intention to introduce similar procedures for corresponding state actions (3.41).

In the Republic of Eire, the Local Government (Planning and Development) Regulations, 1977 require EISs to be submitted for some developments. These regulations require an EIS to be produced by prospective developers if, in the opinion of the relevant planning authority, the cost of development would exceed £5m. Certain types of construction projects, for example public infrastructure developments such as roads, are exempt from these requirements. Consequently, EISs will be prepared only for certain public sector development and for private development above a financial threshold.

## Methods for Impact Analysis

In the initial period after NEPA became law, procedural questions relating to the production and submission of EISs were given prominence over the development of methods for impact analysis. However, once Federal guidelines clarified some of the procedural problems, attention turned towards the adequacy of EISs as a means of providing information for decision-makers and, consequently, to the development of methods for impact appraisal.

The impetus provided by the development of environmental impact analysis in the US stimulated similar activities in other countries. As a result, the formulation of methods for impact analysis has not been confined to the US. In this section a number of different types of methods are discussed. Most of them were developed in the US, but two were developed in the UK and one in Canada. These methods display considerable variety in their conceptual framework, approach to data presentation and technical sophistication. All incorporate means of collecting and classifying material for impact analysis. In addition, methods aid the presentation of results. Generally, all methods share a common objective of ensuring that as many potential impacts as possible are identified, measured and described, although some go further and incorporate means whereby impacts from different project designs can be evaluated and compared. These latter methods not only identify impacts, but also quantify, weight and aggregate them. Many methods have been adapted from other fields, but most of these are useful for only some, rather than all the activities associated with the preparation of an EIS.

Warner and Preston (3.42) state that impact analysis must consider four aspects to comply with NEPA. These are:

1. Impact identification;
2. Impact measurement;
3. Impact interpretation;
4. Impact communication to information users (including the public).

Recently, the importance of monitoring a project has been emphasised. Munn (3.43) and PADC (3.44) consider that this should be dealt with during impact appraisal.

It is only possible to describe a selection of the major methods devised for impact analysis. The methods discussed can be applied to a wide range of the most common types of development. Other methods, for example computerised overlays have been used mainly for linear developments, and have been excluded. In the following

60    Land Use and Landscape Planning

review particular emphasis will be placed on the merits and disadvantages of various methods as practical working tools and on their implications for decision-making. The methods discussed are:

1. Matrices:
   (a) the Leopold Matrix (US);
   (b) the Sphere Quantified Matrix (UK);
   (c) Component Interaction Matrix (Canada);
2. Networks (US);
3. Environmental Evaluation System (US);
4. PADC Method (UK).

The PADC method is included in this section although it differs from the other methods described. It consists of a flexible procedure which includes a generalised interaction matrix.

## Matrices

The pioneering approach to impact analysis was the 'Leopold Matrix' developed by Leopold *et al.* (3.45). This matrix was designed to apply to a number of alternative project designs to ensure that the proposal selected would be not only acceptable, but also the least detrimental to the environment. The Sphere Matrix had a similar aim but was used to assess alternative sites rather than alternative projects (3.46). Both matrices have a similar format since impacts are identified by bringing together project actions and environmental and socio-economic factors. The Component Interaction Matrix (3.47) has a different purpose. It was developed primarily to uncover interactions between environmental components, for example, the dependence of fish species on riparian vegetation via the insect life breeding in the vegetation. Such interactions characterise all environmental systems, and this matrix attempts to uncover these interactions enabling those investigating impacts to follow the consequences of a development action. In this manner indirect impacts can be noted and described.

### THE LEOPOLD MATRIX

In this matrix project actions are related to environmental effects. The matrix consists of a list of development actions and a list of environmental and socio-economic components. The former are ranged horizontally (columns) and the latter vertically (rows) (Figure 3.6). This matrix is of the 'open-cell' type, that is, the cells are blank. An investigator identifies cells where the intersection of a project action and an environmental or socio-economic component is likely to produce an impact. The Leopold Matrix is comprehensive, containing a total of 8800 possible interactions. It is unlikely that all would be relevant for a particular project. Leopold *et al.* indicate that, in practice, the likely number of interactions will range from 25 to 50.

Once likely impacts have been identified they are considered in terms of their 'magnitude' and 'importance'. 'Magnitude' is a measure of the 'degree, extensiveness or scale' of an impact. Importance is defined as 'significance'

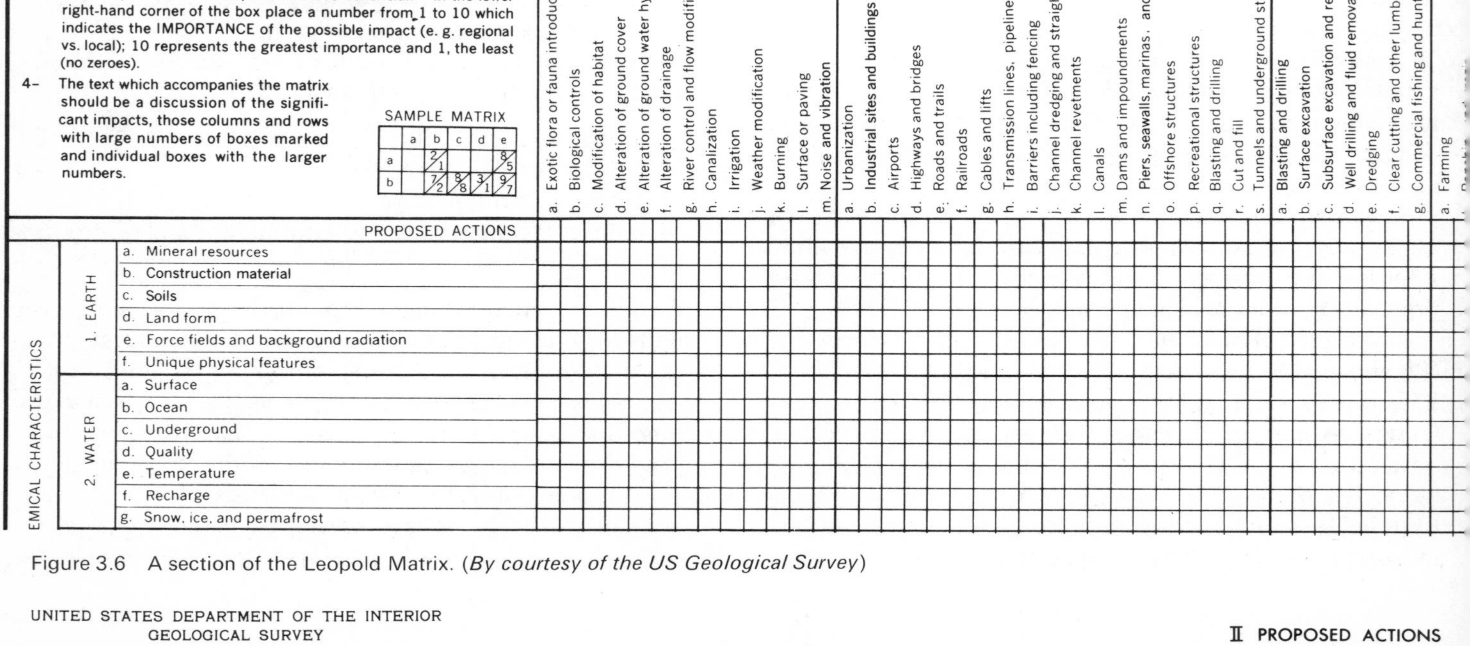

Figure 3.6   A section of the Leopold Matrix. (*By courtesy of the US Geological Survey*)

GEOLOGICAL SURVEY

II PROPOSED ACTIONS

of an impact. Both 'magnitude' and 'importance' are measured quantitatively on scales ranging from 1 to 10. A score of 1 represents least 'magnitude' or 'importance' while 10 represents the greatest. Each cell representing an impact is bisected by a diagonal line, and scores for 'magnitude' and 'importance' are placed in the upper left and lower right sections respectively. An example will clarify the procedure. A specific project might be visually intrusive and the zone of visual influence cover a large area. Consequently, it might receive a 'magnitude' score of 8. The importance of the visual impact may be low, however, and be given a score of 2. This would occur in areas with existing development or in locations where the landscape possessed high visual absorption properties. Values placed in the bisected cells are derived subjectively by assessors as this matrix is not accompanied by rules whereby quantification can be applied in a standardised way. Once the matrix has been completed, particular attention should be paid to cells containing the higher numbers. Also, project actions causing a large number of cells in a column to be marked should be investigated in detail.

The Leopold Matrix has a number of advantages. It provides a comprehensive reference list of possible impacts, and when completed acts as a powerful *aide-mémoire* ensuring that impacts are not forgotten or ignored. In addition, a visual summary of the impacts described in an EIS is provided. This is useful for EIS reviewers and the general public. The main criticisms of this matrix focus on its complexity, its emphasis on first-order direct interactions and the derivation of the numerical components (3.48). Although the list of components is extensive, some are too broad for adequate impact appraisal. Leopold *et al.* suggest that expanded matrices could be constructed for certain impacts to overcome this difficulty. However, a number of different matrices would nullify the visual utility of the matrix approach. Also, different matrices might be needed to show impacts, 5, 10, 20 years from the first fully operational year and the effects of alternative project designs. The additional matrices, which might be needed for analysis, would make comparison and evaluation of alternatives difficult.

Some commentators consider that indirect impacts may be omitted from appraisal because the Leopold Matrix channels thought to the immediate future and only to pairs of interacting components (3.49). This argument, however, disregards the likelihood that experts would be able to uncover indirect impacts with the matrix but not in a manner which would make the direction of links apparent. These could be highlighted in the text, although they would not be obvious from a completed matrix. Consequently, such a matrix would not be very good for communicating impacts to the public.

The use of a subjective ordinal scale (that is, a scale in which the intervals between numbers may not be the same) in assigning scores of 'magnitude' and 'importance' has been criticised (3.50). If such a scale were used, summation of impact scores would be invalid. This fact, however, may not prevent decision-makers from viewing numbers in this matrix as indicating a correct 'objective' assessment of an impact. This assumption may lead them to subtract or add scores for various sets of impacts or alternative project designs, to enable them to make a decision on whether a project should proceed. As standardised weighting is not a feature of the matrix it is impossible to decide the relative importance of different impacts. Also, should alternatives be a subject of comparison this method does not allow a score for different matrices to be derived since the numbers cannot be manipulated arithmetically.

SPHERE MATRIX

Sphere Environmental Consultants Ltd. (3.51) used a quantified matrix to assess sites for the construction of oil production platforms. The principle behind this matrix is similar to that used by Leopold *et al.* The sites are listed horizontally, while 14 environmental and socio-economic factors applicable to all sites form the vertical component of the matrix (Table 3.1). It was known that each of these factors would be affected at each site. Consequently, all the cells indicate an impact. Impacts were ranked by a subjectively derived number on a scale ranging from 0 (very good) to 5 (very bad). As an equal weight was applied to each factor, that is, all factors were considered to be of equal importance, an initial ranking of the sites was obtained by adding the figures representing impacts on each factor for each site. This procedure would appear to be invalid as a means of comparing alternatives as not all impacts are of equal importance.

Sphere tested the applicability of their initial ranking by altering the weights applied to the 14 factors. If different weighting schemes caused large variations in the rankings obtained, it could be assumed that weighting was significant. On the other hand, if little variation occurred, weighting would be insignificant and the initial ranking would represent the best ordering of the sites. The 14 factors were divided into two categories; 'environmental' and 'engineering'. Only the relative weights between factors in different categories were changed. There was no weighting of impacts on factors within these groups, that is, the internal weighting was undifferentiated.

The effects of changing the relative weights of these broad categories were investigated. In all, five different weighting schemes were tested. In one scheme 'environmental' factors were given a zero weighting, while 'engineering' factors retained their original weight and in another scheme this weighting was reversed. Table 3.2 contains the results obtained from the five schemes for all sites. The results in this table were obtained by multiplying the original subjective score for each impact by the appropriate weight. Rankings were obtained for each weighting scheme by summing the appropriate weighted scores for each site. The second column of the table gives the results for the scheme in which 'environmental' factors were given a weighting of zero, while the third column shows the results when this weighting was reversed. The initial ranking

Table 3.1. The Sphere Matrix

| | PORT CAM | CAMAS | RERAIG | W. RUSSEL | RUSSEL BURN | SEAFIELD | ACHINTRAID |
|---|---|---|---|---|---|---|---|
| 1. Visual intrusion | 2 | 4 | 1 | 2 | 3 | 4 | 4 |
| 2. Potential for re-use | 2 | 2 | 5 | 5 | 5 | 4 | 4 |
| 3. Reinstatement possibility | 1 | 1 | 5 | 1 | 1 | 1 | 1 |
| 4. Land use destroyed | 1 | 2 | 4 | 0 | 3 | 3 | 2 |
| 5. Houses directly affected | 0 | 0 | 3 | 0 | 1 | 2 | 5 |
| 6. Houses indirectly affected | 4 | 0 | 0 | 0 | 0 | 2 | 3 |
| 7. Other factors | 2 | 5 | 0 | 2 | 2 | 3 | 1 |
| 8. Road access | 2 | 2 | 5 | 4 | 3 | 3 | 4 |
| 9. Rail access | 0 | 5 | 5 | 5 | 5 | 5 | 5 |
| 10. Sea via rail access | 0 | 3 | 2 | 2 | 2 | 2 | 2 |
| 11. Suitability for labour camp | 2 | 2 | 3 | 3 | 3 | 3 | 3 |
| 12. Site workers | 1 | 5 | 4 | 5 | 3 | 5 | 5 |
| 13. Distance of stage 1 from stage 2 | 0 | 2 | 3 | 2 | 2 | 2 | 2 |
| 14. Ecology | 2 | 1 | 2 | 1 | 1 | 1 | 1 |

| 0 = Very good | 2 = Moderate | 4 = Bad |
|---|---|---|
| 1 = Good | 3 = Quite bad | 5 = Very bad |

Table 3.2. Ranking of alternative platform sites using different weightings

| OVERALL | | ENGINEERING ONLY | | ENVIRONMENT ONLY | | ENVIRONMENTAL FACTORS HALF ENGINEERING | | ENVIRONMENTAL FACTORS TWICE ENGINEERING | | ENVIRONMENT AND ENGINEERING EQUALLY WEIGHTED | |
|---|---|---|---|---|---|---|---|---|---|---|---|
| Categories/A11 | | 8, 9, 10, 11, 12, 13 | | 1, 2, 3, 4, 5, 6, 7, 14 | | | | | | | |
| Port Cam | (19) | Port Cam | (5) | West Russel | (11) | Port Cam | (10) | Port Cam | (26) | Port Cam | (15½) |
| West Russel | (32) | Russel Burn | (18) | Port Cam | (14) | Russel Burn | (24) | West Russel | (37½) | West Russel | (29¼) |
| Camas Russel Burn | (34) | Camas | (19) | Camas | (15) | Camas | (24½) | Camas | (41½) | Russel Burn | (30) |
| Seafield | (40) | Seafield | (20) | Russel Burn | (16) | West Russel | (25) | Russel Burn | (42) | Camas | (30¼) |
| Reraig | (42) | West Russel Achintraid | (21) | Seafield Reraig | (20) | Seafield | (27½) | Seafield | (50) | Seafield | (35) |
| Achintraid | (45) | Reraig | (22) | Achintraid | (24) | Reraig | (29½) | Reraig | (52) | Reraig | (37) |
| | | | | | | Achintraid | (30) | Achintraid | (57½) | Achintraid | (38¾) |

was found to be insensitive to changes in the weights and could provide a ranking upon which to base the decision to develop.

This matrix is accompanied by guidelines for using weights to enable those carrying out analysis to compare alternatives by summing impacts for each alternative. However, it possesses a number of significant disadvantages. It exhibits most of the weaknesses of the Leopold Matrix while possessing few of its advantages. The 14 factors are too broad to be of value. Factors such as

ecology omit as much as they include. This compares unfavourably with the comprehensiveness of the Leopold Matrix. The users of the Sphere Matrix manipulated arithmetically numbers on an ordinal scale invalidating the comparative evaluation of the different sites. Although it was realised that their initial ranking was suspect, the different weighting schemes used to test the sensitivity of the ranking are extremely crude and would be of very little use if a comprehensive impact analysis were required.

## COMPONENT INTERACTION MATRIX

This matrix was devised, by a team working for Environment Canada, to uncover indirect relations between environmental components, and was used in the appraisal of five alternative sites for a log transhipment facility in British Columbia (3.52). In this matrix, project actions are omitted. Both columns and rows list the same environmental components (Figure 3.7). Relations of dependency between different environmental components are noted by placing a 1 in appropriate cells. The row component is dependent always on the column component, ensuring that the direction of the dependency is common for all components; for example, water birds are directly dependent on insects (Figure 3.7). These first-order relations can be used to identify relations of a higher order. Multiplying the matrix by itself gives the number of two-link chains. Multiplying the second matrix by the original reveals dependency chains of three links. For example, a mark in the cell linking song birds to aquatic mammals shows a three-link chain of dependency between them (Figure 3.8). The research team decided that sufficient information was available by the time they had identified five-link chains (Figure 3.8). At this point all cells are completed by inserting numbers denoting the number of links in the shortest chains between two components. This resulting matrix is termed a Minimum Link Matrix.

The impacts of the project on each alternative site were investigated by experts in the research team. The matrix was used subsequently for organising conclusions on likely impacts. Impacts were related only to direct links of dependency as all other dependencies were derived from these primary relations. Consequently, indirect impacts were ascertained from the relations between environmental components uncovered by multiplying the matrix. A ranking system was used to denote the effect of each alternative on every direct relationship between environmental components. The impact of each alternative was entered in the appropriate cell using an ordinal scale ranging from 0 (no noticeable effect) to 3 (severe disruptive effect) (Figure 3.9). The best site was chosen by comparing impacts associated with the sites and ranking each alternative by the amount of environmental disruption.

The main difference between this matrix and the Leopold Matrix is the different emphasis placed on impacts. In the Component Interaction Matrix impacts are related to the connections of dependency between environmental components, thereby allowing indirect impacts to be identified. For example, if a Minimum Link Matrix showed an indirect relation of dependency between pelagic fish and aquatic mammals, those assessing a proposal would be aware that a change in the number of aquatic mammals resulting from a proposed development might affect the population of pelagic fish. In contrast the Leopold Matrix identifies impacts by relating project actions and environmental components. It is difficult to identify indirect impacts using the Leopold method. The matrices developed by Environment Canada are effective in showing environmental complexity to the general public, but are of limited use for impact identification and evaluation.

The components are limited compared to those in the Leopold Matrix, covering only partially environmental and socio-economic factors. A more complex matrix would be

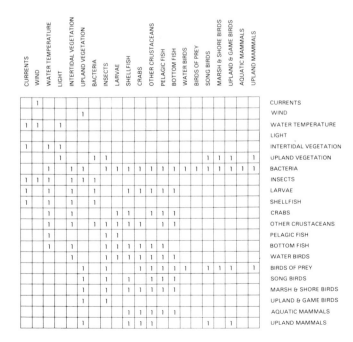

Figure 3.7   Component Interaction Matrix.

(*By courtesy of the Controller of Her Majesty's Stationery Office*)

| | CURRENTS | WIND | WATER TEMPERATURE | LIGHT | INTERTIDAL VEGETATION | UPLAND VEGETATION | BACTERIA | INSECTS | LARVAE | SHELLFISH | CRABS | OTHER CRUSTACEANS | PELAGIC FISH | BOTTOM FISH | WATER BIRDS | BIRDS OF PREY | SONG BIRDS | MARSH & SHORE BIRDS | UPLAND & GAME BIRDS | AQUATIC MAMMALS | UPLAND MAMMALS |
|---|---|---|---|---|---|---|---|---|---|---|---|---|---|---|---|---|---|---|---|---|---|
| CURRENTS | 4 | 1 | 4 | 3 | 4 | 2 | 3 | 3 | 4 | 4 | 4 | 4 | 4 | 4 | 4 | 4 | 3 | 3 | 3 | 4 | 3 |
| WIND | 3 | 3 | 3 | 2 | 3 | 1 | 2 | 2 | 3 | 3 | 3 | 3 | 3 | 3 | 3 | 3 | 2 | 2 | 2 | 3 | 2 |
| WATER TEMPERATURE | 1 | 1 | 4 | 1 | 4 | 2 | 3 | 3 | 4 | 4 | 4 | 4 | 4 | 4 | 4 | 4 | 3 | 3 | 3 | 4 | 3 |
| LIGHT | 0 | 0 | 0 | 0 | 0 | 0 | 0 | 0 | 0 | 0 | 0 | 0 | 0 | 0 | 0 | 0 | 0 | 0 | 0 | 0 | 0 |
| INTERTIDAL VEGETATION | 1 | 2 | 1 | 1 | 5 | 3 | 4 | 4 | 5 | 5 | 5 | 5 | 5 | 5 | 5 | 4 | 4 | 4 | 4 | 5 | 4 |
| UPLAND VEGETATION | 2 | 2 | 2 | 1 | 2 | 2 | 1 | 1 | 2 | 2 | 2 | 2 | 2 | 2 | 2 | 1 | 1 | 1 | 1 | 2 | 1 |
| BACTERIA | 2 | 2 | 1 | 2 | 1 | 2 | 1 | 1 | 1 | 1 | 1 | 1 | 1 | 1 | 1 | 1 | 2 | 1 | 1 | 1 | 1 |
| INSECTS | 1 | 1 | 1 | 2 | 1 | 1 | 2 | 2 | 2 | 2 | 2 | 2 | 2 | 2 | 2 | 2 | 2 | 2 | 2 | 2 | 2 |
| LARVAE | 1 | 2 | 1 | 2 | 1 | 2 | 1 | 2 | 2 | 1 | 1 | 1 | 1 | 1 | 2 | 2 | 3 | 2 | 2 | 2 | 2 |
| SHELLFISH | 1 | 2 | 1 | 2 | 1 | 2 | 1 | 2 | 2 | 2 | 2 | 2 | 1 | 2 | 2 | 2 | 3 | 2 | 2 | 2 | 2 |
| CRABS | 2 | 2 | 1 | 2 | 1 | 3 | 2 | 2 | 1 | 1 | 2 | 1 | 1 | 1 | 3 | 3 | 3 | 4 | 3 | 3 | 3 |
| OTHER CRUSTACEANS | 2 | 2 | 1 | 2 | 1 | 2 | 1 | 1 | 1 | 1 | 1 | 1 | 1 | 2 | 2 | 2 | 3 | 2 | 2 | 2 | 2 |
| PELAGIC FISH | 2 | 2 | 1 | 2 | 2 | 2 | 2 | 1 | 1 | 2 | 2 | 2 | 2 | 3 | 3 | 3 | 3 | 3 | 3 | 3 | 3 |
| BOTTOM FISH | 2 | 2 | 1 | 2 | 1 | 2 | 2 | 1 | 1 | 1 | 1 | 1 | 1 | 2 | 3 | 3 | 3 | 3 | 3 | 3 | 3 |
| WATER BIRDS | 2 | 2 | 2 | 2 | 1 | 2 | 2 | 1 | 1 | 1 | 1 | 1 | 1 | 3 | 3 | 3 | 3 | 3 | 3 | 3 | 3 |
| BIRDS OF PREY | 2 | 2 | 2 | 2 | 2 | 1 | 2 | 1 | 2 | 2 | 1 | 1 | 1 | 1 | 3 | 1 | 1 | 1 | 1 | 3 | 1 |
| SONG BIRDS | 2 | 2 | 2 | 2 | 1 | 2 | 1 | 2 | 1 | 2 | 1 | 2 | 1 | 3 | 3 | 2 | 2 | 2 | 2 | 3 | 2 |
| MARSH & SHORE BIRDS | 2 | 2 | 2 | 2 | 2 | 1 | 2 | 1 | 2 | 1 | 1 | 2 | 1 | 3 | 3 | 2 | 2 | 2 | 2 | 3 | 2 |
| UPLAND & GAME BIRDS | 2 | 2 | 2 | 2 | 2 | 1 | 2 | 1 | 3 | 3 | 3 | 3 | 3 | 3 | 3 | 2 | 2 | 2 | 2 | 3 | 2 |
| AQUATIC MAMMALS | 2 | 3 | 2 | 3 | 2 | 3 | 2 | 2 | 2 | 1 | 1 | 1 | 1 | 1 | 3 | 3 | 3 | 4 | 3 | 3 | 3 |
| UPLAND MAMMALS | 2 | 3 | 2 | 2 | 2 | 1 | 2 | 2 | 2 | 1 | 1 | 1 | 2 | 2 | 3 | 3 | 1 | 2 | 1 | 3 | 2 |

Figure 3.8   Minimum Link Matrix

(*By courtesy of the Controller of Her Majesty's Stationery Office*)

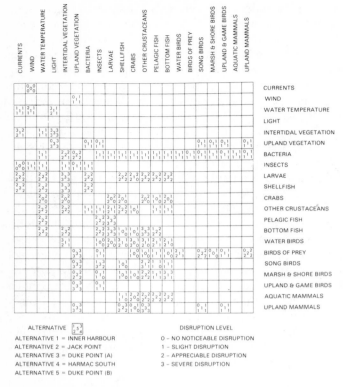

ALTERNATIVE
ALTERNATIVE 1 = INNER HARBOUR
ALTERNATIVE 2 = JACK POINT
ALTERNATIVE 3 = DUKE POINT (A)
ALTERNATIVE 4 = HARMAC SOUTH
ALTERNATIVE 5 = DUKE POINT (B)

DISRUPTION LEVEL
0 – NO NOTICEABLE DISRUPTION
1 – SLIGHT DISRUPTION
2 – APPRECIABLE DISRUPTION
3 – SEVERE DISRUPTION

Figure 3.9    Disruption Matrix

(*By courtesy of Her Majesty's Stationery Office*)

needed to achieve the coverage of the Leopold Matrix. This might be too unwieldy for practical use. Also, the matrices do not indicate the 'significance' or importance of dependencies or relations (Figures 3.7, 3.8 and 3.9). Consequently, the ranking of impacts on specific dependency relations is of little use as the relative importance of the relations of dependency is unknown. Sites cannot be compared meaningfully as the scale of environmental disruption is ordinal. The differences in environmental disruption between sites may vary significantly, even though differences on the ordinal scale may be the same.

The text of the report by Environment Canada raises doubts whether much practical use was made of the matrix, as there are no references to the interactions uncovered by matrix manipulation. Also, the consequences of each alternative are discussed without referring to the Interaction Matrices. Members of the team used their knowledge of the area in an unstructured way to identify likely impacts. For example, impacts on the eelgrass (*Zostera marina*) community were considered to be particularly important and impacts on this community were a major consideration in the final ranking of sites. However, eelgrass is not a component of the matrix, it is subsumed under the heading 'intertidal vegetation'. Similarly, the Disruption Matrix was not an aid to decision-making. Instead, a few key environmental components (fish, shellfish and birdlife) were identified and decisions on the location of the project were based on the degree of adverse impact on these.

## Networks

Networks, like matrices, attempt to incorporate indirect impacts in an assessment method. Sorensen (3.53) developed a method based on a combination of matrices and networks (Figure 3.10). This method was applied to various land use options, such as residential development or crop farms, for a section of the Californian coastline. A list of development actions is linked to a series of 'condition changes' or environmental effects relating to environmental components. In the example illustrated, the effects of residential development on freshwater run-off into an estuary are shown from first-order to second- and third-order 'condition changes' and finally to effects (Figure 3.10). These cause–condition–effect chains were limited to three steps for convenience, but could be extended. After the impact column, a column describing appropriate control mechanisms is added. This method was the first to deal with the post-development situation. At every step in the procedure two questions must be asked. First, whether an identified 'condition change' would induce a further 'condition change'. Secondly, whether the additional change would be sufficiently significant to warrant inclusion in the network.

This method involves the use of existing knowledge to identify likely impacts. Computers are the most efficient means of storing this information and tracing impacts. A network can never be entirely comprehensive, as it is dependent on the quality and coverage of input data, but as a working tool it has two advantages. First, it identifies and lists indirect impacts. This provides a useful *aide-mémoire* to those carrying out impact analysis. Secondly, connections between different condition changes or related impacts are explicit and not subsumed in numerical form as in the Component Interaction Matrix. The nature of connections are stated clearly in the network format (Figure 3.10), whilst the Component Interaction Matrix (Figure 3.7) cannot show such information.

Although networks successfully identify indirect impacts, they give no indication of the relative importance of differing cause–condition–effect pathways. A text is needed to interpret the importance of particular impacts. Also, with increasing detail, networks may become unwieldy and unintelligible to the public. The network approach is useful for assessing a single project and for investigating the likely ramifications of direct impacts. This approach may not be helpful for assessing alternative projects, because decision-makers may have difficulty comparing a number of complex networks.

## Environmental Evaluation System

The Environmental Evaluation System (EES) was devised by the Battelle Laboratories of Columbus, Ohio. The description that follows applies to all versions which have been produced (3.54). EES is based on a checklist of 78 environmental and socio-economic parameters, each represented by a numerical value (Table 3.3). For example,

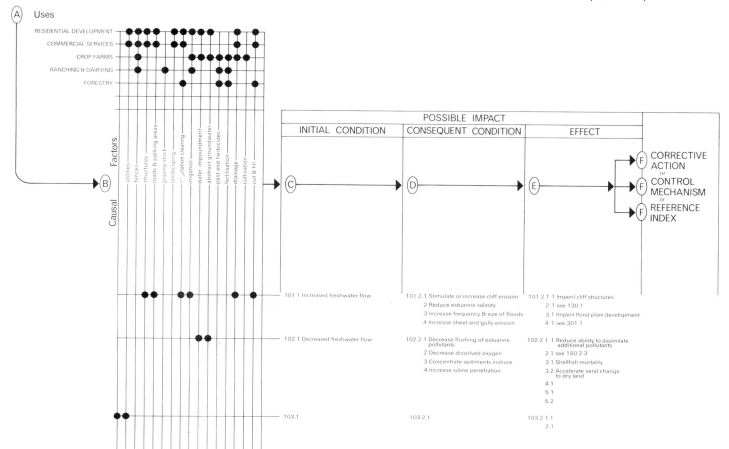

Figure 3.10    The Sorensen Network. (*By courtesy of the Controller of Her Majesty's Stationery Office*)

diversity and aquatic food web indices can be calculated for each aquatic system. These parameters are given weights of relative importance. A group of experts determine these weights by apportioning 1000 points, termed 'Parameter Importance Units', among the parameters (Table 3.3).

Pre-development parameter estimates, for example a food web index, are turned into measures of environmental quality to provide a basis for comparison with the post-impact situation. Environmental quality is scaled from 0 (very bad) to 1 (very good) and has to be defined in a way appropriate to each parameter. Since a parameter estimate for the post-impact situation is related to the appropriate scale of environmental quality, changes which produce a beneficial impact can be taken into account.

Parameter estimates are converted into environmental quality scores using 'value functions' devised for each parameter by a group of experts. Figures 3.11 and 3.12 show the value functions for browsers and grazers in the western United States and for dissolved oxygen respectively. From Figure 3.11 it can be seen that the optimum population of livestock and/or wild herbivores is reached when approximately 50 to 60% of the net annual above-ground production of plants is consumed. When this percentage is exceeded, the stability of the system is disturbed (overgrazed). When it is less, the full grazing potential of the system is not realized. Consumption of only 40% gives an

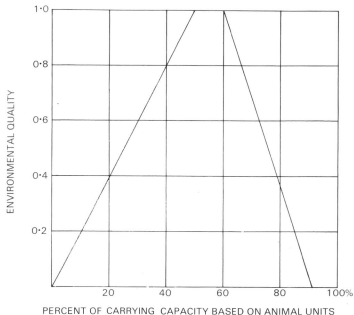

(a) Browsers and grazers

Figure 3.11    Value function for browsers and grazers.

(*By courtesy of the Controller of Her Majesty's Stationery Office*)

Table 3.3. The EES checklist of parameters

ECOLOGY
*Terrestrial Species & Populations*
Browsers and grazers (14)
Crops (14)
Natural vegetation (14)
Pest species (14)
Upland game birds (14)

*Aquatic Species & Populations*
Commercial fisheries (14)
Natural vegetation (14)
Pest species (14)
Sport fish (14)
Waterfowl (14)

*Terrestrial Habitats & Communities*
Food Web Index (12)
Land use (12)
Rare & endangered species (12)
Species diversity (14)

*Aquatic Habitats & Communities*
Food Web Index (12)
Rare & endangered species (12)
River characteristics (12)
Species diversity (14)

*Ecosystems*
Descriptive only

AESTHETICS
*Land*
Geologic surface material (6)
Relief & topographic character (16)
Width & alignment (10)

*Air*
Odour and visual (3)
Sounds (2)

*Water*
Appearance of water (10)
Land & water interface (16)
Odour and floating material (6)
Water surface area (10)
Wooded and geologic
  shoreline (10)

*Biota*
Animals—domestic (5)
Animals—wild (5)
Diversity of vegetation types (9)
Variety within vegetation types (5)

*Man-made Objects*
Man-made objects (10)

*Composition*
Composite effects (15)
Unique composition (15)

PHYSICAL/CHEMICAL
*Water Quality*
Basin hydrologic loss (20)
Biochemical oxygen demand (25)
Dissolved oxygen (31)
Fecal coliforms (18)
Inorganic carbon (22)
Inorganic nitrogen (25)
Inorganic phosphate (28)
Pesticides (16)
pH (18)
Streamflow variation (28)
Temperature (28)
Total dissolved solids (25)
Toxic substances (14)
Turbidity (20)

*Air Quality*
Carbon monoxide (5)
Hydrocarbons (5)
Nitrogen oxides (10)
Particulate matter (12)
Photochemical oxidants (5)
Sulphur oxides (10)
Other (5)

*Land Pollution*
Land use (14)
Soil erosion (14)

*Noise Pollution*
Noise (4)

HUMAN INTEREST/SOCIAL
*Education/Scientific*
Archaeological (13)
Ecological (13)
Geological (11)
Hydrological (11)

*Historical*
Architecture & styles (11)
Events (11)
Persons (11)
Religions and cultures (11)
'Western Frontier' (11)

*Cultures*
Indians (14)
Other ethnic groups (7)
Religious groups (7)

*Mood/Atmosphere*
Awe inspiration (11)
Isolation/solitude (11)
Mystery (4)
'Oneness' with nature (11)

*Life Patterns*
Employment opportunities (13)
Housing (13)
Social interactions (11)

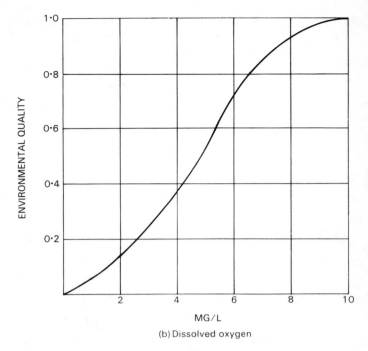

Figure 3.12     Value function for dissolved oxygen.
(*By courtesy of the Controller of Her Majesty's Stationery Office*)

environmental quality score of 0.8. In the case of the value function for dissolved oxygen, a pre-development concentration of 6 mg/l is transformed into an environmental quality score of 0.7. Changes that might occur if development proceeded are projected using predictive techniques. Projected parameter values, for example 4 mg/l of dissolved oxygen, are used to find the post-development quality score. This change of dissolved oxygen concentration would reduce the environmental quality score from 0.7 to 0.38 (Figure 3.12). The procedure is repeated for each parameter. Subsequently, each post-development parameter quality score is multiplied by the number of 'Parameter Impact Units' allotted to that parameter to give a final score for each parameter in terms of 'Environmental Impact Units' (Table 3.4).

Since all parameters are in the same units they can be summed. Consequently, beneficial and harmful impacts of a proposed development can be compared. Similarly, the effects of a development can be compared with the projected situation should the development not proceed. The calculation can be represented by:

$$E_\mathrm{I} = \sum_{i=1}^{m} (V_i)_1 w_i - \sum_{i=1}^{m} (V_i)_2 w_i$$

where $E_\mathrm{I}$ = environmental impact;
   $(V_i)_1$ = value in environmental quality of parameter $i$ with the project;
   $(V_i)_2$ = value in environmental quality of parameter $i$ without the project;
   $w_i$ = relative weight (importance) of parameter $i$;
   $m$ = total number of parameters.

Table 3.4. Selected parameter scores for a water-related development

| PARAMETER | WEIGHT (PIU) | WITH PROJECT (EIU) | WITHOUT PROJECT (EIU) | CHANGE (EIU) |
|---|---|---|---|---|
| ECOLOGY | | | | |
| *Species and populations* | | | | |
| Browsers and grazers | 14 | 14.00 | 14.00 | 0.00 |
| Crops | 14 | 9.24 | 8.12 | +1.12 |
| Sport fish | 14 | 5.74 | 4.90 | +0.84 |
| *Habitats and communities* | | | | |
| River characteristics | 12 | 6.72 | 8.52 | −1.80 |
| ENVIRONMENTAL POLLUTION | | | | |
| *Water pollution* | | | | |
| Basin hydrologic loss | 20 | 15.80 | 17.00 | −1.20 |
| Biochemical oxygen demand | 25 | 18.00 | 21.25 | −3.25 |
| Dissolved oxygen | 31 | 29.45 | 31.00 | −1.55 |
| pH | 18 | 7.20 | 9.00 | −1.80 |
| Streamflow variation | 28 | 19.32 | 8.68 | +10.64 |
| Temperature | 28 | 4.20 | 8.40 | −4.20 |
| Total dissolved solids | 25 | 14.50 | 15.00 | −0.50 |
| AESTHETICS | | | | |
| *Land* | | | | |
| Geologic surface material | 6 | 1.50 | 1.86 | −0.36 |
| Relief and topographic character | 16 | 4.32 | 5.60 | −1.28 |
| Width and alignment | 10 | 3.10 | 4.30 | −1.20 |
| *Composition* | | | | |
| Composite effect | 15 | 7.65 | 8.25 | −0.60 |
| Unique composition | 15 | 0.90 | 2.85 | −1.95 |
| HUMAN INTEREST | | | | |
| *Educational/Scientific packages* | | | | |
| Ecological | 13 | 7.54 | 6.37 | +1.17 |
| Geological | 11 | 2.75 | 3.52 | −0.77 |
| Hydrological | 11 | 2.20 | 1.10 | +1.10 |
| LIFE PATTERNS | | | | |
| Employment opportunities | 13 | 6.76 | 9.10 | −2.34 |
| Housing | 13 | 4.42 | 9.10 | −4.68 |
| Social interactions | 11 | 5.50 | 7.70 | −2.20 |

In addition, a number of alternative project designs can be evaluated by comparing the total number of Environmental Impact Units. The alternative with the lowest total would be preferable.

This method exemplifies the problem of devising appropriate weightings. As Dickert points out,

'. . . . it is hard to believe, for example, that many socio-economic groups (such as low-income groups) would find the Battelle system which assigns over one-third of the possible points to environmental pollution and only twenty-six points (out of a total thousand) to housing and employment opportunities, a good representation of their values' (3.55).

The quantification of all impacts including intangibles, such as impacts on landscape, inevitably distorts and simplifies complex environmental and social systems. Also, the method involves a considerable commitment of resources to impact analysis and is difficult for non-experts to follow.

The main objection to this method, however, lies in its potential for avoiding public scrutiny and debate of major development proposals (3.56). Impacts on different environmental components are reduced to a seemingly neutral, non-controversial number, untainted by special interest, bias or inaccuracy. Laymen, including decision-makers, may believe that social and environmental scientists can predict accurately the impacts of a development. Consequently, they may be inhibited from questioning results obtained from the use of this method. Also, opposition groups or individuals may have to frame their views in terms of this method and might challenge only individual quantitative representations. This may divert attention away from the broad implications of a development. The political implications of this method constitute the most serious objections to its use. If used, elected decision-makers would not fulfil their proper role. This method provides a ready-made numerical answer to all problems of comparative evaluation which leaves no doubt as to the best 'decision'. The result, however, arises from the nature of the method, not the deliberations of decision-makers. Consequently, as a method it removes responsibility for decision-making from the decision-maker (3.57).

## PADC Method

When considering a major development proposal, those assessing a development should ensure that a balanced systematic appraisal of its potential impacts is made. In an attempt to achieve this objective, a method has been proposed which tries to combine best UK local planning authority practice with US experience of impact analysis (3.58). This method was developed for the assessment of major industrial planning applications within the existing UK development control system. The approach is flexible and with some modification could be applied in most planning systems. However, it would be most effective

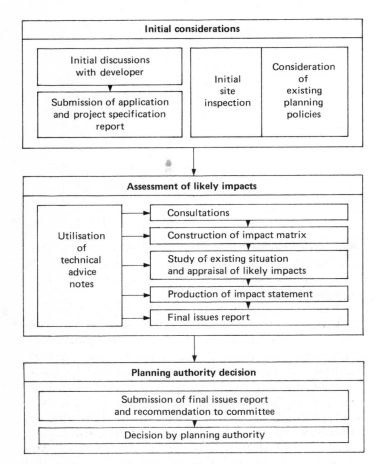

Figure 3.13    PADC structured approach.

(*By courtesy of the Controller of Her Majesty's Stationery Office*)

**Table 3.5. Topics that should be included in a Project Specification Report**

DETAILS OF THE PROPOSED PLANT AND ITS PROCESSES

*Physical characteristics of application site*
  Land requirements
  Site utilisation
  Marine site characteristics

*Employment characteristics*
  During construction phase
  When development is operational

*Financial data*
  Wage and salary levels
  Expenditure on locally produced inputs

*Infrastructure requirements*
  Raw material demand
  Transport requirements
  Water demand
  Electricity demand
  Gas demand
  Housing demand

*Factors of environmental significance*
  Noise levels
  Vibration levels
  Gaseous emissions
  Particulate emissions
  Odours
  Dust
  Discharge of aqueous effluents
  Solid wastes

*Emergency services*
  Fire and medical services
  Hazard
  Control of pollution at marine facilities

under planning systems which require developers to obtain authorisation for development from a central or local government agency. Figure 3.13 shows the proposed method as a series of linked activities, but in many cases, stages may be concurrent.

There are three main activities involved in environmental impact analysis. These are: identifying impacts; predicting the effects of impacts; and presenting results to both decision-makers and members of the public. The PADC Method details means for carrying out these activities. Although the activities are related sequentially, individual components of the PADC Method may be useful at different stages of impact assessment. The method is discussed below in relation to these three major activities. In the following section those with responsibility for assessing proposals and/or authorising development are referred to as 'planning authorities'.

IDENTIFYING IMPACTS

Two elements of the PADC Method are particularly useful in identifying impacts. These are, the Project Specification

Report (PSR) and the Impact Matrix. A prospective developer should be asked to prepare a PSR to be submitted to a planning authority when authorisation for a development is requested. This report provides those assessing a proposed development with a wide range of information which will enable a comprehensive assessment of likely impacts to be made. It is suggested that the information should cover the topics identified in Table 3.5. It may be necessary in some cases, however, for additional information to be supplied at a later date.

Developers may argue that information is not available at this early stage. Experience of major proposals suggests, however, that applicants planning major investments will have gone through detailed investigations of most aspects of a proposed development including siting criteria, labour needs and raw-material requirements. Similarly, levels of emissions may be known from design work and past experience. It is appreciated that in some instances developers may be able to give only approximate figures. A planning authority should attempt to establish which figures are accurate and the degree of confidence that can be placed on estimates. Submission of spurious information can be discouraged by making it known that data from a PSR might be used in framing constraints on development, for example, planning conditions. Information provided by a developer, however, should not remain unquestioned, and independent verification of data included in a PSR is recommended.

Having received a completed PSR a planning authority can identify likely impacts. The completion of an Impact Matrix will help in this activity by systematically relating the characteristics of a proposed development, based on data in a PSR, to the characteristics of a site and its environs. The most effective way of doing this is to use a simple matrix (Figure 3.14). Cells where the intersection of proposed development actions and characteristics of a site and its environs would cause an impact should be identified. Completion of this matrix is not a substitute for analysis, but the first stage of appraisal. Its sole purpose is to aid a systematic consideration of likely impacts. It is important to consider separately the construction and operational phases of development, as some types of impact may occur only in one phase, for example, the effect of a temporary labour camp built to house the construction labour force. This matrix is not comprehensive and should be modified to cater for specific developments.

The Impact Matrix will act as a guide to subsequent

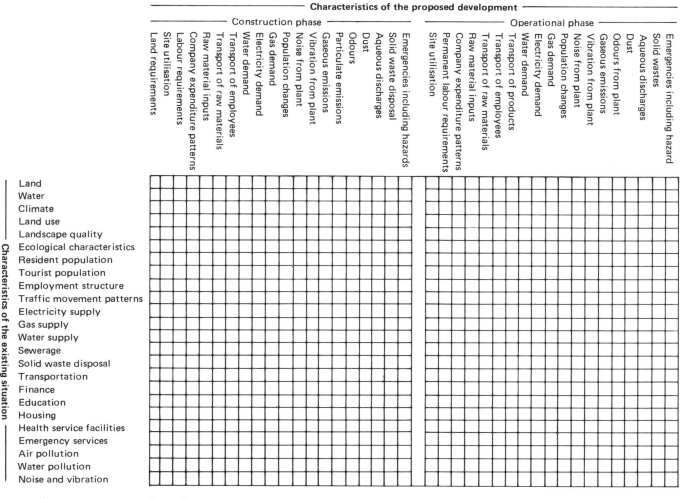

Figure 3.14   An Impact Assessment Matrix.    (*By courtesy of the Controller of Her Majesty's Stationery Office*)

analysis. The method recommends that those assessing a development should contact appropriate experts, specialist groups and organisations to ensure that as many impacts as possible are identified. A copy of appropriate sections of a PSR and an impact matrix should be circulated to each specialist group consulted. Consultees should be asked to comment on the significance of possible impacts identified in the matrix and to identify others which may have been omitted. It may be necessary, however, to obtain more detailed advice from consultees during the assessment of likely impacts.

PREDICTING IMPACTS

While no method can identify and predict all possible impacts of a proposed development, the one outlined below should provide a comprehensive approach of general applicability. Detailed information on the proposed development and data on the existing situation in the area likely to be affected by development should be drawn together. In each instance where a likely impact is identified in an Impact Matrix, an analysis should be made of the scale and significance of potential changes. It is important to establish not only the likely impacts of a development on the local environment and community, but also the extent to which these might impose constraints on the development during both construction and operational phases. This may be particularly important when entering into discussions with an applicant on possible design or layout modifications which would be required before planning permission would be granted.

The assessment of specific impacts is undertaken using the Technical Advice Notes and the List of Questions appended to the PADC Report. Some of the Technical Advice Notes contain detailed techniques for assessing impacts, for example, noise, the zone of visual influence, and the concentration of air pollutants. The remainder provide those assessing a development with a brief introduction to a particular topic such as ecology, and also identify the range of factors that should be considered during appraisal. These Technical Advice Notes would be valuable in briefing consultants and advisers in specialist fields, if relevant expertise were not available in a planning authority. The List of Questions highlights key aspects of the various impacts which might be associated with a development. The ques-

Table 3.6. Questions to aid the assessment of: 1. impacts on land use and landscape; 2. ecological impacts

| 1. LAND USE AND LANDSCAPE | 2. ECOLOGICAL CHARACTERISTICS OF THE SITE AND ITS SURROUNDINGS |
|---|---|
| (i) Is the proposed development compatible with surrounding land uses, such as agriculture, forestry, recreation? | (i) Are the development and the existing habitats compatible? |
| (ii) Will the proposed development substantially alter the landscape quality of the area? | (ii) If 'yes' what conservation methods will be necessary to protect the habitats? |
| (iii) Will the proposed development have a substantial zone of visual influence? | (iii) (a) If the developer described conservation methods that will be used to protect sensitive habitats, are these likely to be successful? |
| (iv) How far are existing land uses within the zone of visual influence compatible with the character of the proposed development? | (b) Are the claims of the developer with respect to these conservation methods realistic? |
| (v) Is the scale of the proposed development compatible with that of the local landscape? | (iv) If the development and habitats are not compatible, what communities will be at risk from: Physical destruction; Changes in groundwater level; Changes in quality of standing or flowing water, oxygen content, salinity, turbidity, flow rate and temperature; Chemical pollution, eutrophication and specific toxins; Changes in silting pattern; Air pollution of both water bodies and terrestrial habitats; Dust deposition; Changes in nutrient status of terrestrial habitats; Opening up of other areas to increased recreation pressure by the construction of access routes, roads and pathways? |
| (vi) Are there any trees or buildings on the site worthy of preservation? | |
| (vii) Are the materials to be used in the permanent structure and buildings of the development in character with those of the local area? | |
| (viii) Are the landscaping proposals submitted by the applicant satisfactory? | |
| (ix) Has consideration been given to a satisfactory scheme for site restoration should the proposed development cease operation? Has an appropriate means of financing the implementation of the restoration scheme been agreed should the company cease to be a viable concern? | (v) In each of the above cases what is the local, regional and national status of any habitats at risk? |
| | (vi) What is the quality of the habitats regardless of status? |
| | (vii) What dependent habitats or communities will also be at risk, including non-residents and migrants? What is their status? |
| | (viii) Can any of these habitats be recreated within a short period (5 to 10 years)? |

Figure 3.15 Impacts associated with temporary work camps for migrant workers are confined to the construction phase.    (*Photo: K. Chapman*)

tions are not exhaustive and may require modifications for specific developments. They illustrate, however, the range of questions which should be considered during appraisal. Questions to aid assessment of ecological impacts and impacts on land use and landscape are shown in Table 3.6.

In analysing probable impacts of both the construction and operational phases of development, it is important to establish their 'magnitude', for example, the number of brent geese that would be affected, and 'significance', for example, the number of geese affected as a proportion of the world population. An assessment should be made of each impact to determine whether it would be:

1. Beneficial and/or adverse;
2. Short term and/or long term;
3. Reversible and/or irreversible;
4. Direct and/or indirect;
5. Local and/or strategic.

Whenever possible, the nature of likely impacts should be explained by quantified information and reasoned argument.

## PRESENTING RESULTS

Results from detailed analysis should be drawn together in

an Impact Statement. In this statement each impact should be described briefly and assessed in relation to the five criteria outlined in the preceding paragraph. Consideration should also be given to the 'no go' alternative by relating existing trends in an area to projections of the situation that would pertain if planning permission were refused. This would identify, for example, areas suffering rural depopulation, falling employment because of decline in a major industry, or environmental degradation from cumulative effects of existing development.

An Impact Statement should include a full description of likely impacts with appended technical reports, summaries of consultations and a discussion of the 'no go' alternative. It should be available for public consultation and should be presented as background material for decision-makers. This material might contain complex data, calculations and technical arguments. Consequently, it would be useful to summarise and interpret the findings of an Impact Statement. Summary Sheets containing brief factual statements of the main impacts can be prepared for this purpose. A discussion of the importance of impacts should not be included in Summary Sheets as this is one of the main functions of an Impact Statement. An example of a Summary Sheet for one aspect of a hypothetical development is shown in Figure 3.16.

| Potential impact of proposed development | Classification of of impact | Description of potential impact |
|---|---|---|
| Airborne fluoride pollution on livestock farming | Indicate where appropriate<br>B = Beneficial<br>A = Adverse<br>St = Short term<br>Lt = Long term<br>R = Reversible<br>I = Irreversible<br>P = Primary<br>S = Secondary<br>T = Tertiary<br>L = Local<br>Sg = Strategic | The proposed plant would cause a significant rise in the level of airborne fluorides in the area. Livestock farming would be impracticable over a large area, because of the risk of fluorosis. This is a crippling disease which causes bone malformation in livestock. The affected area would extend from approximately 600 m upwind (to the south-west) to approximately 1000 m downwind (to the south-east). The profitability of four very productive farms on grade I agricultural land would be adversely affected. At present these farms employ a total of 17 men and have an estimated profit of £140 000. |

Figure 3.16 Summary sheet for a hypothetical development.

# Assessment Techniques

In the previous section a number of methods for impact analysis were reviewed. All methods offer a means of identifying impacts, and some contain guidelines for evaluating impacts. Evaluation, however, requires information on the effects of specific impacts which can only be obtained using specialised techniques. There is, therefore, a conceptual difference between methods and techniques. Methods are concerned with the identification of impacts and the organisation of results, while techniques provide the results. There is an important linkage between methods and techniques. First, impacts are identified using a method, perhaps one of those discussed above. Secondly, techniques are used to predict likely changes. Finally, information and data obtained using techniques can be organised, presented and, in some cases, evaluated according to the guidelines of a particular method.

Techniques for impact assessment can be grouped into a number of subject areas such as hazard, noise, transport, air pollution, ecology, landscape character and visual impact. Landscape planners, ecologists and landscape architects can make a major contribution to impact assessment in three ways; by determining the extent of the area from which an installation can be seen (the zone of visual influence), by assessing the impact of development on the visual quality of the landscape, and by assessing the effect of both on-site and off-site ecological changes. This section contains a description of selected techniques for:

1. Ecological evaluation;
2. Determining the zone of visual influence;
3. Landscape evaluation.

Many of the techniques also are of value for other aspects of landscape planning. The landscape and ecological evaluation techniques described have been developed in the UK to assess the landscape and ecological resources of a particular geographical area. Consequently, it might be impossible or invalid to transfer the techniques to other areas without modification. However, the underlying principles of certain techniques apply regardless of the area being considered so that, after appropriate modification, these techniques could be useful for assessment in different areas.

Techniques are used in appraisal both for assessing the existing situation in an area for which development is proposed and for predicting the effects of development. Most landscape and ecological assessment techniques have been developed to assess the existing situation, such as the ecological value of a site. At present, few techniques exist for projecting changes induced by development. As assessments of ecological value and landscape quality are essentially resource evaluations, most techniques involve an assessment of the extent and quality of available resources over a large area.

## Ecological Evaluation Techniques

Evaluation of wildlife habitats is dependent upon knowledge of the extent, type and quality of habitats. In the UK, this premise is embodied in the criteria used by the Nature Conservancy Council (NCC) in evaluating sites for nature conservation (3.59). These criteria have been discussed by Ratcliffe (3.60). They are: extent; diversity; naturalness; rarity; fragility; representativeness; research and educational value; recorded history; position in an ecological or geographical series; and potential value.

It has been possible for NCC to consider each of these factors in evaluating potential nature reserve sites in the UK because sufficient expertise and time have been available. A more pragmatic approach must be adopted, however, when time or resources are at a premium, for example, during development control procedures or in countries with few ecologists. Frequently, ecologists can determine quickly whether a site needs careful consideration because factors such as rarity, fragility and representativeness can be assessed in the light of past experience. For many sites this may be the most practicable means of assessment. Alternatively, existing large-scale evaluations may be used to identify ecologically vulnerable localities where detailed appraisal of proposed development would be necessary. Most of the survey and evaluation techniques described below are based on one or more of the NCC criteria. Many are habitat evaluations, although several techniques require the identification and recording of individual species.

The eight techniques described in this section were selected because they illustrate the main approaches which have been adopted for ecological assessment. The techniques were developed for:

1. East Hampshire;
2. West Sussex;
3. Cheshire;
4. Groene Ruimte Arnhem-Nijmegen;
5. Evaluating alternative routes of the M6;
6. Evaluations based on higher plant species rarity;
7. Evaluations based on indicator species;
8. Evaluating proposed development sites.

### EAST HAMPSHIRE

The basic technique has been outlined by Tubbs and Blackwood (3.61). This technique was the first attempt to produce a structured ecological evaluation for planning purposes, and has been the model for a number of other techniques. The objective was to divide the study area into a number of zones of different ecological value. Three broad types of vegetation were identified in the study area. These were: plantation woodland, unsown vegetation including non-plantation woodland, and the range of vegetation associated with agriculture (subsequently referred to as agricultural land). Initially, the area was divided into zones according to the presence of these three vegetation types. Areas of unsown vegetation and plantation woodland

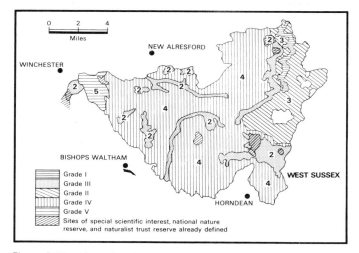

Figure 3.17  Map of ecological value in East Hampshire.

*(By courtesy of Hampshire County Council)*

give a total value for each zone. This was related to the II–V categories of ecological value according to the following scale:

| Score | Category |
|-------|----------|
| 15–18 | II |
| 11–14 | III |
| 6–10 | IV |
| 0–5 | V |

The zones were mapped to give a map of relative ecological value (Figure 3.17).

WEST SUSSEX

The technique used to assess ecological quality in West Sussex (3.62), was similar to the technique discussed above as emphasis was placed on the presence of areas of semi-natural vegetation. Fifteen habitat types were given numerical scores according to a subjective assessment of their relative ecological value (Table 3.7). The distribution of these habitats was determined from aerial photographs and mapped on 2½″ based OS maps. Each one-kilometre square in the area was sampled for habitat type. A standard grid of 16 dots was placed on each kilometre square. The numerical scores of the habitats beneath each of the dots were added to give a total score for each square. This total reflected the value of habitats present. Thus, the maximum score for a square was 160 when all dots coincided with high-grade habitats. Additional scores were given to squares which contained features of particular significance. These were:

1. Continuous high-grade habitat (exceeding 50% of the square–10 points added);
2. Reserves (National Nature Reserve (NNR) or Local Nature Reserve (LNR)–30 points added; Site of Special Scientific Interest (SSSI) or Sussex Trust Reserve–20 points added);
3. Large numbers of fields with associated marginal habitats such as hedgerows and trees (6 to 10 fields–5 points; 11 to 20 fields–10 points; 21 to 30 fields–20 points; and plus 30 fields–30 points).

greater than 25 hectares were distinguished as zones. The remaining area, agricultural land, was subdivided into different zones, for example, valley bottoms, ridges and dip slopes, on the basis of criteria such as topography and soil type. Each zone was ascribed to one of the categories, I–V, on a scale of ecological value where I represented the highest value. The following procedure was adopted:

*Unsown vegetation*: Unsown vegetation of more than 25 ha was assigned subjectively by an ecologist to one of the top two categories of ecological value (I or II). Such factors as rarity of the habitat type and the presence of features of scientific value were considered in the evaluation.

*Plantation woodland*: Plantation woodlands greater than 25 ha were ascribed subjectively by an ecologist to categories II or III. An estimate of the importance of a plantation as a wildlife reservoir was the basis for evaluation.

*Agricultural land*: No agricultural land was placed in category I. Each agricultural zone was assessed for habitat diversity by estimating the quantity of six features. The six features were:

1. Permanent grassland;
2. Hedgerows and hedgerow trees;
3. Banks, cuttings, roadside verges;
4. Parkland and non-commercial orchards;
5. Aquatic habitats such as ditches, ponds and streams;
6. Fragments of unsown vegetation.

The quantity of each of the six features was determined and scored on a scale from 0 to 3 where:

0 = absent or nearly absent
1 = present (but not conspicuous)
2 = numerous (conspicuous)
3 = abundant

The score for each habitat within the zone was summed to

Table 3.7. Habitat scores used in West Sussex study

| HIGH-GRADE HABITATS | OTHERS |
|---------------------|--------|
| Woodland 10 | Parkland 8 |
| Scrub 10 | Orchard 6 |
| Heath 10 | Plantation 6 |
| Unsown vegetation 10 | Improved grassland 3 |
| Tidal mudflats 10 | Arable 2 |
| Sand dunes, sand 10 | Development areas 0 |
| Saltings 10 | |
| Freshwater marsh 10 | |
| Freshwater 10 | |

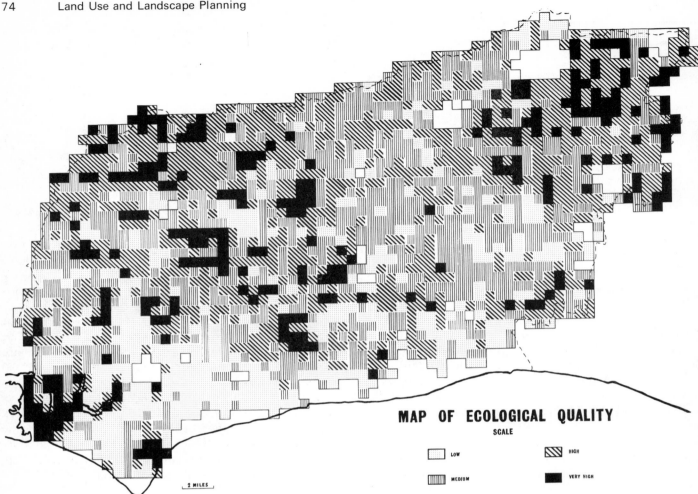

**MAP OF ECOLOGICAL QUALITY**

SCALE

☐ LOW          ▨ HIGH

▥ MEDIUM     ■ VERY HIGH

Figure 3.18     Map of ecological value in West Sussex.

*(By courtesy of West Sussex County Council)*

Scores in the area ranged from 26 to 190 and typical scores included 68 for a square in a mixed farming area and 140 for an estuarine square containing a LNR. These scores were divided by ten and were grouped into four classes to give a more readily interpretable representation of these data. The classes were:

    3–6 = low
    7–8 = medium
    9–11 = high
    11+ = very high

The class of each one kilometre square was mapped to produce a map showing the relative ecological quality of West Sussex (Figure 3.18).

CHESHIRE

The ecological resources of Cheshire have been catalogued in a form which is relevant to both forward planning and to development control (3.63). The object was to identify the ecological assets of the county so that policies and development proposals could be assessed in light of potential impacts on wildlife resources. Initially, the Nature Conservancy Council prepared a map indicating zones of high wildlife interest based on known prime sites for nature conservation in Cheshire, such as NNRs, LNRs and SSSIs. As the map covered less than 25% of the county, NCC carried out an ecological evaluation of Cheshire based on the technique of Tubbs and Blackwood (see p. 72).

These maps were of only limited value for development control, because individual sites were not considered in detail. Consequently, an inventory of important sites was compiled to avoid the problems inherent in attempting to establish the conservation value of a site each time a planning application was received. 387 sites of wildlife importance including 36 scheduled sites (two NNRs, 22 SSSIs and 12 Cheshire County Trust Reserves) and 21 road verges were identified by NCC and the Cheshire Conservation Trust. The remainder were 'sites of biological im-

    Grade A: sites of potential SSSI status;
    Grade B: good examples of particular habitat types
             collectively important on a county basis;
    Grade C: sites of local significance.

Information on all sites of wildlife importance was stored in a computer so that routine screening of development proposals could indicate potential risks to individual sites.

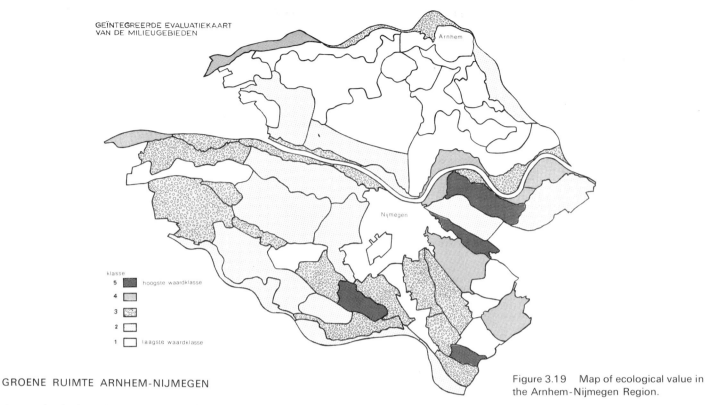

GEÏNTEGREERDE EVALUATIEKAART
VAN DE MILIEUGEBIEDEN

Arnhem

Nijmegen

klasse

5 ▨ hoogste waardklasse

4 ▨

3 ▨

2 ☐

1 ☐ laagste waardklasse

GROENE RUIMTE ARNHEM-NIJMEGEN

Figure 3.19    Map of ecological value in the Arnhem-Nijmegen Region.

An ecological evaluation of the Arnhem-Nijmegen region of the Netherlands has been prepared based on a subjective assessment by relevant experts (3.64). The region was divided into 66 'environmental areas'. For each area, an assessment was made of the abundance of large mammals, reptiles, breeding birds, and winter resident and passage migrant birds. The vegetation was also recorded. From these data mathematical determinations of ecological diversity were made. Each of the 66 environmental areas was assessed subjectively for the ecological value of flora and fauna on a scale of 1–5, in which class 1 was the highest value. Six parameters were used in a subjective evaluation of the vegetation. These were regional rarity, national rarity, representativeness, two attributes of diversity, and reproducibility. Reproducibility is an estimate of the ease with which a habitat can be recreated; for example, agricultural grassland can be created easily, whereas it may take many centuries to produce a mature forest. Zoological evaluations were based on national rarity and abundance. A composite map was made showing the overall ecological value of each environmental area on the five-point scale (Figure 3.19). The value of each area was determined subjectively from the value of the individual components, such as vegetation and mammals.

EVALUATING ALTERNATIVE ROUTES OF THE M6
Yapp developed a technique for evaluating two alternative routes of the M6 through West Cumbria (3.65). The evaluation was based on an assessment of the quality of habitats which would be destroyed along each route. Habitats along each route were assessed using the technique of Tubbs and Blackwood (see p. 72). Yapp proposed a scale ranging from 0–5, in which habitats of the highest value, category I on the Tubbs and Blackwood scale, were given a score of 5. The lowest category, V, was given a score of 1 and the other categories were changed accordingly. In addition, developed areas where new road construction would have little ecological impact were given scores of 0. Thus, semi-natural woodland, part of which was designated an SSSI, and planted woodland were given scores of 5 and 4 respectively. There were four areas of agricultural land present which were assessed according to the presence of the six Tubbs and Blackwood features, such as parklands, hedgerows, banks and streams. On the basis of these features three agricultural areas were given scores of 2, while the fourth area of lower quality scored 1. The score of each habitat was multiplied by the length that would be destroyed by road construction. These values were added to give a measure of the total impact of the road for each of the alternatives (Table 3.8).

This method of assessment has one major disadvantage in that it undervalues high-quality habitats; for example, destruction of 5 km of low-grade agricultural habitat with a score of 1 has an ecological impact equal to the loss of 1 km of high-value habitat with a score of 5. A logarithmic scale to the base 10 is unsuitable, as destruction of 10 000 km of habitat with a score of 1 would be equivalent to the destruction of 1 km of high-grade habitat scoring 5. Consequently, two alternative weighting schemes were used. First, the 1–5 scale was converted to a geometric scale (1, 2, 4, 8 and 16) which gave additional importance to high-quality

Table 3.8. Impact scores for two alternative routes of the M6

| | LENGTH OF HABITAT DESTROYED (km) | HABITAT CLASS (Tubbs & Blackwood) | HABITAT CLASS (Yapp) | HABITAT CLASS (geometric) | IMPACT (Yapp weighting) | IMPACT (geometric weighting) |
|---|---|---|---|---|---|---|
| Route A | 7 | IV | 2 | 2 | 14 | 14 |
| | 5 | II | 4 | 8 | 20 | 40 |
| | 2.5 | I | 5 | 16 | 12.5 | 40 |
| | 3 | II | 4 | 8 | 12 | 24 |
| | 6 | IV | 2 | 2 | 12 | 16 |
| Total impact | | | | | 70.5 | 130 |
| Route B | 15 | V | 1 | 1 | 15 | 15 |
| | 17 | IV | 2 | 2 | 34 | 34 |
| Total impact | | | | | 49 | 49 |
| Ratio of impact A:B | | | | | 1.44 | 2.67 |

habitats. The class for each habitat was multiplied by the length that would be destroyed. The total scores for each alternative were added and the two routes compared (Table 3.8.). Secondly, a more complex weighting system based on a logarithmic scale was developed and the results recalculated. Yapp considered that the geometric scale was the more appropriate.

EVALUATIONS BASED ON HIGHER PLANT SPECIES RARITY

Helliwell has developed an ecological evaluation technique based on botanical surveys. The technique can be used either for assessing large areas from existing floral records (3.66) or for assessing individual sites (3.67). From the surveys an assessment of conservation value is obtained in which species are weighted according to their regional and national rarity. The evaluation of a farm in Cumbria is discussed below as an example.

The 105-ha farm was divided into five habitat types: woodland; re-seeded pasture; permanent grassland; hedgerows; and stream banks. The frequency of occurrence of species in the woodland and grassland habitats was re-corded from random 200-m$^2$ sample plots and from 4-m$^2$ and 1-m$^2$ sub-plots located within the 200-m$^2$ plots. Species were recorded from 16-m long plots located at 200-m and 100-m intervals in the hedgerows and stream banks respectively. Occurrence was weighted according to plot size. Species were given scores of 3, 2 and 1 respectively for each occurrence in a 1-m$^2$, 4-m$^2$ and 200-m$^2$ plot. These scores were added to give a combined total which represented the relative frequency of each species on the farm. The relative frequency of five species is shown in Table 3.9.

The value of each species on a site can be determined by weighting its frequency according to its regional and national rarity. An objective source of data on plant occurrence is the National Mapping Scheme in which presence or absence of each species in the British flora has been determined for each $10 \times 10$ km grid square of the British Isles (3.68). The farm considered by Helliwell is located in a region of 84 grid squares. For each species present on the farm, regional rarity was determined by counting the number of grid squares within the region in which the species occurred. Similarly, national rarity was

Table 3.9. Relative conservation value of selected species

| SPECIES | RELATIVE FREQUENCY ON SITE | PRESENCE IN 100 KM$^2$ SQUARES (regional) | (national) | CONSERVATION VALUE |
|---|---|---|---|---|
| *Agrostis tenuis* | 844 | 77 | 2600 | 30.0 |
| *Lolium perenne* | 16169 | 80 | 3000 | 70.0 |
| *Quercus petraea* | 1260 | 51 | 1300 | 197.4 |
| *Thelypteris phegopteris* | 1.3 | 35 | 600 | 83.2 |
| *Tilia cordata* | 2.0 | 4 | 150 | 635.6 |

assessed from the total number of squares in the British Isles in which each species is found. The regional and national rarity of five species is shown in Table 3.9. The relative national and regional rarity for each species can be calculated from the formula:

$$\text{rarity value} = 1/[e^{(-0.000676y^2 + 0.1613y - 0.1606)}]^{0.64} \times c$$

where $e = 2.71828$
$y = \%$ occurrence (in the region or nationally)
$c = $ a constant, 0.002754

The conservation value of a species is determined from the formula:

conservation value =
$A^{0.36} \times$ (national rarity value + regional rarity value)

where $A = $ relative frequency of the species on the site.

Table 3.10. Relative conservation value of different habitats in the study area

| HABITAT | AREA (ha) | RELATIVE CONSERVATION VALUE |
|---|---|---|
| Woodland | 28 | 2607 |
| Re-seeded pasture | 36 | 518 |
| Permanent grassland | 40 | 1267 |
| Hedgerows | 0.45 | 481 |
| Stream banks | 0.45 | 816 |

This technique can be adopted to assess the relative value of different sites. The conservation value of each species on a site can be added to give a total conservation value and the value of different sites compared. Alternatively, the value of different habitats can be determined. Table 3.10, for example, shows the relative value of different habitats on Beckside farm. It can be seen that the re-seeded pastures make little contribution to the conservation value of the site compared with their total area. Hedgerows and stream banks, in contrast, had comparable conservation value to re-seeded pastures, yet were one-hundredth the area. Woodland and permanent grassland were the most important habitats.

EVALUATIONS BASED ON INDICATOR SPECIES
One of the main functions of ecological surveys for planning purposes is to identify sites which are important for conservation. Peterken has developed a technique for assessing the conservation value of woodland on the presence of indicator plant species (3.69). Primary woodlands, areas with a record of continuous woodland cover through historical times, are the most important woodlands for nature conservation. These woodlands have a distinctive flora and fauna, and many of the species present show little ability to invade newly created (secondary) woodland. These immobile species can be used to identify and evaluate primary woodlands. The pilot study was carried out in

central Lincolnshire. Detailed floral records of 73 primary woodlands were collected and compared with the flora of more than 150 planted woodlands, and several hundred hedgerows. Many of these old mixed hedgerows were remnants of former primary woodland. From the records, 50 primary woodland plant species were identified. These ranged from those plants confined to primary woodlands to those which appear to colonise secondary woodland, but only rarely. Primary woodlands were evaluated by the number of primary indicator species each contained. The highest scoring woodland contained 31 of the 50 indicator species and nine woodlands contained more than 20.

The indicator species identified by Peterken can be used only in central Lincolnshire. In another area appropriate indicator species would have to be identified. A simplified procedure for identifying primary woodland species for any other area of the UK is suggested. From the floral atlas (3.70) all species known to occur in the $10 \times 10$ km grid squares covering the area under consideration should be recorded. Non-woodland species should be deleted from the list. It is recommended that 20 secondary woodlands in the area should be identified, for example, woodlands not present on the *First Edition Ordnance Survey maps*. Species which are found in secondary woodlands also should be deleted from the list. The remaining list gives primary woodland indicator plant species for the area under consideration.

Indicator species have been used in other evaluations. Rose has identified a range of lichen species which may be used as indicators of primary woodland of high conservation status (3.71). Similarly, species indicative of diverse grassland of high conservation status in south Yorkshire and north Derbyshire have been identified (3.72). Ward and Evans used a floral index, based in part on species restricted to limestone pavements, in an evaluation of pavement sites (3.73).

EVALUATING PROPOSED DEVELOPMENT SITES
The procedure for assessing ecological impacts proposed by PADC (3.74) was prepared for use in situations where little is known of the ecological value of a site and its surroundings. The procedure is divided into three phases. First, the existing situation is determined. Secondly, potential impacts are identified. Finally, impacts are appraised. When determining the existing situation the ecologist should produce a habitat map of the proposed site. In addition, surveys should be made of the habitats in the surrounding area, particularly for developments which are likely to produce large-scale impacts over a wide area. It is impossible to predefine the detailed aspects which should be considered, as this will depend on the particular development proposed. Ecologists should assess the conservation status of each habitat considered. At this stage some of the survey and evaluation techniques described above could be of value.

For each of the habitat types identified, an attempt should be made to determine the major factors which control floral and faunal composition. These may be physical,

Figure 3.20 Development of the Zuidoostflevoland in the Netherlands changed an area of open water into a vast reed swamp internationally important for several rare bird species.

(*Photo by courtesy of Rijksdienst voor de Ijsselmeerpolders*)

chemical or management factors. In estuaries, for example, sediment size is important in determining invertebrate fauna and ultimately wading species utilising this food source. Similarly, restricted nitrogen and phosphorus levels are important in oligotrophic lakes and for maintaining the diversity of calcareous and neutral grassland. Past and present management, particularly grazing and burning, is important in many ecosystems. An understanding of the determining factors may aid appraisal of impacts. Ecologists should identify potential impacts from a consideration of survey data on the site and its environs, and a detailed report on the characteristics of a proposed development. Consideration should be given to opportunities for habitat building presented by development. For example, the creation of new polders in the Netherlands has produced a vast freshwater marsh containing several rare bird species (3.75). Major ecological impacts are likely to be associated with:

1. Physical destruction of habitats;
2. Air pollution (heavy metals, sulphur oxides, nitrogen oxides, dust, particulates, pesticides, etc.);
3. Water pollution;
4. Changes in the direction and/or volume of stream flow;
5. Groundwater changes;
6. Management changes;
7. Increased recreation pressure;
8. Erosion;
9. Disturbance of animals by noise.

An assessment should be made of the significance of each potential impact. Initially, it is important to establish the degree to which impacts are reversible. Thus, disturbance (blasting or heavy vehicle movements) during construction might be a temporary reversible change so that animal populations may return to predevelopment levels after con-

struction has finished. In contrast, inundation by a reservoir would be an irreversible change.

An assessment should be made of the magnitude and significance of each irreversible change, and the conservation value of habitats likely to be adversely affected should be determined. In addition, the reproducibility of each affected habitat should be estimated. An indication should be given of whether there are techniques to recreate the habitat on a different site, and the commitment of time and resources necessary to achieve this. Consideration also should be given to the possibility of rehabilitating the site to its former condition once the development has ceased to be operational.

### Determining the Zone of Visual Influence
Visual intrusion is one of the main factors in determining the impact of a proposed installation on landscape resources (see p. 80). It is important, therefore, to establish the area over which a proposed installation can be seen. One simple, but laborious, method of doing this is to draw topographic profiles around an installation. However, Hebblethwaite has developed a technique for a more rapid determination of the zone of visual influence (3.76).

The visual impact of an installation is affected by topography. In a high-relief landscape intrusion may be reduced in a number of ways. First, hills may reduce the extent of the area from which an installation can be seen. Secondly, the location may be selected to ensure that no profile is seen against the skyline. Finally, texture and pattern of vegetation may help to absorb the development visually.

The height of an installation is also important in determining the zone of visual influence. The apparent height of an installation, however, decreases with increasing distance (Table 3.11). Although refractive effects of the atmosphere increase the apparent height, this is exceeded by a reduction caused by the Earth's curvature.

Three pieces of equipment are needed for determining the zone of visual influence—a map (preferably 1:25000 scale) and two pieces of transparent plastic about 15 cm wide and 125 cm long. The contour intervals selected for the map depend on topography. In flat or gently undulating areas, where small changes in topography can influence visual impact significantly, a map with 1 m contours drawn from stereoscopic aerial photographs is ideal. In areas of higher relief, larger intervals can be used. One of the plastic strips, the *sight line plate*, should be marked with a single straight line along its length. On the second strip, called the *height plate*, a number of evenly spaced parallel lines sufficient to cover the required topographic range (for example, 300 m at 5- or 10-m intervals) should be drawn 5 mm apart. These lines should curve slightly downwards with increasing distance to take account of the effective height reduction (Table 3.11).

The sight line plate is placed on the map in the required direction. The height plate is pinned at the site of the installation at a height equal to its altitude plus the height of the proposed installation (Figure 3.22). The height plate is rotated until the nearest rising contour and the line on the height plate equivalent to this altitude coincide with the sight line. Each contour intersecting the sight line is considered in turn working out from the installation. If a contour and the appropriate altitude line intersect above the sight line, the installation would be visible from this point but, if they intersect below the line, the installation would be invisible (Figure 3.23). When an invisible point is reached, the height plate is repositioned so that the altitude line of the previous visible point on the height plate and

Figure 3.21   Visual intrusion of the oil platform fabrication yard at Loch Kishorn.

(*Photo: P. Wathern*)

its contour line coincide with the sight line. By continuing along the sight line as described above, visible points can be determined until the next invisible point is reached, when the height plate must be repositioned. This gives the visible and invisible points in the direction of the sight line. This procedure is repeated at 5° intervals around the installation, noting each point that would be visible. Visible points are linked to show the zone of visual influence.

Visual screening afforded by existing woodlands and shelter belts can be determined by adding tree heights to altitude to show the true OD height of the trees. The effects of planting schemes can also be projected using this technique, if tree heights are taken corresponding to different times, for example after 5, 10 and 20 years.

Table 3.11. Effective reduction of height with distance

| Distance from structure in miles | 2 | 3 | 4 | 5 | 6 | 7 | 8 | 9 | 10 | 15 | 20 |
|---|---|---|---|---|---|---|---|---|---|---|---|
| Effective reduction in height in feet | 2.25 | 5 | 9 | 14 | 20 | 28 | 37 | 46 | 57 | 128 | 228 |

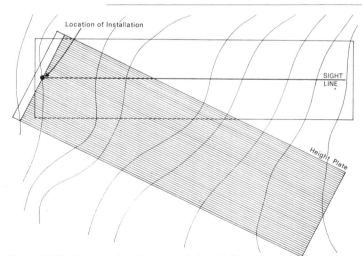

Figure 3.22   Determining the zone of visual influence.

(*By courtesy of the Controller of Her Majesty's Stationery Office*)

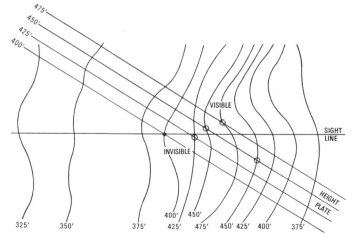

Figure 3.23   Determining visible and invisible points.

(*By courtesy of the Controller of Her Majesty's Stationery Office*)

## Landscape Evaluation

Perception of landscape is the result of an interaction between the physical components of a landscape and a range of personal emotional responses induced by it. Consequently, landscape perception is dynamic, as both the physical components, such as colour and light intensity, and the emotional components vary with time. Evaluation techniques differ in the degree to which the concept of 'landscape as art' influences not only the measurement and evaluation of physical components, but also emotional components (3.77). Some techniques emphasise quantification of the physical components. The basis for other techniques, however, is that the interactions between balance, pattern and form are not considered adequately by quantifying individual components. Generally, these techniques consist of structured subjective evaluations by experts qualified in design.

Landscape evaluation can be divided into two phases. Initially, areas are classified into landscape types. This is a taxonomic exercise concerned with the identification and measurement of diagnostic features. The second phase involves an assessment of the comparative aesthetic value of different landscape types. Such a rigid division may not be possible with certain techniques because features used to derive a classification often are those believed to be important in the perception of landscape. Thus evaluation may be implicit in certain classifications, and high correlations are frequently found between 'landscape type' and 'value'.

Five techniques for evaluating landscape quality are described in this section. These are techniques developed for making a landscape evaluation of:

1. East Sussex;
2. The West Midlands Region;
3. East Hampshire Area of Outstanding Natural Beauty;
4. Scotland;
5. Proposed Development Sites.

No attempt has been made to describe all available techniques, as good reviews of landscape evaluation techniques appear elsewhere (3.78). These five techniques were selected because they illustrate two of the major approaches which have been adopted for landscape evaluation. A third type of approach based on multivariate statistical techniques was developed for the Coventry–Solihull–Warwickshire study (3.79). This technique is not described in this section, because it is given detailed consideration in the previous chapter , p. 40.

### EAST SUSSEX

The evaluation of the landscape of East Sussex (see also page 38) was divided into two phases, a desk study and a field survey (3.80). During the desk study 45 people assessed the quality of 20 selected photographic surrogate landscapes. The photographs were selected to provide illustrations of a wide range of different landscape types. Dunn has shown that the response of people to photographs in preference tests is comparable to

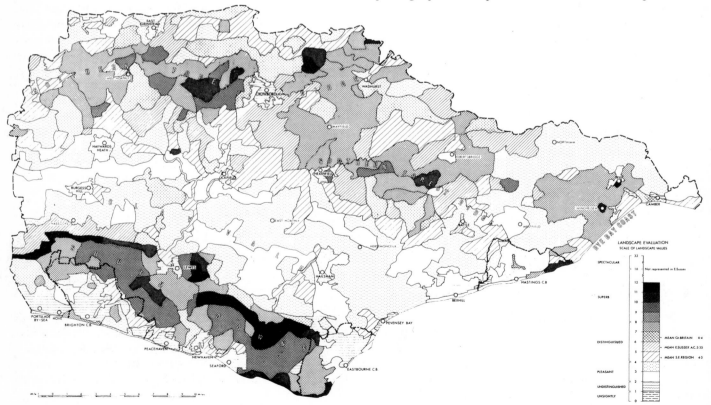

Figure 3.24    Landscape evaluation of East Sussex. (*By courtesy of East Sussex County Council*)

responses in the field (3.81). The assessors gave the 20 photographs numerical scores of value against a reference photograph. Although a similar ranking was produced by each assessor, it was found that 10 people with considerable design experience produced a wider range of scores than the remainder. On the basis of the score range produced by those assessors with design experience, the following scale divided into six classes was devised:

   0 – 1   unsightly
   1 – 2   undistinguished
   2 – 4   pleasant
   4 – 8   distinguished
   8 –16   superb
 16 –32   spectacular

The objective of the field survey was to assess the value of views within the study area on the above numerical scale. The assessors who carried out the field work had considerable design experience and were skilled at map interpretation. Views were assessed from a number of viewpoints. Two viewpoints per kilometre square was found to be an adequate sampling frequency in East Sussex, and these viewpoints were selected to give a broad spectrum of views. At each viewpoint, views were assessed in all directions. Initially, each view was ascribed to one of the classes, for example 'superb' or 'distinguished' and then given a numerical score, to one decimal place, within the range of the class. For example, a particular view in the 'superb' class might be given a score of 11.2. For the purposes of the study a view was defined as the sector of the landscape enclosed within an angle of 60°.

The county was divided into a number of visually discrete landscape areas. The boundaries between these areas were selected to coincide with natural features such as rivers and ridges. View scores collected in the field were converted to composite values for these landscape areas. A view has three components: near views < 800 m; middle views 800 m– 6500 m; and distant views > 6500 m. It was argued that the contribution an area made to landscape quality was determined largely by long-range views into an area, rather than local views within an area. The value of each area, therefore, was assessed from the score of all views in which it featured. In the assessment, views greater than 6500 m were weighted most heavily. Unique views also were given additional weight. The landscape quality of each area was mapped to produce a landscape evaluation map of the county (Figure 3.24).

## THE WEST MIDLANDS REGIONAL STUDY

Three groups of features were assessed in the landscape evaluation produced for the West Midlands (3.82). These were land form, land use and vegetation. The survey area was divided into a number of 2-km grid squares. The character of each grid square was determined with respect to eight features: topography; land; scale; vegetation density (measured as tree cover); buildings; water; detractors; and trespass (the degree of isolation from built-up areas). Each feature was divided into four classes, for example,

topography was divided into flat, undulating, hilly and mountainous. Each class was given a numerical score (Table 3.12). These scores were determined subjectively on the basis of the relative contribution that each class was thought to make to landscape quality. Thus, some features, for example, tree cover and vernacular architecture, make a positive contribution to landscape quality, while others such as derelict land detract from it. For every square, an assessment was made of the appropriate class of each feature which most accurately described the square. Squares were given the score of the appropriate class for each feature; Thus, for example, a square would score 6 if the vegetation density (tree cover) exceeded 50%, and − 8 if detractors were a very large intrusion. Numerical values for each of the eight features were added to produce a total score for each square. The scores were divided into 10 'landscape grades'. The grade of each square was mapped to give the relative landscape quality of the region.

## EAST HAMPSHIRE AREA OF OUTSTANDING NATURAL BEAUTY

The technique of landscape quality assessment developed for the East Hampshire Area of Outstanding Natural Beauty by Hebblethwaite (see also page 39) depended upon a characterisation of the physical form of the landscape combined with an assessment of the influence of land use, visual simplicity and detractors (3.83). Landscape was assessed subjectively and ascribed to one of four quality classes: very high, high, medium and low.

Physical form of the landscape is the primary determinant of quality. Two features are particularly important. These are vertical and horizontal components. There are two types of very high-quality landscape. The first type has strong contrast between horizontal and vertical components; that is, the presence of both is equally important. The second type of very high-quality landscape has no contrast, as only one of the components is present; for example, very high-quality landscape includes marshlands and saltings, which lack vertical elements, and unterraced mountain scenery, which lacks horizontal elements. Between these extremes of strong contrast and no contrast is a range of landforms in which elements are weakly contrasted.

Physical landform and the presence of detractors are considered when assessing landscape quality of different areas. Initially, classes are assessed according to these elements. Very high-quality landscapes have strong contrast or no contrast elements, and lack visual detractors. High-quality landscapes either have weak contrasts between elements and lack detractors or are very high-quality landscapes downgraded by weak detractors. Medium and low-quality landscapes are very high and high-quality landscapes respectively downgraded by the presence of major significant detractors.

The effect of land use is considered during evaluation. Seven types of land use are identified: urban; residential; agricultural; forested; mixed agricultural and forested; special use (for example, golf courses and country parks); and wild areas. The major land uses which are visual

Table 3.12. Score for landscape components

| ELEMENT | DESCRIPTION | NUMERICAL RATING |
|---|---|---|
| *Topography* | Flat land ( < 100 ft altitude difference) | 2 |
| | Undulating (100–500 ft altitude difference) | 8 |
| | Hilly (500–1000 ft altitude difference) | 10 |
| | Mountains ( > 1000 ft altitude difference) | 10 |
| | Open or moorland | 6 |
| *Land* | Cultivated land | 2 |
| | Derelict land | −8 |
| | Parkland | 8 |
| | Domestic (rural farmland with fields) | 2 |
| *Scale* | Perspective over 4 miles | 8 |
| | Up to 2000 ft in height | 10 |
| | > 2000 ft in height | 10 |
| *Vegetation density* (tree cover) | < 2% | 2 |
| | 2–20% | 8 |
| | 20–50% | 10 |
| | > 50% | 6 |
| *Buildings* | Individual dwellings | 0 |
| | Farms | 0 |
| | Villages of traditional materials | 6 |
| | Villages not of traditional materials | 8 |
| *Water* | Stream or small river | 2 |
| | Large river or lake ( > 20 ha) | 8 |
| | Water ( > 25% cover) | 8 |
| *Detractors* | Minor intrusion | −2 |
| | Small but numerous intrusions (e.g. power line) | −4 |
| | Large intrusion | −6 |
| | Very large intrusions (e.g. large spoil heap) | −8 |
| *Trespass* (distance to built-up area) | < 1 km | −2 |
| | 1–2 km | −1 |
| | 2–3 km | 0 |
| | > 3 km | 0 |

detractors include residential and urban development, more than 80% woodland cover (as it limits visibility), and small areas of wild vegetation that look incongruous in a well-managed landscape. Most other general uses do not detract visually, particularly when well managed and maintained. There is also, however, a wide range of specific detractors which must be considered. These include unreinstated mineral workings, refuse dumps, silos, powerlines and industrial buildings. Each detractor is assessed subjectively as very strong, strong or weak. One very strong, two strong, one strong plus two weak, or four weak detractors are sufficient to degrade landscape quality by one class, for example from high to medium quality. In the survey, half-kilometre squares were assessed by inward views from outside the square. These views were taken from many different directions so that the final estimate of quality was based on a number of samples. When assessors felt that the landscape quality of a square was on the borderline between two classes, simplicity of the landscape within the square was considered. Simple large-scale landscapes were upgraded, while small-scale 'cluttered' landscapes were assigned to the lower class.

SCOTLAND

The Countryside Commission for Scotland has published a report which contains a procedure for the assessment of the landscape resources of Scotland (3.84). The suggested procedure would produce both an assessment of landscape character and an evaluation of quality. Initially, the study area is divided into a number of visually self-contained landscape tracts defined on the basis of maps, aerial photographs and fieldwork; for example, a visually contained valley or upland plateau constitutes a tract. The boundaries of these tracts should be drawn to coincide with 1-km grid

Table 3.13. Landscape features for the appraisal of Scottish landscape resources

| LANDFORM | COASTAL |
|---|---|
| *Features* | *Features* |
| cliff | cliffs |
| outcropping rock | beaches |
| peak | islands |
| hill | rocks |
| other | indentation |
| | dunes |
| GROUND COVER | marshes |
| *Moorland* | other |
| heather | |
| bracken | POINTS |
| scattered trees | settlements |
| other | smaller buildings & groups |
| | prominent 'traditional' buildings |
| *Woodland* | (e.g. castles, churches) |
| species distribution | prominent 'non-traditional' build- |
| age distribution | ings (e.g. new hotel, power |
| felling areas | station) |
| edge | tips |
| other | excavations |
| | dams |
| *Farmland* | bridges |
| state of management | masts |
| hedges | eyesores |
| walls | other |
| hedgerow trees | |
| other | NETWORKS |
| | minor roads |
| WATER | main roads |
| *Lakes* | motorway character |
| presence | railway track |
| indentation | H/V wires |
| islands | L/V wires |
| shore | canals |
| water quality | other |
| other | |
| | VIEWS |
| *Rivers* | presence |
| presence | mountains |
| pattern | water |
| islands | distance |
| falls | land beyond sea |
| rapids | (in coastal tracts) |
| water quality | other striking features |
| other | |

squares so that data collected systematically from maps can be related to each tract.

Each tract is classified according to three criteria: landform, relief and vegetation. There are four landform types: valley, plateau, plain and edge. Relief is assessed subjectively on a three-class scale: high, medium and low. Vegetation is determined on the presence of three classes: moorland, woodland and farmland. Each vegetation class is included when it exceeds 20°/₀ of the tract. Consequently, there are seven vegetation types, because combinations of the three vegetation classes, such as moorland/woodland, can occur. From these features a hierarchical classification of character can be produced based on four primary landform elements, three secondary relief classes, and seven tertiary vegetation types.

Seven factors should be assessed in the field to determine quality. These factors are subdivided into 56 features (Table 3.13). For each feature an assessment should be made of its prominence or impact on the landscape.

0   inconspicuous
1   conspicuous
2   very conspicuous

For each conspicuous or very conspicuous feature an assessment should be made of its contribution to landscape quality as follows:

−2   bad
−1   poor
0   neutral
+1   good
+2   excellent

Features which are either inconspicuous or neutral should be given a score of 0. For the remaining features, numerical values indicating the contribution to the landscape and impact are combined to assess each feature; digits are added and the total given the mathematical sign of the contribution to quality. Therefore, a quality score of +2 and a conspicuousness score of 1 gives a combined score of +3. A quality score of −2 and a conspicuousness score of +2 produces a combined score of −4. A record should be made of the combined score for each of the 56 elements in each landscape tract. These scores should be added to give a composite score indicative of the quality of each tract. It is recommended that the composite score for tracts should be grouped into classes of landscape quality for subsequent mapping.

PROPOSED DEVELOPMENT SITES
As none of the published techniques of landscape evaluation were applicable for considering individual development proposals, a procedure was developed by the PADC research team to ensure that appropriate factors would be considered (3.85). A number of key items, acknowledged to be important in determining landscape quality in a number of studies, were identified in order to be considered during appraisal. These items include not only physical components of the landscape but also integrated visual attributes. Initially, the general area in which the installation would be sighted can be divided into landscape tracts. These tracts, visually self-contained units such as valleys, coastal plains or escarpment edges, can be determined from maps and confirmed by fieldwork. In addition, the zone of visual influence should be ascertained. Subsequent appraisal should focus on the tracts wholly or partly within this zone.

A subsequent assessment can be made, particularly by

members of an appraisal team with design experience, of the quality of views into the site. For each tract under consideration, an assessment of both the quality of views into and from the tract and the character of the landscape is required. When data from previous large-scale landscape evaluations are available, these should be utilised. Alternatively, a survey should be initiated using a suitable evaluation technique. If this were not possible, a subjective evaluation should be made of each tract. The factors that should be assessed for each tract are:

1. Topography—value is correlated with increasing relief;
2. Vegetation—vegetation types which enhance the quality of landscape in the UK include woodland, heathland, moorland, downland, hedgerows, shelterbelts and scrub;
3. Water—the presence of water, such as lakes and rivers increases quality;
4. Pattern—the relationship between the tonal and textural elements of the landscape and its scale should be considered. Predefinition of relationships indicative of high quality is not possible, but harmonious relationships should become apparent in the field;
5. Detractors;
6. The type and scale of local architecture and local communities—whether the architecture and scale of local communities is related harmoniously to the surrounding landscape should become apparent from fieldwork.

# Conclusion

This chapter contains a critical evaluation of procedures, methods and techniques which can be used to implement impact analysis. Although it has been shown that these have certain deficiencies, it should not be concluded that impact analysis is of little use. The utility of impact analysis can be illustrated from US experience. Since 1970 more than 7500 draft EISs have been filed. Many criticisms of the effectiveness of NEPA and the associated EIS requirement have been voiced. However, these same critics are the first to defend NEPA when it comes under periodic attack from vested interests opposed to the Act. Most authorities regard impact analysis as a useful, and at times powerful, management tool. It has led to a greater understanding of the potential impacts of major developments and, in a number of cases, has resulted in the modification or abandonment of projects. Perhaps the most significant contributions of impact analysis to environmental planning have been to increase public involvement in decision-making and to encourage Federal agencies to take environmental and social factors into account when formulating their proposals.

Figure 3.25    In developing countries impact analysis would be particularly valuable for the assessment of major developments such as the Cerro de Pasco lead and zinc mine in Peru.

(*Photo by courtesy of P. Hamilton*)

In the development of impact analysis, many attempts have been made to systematise analysis by using complex and sophisticated assessment methods. These have been shown to have a number of important weaknesses. At the present time, flexible means of assessing proposals which can be utilised within the particular political, cultural and economic structure of individual countries are required. In the near future it is likely that impact analyses will be implemented increasingly in developing countries. Multilateral aid agencies are realising that many projects in developing countries have produced serious deleterious consequences which were not foreseen in the project planning stage. Impact analysis is ideal for improving the design and implementation of such projects. For example, the US *AID* agency is sponsoring a detailed impact analysis of the Senegal River Basin Project (3.86).

In the next phase of the evolution of impact analysis, attention is likely to focus on two main issues. First, there is a need for the implementation of comprehensive monitoring schemes to ascertain whether the actual impacts match those predicted during impact analysis. At present, few such comparisons have been made. The results of monitoring exercises could provide useful information for the improvement of predictive techniques. Secondly, impact analysis should not be used only after details of a proposal have been formalised, but should be integrated into plan and policy formulation (3.87). Also it is illogical to consider plans, policies and development in isolation from other proposals likely to affect the same socio-economic and environmental factors (3.88). Impact analysis, therefore, could fulfil a number of roles. It could be used in the preparation of plans and policies, as a means of ensuring the compatibility of different plans and policies affecting a particular area and as a method of assessing the likely impacts of projects, plans and policies.

# References

3.1 The National Environmental Policy Act of 1969, Public Law 91–190; 83 Stat., pp. 852 *et seq.*; 42 USC, pp. 4321–4347.

3.2 COUNCIL ON ENVIRONMENTAL QUALITY, 'Preparation of environmental impact statements', *Federal Register*, **38**, 1973, pp. 20550–20562.

3.3 The National Environmental Policy Act of 1969, Section 101(a), *op. cit.*

3.4 The National Environmental Policy Act of 1969, Section 102(2) (C), *op. cit.*

3.5 CRAMPTON, R. C. and BERG, R. K. 'Enforcing the National Environmental Policy Act in Federal Agencies', *The Practical Lawyer*, **18**, 1972, pp. 79–88.

3.6 COUNCIL ON ENVIRONMENTAL QUALITY, *op. cit.*

3.7 YOST, N. C., 'NEPA's progeny: state environmental policy acts', *Environmental Law Reporter*, **3**, 1973, pp. 50090–50098.

3.8 BURCHELL, R. W. and LISTOKIN, D., *The Environmental Impact Handbook*, Center for Urban Policy Research, Rutgers—The State University, New Brunswick, New Jersey, 1975.

3.9 DELOGU, O. E., 'United States experience with the preparation and analysis of environmental impact statements: the National Environmental Policy Act', *IUCN Environmental Policy and Law Paper No. 7*, International Union for Conservation of Nature and Natural Resources, Morges, Switzerland, 1974.

3.10 VOIGT, H. H., 'The National Environmental Policy Act and the independent regulatory agency: some unresolved conflicts, *Natural Resources Lawyer*, **5**, 1972, pp. 13–22.

3.11 ANDREWS, R. N. L., *Environmental Policy and Administrative Change*, Lexington Books, Lexington, Massachusetts, 1977.

3.12 DELOGU, O. E., *op. cit.*

3.13 ORTOLANO, L. and HILL, W. W., *An Analysis of Environmental Statements for the Corps of Engineers.* Stanford University, Stanford, California, 1972.

3.14 ORLOFF, N., 'The environmental impact process', Paper to the Environmental Impact Statement seminar of the Twin Cities Federal Executive Board, Minneapolis, Minnesota, 6 February 1973.

3.15 The National Environmental Policy Act of 1969, Section 102 (2)(A) *op. cit.*

3.16 ALBRECHT, S. L., 'Socio-cultural factors and energy resource development in rural areas in the West', *Journal of Environmental Management*, **7**, 1978, pp. 73–90.

3.17 JELLINEK, S. D., Introductory lecture, in *The Environmental Impact Statement*, Mitchell, B. (ed.), European Environment Bureau, Brussels, 1975, pp. 4–7.

3.18 COUNCIL ON ENVIRONMENTAL QUALITY, 'National Environmental Policy Act: proposed regulations for implementing procedural provisions', *Federal Register*, **43**, 1977, pp. 25230–25247.

3.19 DOBRY, G., *A Review of the Development Control Process*, HMSO, London, 1975.

3.20 SPHERE ENVIRONMENTAL CONSULTANTS LTD., *Impact Analysis: Oil Platform Construction at Loch Broom*, Sphere Environmental Consultants Ltd., London, 1973.

3.21 SPHERE ENVIRONMENTAL CONSULTANTS LTD., *Loch Carron Area: Comparative Analysis of Platform Construction Sites*, Sphere Environmental Consultants Ltd., London, 1974.

3.22 CREMER AND WARNER, *Application by Cromarty Petroleum Company Limited for a Crude Oil Refinery, Crude Oil Storage, Finished Product Storage and Marine Terminal Facility at Nigg Point, County of Ross and Cromarty. Environmental Feasibility Report 1974.* Cremer and Warner, London, 1974.

3.23 CREMER AND WARNER, *Report on the Environmental Impact of the Proposed Shell UK (Expro) NGL Plant at Peterhead*, Cremer and Warner, London, 1976.

3.24 CREMER AND WARNER, *The Hazard and Environmental Impact of the Proposed Shell NGL Plant and Esso Ethylene Plant at Mossmorran and Export Facilities at Braefoot Bay*, Vols. 1 and 2., Cremer and Warner, London, 1977.

3.25 W. J. CAIRNS ASSOCIATES, *Flotta Orkney Oil Handling Terminal. An Environmental Assessment*, W. J. Cairns Associates, Edinburgh, 1973.

3.26 SPHERE ENVIRONMENTAL CONSULTANTS LTD., *Environmental Impact Analysis: Development of Beatrice Field Block 11/30*, Volumes 1–3, Sphere Environmen‌t Consultants Ltd., Glasgow, 1977.

3.27 SCOTTISH DEVELOPMENT DEPARTMENT, *Appraisal of the Impact of Oil-related Development*, DP/TAN/16, Scottish Development Department, Edinburgh, 1974.

3.28 PADC, *Assessment of Major Industrial Applications—A Manual*, DOE Research Report No. 13, Department of the Environment, London, 1976.

3.29 CATLOW, J. and THIRLWALL, C. G., *Environmental Impact Analysis*, DOE Research Report No. 11, Department of the Environment, London, 1976.

3.30 OECD, *Analysis of the Environmental Consequences of Significant Public and Private Projects. Draft Final Report*, Organisation for Economic Co-operation and Development, Paris, 1976.

3.31 FISHERIES AND ENVIRONMENT CANADA, *A Guide to the Federal Environmental Assessment and Review Process*, Fisheries and Environment Canada, Ottawa, 1977.

3.32 KIFF, J., *A Review of Environmental Impact Assessment and Implications of the Process for CMHC*, Central Mortgage and Housing Corporation, Ottawa, 1976.

3.33 ALBERTA ENVIRONMENT, *Environmental Impact Assessment Guidelines*, Alberta Environment, Edmonton, 1977.

3.34 OECD, 1976, *op. cit.*

3.35 OECD, *Environmental Policy in Sweden.* Organisation

for Economic Co-operation and Development, Paris, 1977.

3.36 OECD, 'Ten recommendations to OECD's environment Ministers', *OECD Observer*, **72**, 1974, pp. 9–11.

3.37 HAMMER, D., 'EEC guidelines for environmental impact assessment', in *Environmental Impact Assessment*, O'Riordan, T. and Hey, R. D., (eds.), Saxon House, Farnborough, 1976, pp. 35–44.

3.38 LEE, N. and WOOD, C., *The Introduction of Environmental Impact Statements in the European Communities*, unpublished report prepared for the European Economic Community, 1976.

3.39 LEE, N. and WOOD, C., 'EIA—a European perspective', *Built Environment*, **4**, 1978, pp. 101–110.

3.40 OECD (1976), *op. cit.*

3.41 HAMMER, D., *op. cit.*

3.42 WARNER, M. L. and PRESTON, E. H., *Review of Environmental Impact Assessment Methodologies*, US Environmental Protection Agency, Washington DC, 1974.

3.43 MUNN, R. E., *Environmental Impact Assessment: Principles and Procedures*; SCOPE Report 5, International Council of Scientific Unions, Toronto, 1975.

3.44 PADC, 1976, *op. cit.*

3.45 LEOPOLD, L. B., CLARKE, F. E., HANSHAW, B. B. and BALSLEY, J. R., *A Procedure for Evaluating Environmental Impact*, US Geological Survey Circular 645, US Geological Survey, Washington DC, 1971.

3.46 SPHERE ENVIRONMENTAL CONSULTANTS LTD., 1974, *op. cit.*

3.47 ENVIRONMENT CANADA, *An Environmental Assessment of Nanaimo Port Alternatives*, Environment Canada, Ottawa, 1974.

3.48 SORENSEN, J. C., Some procedures and programs for environmental impact assessment, in *Environmental Impact Analysis: Philosophy and Methods*, Ditton, R. B. and Goodale, T. L., (eds.), University of Wisconsin Sea Grant Program, Madison, Wisconsin, 1972, pp. 97–106.
WARNER, M. L. and PRESTON, E. H., *op. cit.*
MUNN, R. E., *op. cit.*

3.49 SORENSEN, J. C., 1972, *op. cit.*

3.50 PADC, *Environmental Impact Assessment in the USA: A Critical Review*. DOE Research Report No. 26, Department of the Environment, London, 1978.

3.51 SPHERE ENVIRONMENTAL CONSULTANTS LTD., 1974, *op. cit.*

3.52 ENVIRONMENT CANADA, *op. cit.*

3.53 SORENSEN, J. C., *A Framework for Identification and Control of Resource Degradation and Conflict in Multiple Use of the Coastal Zone*, Unpublished Masters Thesis, University of California, Berkeley, California, 1971.

3.54 WHITMAN, I. L., DEE, N., McGINNIS, J. T., FAHRINGER, D. C. and BAKER, J. K., *Design of an Environmental Evaluation System*, Battelle Columbus Laboratories, Columbus, Ohio, 1971.

DEE, N., BAKER, J. K., DROBNY, N. L., DUKE, K. M. and FAHRINGER, D. C., *Environmental Evaluation System for Water Resource Planning. Final Report*, Battelle Columbus Laboratories, Columbus, Ohio, 1972.
DEE, N., BAKER, J. K., DROBNY, N. L., DUKE, K. M., WHITMAN, I. L. and FAHRINGER, D. C., 'An environmental evaluation system for water resource planning', *Water Resources Research*, **9**, 1973, pp. 523–535.

3.55 DICKERT, T. G., Methods for environmental impact assessment: a comparison, in *Environmental Impact Assessment: Guidelines and Commentary*, Dickert, T. G. and Domeny, K. R., (eds.), University of California, Berkeley, California, 1974, pp. 153–188.

3.56 BISSET, R., 'Quantification, decision making and environmental impact assessment in the UK', *Journal of Environmental Management*, **7**, 1978, pp. 43–58.

3.57 SKUTSCH, M. and FLOWERDEW, R. T. N., 'Measurement techniques in environmental impact assessment', *Environmental Conservation*, **3**, 1976, pp. 209–217.

3.58 PADC, 1976, *op. cit.*

3.59 RATCLIFFE, D. A., *A Nature Conservation Review*, Vols. 1 and 2, Cambridge University Press, London and New York, 1977.

3.60 RATCLIFFE, D. A., 'Criteria for the selection of nature reserves', *Advancement of Science, London*, **27**, 1971, pp. 294–296.

3.61 TUBBS, C. R. and BLACKWOOD, J. W., 'Ecological evaluation of land for planning purposes', *Biological Conservation*, **3**, 1971, pp. 169–172.

3.62 BURROWS, G. S., *Ecological Appraisal of West Sussex*, West Sussex County Council, Chichester, 1973.

3.63 COLLINS, J., *Ecological Appraisal of Cheshire*, Cheshire County Planning Department, Chester, 1974.

3.64 WERKGROEP, G.R.A.N., *Biologische Kartering En Evaluatie Van De Groene Ruimte In Het Gebied Van De Statsgewesten Arnhem En Nijmegen*. Werkgroep G.R.A.N., Nijmegen, 1973.

3.65 YAPP, W. B., 'Evaluation of a linear landscape', *Biological Conservation*, **5**, 1972, pp. 45–47.

3.66 HELLIWELL, D. R., 'The value of vegetation for conservation. I. Four land areas in Britain', *Journal of Environmental Management*, **2**, 1974, pp. 51–74.

3.67 HELLIWELL, D. R., *Beckside Farm: A Botanical Survey and Evaluation*, Merlewood R. & D. paper No. 61, 1974.

3.68 PERRING, F. H. and WALTERS, S. M., *Atlas of the British Flora*, Nelson, London and Edinburgh, 1962.

3.69 PETERKEN, G. F., 'A method for assessing woodland flora for conservation using indicator species', *Biological Conservation*, **6**, 1974, pp. 239–45.

3.70 PERRING, F. H. and WALTERS, S. M., *op. cit.*

3.71 ROSE, F. H., The epiphytes of oak, in *The British Oak: its History and Natural History*, Morris, M. G. and Perring, F. H., (eds.), E. W. Classey, Farringdon, 1974, pp. 250–273.

3.72 WATHERN, P., *The Ecology of Development Sites*, Unpublished Ph.D thesis, University of Sheffield, 1976.

3.73 WARD, S. D. and EVANS, D. F., 'Conservation assessment of British limestone pavements based on floral criteria', *Biological Conservation*, **9**, 1976, pp. 217–233.

3.74 PADC, 1976, *op. cit.*

3.75 WATHERN, P., 'Some aspects of habitat building in the Dutch polderland', *Landscape Design*, **118**, 1977, pp. 20–21.

3.76 HEBBLETHWAITE, R. L., Landscape assessment and classification techniques, in *Land Use and Landscape Planning*, 1st edition, Lovejoy, D. (ed.), Leonard Hill, Aylesbury, 1973, pp. 19–50.

3.77 UNIVERSITY OF MANCHESTER, *Landscape Evaluation*, Landscape Evaluation Research Project 1970–75, University of Manchester, 1976.

3.78 PENNING-ROWSELL, E. C. and HARDY, D. I., *Alternative Approaches to Landscape Appraisal and Evaluation*, Middlesex Polytechnic Planning Research Group, Report No. 11, London, 1973.

DUNN, M. C., *Landscape Evaluation Techniques: An Appraisal and Review of Literature*, Birmingham Centre for Urban and Regional Studies, Working Paper No. 4, Birmingham, 1974.

PADC, 1976, *op. cit.*

3.79 WARWICKSHIRE COUNTY PLANNING DEPARTMENT, *Coventry–Solihull–Warwickshire: A Strategy for the Sub-region*, Supplementary Report No. 5—Countryside, County Planning Department, Warwick, 1971.

3.80 FINES, K. D., 'Landscape evaluation: a research project in East Sussex', *Regional Studies*, **2**, 1968, pp. 41–55.

3.81 DUNN, M. C., 'Landscape with photographs: testing the preference approach to landscape evaluation', *Journal of Environmental Management*, **4**, 1975, pp. 15–26.

3.82 WEST MIDLANDS REGIONAL STUDY, *A Strategy for the West Midlands*, West Midlands Regional Study, Birmingham, 1971.

3.83 HAMPSHIRE COUNTY COUNCIL, *East Hampshire AONB —A study in Countryside Conservation*, Hampshire County Council, Winchester, 1968.

3.84 LAND USE CONSULTANTS, *A Planning Classification of Scottish Landscape Resources*, Countryside Commission for Scotland, Occasional Paper No. 1, Perth, 1971.

3.85 PADC, 1976, *op. cit.*

3.86 LUBIN, S., 'Environmental impact of the Senegal River Basin Project', *KIDMA*, **3**, 1977, pp. 36–39.

3.87 HOLLING, C. S., *Adaptive Environmental Assessment and Management*, PR–6, Institute of Resource Ecology, University of British Columbia, Vancouver, 1977.

3.88 WANDESFORDE-SMITH, G., 'Projects, policies, and environmental impact assessment: A look inside California's black box', *Environmental Policy and Law*, **3**, 1977, pp. 167–176.

CHAPTER FOUR
# LAND USE AND
# AGRICULTURAL CHANGE
John B. Weller

Beef yarding, Monfort, US. Intensive beef production is well known in the United States, especially in the mid-west. Thousands of head are held in corrals and fed from self-unloading trailers. This kind of production depends on climatic conditions as well as on the historical pattern of ranch farming (see page 89)

(*Photo by courtesy of the American Agricultural News Service*)

CHAPTER FOUR
# LAND USE AND
# AGRICULTURAL CHANGE
John B. Weller

## Agriculture: A Changing Landscape

An agrarian landscape denotes a settled people and, as discussed in earlier chapters, agriculture is man's main use of land. It is a hallmark; landscape becomes rural, distinct from the wilderness of lands inhabited by nomadic tribes. Cultivation patterns reflect the evolution of man's technology, and today technology could alter, totally, the patterns of cultivation and of rural landscape familiar to our generation. This is the crux of the problem of agricultural change throughout the world, which has created the need for new techniques in landscape planning. The basic factors underlying this change are clear.

In all countries, both developed and developing, food production techniques are changing with great rapidity and there is no indication that the rate of change will abate. Social issues, such as pollution, may affect the use of certain techniques, but not the basic principles of intensification of output per unit of land and per farmworker. The over-riding need for intensification in food production stems from world population growth and diminishing land resources, coupled with the increased impact of urban communities, especially in developed countries, on rural areas.

Change in farm technology, that is in methods of cultivation and in livestock husbandry, has taken place throughout history. However, the changes in farming methods now taking place can affect the ecological balance and the rural landscape in ways not immediately apparent to the farmer, for farmers and even farmland managers are not trained in ecology and in landscape architecture.

The issue central to agricultural change is the question of priorities in land use, that is, whether the agriculturist should determine the structure of the rural landscape and whether food production, either extensive or intensive, should have

the traditional right of absorbing as much rural land as its owners think desirable.

The historical and social heritage of farmers, except within socialist economies, is three-fold. First they are largely free to choose what food they produce and by what method they produce it, secondly they have considerable freedom in marketing most commodities, and thirdly they have almost complete freedom, either by inheritance or by purchase, in their ownership of a basic resource—land. In recent decades, social pressures have caused some slight change in the traditional patterns. Production techniques are restricted to some extent in relation to pollution and health hazard. Modern marketing of some produce is now with centralised control, sometimes with Government backing. Compulsory land purchase for urban needs has made some inroads into the traditional rights of ownership. All these changes create a degree of tension and resentment.

Any attempt to influence, direct or control landscape planning of farmland would create bitter opposition. The fear of land nationalisation in one form or another, or even of bureaucratic interference with the traditional independence of farmers, makes rational discussion of landscape planning difficult. However, it seems certain that the new situation of population pressure and of modern farm technology makes landscape planning in some form essential.

## Agriculture: The Global Situation

Statistics of the world population are well known and have been discussed in Chapter 1. One-third of the existing population suffers chronic malnutrition, with many dying from starvation; another third suffers poverty and poor nutrition; and population growth tends to be greatest where food resources are most inadequate. Food production remains a major world problem. Its relation to land use planning is critical. Though agriculture is man's primary land use, only about one-tenth of the total land area is used for it (Table 4.1).

Table 4.1. World agricultural land

|  | TOTAL AREA* (ha × 10⁶) | ARABLE AREA† (ha × 10⁶) | ARABLE AREA (%) |
|---|---|---|---|
| Europe | 493 | 145·0 | 29·4 |
| North and Central America | 2242 | 271·0 | 12·0 |
| South America | 1783 | 8·4 | 0·47 |
| Asia | 2753 | 463·0 | 16·8 |
| USSR | 2240 | 227·6 | 10·1 |
| Africa | 3031 | 214·0 | 7·0 |
| Oceania | 851 | 47·0 | 5·5 |
| Total world | 13,393 | 1376·0 | 10·8 |

*Continental area (including inland water)
†Arable land, including fallow, temporary grassland, shifting use
Source: FAO, *Production Yearbook 1972*

Thus, always, there must be a basic aim to increase the agricultural land area. Within the developing world, there is a great potential for increased arable land areas and Table 4.2 shows estimates of the increases of potential arable land use by 1985.

Table 4.2. Percentage of potential arable land in use

|  | % ACTUAL ARABLE LAND IN USE IN 1962 | % ARABLE LAND IN USE PROPOSED BY 1985 |
|---|---|---|
| Central America | 64 | 76 |
| South America | 19 | 26 |
| North-west Africa | 100 | 100 |
| South Asia | 93 | 96 |
| South-east Asia (incl. Sri Lanka) | 44 | 57 |
| Far East | 81 | 97 |

Source: FAO, *Indicative Plan for Agriculture, 1970*

Political, rather than technical, constraints are likely to prevent the realisations of such potential expansions. Equally, reclamation of arid zones could do much to extend the potential arable lands beyond 1985 estimates.

Yield can be increased in terms of land area by '3-D' farming (i.e. trees plus ground crops) and by double crop-

ping where conditions are favourable. Undersowing of a second crop is quite common within developed countries. Controlled irrigation also can be used, particularly in parts of Asia and the Far East. China is particularly well placed, with at least one-half of its rice being irrigated due to the disposition of adequate rivers. Two-thirds of all rice lands are double cropped and some areas, in addition, get a wheat crop from pre-grown plants. In other parts of the world, an International Biological Programme aims to increase productivity from arid lands by 3-D farming (4.1). Certain tree species, such as walnut and carob, can yield 50 t/ha of edible foodstuffs, suitable especially as a substitute for cattle cereal fodder. One of the first experiments of combined forestry and agriculture was in the 1960s and within Kipling's 'great, grey-green, greasy Limpopo River' valley. Here, tree avenues and arable strips alternate so that the tree roots raise the water level and their foliage shades the crops (see also page 130). Trees are selected to yield highly in proteins and carbohydrates, whilst crops are selected for local conditions. At the same time, movable fencing is used for controlled grazing by free-range stock.

Food technology, including field management, also encompasses aspects of ecology, waste, photosynthesis and power fuels (all of which are themselves inter-related) as well as soil science and genetic control. It is a complex subject and only a few examples can be given.

Control over crop wastage, though the latter cannot be eliminated, could do much to reduce food shortages. Wastages, of course, take place both on the farm and beyond the farm gate. The Food and Agriculture Organisation (FAO) reported in 1976 that one-third of the potential food harvest in the world is destroyed annually by pests, weeds and diseases. The estimated value of this loss in 1975 was over 75 billion dollars, equal to the entire grain and potato crop.

Crop loss is critical even within regions of sophisticated agriculture. Within the UK, for example, 70% of all crops are treated by herbicides and 30% by insecticides or fungicides. Of course, as discussed below, these crop treatments absorb 0.5% of all power and energy inputs to UK agriculture—plus 29% for fertilisers—to which has to be added tractor fuels. This is a reason why yields have increased dramatically over the last 25 years; by 60 to 85% in the case of brussels sprouts, cauliflowers, broad beans, carrots and onions. Nevertheless, some two-fifths of all crop values in the UK are wasted between the field and the plate.

Roy has estimated that total losses within the UK could be as high as 42·6%, with wastages as follows (4.2):

'pests and diseases 8%; weeds 5·5%; harvesting 3·6%; farm storage 2·4%; transport/storage 1·5%; processing 5·9%; marketing 1·4%; preparation and cooking 1·4%; kitchen and plate 6·7% overconsumption 3·2%.'

Sophisticated agriculture using power energy liberally, on this basis, perhaps reduces farm production losses from about 33 to 20%. Thus, similar control treatments against crop loss could, perhaps, increase world food production, if uniform elsewhere, by one-eighth, but potential savings are difficult to predict. But, equally within the UK as much loss occurs beyond the farm gate as within production on the farm. Wastage is a serious problem both in terms of energy and of land use.

In terms of world food production, there are many limitations. These have been summarised by Simmons, based on earlier work in 1945 by Pearson and Harper (4.3) (Table 4.3).

Table 4.3. Ecological limits to food production within land area adapted for agriculture

| INDIVIDUAL FACTORS AS RESTRICTION | % USABLE LAND FOR CROPS | % USABLE LAND AFTER RESTRICTIONS |
|---|---|---|
| 1. Adequate sunlight | 35·7 | 100 |
| 2. Adequate $CO_2$ | 35·7 | 100 |
| 3. Favourable temperature | 29·5 | 83 |
| 4. Favourable topography | 22·7 | 64 |
| 5. Reliable rainfall | 16·6 | 46 |
| 6. Fertile soil | 16·3 | 46 |
| 7. Adequate rainfall | 15·5 | 43 |
| *Combination factors* | | |
| 7+1+2 | 15·5 | 43 |
| 7+5+1+2 | 12·2 | 34 |
| 3+7+5+2 | 11·4 | 32 |
| 4+3+7+5+1+2 | 7·4 | 21 |
| All factors | 2·6 | 7 |

The basis of all food production is photosynthesis. All the world has adequate sunlight for this chemical reaction process. But, Simmons has deduced that when all the constraints of temperature, rainfall, topography and fertility are taken into account, the proportion of the terrestrial surface suited to agriculture falls to 7%. Thus, it becomes even more important to eliminate waste and to use land resources selectively.

Agriculture, through plant forms, is the major means of harvesting solar energy. Capacity, both by direct radiation and by plant forms, varies throughout the world. Heslop-Harrison has estimated that within the UK the total incidence of solar radiation in the year averages 100 to 125 J/m²/s (4.4), whole plants only absorb 1% of this total and, of this, but 7% (0.07 J/m²/s) is energy reproduced by the plant. Baxter has suggested that the amount recovered within the harvested crop is only 0·18% of the total incidence (1116 × 10⁹ MJ/yr) (4.5). Therefore, if photosynthesis could be made more effective, energy from food could be increased substantially. Examples of energy production from crops have been given by Duckham and Masefield (4.6) (Table 4.4).

Table 4.4. Energy production as a percentage of annual solar radiation

| CROP | % OF SOLAR RADIATION |
|---|---|
| Rice (Egypt) | 0·17 |
| Cereals (UK) | 0·16 |
| Potatoes (UK) | 0·21 |
| Sugarbeet (UK) | 0·21 |
| *Crops via livestock* | |
| Pig meat | 0·03 |
| Lamb | 0·01 |
| Milk (average) | 0·05 |
| Milk (summer, max.) | 0·15 |

It is well known that livestock is a bad converter of primary energy. Duckham and Masefield calculated that, excluding disease, only 30% of the photosynthate from potatoes was eaten due to respiration loss, unharvested and post-harvest loss and household waste. This represents only 0·21% of solar energy. Grass crops, via beef, yield only 4% of the photosynthate or only 0·02% of solar energy. Mellanby has argued, on this basis, that if Britain became Vegan, using no more energy than at present, 200 million people could be fed (or the present population of the UK on half the energy input) (4.7).

Crop selection is important not only in terms of photosynthetic conversion but also in terms of this conversion as proteins and carbohydrates. Protein can be harvested from a wide variety of plant forms and average yields, together with their effective biological values, are shown in Table 4.5 (4.8).

Table 4.5. Total protein yield

| | kg/ha | % VALUE | EFFECTIVE kg/ha |
|---|---|---|---|
| Forest trees | 2800 | 83 | 2300 |
| Clover | 2000 | 83 | 1700 |
| Maize | 1800 | 83 | 1500 |
| Soya beans | 720 | 65 | 470 |
| Wheat | 450 | 50 | 225 |
| Peas/beans | 400 | 60 | 240 |
| Milk | 110 | 83 | 92 |
| Eggs | 90 | 97 | 88 |
| Broilers | 100 | 75 | 75 |
| Sheep | 35 | 75 | 26 |

Effectively, forests yield ten-fold more protein than wheat per hectare and could be used to increase basic foods. At present, 70% of all the protein used for man's diet comes from cereals and pulses; but, in the United States only 7% of the corn harvest is eaten directly by man, the remainder being used as livestock feed—and, livestock is a bad converter. It is well known that diet is a major cause of land use waste within the developed world. Wilson has suggested that only 11% of the energy, including that in proteins, recovered from the harvested crop is used by man, whilst 70% is used for livestock feed (4.9).

As with proteins, forests can yield ten-fold the quantity of carbohydrate as wheat, and even seaweed yields as much (4.10) (see Table 4.6).

Table 4.6. Annual carbohydrate production

|  | g/m² |
|---|---|
| *Agriculture* |  |
| Wheat | 344 |
| Hay | 497 |
| Beet sugar | 1470 |
| Cane sugar | 3430 |
| Potatoes | 845 |
| *Forest* |  |
| UK pine forest | 3180 |
| Deciduous wood | 1560 |
| *Grasses, etc.* |  |
| *Spartina* grass | 3300 |
| US prairie | 446 |
| Nevada desert | 40 |
| Seaweed beds | 358 |

Agriculture uses power fuels. Within the UK, this has been assessed as only 2·66% in relation to the national consumption (4.11). However, this is use within the farm. From farm to plate, the percentage can rise to 25% within total consumption. The situation was summed up by Bleasdale (4.12):

> 'The production of the major food crops uses one calorie of fuel energy to produce three to five calories of food. But, food processing, handling and storage uses five calories for every calorie of food. In these circumstances, the whole food chain uses more energy than it produces.'

Within UK agriculture, the 2·66% of national power consumption has been estimated as $246 \times 10^9$ MJ/yr (4.13). Therefore, major national savings could not take place on the farm, though other forms of energy consumption, as described above, could make a significant contribution. Artificial fertilisers use 29% of farm energy consumption and much of these could be replaced by recycled farm wastes (4.14). The breakdown of power energy has been given as shown in Table 4.7 (4.15).

Table 4.7. Energy consumed in UK agriculture

|  | ENERGY ($10^9$ MJ) | % |
|---|---|---|
| Solid fuel | 4·1 | 1·67 |
| Petroleum | 84·0 | 34·20 |
| Electricity | 33·1 | 13·48 |
| Fertilisers (nitrogenous) | 63·3 | 25·77 |
| Fertilisers (others) | 7·8 | 3·18 |
| Agrochemicals | 1·3 | 0·53 |
| Machinery | 52·0 | 21·17 |
| Total | 245·6 | 100·00 |

The dependence on fossil fuels and other energy inputs to increase yields has to be related to other priorities for their use. Equally, it is related to any reduction of manpower within food production. Thus, it is likely to become a major international issue within the control and use of power sources. This will affect priorities for land use. It becomes significant in terms of world food resources. In 1968 there were grain reserves to last 80 days, but a decade later this was but 30 days. Equally, the use of land in the production of food can be shown by the UK examples (see Table 4.8).

Table 4.8. UK agricultural land use 1971/72 (million hectares)

|  | TOTAL | FOOD/MAN | FOOD/LIVESTOCK | OTHER |
|---|---|---|---|---|
| Grass | 7·254 | — | 100% | — |
| Cereals | 3·802 | 24% | 70% | 6% |
| Vegetables | 1·016 | 64% | 31% | 5% |
|  | 12·072 | 13% | 85% | 2% |
| Rough grazing | 6·646 | — | 100% | — |
|  | 18·718 | 8·3% | 90·3% | 1·4% |

In 1975, the UK produced 57% of its total food energy requirements. This represents enough food energy produced from each agricultural worker to feed 48 people (4.16).

It is clear that world food production could be increased by an extension of arable land or by increased yields due to better tillage and genetics. But, the issues are more complex.

Food science, nutrition and diet all can be manipulated in such a way that land itself ceases to be the sole factor in the equation as to how to feed the world. Equally, though yields can be increased by the greater use of power fuels, this can impinge on other priorities. Perhaps the central issue is the manner in which the sun's power can be harvested more effectively.

# External Impacts on Agriculture

The taking of land for extractive and service industries, for outdoor leisure, or for forestry will, in general, be impossible without a comparable loss of farmland. Most agriculturalists and farmers are hostile to such loss. Compulsory purchase or free exploitation of farmland for other purposes without the influence of land resource planning is a serious and a deteriorating situation. Purchase of farmland for urban needs obviously may cause hostility on the part of the seller, but it has a deeper significance. Farmers, though aided by their various associations, are not a coherent body. While the decision to take land for mineral extraction or a motorway network may be based on national priorities, land for farming is not related to any accepted national food plan. Thus farmers can never argue that any particular hectare should be inviolate, especially since food production increases in spite of farmland losses. Indeed, they argue from a weak brief against any encroachment.

In addition a new situation is developing. Some farmers recognise their land has a potential other than for food production, particularly for recreational use or in some instances for mineral extraction. Farmers with land of poor fertility or restricted area, where the economics of food production is strained in relation to overheads and to profit, must be tempted to seek more profitable uses for their land. However, changes made without reference to structure and local plans must be detrimental for the environment.

The problem is that no national food or land use plans exist and even in Britain, where there is a longstanding planning legislation, regional, structure and local plans are still in their infancy (see page 14), being almost non-existent in the case of farmland. Structure plans, in terms of agriculture, are discussed later (see page 104). The Government policy statement of 1975 (now being revised), which was dedicated to the expansion of home food production, failed adequately to relate nutrition to food to land within an equation suitable for resource planning (4.17). Thus, by what criteria should a farmer be debarred from realising the full economic potential of his land, and be forced to continue uneconomic food production? What then should be the criteria in land use.

A national food production plan should make sacrosanct viable farmland against other exploitation. A national land use plan, backed by regional and local plans, should make possible alternative uses for farmland rendered uneconomic for food production due to modern technology. This section considers how priorities should be established in relation to the external impacts on farmland. A new type of agricoplanner will be needed to make the land assessment, and new planning procedures will have to be evolved to meet the changing situation. This is essential if the countryside is to absorb the external impacts.

There is no indication at present, that priorities for rural land use and for food production will receive comprehensive evaluation. Agriculturists and planners still consider farmland as the sum of individual farms of indeterminate size, fertility and management, rather than as a resource required to produce an estimated quantity of food of specified quality, albeit within many individual production units. Similarly, the assumption that the countryside should be used for agriculture and for forestry alone, or almost alone, should be re-examined before a true evaluation of rural land resources can be made.

**The Impact of Communications**
The traditional use of highways for farm operations is chaotic. Movement of stock and farm implements along public roads is incompatible with modern transport requirements. Farmland should be self-contained and farm use of highways should be licensed for particular infrequent functions. Similarly, since 30-tonne transporters handling farm materials and produce are becoming common, many rural roads are inadequate. Penalties against poor transporter turnround time, caused by bad access and loading facilities, are normal. Bulk milk collection, for example, may be withdrawn from remote farms with poor road access. It may become essential to locate new farm buildings so that transporters do not have to use the rural road infrastructure. This could restrict certain types of farming in some areas. At present there is no planning strategy at national or local level concerning the location of farm enterprises in relation to communications.

New road networks, with their ensuing farmland losses, create farming opposition. Planning procedures and compensation have improved, but the latter is seldom generous. Though under and over-passes can be provided, the real farm problem is land severance. In motorway planning, farmland should be restructured in field layout; farm roads and buildings and land ownership at least one kilometre on each side of the route should be examined, taking into account land fertility and shape (see also page 204). An attempt should be made to rezone farms into viable units (Figure 4.1). In practice, this does not happen, each motorway creating fragmented farms with compensation only related to actual land acquisition. Rezoning farms would need sound analysis, good public relations and generous compensation.

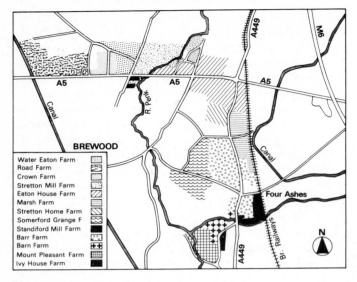

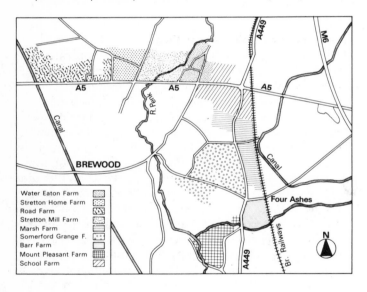

Figure 4.1    Reorganisation of farming estates to avoid conflicts with road traffic. Before reallocation of land (above), two main roads, a canal and the railway crossed the Stretton and Someford estates. The reorganisation so far (below) has removed the worst dangers. When the plan is complete only one farm will be severed by a major road.

## Industrial Impact

The inter-relation between industry and farmland is three-fold. First, as already mentioned, extraction and service industries make a direct impact. Secondly, with industrial redeployment, more factories are being dispersed into rural areas (see also page 231). Thirdly, there is the impact of the service industries on agriculture, together with the distribution of processing factories for its produce. This is a problem which requires further study and research, for it may prove to have more effect on rural land use than any other factor, including the revolution in cropping and field layouts. Aspects of this problem are discussed in more detail elsewhere; but the implication is that agriculture will need quasi-industrial zones, close to road and rail systems,

quite different from the traditional farmstead. The emergence of agrico-industrial complexes, plus urban industries penetrating rural areas, suggests that special zones on poor land should be reserved in regional plans for such development. Location needs new techniques in rural planning.

## Leisure within Agricultural Land

Neither agriculturists nor planners are consistent in their attitudes towards leisure within farmland. Both must establish priorities before proper land use planning is practical. As is stressed in Chapter 6, leisure is a growth activity. A report in 1974 stated that in England and Wales up to 6% of all farms operated leisure facilities, usually for tourist accommodation, and that demand could double by 1984 (4.18). Agriculturists should take heed.

Certain factors seem clear. Intensive farming for specialised crops requires a factory floor of prime land, sized and shaped for optimum production related to mechanisation. Leisure has to be excluded and vandalism prevented. Nationally, in the UK, though not yet assessed, there might be some 6 to 8 million hectares of farm factory floor. No regional plan should be prepared, nor leisure zones discussed, until such areas have been designated. They should be the inviolate base for national food requirements. At the same time, controlled public viewing across such land is desirable, from raised land equipped with map and telescope. These viewing points might be part of country parks. Demonstration farms are also required. These are discussed later (see page 113).

Some farming, based on semi-extensive systems, can traditionally support sports—hunting, shooting and fishing. Agriculturists tend to be irrational towards these sports, being unclear on the interaction between food production and sport. On land poor in fertility, size or shape, sport can provide a better income than food production. Specialist blood sport farms, perhaps including attractive landscapes, woodland and water storage, but where food production is subsidiary, might in Britain total 2 to 4 million hectares. This subject needs careful study. Other forms of recreation do not easily mix with the blood sports. Special recreational farms, with traditional mixed farming in minor key and mainly for produce for visitors, might account for another 2 to 4 million hectares, being suitable for short stays and holidays. This could help fringe farm lands, as discussed later, but land planning would need new concepts.

## Woodland within Agricultural Land

An uneasy alliance exists between farming and farmland forestry (excluding commercial forests beyond the farmgate). Farm woodland is mainly unplanned, being a legacy from where clearances ceased. Modern pressures make farmers question this legacy and this makes conservationists wary. Land of steep profile or poor fertility may remain wooded since reclamation has no value. Other old woods, covering potential food cultivation land, in varying amounts in different regions, still exist for three main reasons. First, farmers may not have wanted or been able to afford to extend their cultivated land. Secondly, sporting farmers value such woods as game reserves and, thirdly, some woods have given shelter for grazing fields. Modern economics make their continued retention uncertain except within semi-extensive farmlands where sport may be developed as a cash crop. The situation is aggravated by recent fiscal and tax policies which make long-term investment of doubtful value. Though field windbreaks are still needed, as discussed later (see page 119 and 130), old woods are often wrong in location and in size. However, some farm woodland is managed as a crop within the overall land policy, often as coppices on wet land. Such woodland may provide both shelter and wildlife reserves.

The problem of farm woodlands is two-fold. First, most form neither part of a regional nor a farm plan and, secondly, few are available for public use. These are problems of land use. Some woodlands should be wildlife reserves, others should have a recreational use, perhaps providing link paths across the country, and others should be shelter belts and coppices. In some cases, there should be co-operation between landowner and planning authority for retaining or planting woods for amenity reasons (see Chapter 5). Old woods should be felled only within a regional policy.

# Internal Change Within Agriculture

The impact of external pressures on agriculture has coincided with a revolution in farm technology and management—what often is termed 'the second agricultural revolution'. This has taken many forms, being part of wider changes is world technology.

In most developed countries, the pattern follows four overlapping stages. First, a mechanical revolution, followed by electrical power distribution throughout the countryside which made practical intensive crop storage and livestock housing. Thirdly, with these changes in efficiency, agriculturists begin to adopt the management techniques used in industry. In addition, raw materials are improved with better stock genetics, seeds and fertilizers. Finally, the managerial revolution includes the growth of automation and computer planning. We are in the midst of this phase and it is likely to prove the most significant both in terms of productivity and of landscape. An example of the rapid change in productivity in US produce, which reflects this period of four technical changes is shown in Figure 4.2.

This makes the introduction of new planning techniques more urgent. The impact of the four stages on the landscape can be given briefly. However, when viewing the rapid changes in farm technology, it should be stressed that, though output increases, the position of agriculture within the gross national domestic product (GDP) continually declines.

The agricultural percentage of GDP in most countries will have been halved between 1958 and 1978. The actual percentage varies, depending on the agricultural base. Within the UK, the decline is from 4·5% GDP in 1958 to 2·5% in 1976, and in Italy, for the same period, from 17 to 10%. The decline in the position of agriculture represents, also, loss of status and political influence. The issue is one related to industrial wages. The time taken by the average wage-earner to be able to buy certain foods also generates national attitudes about the value of farming. Equally, the relative capacity of each country to be self-sufficient in food production can help counter-balance the political respect for agriculture. These matters are illustrated in Tables 4.9 and 4.10. It is clear, as experience has shown, that the United Kingdom is particularly vulnerable.

Table 4.9. EEC: Minutes worked to earn food; 1976 average wages

|  | MILK (1 litre) | FILLET BEEF (1 kg) | PASTURISED BUTTER (1 kg) | BEER (1 litre) |
|---|---|---|---|---|
| Belgium | 5 | 120 | 54 | 11 |
| Denmark | 4 | 137 | 39 | 13 |
| France | 8 | 166 | 80 | 14 |
| West Germany | 6 | 144 | 57 | 18 |
| Irish Republic | 6 | 103 | 44 | 28 |
| Italy | 9 | 184 | 109 | 21 |
| Netherlands | 5 | 100 | 62 | 9 |
| UK | 7 | 147 | 35 | 24 |

Source: Barclays Bank, *Agricultural Common Market 1977* (based on Agra Europe).

The future of the Common Agricultural Policy within the EEC cannot be clear; even less can be its effect on agricultural land use. It is probable that the UK aim to be self-sufficient in food production (4.19) may be weakened by pressure on each member country to produce what is best suited to its land. For England, this might make a shift towards intensive grassland and permanently housed livestock (4.20). There is a current trend for arable production to expand in eastern England, with livestock to be grouped westwards. In turn, this moves straw away from livestock areas and leaves farm wastes where effluent is less beneficial for the land (4.21). Thus, pressures without and within do affect the landscape.

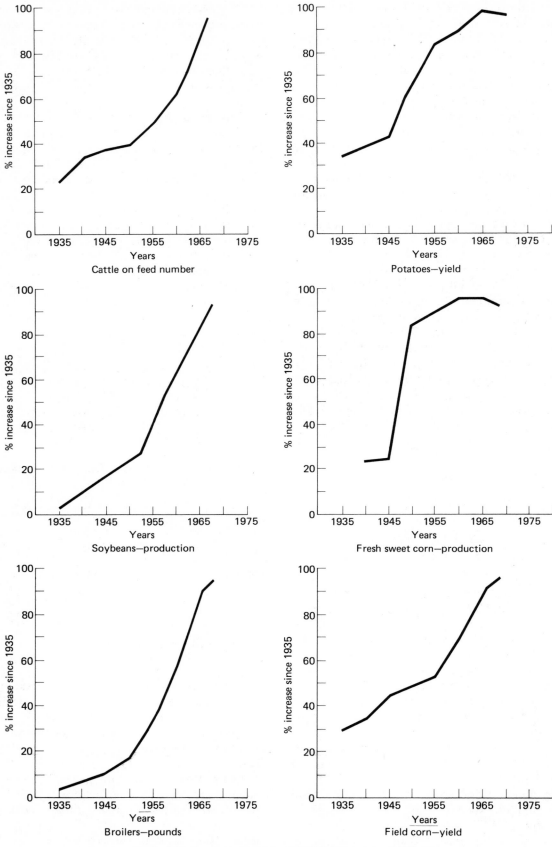

Figure 4.2    Increases in productivity in US produce, 1935–67.

(*Source:* US Yearbook of Agriculture, 1970)

Table 4.10. EEC: Home supply and consumption by member States, 1972

|  | GRAINS | SUGAR | POTATOES | MEAT | BUTTER | CHEESE | VEGETABLES | FRUIT |
|---|---|---|---|---|---|---|---|---|
| EEC | 91 | 89 | 100 | 94 | 92 | 100 | 97 | 81 |
| Belgium | 45 | 173 | 96 | 122 | 107 | 50 | 118 | 66 |
| Denmark | 101 | 118 | 102 | 358 | 297 | 244 | 88 | 68 |
| France | 164 | 150 | 104 | 96 | 111 | 114 | 96 | 101 |
| West Germany | 83 | 94 | 94 | 85 | 101 | 86 | 45 | 53 |
| Irish Republic | 80 | 108 | 105 | 271 | 196 | 485 | 103 | 23 |
| Italy | 69 | 74 | 97 | 71 | 68 | 85 | 112 | 121 |
| Netherlands | 36 | 113 | 123 | 175 | 373 | 230 | 183 | 82 |
| UK | 65 | 35 | 96 | 68 | 17 | 52 | 82 | 42 |

Note: Break-even point = 100.
Predominant food importers: UK, West Germany, Italy.
Export surplus for some items: France, Netherlands, Irish Republic, Denmark.
Source: Kennet, W., *The Futures of Europe*.

## Farm Size

The structure of farm size, often of management, varies throughout Europe, and in this the United Kingdom is more industrialised, working within larger units (see Table 4.11.). The rapid change in size of holdings within the UK can be seen from Table 4.12, which shows the change for the decade 1964–73.

Thus there has been a marked swing to farms of over about 120 ha. In turn, this is reflected in larger managerial units, using more sophisticated techniques. Though only 8% of holdings were of this size, they represented about two-thirds of the assets as shown from Table 4.13.

Table 4.11. Size of farm holding within the EEC

|  | TOTAL HOLDINGS (1000s) 1975 | | | AVERAGE SIZE (ha) | TOTAL NUMBER |
|---|---|---|---|---|---|
|  | >1 <20 | >10 <50 | >50 | | |
|  | (breakdown by hectares) | | | | |
| Belgium | 3·3 | 47·3 | 54·9 | 13·4 | 105·5 |
| Denmark | 10·1 | 79·1 | 40·6 | 22·1 | 129·8 |
| France | 143·0 | 650·0 | 432·0 | 23·5 | 1225·0 |
| West Germany | 26·2 | 387·8 | 490·6 | 13·5 | 904·6 |
| Irish Republic | 14·9 | 140·9 | 111·0 | 17·7 | 266·8 |
| Italy | 36·8 | 262·4 | 1874·2 | 7·7 | 2173·4 |
| Luxembourg | 0·5 | 3·3 | 1·8 | 22·4 | 5·6 |
| Netherlands | 3·2 | 74·1 | 66·5 | 14·2 | 143·8 |
| UK | 83·3 | 116·3 | 73·7 | 64·2 | 273·3 |

Source: *EEC Yearbook of Agricultural Statistics 1976*

Table 4.13. Capital size of holdings in the UK, 1974

| CROPS AND GRASS (acres) | HOLDINGS (No) | (%) | AREA (acres) | (%) | TOTAL ASSETS (£m) | AVERAGE ASSETS PER HOLDING (£) |
|---|---|---|---|---|---|---|
| <50 | 132,800 | 48 | 2600 | 9 | 1690 | 12,700 |
| >50 <150 | 89,200 | 32 | 8100 | 27 | 5270 | 59,000 |
| >150 <300 | 34,800 | 12 | 7400 | 25 | 4820 | 138,500 |
| 300 and over | 21,200 | 8 | 11,700 | 39 | 7600 | 358,500 |
|  | 278,000 | 100 | 29,800 | 100 | 19,380 | |

Source: de Paula, F.C., *Farm Finance and Fiscal Policy*

Table 4.12. Changes in farm holding sizes between 1964 and 1973

|  | SIZE OF HOLDINGS (ACRES) GRASS AND CROPS | | | | | | |
|---|---|---|---|---|---|---|---|
|  | <5 | >5 <30 | >30 <100 | >100 <150 | >150 <300 | >300 <700 | >700 |
| 1964 | 66,004 | 93,641 | 88,422 | 27,957 | 32,079 | 12,798 | 2166 |
| 1973 | 18,295 | 54,681 | 66,399 | 23,966 | 28,994 | 14,163 | 3415 |

Source: *Agricultural Statistics England and Wales*, HMSO, 1973.

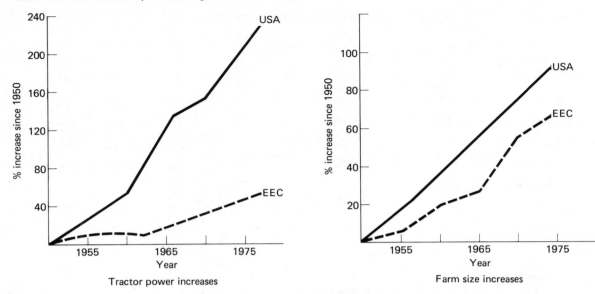

Figure 4.3    Increases in tractor power and farm size in the US and EEC countries, 1950–75.

De Paula has estimated that the total UK agricultural and horticultural assets in 1974 were over £21,000m, of which nearly four-fifths were landlords' assets and the remainder tenants', but of which only 8% were under long- or short-term loans. Thus farmland represents a vast underused financial asset. This is partly why—though there has been a major expansion of owner-occupied farms from 12% in 1911 to 54% in 1976—there is a growth of institutional land ownership. In 1971, this was estimated at 8·8% of all farmland in England and Wales and 9·2% in Scotland (4.22), and totalled just over 1·5 million hectares. The matter, at present, is being examined by a Government committee, together with the incidence of foreign purchase of farmland. Taxation policy has encouraged institutional investment, and comparatively low land prices make large private farms and father/son inherited farms unlikely to survive in their present form. Most opinions stress that there is likely to be a major change in land ownership structure which could affect both farm size and management.

Farm size expansion has been more rapid in the US than in the EEC, though less dramatic than in the UK. What is more implicit to land management change is the investment in tractor power (see Figure 4.3). The implication of energy inputs to food has already been discussed, but machinery power and concentration of livestock in big units are fundamental factors which control field size and layout, as well as those of farmsteads.

### The New Scale Farm

The effect of changes in cultivation and harvesting equipment on field patterns is discussed in the next section. There is also, however, radical change in the 'farmstead', and specialised farm building units are a phenomenon of our times. Central grain silo units, to which several thousand hectares may be contracted, have been common in Europe,

the United States and other parts of the world for decades. The example of such a silo group in France (Figure 4.4) is typical. It seems probable, following surveys of the UK grain industry, that similar ventures will be created in England. Indeed, large central storage already exists in parts of the Fens. The impact of such extensive and tall buildings on a small-scale or traditional English landscape may prove severe. Set in the prairies, of course, they can provide a foil to the vast open horizons of the grain belt. However, such buildings can be acceptable if designs are functional and scales are in sympathy with the landscape. It is essential to find a formula for creative control over design.

Figure 4.4    A group of grain silos, which is a typical example of cooperative storage in the French landscape.

(*Photo by courtesy of* World Crops)

Figure 4.5 Rows of cattle pens at Monfort. The feedlot comprises 100,000 head of steers and is run on modern management principles. Dust and run-off water are both controlled.

(*Photo by courtesy of the American Agricultural News Service*)

Large concentrations of livestock into one area, as practical with modern forms of management, will engender their own side-effect problems. The visual problem will depend on location and landscape as well as the nature of the building requirements and the degree of external control over the layout and buildings. Intensive beef units in corrals do not pose much problem in this respect, nor in terms of the other basic problem, that is, pollution from effluent. The aerial view of the feedlot in Monfort (Figure 4.5) makes it clear that such landscapes can absorb both the yards and silo unit required for 100,000 head.

Dairy cattle, too, can be managed in large units. Again, in warm dry lands, open yards are practical as shown in Figure 4.6. In other parts of the world, with more severe winters, different systems prevail. In the United Kingdom, the tradition is for summer grazing followed by four to six months within buildings. Unit size, in consequence, tends to be restricted to around 80 to 150 head—though the average herd size is still less than 50. Nevertheless, practice is changing and the multi-hundred-head units are beginning to appear, some of which are permanently housed. In Eastern Europe, the tradition of the small farm unit has been broken. The dairy unit near Prenzlau, East Germany (Figure 4.7) is typical of several now built. There are political and economic reasons why such layouts have not been built in Western Europe, but already dairy units of 600 to 1000 head are not uncommon. Multi-thousand-head units for the smaller animals, that is for poultry, pigs, calves, rabbits, etc., are commonplace. Since they are smaller, the buildings are less dominant, but can equally create a visual hazard to pleasant landscape. Moreover, the traffic generated by units of this size may well prove to be more than the rural infrastructure of roads can absorb. This is discussed further below.

Intensive livestock housing, in all developed countries, has been a consistent trend. It seems probable that in many parts of the world a situation will prevail, certainly within

Figure 4.6 Dairy unit in California; milk production with feed yards, silo feed storage, feed mixing unit and milking parlour for several hundred head.

(*Photo by courtesy of Gordon Craddock*)

Figure 4.7 Dairy unit near Prenzlau, East Germany. The model of this unit at Dedelow, with cattle housing, tower silos, plus slurry storage tanks at the far side, is typical of many dairy schemes for 1000 or 2000 cows. Such schemes are not always as labour-intensive in terms of output per man as smaller units in other countries.

(*Photo by courtesy of* Farmers Weekly)

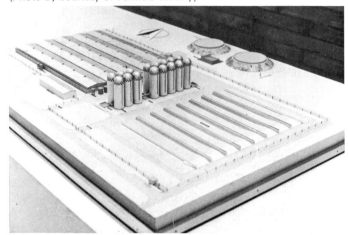

this century, when nearly all farm stock are housed permanently, or for the greater parts of their lives. In many cases, units will be large, though some smaller layouts on specialised, part-time farms will prevail. Consideration of trends in farm buildings is difficult, since all pointers suggest a kind of science-fiction situation evolving.

## New Methods of Handling Raw Materials and Produce

Logistics of handling materials in the production of food have been left unstudied. It seems certain, as pressures on farming increase and more sophisticated management techniques are used, that this will become a critical issue, especially to any improvement in landscape planning. Traditional farming has been based on the two concepts—that it is cheaper to take animals to their feed in the fields than feed to them at their housing and, secondly, it is cheaper to take stock and produce from the farm to distant processing factories than it is to site stock housing and crop storage near the abattoir and factory. Both concepts need re-examining.

There is growing evidence that moving stock creates stress which has a measurable effect on their sale value. In fatstock this is shown in a reduction in liveweight and by a discoloration in the meat. In large units, when costings are managed by computer control, the effect can be serious. Two factors appear as critical. For health reasons, there may be an advantage to break the life cycle between the initial growing stage and the fattening period. But, journey time between the two units should be restricted and a distance of 30 to 40 km should be the preferred maximum and 80 km the absolute maximum. If this is accepted, present practice of moving stock over great distances, often from uplands to lowlands, cannot be justified—especially if transportation costs are studied. In the same manner, distance from fattening house to abattoir should be restricted also to 30 to 40 km and batches of stock should be slaughtered with the minimum of time at the lairage. Similarly, the location of abattoirs needs re-appraisal so that fatstock units and the slaughterhouse may be brought into a planned relationship, the latter being sited near a road and rail network for distribution of processed food to the urban areas.

The scale of modern abattoir and dairy, to be economic, also has to be increased and modern units need to serve a population of at least one million, possibly made up of several towns. The plan diagram (Figure 4.8) indicates the kind of relationship which might exist. If this kind of pattern is economically correct, landscape planning techniques should assist the best zoning for the component parts. This kind of planning process relating food production to urban area still has not been resolved.

The concept was taken further in a thesis by Thompson and Jarvis (4.23), as shown in Figure 4.9. This study showed how a large tract of prime farm land near Hull might be restructured in conjunction with the Humberside urban ex-

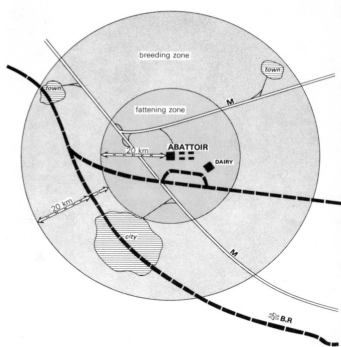

Figure 4.8   Modern abattoirs and dairies should be sited, together with their by-product factories, close to a road-rail network, around which in a 20 km radius would be the livestock-fattening units and beyond which would be the breeding zones and the points of consumption.

Figure 4.9   Conveyors from arable production zones take grass and grain to livestock production buildings, divided from the abattoir and by-product factories by a railway. The units are also sited close to a motorway.

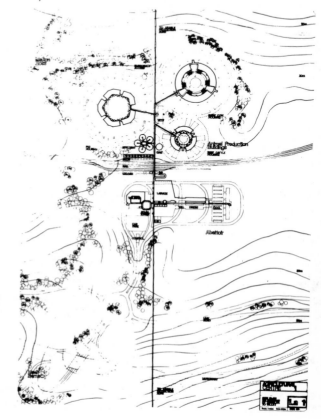

pansion plan. Mechanical conveyance tracks from 'field' to processing plant would be a logical step in materials-handling, removing much of the bottleneck in many farm operations. Since irrigation and effluent pipelines already exist, once production areas are large enough, other field conveyors may be developed. Concentrations of stock require first-class administration and management, backed by veterinary and other skills. To support such facilities, units would have to be larger than today, and a development along the lines described in the thesis seems probable, especially as labour costs rise.

The ultimate form for agriculture and, therefore, for the rural landscape is a matter of speculation. One thing is certain however—the present change within agriculture is accelerating.

## Farm Manpower

The second agricultural revolution is changing the structure of farm manpower. It is true both of farmers and of farm workers, and the change is significant in a number of respects.

Mechanisation and farm amalgamations have reduced manpower substantially in all developed countries. The 'drift from the land' has become a hackneyed term. In most countries, the reduction in farm manpower has been a natural process so that redundancy, unlike the experience in some industries, has been rare. It is one mark of industrialised countries that the percentage of the working population directly engaged in food production is not only small but is further diminishing. This decline is shown for some European countries in Table 4.14.

Table 4.14. Workforce in agriculture, fishing and forestry in EEC countries

|  | TOTAL WORKFORCE (1000s) | | PERCENTAGE OF TOTAL WORKING POPULATION | |
|  | 1966 | 1975 | 1966 | 1975 |
|---|---|---|---|---|
| Belgium | 219 | 136 | 5·9 | 3·6 |
| Denmark | 315 | 228 | 14·2 | 9·8 |
| France | 3333 | 2351 | 17·2 | 11·3 |
| West Germany | 2790 | 1822 | 10·6 | 7·3 |
| Irish Republic | 334 | 252 | 31·6 | 24·5 |
| Italy | 4589 | 2964 | 24·9 | 15·8 |
| Luxembourg | 15 | 9 | 11·1 | 6·0 |
| Netherlands | 375 | 299 | 8·5 | 6·6 |
| UK | 910 | 667 | 3·7 | 2·7 |

Source: 1966: *OECD Labour Force Statistics 1963–74*
1975: *EEC Yearbook of Agricultural Statistics 1976*

The decline of work directly connected with rural land is dramatic. It reflects the Common Agricultural Policy of the EEC in which Article 39 stated:

> 'to increase agricultural productivity by promoting technical progress and by ensuring the rational development of agricultural production and the optimum utilisation of the factors of production, in particular labour . . .'.

An EEC Directive (No. 160) of 1972 went further, for it concerns:

> 'measures to encourage the cessation of farming and the re-allocation of utilised agricultural area for the purposes of structural improvement . . .'.

Thus, both within and without the EEC, it is not surprising that the International Centre for Conservation, based in Rome, is concerned that Europe has 10,000 derelict villages. In addition, many rural areas have severe socio-economic problems, especially within uplands and agricultural fringe areas.

In the United States, trends are similar with today only 3·3% of the total labour force of 84 million still engaged as farm workers. This contrasts with the traditionally peasant population of the USSR, where 20% of the 135-million labour force are in agriculture, and within the Third World, where 80% may work on farms.

The balance between farmer and farmworker, also, is significant within the rural economy (Table 4.15). With the exception of Italy, full-time employed staff are fewer in number than the farmers themselves. Within the US, where 4·3 million worked in agriculture in 1974, some 3·2 million were farmers or their families. Thus, within developed countries, agriculture is not a generator of rural employment, except within the support industries for servicing and for processing, much of which may be based in country towns.

Table 4.15. Agricultural labour force in EEC countries in 1975

|  | FARMERS | FAMILIES (1000s) | EMPLOYEES |
|---|---|---|---|
| Belgium | 85 | 27 | 6 |
| Denmark | 130 | 7 | 19 |
| France | 791 | 481 | 200 |
| West Germany | 480 | 580 | 100 |
| Irish Republic | 209 | 209 | 34 |
| Italy | 622 | 399 | 809 |
| Luxembourg | 5 | 7 | 1 |
| Netherlands | 148 | 65 | 32 |
| UK | 280 | 82 | 227 |

Source: *EEC Yearbook of Agricultural Statistics 1976*

Table 4.16. Size and output of UK farms in 1974

| PERSONS ENGAGED (full-time) | NO. OF HOLDINGS | % TOTAL HOLDINGS | FINAL OUTPUT PER ANNUM (£m) | (%) | AVERAGE OUTPUT PER HOLDING (£/annum) |
|---|---|---|---|---|---|
| Less than 1 man | 115,400 | 41 | 256 | 6 | 2200 |
| 1 or 2 men | 66,500 | 24 | 655 | 15 | 9850 |
| 2 to 4 men | 55,000 | 20 | 1078 | 24 | 19,600 |
| More than 4 men | 41,100 | 15 | 2500 | 55 | 60,830 |
| | 278,000 | 100 | 4489 | 100 | |

Source: de Paula, F.C., *Farm Finance and Fiscal Policy*

The size of farm unit is small compared with most industries as shown in Table 4.16. This table reveals how output per man rises sharply as the size of holding (and of capital investment) increases. All farming does tend to be based on small teams, often family-based, except on the collective farms in certain parts of the world. Some types of farming have seasonal labour requirements, providing part-time work, particularly at harvest. In the US, for example, some 2·5 million, in addition to the full-time workforce, do some hired farm work, although two-thirds are employed for under three months.

The change in farm manpower has several consequences. Traditionally, the farm gave employment to the slow of wit, thus creating the image of the dull yokel. Today, skills of livestock management, of fieldwork and of machine maintenance need exacting standards. Moreover, farmworkers are responsible for higher capital investment *per capita* than in most other industries. There is no place for the unskilled labourer on the modern farm. However, as the farm labour force declines, the need for skilled services to agriculture has increased. These include advisory services, both Government and private, as well as machinery, feed and fertilizer, and transport service industries.

Developing countries have a different manpower problem since, as mentioned above, in many cases up to 80% of the working population are on the land. With low industrial growth rates, it is unlikely that agricultural mechanisation will be as rapid as in Europe and North America. However, the 'green revolution', with increased crop yields of rice and wheat, has shown signs of reducing the number of farm jobs. Most sociologists believe that the shift from oxen to tractors should not be rapid. Economically, this must be so. Nevertheless, the medium term aim must be to intensify food production by mechanisation, thus reducing farm labour. In the long term, there seems little reason why the farm labour force will not drop dramatically, especially if other forms of food, such as hydroponic crops, synthetic proteins and fish farming are developed to aid the feeding of undernourished peoples.

# The Role of Planning Authorities in Food Production Planning

Planning Authorities in Britain, since the 1947 Act (page 14), have had responsibility for zoning land between different uses. This created zones for housing, for industry, etc., with the green belts and *white areas* set aside for farming. In urban areas, control has been quite detailed, even to determining basic industrial layout and building design within designated factory estates (see Chapter 8). However, once land has been designated for farming, there has been little control over detail, except for some aspects of planting and of design for larger farm buildings, access on to highways and, in a few cases, of tree preservation orders. Planners have made little impact on the physical appearance of the agricultural landscape. Indeed, few would assume they should do so. This situation now needs critical re-appraisal in view of the pressures on land use, together with such side effects as pollution.

Within recent years, there has been a spate of regional or county planning reports. In particular, county structure plans have been prepared (see page 14). Without exception these reports have proved negative with regard to food production planning. Most accept, without real analysis, the need to keep existing farmland for farming. In 1967, the Strategic Plan for the South East (4.24) emphasised the situation:

AIMS OF STUDY RELATED TO THE COUNTRYSIDE
1. 'To relate the needs of urban growth and the countryside...
2. To provide for appropriate use and development of the countryside's resources—agriculture, minerals, heritage and recreation...
3. To devise a comprehensive countryside policy.'

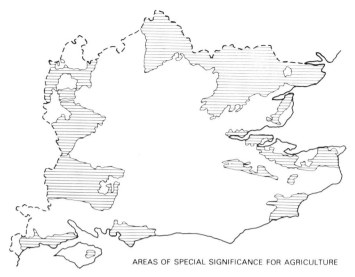

AREAS OF SPECIAL SIGNIFICANCE FOR AGRICULTURE

Figure 4.10   Areas of special significance for agriculture in south-east England.

(From the Strategic Plan for the South-East)

## AIMS OF THE STUDY RELATED TO AGRICULTURE

'...occupies over 60 per cent of the land surface...contributes significant proportions of the national output of fruit, hops, pigs and poultry as well as wheat and barley... well suited to meet the challenge of possible change in the political and economic context in which it must operate....'

'...objective for the regional strategy should be to identify those areas where conditions are particularly suitable for the further promotion of agricultural productivity by virtue of their existing and prospective farm structure, productivity levels and specialisation, land quality, and immunity from present and foreseeable urban intrusion...but, where land and farm structure is less well suited for capital-intensive farming, the needs of agriculture would have to be met in the context of other competing needs for land... it would be the task of the local planning authorities to reconcile conflicting claims, bearing in mind that generally agriculture should continue to be the main land use in the region.'

Though agriculture accounted for 60% of the land resource, it was given only one page out of the 150 in the report. As in most reports, need was expressed for safeguarding the best farm land but, expressed more clearly than most reports, was the acknowledgement that lower-quality land would have to compete with urban and other needs.

In 1975 Essex County Council produced the first part of its Structure Plan for North and Central Essex (4.25). This was an 158-page report which concerned one of the most fertile parts of England. A total of 7 pages, plus another 3 pages of charts and maps, was devoted to 'countryside and coastline'. It included an interesting analysis of those 'areas of special significance for agriculture', but was based on data from the Ministry of Agriculture derived almost a decade earlier in 1966:

'...and included farm size in relation to type of farming, viability of farms, quality of land, degree of

specialisation and areas with potential for future production...but delimitation of these areas should not be taken to imply that land elsewhere is necessarily of less importance since smaller areas may also be of significance at the local level.'

Thus most of north and central Essex had agricultural significance (Figure 4.11), but equally important is the relation of this land to values other than for food production as 'protected land' (Figure 4.12):

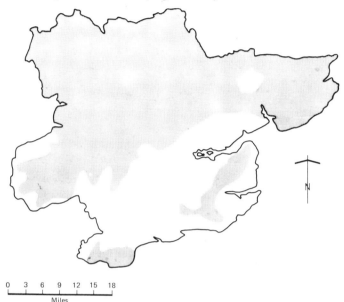

0  3  6  9  12  15  18
Miles

Figure 4.11   Areas of special significance for agriculture in Essex.

(By courtesy of Essex County Council)

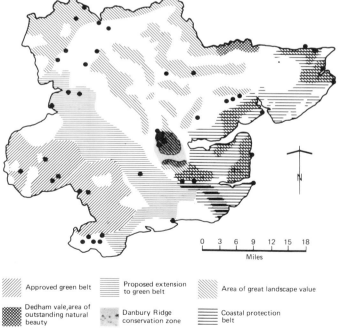

0  3  6  9  12  15  18
Miles

Approved green belt — Proposed extension to green belt — Area of great landscape value
Dedham vale, area of outstanding natural beauty — Danbury Ridge conservation zone — Coastal protection belt
● Site of special scientific interest

Figure 4.12   Protected and valued land in Essex.

(By courtesy of Essex County Council)

'... Areas of Great Landscape Value ... particularly good examples of characteristic landscape and known to attract visitors. Care to avoid inappropriate development ... it is implicit that a detailed analysis of particular areas would be made when specific proposals for development emerged.'

From this analysis the report suggested that land use planning could be based on two evaluations, both requiring further research:

'*Single-use areas*
The county could be divided into single-use areas with, for example, agriculture dominant in areas of exceptionally productive farmland. This would obviously involve a far more detailed evaluation of agricultural potential by the Ministry of Agriculture, Fisheries and Food and would have to be constantly reviewed in the light of improved management techniques and changes in food production demands ...

*Multiple-use areas*
In these areas, recreation and conservation would be more closely integrated with farming ... land management schemes could be drawn up involving the user interests to highlight conflicts and arrive at a workable solution on access and conservation ....'

This concept of zoning white lands is correct—but the report makes clear that there is no way, at present, to implement the policy. Moreover, the report does not examine the actual or potential value of the land in terms of specific objectives for food production. The situation is even less clearly defined within the 1974 Leicester and Leicestershire Structure Plan prepared by the county council within a survey of 300 pages and a written statement of 120 pages (4.26). Within this bulky report, though agriculture is acknowledged as important, only 7 pages (plus charts and maps) is devoted to its survey, generally as follows under 'countryside, landscape and agriculture':

'Agriculture: one of the most important activities in Leicestershire ... occupying about 80% of its land ... associated with extensive rather than intensive methods of farming with a concentration on livestock and cereal production ... mixed farms which make up so substantial a part of agricultural holdings ... most is classified as Grade II ... farms need considerably amended services ... with large tank lorries (within) relatively narrow access roads ... a solution will be found as the County Council adopts a policy of strict rural traffic management.'

And, the agricultural statement is contained within less than 2 pages, within a series of vague statements of good intent:

'... The Authority will generally permit new isolated dwellings in rural areas only where such a dwelling fulfills 'agricultural need'

To preserve as far as possible areas of highly productive agricultural land within the County in their present use

To concentrate recreational facilities on the urban-rural fringe and on poor quality farmland where possible

To encourage ... new planting of trees in any small areas of otherwise unworkable land on farms ...

To discourage the sale of plants and produce directly from farms, market-gardens and nurseries to the public where this may create traffic or other hazards but otherwise to accept that this is generally an integral part of agricultural and horticultural operations

To minimise the impact on the road system of heavy vehicles servicing farms.'

The failure to grasp what food production and land use should be about within structure planning of resources is revealed in county after county. In the County Structure Plan for Bedfordshire in 1976 (4.27), only one page plus a map is devoted to the 'agricultural survey' within the 186-page Report of Survey: Consultation Draft, in spite of recognising:

'Over three-quarters of land is down to agriculture and 44% of this falls within Grades I and II of the Ministry of Agriculture's land classification (compared with 17% in England and Wales as a whole) ... but the acreage of land in agricultural use from 1950–1970 was reduced by over 7% (2.7% in England and Wales) ... preservation of Grades I and III of paramount importance acting as a significant constraint against future development.'

The survey was followed up by an 115-page Written Statement: Draft Consultation Report, also in 1976. This contained a number of policy statements to protect agricultural land:

'*Policy 73*
The local planning authorities will seek to minimise the overall loss of productive or potentially productive agricultural land to other forms of development.

*Policy 74*
The local planning authorities will not permit new residential, industrial or recreational development on land classified as Grades I and II.

*Policy 75*
There will be a general presumption against the development of land classified as Upper Grade III unless special justification can be shown in a particular case.

*Policy 78*
The County Council will initiate and maintain a forum wherein the requirements of agriculture and current agricultural practice may be discussed.

*Policy 80*
The local authorities will not permit recreational proposals which would conflict with the efficient operation of agricultural practices. However, countryside recreation of a quiet nature and low intensity will be encouraged, where appropriate.

*Policy 81*
Throughout the County, the local authorities will aid agricultural efficiency by the definition of more precise management measures on the periphery of towns and villages...

*Policy 84*
The County Council will promote the principles of landscape management put forward by the Countryside Commission in the consultative document "New Agricultural Landscapes".'

It is essential to protect good food-producing land, but these examples make clear the continued demarcation between planning resources within the framework of town and country planning, and actually examining the nature of the resources themselves, let alone within a strategy for national nutrition. Planning, basically, is reduced to cosmetics. Though important, it is not the crux of the problem of land use priorities. As discussed later, farm and soil structure are the real issues, and in these there is a tension between the planner and the farmer. The Ministry of Agriculture's Classification of Agricultural Land (see page 95) has been criticised. The reaction to this criticism that such classification '...is not readily understood by planners and therefore does not rate highly as a total in land-use decisions...' was typical amongst farmers, as expressed by a leader in the *Farmers Weekly* (4.28):

'Planners are not farming's favourite people...(the report) assumes, as do too many planners, that by mathematical calculation one can show whether a decision to turn a particular piece of land from an agricultural purpose to a residential or manufacturing one will be economically good or bad.'

Planners are aware that farmers do not want to be 'planned', and all the structure plans reflect a desire, agriculturally, to be negative towards resource evaluation.

The situation in the United States is different. Land use planning has not had the same base. However, farmland is protected from development in many states. The rapid change from food surplus to shortage in the 1970s has increased such protection. California had a Land Conservation Act in 1965 by which land threatened by urban expansion received preferential tax treatment if it remained in agriculture. By 1975, one-third of the state's farmland was under contract to remain in food production. New York State with Suffolk County has Agricultural District Law and their Agricultural Resources Commission in 1968 created 'agricultural districts' between local and state government and the farmer. By 1975, one-half of the full-time farmland was within 200 protected districts (4.29).

In 1975, a major seminar was held in the United States on the 'Retention of Prime Lands' and it was recommended that a Land Resources Council, similar to the US Water Resources Council, should be established (4.30). The Council would support land use committees within each state which would be responsible for soil and land surveys, to ensure that the 'location and amount of prime and unique farmlands' should be recorded, and for research 'to improve agriculture productivity', since 'evidence indicated we have reached the point where decreases in land in production may no longer be balanced by increases in productivity'.

Figure 4.13 Location of agricultural districts in New York with respect to major urban centres.

(*By courtesy of the* Journal of the American Institute of Planners)

## The Role of the Ministry of Agriculture in Rural Resource Planning

While country planning has had little impact on food production problems in Britain, the Ministry of Agriculture has made little contribution to the planning of rural resources, particularly of land. The history of the Ministry is such that this is not surprising. The first Board of Agriculture was created in the Napoleonic Wars and was responsible only for farm statistics. The Board gave way in 1919 to the first Ministry of Agriculture and Fisheries, with State guidance, even control, over agriculture increasing in the Second World War. Government policy for food production was set out in the Agriculture Act of 1947 which, like the Town and Country Planning Act of the same year, still is the basis of much official thinking. The Act promised to maintain 'a stable and efficient agricultural industry capable of producing such part of the nation's food and other agricultural produce as in the national interest it is desirable to produce in the United Kingdom'. This has proved to be a flexible objective, not only from the farmers' viewpoint, but in terms of research and development in basic resources. In 1954, the separate Ministry of Food was amalgamated to form the Ministry of Agriculture, Fisheries and Food. This was a logical link between primary production and consumer.

The combined Ministry gained an international reputation in many aspects of food production and hygiene, particularly in its farm advisory services (Agricultural Land Service and National Agricultural Advisory Service) which did much to help farmers master the second agricultural revolution, creating remarkable increases in farm productivity in terms of labour and of yield. The twin advisory services were amalgamated into the Agricultural Development and Advisory Service, with the emphasis on collective development rather than on unlimited advice on every farm. However, the Ministry has made little impact on resource planning in its three main attributes of land use, food logistics and food technology. Such objectives are not within its main terms of reference.

By definition, a Ministry of Agriculture, Fisheries and Food is unlikely to concentrate effort on rural land as a national resource. Moreover, any industry, such as farming, made up of fragmented production units, is unlikely to co-operate with a Ministry devoted to collective efficiency in terms of overall resources such as land use and logistics. There has been a basic tension with MAFF's relationship with farmers between the command in the 1947 Act for a 'stable' and an 'efficient' agricultural industry since the two are not always synonymous. There is also a tension between MAFF and land users other than farmers.

One effect of the Scott Report of 1942 (4.31) has been that it is:

'an integral part of the Government's planning policy that the better agricultural land should not be taken for other use if there is less valuable land that would serve the purpose. The Ministry of Agriculture, Fisheries and Food assists in carrying out this policy in England and Wales by providing expert advice to planning authorities and other departments on the implications, from the standpoint of the public agricultural interest, of all substantial proposals to take agricultural land for other purposes.'

It has been integral to this planning policy that responsibility for change in land use is vested in other Ministries, such as Housing and now within the Department of the Environment. Expert advice from MAFF has been used both in the preparation of outline plans for location of new towns and national services, and in public appeals against planning proposals. However, MAFF has never had the brief to form a top-level 'Land Resource Planning Unit' (of whatever title) directly responsible to the Deputy Director of the Ministry. This has meant, for example, that MAFF has never had the power to collect data from county planning authorities on changes in land use. Therefore, when MAFF has presented advice on a particular proposal to take a large block of agricultural land into other use, it has been impossible to relate the proposed change to national annual trends in loss of farmland, both in terms of quantity and of quality.

The limited impact of MAFF on rural resource planning is emphasised by a study of *The Sourcebook of Planning Information* (4.32). Out of 600 text pages, MAFF is indexed to four references and not once to the sections on rural planning, land use and countryside. Three of the references are to farm statistics. They have a real use in understanding food productivity, but they are not the basis for rural resource planning, particularly in matters of land use. The fourth reference is to the Agricultural Land Classification Maps which are discussed in Chapter 2. It is clear that the Ministry has not made a fundamental impact on the source of rural planning information.

In addition to land use, studies of rural resources planning should be concerned with the study of the logistics of food production, processing and distribution, together with those of the service and by-product industries. As already stated (see page 107) these have had little or no co-ordinated study and there has been no attempt to relate production zones to transportation policies within Government policies expressed through MAFF or the other planning Ministries.

Although the Ministries of Agriculture and of Food have been combined for nearly two decades, the overall problem of food technology has never been integrated, especially in relation to rural resource planning. For example, though MAFF may be asked to give evidence concerning potential loss of farmland by a proposed designation order for a new town or city, the technical problem of planning resources for feeding the proposed population has never been discussed. Such resource planning has never been the responsibility of MAFF. This is discussed further in the section dealing with regional development plans. At the national level, the Ministry has never been required to examine the relation between land use and population diet. Thus, the location of production zones for different foods and the potential needs for certain classes of land for particular foods has never been part of the structure of MAFF's brief.

It seems essential that in any crowded industrial country, where land is a heavily exploited resource but where 80% of the total area is devoted to agriculture, the Ministry of Agriculture and Food should be concerned with food technology *and* with rural resources. If this chapter on agriculture's relation to landscape planning techniques has any basic plea, it must be that industrial countries with restricted land resources should have a Ministry of Rural Resources and Food Technology. The concept of 'agriculture' being divorced from 'land use' cannot be sustained.

As previously discussed, European agriculture is being integrated within the EEC's Common Agricultural Policy. To this extent, MAFF is no longer a free agent. The policy base, anyway, is widened to include socio-economic advisory services. It is probable that it will be widened again to include wildlife conservation. The Porchester Report with regard to Exmoor has suggested that certain areas should be inviolate against further agricultural improvement (4.33). This has profound implications regarding the directions made after the 1947 Act.

All over the world, ministries responsible for food production tend to be in evolution. The US has made a significant change towards retention of prime lands (4.34). In addition, it has developed a network of ecological advice. Major Federal and some state developments, within a strategy requiring impact analysis reports (see pages 54 to 56), have to examine potential effects on wildlife and agriculture.

Many countries with arid zones have major departments for developing agriculture. For example, the Libyan Arab Republic has a Council for Agricultural Development which, in 1974, produced a wide-ranging development study for Jabel el Akhdar, covering 2000 farms of 25 to 80 ha within an aim of 'creating a settled society by establishing completely equipped up-to-date farms to be put under

scientific dry farming with supplementary summer irrigation' backed by full extension services for 'pilot and experimental areas... training... servicing... supporting co-operatives... marketing'. All oil revenue states have ambitious plans for new agricultural and rural settlement expansion. Many are pioneering new ideas of land management. And, even within other types of land economy, major developments are promoted by central Government. The Indian Government has several schemes such as the Khadi Village Industry Commission, Bombay, where since 1960 small methane plants have been installed so that each cow's effluent can produce enough gas for one person's cooking requirements (4.35) (Figure 4.14).

One of the most dramatic developments, again in Libya, is the Kufra Production Project which covers 10,000 ha, and which is based on 100 wells, some 400 m deep, tapping the great underground water basin discovered during oil explorations. Each circle of 1100 m diameter covers 100 ha, irrigated from a rotating boom attached to the well; the boom rotating between 20 and 80 hours depending on need. Forage and grain is produced to feed Barbary sheep; some 80,000 ewes and their lambs when the project is fully developed. This is the first of several similar projects (4.36).

## The Farming Fringe

Farmscape, defined as being agricultural areas of improved and unadulterated farmland, can degenerate into two types of fringe land (4.37):

> '*rurban*: rural-urban zone in which sprawling settlement fragments farmland and causes it, in time, to degenerate into idle wasteland;
> *marginal*: mixed zone where land fluctuated between improved and un-improved status according to climate'.

Town planners have always been concerned by the urban fringe. In Britain, one of the great post-war planning concepts has been the green-belt principle of restraint to urban growth. Green belts may have restrained sporadic changes of land use, but such areas are stressed by urban activities and, today, often come under attack as a principle which restricts developments and inflates costs.

Agriculturists believe problems of the farming fringe areas, as defined above, are becoming insoluble. Planners have produced no solution for these areas; indeed, such is the divorce between *town* and *country* planning, that there is a tendency for planners to indicate it as an agricultural and not a planning matter. It is relatively easy to formulate laws which prohibit urban development within green belts and which designate white areas of countryside as farmland. It is much harder to make farming practical in all such areas: if impractical, should this be of concern?

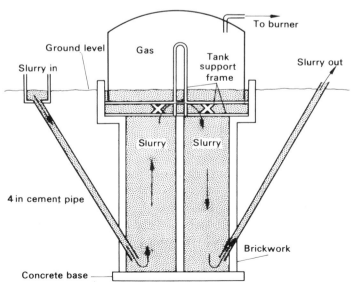

Figure 4.14   Section of methane plant, Gabor Gas Scheme.

(*By courtesy of* Farmers Weekly)

## The Rurban Fringe

In traditional planning there is a clear-cut division between town and country. Much post-war development has been on this basis. At the edge of the last housing estate around every town is a garden boundary, beyond which farmland produces food. Such an idea has much, in theory, to commend it having an historical basis in town evolution. With extensive traditional farming, when small herds and flocks grazed under-productive permanent pastures, given some tolerance from the farmers, it was a reasonable basis for planning. However, it no longer works. As soon as farmland is managed as a business, with every hectare planned for intensive production, there can be no such tolerance. Such farmland cannot be used for random recreation; but the clear-cut green-belt boundary, though building is restrained, cannot prevent trespass. The urban pressure for recreation around every town is too great. Trespass, with the associated risks of damage and of serious vandalism, dominates farming around the main urban areas. The problem, perhaps insoluble, is how to resolve the rural planning and agricultural issues within the green-belt concept.

Urban damage to farming processes takes many forms. Theft is a growing problem. Indeed, rustling within the proximity of motorways is becoming serious. Hedges and fences are damaged and, where stock is kept, gates left open. Junk is placed in every ditch and corner. Plastic and metal litter is dropped in fields to the danger of machinery and livestock. Crops are damaged and, sometimes, sporting guns used unwisely. Trespass can lead to fire risks, even buildings being burnt. Many farmers close to urban areas have to modify their management because of such abuses, and land values may be prejudiced. The situation seems to be deteriorating and the farming community is apprehensive.

The Ministry of Agriculture made an investigation of farm problems around the North-East conurbation in 1973 (4.38). Of 91 holdings within the survey, 84% recorded some trespass damage over the previous three years. Almost half of the holdings had severe problems with at least 20 incidents of damage, or an estimated £100 total damage, within one year. Moreover, 14 enterprises had been discontinued and six reduced in scope because of trespass. A similar degree of trespass damage was revealed by a Countryside Commission survey in 1975 (4.39) amongst 69 holdings adjacent to the urban areas in Hertfordshire, and where 88% had trespass and 78% suffered damage, generally as follows:

| | |
|---|---|
| Rubbish dumping | 71% |
| Horse riding damage | 36% |
| Livestock worrying | 29% |
| Gypsy nuisance | 26% |
| Theft of crops or livestock | 16% |
| Unauthorised shooting or poaching | 14% |
| Motorcycle damage | 14% |

The nature of the problem is obvious. Urban pressures must have a safety-valve between housing and productive farmland. At present, there is no legislation that can cope with the situation. New concepts must be developed. In the long term, social education may reduce actual damage to farmland. The immediate problem is how to disengage food production from the urban fringe and, having done so, how to devise new forms of land management for it. In many cases, land close to urban areas is top-grade farmland. In such situations, it must be kept for food production with stiff legislation against trespass. Thus, incentive must be made for recreational interests to be oriented to those urban boundaries where land quality is second-rate.

There is a natural desire to form the fringe areas as a traditional country house park or extensive farm, so that land is maintained by farming but free for recreation. Even with subsidised farming and compensation against damage, this is unlikely to prove practical. The system works only when recreational use is infrequent. With normal urban pressures, neither crops nor grazing stock could be managed. It might prove practical to farm extensively on a rotational basis, with land open for walking and other simple pursuits at clearly stated intervals, after which a 'warden' would inspect, clear rubbish and make repair before the land reverted to a period of grazing or cropping. Even this mixture of recreation and quasi-farming is unlikely to be practical close to an urban boundary; however, it should be tried experimentally.

Figure 4.16 shows a different concept for the urban fringe. The city region would be surrounded by a ring road and a recreational zone. The latter might be some 3 to 8 km wide,

Figure 4.15   A common near Bridgend in South Wales protected by the Coity Wallia Common Act 1976. Here vandals have left their mark and the rubbish is a danger to sheep.

(*Photo by courtesy of* Farmers Weekly)

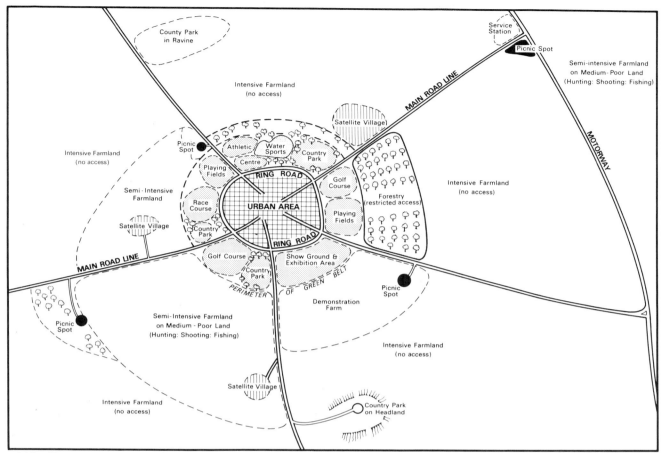

Figure 4.16    The rurban fringe. A plan showing a possible land use pattern for the rurban fringe around a city region.

depending on land and other circumstances. It would contain a wide range of open-air and showground activities, including water sports. There would be landscaping and tree planting; some housing could be included.

Around the recreational zone, where farmland was not top-grade, semi-intensive farming could be carried out. This would include controlled recreational use, such as traditional blood sports. There could be satellite villages and picnic spots within these lands, but other access would be restricted to whatever a farmer might permit and, probably, for which he could make a charge. On all first-class land around the city, intensive farming would be practised without public admittance. This might mean the loss of existing footpaths and even country lanes. By degrees, dwellings in these areas might be reduced in number. If, within this land, some terrain was not suitable for intensive fieldwork, it might be practical for country parks or viewing areas to be formed. These would need careful siting and design to prevent risk of trespass into the farmland. A demonstration farm would be formed somewhere suitable near the city (see page 96 and page 113).

At present, such a concept as that shown in Figure 4.16 is impossible. Neither agriculturists nor city authorities would find it practical or desirable, the former because of the control implied over the freedom to farm without the zoning of activities that at present exists, and the latter

because of the financial and managerial problems involved. In any case, present planning legislation could not cope with such far-reaching control over land use.

The Countryside Commission has conducted three surveys between 1972 and 1979 within different types of rurban fringe (Bollin Valley, south of Manchester; Hertfordshire/Barnet; Havering, London), introducing some management and grant aids to alleviate the tensions from public pressure, but without fundamental change in land structure (4.40, 4.41).

## The Hill and Upland Fringe

All advanced agricultural countries find their upland and hill farming both uneconomic and a social embarrassment. The latter is for two reasons. First, there is a legacy of support for these areas which cannot be easily terminated. Secondly, if terminated, many people consider the ensuing scrub to be unacceptable, an acknowledgement of defeat after years of toil. One-third of the farmland of Britain is in this category. Though it produces only some 6 to 8% of total farm output, it has absorbed up to one-fifth of Government support to agriculture. Even so, few upland or hill farmers make an adequate living and their situation is getting worse—their standards of living declining. The picture in the UK is made confusing since half the sheep breeding stock and half the wool clip comes from these farms, together with production of most of the store sheep and about one-seventh of the store cattle.

The basic upland problem is fragmentation of holdings, often enforced by terrain making amalgamation difficult, coupled with vagaries in the weather. There tends to be high stock mortality and low fertility compared with lowland farming. Work imposes long hours and physical hardship. Average age of those farming tends to be high, yet there are insufficient younger men to make natural retirement a solution to the problem. Social services, of course, diminish even faster than in lowland areas and this encourages young families to quit. In financial terms, greater benefit to food production would be gained by closing hill farming and using the same aid to improve lowland farming. However, in landscape terms, random and unplanned retraction of upland farming would be no solution.

Throughout Europe, measures exist to assist some production from upland areas, and the EEC is introducing measures to assist these 'disadvantaged regions'. However, the upland farm problem seems intractable. To withdraw grazing by sheep and cattle would create, within a few years, scrub and wastelands, diminishing the value of these areas for recreation. Forestry is a natural option for upland development and, indeed, it absorbs more labour than agriculture. It is a long-term solution, generating no income for more than a generation, so it is no help for small and impoverished farmers. Moreover, the seasonal nature of the work tends to encourage mobile gang labour rather than providing work locally. Politically and economically, it seems unlikely that afforestation would replace upland farming on the vast scale necessary to stabilise the social problem. The main hope expressed for the upland fringe is in recreational use. This, however, also creates problems for land use and financial planning.

In Britain the Country Landowners Association is concerned by the problem of hill farming and, in 1972, it stated that the Government should undertake an inquiry into possible solutions within five main terms of reference (4.42).

1. To make recommendations as to the part which the hills should play in the future production of food and timber.
2. To examine what can be done by those living in the hills to help themselves and what degree of Government support is necessary.
3. To recommend whether or not new and developing towns based on light industry and tourism can or should be established close to, or within, the hill areas and can provide employment for those working in the hills.
4. To establish how the hills can add to the quality of life of those urban people wishing to visit them.
5. To advise how any solutions recommended can be implemented at local level.

This is a sensible basis for examining the problem and, as the CLA indicates, the inquiry is pertinent to all European countries with uplands. However, it should not have been necessary to request a Government inquiry. The difficulty of upland farming has been known for many years. If rural resource planning had been developed as part of town and country planning, these problems would have been investigated and possible solutions tried in practice.

The Countryside Commission is conducting several experiments in upland areas, the first of which was in the Lake District (4.43). A major report on upland landscape is being prepared. Earlier, it was recognised in Wales that subsidies gave a substantial part of farmers' net income in upland areas where integration between farming and other land uses seemed essential (4.44).

The Ministry of Agriculture is preparing survey maps, taking into account vegetation, gradient, irregularity and wetness of all uplands (enclosed and wholly or partially improved land) and hills (unimproved areas covered by natural vegetation). Hills will be evaluated from H1A (generally improvable and of high present grazing value) in seven stages to H4 (generally not improvable and of low grazing value). Similarly, uplands will have five grades from U1 (generally suitable for grazing, mowing and occasional arable cropping) to U4 (mostly rough grazing and not generally improvable). This mapping has started, and a Countryside Commission report on upland management will soon be published; but many problems remain unresolved. For example, the Development Board for Rural Wales, established in 1976, has no function to relate 'development' to agriculture or forestry.

There are sound reasons why forestry should be extended within Britain, especially in the hills and uplands. The problem is to assess the extent and location of planting, within a programme over the next decades, together with the extent to which recreation can be included. Farming policies are more difficult. There seems little economic, social or even landscape reason why substantial areas should not be selected to revert to natural scrub. Secondly, it is probable that farm grazing lands should be under ranch control, managed with mobile labour backed by air inspection. As with lowland recreational areas, grazing and people should not mix in concentrated numbers. Therefore, there might have to be rotational use between these interests. Traditional farmsteads could become holiday centres with their managers acting as wardens, few of them farming other than for 'allotment' support to feed those on holiday. In all three developments (forestry, ranching and recreation) fundamental changes in rural resource planning and in Governmant aid would be necessary. Unfortunately, however desirable, such change would be resisted. Traditional farmers are not adaptable to new situations. The social problem may have no solution.

### Socio-economic Advice

The EEC recognises that there are many social problems in farming, partly due to small sizes of holdings but also due to stress of income within fringe farmland. The Council Directive 72/161 concerned 'the provision of socio-economic guidance for and the acquisition of occupational skills by persons engaged in agriculture'. An earlier Directive, reconfirmed in 1975 (75/268) (4.45), for farming in hills and less-favoured areas, is aimed:

> 'to assist the maintenance of agriculture in such areas for reasons which include the conservation of the landscape, to foster their non-agricultural developments (e.g. through tourism and craft industries which involve the farming community) and to give special aid to farmers who are in a disadvantaged economic position due to the nature of the physical environment . . .'.

The Directive 72/161 is set out under titles or sections:

1. Provision of socio-economic guidance for the agricultural population;
2. Acquisition of occupational skills by persons engaged in agriculture;
3. Vocational retraining for those wishing to leave agriculture;
4. Financial and general provisions.

Thus, modern agricultural advice has been extended beyond food production to include social issues and multi-occupational skills. This could change attitudes to land use.

## The Fertile Fringe

Few areas of agricultural land can be put to productive use without pockets, often considerable in extent, of unproductive land. Fringe land within fertile land is not recognised as a main classification in terms of mapping. Nevertheless, such lands need to be considered. They may be caused by changes in soil or terrain, especially where there are geological faults. They can be caused by land shape, where rivers and roads, or other developments, break the area that is economic to cultivate with large machines. Fertile land has many fringes where dereliction, in terms of food production, occurs. In the past, many of the geological faults became copses and it is probable that this should be perpetuated, forming wildlife reserves. The traditional use for other waste areas was as grazing land. Even today, some farm policies include stock for grazing land that cannot be used by machines, particularly river meadows liable to flooding. Economically, this becomes questionable and, as fieldwork becomes more intensive in the use of specialist machinery, there will be more land both ungrazed and untilled. Perhaps, much of it could be tree-planted and some of it permitted to become scrub, though only when weeds are no hazard to adjoining fields.

The central issue, in terms of rural planning, is the extent to which these fringe areas may be permitted to become derelict without public control and, secondly, to what extent they should remain in private ownership. If it is accepted that the most fertile land, perhaps within large areas, is exclusive to farming without rights of access, then it may be that many of the waste corners should provide public recreation. Some, close to roads, might form country parks and picnic sites. Others might be linked with footpath routes for hiking. The problem of free access to such areas may prove difficult. It seems probable that some fringe areas could be made available for recreational use on a limited 'club' basis. Thus, abuse of access close to productive areas would be governed by a club committee, the farmer having control via the committee with the right, perhaps, to be a member.

As previously stated, the farming fringe areas are likely to prove one of the most important and difficult planning problems to resolve in the next decade.

## Demonstration Farms

Rural planning should provide for special facilities to demonstrate the cause and effect of modern agriculture to an urban public. Farmers are not orientated towards creating good public relations. Indeed, public intrusion onto farm land seems incompatible with intensive management. In consequence, loss of hedgerows, permanently confined animals and chemical pollution cause public apprehension—even hostility. A new form of demonstration farm is required, but the prevailing situation in the UK does not encourage their creation.

Agricultural colleges have a tenuous link between education and practice, both in terms of farming and of estate management. Their farms are not designed specifically for student tuition, let alone for public demonstration. Agricultural shows, though popular with the public, confuse traditional rural values and entertainments with a forum for selling new equipment and techniques to farmers. Certainly, the public is not educated in intensive farming methods. The British Royal Agricultural Society has a permanent showground in Warwickshire—its scope being diversified to include public education in modern rural life as well as intensive farming demonstrations. This is a small beginning. Unfortunately, on commercial farms, the farm improvement grant procedure is based on helping food production modernisation within 'prudent landownership'. This is interpreted to be the narrow concept of farmland in terms of food production. A landowner attempting to create new farm buildings with facilities for public demonstration might find his proposals outside the scope of grant allowances. Similarly, the use of food production for education, including the provision of facilities for parking, refreshment and demonstration, perhaps with residential accommodation, might run counter to the planning authorities' concept of the white areas devoted to food production. Concepts of rural land use tend to be rigid within the existing framework of planning.

Indiscriminate provision of hostels for students of rural life and the creation of demonstration facilities in the

Figure 4.17 Flevohof, Netherlands. Aerial view of the demonstration farm. The foreground shows the extensive lakes, partly used for boating. On the right is a group of farm buildings housing a dairy farm of 100 cows and calves, plus 36 sows and progeny, and 5000 hens. On the left are glasshouses for horticulture plus, by the lake, demonstration buildings for food-processing techniques with administration areas near the plantations. Recreational and children's play areas are sited in the latter.

(*Photo by courtesy of Stichting Nationale Landbouwmanifestatie— Flevohof*)

countryside, as at present constituted, could be wrong. An overall concept of rural resources must predominate. Yet, the concept of residential demonstration farms, including educational, recreational and agricultural interests, should be an essential element of rural planning.

Flevohof, in the Netherlands, is an example of a demonstration farm of some 140 ha within the reclaimed polders of the Zuyder Zee, set apart from urban pressures, screened by extensive plantations, but close to the main highway routes (Figure 4.17). The farm itself is commercial, but with the concession that space is provided for spectators and that 'fringe' areas are used for recreation. The demonstration shows how crops and livestock are managed, through the various processes, to provide meals ready for consumption with good standards of hygiene.

The layout aims to provide an educational link between country and town life, providing at the same time recreational facilities for the urban family to enjoy an outing to the countryside. The concept took about a decade before the first ideas became operational in the spring of 1972; the cost was less than £2 m. Within the first year, income from visitors was substantially above expectation.

Flevhof demonstrates a principle which should be a prototype for every urban country. Indeed, with some variation of scope and scale, this type of agricultural centre should be available regionally. One of its successes has been the skill in layout and in detail design, executed within a 'master' plan. It is essential to appreciate that this kind of venture is a skilled planning exercise. Its benefits to the community for education and recreation can be considerable. The location of such centres needs careful regional planning, and it is doubtful whether this should depend on the whims of a free market and private enterprise, even if under the control of normal planning procedures. Location, as for a new town, reservoir or airport, should be a planned operation within a regional framework with the execution of the project under strict control within a master plan.

Such regional demonstration farms should be backed with 'outriders', probably located around conurbations, but technically linked to the regional concept. These additional farms could be private units where demonstration facilities are permitted, but under supervision or control from the regional centre. Demonstration farms could be an important element of planning the urban fringe areas and, with less commercial food production value, in uplands.

The Countryside Commission has made a particular study, backed by development projects, of access into farmland. This includes a policy for demonstration farms, though not on the scale of Flevohof. A need exists to provide interpretation of farm practice to the general public. Historical and modern techniques are to be set up and contrasted at Shipley, Derbyshire. Experiments in modern farm landscape within commercial practice, plus a balance for wildlife and landform, are being set up in 10 lowland farms of different location and type. These will open to show other farmers what can be achieved. In addition, for the public there are to be many farm trails and farm open days. So great is the interest in the subject that the Commission helps and supports the Countryside Research Advisory Group and a Countryside Recreation Management Association. These relate also to the new socio-economic Ministerial policy. Many commercial farmers exploit the situation and make provision for visitors to make regular, occasional, or residential visits to see how their farms work. This will have a profound effect on rural land use.

## Field Management and Landscape Values

Visual changes within the agricultural landscape have become of public concern. Traditional countryside, at least in European countries, is largely man-made since the 18th century enclosures. Some areas do have much older, basic landscapes, and to the historian and ecologist it is important to differentiate between the enclosures and medieval or even Roman field patterns. Field patterns evolved as a result of local topography and field management. The latter depended partly on shelter and water being provided for small herds of grazing stock and partly on the teamwork of horse-ploughing, fields often being sized in relation to a day's work. Some field patterns reflect particular management problems, such as in upland areas where sheep grazed the moorlands (outbye), but had intensive pasture (inbye) near the farmstead, and between which were extensive enclosed pastures (fridd).

Lambs produced from these marginal farms have been the mainstay for lowland fat lamb enterprises for centuries and this relationship in production is a feature of landscape evolution. Such factors created a legacy of some visual attraction in a patchwork of small fields, trees, copses and undulations, where a ten-acre enclosure became a noteworthy exception. In contrast, the downland sheepwalks, the river flood meadows and the uncleared woodlands gave a relief in scale. All this has changed—and changed within three decades.

The traditional pattern tended to be repeated in other lands settled by Europeans. However, the climate and scale of some countries, particularly in the open lands of the mid-west in the US, in Australia and in similar terrain elsewhere created a dissimilar pattern of agriculture. In these larger-scale landscapes, the tension between urban planning interests and the farming community is less acute, though the memory of the dust-bowls still lingers. The image of the prairie landscape is unpopular in urban Europe and the risk that its landscape may become as open and as dull, with erosion risks also increased, has lead to thoughts of urban control over farming activities.

As discussed earlier, the last decade has been significant in that business management techniques used in urban industries have been applied to fieldwork in terms of man/machine efficiency, backed by chemical aids to crop control. Thus, the traditional structure of field patterns was found to be an anachronism and in many parts it became essential to restructure the landscape, often with the backing of Government grants to promote a more efficient agriculture. Landscape values in terms of topography and of ecology, let alone any historical connections, were not considered in such change. Naturally, farmers were concerned by the dangers of soil erosion, but these tend not to be significant except for light soils and even there the risks were not fully understood or proven.

Figure 4.18    Tractor-drawn cultivator with a span of 5.5 m can prepare a seed bed at a rate of 6 ha per hour—provided the fields are large enough.

(*Photo by courtesy of Ransomes Sims and Jefferies Ltd.*)

It has become fashionable to question field changes and, certainly, unco-ordinated change has risks to the environment. In landscape planning it is important to understand the needs of modern field management and, more particularly, to forecast future techniques.

There seems a consensus of engineering and estate opinion that modern fieldwork should be based on units of some 20 ha (within normal limits of 15 to 25 ha). This suits modern machine sizes and the cropping programmes, given soil and fertility uniformity over such an area. However, such field sizes would create a landscape different in scale from that of today but, in itself, not disastrous in landscape value provided the overall landscape is replanned (see page 109). There could be, of course, consequential historic losses even if the ecology of the locale is balanced by new planting. In the ideal layout, each field would be rectangular in an approximate proportion of 1:4, with headlands at the narrow end with minimum falls, probably draining to deep-laid pipes along the flank.

The basic field would not vary for most requirements. Even in the few cases where cattle might graze, the field would be divided by temporary electric fencing. For corn, most root vegetables, legumes and for harvested grass, the long rectangle up to 25 ha in area would suit both modern tractors, cultivators and harvesters. Access would be from one headland where turning space would be provided. Divisions between fields along the flanks would need to be low, either wire fencing, mechanically cut hedges (without trees) or banks to a lower level, except in the cases where the flanks lay against tree shelter belts or public highways. In the former case, the belt would be planned on a long-term coppicing programme and its relation to air turbulence would need to be considered (see page 119). In the latter case, the effect of lead pollution from traffic fumes has to be considered, penetration being serious for up to 100 m.

In the zones where intensive farming is to be encouraged, field patterns must be permitted to change into modern management layouts provided provision is made for district topography, ecological balance and protection of certain historic landscape features. The rigid mathematics of such concepts could be modified by local topographical 'difficulties' which could be exploited. However, the district planning should not be left only to the pressures of individual farm planning but must come within the guidance or control of a regional rural landscape planner. The extensive farming areas pose different problems, both in scale and in technique, which are discussed elsewhere.

Consideration of future field machinery techniques verges towards the realms of science-fiction. The danger is to assume that such fiction will not become reality. It seems probable that within 10 years, at most 20, remote con-

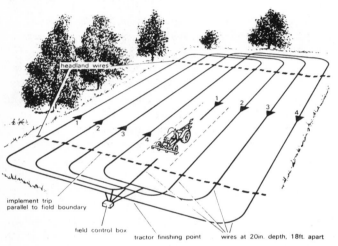

Figure 4.19 Two examples of automatically controlled tractors. *Above*: the tractor is radar controlled. *Below*: control cables are buried underground.

(*Photo and diagram by courtesy of the National Institute of Agricultural Engineering*)

trolled fieldwork will be the norm (Figure 4.19). There is no technical reason why this should not be so and in human terms, since fieldwork can be thought tedious or unpleasant, it could be desirable. The main restriction is the present level of agricultural wage but, as the latter increases to industrial standards, pressure for automation will increase in proportion. The real uncertainty is to forecast which technique is likely to prove the most efficient and viable. At present, this cannot be hazarded; but, in any event, there are two implications.

First, automated fieldwork will make streamlined field patterns more necessary, probably with a premium for best-quality land in units of 100 ha rather than of 15 to 25 ha. Secondly, control gear may make a visual impact, in addition to changes in field size, particularly in the case of gantry techniques. If it is socially desirable, for several reasons, to permit, even promote, the most efficient mechanised agriculture, then it is pertinent to keep fertile land of adequate size and shape in zones free from urban change. At present, this is not so, since land, however fertile, may be fragmented by services and roads, let alone by actual building—the criteria not having been established to give realistic protection in terms of fertility and viability. Moreover, if new field patterns of this type are to evolve, with dramatic change for landscape values, then procedure to direct such change within clear policies for rural resources must be given priority.

### Soil Structure, Drainage and Farming Technique

The debate concerning modern farm techniques and the long-term fertility of agricultural land will be keen for many years. Indeed, such debate if based on a rational assessment is vital if mistakes are to be checked before irrevocable harm occurs. There must be a continuous watching brief, based on inspection and research. In Britain the Agricultural Advisory Council's report for England and Wales (4.46) is a turning point for such debate. For the first time a national assessment has been made since the effect of the second agricultural revolution, with its heavier field machinery, caused concern. It is clear from the report that more needs to be known concerning the relation between machine design and fieldwork planning. The report indicates that 'a whole range of soils is suffering from the effects of the passage of heavy machinery over them in unsuitable conditions. This is often due to the adoption of tight cropping sequences on difficult land in areas of medium or high rainfall, especially in the absence of leys'. But the report found that, though compaction, deformation and smearing of soils by machines can be damaging, there was no instance found where recovery had not taken place, given time, suitable weather and proper treatment. Indeed, larger machinery can reduce the total area of wheel impact and the frequency of passes. It seems probable that, provided inspection, research and development are co-ordinated, there is no reason why intensive mechanisation should not continue.

Soil structure also depends on organic content—the

Figure 4.20    The effect of proper drainage on a Yorkshire farm of 36 ha. The photograph above shows the land before drainage and the photograph below the land two years after drainage.

(*Photo by courtesy of A. N. Ede*)

traditional humus. However, the report acknowledges that this is difficult to evaluate and observational evidence is conflicting. This is another matter where land conditions should be monitored and research co-ordinated. In addition, techniques for applying organic manures from livestock, whether as solids, semi-solids or liquids, also need study. The report suggests that 'some soils are now suffering from dangerously low levels of organic matter' but equally that 'there is no evidence to show that the disappearance of livestock from certain areas, and the replacement of ley-farming and farmyard manure by chemical fertilisers, has led to any inherent loss of fertility. Nor is there any evidence that organic matter is intrinsically a better source of nutrients... but soil structure is another matter. On unstable soils, the influence of organic matter is all-important.' The acidity of the soil can be a matter for concern, and in some areas liming should be increased since the rate of loss of lime from soils by drainage and crop removal increases. Equally important, the report found that all-arable rotations could be satisfactory on stable soils, such as in some parts of eastern England, but there could be concern for their effect on weaker soils such as in parts of the Midlands. Continuous corn growing is not common, but corn cropping with break crops is increasing.

The evidence suggests that modern field techniques, with some limitations and with careful inspection, need not give long-term harm. There is great importance, however, in the provision of correct and adequate land drainage. The Romans practised land drainage, both with tiles and with ditches. Medieval ridge-and-furrow and boundary ditch drainage is a feature of the Midlands. Modern drainage became important with the enclosures. Annual drainage of England and Wales is around 70 000 ha at an average cost of £50 per ha. It is thought that some 3 million hectares

Figure 4.21    Lettuce production in the Florida Everglades. The swamps were drained and cleared in the 1960s to produce some of the largest fertile fields for vegetable production. However there have been side-effects—the swamp habitat, important to many species, has been destroyed, and there have been climatic changes.

(*Photo by courtesy of* Farmers Weekly)

is in urgent need of drainage and at present drainage rates, as the report states, 'it could well take another 40 years—to 2010 and beyond—before the improvements that are considered necessary now are completed; and in the meantime some existing systems, even some post-1945 ones, will break down and need replacing'.

Proper drainage could provide an untapped land resource in Britain. In terms of planning rural and food resources it is vital and the contribution to landscape character is significant. The problem of estimating farmland requirements in terms of food production and in terms of viable blocks of farmland is made difficult due to lack of knowledge of potential fertility which could be gained by adequate drainage. The question is posed that if the investment rate was increased tenfold, to drain three-quarters of a million hectares in the next decade, by how much would food production increase—would it double?

It is the intensification of farmland use, by drainage and by restructuring field patterns, that makes it possible to forecast that there need not be a shortage in food production in spite of considerable losses of farmland to urban need. However, it is essential, by establishing a land fertility/viability classification, to reserve the most valuable farmland for food production. The techniques for this assessment are still un-coordinated and unproven, and the responsibility of no central authority.

### Field Hedges

Field hedges and trees are part of the legacy of the enclosures, though a few date from earlier times. In terms of agriculture, the high maintenance cost and the need for larger fields, with less need for livestock shelter, has made their presence an anachronism. Most of the field study concerning hedges has been made from the Nature Conservancy Council's Experimental Station at Monks Wood, Huntingdon, by Dr. M. Hooper. It is thought that some 650,000 km of hedgerows remain in England and Wales, but these have been grubbed out at a rate of 8000 km each year, especially in the lowlands, until very recently when field amalgamation has declined. This has caused national concern. Hedge removal is essential for modern intensive farming. The real problem is that removal is based on individual farm need, usually without consultation beyond an examination of machine and crop programming, and that other factors do not get considered. More particularly, there is no thought for the effect within a district or region if a number of individual farmers remove hedges without relation to each other. Hedgerows, like buildings, should be inspected as a national asset, then classified for their value, certain groups being scheduled for protection unless particular reasons given by a farmer or developer—whether private or Government department—make their removal in the national interest. A number of factors should be considered in the assessment.

The ecological balance of the countryside is important and is gaining public recognition, though evaluation criteria are still largely unproven. Hooper has shown the significance of hedges for wildlife habitats in lowland areas. Many species use them for breeding, though not always commonly, including amongst those species found in lowland areas all 6 of the reptiles, 21 out of 28 mammals, 65 of the 91 birds, and 23 of the 54 butterflies. Moreover, hedgerows are corridors of wildlife movement, especially linking woodlands. Equally, they have immense value for the flora of a district. Ideally, hedgerows should be 'A' shaped, with a wide and sheltered base. The ecological value of a hedge may be reduced by drift of chemicals from field spraying. It is not easy to assess which hedges are vital ecologically, but if too many are lost within any district great harm can be done. It is also important to assess the value of roadside verges since these, too, are both havens and corridors for certain species. Spraying and spring cutting can cause great damage, yet when maintained at some cost and care the verges may counteract much of the harm caused by hedgerow losses between fields (see page 131). Yet, a decision to spray a verge, which is undertaken by highway authorities, is not related to field planning which is the concern of a farmer, possibly with advice from the Ministry of Agriculture. Neither is the province of country planning within the planning departments and neither is likely to be the concern of landscape architects.

The planting or removal of hedges is seldom considered in visual terms. The landscape architecture, if that is the correct term, of the countryside is almost completely neglected. Yet, some hedgerows are vital in their contribution to the landscape. Some hide eyesores, others act as link elements between other features, whilst some soften or delineate the land contours or lines of communication. Part of the classification of hedge values should be a visual assessment by those trained to understand the components and topography making a landscape.

Hedges, in some cases, have great historical value. Hooper has shown that there is a relation between the age of a hedge and the number of species forming it. Many hedges are of great age, marking the historic boundaries of administration, dividing the hundreds and the parishes of Medieval Britain. Other boundary hedges mark the division of land ownership or delineate the old drove-roads and country tracks. Many hedges have made significant contributions to the development of famous battles, sometimes proving to be turning points in history. Yet, historical value is seldom held to be important when fields are amalgamated and hedges destroyed.

One landowner has appointed for his estate at Rougham, Suffolk, a conservancy officer and a historian to evaluate all his hedges. The preliminary report (4.47) has classified nearly 30 km of boundaries within some 550 ha, which is the main area of the estate. From this evaluation, it will be possible to restructure the field layout in future years with the least harm to historical and biological interests. It seems incredible that this care is not taken throughout the farmland of Britain. There is great need for a comprehensive survey to be made and for responsibility to be co-ordinated.

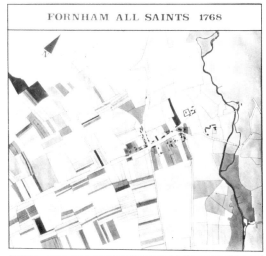

Figure 4.22   Fornham All Saints, Suffolk. Field patterns 1768, 1804, 1966. The map of 1768 shows the village near the river crossing with the open-strip fields typical of the period divided into many lots, several owned by one man. By 1804 land ownership had changed, and the strips had been regrouped into block holdings. By 1966 further change had brought ownership into 'structural' blocks around the highways. Tones on the maps indicate ownership.

*(Photos by courtesy of J. M. Gorst)*

Principles for approximate dating were established by Hooper, who showed that an average of one species per 100 years of history became established within about 30 m of hedge (4.48). Though many studies have been made, these have not been collated. Many hedges are being lost due to ignorance. The matter is too important to be left to individual farmers, many of whom may be ignorant, indifferent or even hostile concerning the importance of conservation for ecological, visual or historical reasons. There is some move towards accepting public contribution to the cost of hedge maintenance where hedges have a community value. Compensation is beginning to be paid in a few cases. It is not clear yet whether this will become a national trend nor what the limits of compensation should be.

Hedgerow trees, equally, are a vital component in most farm landscapes. Many have gone, and most are past their prime in many areas. For natural regeneration, the Forestry Commission suggests that for every mature tree there should be six semi-mature and 12 saplings for many species. However, surveys of lowland farms have shown that this can be down to a 1:1:1 ratio in some areas, which represents a landscape in serious decline (4.49).

**Shelter Belts and Soil Erosion**
Ecological changes caused by new farming techniques can be harmful and, since extremes can be disastrous as in the formation of dust bowls, sudden and dramatic change from a *status quo* should be treated with caution. The loss of trees and of hedges can be a matter of concern, as discussed above and in Chapter 5, and this is one of the central issues in the formation of new landscapes to suit mechanised farming. Soil erosion can be caused by water or by wind. Trees are valuable conservers of water and their loss can lead to waterlogging of land, eventually to flooding. This may cause soil to clog or, in light soils, the humus to be eroded into streams. Wind erosion has become a particular fear, especially on peats and sands, as hedges disappear.

The effect of wind plus soil velocity can move topsoil with the same chain reaction as an avalanche, with the finer material uplifted as dust and coarser matter moving until it lodges in ditches or against other barriers. Maximum velocity in soil movement can be reached within 70 m on light soils, or 350 m on medium land, but needing more than 1000 m in heavy lands. US research has shown that soil particles do not blow until wind velocity is 21 km/h about 3 cm above the ground, and this is known as the threshold velocity (4.50). Moreover, the lighter particles which get blown can hold up to 20 times as much humus and phosphate as those which remain. The wind capacity to carry soil is proportional to the cube of the wind velocity and, therefore, stronger winds carry proportionally more soil. Windblown soil can block drains and ditches, and drift to bury verge plants and roads like snow.

The loss or drifting of topsoil obviously is serious but,

Figure 4.23  Farmstead shelterbelt in the Yorkshire Wolds. A farm landscape planned 150 years ago and now in its maturity. The open sheepwalks were reclaimed and divided into large open fields generally running with the contours. The farmstead was protected by a 'U' deciduous plantation, open to the south and linked with a shelterbelt along the headland. The belts are some 30 m deep. A natural tree belt has been left along the valley watercourse.

*(Photo by courtesy of E. W. Hart)*

Figure 4.24  Tamora, Nebraska. An open-land shelterbelt. Open farmland and a highway with a ten-row shelterbelt planted in the 1940s and photographed 18 years later. Additional shelterbelts protect buildings adjacent to the road.

*(Photo by courtesy of* Farmers Weekly*)*

equally, the effect of sand-blasting of flora and crops is dangerous. The situation can be improved in a number of ways. In some cases, deep ploughing can mix clay into the lighter topsoil to form a heavier humus. Marling has been a traditional technique in light soil conditions. Similarly, emulsion waste can be spread and mixed to form a heavier topsoil. This is practised in Britain, but more dramatic results are being gained in re-afforestation of deserts by fixing the dunes with oil by-product wastes. In some situations, minimal cultivations may prove to be the best solution but experience of the technique is still limited. Obviously, if it is possible to plant, fertilize and eventually harvest crops without ploughing, through retarded grass ground cover, then wind erosion is of limited risk.

Shelter belts, in visual terms, are the most important landscape contribution that also may restrict, though seldom prevent, the risk of wind erosion. Windbreaks, such as hedges and hurdle fences, probably do no more than create harmful air currents and eddies which damage crops. Tall hedges may provide shelter from sun and wind close to their lee for grazing stock, but this is becoming less important with permanent stock housing. But, in an open and stockless landscape, the use of shelter belts can be desirable to reduce erosion and to improve the appearance of landscape (see also page 131).

Landscapes planned with shelter belts of trees have a long history. Figure 4.23, showing the Yorkshire Wolds, is typical and other examples can be found in Normandy and other European fertile plains, cultivated for several centuries. As discussed below, this kind of tree belt is too uniform and dense, however grand in visual terms, but in principle this shows the openness of the future landscape with buildings enclosed by trees, rectangular belts normally

placed at right angles to the prevailing wind, and free-shape belts along the water-courses where recreation also may be provided. The modern shelter belt in Nebraska (Figure 4.24) is typical of wide-open terrain in many lands without rapid changes in topography and a long tradition of agriculture. Visually, such a landscape is a disaster, and a

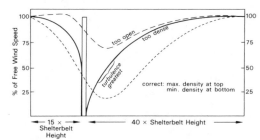

SECTION WIND REDUCTION AND SHELTER BELT INTENSITY

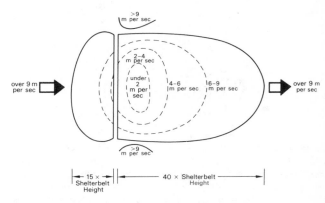

PLAN: REDUCTION IN WIND FROM A GOOD SHELTER BELT

Figure 4.25    Reduction in wind effects by a shelterbelt.

*(Based on E. Long, 'Shelter belts' Farmers Weekly, 4.10.68)*

single shelter belt insufficient to protect the production areas. In restructuring old farmlands, the complete prairie situation must be avoided, even when soils are heavy. An ecological and visual balance must be encouraged, even deliberately planned.

The design of shelter belts depends on many factors aimed at slowing down wind flow and redirecting it over croplands. Thus, the belt should be a filter and not an impermeable barrier. The effect of wind reduction and shelter belt planting is shown in Figure 4.25. Wind angle, exposure, soil type and fertility have also to be taken into account, and species will depend on locality. To permit about 50% wind permeability, a mixture of conifer and deciduous trees is to be preferred. It is probable that the land should be designed so that belts provide some commercial timber and, therefore, the planting of belts will be on a rotational basis. Visually, the landscape will change every decade.

### Planting Field Corners

Field cultivation leaves headland problems where machinery has to turn. Even with well-planned machinery circulation, there can be wastage some 4 to 8 m wide. This is why rectangular fields are preferred. Likewise, at field corners, there is greater wastage, often dereliction. A vehicle with a 30 m turning circle, which is not uncommon, can leave an area of some 80 m$^2$ in each corner. These waste corners can be valuable assets for wildlife. Figure 4.26 shows the kind of planting favoured by Ministry, Agriculture and Forestry advisors. Such a corner could take some 25 trees and bushes. The aim is to provide mixed cover so the plantation should be formed as a pyramid. Species will depend on locality. In most situations there will be two or more corners coming together. If farmland has to be restructured, with considerable loss of hedges and hedgerow trees, this can be mitigated by using the waste areas, such as field corners to provide wildlife habitats and amenity interest. Travelling around the countryside, it is clear that this kind of planting is rare. Yet, grubbing out hedges is not controlled. Somehow, by education or by control, field shapes must be restructured, but new wildlife habitats also created.

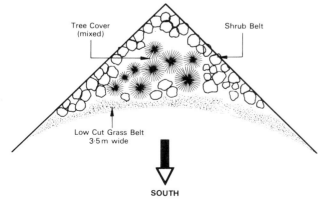

Figure 4.26    Diagram of planting in a field corner.

## Preserving the Historic Landscape

Agricultural landscapes form part of the social and historic fabric of any country. In Britain, this is largely the pattern created by the enclosures, entrenched in which are remnants of earlier land uses. Prehistoric barrows and Iron Age ditches are obvious examples. Equally, the remnants of royal or monastic forests, the few remaining village strip fields, such as Laxton in Nottinghamshire, and the more numerous ridge-and-furrow patterns from early plough systems, all are an important part of historic heritage.

Planning legislation has made considerable impact within historic towns and villages. The designation of conservation areas, the scheduling of buildings and the preparation of detailed development plans, backed by active local amenity societies, have done much to save part of the architectural and historic heritage—though few would be complacent in view of the many losses and the constant threat of despoliation. However, within agricultural countryside the concept of conservation, in planning terms, is almost alien. Since European Conservation Year 1970, there has been a growing awareness for the need of ecological conservation and a tentative move towards better protection of some features. However, notwithstanding national parks and areas of outstanding natural beauty, the problem of comprehensive conservation remains neglected. This section can highlight only a few factors within a subject of profound importance to the theme of the book. The problem of the agricultural landscape is, in principle, four-fold—it concerns dwellings, farm buildings, agricultural practice and historic events—each of which still needs fundamental research to evaluate its contribution to the landscape, especially in terms of conservation (4.51).

The problem was recognised in 1962 by UNESCO, which recommended 'the preservation and, where possible, the restoration of the aspect of natural, rural and urban landscapes and sites, whether natural or man-made, which have a cultural or aesthetic interest, or form typical natural surroundings'. The International Council on Monuments and Sites (ICOMOS) defined historic landscapes in 1964 as follows:

> 'The concept of an historic monument embraces not only the single architectural work but also the urban or rural setting in which is found the evidence of a particular civilisation, a significant development or an historic event.'

St Bodfan Gruffydd, based on UNESCO and ICOMOS evaluations, has defined rural landscapes as *protected* or *unprotected* (4.52):

*Protected*:
Natural landscapes:    limited wilderness areas
                                    features of antiquity

Archeological
landscapes:
 primitive topographical items
 hill fortifications and
  earthworks
 Roman and Saxon settlements
 Medieval farms and forests
 historic agricultural features

Historical
landscapes:
 town/country relationships
 battlefields
 historic sites or events
 industrial archaeology

*Unprotected*:
 park and garden landscapes,
  rural landscapes planned for
  visual effect.

Within these definitions there is need for a policy to protect, to finance and to restore such landscapes, many of which lie within agricultural areas.

The speed of agrico-technical change is so great that no building erected before 1960 has much productive value on a progressive and well-managed farm or estate. This means the legacy is redundant.

The Essex farm building group (Figure 4.27) makes the point: such buildings are an embarrassment, fit only for demolition. A small part of the legacy has a partial value for storage, and the best barns and courtyards can be adapted as a machinery and workshop complex for larger estates. A few of the older stock buildings can be converted into isolation quarters, particularly for calves, and some courts may be useful for special stock groups such as dry cows in a dairy unit or as gilt yards in a sow unit. However, the number of special cases is limited and in most such cases the old buildings are used because they exist rather than from any

Figure 4.28  Bradfiled Woods, Suffolk. The remaining 65 ha of monastic woods, once owned by the Abbey of Bury St Edmunds, is the largest unspoilt boulder-clay wood in Suffolk which suffered partial clearance for agriculture (as seen in the foreground) before being saved by public appeal to become a nature reserve under the support of the Society for the Promotion of Nature Reserves.

*(Photo by courtesy of the Royal Air Force)*

analysis of efficient management. Timber, cob, clay lump, and thatched buildings quickly fall into decay and are easy to demolish. Such redundancy can be seen throughout southern England. Brick, and more particularly stone, buildings are more durable, especially as long as the roofs are sound. It is not difficult or particularly expensive to replace defective slates or tiles with corrugated sheeting (as in the Essex group), which gives such structures a longer life. But even this cost is more than the value of many of these buildings.

Though most farm improvement schemes pass through the administration of the Ministry of Agriculture and a small number, probably less than 10%, through the Department of Environment, in the form of planning applications (though the mechanism of these applications has only a tenuous link with the DoE), there is no authority keeping a watching brief on the dwindling stock of traditional farm buildings. Indeed, demolition can be unrecorded except for the few scheduled buildings. A personal estimate is that fewer than 20% of the existing stock of pre-1940 farm buildings will remain in a recognisable state at the end of this century. It seems most unlikely that the loss will be recorded.

The history of agricultural development is witnessed both in farm building design and also in the fields, meadows and woodlands. If the threat to the former is urgent, that to the latter equally is critical.

The fame of the strip fields at Laxton, Nottinghamshire, let alone statutory protection, may succeed in keeping this record of early farm technique for posterity. Some other remnants of open field layouts that remain in other parts of the country may not be as fortunate. The ridge-and-furrows of the Midlands are at risk, though it seems unlikely that all

Figure 4.27  Redundant farm in Essex. This view is typical of redundant farm building groups. The original thatched or tiled weather-boarded barn, with outlying shelters and yarding, may have been attractive and an important contribution to the landscape.

*(Photo by courtesy of* Farmers Weekly)

record could be obliterated. But when a national record of farming systems is considered, it is obvious that there is neither knowledge of what ought to be kept nor any procedure for identifying the best locations of each system still surviving, let alone any system of control for preservation, similar to that for historic buildings.

Besides agricultural needs, in buildings and in field systems, farmland also includes evidence of a country's history. Much of prehistory, particularly barrows and other simple earthworks, has been erased by modern farming and only a small percentage of those that survived to this century will remain intact at its end. Destruction became acute not only because of increased power in field machinery but also in the extension of cultivation into old pastures, particularly into virgin chalk downlands where prehistory and traditional flora had been undisturbed. However, recent development of deep ploughing means that remains below the land surface now are threatened.

Ancient landmarks within farmland are now semi-protected under the Field Monuments Act of 1972 (4.53). This Act has created a new situation by providing compensation to the landowner or farmer for production losses due to keeping the scheduled remains. This may save from destruction many landscape features, but hardly will protect many of the known, let alone the unknown, buried remains. Moreover, the technique for recording history in terms of existing topographical and landscape features, such as battle-grounds, hardly comes within the scope of the Act.

# Agriculture: A Planning Framework

No regional or local land use plan for the countryside can have meaning until there are changes at national level in basic planning concepts.

The first essential is that the present divorce of agriculture from country planning must be overcome. As long as farmers and planners are not from the same basic training, with the same outlook, there must be friction and misunderstanding. It is essential there should be a new 'agrico-planner' whose training should spring both from the tradition of farm estate management and from land use planning colleges. It should be the aim of national Governments, preferably within an international code of parameters, to establish training for this new kind of agrico-planner. This would take a generation to reach maturity, by which time much harm will have occurred to rural landscapes, thus new forms of curricula should be prepared as a priority. For the short term, other national action is required.

Coupled to education, there is the need to perceive that 'farming' must be understood in terms of 'food technology and nutrition'. As a corollary, farmland must be seen as a 'factory floor' that can be planned for specific levels of production, whereas other rural land is an 'amenity floor' that can be used for ecological and recreational needs. This understanding will evolve within national consciousness only when Governments fuse food technology (farming) with rural land use (country planning) within one Ministerial framework. Only after such fusion will rural land be understood to be a national resource similar to other resources, such as energy or materials, from which priorities for its development and its use may be determined.

Rural land is a resource for many activities other than farming. It is, of course, a resource for wildlife, and ecological balance is vital, not only in terms of soil stability, but also as a spiritual base for man's inspiration. Ecological balance does not mean that culling of some life from some areas of land is wrong. Agriculture implies that culling is essential to achieve any crop. There is awareness today that areas that sustain habitats for species must be permitted. The right balance of land use will need generations of study to achieve. There will be mistakes, but these must be short-term. Therefore, all agriculture—and forestry and fishing—must be monitored and there must be capacity to correct mistakes. Reclamation of the Sahara Desert is to correct a mistake nearly 2000 years old. Spiritual balance usually implies both diversity of landscape, with access to it, and an awareness of historical evolution. Thus, though change is essential for evolution to continue, it is essential also that some retention of old settlement patterns is made.

Resources from land are material for man's physical needs. These include both food and water, as well as fuel and power, the latter coming sometimes from water. If extracted, the latter are finite, but some may be regenerative if they are derived from plant forms. Land, too, is a resource for settlement and for communication. It is probable that food production will always be the major land use, except where 'wildscape', by the nature of the terrain, dominates. However, the equation of how much land is needed to feed any population is not static. It is a matter of technical progress. Equally it can be one of social objective. Both are subject to political influence and, in this, are many tensions. The objective of any planning framework should be to relieve such tensions. In reality, this is an issue where much needs to be learnt.

Priorities, at national level, must be established for rural land in terms of food production and of recreation. This must be based on a national food plan, based in turn on assessments of population, nutrition and the degree of self-sufficiency in food production required—all of which are not fixed estimates but need to be under regular revision. These estimates can be converted into land use production requirements, related to potential fertility (allowing for drainage, modern management and farm structure, etc.), to viability (allowing for mechanised production unit size), as well as to location (allowing for materials handling and processing). This assessment would need all the resources of modern planning techniques. But from this analysis, within estimates of food requirements (allowing for political instabilities), a national strategy for reservation of prime farmland could be made equal in 'power politics' to other resource planning, such as fuel or communications. This reservation of prime land could be linked to ecological and to recreational strategies, but the latter would be allocated mainly to non-prime farmland.

Any strategy for agricultural land, backed by Ministerial and educational frameworks, must be based on legislation, on research and on monitoring policies. Legislation would set out the processes for making structure plans at various levels and for permitting changes in land use. Research would make surveys of logistics in food production and in the methods of production, including such matters as genetics of livestock. Monitoring processes are vital for recording such items as changes in land use, as well as in health hazards and ecological side-effects caused by such changes. From national integration of land use and food production into one framework, such matters as population growth, industrial development and transportation patterns could be examined in relation to the policy for rural land requirements.

### Regional Planning
With a national strategy for rural land established, it would be practical to create regional plans in which agriculture could be integrated with other planning requirements. For the first time, regional plans would have a real meaning for the 'white areas' of the countryside. It is not sufficient, in planning terms, to assume all land between settlements is left white on the maps—like unexplored territory—for food production. The open spaces are a resource which can be used according to the land potential within a scale of priorities. Within a national strategy farmland would no longer receive protection, as at present, largely out of sentiment, just because of its historical occupation of certain areas; nor would it be selected for compulsory acquisition for other requirements such as roads or towns, as at present, largely on the basis that there seems to be plenty of other land available elsewhere for farming. For the first time, because of national research and monitoring, there would be a proper basis for evaluating rural land. The regional planning office would be responsible for the research and monitoring studies demanded by the national strategy requirements. This office would include experts in all rural land use problems, including those of agriculture. In turn, the regional office would give instruction for local plans.

### Local Planning
Local plans for the countryside should be prepared in the same manner as is common for city and town. Rural land would be examined and evaluated as a basis for zoning between food production, amenity, communications, forestry, mineral extraction, etc., in the same way as urban areas are zoned for residential, industrial, commercial, and recreational requirements. Certain prime farmland could be protected from other exploitation as might the commercial heart of a city be zoned to prevent the intrusion of industry. Other lands could be zoned as 'conservation areas' in which related features, such as historic farm buildings, topography, historical farm techniques, could be protected from sudden and irrational change.

### Co-operation in Rural Planning
The present structure in rural planning, at all levels, does not promote confidence. Techniques for planning agricultural land are ill-defined. However, change in farming practice is so rapid that, unless new forms of planning are evolved quickly, it may prove too late to attain a sound balance between change and its side-effects. Until agrico-planners are trained and until a national food plan is prepared, it is essential that within the existing framework of planning co-operation should be promoted between interested parties. Every planning office should employ an agriculturist, probably with an estate management training. Similarly, every Ministry of Agriculture office should employ a planner or landscape architect. This should be mandatory at both national and regional level and, as soon as practical, at local level. In the meantime, at local level there should be a joint advisory panel of all those with a stake in the development of the countryside. In some parts, panels of this kind are evolving but their link with the preparation of landscape plans tends to be tenuous.

Patterns of rural land use and planning vary in many parts of the world. There can be no single formula. Historical and social evolution in land tenure, amongst other factors, makes this so. However, what is constant is two-fold. First, strategy for priorities in land use needs to be set within (inter)national, regional and local assessments, with or without state control. The latter is a social matter of Government. Secondly, the discipline of work within rural areas needs to be broad, especially if planning is to be effective. Food is an essential for man, but much else has to be achieved from rural land. In developing countries, especially where agriculture is the objective within arid, forest or swamp land, it is vital to understand that ruthless food production alone will not be the best long-term objective. Within industrial nations, with large populations, the social needs for land must also find relief, and a traditional farm-based land ownership may not be broad enough in its social awareness. Co-operation between many disciplines is vital and this may well need direction, through land use planning, from national organisations and Governments.

## References

4.1 INTERNATIONAL COMMISSION FOR APPLIED ECOLOGY, *Report*, UNESCO, Paris, 1976.
4.2 ROY, R., *Wastage in the UK Food System*, Earth Resources Research, London, 1976.

4.3 SIMMONS, I. G., *Ecology of Natural Resources*, Edward Arnold, London, 1974.

4.4 HESLOP-HARRISON, J., 'Crops, commodities and energy capture', *Biologist*, **22**, 1, 1975.

4.5 BLAXTER, K. L., 'The energetics of British agriculture', *Biologist*, **22**, 1, 1975.

4.6 DUCKHAM, A. N. and MASEFIELD, G. B., *Farming Systems of the World*, Chatto and Windus, London, 1970.

4.7 MELLANBY, K., *Can Britain Feed Itself?*, Merlin Press, London, 1975.

4.8 *Greenplant Report*, Vegetarian Society, London, 1976.

4.9 WILSON, P. N., 'Introduction to energy use and British Agriculture', in *Energy Use and British Agriculture*, Bather, D. M. and Day, H. I. (eds.), Reading University Agriculture Club, Reading, 1976.

4.10 *Report of Energy Working Party*, Joint Consultative Organisation, Research and Development in Agriculture and Food, Report No. 1, London, 1974.

4.11 *Report of Energy Working Party, op. cit.*

4.12 BLEASDALE, J., Annual Address to the British Association for the Advancement of Science, Cambridge, 1977.

4.13 *Report of Energy Working Party, op. cit.*

4.14 WELLER, J. B. and WILLETTS, S. L., *Farm Wastes Management*, Crosby Lockwood Staples, London, 1977.

4.15 *Report of the Energy Working Party, op. cit.*

4.16 BLAXTER, K. L., *op. cit.*

4.17 MINISTRY OF AGRICULTURE FISHERIES AND FOOD, *Food from Our Own Resources*, HMSO, London, 1975.

4.18 COUNTRYSIDE COMMISSION, *Farm Recreation and Tourism in England and Wales*, Countryside Commission, Cheltenham, 1974.

4.19 MINISTRY OF AGRICULTURE FISHERIES AND FOOD (1975), *op. cit.*

4.20 DAVIDSON, J. and WIBBERLEY, G., *Planning and the Rural Environment*, Pergamon, Oxford, 1977.

4.21 WELLER, J. B. and WILLETTS, S. L., *op. cit.*

4.22 GIBBS, R. and HARRISON, A., *Land Ownership by Public and Semi-public Bodies in Great Britain*, Department of Agriculture Economics, University of Reading, Reading, 1974.

4.23 THOMPSON, R. F. and JARVIS, C. A., *An Agricultural Centre*, Architectural Thesis, University of Leeds, Leeds, 1970.

4.24 MINISTRY OF HOUSING AND LOCAL GOVERNMENT, *Strategic Plan for the South-East*, HMSO, London, 1967.

4.25 ESSEX COUNTY COUNCIL, *Structure Plan for North and Central Essex*, County Planning Offices, Chelmsford, 1975.

4.26 LEICESTERSHIRE COUNTY COUNCIL, *Leicester and Leicestershire Structure Plan*, County Planning Offices, Leicester, 1974.

4.27 BEDFORDSHIRE COUNTY COUNCIL, *County Structure Plan for Bedfordshire*, County Planning Offices, Bedford, 1976.

4.28 Leader, *Farmers Weekly*, 24 March 1978.

4.29 'Agriculture and urbanization', *Journal of American Institute of Planners*, November 1975.

4.30 US DEPARTMENT OF AGRICULTURE, *Perspectives on Prime Land*, US Government Printing Office, Washington DC, 1975.

4.31 SCOTT (Chairman), *Report of the Committee on Land Utilisation in Rural Areas*, HMSO, London, 1942.

4.32 WHITE, B., *The Sourcebook of Planning Information*, Clive Bingley, London, 1971.

4.33 PORCHESTER, LORD, *A Study of Exmoor*, Report, HMSO, London, 1978.

4.34 US DEPARTMENT OF AGRICULTURE (1975), *op. cit.*

4.35 WELLER, J. B. and WILLETTS, S. L., *op. cit.*

4.36 ALEXANDER, F. R., 'Full circle', *Farmers Weekly*, 4 June 1976.

4.37 LAND COUNCIL, *Report*, London, 1978.

4.38 MINISTRY OF AGRICULTURE FISHERIES AND FOOD, *Agriculture in the Urban Fringe—a Survey in the Metropolitan County of Tyne and Wear*, ADAS Technical Report 30/1, 1976.

4.39 COUNTRYSIDE COMMISSION, *Urban Fringe, Countryside Recreation Review*, Countryside Commission, Cheltenham, 1976.

4.40 *Ibid.*

4.41 COUNTRYSIDE COMMISSION, *Bollin Valley Study*, Countryside Commission, Cheltenham, 1976.

4.42 COUNTRY LANDOWNERS ASSOCIATION, *Report on Hill Farming*, London, 1972.

4.43 COUNTRYSIDE COMMISSION, *Lake District Upland Management Experiment*, Countryside Commission, Cheltenham, 1976.

4.44 WELSH COUNCIL, *A Strategy for Rural Wales*, HMSO, London, 1971.

4.45 JONES, G. E., *Socio-economic Advisory Work—The Policy of the European Communities and its Implementation in the UK*, University of Reading, 1977.

4.46 MINISTRY OF AGRICULTURE FISHERIES AND FOOD, *Modern Farming and the Soil*, HMSO, London, 1971.

4.47 RANSOM, C. E. and DYMOND, D., *Suffolk*, Private Report, 1972.

4.48 HOOPER, M. D., *Hedges in Local History*, National Council for Social Services, London, 1973.

4.49 WESTMACOTT, R. and WORTHINGTON, T., *New Agricultural Landscapes*, Countryside Commission, Cheltenham, 1974.

4.50 US DEPARTMENT OF AGRICULTURE, *Windbreaks for Conservation*, US Agriculture Information Bulletin 339, US Government Printing Office, Washington DC, 1974.

4.51 STAMP, L. D. *Britain's Structure and Scenery*, Collins, London, 1946;
HARVEY, N. H., *A History of Farm Buildings in England and Wales*, David and Charles, Newton Abbott, 1970;
HOSKINS, W. G., *The Making of the English Landscape*, Hodder and Stoughton, London, 1955;
HOSKINS, W. G., *Fieldwork in Local History*, Faber

and Faber, London, 1967.
4.52 St. Bodfan Gruffydd, B., *Historic Landscapes*, Landscape Institute, London, 1978.
4.53 *Field Monuments Act*, HMSO, London, 1972.

# Bibliography

Agricultural Advisory Council, *Modern Farming and the Soil*, HMSO, London, 1970.

Allaby, M., *World Food Resources*, Applied Science Publishers, Barking, Essex, 1977.

Appleton, J., *The Experience of Landscape*, Wiley, London, 1975.

Ashton, J. and Long, W. H., *Remoter Rural Areas of Britain*, Oliver and Boyd, London, 1972.

Bather, D. M. and Day, H. I., *Energy Use and British Agriculture*, Reading University Agricultural Club, Reading, 1976.

Best, R. H. and Coppock, J. T., *The Changing Use of Land in Britain*, Faber and Faber, London, 1962.

Centre for Agricultural Strategy, *Land for Agriculture*, University of Reading, Reading, 1976.

Cherry, G. E. (ed.), *Rural Planning Problems*, Leonard Hill, London, 1976.

Countryside Review Committee, *Food Production in the Countryside*, Topic Paper No. 3, HMSO, London, 1978.

Davidson, J. and Lloyd, R., *Conservation and Agriculture*, Wiley, Chichester, 1977.

Davidson, J. and Wibberley, G., *Planning and the Rural Environment*, Pergamon, Oxford, 1977.

de Paula, F. C., *Farm Finance and Fiscal Policy*, Agricultural Mortgage Corporation, London, 1976.

Duffey, E. *et al.*, *Grassland Ecology and Wildlife Management*, Chapman and Hall, London, 1974.

Edwards, A. and Rogers, A. (eds.), *Agricultural Resources —An Introduction to the Farming Industry of the UK*, Faber and Faber, London, 1974.

Edwards, A. and Wibberley, G., An agricultural land budget for Britain, 1965–2000, Wye College, London, 1971.

Harrison, A., Farmers and farm businesses in England, University of Reading, Reading, 1975.

Hearne, A., Bell, M. and Rest, D. van, Physical and economic impact of motorways on agriculture, University of Aston, Birmingham, 1977.

Hill, B. E. and Ingersent, K. A., *An Economic Analysis of Agriculture*, Heinemann, London, 1977.

Jones, G. E., Socio-economic advisory work, University of Reading, Reading, 1975.

Kennet, W., *The Futures of Europe*, Cambridge University Press, Cambridge, 1976.

Large, B. and King, N., *The Integrated Use of Land for*

*Agriculture and Amenity Purposes*, Grassland Research Institute, Berks., 1978.

Leach, G., *Energy and Food Production*, International Institute for Environment and Development, and IPC, Guildford, 1976.

Ministry of Agriculture Fisheries and Food, *Type of Farming Maps for England and Wales*, HMSO, London, 1971.

Ministry of Agriculture Fisheries and Food, *Agriculture in the Urban Fringe*, HMSO, 1976.

Ministry of Agriculture Fisheries and Food, *Definitions of Terms Used in Agricultural Business Management*, HMSO, 1977.

Morgan, W. B., and Munton, R. J. C., *Agricultural Geography*, Methuen, London, 1971.

Natural Economic Development Office, *Agriculture into the 1980s*, London, 1977.

Nature Conservancy Council, *Nature Conservation in Agriculture*, London, 1977.

Organisation for Economic Co-operation and Development, *Land Use Policies and Agriculture*, Brussels, 1976.

Pollard, E., Hooper, M. D. and Moore, N. W., *Hedges*, Collins, London, 1974.

Potter, D. (ed.), *Social Sciences Decision Making in Britain III*, Parts 1–6, Agriculture, Open University Press, Milton Keynes, 1972.

Roy, R., *Wastage in the UK Food System*, Earth Resources Research, London, 1976.

Royal Institute of Chartered Surveyors, *Future Pattern of Land Ownership and Occupation*, Royal Institute of Chartered Surveyors, London, 1977.

Rural Planning Services (ed.), *The Classification of Agricultural Land in England and Wales—A Critique*, Ipsden, Oxford, 1978.

Soil Conservation Society of America, *World Food Situation—Implications for Land Resource Conservation*, 1975.

University of Manchester, *Landscape Evaluation*, Landscape Evaluation Research Project 1970–75, Manchester, 1976.

US Department of Agriculture, *Perspectives on Prime Lands*, US Government Printing Office, Washington DC, 1975.

US Department of Agriculture, *Recommendations on Prime Lands*, US Government Printing Office, Washington DC, 1975.

US Department of Agriculture, *Fact Book on US Agriculture*, US Government Printing Office, Washington DC, 1976.

Weller, J. B. and Willetts, S. L. *Farm Wastes Management*, Crosby Lockwood Staples, London, 1977.

Westmacott, R. and Worthington, T., *New Agricultural Landscapes*, Countryside Commission, Cheltenham, 1974.

Woodruffe, B. J., *Rural Settlement Policies and Plans (Theory and Practice in Geography)*, Oxford University Press, Oxford, 1976.

CHAPTER FIVE
# FORESTRY AND LAND USE
Sylvia Crowe

Riverside trees conserve the banks and are a typical feature of
valley landscapes

*(Photo by courtesy of the Forestry Commission)*

CHAPTER FIVE
# FORESTRY AND LAND USE

## Historical Background

Over all land areas where soil and climate favour the growth of trees, forest is the natural climax vegetation. This means that if the land is left to nature, trees of one species or another will establish themselves as the dominant plant culture, containing within their shelter all the wild species of plant and animal life which are natural to the locality and forest conditions. These natural forests once covered the greater part of Europe, the Middle East and North America as far north as the Arctic Circle, as well as large areas of Asia, Africa and Southern and Central America. The extent, species and positions of forest lands have shifted through geological time with the changing land masses and climate. The forests receded south at each ice age and then spread north again during warmer periods.

The aridity of climate over many desert areas has increased within historical time. But the greatest change over the last few thousand years has been caused by man.

As mankind has increased, forests have been destroyed, until today few virgin forests remain. The Amazon rain forest is one of the largest surviving examples and that is now under threat. Some forest destruction by men occurs in the earliest stages of civilisation and even before. Clearings are made for settlement and agriculture, and there is damage by the overgrazing of nomadic flocks, or the burning of forests by hunters to drive out the prey. But it is when the numbers of men increase, whether nomadic or settled, that serious destruction of the forest begins.

The pressure on the forest comes from two motives; the wood is required for building and fuel, and clearings are needed in the forest to make room for settlements and crops. Sometimes also the element of fear comes in and forests are destroyed to eradicate the threat of wild beasts.

A typical sequence in deforestation is first the felling of trees for fuel and building, and the clearances for agriculture, accompanied by the prevention of regeneration by the overgrazing of domestic animals (see page 6). Variations on this sequence can be traced in almost all parts of the habitable earth. It contributed, in conjunction with climatic changes, to the formation of the deserts of North Africa and the Middle East. Once both these regions were well timbered and fertile.

The Mediterranean basin, including the Greek islands, were wooded in Homer's time and Plato mourned the destruction of the forests. One factor in the present lack of trees in the Mediterranean region has been overgrazing by the black goat, which effectively prevents the growth of any tree seedlings. This animal has been outlawed in several countries where reafforestation is in hand. Britain was at one time almost wholly forest. In lowland Britain most of the forests have been replaced by agriculture, augmented, particularly in recent years, by building and industrial inroads. But in highland Britain the Mediterranean pattern has been repeated. During the 17th and 18th centuries the trees were taken, mainly for fuel, including smelting, and re-growth has ever since been prevented by grazing animals, particularly sheep, leaving a land of bare hills of low agricultural value (Figure 5.1).

The merciless lumbering of North American forests for timber is well known, and vast clearances have been made for agriculture. In Australia great numbers of trees have been, and still are, destroyed to give uninterrupted fields and sheep runs. Some farmers are now realising the benefit of shade and shelter which the trees gave and are beginning to re-plant.

Some clearance of forest is necessary, to allow for the settlement of men and the growth of their crops. The fault lies in too drastic and thoughtless a clearance. Equally,

Figure 5.1    Centuries of over-grazing have denuded the hills in southern Scotland. Erosion gullies can be seen on the steep scarps. Both land use and wildlife will be improved by afforestation.

(*Photo by courtesy of the Forestry Commission*)

wood is a valuable raw material which can benefit men in countless ways, but is a renewable, permanent asset to be harvested as a crop, and not destroyed.

In all cases cited the destruction went too far, and the evil consequences have included the deterioration of climate, soil and environment, and the increase of flood and drought (see page 5).

# The Functions of Trees and Forests

Since righting the present imbalance between trees and men should be one of the objectives of planning, it is important to understand the part which trees play in the functioning of the landscape. The contributions which they make to life on this planet and to our civilisation, can be summarised under the following headings:

   1.  Amelioration of climate;
   2.  Soil improvement and conservation;
   3.  Water conservation;
   4.  Wildlife conservation;
   5.  Atmospheric purification;
   6.  Timber and food production;
   7.  Visual and aural improvement of the environment;
   8.  Recreation.

## Climatic Amelioration

Trees contribute to this in several ways. The most important are wind shelter and shade, but trees also have the effect of modifying climatic extremes and countering aridity, by checking the wind, and holding a body of humid air within their canopy. This reservoir of air acts as an equalising agent. Considerable afforestation has been carried out in Israel, with the purpose of influencing the climate.

### WIND SHELTER

In the majority of climates, wind shelter adds to the comfort of living and to the range of crops which can be grown. In cold or windswept localities this shelter may make all the difference between a land being habitable and productive, or being barren and useless.

The shelter may be in the form of woodlands, shelter belts or hedges or even single rows of trees (see page 120).

The stronger the winds, the more substantial and closer together the shelter belts must be. It is therefore impossible to lay down a hard-and-fast formula applicable to all parts of the world. But some examples may be given as a guide.

*Shelter Belts and Windbreaks* by J. M. Caborn (5.1) goes into the technique and theory of shelter belts in detail, and cites evidence of the advantages to be gained by the provision of shelter.

In moist climates, such as that of Great Britain, the chief advantage to crops and stock is the rise in temperature caused by checking the wind velocity. In the USSR, USA and Canada, the greatest advantage is due to the reduced velocity checking the evaporation and conserving moisture.

Crop improvements of 45% in parts of the USA are recorded in a zone extending four to five times the height of the wind break.

Noticeable climatic amelioration extends over a distance of 10 to 12 times the height of the shelter. Thus a windbreak 20 m high would provide a sheltered zone 200 or more metres wide. While one 15 m high would give shelter to a width of 150 m. The necessary width of the shelter belt depends on climatic conditions, but is usually 10 to 20 m. In very windy positions sufficient width must be given to allow the leeward trees to reach the desired height; they will only do this if they are sheltered by lower trees and shrubs on the windward side, the top of the shelter belt following the angle at which the wind clips off the growth.

Species for windbreaks must obviously be wind-hardy, growing well in the particular locality. The best results are obtained by an admixture of undergrowth, which will help to filter the wind and slow it down. The siting of the shelter belts must be carefully related to the prevalent, or the strongest, winds, or shaped so that they give shelter in all directions. In hilly districts they should be sited to take advantage of the natural topography.

In some cases, their effectiveness can be increased by planting them on banks or artificially formed hills. These earthworks can also be used to give initial shelter when establishing the belt in very bleak positions.

Figure 5.2 Hedgerow trees comprise a high proportion of Britain's hardwood timbers—they give shelter to fields and buildings, and add to the wildlife and beauty of the landscape.

(*Photo by courtesy of the Forestry Commission*)

In lowland Britain the old patterns of hedgerows which developed over centuries of increasing enclosure from the Middle Ages to the 19th century provided excellent shelter. The recent and continuing removal is causing anxiety. There can be no doubt that the original fields were far too small for the operation of farm machinery and that the removal of some hedges was inevitable and in the interests of good farming, but in some districts, particularly where the soils are light and the winds strong, there have been cases of loss of top soil by wind. This is only one of the ill effects which may be attributed to a wholesale loss of hedges and hedgerow timber, for the old system made a very pleasant and habitable land, extremely rich in wildlife and having a high degree of ecological equilibrium.

It is certainly desirable that the benefits once provided by the hedgerows should be retained or restored, albeit in many cases in a different form.

In East Anglia, where the removal of shelter causes the greatest damage, the Ministry of Agriculture has long advocated the planting of shelter belts. Owing to their greater height they can be more widely spaced than hedges, thus giving larger fields. They can also produce some value in timber.

There are many parts of the country where shelter belts, coppices and woodlands may be a more practical solution than the retention of hedges. They can for instance be sited on poor land or corners of land fragmented by roads or other boundaries. The best solution will vary in each locality in accordance with geology, topography, climate and land use. The important point is to ensure that, by one means or another, there is sufficient tree cover to keep the land in good health and habitable for man and beast.

A striking feature in almost all parts of Britain is the way in which old farmsteads are always sheltered by trees in one formation or another. A perpetuation of this tradition alone would go some way to restoring the well-being of the rural landscape, both visually and as a habitat.

The damage caused by the removal of trees and hedges in Britain has been minimised by the quality of the soil and the equable climate. To see the full effects of neglecting wind shelter, one should study the history of the dust bowls in America and many other parts of the world.

The value of trees for shade is naturally of the greatest importance in making living conditions tolerable in tropical climates, although even in temperate climates they have their value both for human comfort and for stock. Shade for stock was the chief reason for the hedgerow trees in the English countryside.

A special case of combining the value of shade and shelter can be seen in the rows of trees planted along irrigation channels in the desert. These check the evaporation both by shade and shelter.

Figure 5.3 *Tamarix* windbreaks established on loose sand stretches between the sea and the edge of the Gaza Forest Reserve.

(*Photo by courtesy of Ilanot Forest Research Division, Agricultural Research Service, Israel*)

In Egypt's Liberation Province, reclaimed from the desert, rows of *Casuarina* trees form avenues down the irrigation channels which water the citrus orchards.

In the Negev Desert *Eucalyptus*, *Tamarix* and *Acacia* are grown in strips 4 trees wide round fields of 10 ha. This checks evaporation and erosion. The windbreaks of the Gaza Forest Reserve are a further example (see Figure 5.3).

In parts of tropical Africa crops are grown under the shade of the high forest trees. Where this over-storey is removed the sun dries out the fine laterite soil, which may then blow.

### Soil Improvement

Fertile soils are built up over long periods under forest conditions. The valuable brown earths, which constitute the richest and most stable agricultural soils of Britain and much of Europe, were formed under forest conditions. The action of forests in creating and maintaining soil fertility is three-fold:

1. The root action of trees causes a cycling of soil nutrients. The minerals needed for plant growth are drawn up from the lower layers of the soil and returned, through leaf fall and decay to the surface layers where they become available to a wider range of plant growth. At the same time the moisture lying at the lower levels is also circulated. The greatest utilisation of soil, water and nutrients will thus be effected by a mixture of plant species having different rooting depths. An interesting use of this principle is the traditional growing of *Populus* (which is deep rooting) with *Vitis* (which is shallow rooting) in parts of Portugal. The *Populus* acts as a water-pump to bring the moisture within reach of the *Vitis*.

   The penetration of roots also causes soil aeration. Some species, e.g. *Robinia*, further enrich the soil by means of nitrogen-forming nodules on their roots, and are therefore particularly valuable in the reclamation of derelict and infertile land.

2. Leaf fall and decaying wood feed the soil with nutrients and humus, and encourage earthworms, which further enrich and aerate the soil.

   There is considerable difference in the humus-forming value of different species. For example, *Quercus* is rich, and *Eucalyptus* poor. In general, deciduous trees are better humus providers than evergreens.

3. Trees prevent loss of fertility by checking erosion.

PREVENTION OF EROSION

The stability of the root system of trees and the protection from wind and torrential rain given by their canopy stabilises soils and prevents erosion by wind or water. This

Figure 5.4    Young afforestation can be seen on this eroded hillside in Scotland. The hardwoods, which have survived in the valleys should be kept and augmented, but the crop will be coniferous because of the difficult conditions.

(*Photo by courtesy of the Forestry Commission*)

factor is of particular importance on steep slopes and on light soil.

### Restoration of Waste Land

The soil-forming function of trees can be put to good use on waste land, whether it be natural waste, such as sand dunes, or man-made waste such as spoil heaps (as discussed in Chapter 8).

It must be realised that the creation or restoration of soil fertility is a long process, and requires patience.

There are many examples of the stabilisation of shifting sand dunes by afforestation. In every case it is necessary to build up the right growing conditions by first checking the actual movement of the sand. This is often done by thatching the surface of the sand with brushwood, amongst which the trees are planted. Use is also made of the natural sand-stabilising properties of *Ammophila arenaria* and *Hippophae rhamnoides*. In Britain the pioneer tree for afforesting sand dunes is usually *Pinus laricio*. Timber crops are harvested from some duneland forests, but their chief value is in protecting the lands bordering the coast from the effects of blowing sand. A hundred years ago, a poverty stricken stretch of land along the Norfolk coast in England was turned into valuable farmland by the stabilisation and afforestation of the coastal dunes. In the Norfolk Breckland over 20 000 ha of sandy land, too poor for agriculture, was planted about 40 years ago with pine. It is now a thriving forest, and broadleaf trees are appearing within the conifer stands. The reclamation of desert by afforestation comes midway between the restoration of natural and of man-made waste, since often desert conditions are due partly to past human mismanagement and partly to changing climatic conditions, which may have deteriorated over the centuries.

Reafforestation is taking place in many countries of the Middle East, but this represents only a minute proportion of the lands which might be brought back to fertility by this means.

Most of the old industrial countries have begun to restore some of the waste lands created by extractive and industrial processes (see Chapter 8).

Unfortunately this reclamation is not keeping pace with the new waste lands which are continuously being produced. A far more determined effort is needed before the process can show a gain of restored land over that being destroyed. However, the work of the last two decades has built up a body of expertise which could now be used on a wider scale.

Energetic government action, at both national and local levels, is required to combat land dereliction. Parallel with a drive to restore old dereliction, there should be a tightening of legislation to ensure that all land is returned to beneficial use as quickly as possible after disturbance by mining or any other industrial process.

In many cases, planning permission to win minerals is only granted on condition that plans for restoration of the land after working are agreed with the local authority. This condition should be universal, and stronger safe-guards are needed to ensure that the restoration plans are adequately executed and the trees properly maintained.

Figure 5.5, 5.6 and 5.7    The reclamation of Culbin Sands.

Figure 5.5    Before reclamation—these blowing sand dunes roll across farmlands near the coast and cause increasing destruction.

Figure 5.6    The first stages in the reclamation of sand dunes—the loose sand is thatched with branches and the gullies are stopped with wattle fences.

Figure 5.7    Pine forests maturing on the sands after reclamation.

(*Photo by courtesy of the Forestry Commission*)

Afforestation is often found to be the best after-use for slag and other spoil heaps. The growth of trees sets in motion the cycle of fertility and gradually over the years builds up the quality of the soil. As the waste areas are usually in the neighbourhood of densely populated areas, the formation of woodlands can do much to improve the quality of the environment for living. An example where this has been achieved is Swansea, where young forests are now growing on part of the derelict Lower Swansea Valley.

Many tree species show a remarkable tolerance of the difficult growing conditions on spoil heaps. Success lies in first investigating the growing conditions of the tip and then discovering the pioneer tree, shrub or herb most likely to survive; this is discussed in greater detail in Chapter 8. In different parts of Britain *Alnus, Larix, Robinia* and various species of *Pinus* have succeeded in growing under difficult conditions. Once the growing conditions have been improved by the shelter and soil amelioration provided by the pioneer crop, it may be possible to introduce other more desirable species.

Some of the largest-scale reclamation schemes on industrial waste-land are being carried out in West Germany, notably in the Saar and Ruhr districts. Here, immediately open-cast coal mining is completed, the land is formed into a recreational landscape of lakes set in forests. Such a scheme is described by Professor Olschowy (see Case History 3).

### Water Conservation and Flood Control

There is considerable controversy as to the effect of forests on water conservation and availability. The effects on availability undoubtedly vary according to age of forest, species and climatic conditions.

The tree canopy causes less water to fall on the surface of the soil than would be the case over open grassland. This is due to the evaporation of the water as it is checked and held by the tree canopy, the tree foliage having a high rate of evaporation. This loss is said to be greater under conifer forest than deciduous; it is evident that the interception and evaporation will be less when the leaves have fallen and the canopy consists only of bare branches.

It is also true that in the first few years after new forest planting, where the ground has been prepared by ploughing, there will be increased run-off as opposed to absorption of water. This effect, however, is temporary and only applies when the furrows run across the contours. Contour or all-over ploughing tends to check run-off.

The great value of established forest is that it equalises the water regime. This is usually more important than the actual amount of water which reaches the surface of the ground. A large proportion of rainfall is lost in run-off, and this is most serious in climates where the rain falls in torrential downpours, as it often does in areas of low annual rainfall. The run-off is also aggravated by steep gradients, and there are examples all over the world of erosion gullies being made

ever wider by the water running unchecked down them, causing loss of water, flooding and loss of top soil (see also page 5).

Afforestation prevents this condition. It breaks the velocity of the falling rain so that it reaches the ground more slowly and can sink in. The run-off of the water will be further reduced by the vegetation of the forest floor, and the root systems of the trees tend to form an underground reservoir for the retention of moisture. The tree roots also bind the soil together, preventing the formation of gullies.

Many floods are due to the deforestation of the lands surrounding the headwaters of rivers.

The disastrous floods of the River Arno in Italy have been recurrent over hundreds of years, ever since the Tuscan woods were destroyed. The repeated recommendations to re-afforest have not so far been implemented.

The important positions for afforestation in the interests of water and flood control, are on steep slopes, and at the headwaters of rivers. Planting along the contours to form a series of water-catchment terraces is a valuable method of conserving water and preventing erosion.

Trees and shrubs planted along river sides have the effect of slowing the water flow as well as strengthening the banks; they also conserve water by checking evaporation. Considerable work has been carried out in Germany on the protective use of river-side planting. Trees are often cleared from river banks to facilitate access for machines. Even where this is necessary they need only be cleared from one bank. As the trees' shade is beneficial they should preferably be retained on the southern bank.

In countries prone to avalanches, forests play a vital part in counteracting the danger. In Switzerland, for example, this is regarded as one of the most important functions of the forest. A belt of forest on the lower mountain flanks, protects the valley villages and farmlands from the snow on the higher open mountain sides. The forest is managed under a forest officer for the canton, in the best interests of all the land owners and of all land uses.

### Wildlife Conservation

As so great a proportion of the Earth's surface was once forest, it is natural that a vast number of wild species should be forest dwellers. Some, like the red deer, have adapted themselves to open country, but with the reappearance of forests are once more availing themselves of the shelter.

The extent of forest required as habitat by different species varies from the modest requirements of some small woodland birds (who will make do with the shrubs of a suburban garden) to the great areas required by such beasts as the wolf and tiger, who need for their survival the complex animal population which can only build up in a huge tract of land containing diverse habitats.

It follows that the conservation of wide forest areas in Asia and Africa and the far north of the American continent is essential for the survival of some of the Earth's finest beasts.

Figure 5.8    An ecological reserve in the New Forest, Hampshire.

(*Photo by courtesy of the Forestry Commission*)

But even in Europe where long settlement and deforestation has caused the disappearance of most of the larger wild animals, forest conservation of wildlife can do much not only to preserve existing species but to encourage their increase.

For instance, in Britain the recent formation of new forests has added considerably to the population of deer, and of many species of birds, some of which had become almost extinct. While broadleaf woodlands are in general richer in wildlife, certain species, such as firecrests, crossbills, black game and capercaillie, favour the conifer forests (5.2). However, the richest habitat is provided by forests of mixed species and mixed age.

Foresters in general have a conservationist attitude to wildlife, treating deer not as pests but as welcome denizens of the forest, and by careful and humane culling they keep their numbers to a level which ensures the health of both deer and forest.

The provision of appropriate wildlife habitats should be part of forest management. This will include:

1. The provision of food plants by encouraging whatever the local source of food may be, such as *Rubus, Rosa, Crataegus* and *Sorbus*, and even the retention of an occasional dead tree for the benefit of woodpeckers. In the New Forest glades are left open for grazing deer and are known as lawns. These add immeasurably to the beauty of the forest and to the pleasure of its many visitors.
2. The provision of wildlife habitats within the forest will ensure that birds have suitable nesting sites and that every species has the living conditions and degree of seclusion which it requires.

These needs will have to be considered in planning all forest operations and in public access and recreation plans.

Areas of undergrowth will be needed for nesting, and there must be provision of the 'edge' habitat which is popular with many species of birds and plants as well as with man. This means treating the edges of clearings, rides and boundaries generously, allowing space for the development of the plant growth which is natural to such positions, and encouraging the penetration of light into the forest.

Forest management can encourage flora as well as fauna. Many of the well-known spring flowers, such as primroses (*Primula vulgaris*) are dependent on a degree of light and sunshine penetrating the forest canopy. They will flower abundantly in the first few years after a clear felling, and may then be suppressed until thinning again lets in the light. The same generous treatment of rides and margins which favours wildlife will equally favour forest flowers.

In Friston Forest, on the South Downs, wide rides (treated under various regimes of cutting) have encouraged a remarkable diversity of chalkland flowers along the margins. These in turn have encouraged many species of butterfly, which have become scarce on the open downland since intensive agriculture has replaced sheep grazing.

Water edges are particularly rich habitats, and again sufficient space should be allowed for the development of waterside flora. It is often possible to create new ponds by the damming of streams or scooping out a hollow in boggy ground. As well as being useful for fire fighting, these areas of water, however small, will attract wild fowl, and often bring the deer to drink.

A rich wildlife should be an essential part of any forest, whatever the main function of that forest may be. It is worth while for its own sake, but it is also an important economic asset. This perhaps is realised best in India and Africa where the wildlife forms the chief tourist attraction in national parks.

There is also a largely underdeveloped source of protein

which can be culled from the forest wildlife. Provided this is done with humane and wise restraint, the numbers of the wild animals always being kept at their optimum for the habitat, much good could result. As an example, considerable quantities of venison are now produced from the British forests. In countries where there are difficulties in farming domestic cattle, for instance in areas infested by tsetse fly, the farming of forest fauna has great possibilities.

### Atmospheric Purification

The physiological action of trees makes them of great value as an antidote to pollution caused by the human race.

Photosynthesis, the process carried out by the chlorophyll in green leaves, absorbs carbon dioxide from the atmosphere and gives off oxygen—the opposite process to that of breathing, which absorbs oxygen and gives off carbon dioxide.

This fact alone underlines the necessity for extensive tree planting in populated areas; the larger and more densely populated the area the greater the need for trees.

But in addition to photosynthesis, trees can purify the atmosphere in other ways. They are valuable as screens to sift dust particles out of the air, and by means of the air currents which they induce, polluted air can be lifted to a higher stratum, where it will tend to disperse.

These attributes make tree belts very beneficial when they are sited between industrial areas and dwellings. Considerable research has been done on this subject in Germany.

### Visual and Aural Values

While there can be grandeur in a completely wild treeless landscape, as soon as men and their works enter into the picture the lack of trees is felt as a deprivation. A humanised agricultural landscape needs at the least sufficient trees to give adequate shelter from wind and sun and to supply that diversity of habitat which gives interest and variety to the landscape, as well as an ecologically balanced countryside.

But it is when the number of men and the scale of their works increase that the visual need as well as the physiological need for trees is felt most strongly. Sometimes the sheer bulk and quantity of human structures becomes overpowering, at other times a particular land use or structure is ugly in itself. In both these cases, trees form the best screens and antidotes. One of their great virtues is that they reintroduce the organic scale into megalopolis. They reconcile the scale of the individual, who feels at home amongst the trees, to the scale of city civilisation. The town forest, merging together the disparate elements of the city, will cure the restlessness which is one of the ugliest features of our present urban surroundings. Carried into the city in the form of linear parks and tree-planted streets and gardens, the whole town can be made habitable and beautiful. One of the finest examples of the use of town woodland and penetrating parks is at Stuttgart in West Germany, where the surrounding hills serve as a town forest for the people's recreation, and the trees drift down into a long central park which brings peace and refreshment into the centre of the city.

Another fine example of a city forest is the Forêt de Soignes outside Brussels, where wildlife, timber production and quiet recreation all find a place. The sheer beauty of trees and their response to the rhythm of the seasons, are reason enough to make them a part of everyday city life.

A completely man-made and comparatively recent example is the Amsterdam Bos. Here every kind of recreation is carried on within 895 ha of woodland, planted on land which was reclaimed from the sea. This is a remarkable testimony to the value of town woodlands, carried out by a people as efficient as the Dutch, who considered it worth while to use this huge area of expensively reclaimed land for the purposes of recreational forest.

The quietness to be experienced within a forest is one of its greatest blessings in the noise-shattered world in which

Figure 5.9    Cannop Ponds in the Forest of Dene where economic forestry gives way to landscape and conservation.

(*Photo by courtesy of the Forestry Commission*)

so many of us live. Again it is where men are most numerous and active that we most need the relief from noise which trees can bring.

A very wide belt of dense planting is needed to deaden completely the traffic noise of a motorway but considerable psychological relief is given by concealing the noise source —the thicker and denser the leaf barrier the more the sound will be diffused.

### Recreation

The special attraction of forests for recreation includes:

1. Wildlife interest;
2. Visual variety and beauty;
3. Powers of crowd absorption.

1. Wildlife conservation in the forest has already been discussed. The contribution which it makes to recreation and education is very great, and facilities to enjoy it are being increasingly developed all over the world.

Children, and indeed adults, who have grown up in cities may be totally ignorant of the flora and fauna of their own country. To awaken their interest, simple nature trails are planned through many forests, with a leaflet to explain the plants and other things of interest they may see. Often a small forest museum will help the explanation, and show them the birds and animals they may hope to see.

Many schools have centres in the forests where groups of children can stay and study natural sciences on the spot.

Figure 5.11    Falling Foss waterfall, Langdale Forest close to the car park and forest trail.

*(Photo by courtesy of the Forestry Commission)*

Figure 5.10    The visitor centre at Weston Birt Arboretum which is a focal point for the interpretation of forestry to the visitor. (Architect: Andris Berzins; landscape consultant: Cliff Tandy)

*(Photo by courtesy of the Forestry Commission)*

Figure 5.12 Deciduous trees and native plants along the roads and rides contribute to conservation and to the pleasure of walkers.

(*Photo by courtesy of the Forestry Commission*)

Developing from this early interest is an ever-growing body of bird watchers and naturalists in different fields.

The future welfare of the landscape will depend on the interest and understanding of the generation which is now learning to appreciate nature.

2. The attraction of forests is shown by the numbers of people who visit them to walk, ride and picnic. To these the conservation of a forest in its full beauty is paramount. For instance, in the zone of broadleaf forests, they will come to enjoy the delights of the changing seasons, the opening of the spring buds and flowers and the colours of autumn. They will usually welcome a proportion of conifer planting for its contrast and winter interest, but only if it leaves the beauty of seasonal deciduous trees unimpaired.

3. The degree to which woodlands can absorb crowds without detriment is becoming an ever more important factor in this overcrowded world. It must, however, be realised that forests have a saturation point, beyond which the health as well as the enjoyability of the woods will decline.

The first sign of over-wear is cessation of natural regeneration as treading feet destroy the seedling trees. In urbanised and heavily used districts this often has to be accepted, and counteracted by artificial replanting or by the exclusion of the public from an area while it regenerates.

The next sign of over-use is compaction of the soil over tree roots or erosion following the treading out of the forest floor. At this point steps must be taken to reduce the numbers of visitors, or purely artificial means of access must be provided, such as pathways raised off the forest floor by wooden slats or logs. These extreme cases of over-wear are only likely to occur in town woodlands or at overloaded points of access or special view-points in larger forests.

The forest's powers of crowd absorption are partly due to

Figure 5.13 A well sited car park amongst larches on the Cwm Carn Scenic Forest Drive in Eddw Forest, South Wales.

(*Photo by courtesy of the Forestry Commission*)

the natural screening effect of trees. It is possible to feel alone in a forest when in fact there are enough other people in the vicinity to appear as a crowd if seen in open country.

Fortunately different people look for different things in their recreation. Those who want solitude may wander down the lesser woodland paths, while the gregarious congregate in woodland clearings near the access points and car parks. Good planning in the forest will ensure that the desires of both can be satisfied. Good planning will also ensure that the most used paths leading from the car parks do not lead too close to the wildlife sanctuaries.

The screening value of the forest is also valuable in providing unobtrusive sites for camps and car parks (see also page 173). The ideal sites for these are either in areas of very open woodland, or in small clearings within the wood (Figure 5.13). Vehicles must not be parked so close to the trees that they cause damage either to the trunks or to the roots by compaction of the soil. Well-placed logs at strategic points on the forest floor form effective yet unobtrusive car-stoppers. Impaction can be minimised by a layer of blinded hard-core over the extent of root-spread within the car parking area.

Another factor in the suitability of forests for recreation is that reasonable public access does not conflict with good forestry. Fire danger, which is sometimes cited as a reason for the exclusion of the public, is at its greatest when the crop is young, and the risk decreases when the trees have grown out of the thicket stage. It never, of course, disappears, and it is vital to educate the public to take the utmost care.

The acceptability of the public in forests contrasts with the greater difficulties of accommodating them in open countryside, as the extent and intensity of agricultural operations increase. Open country to which there is access, such as heathlands and hill-grazing and mountains above the tree line, can soon lose its look of majestic wilderness if invaded by too many people, and even more by camps and car parks. Forests can therefore form very useful buffer zones adjoining the wilder areas of national parks.

An interesting example of this is the wooded area bordering the south rim of the Grand Canyon. Within this wood are absorbed the camps, car parks and buildings needed for visitors to the national park, without impinging on the grandeur of the Canyon.

Nevertheless, forests should not be degraded into hiding places for unwanted and unrelated objects. Anything sited within them should partake of the forest character and impinge as little as possible on unmolested woodland.

This applies both to the design of all artifacts within the forest and to their numbers and extent. The appeal which forests have for people does not consist wholly of static views. An even greater pleasure is found in walking within the forest, sensing the peace and atmosphere which is a complete contrast to the busy world outside. To appreciate this to the full requires large areas of forest free from urban reminders. Equally the wildlife of the forest, which contributes so much to its attraction, requires ample areas of undisturbed habitat, varying in size according to the species.

## Forest Products

In the past, wood was used for fuel and for building. Now the chief demand is for pulp and fibre. Future uses can only be surmised, but may well include large-scale food production.

Every change in use demands change in management and species. A classic example is the old coppice and standard method in England. The coppice, usually hazel (*Avellana*), hornbeam (*Carpinus*), or sweet chestnut (*Castanea sativa*) was used mainly for fuel and fencing. The standards (usually *Quercus robor*) were widely spaced and therefore developed the elbowed character required for ship's timbers. The method has no relevance to modern timber demands although where it remains it forms a very beautiful and floriferous woodland.

Recently an area in the Wye Valley was re-coppiced after a lapse of some 30 years. This was carried out in the interests of conservation, but some use was found for the cuttings as pulp wood. In many private woodlands coppice is used for estate fencing, and the widely used chestnut-pale fencing comes from sweet chestnut coppice. At the other end of the scale, large timber of high quality can be obtained from individual trees in forests managed on a selective system. A far greater diversity of management is possible if these small-scale opportunities are taken to use timber for specialist purposes rather than for the mass production of wood for the pulp mills. To meet our present needs, both types of management, extensive and intensive, are required.

In view of the long maturation of timber crops, the possibility of changing requirements should always be borne in mind, and the maximum diversity and flexibility maintained. Soil kept in a high state of fertility by far-sighted forest management will always be an asset, no matter what type of wood product is required, or even if the land is turned to agriculture use.

The maintenance of soil fertility should therefore receive priority and not be sacrificed to the immediate attraction of crop values which may prove transitory.

The use of leafy tree branches for fodder has a long history and is still practised in parts of the world. *Salix* is used in this way in Kashmir. The use could well be extended in the future and experiments on the extraction of protein for human use are under way. With the growing pressure on the world's food supplies, such a development would be welcome, and would certainly seem a better use of trees than turning them into pulp for Sunday Supplements. It does in any case emphasise the need to keep an open mind on the type of tree for which there will be the greatest demand in the future, and underlines the necessity to keep reserves of all types of forests and all species.

The importance of maintaining the full range of the Earth's stock of species, both flora and fauna, is at last being realised, and forests have perhaps a greater part to play in this policy than any other type of ecosystem. However, such policies require farsightedness, for forests, if destroyed or damaged, take generations to replace.

## Multi-use of Forests

Since woodland serves so many diverse ends, it is, by its very nature, multi-purpose. Every forest must, at the least, affect soil and climatic conditions, and harbour wildlife.

In planning for the best use of forests, the prime object of the forest in each case should be identified, and then combined as effectively as possible with other benefits. Sometimes the collateral benefits can be achieved without any reduction of the prime object, or may even enhance it. In other cases it may be necessary to depart from the 100% attainment of the prime object in order to achieve optimum all-round benefit to the landscape and community.

An example of improving the prime object by paying attention to a subsidiary one, is the use of undergrowth in shelter-belts for the encouragement of bird life. The undergrowth will at the same time increase the efficiency of the windbreak (see page 120).

Recreation can be inimical to wildlife if too many people are allowed near the habitats. On the other hand, forest recreation would lose its greatest appeal if there were no wildlife. It is therefore in the interests of both that undisturbed zones should be assured to the birds and animals; above all, for their breeding grounds. This can be achieved by careful zoning and routing of paths.

Commercial timber production, if carried to the point of maximum short-term cash benefit, usually cuts across other forest values. But small concessions are often sufficient to achieve optimum benefit. In many cases, if the long-term view is taken, and continuing soil fertility and biological health assured for the future, the concessions may represent no loss at all. The greatest potential loss to landscape quality

and to biological values is where the economic crop is of even age and single species. This can be particularly damaging if the species is a light-excluding conifer.

This position has arisen in many of the newly planted forests in northern Britain. They are planted on degraded soils under difficult climatic conditions. On the more difficult of these sites, no broadleaf will produce timber, whereas some of the North American conifers, notably Sitka spruce, will grow remarkably well. It is therefore inevitable that these be used as the crop tree.

But it is not inevitable that they extend unbroken over every acre of forest land. On some sites [often indicated by the growth of bracken (*Pteridium aquilinum*)] larch (*Larix*) can be grown and, although less economically attractive, it will produce timber. While still coniferous (and an alien to Britain) the *Larix* is deciduous and has exceptionally beautiful spring and autumn colouring. Throughout the year it can lighten the dark spruce forest, and its range of colouring links with the yellow-greens and russets of the native hills. In its later stages *Larix* also develops a richer forest floor by letting in more light then the *Picea* (spruce). Comparatively recent introductions from Chile, *Nothofagus procera* and *N. obliqua* are being tested and give promise of being valuable timber trees, adaptable to many upland areas where previously spruce has been the most valuable crop-tree. The *Nothofagus* are trees of great beauty and will give that deciduous relief so much needed in our predominantly spruce forests. *Betula* (birch), *Sorbus aucuparia* (rowan) and *Quercus sessiliflora* (oak) are all native to these highland sites. None of them produces timber, but all are very beautiful and ecologically important. Some old woods of sessile oak remain, and many are being preserved, but the grazing sheep prevent their natural regeneration. They often survive in gullies, whose steep sides have protected

Figure 5.14 Dundeugh Forest, Galloway, south Scotland. This coniferous forest is a good example of planting to topography and enhances the recreational amenity of the reservoir.

*(Photo by courtesy of the Forestry Commission)*

them from the sheep. Where these gullies fall within the land to be afforested, the oak can remain, with little economic loss. Similarly, rocky areas, where the growth and extraction of timber would be difficult, can be left to the birch and rowan.

As these native trees will be protected from grazing by the forest fence, they will multiply and thrive. Similarly the crop trees can be kept well back from the sides of streams, letting light into the water and encouraging the native waterside growth. Rides and clearings related to the topography can break the monotony of the mono-culture crop.

These measures are little more than common sense involving the expenditure of thought rather than money. If to these is added the very small expenditure of planting a few drifts and inter-mixture of native broadleaves, related to the rides and clearings and linking with any farmland there may be in the valleys, then the timber crop will be assimilated into the landscape, the wildlife will be encouraged, and the deciduous leaf fall will aid the long-term regeneration of the soil, whose present degraded condition dates back through centuries of tree clearance and over-grazing.

## Planting to Topography

In forestry as in all landscape planning, the land itself must be allowed to speak. Fine landscapes result from men working through, and in sympathy with, nature, not by imposing on her a preconceived pattern.

The result of this latter course can be seen in harsh rectangular blocks of forestry, drawn on a map far from the site and imposed on a hillside without regard to the topographical modelling, the local soil changes, or the changes in microclimate given by bluffs and natural wind deflections (Figure 5.15).

In many parts of Britain, the topography is so varied, the geological formation so broken, that simply following the indications of the ground is enough to give a planting line which will fit the landscape with that appearance of inevitability which is the hallmark of good design. Looking at a hillside one can see where ribs and outcrops of rock make planting difficult and of doubtful value, while between the rocky outcrops flushes of grass, usually coinciding with the more sheltered hollows, suggest where planting could be carried further up the hillside.

If the upper boundary of the plantation adheres rigidly to a given contour, it forms a harsh and artificial line which contradicts the land form, and would never be found in a natural forest. In nature, even on a featureless even hillside, the trees would gradually die out as they reached the upper limit of growth and become intermingled with some stunted scrub. The same effect can be obtained in planted forests by following every indication of the ground, and by sparser planting of the trees as they reach the upper tree line.

Figure 5.15   A plantation ignoring the landform and cut into square compartments. This rigid pattern is now being replaced by a greater regard to the landscape.

(*Photo by courtesy of the Forestry Commission*)

Figure 5.16   Snowdonia—species selected for their suitability to the changing terrain with old hardwoods retained in the valley and on the rocky knolls.

(*Photo by courtesy of the Forestry Commission*)

Other factors which relieve the monotony of unbroken conifer forests, are the needs for open strays for sheep to reach the hill pastures. These can be shaped to give the best visual as well as practical results.

Landscapes where farm and forest are integrated into a pattern of sheltered open space, contrasting with the solidity of forest, are some of the most beautiful in the world.

Planning forests for the combined uses of timber production, conservation, shelter and human enjoyment will create a new beauty in the landscape, and by combining all these functions will make the best use of the Earth's limited land surface.

## Integration of Forest and Agriculture

The value of integration between farm and forest is a hotly argued issue. The degree to which it is desirable varies according to soil, climate and the type of farming which is practised (see page 96).

As we have seen, some element of tree growth within the agricultural landscape is always desirable for reasons of shelter, ecological diversity and the habitability of the land.

An interesting vindication of this is supplied by the policy adopted in the more recently reclaimed polders of the Netherlands. Despite the very high cost of the reclaimed land, between 10 and 20% is being planted as woodland, not primarily for timber production, but for wildlife, shelter and the pleasures of living.

In many schemes for the recasting of farm holdings in other parts of Europe, including France and Germany, woodland areas and shelter belts are planned as part of the new agricultural pattern.

There is a tendency for the farmer to demand that all the land shall be available for his crops and grazing, while the forester wants to plant all available lands with solid forest, but where the two interests have got together, to form a combined landscape, the results have been spectacular, not only in the literal sense of creating a magnificent landscape, but also in the practical results obtained.

On the windy highlands and islands of Scotland, shelter can play a vital part in making farming (and indeed living) a kinder proposition than it has been for the last few hundred years. Shelter planting is being established on many of the islands more for the sake of the farming crofts than for the timber. But in the majority of cases the forestry and the farming are both viable, and benefit each other. Any increase and diversity of employment is helpful to the communities in remote areas, and the forest workers enrich the community, while the forest roads can also serve farms which

Figure 5.17   Valley farmlands can be improved by the shelter of forested hills. These Welsh hilltops are used for sheep grazing (and hill walking). A sheep stray connects the valley fields to the hilltops.

*(Photo by courtesy of the Forestry Commission)*

could not afford them on their own account.

The increase in stock bearing which can be brought about by the provision of shelter in really bleak districts, is illustrated by a case in Wales (Figure 5.17).

On an estate of 1616 ha previously used wholly for sheep grazing, 767 ha were afforested. Thanks to the shelter provided by this afforestation, more sheep can now be grazed on the remaining 849 ha than were previously grazed on the whole estate.

Strong opposition to the introduction of forestry or indeed of any tree planting can arise in countries where there are heavy demands on land space, and where there is a natural desire to devote any available land to agriculture.

In some countries, such as Japan, the topography of the land offers the solution, allowing the steep hills to remain in forestry, while the valleys are developed for intensive agriculture and urban uses. As a result, 65% of Japan, despite its high population density, is still under forest, and three-quarters of this is still natural forest. It is interesting that the majority of Japanese woodlands are owned by farmers, who welcome the augmentation of their income.

In other countries, such as part of the USA, the past experience of dust bowls has shown the value of tree planting, which is now being used widely as a remedial measure. The US Conservation Service has achieved remarkable results by contour planting on land where deforestation and over-cropping had caused erosion. Worn out cotton-growing land in the Southern States has similarly been restored.

Lowland Britain represents a country where stable soil and a temperate climate prevent the more spectacular ill effects of deforestation and where the farmer is anxious to bring every hectare of good agricultural land under the plough. Although Britain has one of the lowest percentages of afforested land in Europe, the country had, until recently, a generally well-treed appearance because of the number of hedgerow and park trees. Before the onset of Dutch Elm Disease 90% of the mature hardwood timber in Britain consisted of hedgerow trees. The devastation caused by DED, added to the removal of hedges for agricultural purposes, and the further loss of hedgerow trees by the use of mechanical hedge-cutters, has destroyed the once tree-clad appearance of many parts of the country. Unless the lost trees and hedges are replaced by equivalent tree cover, the loss to the countryside will be greater than is now realised. The replacement need not necessarily be in the same pattern of hedged fields, and a landscape of larger fields, with groups and spinneys of trees, may well evolve (see page 120). The wholesale hedge clearance has been in aid of mechanisation, but the human as well as the ecological factor must be remembered. Not only is a treeless landscape inhospitable to live in, but even working conditions can suffer. A case has been reported of a ploughman in East Anglia who abandoned his tractor in despair at the sight of a 300-ha field stretching before him waiting to be ploughed. Wild animals are not the only creatures who need woods as part of their habitat.

# Species

The types of forest found in different parts of the world fall into broad climatic zones. In the cold regions towards the most northerly limit of tree growth, are the conifer forests, such as cover great areas of Scandinavia and the northern regions of the American continent. There are few deciduous trees, that growing furthest north being *Betula*.

South of this comes the more temperate zone of the deciduous and mixed forests, which once covered most of Europe including the British Isles.

Southward again, under more arid conditions comes the Mediterranean vegetation with a high proportion of broadleaved evergreens with small leaves. In the tropics the forests are of large broadleaved evergreens.

The actual species native to different countries, while falling within this general classification, vary considerably according not only to local climate and soil, but to the chances of geological history. Great Britain for instance is poor in native species because it was severed from the main European landmass before the spread northward of many species which re-established themselves in the European mainland after the retreat of the last ice age. Norway spruce (*Picea abies karsten*) for instance was native to Britain in interglacial times, but did not return after the final glaciation.

Under these circumstances it is not surprising that there has been massive introduction of species from other countries, and in this respect Britain is merely an acute example of what is happening in other parts of the world.

It is therefore worth considering the pros and cons of using introduced tree species.

Where an indigenous species meets the requirements for which a forest is established or perpetuated, it should be given preference. There are several reasons for this. The native trees are an established part of the ecological situation in the country, therefore the risk of unforeseen side-effects is removed. It is also the longest-established species which have developed the greatest number of associated organisms and therefore add most to the biological richness of the habitat. Native trees are visually an ingredient of the landscape, and in this age when there is a tendency to make all lands look alike, individual character is very precious and should be preserved.

However, there are many cases where an exotic tree will serve the prime purpose of a forest better than any indigenous species. Obvious examples are the North American conifers, which will grow and produce timber on the bleak peat-covered hills of Britain where no native timber can be produced. The use of imported crop trees is analogous to the use of imported food crops and grasses. But it brings with it an equal need to ensure that the native species and associations do not disappear. On the whole, agriculture has not met this responsibility, but it is vital that forestry should do so.

While the use of alien species is often justified, it involves a responsibility to study and watch for any undesirable effects on the ecology or the appearance of the landscape. For instance, there is considerable misgiving on the results of the wholesale planting of *Eucalyptus* in the Mediterranean basin. Their water-greedy roots can increase aridity, and their leaf fall does little to enrich the soil.

Some species on the other hand, like the nitrogen-fixing *Robinia*, may do more for the improvement of infertile soils than a native species. *Alnus incana* has been found of particular value in the reclamation of industrial wastelands, and there are certain trees particularly well-suited to growth under urban conditions which may well be introduced from one country to another. Norway maple (*Acer platanoides*), plane (*Platanus acerifolia*) and *Jacaranda* are all species which enrich cities far from their place of origin.

The first consideration in choosing species for any type of planting is to select those which will thrive in the soil and climate. From amongst the possible species, those best fitted to the particular purpose of the plantation can be selected, and this will often mean selecting a species capable of good timber production. But as we have seen, there is always an element of multipurpose use within any forest, so that to the main species there may be added others, equally able to thrive, but of less timber value, for the sake of the contribution they can make to wildlife, fertility and the beauty of the landscape.

Mixed forests are often of great beauty and are a feature both of the tropics and of areas of temperate climate and good growing conditions. In Japan, with its moist temperate climate, the hills are clothed in forests of great beauty, comprising hundreds of species and varieties of trees. The dark majesty of the *Cryptomeria* is relieved by the great variety of *Acer*, with their glorious autumn colour and by many spring flowering trees.

The same beauty and variety can be seen in the Great Smoky Mountains of Tennessee, with their wonderful stands of *Liriodendron* and understorey of *Kalmia* and *Azalea*. Forests of more uniform species are found in the harder growing conditions of the north, where the conifer predominates, and in more arid regions, where only a few species will withstand the lack of moisture.

Examples of natural monoculture are found where a light-excluding tree such as *Fagus* has become the dominant species and by its deep shade inhibits the growth of other trees or undergrowth. *Quercus* and *Fraxinus* on the other hand encourage a rich understorey of forest floor and shrub layer, as well as the intermixture of other tree species.

In Great Britain, beech (*Fagus*) forms the natural climax forest on the thin chalklands and despite the lack of shrub layer provides spectacular beauty in the spring when the opening leaves coincide with sheets of bluebells (*Endymion non-scriptus*), and again in the autumn and early winter when the leaves first turn golden and then fall to form a carpet of deep russet, which remains until the spring. The woods of oak (*Quercus robor*) which form the natural climax on the clay lands of southern Britain are no less beautiful in a quite different way. Their rich shrub layer and flora give immense variety and their bird life is far richer than that of the beech woods.

Every type of forest has its particular beauty, and uniformity of type should be avoided. Beautiful though a mixed forest may be, a general mixture of species should not be allowed to replace the distinctive natural types.

In establishing new forests, trees are often planted in mixtures, sometimes with the intention that the final forest shall be a mixture of species, sometimes with the purpose of using a quick-growing species as nurse crop or for early harvesting. Examples of the latter practice is the planting of a conifer crop as nurse to the frost-tender beech (*Fagus*). The conifers, reaching marketable size long before the beech, are removed to leave the beech as the final crop.

Man-made forests are often deficient in shrub layer, and although there is great beauty in a clean-boled stand of high forest, there is also beauty, and great conservation value, in the shrub layer found in all natural forests formed of light-demanding trees. The shade-bearing trees themselves cast heavy shade and therefore inhibit shrub layer and forest flowers. The light-demanding throw a lighter shade and thus encourage undergrowth.

# Types of Forest Management and their effect on Landscape and Land Use

Selecting the correct method of forest management is an essential factor in integrating woodlands, whether new or existing, into the landscape plan.

The plan must identify the particular use, or range of uses, appropriate to each woodland.

It is evident that a woodland whose chief function is shelter will require quite different management from one used primarily for timber production.

In deciding on the best regime the following aspects must be stated in the plan.

1. The nature of the woodland, its age structure and species;

2. The visual contribution which it makes to the landscape;

3. The desirable uses of the woodland;

4. The resources which will be available for its management.

In the light of these considerations the different possibilities of management should be considered, and the best method chosen.

## Selection and Regeneration

Selection produces a mixed-age forest and maintains a continuous canopy. It has many amenity advantages. It gives the endless variety of different-aged trees; it is conducive to a wide range of wildlife, and it ensures continuity in the appearance of the landscape.

Its practical value includes providing continuous protection and cover to the soil. For the latter reason it is the method used in the Swiss forests, whose chief function is to provide protection, especially from avalanches (see page 134). It is, in fact, widely practised throughout Europe.

A selective forest is the nearest approach to natural forest conditions, but the success of regeneration can be jeopardized by too many grazing animals, wild or domestic.

## Clear Felling

Clear felling is often favoured for economic reasons. It usually poses more problems for the landscape planner than selection felling. The dangers to be avoided are both visual and ecological. There is the risk of removing shelter, which may expose adjacent crops to wind blow, and under some soil and climatic conditions the overexposure of soil may result in erosion or, if carried out on a large-enough scale, in flood danger. All these factors must be understood and taken into account, and they are equally relevant whether the forest is being felled for re-planting or for some other land use. If the clear-felled area is to remain as forest it must be re-planted, or managed for regeneration immediately and never be left derelict.

Clear felling can give ugly results in the landscape, but need not do so (Figure 5.18). The worst cases are when the trees are felled in harsh rectangles or shapes unrelated to the topography. The same principles apply in felling as in planting; the shape and nature of the ground must be the guide. There is often some natural line related to the terrain. But even where no strongly marked feature governs the shape, coups of a natural gladelike form can be felled, leaving groups or promontories of wind-firm trees standing out from the surrounding forest. In some cases it is possible to pre-thin the line of severance so that a wind-firm and well-furnished edge to the standing forest will be revealed. One of the ugliest features of planted (as opposed to natural) forests, is the solid wall of the forest edge, unbroken by light or undergrowth.

Careful attention to the shape of fellings will help to build up a mixed-age forest for the future, allowing some of the finest trees to remain to a greater age than the main crop (Figure 5.19).

If the harsher effects of clear felling can be avoided, there are also advantages. New views can be opened up which often reveal unexpected beauties to those using the forest for recreation. Well-shaped coups within the forest give vistas down into the interior which add beauty and interest to the forest rides. The flush of wild flowers which appears in the first few years after felling can be spectacular.

In forests used for recreation, the paths and nature trails can from time to time be re-routed to take full advantage of these benefits. The most attractive types of forest to walk through are either those of mixed age and species, or plantations which are nearing maturity, with the light coming through their trunks, or a varied woodland giving a proportion of glades and open views alternating with high forest. The most monotonous paths are those leading through any species in unbroken stands at the thicket stage (which is usually the first 15 to 20 years of their lives).

It should be noted that clear felling is not entirely alien to natural forests, as it can result from fire and wind blow.

## Group Felling

Group felling consists of taking out sufficient timber to open up a small space in the forest canopy. It can be valuable in allowing the gradual regeneration of a closed-canopy forest

Figure 5.18    Clear felling can be tempered by leaving groups and promontories of the old groups.

*(Photo by courtesy of the Forestry Commission)*

Figure 5.19    Felling to a broken edge, instead of to a hard line, gives a better forest landscape. The new crop will interpenetrate with the old, and a mixed-age forest will develop.

*(Photo by courtesy of the Forestry Commission)*

where the more drastic method of clear felling is undesirable. This often applies to woodland whose prime purpose is amenity, or where the wood forms a windbreak or essential clothing to a slope or skyline.

## Overstories on Felled Areas

Occasionally a few trees are left standing in a clear-felled area. These may serve as protection for the young crop or as seed parents, or they may be left purely for amenity. The visual success of this measure depends on the density, position and condition of the trees left. If they are well-formed, wind-firm and not too isolated they may look well and serve a useful silvicultural purpose. But if they are spindly and windblown, they achieve little. They often look best if left in groups rather than as isolated specimens.

## Treatment of Old Forests

In the case of virgin forest, or forests which, although once planted or managed by men, have taken on a natural character, management will depend on the composition of the forest and on the purpose for which it is to be managed.

The total destruction of a forest by clear felling without any steps being taken to regenerate it or put it to new use, is a crime against the landscape, and has resulted in degraded landscapes in many parts of the world. The second growth which may come from the cut stumps of the old forest usually form very inferior trees, and poor scrub growth. Even where this has happened, subsequent good management can do something to retrieve the position. An interesting case study was made by Harvard of an area in New England. When the settlers came they found virgin forest of mixed species with a high proportion of white pine. This was cleared to make way for fields and to provide building material and fuel. When the richer lands to the West were opened up, the settlers left the poor stony ground, and the fields reverted to forest. This second growth forest is of poorer quality than the original virgin forest, but by careful management it is being nursed back into a timber crop. This sequence has also provided wooded residential sites, where houses can be set amongst the groves of second growth forest.

These rescue operations do not however excuse the initial destruction.

Legitimate methods of dealing with natural forests are:

1. To keep them as they are, as conservation areas. This is desirable where the forest represents a particularly interesting or locally rare type of woodland.

2. To harvest their timber and perpetuate the crop by good management. This is applicable where the wood has good timber potential.

3. To convert the forest to some other species, which has more value.

This method has been used to underplant trees lacking timber value with a more productive species. It is a method to be used in moderation and with caution, lest all natural woodlands are gradually destroyed. The danger of this has been recognised in a recent policy decision by the Forestry Commission to encourage broadleaves where they will thrive. It is also possible to replace the old trees with a better strain of the same species. Particularly fine trees are selected as seed parents, and the seedlings grown to replace poorer strains.

4. Where the forest use is to be primarily for recreation, it is probable that the best treatment will be a limited opening up of rides and views, without destroying the essential character.

There is danger in assuming that an old wood will necessarily survive if it is not managed at all. Some new ecological factor may prevent the regeneration of the old trees. This has occurred in the Black Forest of Caledonian pine (the original native strain of *Pinus sylvestris*), where deer have prevented the growth of seedlings, and the forests are now being artificially regenerated by young trees raised in nurseries from the Caledonian's seed, and planted out with protection. Grazing animals and rabbits will often make this type of management necessary if the old natural woodlands are to survive after the lifetime of the present trees.

# Afforestation as a Planning Process

Since the natural climax vegetation of a large proportion of the Earth's surface is forest, it follows that an increase in the depleted forest area will add to the stability and health of the environment.

As we have seen, trees are the natural antidote to pollution caused by too great a number of the human species, and for this reason the more people there are, the more need there is for trees. The problem in achieving this is the shortage of land space; the very conditions which demand more trees making it more difficult to find space for them. Tree planting should therefore have a high priority in areas where they can be established.

Positions where they may be of particular value include:

1. *Land of low fertility.* Trees of the right species may succeed better than any other crop on inhospitable land and, at the same time, may improve conditions by gradually increasing fertility and providing shelter.

2. *Steep slopes, particularly where there is danger of erosion or flood run-off.* Tree cover will check both these dangers. The angle of slope at which afforesta-

tion is desirable varies according to climatic and soil conditions, but any slope greater than 1:6 should be considered for tree cover, with the proviso that existing ecosystems of special value are not thereby destroyed.

3. *Exposed positions needing shelter whether from wind or sun.* This is equally important for the shelter of farmland and for habitation, where shelter may make all the difference between pleasant living and hard conditions.

4. *Derelict industrial land.* Trees are often the best means of reclamation as well as providing the best after-use in the provision of recreational forests.

5. *Town forests.* The creation of woodland for town recreation areas has everything to commend it (see page 136).

   It is a far more creative act of planning than the half-hearted areas of downtrodden fields which often form the bedraggled edge between town and country. As we have seen (page 138) forests have greater absorption capacity for crowds than open land, as well as the power to counteract pollution and deaden noise.

6. *Land cut up by development.* Many urban developments, notably motorways, leave strips and pockets of land disconnected with surrounding land uses. These are often put to the best use by tree planting. The trees give a visual unity to the fragmented scene and add a positive landscape value to what may otherwise be a non-landscape. They foster wildlife, and in the case of motorways, form linear nature reserves running right through the country. In these cases also their virtues of air purification and noise absorption are particularly valuable, considerably lessening the pollution effect of motorways on the surrounding land.

# The Visual Qualities of Forestry

Forests at one time formed an unbroken cover over large areas of the earth.

Gradually holes were carved in this cover for men's settlements and agriculture. These clearings have increased until in most countries where civilisation has been long established the pattern is reversed, showing either vast areas of bare ground or at the best building and agriculture within a sparse pattern of woodland.

In those lands where the denudation has gone furthest, the process should now be reversed and the tree cover increased. But what pattern will evolve from this new trend? The landscape planner must face this question and find an answer in positive terms.

We have seen what an important role trees have in urban life. Therefore, wherever there are cities, industries and dwellings, these should be set within a complex of trees—trees permeating the towns and thickening into the woodlands which will form the buffer and transition between urban settlements and open or agricultural country.

In the countryside the pattern will have infinite variations according to the topography, geology and climate of the region. In fertile agricultural country, the woodlands may be mainly in the form of shelter belts, forming a network over the country and thickening into larger woodlands on areas of poorer soils, on steep slopes, and on bleak uplands.

In a topography of hill and valley, the slopes may be wooded, sheltering the agricultural valley with open hilltops above the tree-line. The altitude of the timber line above which trees will not thrive varies according to latitude and wind exposure. In northern Britain it is about 530 m, in Switzerland and Germany it is far higher.

The relationship between the tree-line and the topography is obviously a deciding factor in the forest pattern. Where the tree-line is higher than the hills, it is usual to find a pattern of completely wooded hills and open valleys. In very exposed situations trees may grow only in the valleys. In arid lands they may only follow the water courses. On some of the foothills of the Himalayas in northern India, trees grow only on the northern faces. The patterns are endless and they reflect on one hand the natural condition of the sites, and on the other the special needs of the people inhabiting the land.

If these two factors are brought together, trees will contribute their maximum benefit to the environment, and will supply that sense of place, the individuality of different landscapes which we are in danger of losing.

In the proper use of this element of the landscape, the planner has a powerful tool to regenerate the environment. But to do this he has to appreciate the visual value not only of forests, but the whole tree-content of the landscape. To do this he must develop an objective and analytical approach.

The role of trees varies from one landscape to another In exposed areas, and typically in northern England, the wind-clipped shelter belts and small woodlands form solid clear-cut shapes, contrasting with the surrounding open ground. In the more sheltered South, the effect is more of a network of trees lying loosely over the landscape. This is the pattern which is being eroded in many districts by the loss of hedgerow trees.

In whatever formation the trees may grow, they provide a vital space-division in the view. In some of the east Midland counties great tracts of featureless and treeless country lack all sense of form. While adjacent to them the same relatively featureless topography is transformed by the hedgerows and spinneys which provide space containment and perspective.

The species of trees are as important a visual factor as

Figure 5.20   Scarps are often too steep and thin-soiled for agriculture; their afforestation makes a typical scarpland landscape. The trees prevent run-off and erosion and shelter the valleys.

(*Photo by courtesy of the Forestry Commission*)

their grouping and both factors influence each other.

The visual effect of a light network of trees, can only be attained by certain broadleaf species, including the elm, the ash and the oak, while conifers can be more easily accepted in the more solidly shaped patterns of the North. The argument between the use of conifers and broadleaf is often emotive, and should be coolly analysed. There are three visual factors, their shape, their texture and their seasonal colouring. The value of these in each particular landscape must be weighed. In Britain the value of the changing colour of deciduous trees is particularly high, because of the long duration of Spring and Autumn which provides a pageant of slowly changing colours over half the year.

The shape of trees, either singly or in groups, can be typical of certain landscapes, and has a rightness which should not be ignored. The Caledonian pine of the Highlands, the beech of the chalk downs are two examples which a planner should recognise as of equal, or greater, importance than a region's historic buildings. Unlike buildings they need, not just preservation, but renewal and continuity.

Figure 5.21   The exposed, rocky hilltop is afforested while farming continues in the more fertile and sheltered valley.

(*Photo by courtesy of the Forestry Commission*)

# Conclusions

Trees and woodlands are a vital element in landscape planning. In Britain, at least, they are not considered in a sufficiently positive manner.

A few trees or woodlands may be protected by a Tree Preservation Order, and occasionally planning approval for a building may be dependent on the planting of a tree screen. There is sometimes negative provision in that certain areas in national parks are placed in a category of open land on which no afforestation should take place.

But there is seldom an analysis of how land use and ecology will develop in an unplanted area, nor plans for the ultimate replacement of trees placed under Tree Preservation Orders. Nor is sufficient thought given to establishing new woodlands as a constructive part of the planning process.

To achieve positive action, the landscape survey and analysis (Chapter 2) should record the relevant facts, i.e.:

1. Existing trees and woodlands, their species, age, condition, present method of management. The function they serve (e.g. shelter, wildlife), their interference with present land use, if any. (This might apply to hedgerow trees in heavily timbered farmland.) Their visual contribution to the landscape.

2. Soils more suited to forest than agriculture;

3. Slopes, water courses, gathering grounds needing tree cover for protection;

4. Exposed areas needing wind shelter;

5. Visual features which could be improved by tree planting;

6. Derelict or degraded land which could be improved by tree cover.

The landscape plan should recommend the subsequent actions. This may include:

1. Afforestation of areas where this would achieve all or any of the following objectives:
Better land use;
Conservation of water;
Conservation of wildlife and other biotic factors;
Improvement of degraded soil;
Provision of woodland for recreation;
Visual improvement of the landscape.
The last listed is of particular value where an open landscape has been fragmented by workings or structures.

2. Remembering that a forest takes 20 to 30 years to gain the appearance of a woodland, the plan should look ahead and establish woodlands where future development, and particularly châlet or caravan development, may occur.
Similarly town forests should be established ahead of the development of new towns where this is possible. But existing towns should also be provided with their town forests.

3. Where the survey has revealed that trees, important in the landscape, are nearing maturity, new trees should be planted to perpetuate the landscape value. This is not always easy, as the young trees, unless they are shade-bearers, such as *Fagus* will have to be planted clear of the shade thrown by the mature trees. In some cases they can be planted on an adjacent piece of land, in other cases, selected mature trees may have to be felled to make space for the replacements. Avenues can be perpetuated by replacing trees gradually over the years, or even by taking out and replanting alternate trees. A policy of replacement must be put in hand at least 50 years before the original trees near the end of their life span.

4. Where existing trees are found to be genuinely incompatible with the land use, positions for at least an equivalent number of new trees should be found.

5. The landscape plan must specify the type of woodland to be planted, the species and the method of management.
It must be made clear whether it is to be economically viable as a timber resource, whether the timber value is to be subordinated to other uses, or whether timber value should be ignored. Where a large area is involved it will almost certainly need to be economically viable. In this case the steps necessary to make it acceptable both visually and for conservation, should be stated. If the timber is to do little more than pay maintenance costs, there will be more latitude in the species which can be chosen.

Two cases in which there will be virtually no timber consideration, will be nature reserves and town woodlands.

Nature reserves are most likely to be designated in old-established woodlands, and the plan should state that management is to be to this end, and will probably be undertaken by the Nature Conservancy Council or a Naturalists Trust.

The landscape plan should ensure that each type of woodland is of a viable size for its particular function and that the correct degree of maintenance will be available and financially possible. It has to be realised that no land, whether open or wooded, can be left to look after itself. Men have interfered so drastically with the ecology by, for instance, eliminating the wolf and introducing the grey squirrel, that some conscious control is necessary.

For this reason, trees and woodland must be incorporated into the plan with as much care and discrimination as housing or industrial development.

## References and Bibliography

5.1 CABORN, J. M., *Shelter Belts and Windbreaks*, Faber and Faber, London, 1965.
5.2 STEELE, R. C., *Wildlife Conservation of Woodlands*, HMSO, London, 1971.

COLVIN, B., *Land and Landscape*, John Murray, London, 1970.
CROWE, DAME SYLVIA, *The Landscape of Forests and Woods,* Forestry Commission, HMSO, London, 1979.
FRASER DARLING, SIR FRANK, 'The forest and the global environment', *Scottish Forestry*, **29**, 1, 1975.
HARVARD COLLEGE, *The Illustrated Account of Models Designed to Show the History and Silviculture of New England Forests,* Harvard College, Petersham, Mass., 1941.
HOLMES, G. D., WAREING, P. F. and HARLEY, J., 'A discussion on forests and forestry', *Philosophical Transactions*, Series B., **271**, 911, 1975, pp. 45–232.
MILES, R., *Forestry in the English Landscape*, Faber and Faber, London, 1967.
USDA FOREST SERVICE, *National Forest Landscape Management,* 2 Vols., US Government Printing Office, Washington DC, 1975, 1977.

CHAPTER SIX
# LEISURE PROVISION AND LANDSCAPE PLANNING
John Foster

GRAFHAM WATER, HUNTINGDONSHIRE. Sailing and fishing are
compatible recreational activities on a reservoir when they are
adequately controlled by the water authority

*(By courtesy of the Great Ouse Water Authority)*

# LEISURE PROVISION AND LANDSCAPE PLANNING

## Growth of Leisure

Leisure—the time available to us when the disciplines of work, sleep and other basic needs have been met—is a highly significant factor of life today. Despite the current situation of inflation in many countries, higher incomes, more free time, greater personal mobility and better education are all contributing to an increasing demand for outdoor recreational facilities.

The implications of this demand on the countryside are tremendous—conflicts with traditional rural land uses, congestion on country roads, overcrowded coasts, wilderness characteristics disappearing, sensitive flora and fauna at risk, and pollution of the air, water and soil are common occurrences. Is it possible, by careful planning and landscape design, to reduce or even eliminate some of these problems and to accommodate more recreation in the countryside without damaging its essential character and quality?

The Americans have taken a hard look at the future shape of outdoor recreation in their country (6.1). Their population, it is estimated, will double by the end of the century, but by then outdoor recreational demands are likely to have quadrupled. Here is a pointer to the future which must not go unheeded by other developed countries of the world. In Britain, action is imperative for, while the population may not be much greater by the year 2000, with an overall population density of more than two people per hectare (for England and Wales alone the figure is nearly four people) the country is already crowded by comparison with America.

## Early Developments

If today we take leisure for granted as an important and necessary part of life, we do not have to look far back into history to be reminded that, for all but the powerful and the rich, it was a luxury which could only rarely be enjoyed. While the hunting forests and the sporting estates of the wealthy indicate a highly developed interest in leisure activity in their day, they were enjoyed by only a tiny proportion of the population. True, the village greens and common land offered opportunity for the working man to spend leisure time out of doors, but the fact remains that he was often more concerned to use these for his farming interests than for recreation.

The effect of the Industrial Revolution in many European countries was to produce a new set of conditions—long hours in factories, child labour, bad housing and a whole range of social problems of a population moving from rural to urban life. In a sense it was the very magnitude of these problems which stirred national consciences and produced the first tentative steps towards the provision of recreation facilities and the time to enjoy them.

In Britain, initially the facilities were little more than the development of parks from common land and other open spaces close to towns, and the time available for recreation no more than the recognised annual religious festivals, until the four Bank Holidays were established in 1871 and later the weekly half-holiday.

As the railway system developed, mobility began to become a significant factor. People moved between towns and to inland and coast resorts in greater numbers than ever before, and the cheap excursion—a notable feature of rail travel from earliest times—opened up new horizons for many working families. While much of this movement was through countryside, most people went to towns rather than the countryside itself. This era saw the development of many of the major resorts which today are in difficulties because of the greater mobility produced by the motor car.

The countryside itself remained largely untouched by recreation, apart from an interest in hill walking, notably evident in the industrial cities of the north of England from which at weekends numbers of hardy walkers moved out to the high moorlands of the Pennines. The need to ensure that right of access was available was soon recognised and one of the oldest societies dedicated to this task—the Manchester Association for the Preservation of Ancient Footpaths—was founded as long ago as 1826.

The first national park in the world was established at Yellowstone in the United States in 1872. Its purpose was not so much to provide space for recreation—there was plenty of that in America—as consciously, to protect an area against the widespread inroads into the natural environment being made at the time by the pioneers engaged in opening up the country.

Other national parks followed, not only in the United States, but in Canada, New Zealand, Australia and other then developing countries, their objectives generally being, first, to conserve and, secondly, to provide for the enjoyment of the public. In Britain, a reflection of the Yellowstone idea came in 1884 when James Bryce, a one-time British Ambassador in Washington, promoted a Bill in Parliament to give the public right of access to mountain land in Scotland. Although his effort was unsuccessful, it was an important milestone in the development of a wider interest in the use of the countryside for leisure.

Parallel with this interest in recreation was the awakening recognition of the need to protect countryside against increasing attacks on its established character. Pressures were first evident around the expanding industrial towns and an early response, in Britain, was the establishment of the Commons, Open Spaces and Footpaths Preservation Society in 1865. However, it was in other European countries, notably Germany, Italy and Sweden, that legislation developed in the second half of the 19th century empowering municipalities to sort out some of their problems of housing and urban development, thereby giving some protection to surrounding countryside.

## Developments during the First Half of the 20th Century

In Britain, Ebenezer Howard, a Londoner who had spent part of his early life in the United States on the land, founded the garden city movement at the turn of the century, introducing the concept of new and self-contained towns, limited in size and population and protected by green belts, thus combining town and country advantages and conserving land values for public purposes. Letchworth, the first garden city, was founded in 1904, and many ideas developed from it have been embodied in new urban communities in many countries, including the post-1945 new towns in Britain.

The Housing and Town Planning Act 1909 gave statutory recognition to urban planning in Britain, but did nothing to ease the developing pressures on the countryside. Theoretically, the Town and Country Planning Act 1932 made planning control possible outside towns, although in fact the Restriction of Ribbon Development Act 1935 proved a rather more effective instrument in checking the outward sprawl of urban development at that time.

While statutory planning was dragging its feet in relation to the countryside, more people, with the freedom of the motor car at their disposal, were spending more of their leisure time there. From a mere 100,000 motor cars in Britain at the end of the First World War, car ownership had risen to 2 million by 1939. Walkers, too, were on the increase, helped in their interest by the creation of the Youth Hostels Association in 1930, and open conflicts with landowners were becoming common.

However, the National Trust for Places of Historic Interest or Natural Beauty, founded in 1895, was by now a well-established instrument in England and Wales* for the conservation and protection of important buildings and land by their acquisition and management. Many local preservation societies came together in 1926 and formed the Council for the Preservation (now Protection) of Rural England (CPRE). Primarily concerned about bad development in the countryside, the Council pressed with some success for the setting up of national parks to protect the most beautiful parts in England. An official report on national parks published in 1931 (6.2) might have been acted upon had the Governments at that time not had to turn their attention to the gathering clouds of war.

## After the Second World War

The post-1945 flood of legislation bore on its crest enactments of far-reaching importance to countryside and coast. The Town and Country Planning Acts of 1947 made planning mandatory throughout Britain and required county councils to prepare development plans for their areas (see page 159). However, the small scale (1:63,360) at which the development plan maps had to be produced was such that they were blunt instruments in relation to the countryside. They could, and did, establish Areas of Great Landscape, Historic and Scientific Value, but in practice the degree of protection given by this designation was not great.

The inter-war pressures of the CPRE and others bore fruit in 1949 when the National Parks and Access to the Countryside Act† was passed.

The National Parks Commission was set up and, over a period of six years, 10 national parks were established, covering about 9% (1,361,820 hectares) of the area of England and Wales. An eleventh national park was proposed in mid-

---

*The National Trust for Scotland was founded in 1931.

† There is no comparable legislation for national parks in Scotland.

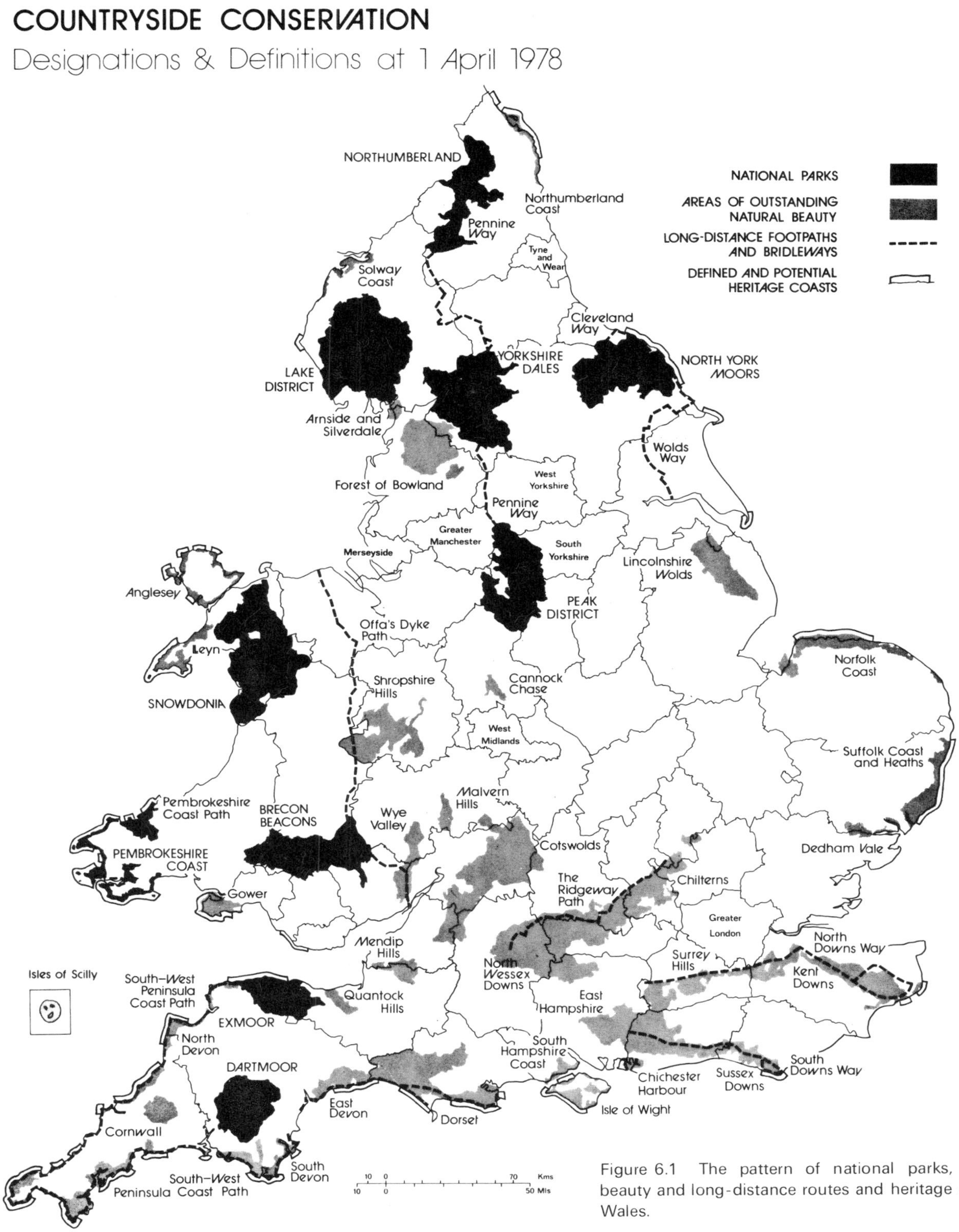

# COUNTRYSIDE CONSERVATION
## Designations & Definitions at 1 April 1978

NATIONAL PARKS

AREAS OF OUTSTANDING NATURAL BEAUTY

LONG-DISTANCE FOOTPATHS AND BRIDLEWAYS

DEFINED AND POTENTIAL HERITAGE COASTS

Figure 6.1   The pattern of national parks, areas of outstanding beauty and long-distance routes and heritage coasts for England and Wales.

Wales in 1972, but was not adopted. The same Act enabled the designation of areas of outstanding natural beauty, and by the end of 1977 there were 33 of these, covering a further 9·6% (1,447,500 hectares) of England and Wales (Figure 6.1). Long-distance routes were established, of which the Pennine Way is the longest and best known; again, by the end of 1977 there were nine such routes with a total length of 2528 km (6.3). In Scotland one long-distance route had been designated at the end of 1977—the West Highland Way—with a length of 147 km.

The Sports Council, set up in 1965, added its weight to the call for more physical recreation provision in the countryside as well as in the town. In 1967 the Government promoted a recreational role for waterways in a White

Paper. In the same year the Countryside (Scotland) Act was passed, with the Countryside Act (for England and Wales) following in 1968. These two Acts promoted the concept of country parks and made possible the provision, by local authorities, of a wide range of informal recreation facilities in the countryside, with some finance both to local authorities and private interests for this work.

The series of Town and Country Planning Acts of the late 1960s and early 1970s altered the basis for development plan preparation (see page 14). The overall development plan (structure plan) now deals only with major policy subjects, including communications, population and employment, and requires the formal approval of central Government. Thereafter local planning authorities can prepare—and themselves adopt—local plans. These are mainly of two kinds: district plans, involving medium-term periods where the timing of change is not readily predictable; and action area plans, where intensive change will be undertaken in the short term (see page 14). Taken in conjunction with recent reforms of local government, including in the case of Scotland a regional level of government, this new planning system offers a useful means of getting recreational needs and landscape policies identified and worked into a planned programme of development and conservation.

So much for the legislation which bears on leisure in the countryside today—what about the activities themselves? In 1965 a pilot national recreation study produced some useful indicators (6.4).

This survey put 'disposable' time—the time available for leisure—at between 40 and 50 hours on average per week. More than half of this time is taken up with activities in and around the home, such as gardening, do-it-yourself, reading and watching television. Of the remainder—leisure activities away from home—on average between 10 and 15% is spent in outdoor recreation, some of it in the countryside. This latter is the part of leisure with which we are mainly concerned here.

The range of activities undertaken within the countryside is wide, and many of the individual activities are increasing in scale. Pleasure motoring, according to the 1965 survey, is the activity most frequently indulged in and taking up most time.

The survey lists a number of activities which have increased in popularity. Swimming and fishing are at the top, with walking, camping, sailing and golf all following closely behind. Specialised activities too, such as rock climbing, caving, water-skiing and riding, have all gained in popularity in recent years and there has been an increasing interest in the study of natural history and archaeology in the countryside.

The factors of increased mobility, free time and disposable income in recent years have combined to increase interest in second homes in a number of countries, and these are now producing a whole series of new planning considerations and problems. In Sweden and Norway, where about one-fifth of all households are second-home owners, there are acute problems in places (particularly on the coastline) arising from development which is visually unsympathetic to its surroundings and which poses severe servicing and public health burdens. In the United Kingdom, on the other hand, where second-home owners represent only about 3% of all households, most of these problems lie in the future, and there is opportunity to plan ahead thoughtfully and to good standards (6.5). An important general point about second homes is that they transfer to new locations—sometimes quite remote—not only recreational activities which might otherwise have taken place much nearer home, but also some leisure-time activities normally associated directly with the first home, such as gardening, and house care and maintenance.

### Leisure and Landscape

The effect on the landscape of all this leisure activity is inevitably of increasing significance. The intention of this chapter is to examine leisure in relation to land as a resource—in four main situations—on the urban fringe, in the wider countryside, in remote areas and on the coast. First, however, we shall look at the effects or impacts—good and bad—of leisure activities on the landscape and at some of the reasons why we need to plan positively for leisure in relation to the landscape.

# Impacts of Leisure

Leisure activities can affect the countryside in a number of different ways. The landscape—in a visual sense—can be altered by development, its ecology can be changed, traditional social systems can be radically altered by an influx of visitors, and local economic conditions can quickly vary with changing leisure habits.

In terms of their effect on the countryside, some of these impacts are good and some are bad. What is important is to be able to anticipate them in planning for leisure, so that those which have a beneficial effect can be exploited and those which would be detrimental can be avoided or minimised. In this way leisure planning can make its most effective contribution within the broader framework of land use planning.

### Visual Impacts

We must distinguish at once between badly sited or designed development in the countryside, which has an adverse effect on the enjoyment of the prospect to visitors, and the ill effects on the quality of scene arising from over-use by visitors themselves.

Planning authorities have to take into account a number of considerations when deciding whether or not to approve particular proposals for development. Landscape quality should be one of these considerations, but there will be others, including employment opportunities, traffic flows, availability of services and so on. In national parks and other areas designated for special protection of their scenic character, landscape considerations may take precedence; elsewhere they may be felt to be of relatively less importance. Achieving the right balance is difficult, but could be helped by two things. The first is the development of environmental impact assessment techniques and the use of landscape assessment and classification methods (Chapters 2 and 3), and the second is the inclusion of countryside recreation as a significant element in the statutory land use planning process.

A third factor which is becoming increasingly important is the attitude of the general public. As more people use the countryside in their leisure time, public support for conservation of fine scenery—and the improvement of degraded landscapes too—is likely to increase. This is a benefit of the leisure use of the countryside which has yet to be appreciated and exploited.

The adverse effect which visitors themselves can have on countryside manifests itself in various ways. Visitor provisions, such as hotels, caravan and camping sites, marinas and the like, may be badly sited in relation to landscape interests or well sited but badly designed (or both). Over-use or careless use of the countryside can show itself in scars of worn vegetation, erosion channels, conspicuously parked cars and derelict buildings. In remote areas, where the quality of the recreation experience lies in the feeling of being alone, the presence of too many people may even be felt to be detrimental. The solutions to these particular problems lie in the preparation and the implementation of adequate recreation plans and the proper management of recreation provision thereafter, including limitations on use where this is necessary.

Leisure can have beneficial impacts on landscape too. Well designed development may, on occasions, enhance a scene, or the demand for weekend cottages may result in previously derelict buildings being rehabilitated and their surroundings tidied up.

## Ecological Impacts

Some leisure activities can produce far-reaching changes in the ecological system. In planning for recreational use it is essential to be able to identify situations where the eco-system is resilient and can stand up to hard wear, and where it is sensitive and would break down easily. We must also try to assess how much pressure a given area will withstand, so that over-use can be avoided by planning diversions and alternatives.

Our concern here is primarily with carrying capacity in the physical sense. At one end of the scale are the hard rocks

Figure 6.2   Severe damage to soft coastal grassland (traditionally used for grazing) arising from uncontrolled use as a caravan and camping site during the summer months. Remedial action is now being taken here to prevent the grass disappearing and the sand beach extending over the whole area.

*(Photo: John Foster)*

Figure 6.3   Gullane, East Lothian. The foredune is being reformed using brushwood to provide sheltered embayments in which marram grass has been planted. Access through the foredune is restricted to the point where the black diamond on the post is located.

*(Photo by courtesy of East Lothian Planning Department)*

Figure 6.4   Aerial view of coast showing extensive re-establishment of the foredune coupled with planting of the open sand area behind.

*(Photo by courtesy of East Lothian Planning Department)*

of parts of the coast and mountain country. At the other end are the soft coastal dunes (Figure 6.2) and margins of inland lakes and rivers where even relatively light recreation use can reduce stability very quickly. Between these extremes lie many types of countryside and coast where erosion and deterioration may be started by varying degrees of recreational use.

Practical experience in the rehabilitation and management of soft countryside and coast is now considerable, and useful work is being done in a number of places in Britain, notably in some of the dune areas of the east coast (6.6). Prevention is better than cure, however, and techniques for assessing the sensitivity of soft countryside and coast are being explored so that positive policies for development (or non-development) and management can be worked out in advance of recreation pressures. For example, extensive studies of the beaches of the north-west Highlands and Islands of Scotland (6.7) have been carried out for the Countryside Commission for Scotland to guide the preparation of recreation development and management plans for this still relatively remote part of Britain. The problems of recreational pressures on footpaths in various kinds of situations have also been studied, and practical guidance is available on the management of existing paths and the development of new ones (6.8).

Leisure activities may upset important ecological systems by destroying flora through trampling and driving away sensitive wildlife. This not only may adversely affect conservation interests, but also may reduce important research possibilities. In Britain the Nature Conservancy Council, through its system of national nature reserves and sites of special scientific interest, has secured useful protection for important habitats, and typical examples of a range of physiographical conditions. However, this protection cannot be complete either as to what is included or as to the degree of protection afforded, and valuable work is also being done by voluntary bodies such as the County Naturalists Trusts in England and Wales and the Scottish Wildlife Trust.

The developing public interest in conservation, manifest in voluntary bodies like these Trusts, perhaps offers one of the best prospects for safeguarding ecological interests in the future. As more people use more of their leisure time in studying nature, so their perception will increase and their demands for the proper conservation and management of land are likely to become more insistent and effective.

### Social Impacts

More people using countryside and coast for leisure activities can have significant consequences on established social structures. On the one hand the potential prosperity arising from more visitors is an opportunity to be used to advantage; on the other this influx can change radically the social character of a place and, unless great care is taken, submerge one of the very attributes which made it so attractive in the first instance.

On the credit side there are the new employment opportunities created in servicing visitor interests, ranging from the provision of accommodation to the manufacture and sale of local craft goods. Where leisure activities increase the size of the resident population in a community it may become possible to provide social and other services which were not previously economic. This is particularly important in relatively isolated communities where the re-establishment of a local bus or rail link may hold people who would otherwise leave the district for good.

On the debit side new patterns of holidays and leisure activity, including the demand for self-service accommodation rather than fully serviced hotels and boarding houses so popular in the past, may adversely affect established resorts and reduce employment opportunity in them. The social problems arising from this sort of situation have been particularly acute in the traditional coastal and inland resorts; their solution is no easy matter and trying to attract light industry to provide alternative employment is all too seldom a real answer.

The developing popularity of second homes is also impor-

Figure 6.5   A traditional country cottage near Ruthin, Denbighshire, reconditioned and now used as a second home.

(*Photo by courtesy of Denbighshire County Planning Department*)

Figure 6.6   Purpose-built second home in the countryside, sympathetic in form and colour and texture of external materials to local traditional building.

(*Photo by courtesy of Denbighshire County Planning Department*)

tant. While the acquisition of empty property and its subsequent improvement can be a definite advantage in a declining community, on occasions competition between local people and would-be second-home owners (often with deeper pockets) can effectively prevent the former from buying houses for their own needs. Unless a local housing authority is alive to this, and sympathetic, serious social problems may develop. Some communities in remote areas have now reached the stage where so many of the existing dwellings are in second-home use that the resident population remaining simply can no longer support all-year-round community services and, as these are progressively withdrawn, so more local people leave the district.

### Economic Impacts

Leisure is an important factor today in the economy of most countries, and certainly this is so of Britain. Tourism is a significant source of foreign exchange, and provides new economic opportunities for many local communities previously stagnating or declining. Day recreational activities, too, are producing economic opportunities as people become more willing to pay for facilities in the countryside. The success of the opening of many castles and famous gardens is just one example of this.

In providing facilities for leisure—whether for tourism or day recreation—there is frequently an important economic problem to be faced. While the private sector can often shoulder the capital cost of providing the facilities, whether they be hotels, mountain transport systems, or game parks, the cost of the essential infrastructure, such as access roads and services, may be considerable and may have to be met out of public funds. As leisure activities increase, public money may also be needed to mitigate the damage done to established rural interests by increased pressure of visitor use, and the likely cost of preventing damage arising from all the impacts already discussed needs to be taken into account at the planning stage.

## Planning for Leisure

Recreation is any pursuit we engage upon during our leisure time, other than those to which we are normally highly committed, such as religion, politics or further education (6.9). The last thing we want is to be told what to do with our leisure time.

However, we have already seen that recreation has significant impacts on countryside and coast, and that an important body of legislation bearing on it has developed in recent years. The planning we are concerned with is not for the purpose of directing the use of leisure time, but rather is for anticipating the scale and character of recreation

Figure 6.7   Heavy and indiscriminate car parking is frequently increased when there is the added attraction of the recreational use of water.

(*Photo by courtesy of the Peak Park Planning Board*)

demands, relating these to available resources and ensuring that those resources are not impaired.

Planning must involve provision in the right place and at an adequate scale to absorb people into the countryside without detriment to it, and must be able to recognise optimum conditions where diversion rather than further provision is the right course. Recreation facilities today can cost a great deal—and this is often public money—so planning must also concern itself with securing the most effective cost-benefit situation and the best integration with other demands on resources.

Let us look briefly now at the main factors which affect demand for recreation and the supply of resources, and consider how they relate to each other in planning for leisure.

### Demand Factors

The time available for leisure activity influences demand and in Britain, as in many other countries, the number of hours worked per week (excluding overtime) continues to decrease. Also relevant is the fact that the working week is now concentrated within five days, making longer recreation trips a regular possibility. The prospect of greater automation may soon make the four-day week a reality for many people. Additionally, annual holidays, now generally with pay, have become longer, making travel further afield practicable, and second and third holidays away from home more common. Despite inflation, real income has also risen and most people spend part of it in satisfying leisure interests, either directly on holidays away from home or indirectly in acquiring and learning how to use sometimes highly sophisticated recreation equipment. Economic security in retirement, and earlier retirement coupled with a longer life span, are further increasing leisure activity possibilities for more and more people.

With over 14 million private cars in Britain in 1977 and

Figure 6.8  Cars are a particular problem in narrow streets not designed for motor traffic, as here at Robin Hood's Bay on the Yorkshire coast.

(*Photo : John Foster*)

the likelihood of there being about 24 million by the year 2000 (allowing for increases in fuel and other costs), car ownership is undoubtedly one of the most significant factors to be taken into account. The motor car is more than just a means of seeing the countryside, however, and is increasingly being used as a means of transport to get to specific locations for other activities. In fact it has set up a whole range of new demands on the countryside by making it possible to carry out recreational activities in completely fresh and sometimes remote and highly unlikely locations.

Today there is a noticeable movement towards individual participation in recreational activities and away from interest in mass spectator sports, recently so popular. More people, with the benefit of better education, want to do more things themselves rather than watch others doing them, and this inevitably means greater pressure for land for recreational purposes.

Beyond this, recreation demand is affected by a range of interacting factors related to occupation and social class, deriving from the way people live in various social groupings and the recreational interests they are drawn to on that account. Allied to this is the change in pattern of activity during

life—the mobility of single status, the ties of marriage in its early stages of raising a family, the greater mobility of middle life (often with the benefit of higher income) and finally the return in old age to relatively restricted movement.

## Supply Factors

Here we are concerned with the range of natural and man-made resources which are available for recreation, either completely or in association with other land uses such as farming, forestry and industry (see Chapters 4, 5 and 8). We need first to identify what are the physical resources within any given area and then to classify them in terms of their character and quality, and their capability for taking recreation use, either alone or in association with other uses.

It is not enough, however, simply to catalogue the nature and capability of resources and assume that this represents the supply side of the equation. Other factors affect supply—for instance, location of resources relative to demand, degree of accessibility, and the cost of using facilities. A remote natural lake, accessible along a narrow rough track, with expensive launching charges may well be much less used for sailing than a flooded gravel pit, adjoining a convenient main road, where launching is free.

If recreation development is not to reduce the quality of the environment, the supply of resources will also be conditioned by the factor of carrying capacity (see also page 27). This is simply the level of recreational use an area can sustain without an unacceptable degree of deterioration of the character and quality of the recreational experience or related land uses. The carrying capacity is conditioned by the four main types of impact already described—visual, ecological, social and economic. The fourth type—economic capacity—arises where an area also has a use other than recreation, maximum capacity being reached when damage to the non-recreational activity becomes economically unacceptable from a management point of view.

Where there exists a hierarchy of designated areas at national, regional and local levels this will affect the supply of recreation resources. Recreation provision in national parks or areas of outstanding natural beauty (in England and Wales) will be limited to that which is sympathetic in scale and character to their outstanding landscape qualities. Similarly, in the forest parks of the Forestry Commission recreation must fit in with timber production, and in some national nature reserves minimal access for recreation may be the appropriate policy in order adequately to protect their particular scientific interest.

## Research

Being able to identify and, where appropriate, quantify factors of demand and supply is an important step in planning for leisure activities, but it is not enough in itself. There is an inter-action between these factors which must be taken into account and, in the wider context of country planning, the effect of recreation activity on other land uses must also be assessed.

Until quite recently there has been all too little research in the recreation field. However, public bodies, universities and individual researchers are now making up for lost time. In Britain progress has been helped by the Countryside Recreation Research Advisory Group established in 1968 and by the work of the Countryside Commission in the preparation and publication of its Research Register (6.10).

Of the studies undertaken in the mid-1960s, two were particularly useful attempts to bring together and analyse the relevant factors of demand and supply in relation to a specific area, and to produce a credible planning policy therefrom. The first was a study of the County of Donegal undertaken for An Foras Forbartha by a specially appointed team of investigators (6.11). This tried, possibly for the first time, to measure the capacity of different elements of countryside and coast to take human use without damage. Inevitably some of the measurements had a subjective base and were criticised for this, but the study nevertheless opened up a new avenue which later researchers have developed. The study also explored the idea of posing options for action and development, and formulated a type of budget to show the impact of each option, not only on the financial and human resources, but on the land resources too.

The other study—of the East Hampshire Area of Outstanding Natural Beauty (see pages 39 and 72) by a combined team from central and local government agencies (6.12)—was more wide-ranging. It sought to identify types of land uses and methods of management and to record their inter-relationships as a basis for securing the maximum fulfilment of demand on the countryside compatible with other demands and in accord with national and regional policies. The study was time-consuming and hardly a practical proposition for use other than in an area with specially difficult planning problems. To widen this experience and in search of ways of simplifying methodology, the Countryside Commission initiated a similar study in 1969 for the Sherwood Forest area (in collaboration with Nottinghamshire County Council) (6.13), and more recently a comparable study in the South Pennine Uplands (6.14).

In the early 1970s other kinds of research were initiated in Scotland in an effort to look more generally at planning for recreation, with the importance of resource conservation much in mind. Two studies were sponsored jointly by a group of national agencies with a common interest in tourism and recreation. These were the Tourism and Recreation Inventory Package (TRIP) and the Scottish Tourism and Recreation Study (STARS). The former is essentially a computer data bank system for recording relevant physical resources, not only their presence but, where possible, their capacity and constraints on their use and development for recreation (6.15). The second project is concerned with the scale, nature and geography of recreational demand, and its results are derived from a national interview survey undertaken in 1973 (6.16).

These two studies, valuable though they are, were not specifically designed to link the supply/demand equation and a further major research project was undertaken, called the Scottish Tourism and Recreation Planning Studies (STARPS). This involved first the collection and marshalling of data and the formulation of national policy ideas; then the preparation of policies for tourism and recreation for each of the 12 regional and island authorities in Scotland and steps to secure these policies as significant elements in the relevant structure plan strategies (6.17).

It is hoped that these Scottish studies, along with other research going on elsewhere, will produce techniques for a system which can be used over a wide range of geographical situations, bringing together supply-and-demand considerations and establishing alternative planning solutions, which have regard both for local resource interests and existing land uses and for national policy thinking. The application of systems analysis can have a useful part to play in this, as has been successfully done in the systems model (RECSYS) set up by the Michigan Departments of Conservation and Commerce in conjunction with the Michigan State University (6.18). This model links the three basic elements of origin, destination and inter-connection to resource inventories, visitor origins and statistics of use and, by the application of attraction indices, predicts new patterns of demand.

A few years ago a procedure was worked out in the United States for assessing the impact of specific major developments on their environment (6.19). The analysis is made with a matrix which sets out on one axis the actions which produce environmental impact and on the other the existing environmental conditions. This has the advantage of separating off factual information on the magnitude of each type of impact from the more subjective evaluation of the relative importance of the impact, thus making possible a more meaningful overall assessment of the environmental effect of a particular development proposal. Acceptance of the idea of environmental impact analysis has gained ground in Britain since the recent publication of a Government report on the subject (6.20), and an official manual prepared by Aberdeen University for the guidance of local authorities and others (6.21) (see Chapter 3).

## A Recreation Planning System

In Britain, as in many countries, the recreational use of countryside and coast is increasing significantly. There is now a body of legislation—albeit not perfect—bearing on the planning and provision of recreational facilities, and expertise is developing fast in the use of land and water resources in relation to demands on them.

The aim now must be to develop a workable and adequate recreational system, like that which already exists in the Netherlands, whereby the best overall range of recreational provision can be made, at a scale adequate to meet demands, with a maximum co-ordination of public and private interests, a minimum of conflict with other land uses, and a high standard of landscape design throughout. This system must be flexible enough to take account of future changes in the pattern of recreational demand and land use, and also be capable of being integrated with other land uses.

The kind of situation which exists in Britain is common to many countries and presupposes positive and continuing commitments at national, regional and local levels of the public sector. Central Government has a responsibility to produce a broad national strategy for locating the main elements of recreation provision in relation to population, communications and landscape quality. Authorities at the regional level have the responsibility of developing positive recreational strategies for their areas which will both fit in with the national planning level and, at the same time, provide a practical framework into which local authorities can fit smaller-scale recreational provisions, such as country parks, picnic sites and footpath networks. Authorities at the local level have a particularly important responsibility in drawing together the major national and regional elements of recreational provision by linking and complementing these on the ground so that the overall pattern can best meet the scale and diversity of demands on it.

Provision for the recreational use of the countryside must therefore be an important element in its own right in the statutory planning system of any country. In the context of the British system, structure plans must include a broad strategy for recreational use appropriate in character and scale to the nature of the area and the anticipated demands on it, incorporating major designated areas such as national parks and forest parks, and making proposals for major new areas and the main elements of linear networks such as long-distance routes. Local plans must further develop the recreational strategies in terms of a specific land use pattern related closely to the availability of recreational resources and the feasibility of developing them. Action plans can then further refine the pattern by relating the proposals to a time programme for implementation.

While we are concerned here primarily with techniques for planning for recreation, management after provision must also be adequately anticipated at the planning stage. It is important to ensure that, in planning for recreation, situations are not allowed to arise which will pose insuperable management problems later.

Adequate regard to capacity at the planning and design stages can reduce a whole range of potential management difficulties. The choice of sites for recreational development (away from scenically or scientifically sensitive areas) which will not set up difficult traffic situations will also help towards smooth management. Assurance of the practicability of providing adequate landscaping of the right kind is important, too—there is no point in planning a caravan park behind an open beach on the basis of landscaping the site extensively when in fact the climate will make the successful planting and management of trees impossible.

# Leisure on the Urban Fringe

Although we are not strictly concerned with the urban situation, the point is relevant that the quality of town environment affects people's attitude towards the countryside. If townspeople live in well-planned urban surroundings, their decisions to visit countryside or coast are more likely to be consciously taken with a purpose in mind rather than simply as a means of escape.

But however satisfying the urban scene, people will increasingly want to move out of it for a variety of leisure activities. For brief visits their first interest will be in the countryside lying immediately beyond the edge of the town. The outer limit of this will vary from place to place, depending on the physical character of the countryside and of the town itself, but for our purposes it is convenient to think of urban fringe countryside as that which can be used for recreation on a half-day or evening visit—not more than say about half an hour's driving from the town on local roads.

Where the boundary of town development is well defined or sharply cut off, it is possible to be in countryside quickly, but where a town straggles out through suburban sprawl the feeling of being in countryside may not be achieved for some distance. In the latter situation farming may be fighting a losing battle against urban pressures and this urban/rural fringe may be a particularly depressing place in consequence.

## Nature of Activities

Recreation and sports grounds are a common feature on the periphery of many towns and cities and in the green belt land close to some major cities. Sometimes they are run by public bodies, including education authorities, and sometimes by industrial and commercial organisations for their own workers. They provide facilities for a wide range of activities—football, volleyball, hockey, tennis, bowls, archery, and track and field athletics—and, together with their pavilions and car parks, are often a significant category of land use. Golf courses, too, take up substantial areas of land near towns, providing their users with a feeling of being in the countryside while still near home.

Although spectator sports do not play such an important part in leisure today, a few—such as stock car racing and go-karting—are good business and their promotion close to major towns offers a fair prospect of commercial success. There are also long-established motor racing circuits and horse racing tracks still doing well close to some towns.

The existence of small lakes or reservoirs, or of canals or rivers close to towns makes possible a further range of recreational activities. Sailing, rowing and canoeing are popular, power-boating and water-skiing are on the increase and—most important of all in terms of numbers—is

Figure 6.9    Some specialist recreational interests require space; flying model aircraft on Epsom Downs.

(*Photo: John Foster*)

fishing. Competition for the recreational use of the water is nowhere greater than near urban centres, with the added complication that some of these activities simply do not get on together.

Sport, because it is organised, can often compete more successfully than informal recreation activities for the land it needs on the urban fringe. Horse riding and walking require space on open land or the continuity of tracks. More specialist interests, such as flying model aircraft or nature study, also need open country. Even picnicking cannot really be enjoyed without space, and a place to leave the car safely off the road.

The pressure of demand for recreational land and water on the urban fringe is heavy and its diversity may well be greater than in the wider countryside. This situation offers opportunities for developing and applying landscape planning and management techniques which will not only increase the recreation potential of urban fringe countryside but also improve its environmental quality as a setting for the town.

## Strategy Considerations

Two main problems arise in relation to recreation in urban fringe countryside: the first between recreation and other established land uses, mainly farming; and the second within recreation itself between incompatible activities.

In fitting recreation in with other land uses it is important at the outset to establish the character and extent of existing farming activities. If farming is dominant and thriving, there is much to be said for securing its interests and fitting recreation activities around it so that it can continue to thrive. Alternatively, if farming is struggling, either because of the fragmentation of holdings by roads and other development or because of the pressure of people trespassing, a deliberate policy of cutting back on farming in

favour of recreational and other urban fringe activities may be preferable (see page 110).

A policy of retaining farming as the dominant use would be likely to strengthen existing landscape character, whereas recreation as the dominant use could result in the development of new landscapes, particularly if there is derelict land. In urban fringe countryside one policy may be appropriate in one place and a different one in another. What is important is that each segment (or area) around a town is significant enough in scale to be able to apply to it an effective policy of design and management.

Where farming can be successfully retained there may still be pressure from people wanting to use parts of the land in their leisure time. If farming is to survive in these areas, adequate and convenient recreation space must be provided elsewhere, and the roads through the farmed areas designed to encourage people to keep moving on to those places.

Where recreation is the dominant land use, the extent of landscape planning opportunities will depend much on existing character. If this is good—for instance, established parkland—it should be retained in the new pattern of recreational use, possibly developing the open land for sports activity where it is flat enough, and elsewhere promoting access for informal recreation. Parkland and woodland belts can provide a useful basic pattern for separating off recreational uses that are visually incompatible, for instance spectator sports from picnicking or fishing. New planting can help to create a series of distinctive areas, each with its own character in sympathy with the kind of activity to be carried on in it and pleasant in its own individual way.

Where this sort of recreation-dominated countryside contains a mixture of public recreational areas (e.g. commons) and areas developed for private recreation (e.g. works sports grounds), an adequate network of access between the former must be developed if trespass is to be avoided on the latter. Opportunities include footpaths and riding tracks along river and canal banks and through woodland strips, and picnic sites where there are good viewpoints or particularly attractive vistas. More people today are using cars to get to their particular recreational interests and adequate road access to and within these areas is essential, with sufficient car parks provided either in secluded locations or well landscaped.

Derelict land of many different kinds exists close to towns, ranging from run-down farmland, through a variety of types of factory dereliction to the spoil tips and holes of past mineral operations. This offers a particularly valuable reserve of land for recreational development and an opportunity to achieve the distinctive 'green-urban' landscape which Nan Fairbrother saw as the solution to the present drabness of so much countryside around towns (6.22).

Turning now to the second main strategy problem, that within recreation itself between incompatible activities— this can be minimised by using features such as woodlands to separate off different uses from one another. Natural contours can also help, and the making of new landforms from heaps and holes is well worth while. These devices can be used to reduce noise as well as eliminate view, although with some organised sports like stock car racing, unless the use is very infrequent, relative isolation may be the only satisfactory solution. Many spectators in any case do not have much awareness of the quality of their surroundings, nor is this particularly necessary to their enjoyment. While this is not an argument for putting these activities in rural slums, it allows more freedom to locate them without harm in areas of relatively low scenic quality.

Another problem is that of under-use of recreational facilities. Education authority playing fields are an example of this, and their use by other organisations out of school hours or at holiday times could make a useful contribution towards satisfying demand under pressure conditions on the urban fringe. Golf courses, too, offer possibilities of greater use by the provision of footpaths through them, at no loss to the efficiency of their primary purpose.

## Providing Comprehensively

In the face of the increasing scale of recreational activity close to major towns and cities, demand needs to be met comprehensively, rather than simply at locations where the chance occurs for a public authority to acquire land or where a private operator sees a commercial opportunity. This is becoming increasingly important as rising fuel costs tend to reduce the average length of recreational trips and,

in consequence, to increase still further pressure for recreational provision close to home and, where possible, served by public transport.

The Lee Valley Regional Park project (6.23), extending for 37 km from north London out into rural Hertfordshire, is a good example of the co-operative development, by three county councils, of a continuous linear park from mainly run-down land, providing for a wide variety of recreational activities. The overall concept is a number of wide-ranging sports and recreation centres convenient to urban concentrations, with areas of quieter activity between them, the whole linked together by the continuity of the river.

This is also the theme of the Tyne Recreation Study (6.24), which proposes for a length of about 23 km of the Lower Tyne, centred on Newcastle, three major parkland areas comprising a countryside park, a water park and a city exhibition park, all linked together by a continuous open space and footpath system. The project emphasises the river corridor as a landscape entity and envisages a significant upgrading of environmental quality by removing dereliction and reducing river and atmospheric pollution. Successful work of this kind has already been done in several countries, for instance the Delaware Waterfront project and the Rotterdam and Cologne waterfront recreation developments.

In the older coalfields of the north of England and of Scotland, the past dereliction of mining tips and subsidence areas has been successfully converted into recreational and amenity areas, sometimes combining both land and water

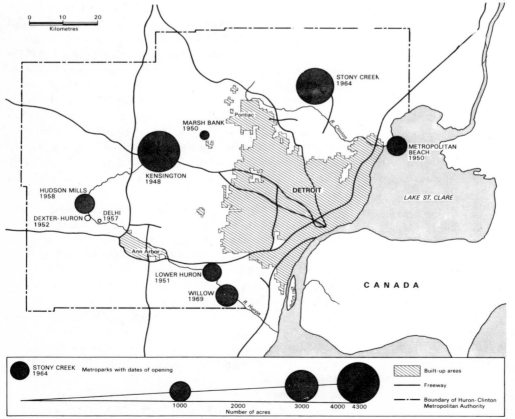

Figure 6.10   The park scheme of the Huron-Clinton Metropolitan Authority demonstrates useful co-operative action by five major public authorities to provide a viable pattern of open spaces on a regional scale, well related through the freeway system to the needs of the main urban concentrations of Greater Detroit.

(From *Land and Leisure* by J. Alan Patmore, with the permission of the publishers, David and Charles. Data supplied by the Huron-Clinton Metropolitan Authority)

activities as at Strathclyde and Lochore Meadows (Fife) Country Parks, which have been converted from derelict and dangerous areas into pleasant and useful recreation parks by the local authorities during the past decade.

Comprehensive planning and provision of the kind needed is well demonstrated in the park system of the Huron-Clinton Metropolitan Authority in Detroit (6.25) which was set up in 1940 by the five major public authorities in the greater Detroit area (Figure 6.10). The system of parks is linked to the freeway system and they are so distributed that there is one within easy reach of all residents. Attractive river valley locations have been used where possible and facilities range from simple picnic provision to sophisticated marina development; nature centres and trails have been provided to stimulate a positive interest in nature study and conservation. The nine parks vary in size from about 80 to 1700 hectares and together record over 6 million visits a year.

This comprehensive provision for countryside recreation on the urban fringe has its counterparts in Europe in the town forest lands adjacent to cities such as Stuttgart, Brussels and Amsterdam (see page 136). In Britain the makings of such a system already exist around a number of major urban areas. The commons and significant open spaces, like Epping Forest, on the periphery of the Greater London area, coupled with projects such as the Lee Valley Regional Park and the new country parks, could readily be developed into one integrated recreational system. Not only is provision planned on this wider geographical basis more likely to satisfy demand adequately close to town, but it is also capable of helping to draw off some pressures from the wider countryside which may be less able to withstand the heavy recreational use it would otherwise get.

# Leisure in the Wider Countryside

Here we are concerned with the widely ranging countryside which stretches from the outer limit of the urban fringe to the remote mountain and hill land. In Britain, as in many other European countries, it carries most of the farmland and a good deal of the woodland, and increasingly is coming under pressure from urban populations who also see it as their playground. In small heavily populated countries such as Britain, the pressure on the wider countryside for recreational use is frequent as well as heavy, since much of it derives from day and weekend visitation rather than holiday use from distant towns and cities.

While farming and forestry in the immediate future are likely to take precedence, with other uses (including recreation) being fitted in to the established pattern, in the longer term this may not be so. The European Economic Community and the development of new techniques of food production (see Chapter 4) may reduce the need for land for farming in the future. Fiscal changes too, such as capital transfer tax and the possible wealth tax in Britain, may result in new land management policies flowing from the break-up of major estates and large single landholdings.

In the face of the increasing demand for outdoor recreation, reductions in the needs of traditional land uses and new ideas for management of land will potentially offer an opportunity to develop new uses and management techniques. If we want the established characteristics of the wider countryside to be retained in the future as desirable attributes, the changes will require to be wrought with great care. On the other hand, where change is acceptable, there will be opportunities for developing exciting new landscapes.

## Nature of Activities

Demands on the wider countryside for recreation, like those in the urban fringe, vary greatly in range, character and scale. Some are similar, but the general emphasis is away from sports activities (other than traditional rural sports such as hunting and shooting) towards informal recreation, both active and passive.

Some active recreation, like walking, cycling and riding, requires access either along tracks or over open stretches of countryside. Other activities, including rock climbing, fishing and boating, produce more localised demands, which can be heavy and can raise incidental problems of access through adjoining land.

Passive recreation for most people means motoring for pleasure to enjoy the general countryside scene and to stop periodically at vantage points and places of interest. The motorists' needs are for adequate roads, parking space at beauty spots and land for picnicking. However, these needs have significant peak-period characteristics and can produce serious problems of trespass, over-use and sometimes mis-use of land. Indeed the point is relevant that the freedom of the motor car to move about the countryside will have to be curbed in the future, as is already the pattern in towns and cities.

Although much recreation in the wider countryside is on a day-use basis, either by residents of nearby towns or by holidaymakers driving out from established resorts, recreation involving an overnight use is nevertheless a significant element. Tented camping, caravanning and hostelling all make demands on land, both for accommodation and access. While, as was mentioned earlier, the demand for second homes is at present being met to some extent by rehabilitating existing cottages in villages and converting barns and similar buildings in the countryside, substantial areas for new second-home settlements in open country will soon be needed.

Tourists and holidaymakers in transit pass through the wider countryside on main roads en route for their destinations. Their basic needs are relatively limited—mainly roadside reception facilities with lavatories, picnic accommodation and rest areas away from the noise of traffic. If their movement is at a leisurely pace, they will use the other facilities for countryside recreation which already exist for the benefit of day visitors, just as the latter will use roadside reception facilities provided for long-distance travellers if this is convenient for them.

## Strategy Considerations

Before a planning authority can determine a strategy for developing recreation in the wider countryside, the existing pattern of land use needs to be established and its economic condition assessed. From this can broadly be determined the character and scale of recreational activity which can be grafted on to the existing land use pattern without adversely affecting its economic future or damaging its environmental quality. Such a fundamental examination would also show where recreation provision might positively improve a situation economically or environmentally.

The extent and location of resources of specific recreational value need to be mapped, including water in lakes, reservoirs, rivers and canals, open country and common land, recognised places of interest, viewpoints, footpaths and places with potential for specialised activities like rock climbing and caving. The degree and convenience of existing access to these areas should be recorded, both from the nearby towns and from the public highways to the sites themselves. The extent to which the resources are already used, and whether or not with difficulty, needs also to be related to the scale of demand.

From basic information about the resources, their availability and extent of use, and the demand for them a recreation planning strategy for an area, which will protect existing land uses and the quality of the environment, can then be developed.

Provision for active recreationists will be conditioned by the availability of the particular resources they need—water space for sailors, rock faces for climbers and so on—and planning must be directed to developing or extending their use with the minimum effect on adjoining land uses.

Visitors bent on passive recreation raise a different range of problems, not least because of their significantly greater numbers, and providing for them must inevitably be a major preoccupation in planning for recreation. While these visitors are anxious to see pleasant countryside, fortunately they seldom want to do this in complete isolation from their fellow men. This makes possible the adoption of a policy of moderate concentration into planned and adequately equipped attraction areas, and avoids the need for wide dispersal over farmland, with the consequential risk of trespass and damage.

An overall strategy for recreation provision in an area has therefore two main aspects; first, developing the resources of the area for the active recreationists and, secondly,

providing moderately concentrated facilities for passive visitors. In the first case the amount of the resources is finite unless, say, a new reservoir is built on which sailing or fishing can be developed. In the latter case provision may be extended as required provided this can be done in reasonably attractive countryside and at minimal loss to existing land use interests.

There is a third aspect of strategy, literally linking the other two together. This is the network of roads and paths which provides access into and through the countryside and to individual recreational provisions. The more efficiently and pleasantly this network can join up all the various units of provision—particularly those with a common interest—the more successful is likely to be the overall recreation strategy.

## Local Attraction Areas

Visiting a castle or a stately home in its landscaped parkland is no new experience. In Britain, Chatsworth House, Derbyshire seat of the Dukes of Devonshire, has been open to the public for well over a century. Today such private estates serve a valuable purpose in giving some experience of countryside to large numbers of people. Many public authorities too have held recreational open space in the countryside for a long time.

However, although the concept is not new, in Britain it was not until the Countryside Acts in 1967 and 1968 that the development of 'country parks' as such was put on a recognised footing. Their function is to provide or improve opportunities for the enjoyment of the countryside by the public, and to do this in such a way as to take pressure off sensitive farmland and more remote and solitary places. Generally, but not always, they are situated conveniently to towns to avoid the need to travel far and to help reduce congestion on the roads (6.26).

By the end of 1975 there were 147 designated country parks in Britain, varying in size from 7 to 1500 hectares

Figure 6.11  Visiting stately homes like Castle Howard in Yorkshire is a long-established recreational activity which has become significantly greater in scale as personal mobility has increased.

(*Photo: John Foster*)

(6.27) and in character from formal gardens and parkland to woodland and rough moorland. The retention of some degree of rural activity in country parks is important, for instance sheep grazing or an element of forestry, if people are to feel that they are in the countryside and not just in an urban park which happens to be surrounded by open land.

Because of the intensive nature of the recreational use of country parks, parts of them may require to be rested periodically to allow the land to recover from the worst effects of trampling. This could well provide the opportunity to promote the element of traditional farming use so important to their overall character. To facilitate easy switching from recreation to another use and back again, a good overall network of services is necessary throughout each park, to which mobile recreation equipment can be plugged in when required and removed to another site when not in use.

Culzean Country Park on the Ayrshire coast—the first to be designated in Scotland—encompasses the traditional concept of a large house open to the public, with an extensive area (220 hectares) of open farmland and woodland where public access is being positively developed (Figure 6.12). Some farming is deliberately maintained for educational purposes and motor vehicles are carefully channelled so that their presence does not reduce the quality of the countryside experience within the park.

Culzean and many other country parks are of rectangular shape but there is no reason why country parks should not be linear too, based on a river or canal or a disused railway line. One of the first country parks to be established in England, the Wirral Way in Cheshire, comprises about 19 km of old railway line made usable for walking or riding, with the station sites converted into centres for car parking and picnicking (Figure 6.13). The Tissington Trail in the Peak National Park exploits the same situation of a disused railway line and station sites located in countryside of high scenic quality.

The legislation which established country parks also provides that urban authorities can finance them either wholly or in collaboration with the rural authorities in whose areas they are located. This makes it possible to develop country parks around major urban centres where they are most needed and in the most efficient relationship to other land uses and to access, without the cost being entirely a burden on the rural receiving authorities. Co-operative effort of this kind has been further successfully developed in Bavaria where, at Nuremberg, the city council and the three county authorities adjoining it pay about 0.5 DM per person per year into a common fund for land acquisition and the provision of recreation facilities in the countryside which will be in their joint interests.

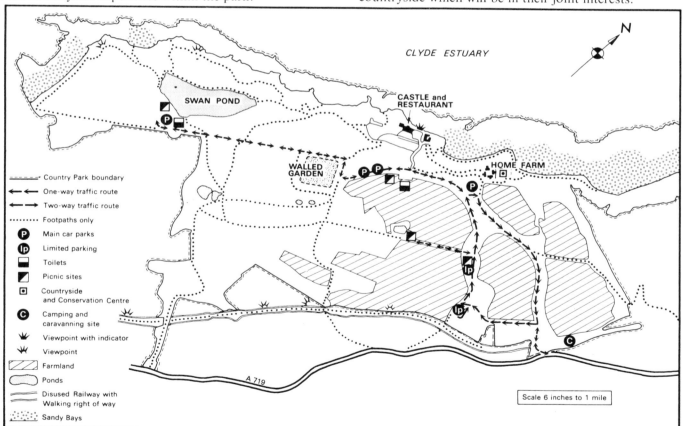

Figure 6.12   Culzean Country Park offers a diversity of countryside recreational interest, including sea coast, woodlands, farmland and—adjoining the Castle—formal gardens. Motor traffic is limited to a one-way system serving a main car park at the Home Farm (now developed as a major visitor centre) and beyond this to one main access serving a series of smaller car parks. Elsewhere in the Park, particularly in the main western woodland area, movement is on foot only.

(*By courtesy of the National Trust for Scotland*)

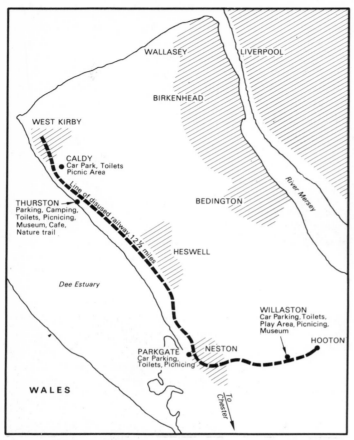

Figure 6.13    The Wirral Country Park comprises a length of disused railway line between West Kirby and Hooton in North Cheshire to which is linked a number of major recreation areas, all conveniently sited in relation to local urban areas.

(*By courtesy of Cheshire County Council*)

Figure 6.14    The old rail bed in the Wirral Country Park is now soiled over and seeded, and is used extensively for horse riding.

(*By courtesy of Cheshire County Council*)

Figure 6.15    The Tissington Trail in the Peak National Park comprises a 12-mile length of disused railway line, now converted into a pleasant grass-covered walkway, and much used by visitors in association with car parks and picnic sites developed at the old railway station locations.

(*By courtesy of the Peak Park Planning Board*)

## Regional Attraction Areas

Country parks are relatively small intensively used areas of countryside located fairly near to towns. As one moves further out into the countryside, and particularly away from areas of intensive farming, it becomes possible to develop larger blocks of land for recreation on the basis of some degree of multiple use. Such areas may have more than a local connotation and, although the term 'regional park' has no statutory significance in Britain, they may be providing a regional function in all but name.

A regional attraction area could comprise one large area of land, possibly either open common land or forest or a combination of both, where recreation provision is spread fairly evenly over the whole of the area, or it could be made up of a number of smaller blocks of recreation land linked together through enclosed farmland in a planned way by a system of access roads and footpaths.

This latter concept has been well developed at Cannock Chase in Staffordshire where the County Council, the Forestry Commission and the National Trust all have extensive land holdings within a designated area of outstanding natural beauty, and have promoted a joint policy of recreation provision which allows of a maximum degree of public access coupled with forestry and some farming activity. The area is under heavy pressure from surrounding towns, and part of its heartland has been made a motorless zone served by peripheral car parks. At the Clyde/Muirshiel Regional Park in Scotland the same concept of relatively small areas of intensive recreational use, linked together by walking routes through farmland and over open hill country, has been successfully developed over a period of years by the local authority.

Figure 6.16. Forestry Commission car park and picnic area, Dartmoor. Conveniently situated at the beginning of a forest walk, this parking and picnicking area is small in scale and secluded from general view by the screen of trees on the woodland edge.

(*By courtesy of the Forestry Commission*)

Figure 6.17 Woodland on the edge of Haarle Forest, Netherlands, near the German border, used to good effect for parking cars inconspicuously. The attraction here is a viewpoint off the bottom right-hand corner of the picture, approached across the open heathland by a footpath fenced off to prevent damage to the vegetation. Cars are not permitted to stop on the main road in this vicinity.

(*By courtesy of the Netherlands State Forest Service*)

Woodlands provide a useful opportunity for developing recreation facilities on a significant scale without undue impact on the landscape. The Forestry Commission, with over 1·2 million hectares of land, including seven Forest Parks, recognises this and in 1971 published a policy document in which it stated its intention to develop the unique recreational features and potential of its forests (6.28). On the ground this means access freely on foot along its 26,000 kilometres of forest tracks, with special provision for scenic motor drives in a few places, and increasing provision for picnicking, camping and caravanning. The importance of conservation is recognised and facilities have been developed so that people can enjoy forest walks and nature trails with the opportunity of seeing interesting wildlife. To a lesser extent private woodland owners too are accepting public access as something which need not just be tolerated, but rather can be a positive means of securing public co-operation and goodwill. The Dutch Government have taken this a stage further and will pay an annual sum per hectare to private woodland owners who are prepared to allow public access on their land. This payment is in effect for meeting the cost of such warden supervision as may be necessary and the expense of making good any damage done by the public.

In open upland country, there is opportunity to provide public access over extensive areas through formal agreements made under the National Parks and Access to the Countryside Act 1949* between local authorities and private landowners (6.29). These agreements give the public the right of access for open air recreation, in return for which landowners have the protection of bye-laws and a warden service to enforce them. This particular device has a potential, by no means fully exploited yet, for securing recreation as one element in a multiple land use system which may also include sheep, grouse and water catchment.

*In Scotland, under the Countryside (Scotland) Act 1967.

## Water Recreation

Unlike many other kinds of outdoor recreation, which can be enjoyed widely over the countryside, water recreation is obviously limited to those places where usable water exists and, apart from those in the Lake District, the main natural inland water areas in Britain are the lochs of the Scottish Highlands which are a long way from the heavy population concentrations of the Midlands and South East England. Upland reservoirs also tend to be well removed from major towns and cities and, in any case, where the water is being impounded for supply, their use for recreation is often restricted. Water in linear form—in rivers and canals—is more widely distributed, but the range of recreational opportunities on it is more limited in scope.

The demand for facilities for water-based recreation has increased greatly in recent years and the rate of increase is likely to continue. The range of interest is wide and, as we have already seen, some types of water recreation simply must be separated from others. Demand can be helped in three ways, (a) by securing recreational use on new water areas when they are formed, such as new reservoirs or flooded gravel pits, (b) by securing recreational use of water areas hitherto not used, and (c) by stepping up the intensity of use on water already available for recreation.

Fortunately the very restrictive attitude towards public access to water supply reservoirs is now easing as adequate treatment systems are developed (6.30). In the case of new upland reservoirs, like the Derwent Reservoir in Northumbria, recreational provision is now generally built into their basic design and, in addition to public access on the open country parts of their gathering grounds, sailing under the aegis of a club and fishing on a controlled ticket basis are provided for. New lowland reservoirs can also be designed to include provision for leisure activities, as at Grafham Water, in Huntingdonshire, where a major new reservoir completed in 1966 provides three large picnic areas with car

parks, facilities for a sailing club, trout fishing from boats and from the bank, a nature reserve and a residential training centre for teaching sailing to young people (Figure 6.18). (See also page 178).

The provision of recreational facilities on water not hitherto used offers possibilities for the future, but must be handled carefully in relation to landscape interests. The attraction of many natural lakes and some long-established reservoirs lies in the quiet beauty of their setting, and this in turn sometimes derives from their relative inaccessibility. Before new access roads are made and active recreation developed in such places it is important to examine the quality of the landscape resources, and balance it against the availability of other convenient water areas and the pressure of recreational demand. If the balance favours development, the compatibility of the various possible uses must then be studied. Conflict can arise between sailing and fishing on occasions, but more often it will arise when power boats are introduced, either for use in their own right or for water skiing. Zoning of parts of lakes and reservoirs for different uses is one solution as at Loch Earn in Scotland where this has been done by the riparian interests and water users themselves forming an association. Separation of different uses on a time basis is also a possibility, but more difficult to handle unless all users are thoroughly familiar with the details of organisation.

In planning for the recreational use of water areas account must be taken of likely spectator interest and adequate provision made for access to the vicinity of the water, with parking and picnicking facilities strategically placed for viewing, but not dominating their surroundings. A good example of this kind of provision is that which has been made at the Chew Valley Reservoir in Somerset.

When a new reservoir is to be constructed, landscape and recreation planning interests should work in close cooperation with design and construction engineers from the

Figure 6.18 Water is as much an attraction in the Netherlands as it is elsewhere, and its use for recreation is highly developed. This picnic site and paddling pool were made from a disused pit from which sand had been dug for the nearby Amersfoort-Zwolle motorway. Today the facility is well provided with screened car parks, and the beach is popular for picnicking and day camping.

(By courtesy of the Netherland State Forest Service)

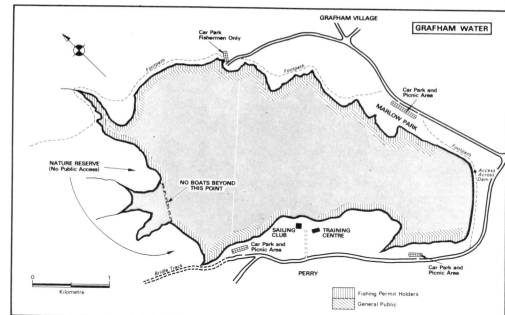

Figure 6.19 Grafham Water, Huntingdonshire, recreation plan. The Great Ouse Water Authority designed recreational use into this project at the outset. The plan shows the wide range of recreational opportunities available to the public and the substantial extent to which they have access to the water's edge.

(*By courtesy of the Great Ouse Water Authority*)

outset. The Errwood Reservoir in the Peak National Park is a good example of this. Here the existing landscape was examined in detail at design stage and a new landscape pattern devised which took account of the existing situation and sought to reinforce its best attributes, at the same time introducing new elements and fitting into the scene a good range of recreation facilities.

Water in linear form can provide a useful element of network link, although this link interest may often relate to the possible continuity of bankside access rather than to the waterway itself. Rivers in the wider countryside, unless in their lower reaches where their breadth and slow current make some boating possible, are mainly of interest to fishermen and canoeists, who do not operate particularly well together unless the river is fairly wide. The right to fish

from the bank is the prerogative of the riparian interests who may retain it for their own private use, let it on a day ticket basis or lease it either to a private individual or a club. Although the canoeists' interest is primarily one of passage, canoes have to be launched and proper access to the water must be provided for this purpose if trespass is to be avoided.

While the length of the canal system in Britain has shrunk in recent years, the interest in canals for pleasure cruising has been increasing. The British Waterways Board, faced with a difficult economic situation, balanced the relative extent of the major uses of waterways for commercial transport, water supply, cruising and general recreation, and refined the canal system to produce a network which for England and Wales is around 2200 kilometres (6.31).

Figure 6.20 In Britain parts of the canal system are becoming increasingly used for recreation, with botel units providing sophisticated accommodation in traditional narrow boat form.

(*Photo: John Foster*)

Figure 6.21 The Dutch canal system, as here at Alkmaar, is well maintained and extensively used for recreation as well as the transportation of goods.

(*Photo: John Foster*)

Because of the commercial origin of canals, this network has the advantage of being conveniently situated in relation to urban areas, and its maintenance can therefore offer a useful recreational opportunity, not only for cruising but also for land-based activities which can utilise the continuity of the towpaths. Useful recent studies have included one of the Leeds and Liverpool Canal as a recreational resource (6.32), and in Scotland one of the Union Canal (6.33).

The rehabilitation of lengths of canal which have fallen into disuse is well worthwhile, partly of course as elements of an overall cruising network, but again also as local areas of quiet informal recreation. Where the landscape character of a canal is pleasant this should be positively maintained and wherever possible enhanced; on the other hand where the canal passes through derelict land or land of low amenity there is useful opportunity to upgrade its landscape corridor. While the future of the present limited canal network in Britain is seen primarily as recreational, the possibility of a greater use again for commercial transport need not reduce the recreational interest (see also page 220). On the contrary, the possibility of seeing commercial barges operating on a canal could be a leisure attraction in itself. This successful multiple use of canals is well seen in the Netherlands where they have an important drainage function as well.

### Linear Network

The roads, bridleways, footpaths and in some instances waterways which link attraction areas and other recreation features are an important element in the recreation system of the wider countryside and, if adequate and convenient, can positively help both countryman and visitor.

In planning for recreation an appraisal of the existing country road network is necessary to establish its convenience and adequacy in relation to existing and proposed recreation areas. If the network is inconvenient in that it results in heavy recreation traffic passing through sensitive farmland or is inadequate in terms of road widths and alignment, the re-routing of this traffic on to other more suitable roads or constructing completely new tourist roads must be explored.

The idea of road building specifically for recreation traffic is fairly novel in Britain and, apart from some new roads associated with reservoir development and particular recreation facilities such as skiing on the Cairngorms, little has been done. However, there is ample precedent elsewhere, particularly in the United States where scenic roads like the Blue Ridge Parkway on the Appalachians were constructed as tourist routes and are equipped to handle leisure motorists in large numbers (6.34). The Forestry Commission has developed this idea and makes a small charge for cars using some of its forest roads such as Pickering and Hamsterley Forest Drives in Yorkshire. However, the idea could be developed further as a positive element in recreation planning strategies, meeting capital and maintenance costs from charges on vehicles.

Figure 6.22  In Forestry Commission woodlands, popular and well-marked trails have been developed in extension of the traditional footpath system of the countryside.

(*Photo: John Foster*)

Within the existing system of country roads, quite apart from constructing new routes, much can be done to help the movement of visitor traffic through sensitive farmland by designing the roads to discourage stopping and verge parking and providing adequate signposting leading on to places of interest where parking accommodation is available. Where these roads have a through route function, roadside reception areas at intervals on them will reduce indiscriminate stopping and parking.

Public rights of way for use on horseback or on foot must be registered in England and Wales (although not in Scotland) and consequently for the first time their pattern has been recorded comprehensively on maps. Largely this is a traditional pattern deriving from the need to get conveniently from place to place in the days before the motor car, but its attraction today is still great, providing as it does opportunities for getting completely away from traffic.

The recreational value of particular bridleways and footpaths will much depend on the convenience of access to them, and the availability of car parking facilities may determine how well a particular route is used. In developing the footpath network in an overall countryside recreation plan, provision should be made to establish new links where these would improve continuity in non-sensitive areas. As more and more people begin and end their walks at their cars, adequately waymarked circular and loop routes need to be devised, with convenient parking facilities associated with them. Again, the Forestry Commission has produced useful way-marked footpath systems in its forests, which are now well used by the public.

### Leisure Accommodation

In intensively farmed countryside, opportunities for providing caravan sites and second homes will be limited. Elsewhere the possibilities should be related to the importance of

Figure 6.23   Caravan and camping site at Woutershok, Netherlands, developed in clearings cut in an existing woodland. The site is inconspicuous in the general landscape and the arrangement of a series of separate clearings—some for caravans, some for tents, others for organised groups—ensures interest and variety within the overall boundary. One of the clearings is set aside for visitors with dogs.

*(By courtesy of the Netherlands State Forest Service)*

farming and the weight of demand for accommodation, the latter being some guide to economic opportunity.

Caravan sites can vary greatly in size and character from small transit sites for touring caravans to large sites containing a predominance of static vans. Insofar as transit sites are for caravanners truly on the move, they need to be located on or near main roads, and their size related to the scale of demand and the capability of the landscape to absorb them visually. They are difficult to operate economically and increasingly may have to become the responsibility of public authorities.

Of more direct impact on the wider countryside is the demand for caravan sites for holiday and seasonal use, ranging from periods of a few days to six months or more. They need to be located where they will not be conspicuous or adversely affect other countryside activities. They require

reasonable access and a choice of location which takes advantage of landform and woodland cover for seclusion.

As well as relationship to the overall landscape, the layout within the sites themselves is important. Putting caravans a minimum distance apart in an open field offers little amenity for the caravanners. Informal grouping is essential, utilising landform and trees to the best advantage and undertaking new planting where necessary. Caravan sites have been extensively developed within woodland in some countries where a reasonably dry climate exists. In modified form, by grouping caravans in woodland clearings rather than under trees, this principle can be usefully adapted to the British situation.

The caravan is essentially a mobile unit and, fixed in one place with its wheels removed, it cannot but look out of character in the countryside. For permanent use, where new

Figure 6.24   Forestry Commission caravan site in the Forest of Dean. A secluded site in a woodland clearing, but with enough space for caravanners not to feel crowded together.

*(By courtesy of the Forestry Commission)*

Figure 6.25   As well as location and layout, detail is also important in the development of caravan sites: a well-designed water supply and litter collection point on a site near Perth in Scotland.

*(Photo: John Foster)*

Figure 6.26   The Forestry Commission in Britain has begun to develop holiday chalet sites on their land in scenic areas, using log-faced buildings to fit in with the woodland environment.

(*By courtesy of the Forestry Commission*)

structures are required, cabin or chalet-type buildings are a preferable alternative, provided that their shape and the colour and texture of their external cladding materials are sympathetic to their surroundings. Although higher in first costs, from an investment point of view these have a longer life than caravans, involve less maintenance and can be let at a higher rent over a longer season.

As the existing stock of old cottages and other buildings in the countryside becomes converted to second homes, the demand for sites for new structures is likely to increase. Unless a rash of new holiday development is to be accepted, planned concentration will be essential. Proximity to inland water, villages of character and locations with good views are all important attractions, but care is necessary to ensure that new second-home settlement does not dominate these and thereby reduce their attractiveness. In Wales, Denbighshire County Council studied the problems and opportunities of second homes in some depth a few years ago and established useful planning policies in relation to existing land uses and landscape considerations within their area (6.35).

Experience in the United States, Scandinavia and elsewhere has shown the importance of securing that the development of second-home communities is planned as a whole, and that there is adequate control over the layout of their various parts and the design of individual buildings. This makes a strong argument for acquisition of the land and comprehensive development by one agency, adequately provided with landscape expertise, rather than development by individual interests without regard to overall character and quality. In Britain the Forestry Commission has begun to explore the possibilities of this kind of development on its land and at Strathyre in Perthshire has already developed a well-laid out cabin site with log-faced buildings of design appropriate to their locality.

## Leisure in Remote Areas

Remoteness is relative, and neither scale nor distance is necessarily its true measure. Rather it is a quality of experience and one which is becoming increasingly sought after in the crowded conditions of modern life. Remoteness is sometimes equated with difficulty of access. If a piece of moorland or a mountain is well removed from roads and the only approach to it is on foot, then it is more likely to be felt to be remote than if one had just stepped out on to it from a car.

Intensity of use also has a bearing on whether or not a place feels remote. Well-farmed country, although far removed from town, would be felt by most people to be less remote than high fells or moorland where grouse and deer are the only crops, even though the latter is perhaps only a few miles from a town. Isolation too may be a factor of remoteness on occasions. It is quite possible to feel cut off from the world in a community, as well as on a mountain peak, if that community is itself isolated from others.

In any considerations of the leisure use of remote areas the expectation of visitors that they will be able to find this special kind of experience is very important in planning for the right scale and type of recreation provision and subsequent management policy.

### Nature of Activities

In remote areas recreation possibilities are much taken up with physical activity, some of it demanding a high degree of skill. Hill walking, mountaineering, rock climbing, pony trekking and skiing are all popular activities which presuppose freedom of movement over open country. The traditional sporting activities—fishing, stalking and shooting—also need space, and at certain times of the year come into sharp conflict with other recreational interests.

The degree to which passive recreation, mainly motoring for pleasure, is possible will largely depend on the existence of a road pattern. This pattern is not likely to be extensive, otherwise an area would not retain the quality of remoteness. The roads, too, will generally be narrower and less well aligned and surfaced than main roads elsewhere. Nevertheless this is just the kind of country which attracts some leisure motorists, for it offers them the experience of enjoying high-quality scenery with a spice of driving adventure thrown in.

Because of their character, remote areas will increasingly be sought out by people on holiday as well as by casual day visitors. Overnight accommodation will therefore be in demand, ranging from camp sites and hostels well away from public roads to caravan sites and hotels in the small communities on the perimeter of the areas or isolated within them. Sites for second homes will also be in demand, particularly in sheltered places where local climatic conditions are favourable.

## Strategy Considerations

A strategy for recreation in remote areas will have some of the characteristics of that for the wider countryside, but should place greater emphasis on conserving landscape quality and in maintaining the distinctive characteristics which identify one place from another. Farming is unlikely to be so dominant and other uses, such as forestry, may already be producing social and economic changes. An important consideration of a planning authority in developing a recreation planning policy must be to try to make recreational activities positively contribute to the local economy without reducing the distinctive attractiveness of the resource.

Recreation pressures must be kept below a level where they would damage the ecological quality or the visual character of an area. The rutted tracks and worn patches of vegetation caused by cars on open moorland away from roads in Dartmoor or the Yorkshire Dales demonstrate in one example both kinds of damage. Capacity potential needs to be assessed and when new recreation provision is made, particularly where it is concentrated as in a winter sports centre, there must be a continuous monitoring process thereafter to identify and correct damage arising from overuse.

Where the established land uses of hill farming or sport operate with economic benefit to local populations and there is also pressure for public access, a formal access agreement between the local planning authority and landowner is now a well-tried device. This provides for controlled access by the public who are subject to bye-laws and the oversight of a warden or ranger service, with the ability

to close areas at special times, as for instance during lambing in the spring or grouse shooting after Twelfth August.

In some areas which possess particularly fine wilderness characteristics, road access and development of any kind may need to be avoided. To secure this end the responsibility of public ownership may have to be accepted where the land will be left with no economic future in consequence of the adoption of a wilderness type of policy. Alternatively, as is now being done in parts of Western Germany, hill farmers could be subsidised to maintain a traditional landscape character in hill country of scenic importance where farming as such is no longer economic and where there is strong public sympathy for the established appearance of the place.

If recreational planning and management strategies for remote areas are to operate successfully, the administrative units must be large enough to be meaningful. In this respect, the recent re-organisation of local government in Scotland, which established units on a regional scale, has much to commend it. Where local government boundaries cut across remote areas, joint administration and management across those boundaries must be established. Joint administration of another kind is also valuable, namely through a consortium of public authorities, private landowners and conservation interests. This will minimise conflicts between landowning and user interests, and allow the best use to be made of public and private funds available for the development and control of recreation.

## National Parks

In the wider countryside we have seen the value of developing the concept of country and regional parks as specific attraction areas to take pressure off more sensitive places. Logically, national parks would be the comparable attraction areas in remote country, and in some respects the 10 national parks in England and Wales are just this. However, it is important to remember that, while country parks and regional parks would be designated to have a recreational function, national parks are designated primarily for their distinctive quality of landscape beauty. The dilemma of protection and development which arises in consequence is nowhere more evident than in the Peak National Park (140,000 hectares) which has a population of over 17 million people living within 100 kilometres of its boundary and an annual visitation of over 10 million.

While some national parks have spare recreation capacity which could be developed with care, others need a deliberate diversion of visitor pressures away from them. Where the latter is the situation in some United States national parks, 'house full' notices are put up at road entrance points when the car parking and road capacities in the back country are known to be at their environmentally safe limit. In these situations it is seen as important to tell the recreationist positively where he can get entry to an alternative area of the kind of country he wants to visit.

The French national parks have adopted a useful system which provides for an inner zone or core—the most remote country which is kept inaccessible to all but the visitor on foot or pony—and an outer zone containing some road network and a variety of accommodation centres. An intermediate zone of moderate penetration makes a useful transition from the outer to the inner zone. This system has great potential, particularly where major new recreation development can be concentrated in peripheral locations round a core of wild country with good road communications built to them but not penetrating beyond.

The method adopted for securing adequate protection with the best provision of resource-based recreation must depend on the particular circumstances of each case. However, if anything is to be learned from the experience of the past 25 years of national park administration in England and Wales, it is that policies for protection through planning control alone are not enough; they must be matched by complementary action for the enhancement of landscape beauty and the development of suitable kinds of recreational facilities, always bearing in mind the economic interests of the indigenous population. This means a willingness on the part of Government to make adequate funds available and to establish policies that truly represent the national interest of these areas.

A recent report to Government by an official National Park Policies Review Committee (6.36), recognising the problem of rationalising the two statutory purposes of national parks, namely to preserve their natural beauty and to promote their enjoyment by the public, recommended that the legislation be altered to make absolutely clear that the public enjoyment of national parks should be such as to leave their natural beauty unimpaired for the enjoyment of this and future generations. This principle of handing on— the concept of trusteeship—the Committee saw as necessary for safeguarding the integrity of national parks in the future.

**Motor Traffic**

While the road network will restrict the penetration of motor cars into remote areas where recreation pressures are heavy, there may nevertheless be severe problems of congestion on approach roads and at the heads of valleys where cul-de-sacs peter out.

The provision of better parking facilities and turning spaces at road ends may be a solution, but this will only be so in circumstances where moving traffic on the road itself is not congested at peak times and where the extent of use is not likely to increase significantly as a consequence of the further provision. The inherent problem in providing parking space in these circumstances is that it will inevitably draw new traffic to the area and may set up a situation of congestion which did not exist before.

On the other hand the curtailment of traffic by deliberately

Figure 6.27  A crowded road through the Goyt Valley, subject to heavy verge damage and dangerous for walkers.

(*By courtesy of the Peak Park Planning Board*)

Figure 6.28  Walkers enjoying the Goyt Valley road, traffic-free after the establishment of restrictions on the movement of cars. A regular service of minibuses looks after those who do not want to walk.

(*By courtesy of the Peak Park Planning Board*)

Figure 6.29  Coastline is particularly sensitive to lack of control; derelict vehicles on an open stretch of shore on the Clyde Estuary.

(*Photo: John Foster*)

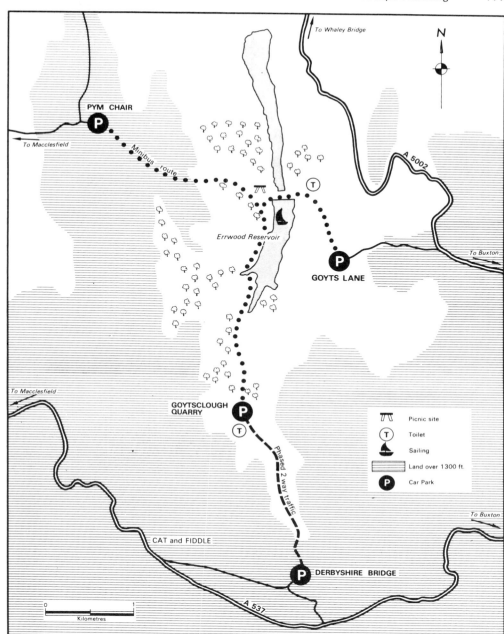

To Whaley Bridge

N

PYM CHAIR

To Macclesfield

Minibus route

A 5002

T

Errwood Reservoir

To Buxton

GOYTS LANE

To Macclesfield

GOYTSCLOUGH
QUARRY

T

Phased 2 way traffic

Picnic site

Toilet

Sailing

Land over 1300 ft.

Car Park

To Buxton

CAT and FIDDLE

DERBYSHIRE BRIDGE

A 537

0                1
Kilometres

Figure 6.30 The Goyt Valley traffic experiment of 1970 and 1971 proved that the public is willing to accept that cars have to be restricted in their movement on occasions for the benefit of everyone. On Saturdays and public holidays the roads linking Goytsclough Quarry, Goyts Lane and Pym Chair were completely closed to traffic and a free minibus service operated between the terminal car parks.

(*By courtesy of the Peak Park Planning Board*)

not providing parking space may be a real hardship to many people for whom strenuous walking is not a feasible alternative. The solution of closing roads completely to private traffic and providing a public transport service is now actively being tried out in a number of countries. In Britain the Goyt Valley experiment of 1970 and 1971 in the Peak National Park has provided useful information from practical experience (Figure 6.30) (6.37). Here access along three previously heavily congested hill roads into a remote valley was restricted at weekends in the summer and the options were available of either walking or using a free mini-bus service. Surprisingly, so far there has been little follow-up on this experiment elsewhere in Britain.

Where it is desirable to provide for the motor car in remote country, particular skill must be exercised in fitting parking spaces into sheltered areas where adequate screen-

ing can be obtained either by landform or trees (see also page 138). Individual parking areas should never be large, although a maximum acceptable size will depend on the particular conditions of each situation. In general terms a scale of say 10 to 20 cars is of the right order unless within woodland or exceptionally well sheltered from view. Good design is highly important and layouts should be informal to avoid cars being parked in straight lines or geometrical patterns. Gravel surfacing or reinforced grass is to be preferred to tarmacadam or bare concrete, provided that it can be adequately drained to stand up to hard wear. Kerbing, where it is necessary, should be turfed over to show a soft edge of vegetation rather than a hard line of concrete. Any new trees planted for screening should be suitable for the local environment, always avoiding exotic species more appropriate to urban situations.

## Accommodation

Two factors are particularly important in planning for leisure accommodation in remote areas—those of location and scale. In other than heavily wooded country the scattering of second homes or caravans sporadically over an area should be avoided. Likewise isolated development conspicuously sited in hill country is better avoided, or at least should be sited very sensitively. The view from a group of mountain chalets may be fine looking out from within, but the buildings may change quite dramatically the scale and character of their setting.

The scale of individual buildings in relation to the traditional building forms of an area and in relation to the scale of the landscape itself is important (6.38). Scale is also relevant in relation to existing communities to which new recreation development may be attached. The social consequences of a very large caravan site or second-home development beside a small hamlet can be as damaging as its visual consequences. If pressures demand provision on such a scale, there may be merit in establishing small holiday communities quite on their own, as has been successfully done in the hill country of Provence, adapting sheltered sites for them well linked to the existing public highway system.

## Leisure on the Coast

The coastline of Britain is extensive relative to the land area and few parts of the country today are more than two or three hours' drive from the sea. Coupled with the high density of population, this has helped to establish the coast as a recognised leisure destination for the masses.

However, although these pressures are heavy in places and bad development has damaged some fine natural coastline, the situation is nowhere as bad as that along so much of the Mediterranean coastline. There the relatively short lengths of seaboards compared with the vast population of the European hinterland and the much more favourable climatic conditions which exist have combined to produce situations of gross over-development in many places. Providing for leisure in these circumstances of great and increasing demand and good climate is a highly profitable business and private interests have cashed in, apparently with little regard either for the quality of the natural environment or—in some places—the appearance of the development carried out.

In Britain limited access and relative remoteness have so far saved a good deal of the coast from being extensively developed, and a national policy could still be worked out to protect those lengths which have a special scenic or scientific interest while at the same time allowing the careful development of some other parts to a good standard. Improvement of already damaged coastline also needs to be tackled by a positive programme to remove derelict industrial and war-time eyesores.

## Nature of Activities

Leisure activities on the coast range widely, depending on its character and the extent of shelter. Sandy beaches are the traditional attraction for families wanting to bathe, picnic and play beach games. But rocky shores also attract families, and many children find as much to interest them among the rocks and pools as they would on a sand beach. Headlands, cliffs and coves, too, draw people who want to enjoy fine views, sometimes on foot, often well away from crowded beaches.

With the upsurge of interest in water recreation, sheltered estuaries and bays are increasingly being used for sailing, power-boating and water-skiing, as well as for the traditional activities of fishing and bathing. In open-sea situations, under favourable conditions, surfing is also increasing in popularity. The development of associated land-based facilities, ranging from single slipways for launching to sophisticated marina complexes is good business, and demand in places outstrips supply.

With 70% of all holidays in Britain being taken at the coast, the provision of accommodation makes important demands on land. While the desire for serviced holiday accommodation is declining, the popularity of self-catering holidays, particularly in caravans and chalets, is on the increase, and the mobility of the motor car has already produced a wide scattering of recreation development along the coastline.

## Strategy Considerations

Two reports by the Countryside Commission in 1970 (6.39), describing the situation on the coast of England and Wales with regard to holiday accommodation, day-use recreation and industrial and other dereliction, serve to demonstrate the complexities of the problems common to countries with a significant length of coastline. About 75% of the total length of 4384 km of the coastline of England and Wales is still undeveloped and, of this, 1168 km is promoted in the report for special designation for its high scenic quality, thereafter to be planned and managed as Heritage Coast for protection of its character. A study of the Scottish mainland and islands coast in 1974 (6.40), primarily in relation to onshore oil-related development pressures, predictably showed a predominantly undeveloped coastline with a substantial proportion of the total of 10,080 km of a Heritage Coast category of quality.

Any strategy for recreation on the coast must accept that pressures will continue to build up. On developed coast opportunities must be taken to adapt established resorts to present-day needs. Those which can offer weekend and day visitors a good variety of recreation opportunities and which can switch some of their accommodation to self-catering types will help their own economic prospects and may also help to relieve pressures on more sensitive coastline elsewhere. If they are also capable of some peripheral expansion or intensification of development without detriment to their character, they will be better able to develop and sustain a good range of visitor facilities.

A recreation strategy for coastline outside the established resorts must be related to the quality and sensitivity of existing scenic character, and the extent to which new or more intensive recreational uses would adversely affect existing land uses or cause physical erosion. Where the situation favours further development, and the coastline is not of outstanding scenic quality, planned attraction areas, such as coastal parks and new holiday settlements, can be established. On coastline of high amenity the major objective of planning policy should generally be conservation, with provision only for access and types of activity consistent with maintaining the quality of the environment.

In evolving a strategy for recreation it is important that a significant length of coast is planned at any one time, and that it is linked with its hinterland to help diversify recreational interests and avoid the over-use of a few traditionally popular locations. The development of a strategy on an adequate scale will also help the integration of recreation with other land uses.

## Attraction Areas

Because of the great recreational pressure on parts of the coastline there is a need to establish specific areas of attraction in the form of coastal or regional water parks, and also to develop new centres for holiday accommodation and second homes to supplement the growing demand in existing resorts.

Coastal parks would be, in effect, country parks on the coast and would comprise relatively short stretches of shore with some hinterland, on which intensive provision would be made for informal outdoor recreation. This would include car parks, picnic areas and access to beaches, with the support facilities of cafes, shelters and lavatories essential for day use. These parks would not cater for overnight accommodation, other than possibly space for some simple camping as in the proposed Great Kills Park on the Staten Island waterfront, New York (Figure 6.33).

Since a coastal park would be a relatively small element of recreation provision, there is a case, particularly in the context of a river estuary or a bay, for developing a number of such elements, integrating them with other land uses and using the adjoining water area to pull everything together into one unit. This would make it possible to regulate different kinds of recreation uses to avoid them conflicting with one another or adversely affecting existing farming, fishing or scientific interests. Chichester Harbour would make a compact regional water park of this kind, and on a larger scale the Menai Straits and parts of the Clyde Estuary could benefit from such a comprehensive treatment. Where new coastal water is being created by barrages, as suggested for Morecambe Bay and the Solway Firth, recreational use of the water surface and the new coastlines should be planned into the project from the outset.

Regional water parks could provide a diversity of recreation opportunities and, comprehensively planned, could make better use of resources than would a number of unconnected recreational provisions. A logical zoning of the water area would be possible, keeping power boats and sailing craft apart from one another and away from areas of important natural history interest. This zoning pattern could be strengthened by (a) ensuring that different kinds of shore-based recreation development are located to fit logically into the pattern and, (b) controlling the scale of development in relation to the extent of water available for different uses.

Policies for concentrating at least some holiday accommodation development into new holiday settlements must be undertaken. While these might sometimes utilise virgin sites, there are advantages in building onto existing nuclei, and particularly in up-grading and expanding some of the less satisfactory caravan villages which developed before planning controls existed. Derelict war-time sites also offer useful opportunities—sometimes with the advantage of services already laid on—provided they are satisfactorily located from access and landscape points of view.

Figure 6.31    Major recreational development at Le Lavandou on the Mediterranean coast, with extensive ranges of flats located around new mooring basins for pleasure craft.

(*Photo: John Foster*)

Figure 6.32    Cote d'Esterel, a self-contained holiday settlement with its own private boat harbour, adopting a high-density pattern of layout closely contained by woodland and sea.

(*Photo: John Foster*)

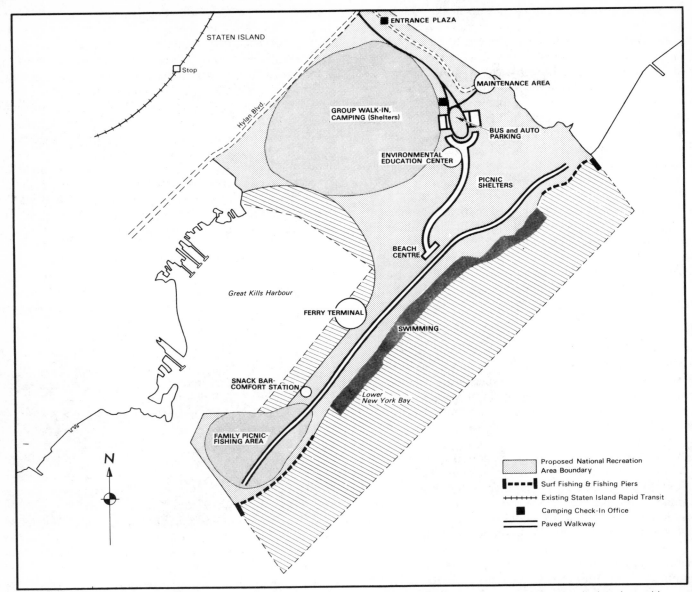

Figure 6.33   The Great Kills Park on Staten Island, is one of five units of the Gateway National Recreation Area Project of the US National Park Service and Bureau of Outdoor Recreation. It would take in about 520 hectares of land and water and would be developed for boating, fishing, swimming (when pollution in the bay area has been reduced), picnicking and environmental education, with an area set aside primarily for group camping.

(*By courtesy of the US National Park Service and Bureau of Outdoor Recreation*)

New holiday settlements will need a good range of types of accommodation; for the mobile visitor—motels and caravan and tented camping sites; for the static holidaymaker—holiday chalets, cottages and flats. They should also include adequate support facilities—catering establishments, shops, car parks, access to beaches or shores and, if their scale justifies it, some entertainment provision. The increasing demand for second homes makes it possible to contemplate these settlements as containing some owner-occupied accommodation as well as holiday letting accommodation. How far the privately owned element could be permitted to become permanently occupied, for instance by retired people who have sold their main homes, would depend on circumstances. If a settlement is designed purely

as a holiday village, then permanent occupation would be unlikely to be satisfactory, but if it is laid out to more generous standards, as are some of the new holiday villages on the south coast of France, then there could be some degree of permanent occupation.

The layout and design of coastal and regional water parks and new holiday settlements will raise many landscape problems. Development should not bring pressure on visually or ecologically sensitive areas, and layouts should ensure that visitors are channelled away from places where they could cause damage. The Dutch are particularly good at this, both in their skill in making facilities so attractive that they positively draw people to them and also in devising telling notices about behaving responsibly towards the environment. Buildings must be designed so that they are not obtrusive. Caravans are specially difficult in coastal locations and there is a strong case for developing more extensively the use of chalets of good design in place of static caravans.

Coastal parks, like country parks, would generally be the responsibility of local authorities and can be established under the Countryside Acts. Regional water parks are more difficult and there is no legislation at present in Britain which provides for their designation or administration. They could well be within the areas of a number of public authorities and some form of joint administration and financing needs to be devised if they are to be developed comprehensively. There could well be a substantial element of private capital involvement in regional water parks, as there would certainly be in new holiday settlements. The system already described of using this capital for developing the recreation provisions, with supporting public finance for the infrastructure of roads and services, would have merit.

### Undeveloped Coast

By developing attraction areas, such as coastal parks and new holiday settlements, it would become more feasible to limit activities elsewhere to those consistent with maintaining environmental quality, leaving some parts of the coast completely undeveloped for those who value remoteness and are prepared to make some effort to find it.

The problem then arises of how to zone undeveloped coast to make the best use of it, having regard to its particular qualities of landscape character and scientific interest, its vulnerability to erosion, and the degree to which it is already used by people. The capacity of coast to absorb people without loss of visual or ecological character will help to establish a basic zoning pattern of optimum use, but there may be places where recreational use should be kept at a level well below this optimum. Farming may be an important land use to be protected in the immediate hinterland, for instance, or existing access roads to the coast may be narrow and dangerous for visitor traffic.

If zoning policies are to be successful for areas already under pressure, they will have to look to methods of positively controlling the extent of recreational use. The prevention of indiscriminate parking, limitations on the size of authorised parks and fluctuating parking fees are all devices which allow access to cars, but control their numbers. Sometimes, however, cars may have to be banned altogether or held at points some distance back from the coast as, for instance, where their appearance on an open headland would spoil the view or their presence among sand dunes would accelerate erosion.

It may be necessary, for instance where arable farmland or soft dunes abut the shore, to channel people along specific routes, as is done at the Gibraltar Point Nature Reserve in Lincolnshire, from the car park through the dune system to the beach. In this kind of situation the willingness of people to accept the restriction will depend on how attractive the

Figure 6.34   Fenced way through to the beach at Gibraltar Point, Lincolnshire, protecting sensitive dunes in a local nature reserve from trampling.

(*Photo: John Foster*)

approach to the beach can be made. At Gibraltar Point the device adopted of making the fenced track through the dunes into a self-guiding nature trail works well.

On the more remote coast where there is no convenient road access, there may be a strong presumption in favour of maintaining this situation and establishing quiet zones for recreational use on foot only. In these circumstances it becomes important to ensure that there is a reasonable public footpath to and along the shore or cliff top and that information is available to visitors about local items of natural history interest.

In designing recreation facilities on undeveloped coastline, good basic siting, using landform to hide cars and buildings from conspicuous view, is better than any attempt to provide screening with trees which themselves may look out of place in an open wind-swept situation. Buildings should be grouped together, modest in scale, of simple design and in sympathetic colours; their function should be to service the essential needs of visitors—no more than simple catering facilities, information points, shelters and lavatories.

On undeveloped coastline which is not of particularly high scenic quality or specially vulnerable and where there is good natural cover, there may be places where small caravan sites or groups of chalets could be established. However, this must be done with an eye to any consequential pressures and demands the development would impose on the coast in the vicinity. The result of allowing too great a freedom for this kind of development is all too obvious on the Mediterranean seaboard and, to a lesser extent, in Scandinavia. Recent legislation in Norway, which severely restricts the freedom to build within 100 metres of the sea, is designed to curb the uncontrolled spread of second homes along open rocky coasts where they are already spoiling the character. In Britain, the comprehensive nature of statutory planning control powers is helpful, but local authorities nevertheless need to develop and enforce strict planning policies if the character of the coastline is not to be lost through inappropriate development.

# Leisure with a Purpose

How people use their leisure time could in most respects be said to be their own affair, but when they are in the countryside they have some responsibility to ensure that they do not damage its interests. The trail of litter and other destruction which so often follows heavy recreational use makes it plain that this responsibility is far from understood. Perhaps this is not altogether surprising, for Britain is an urban nation with four out of five of its population living in major towns and cities. In their daily experience and attitudes these people are far removed from the countryside, and to them a secluded ditch may seem as reasonable a repository for litter as the bin on the street corner at home, or a field of mowing grass as logical a picnic place as the town park.

People visiting the countryside for leisure may or may not have a positive purpose in mind. The former—the positive users—can be actively involved in walking, camping, canoeing or the like, or can be passively driving for pleasure or enjoying the fine scenery. To some of them the countryside will simply be a backcloth to their activities; to others its qualities will be why they are there at all. Those who are in the countryside without a specific purpose in mind may be enjoying their visit, but it may not be very important to them where they go or what they see.

If the positive users observe the country code they will be able to follow their interests without causing trouble to the countryman. If the lack of purpose of the other type of user is due to a lack of understanding then, not only will they be more likely to cause damage, but they will be missing out on an important opportunity to increase their enjoyment. This is not to say that everyone using the countryside for leisure must always do so with a purpose. Just looking around with no particular goal in mind can be enjoyable on occasions.

As recreational pressures on the countryside increase it becomes even more important to ensure that urban visitors understand something about rural life and how they can often, quite inadvertently, cause damage to it. In learning about the countryside there is a bonus, for knowledge sharpens appreciation and this in turn helps to produce an all-important attitude of protection.

## Conservation Education
There is no doubt that countryside and coast are capable of absorbing more recreational use without detriment to character or quality if visitors understand something about conservation. Knowing the country code is an important first step, but more can be done to promote understanding by deliberately providing something to do for people who are in the countryside and working into this a conservation message.

The national park authorities in England and Wales have been doing this work for some years through countryside information centres and warden services. Many organisations, including the Nature Conservancy Council and the Forestry Commission, have developed useful self-guiding nature trails and forest trails. Local authorities and voluntary bodies have encouraged people to take a direct interest in wildlife, and have found people more than a little keen to do this. At Gibraltar Point in Lincolnshire more than a quarter of a million people visit the local nature reserve on the salt marshes every year, and at Loch Garten in Inverness-shire over 100,000 visitors annually make the trip to the hide to view ospreys at close quarters through binoculars.

An encouraging development has been the willingness of some landowners and farmers to show visitors around their estates and farms, explaining to them the special problems of operating in conditions of recreational pressure (6.41). Some landowners have set up estate and farm trails and encouraged schools to visit them and field study centres to use them for teaching purposes. The importance is also being recognised of getting townspeople interested in conservation before they ever leave their urban surroundings. Many cities are developing nature trails and countryside centres in their town parks, and are providing expert staff to promote programmes for their use, particularly by young people.

## Countryside Interpretation
Countryside interpretation is simply the task of explaining the countryside to visitors so that they come to understand the deeper significances of the places they visit. In doing this it is important to point out the impact that man has had on his environment in the past and the effects he can have for good or ill in the future.

Countryside interpretation is still relatively new in Britain, but it has been extensively and successfully used for many years in the United States, particularly in national parks, as a means of capturing the interest of visitors and making them more aware of their environment and the need to look after it.

Provision for countryside interpretation can vary greatly in character and scale, from major visitor centres through a wide range of outdoor facilities, including open-air museums, trails and panorama viewpoints, to simple notices at points of interest (6.42). The range of subjects, too, can be great, for environment is not simply that which we think of as 'natural'. It also covers a whole spectrum of interest in archaeology and social and industrial history. Through the presentational skill of the interpreter, people can be attracted in many different ways to take an interest in what is around them. It is then for the interpreter to put over a story which leaves the visitor with some positive and sympathetic feeling towards the environment.

The extent to which specialised natural history interests are interpreted is now considerable in Britain. Peter Scott's Wildfowl Centre at Slimbridge is perhaps one of the best

Figure 6.35 The on-site interpretation of the life of a rural community—as here at the Auchindrain crofting township in Argyll—is a particularly worth-while activity which is becoming more and more popular.

(*Photo: John Foster*)

known of a number of places where a particular aspect of natural history is explained to the general public. More places like Slimbridge are needed, however, and many organisations, both national and local, are active in providing them, with some support from public money.

Outside the immediate natural history field in recent years there have been useful new developments. The open-air museum type of provision, already well developed in the United States and Scandinavia, is now making progress in Britain. At the Welsh and Ulster Folk Museums and at the Weald and Downland Open-air Museum in Sussex, examples of local vernacular buildings have been re-erected on parkland sites and furnished in the style of their times. Similar work of rescue and re-erection is being done at the Avoncroft Museum of Building in Worcestershire. A variant of this theme is the restoration of groups of buildings on their original site, recreating the communities themselves in their own historical environment. This is particularly appropriate in the case of small farming and crofting communities where the surrounding landscape has been little changed by development since the time they were occupied.

In Denmark, at Moesgard, near Aarhus, and at Lejre, near Roskilde, a further interesting type of development is taking place. Prehistoric dwellings are being constructed in the forms and materials of their times from the best available archaeological knowledge. Some of them are then used in an imitative context; young people occupy them for short periods, wearing clothes and preparing and consuming food appropriate to the period. In this way many people—both those taking part in the living experience and visitors observing it—are able to gain a much better understanding of the past then by simply displaying the dwellings as museum pieces.

A new dimension was added to countryside interpretation in 1970 when the Landmark Visitor Centre was opened at Carrbridge in Inverness-shire. Here, using multi-screen

Figure 6.36 Reconstructed prehistoric dwellings at Moesgard in Denmark. Young people stay for short periods to experience the living conditions of early times.

(*Photo: John Foster*)

Figure 6.37 Similar work to that at Moesgard is being done at the Butser Iron Age Farm in Hampshire.

(*Photo: John Foster*)

Figure 6.38 Landmark Visitor Centre. The long low lines of the building contrast well with the tall pines in the background. The woodland is used to good effect for car parking and picnicking, and a nature trail runs through it.

*(By courtesy of Visitor Centres Ltd.)*

projection in a circular auditorium, visitors can learn in pictures and music about the history of this part of the Highlands from earliest times. In an environmental exhibition they can see how the Highlander lived 200 years ago and, outside, a nature trail introduces them to the old Caledonian Pine forest and the animals and plants that live in it. This type of interpretive provision has been repeated elsewhere, but it is expensive and can only be established at key places in the countryside. However, it can serve as an important focal point for a range of more modest interpretive facilities, introducing knowledge of their existence, what they are about and how to get to them.

Interpretation provided on this basis requires thorough overall planning so that the various themes within an area or region are complementary to one another and not repetitive (6.43). Visitors can thereby get a wider range of experience, greater enjoyment from what they see and, at the end of the day, they can have a broader understanding of the countryside around them. The idea of bringing public and voluntary specialist bodies together to prepare and implement regional interpretive plans has been developed by the Countryside Commission for Scotland, with the long-term intention of putting the whole regional organisation of interpretive plans into a national framework so that people will be served by a network of interpretive centres whose themes will range widely over countryside subjects.

### Relevance to Landscape Planning

Recreational planning policies can benefit from taking account of the interpretive potential of an area and developing countryside interpretive facilities as fully as possible. This has the double advantage of improving protection standards through greater knowledge of the countryside and securing a higher degree of control by directing people's attention towards specific locations geared to receive them.

In the process of developing a recreational planning policy for an area, the interpretive input follows the stage when the resource survey has been analysed and a broad conservation and recreational policy worked out. At that stage an inventory of basic information about interpretive potential is drawn up from available documentary and site information, and the essential theme or story is selected which will demonstrate the significance of the place. Where the theme chosen needs supporting information, which has not been studied in the past, new research information may be commissioned; hence these plans can add significantly to knowledge of an area. The theme is then developed into an interpretive plan and decisions are taken on how best to communicate the story to the public— whether in a building or by trails, viewpoints, guided walks or ranger service activities or, as is frequently the case, by a variety of different media.

The execution of interpretive facilities on the ground provides useful opportunities for landscape design ingenuity, such as the development of techniques for making hard-wearing surfaces which are appropriate in appearance to situations of high landscape quality. The paraphernalia required—notice-boards, signposts, viewpoint indicators and so on—also need to be of design and materials which will withstand hard weather and rough treatment (6.44).

Interpretive facilities will vary greatly in operation. Where interpretation is undertaken within a building there is likely to be staff supervision, although the exhibits themselves may

Figure 6.39    A story to tell

(i) A timely warning—strikingly portrayed—to visitors to the Gibraltar Point nature reserve in Lincolnshire
(ii) The story of East Linton, in East Lothian, told on a hard material which will stand up to weather and malicious damage
(iii) The Forestry Commission have adopted a particularly fitting

timber sign as their standard—here in Grizedale in the Lake District gently reminding visitors not to leave litter
(iv) A simple footpath sign, modest in scale and well executed in local slate

(*Photos: John Foster*)

not necessarily involve staff time in operating or demonstrating them. Indeed, a basic keynote of self-instruction has much to commend it; people like to learn by doing things themselves, whether this is simply the operation of a series of question and answer buttons or the hard physical exertion of grinding corn by hand in a quern. Outside, there is likewise much to be said for the self-guiding type of exhibit or trail, provided the route is well planned both in time and space and the explanatory material is attractively and clearly set out.

In using purpose-built visitor centres, as opposed to buildings which have an intrinsic role in the site interpretation, e.g. country house or open-air museum buildings, the objective should be to simulate within them aspects of the environment in such a way as to gain the interest of visitors and whet their appetites for the outdoor experience of evidence at first hand. In such cases interpretive centres should make visitors positively want to move out to see the reality of what they have learnt within the building. In the case of school groups, however, the use may be reversed and buildings are probably better used after, rather than before, for summing up or carrying out concluding exercises. Because of these differing needs it is very difficult to design

Figure 6.40    At the headquarters of the Countryside Commission for Scotland near Perth, recreational equipment and constructional techniques are on display, with back-up information, to help people making recreational provision in the countryside to choose what is most appropriate for their particular need.

(*Photo: John Foster*)

interpretive centres which cater satisfactorily both for general visitor use and for use by school parties.

Conservation education, and countryside interpretation as a tool in putting it over, has only been described here to the extent necessary to demonstrate the idea of leisure with a purpose as a positive contribution to countryside recreation planning. Beyond the actual facilities on the ground is the possibility of a whole range of support provision through the formal educational system, both at day school and at adult education levels, and the activities of voluntary bodies in orientating public attitudes towards using the countryside for recreation with greater purpose.

# In Conclusion—Priorities and Opportunities

We have seen that in a situation of limited land resources and rising demand for leisure provision, as is the case in Britain and many other countries today, it is essential to develop a recreational system, adequate in scale and sufficiently flexible to meet the future changes in the nature and geography of demand. Such a system, we have already established (see page 161), presupposes involvement in the planning process by all levels of government, in a properly integrated manner.

At the *national* level broadly these responsibilities of Government are:

1. To develop, through the appropriate agencies, research into recreational demand factors and recreational planning techniques likely to have widespread application;
2. To produce an overall strategy for the disposition of the main elements of recreational provision of national significance in relation to major population, communication and landscape quality interests;
3. To secure the integration of this overall strategy within the recreational strategies being planned by authorities at regional and local levels, and to establish a co-ordinated programme for implementation;
4. To provide adequate finance both direct to the national elements in the recreational system (e.g. national parks) and to statutory bodies and local authorities for their contributions;
5. To foster high standards of siting, layout and detailed design in all recreational provision in the countryside whether carried out by public or private agencies.

At the *regional* level the appropriate authorities have the responsibility of planning recreational strategies which will both fit in with the national strategies of central Government and provide a realistic framework into which local authorities can fit smaller-scale recreational provisions. Regional level authorities also have to establish priorities for capital expenditure and ensure that adequate finance is available for subsequent management of those recreational facilities which are not economically self-supporting.

Authorities at the *local* level have the important job of drawing together the major national and regional elements of recreational provision by linking these and complementing them on the ground, so that the overall pattern of facilities will be as effective as possible. Many of the provisions they will be called upon to make will be unlikely to produce much direct income; therefore, there rests upon local authorities special responsibility for maintaining a continuing high standard of management as well as good design in the first instance.

In Scotland, where there are no national parks at present, the need to develop recreational opportunities in a systematic way was recognised in a report published by the Countryside Commission for Scotland in 1974. This report, *A Park System for Scotland* (6.45), has now been accepted in principle by Government as a basis for legislation. It envisages a system comprising urban parks, country parks and regional parks, with a fourth element (given the working title of *special parks*) providing for particular recreational requirements on a national scale. Within all of these categories there would be conservation of the landscape to a degree appropriate to its character as a recreational resource, with adequate finance both to secure the appropriate level and spread of recreational facilities within the elements of the park system and to ensure their continued management in the public interest.

We conclude now with a brief look at some of the main factors which contribute towards a successful recreational system—from research through the stages of planning and implementation to on-going management—and at some of the priorities and opportunities for action which exist in relation to the landscape aspect of recreational planning and provision.

**Research**

Here we need to develop knowledge of the nature and scale of recreation demand and the capacity of different kinds of countryside and coast to take leisure uses—relating these to each other and anticipating the effect of recreation on other land uses. Practical methods need to be refined for identifying significant management factors at the planning stage, for managing various kinds of recreation provision, and for monitoring recreation activities to assess their effects on the environment. All research agencies must work to a fully co-ordinated programme, drawing from relevant experience in other countries and disseminating the results of their work as widely as possible.

Further study and experiment is necessary on the feasibility of putting recreation facilities on a more economic footing so that new countryside provision can be made self-supporting (or nearly so). Significantly more private capital for this kind of development would then become available, with the consequent possibility of spreading more widely the use of public funds.

## Planning

Provision for the leisure use of the countryside must become an important element in its own right in the statutory planning system. Structure plans must include a broad strategy for recreational use appropriate in character and scale to the nature of the area and the anticipated demands on it, incorporating major designated areas such as national parks and forest parks, and proposing major regional attraction areas and the main elements of linear network such as long distance routes.

Local plans must further develop the recreation theme in terms of a specific land use pattern related closely to the availability of recreation resources and the feasibility of developing them. Proposals for local attraction areas, such as country parks, should be set out, along with the detailed network pattern of linking roads and paths and the provision for specialist activities such as camping and caravanning, sailing and fishing. Action plans can further refine the pattern by relating the proposals to a time programme for implementation.

The absence of a recognisable category of recreational land use at the regional scale is an important gap in the countryside recreational hierarchy at present. Neither country parks, at one end of the spectrum, nor national parks at the other meet this need. The ability to establish regional parks, ranging in size from 10,000 to 100,000 hectares, in the wider countryside could effectively draw together heavy recreational pressures which otherwise would cause problems spread over the countryside at large. While the recreational facilities within such regional parks could be developed and run by local authorities, their distribution and establishment require at least some policy guidance at national level.

Co-operation at all levels of interest is essential. Government agencies require to work closely together on national policy issues; the same agencies must collaborate at regional level and link closely with local authorities and private interests, and the co-ordinating machinery must be capable of reflecting national policy thinking and decisions down through the whole system to the smallest public authority and commercial operator in the field.

## Implementation

The implementation of recreation projects requires as careful planning as their location, so that the best use is made of available capital in relation to the priorities of demand. In the future, public and private enterprise action must be co-ordinated to the limit to avoid unnecessary replication of provisions on the ground and waste of public money.

Implementation is the stage when landscape design skill can complement the earlier planning skills which (hopefully) chose well the locations of projects in the first place. In countryside near towns, opportunities will arise for improving landscape quality where land has become run down or completely derelict. In much of the wider countryside and coast and in remote areas the existing character of the landscape will be attraction enough in itself, and the skill will be to fit needed recreation uses unobtrusively into their surroundings.

Design for leisure also requires a high degree of skill in detail as well as overall layout, and techniques for quickly producing new landscape features within recreation sites need to be developed and tried out.

## Management

Management has two aspects—management of land for people and management of people themselves.

If location and design are right, land management can start off with a situation which will be basically favourable to it. In intensive recreation situations particularly, such as country parks, management must be a continuous process in the hands of skilled people, with an important monitoring function to detect over-use quickly and deal with it.

Management of people needs to be both firm and friendly, so that people are drawn naturally and easily towards the areas that are equipped to handle them and away from the sensitive places where their presence would cause damage. Countryside interpretation is a valuable tool, with the double advantage of helping to protect the countryside from damage and at the same time increasing people's enjoyment of it.

Management expertise must also extend to the increasingly sophisticated equipment which is now commonplace in recreation. Cars, caravans, power boats, sailing dinghies, gliders and so on produce many problems. New techniques need to be devised for concentrating their use at suitable places and limiting them at others, using zoning in time and space, and systems of public transport to reduce congestion and other ill-effects.

## The Longer Term

Before the end of the century the land requirements of agriculture and forestry may be very different from those we know today. Already some European countries are contemplating a substantial switch from farming to forestry, incorporating a useful recreation element into new woodlands, but leaving some large-scale management problems as yet unresolved.

The expectation is that farming in Britain will become more intensive on the good land—so much so that its workshop character may render it both unsuitable for recreation and unattractive to the recreationist. How far forestry will take up the less good land which becomes redundant we do not know. However, it is likely that some land with recreation potential will be available, and some of the multiple-use problems of today could be replaced by problems of finding a suitable single use for redundant land.

We need to be ready to exploit the recreational possibilities of this land so that it will continue to have a use of sufficient economic value to ensure its satisfactory management. The sporting potential of some hill land may secure this, but in many places where public access on foot will be the main use, lack of management for farming purposes could produce, not an exciting wilderness condition, but rather the desolation of neglect.

On the other hand demands to use limited resources for water recreation and specialist activities such as caving and rock climbing will undoubtedly continue to increase. There is no reason to believe either that passive recreation—motoring included—will become less popular and ways of managing people and their recreation equipment in large numbers in the countryside will also have to be developed to a scale at present not fully comprehended.

These may be felt by many to be problems for tomorrow and therefore of little concern to us today. If we want our environment to survive the pressures of leisure into the next century, however, we must anticipate now the situations which will arise and develop the knowledge and expertise—by study and experiment on the ground—to handle them successfully.

# References

6.1 OUTDOOR RECREATION RESOURCES REVIEW COMMISSION, *Outdoor Recreation for America*, US Government Printing Office, Washington DC, 1962.

6.2 *Report of the National Parks Committee*, Cmd. No. 3851, HMSO, London, 1931.

6.3 COUNTRYSIDE COMMISION, Tenth *Report*, HMSO, London 1978.

6.4 BRITISH TRAVEL ASSOCIATION/UNIVERSITY OF KEELE, Pilot National Recreation Study; Report No. 1, 1967; Pilot National Recreation Study; Report No. 2, 1969.

6.5 DARTINGTON AMENITY RESEARCH TRUST, *Second Homes in England and Wales*, Countryside Commission, Cheltenham, 1972.
DARTINGTON AMENITY RESEARCH TRUST, *Second Homes in Scotland*, Countryside Commission for Scotland, Perth, 1975.

6.6 TINDALL, F. P., *Dune Conservation; A twenty year record of work in East Lothian*, East Lothian Council, 1970.

6.7 ABERDEEN UNIVERSITY GEOGRAPHY DEPARTMENT, Series on the Beaches of West and North Scottish Mainland, and Western and Northern Isles (13 Volumes), University of Aberdeen, Aberdeen 1969–75.

6.8 HUXLEY, T., *Footpaths in the Countryside*, Countryside Commission for Scotland, Perth, 1970.

6.9 COUNTRYSIDE RECREATION RESEARCH ADVISORY GROUP (CRRAG), *Countryside Recreation Glossary*, Countryside Commission, London, 1970.

6.10 COUNTRYSIDE COMMISSION, Research Register No. 9, Countryside Commission, Cheltenham, 1977.

6.11 AN FORAS FORBARTHA, *Planning for Amenity and Tourism*, Government of Ireland, Dublin, 1966.

6.12 HAMPSHIRE COUNTY COUNCIL, *East Hampshire Area of Outstanding Natural Beauty— A Study in Countryside Conservation*, Hampshire County Council, 1968.

6.13 ZETTER, J. A., *Planning for Informal Recreation at the Local Scale; Sherwood Forest Study*, Countryside Commission, London, 1973.

6.14 WEST RIDING COUNTY COUNCIL, *Recreation in the South Pennines; An interm Report*, West Riding County Council, 1973.

6.15 TOURISM AND RECREATION RESEARCH UNIT, TRIP Series, No. 1 System description, University of Edinburgh, Edinburgh, 1974.

6.16 TOURISM AND RECREATION UNIT, STARS Series, No. 1 Survey Description, 1975; No. 2 Summary Report, 1976; No. 3 The Holidaymaker in Scotland, 1976; No. 5 Patterns of Outdoor Recreation in Scotland, 1977; No. 7 Tourism in the Highlands and Islands, 1977; University of Edinburgh, Edinburgh.

6.17 SCOTTISH TOURISM AND RECREATION PLANNING STUDIES, *Planning for Sport, Outdoor Recreation and Tourism*, No. 1 Strategic Issues, No. 2 A Guide to the Preparation of Initial Regional Strategies, 1976; Countryside Commission for Scotland, Scottish Sports Council, Scottish Tourist Board and Forestry Commission.

6.18 MICHIGAN DEPARTMENT OF CONSERVATION, *Outdoor Recreation Planning in Michigan by a System Analysis Approach*, Part I—A Manual for Programme RECSYS, Technical Manual I, Michigan Department of Conservation, 1966.

6.19 DICKERT, T. G., *et al.*, *Environmental Impact Assessment; Guidelines and Commentary*, University of California, Berkeley, 1974.

6.20 CATLOW, J. AND THIRLWALL, C. G., *Environmental Impact Analysis*, DOE Research Report No. 11, Department of the Environment, London, 1976.

6.21 PADC, *Assessment of Major Industrial Applications*, DOE Research Report No. 13, Department of the Environment, London, 1976.

6.22 FAIRBROTHER, N., *New Lives, New Landscapes*, Architectural Press, London, 1970.

6.23 LEE VALLEY REGIONAL PARK AUTHORITY, *Report on the Development of the Regional Park*, Lee Valley RPA, 1969.

6.24 THOMAS, D. J. and ROBERTS, J. T., *Tyne Valley Recreation Study*, University of Manchester, 1969.

6.25 HURON-CLINTON METROPOLITAN AUTHORITY, *Park Users Survey*, Detroit, 1965.

6.26 COUNTRYSIDE COMMISION, *Policy on Country Parks and Picnic Sites*, Countryside Commission, London, 1969; COUNTRYSIDE COMMISSION FOR SCOTLAND, *Policy on Country Parks for Scotland*, Countryside Commission for Scotland, Perth, 1972.

6.27 COUNTRYSIDE COMMISSION, *Tenth Report*, HMSO, London, 1978; COUNTRYSIDE COMMISSION FOR SCOTLAND, *Tenth Report*, Countryside Commission for Scotland, Perth, 1978.

6.28 FORESTRY COMMISSION, *Fifty-sixth Annual Report*, HMSO, London, 1977.

6.29 COUNTRYSIDE COMMISSION, *Access to Open Country; Model Clauses for Access Agreements*, Countryside Commission, Cheltenham, 1970; COUNTRYSIDE COMMISSION FOR SCOTLAND, *Access Agreements*, Countryside Commission for Scotland, Perth, 1971.

6.30 INSTITUTION OF WATER ENGINEERS, *Recreation on Reservoirs and Rivers*, Institution of Water Engineers, London, 1972.

6.31 BRITISH WATERWAYS BOARD, *Recreational Use of Inland Waterways; Data 1967/74*, British Waterways Board, London.

6.32 MCLAUGHLIN, G. AND BLAIR, J., *It Lends Itself Naturally; A study of the Leeds and Liverpool Canal as a Recreational Resource*, British Waterways Board, London, 1973.

6.33 INLAND WATERWAYS AMENITY ADVISORY COUNCIL, *Scottish Waterways; Forth and Clyde Canal; Union Canal*, Inland Waterways Amenity Advisory Council, London, 1974.

6.34 CARTER, R., 'Scenic routes; Roads for pleasure,' *Surveyor*, **138**, 4125, 1971, pp. 26–31.

6.35 JACOBS, C. A., *Second Homes in Denbighshire*, Denbighshire County Council, 1972.

6.36 SANDFORD (Chairman), *Report of the National Parks Policies Review Committee*, HMSO, London, 1974.

6.37 MILES, J. C., *The Goyt Valley Traffic Experiment*, Countryside Commission and the Peak Park Planning Board, 1972.

6.38 KNOWLES, P., *Building Design Guide; Peak National Park*, Peak Park Joint Planning Board, 1976.

6.39 COUNTRYSIDE COMMISSION, *The Planning of the Coastline*, HMSO, London, 1970; COUNTRYSIDE COMMISSION, *The Coastal Heritage*, HMSO, London, 1970.

6.40 SCOTTISH DEVELOPMENT DEPARTMENT, *North Sea Oil and Gas, Coastal Planning Guidelines*, Scottish Development Department. Edinburgh, 1974.

6.41 DARTINGTON AMENITY RESEARCH TRUST, *Farm Open Days for the Public; A Guide to Organisers*, Countryside Commission, Cheltenham, 1974.

6.42 BEAZLEY, E., *The Countryside on View*, Constable, London, 1971.

6.43 COUNTRYSIDE COMMISSION/COUNTRYSIDE COMMISSION FOR SCOTLAND, *Guide to Countryside Interpretation; Part I, Principles of Countryside Interpretation and Interpretive Planning; Part II, Interpretive Media and Facilities*, HMSO, London, 1975.

6.44 BEAZLEY, E., *Designed for Recreation*, Faber and Faber, London, 1969.

6.45 COUNTRYSIDE COMMISSION FOR SCOTLAND, *A Park System for Scotland*, Countryside Commission for Scotland, Perth, 1974.

# Bibliography

APPLETON, I., (ed.), *Leisure Research and Policy*, Scottish Academic Press, Edinburgh, 1974.

BELL, M., (ed.), *Britain's National Parks*, David and Charles, Newton Abbott, 1975.

BONHAM-CARTER, V., *The Survival of the English Countryside*, Hodder and Stoughton, London, 1971.

BRACEY, H. E., *People and the Countryside*, Routledge and Kegan Paul, London, 1970.

BROCKMAN, C. F., *et al.*, *Recreational Use of Wild Lands*, 2nd ed., McGraw-Hill, New York, 1973.

BURTON, T. L., (ed.), *Recreation Research and Planning*, Allen and Unwin, London, 1970.

CHERRY, G. E., *Environmental Planning 1939–1969*, Vol. II: National Parks and Recreation in the Countryside, (Peacetime History), HMSO, London, 1975.

CHERRY, G. E., (ed.), *Rural Planning Problems*, Leonard Hill, London, 1976.

CLAWSON, M., *Land and Water for Recreation*, University of Chicago Press, Chicago, 1963.

COPPOCK, J. T. and DUFFIELD, B. S., *Recreation in the Countryside: A Spatial Analysis*, Macmillan, London, 1975.

COUNTRYSIDE COMMISSION, *The Weekend Motorist in the Lake District*, HMSO, London, 1969.

COUNTRYSIDE COMMISSION, *The Demand for Outdoor Recreation in the Countryside*, Report of a Seminar, Countryside Commission, London, 1970.

COUNTRYSIDE COMMISSION, *Disused Railways in the Countryside of England and Wales*, HMSO, London, 1970.

COUNTRYSIDE COMMISSION, *Upland Management Experiment: A Report*, Countryside Commission, Cheltenham, 1974.

COUNTRYSIDE COMMISSION, *Waymarking for Footpath and Bridleway*, Report of the Waymarking Study Group, HMSO, London, 1974.

COUNTRYSIDE COMMISSION FOR SCOTLAND, *Scotland's Countryside*, Countryside Commission for Scotland, Perth, 1977.

COUNTRYSIDE COMMISSION FOR SCOTLAND, *The Speyside Way; A Report on a Proposed Long-Distance Route from Spey Bay to Aviemore*, Countryside Commission for Scotland, Perth, 1977.

COUNTRYSIDE RECREATION RESEARCH ADVISORY GROUP, *Research Priorities*, Countryside Commission, London, 1971, 9pp.

COUNTRYSIDE RECREATION RESEARCH ADVISORY GROUP, *Recreation and the Urban Fringe*, Proceedings of a Conference held by CRRAG in Cheltenham, September, 1975, Travis, A. S. and Veal, A. J., (eds), University of Birmingham, Centre for Urban and Regional Studies, Birmingham, 1976.

DARTINGTON AMENITY RESEARCH TRUST, *Farm Recreation and Tourism in England and Wales*, DART, 1974.

DARTINGTON AMENITY RESEARCH TRUST, *Public Transport for Countryside Recreation,* Countryside Commission, Cheltenham, 1976.

DARTINGTON AMENITY RESEARCH TRUST, *Second Homes in Scotland,* A Report to Countryside Commission for Scotland, Scottish Tourist Board, Highlands and Islands Development Board, Scottish Development Department, DART, 1977.

DERBYSHIRE COUNTY COUNCIL/PEAK PARK PLANNING BOARD, *Sailing on Reservoirs,* Derbyshire County Council, 1967.

DOUGLAS, R. W., *Forest Recreation,* 2nd ed., Pergamon Press, Oxford, 1975.

DOWER, M., *The Fourth Wave: The Challenge of Leisure,* Civic Trust, London, 1965.

DUFFELL, J. R., *Car Parking and Pleasure Travel in the Countryside,* Institution of Municipal Engineers, London, 1974.

FAIRBROTHER, N., *The Nature of Landscape Design,* Architectural Press, London, 1974.

FISCHER, D. W., LEWIS, J. E., and PRIDDLE, G. B., *Land and Leisure: Concepts and Methods in Outdoor Recreation,* Maaroufa Press, Chicago, 1974.

FORESTRY COMMISSION, *Public Recreation in National Forests,* HMSO, London, 1968.

FORSTER, R. R., *Planning for Man and Nature in National Parks; Reconciling Perpetuation and Use,* International Union for Conservation of Nature, Morges, 1973.

HALL, A., *The Bollin Valley;* A Study of Land Management in the Urban Fringe, Countryside Commission, Cheltenham, 1976.

HOOKWAY, R. J. S., European Conservation Conference: Report on Theme IV—Leisure, Council of Europe, Strasbourg, 1970.

LAND USE CONSULTANTS, *A Planning Classification of Scottish Landscape Resources,* Countryside Commission for Scotland, Perth, 1971.

MARLOWE, O. C., *Outdoor Design: A Handbook for the Architect and Planner,* Crosby Lockwood Staples, London, 1977.

MILLER, T. G., *Long-Distance Paths of England and Wales,* David and Charles, Newton Abbot, 1977.

NEW FOREST JOINT STEERING COMMITTEE, *Conservation of the New Forest;* Final Recommendations, New Forest Steering Committee, 1972.

ORRAM, M. H., Recreational Use of Forests in Holland: Research and Development Paper No. 48, Forestry Commission, London, 1967.

PARHAM, E. T., *The Deeside Railway Line: Its Potential Use,* Countryside Commission for Scotland, Perth 1971.

PARHAM, E. T., *Disused Railway Lines in Scotland, A Strategic Appraisal,* Countryside Commission for Scotland, Perth, 1973.

PATMORE, J. A., *Land and Leisure,* David and Charles, Newton Abbot, 1970.

PEAK PARK PLANNING BOARD, *A New Look at Water Resources,* Peak Park Planning Board, Bakewell, 1971.

RAPAPORT, R. and R. N., *Leisure and the Family Life Cycle,* Routledge and Kegan Paul, London, 1975.

SCOTTISH DEVELOPMENT DEPARTMENT, Report of the Technical Group on the Cairngorm Area, HMSO, Edinburgh, 1967.

SCOTTISH TOURIST BOARD, *Tourism in Scotland,* Scottish Tourist Board, Edinburgh, 1970.

SIDAWAY, R. M., *Organisation of Outdoor Recreation Research and Planning in the Netherlands,* Forestry Commission, London, 1974.

SIMMONS, I. G., *Rural Recreation in the Industrial World,* Edward Arnold, London, 1975.

SKINNER, D. N., *The Planning and Design of Rural Roads: The Implications of Landscape and Recreation,* Scottish Tourist Board and Countryside Commission, Scotland, Edinburgh, 1976.

TILDEN, F., *Interpreting our Heritage,* University of North Carolina Press, Chapel Hill, 1969.

TIVY, J., *The Concept and Determination of Carrying Capacity of Recreational Land in the USA: A Review,* Countryside Commission for Scotland, Perth, 1972.

TRAVIS, A. S., *A Strategic Appraisal of Scottish Tourism,* Scottish Tourist Board, Edinburgh, 1974.

TRAVIS, A. S., *et al., Recreation Planning for the Clyde,* Scottish Tourist Board, Edinburgh, 1970.

US DEPARTMENT OF THE INTERIOR, Bureau of Outdoor Recreation, *Outdoor Recreation: A Legacy for America,* US Government Printing Office, Washington DC, 1973.

ROBIN WADE DESIGN ASSOCIATES, *Proposed Development of an Interpretive Centre at Clumber Park, Nottinghamshire,* Countryside Commission, Cheltenham, 1976.

WESTMACOTT, R. and WORTHINGTON, T., *New Agricultural Landscapes,* Countryside Commission, Cheltenham, 1974.

WHITBY, M. C., *et al., Rural Resource Development,* Methuen, London, 1974.

CHAPTER SEVEN
# COMMUNICATION SYSTEMS IN THE LANDSCAPE

Derek Lovejoy

M6 MOTORWAY in the Lune Valley, Westmorland. A nation's life line; a greedy consumer of a nation's most reliable resource—land—which could either scar the landscape and lower quality of life, or by using all professional skills be an object of grace and beauty to enhance and not despoil the landscape

# COMMUNICATIONS SYSTEMS IN THE LANDSCAPE

## The Communications System

In planning terms, the aim in creating any communications system, whether for the movement of people and freight, the transport of materials through pipelines, or the transmission of power by cable, is to obtain maximum co-ordination and maximum socio-economic benefit with minimum disturbance to the environment.

Ideally, the various components of a nation's communications network must operate as a co-ordinated and integrated whole. Those countries which have established their communications systems as a composite part of their overall planning have considerable social and economic advantage over those whose systems are fragmented.

The aspects of communication of major concern in this chapter are, quite obviously, those relating to land use and landscape planning, but these cannot be discussed in isolation from other considerations, in particular:

1. The need to complement the economic and growth policies of a nation or a region;
2. The 'planning' of the system and the adaptability of the plans to unforeseen changes;
3. Socio-economic effects of the system;
4. Environmental impacts.

### 1. The System as a Complement to Economic and Growth Policies

The economic growth and the development of a nation or region, and consequently of all its resources, are closely related to an infrastructure, within which the overall communications system is of fundamental importance because of its close relationship to economic activity. Since the costs of communication and transportation are components of the aggregate cost of development and the conservation of resources, higher efficiency of the system will be reflected in lower cost of development and in conservation of resources. An example of this point is, surely, the question of containerised freighting discussed later in this chapter.

The analysis of any system should identify the priority ranking for its improvements. Evaluation of this ranking on the basis of such parameters as time and capital will result in assessment of deficiency and will assist in formulating plans to reduce this deficit. However, in any such scheme of improvement, a careful watch must be kept on investments.

### 2. The 'Planning' and Adaptability of the System

The need for an integrated communications network has already been stated; the need for planning this system is obvious.

The communications requirements for different regions must be studied case by case in order to provide an optimal combination of different means of transport and related facilities. Such complex infrastructural combinations must be conceived as integrated wholes, even when they are to be brought into operation gradually.

In terms of planning strategy, the hazards of long-term planning and forecasting introduce logistic constraints. Planning studies may reveal that for different growth rates, different strategies are required. It is extremely difficult, if not impossible, to switch from one strategy to another. If the growth rate is changed, selected strategies must be sufficiently flexible to be adaptable to change at any stage.

### 3. The Socio-economic Effects of the System

Until comparatively recently the co-ordination and routeing of major communication and transportation facilities, such as roads, canals and railways, and all forms of transmission lines and pipelines (see Chapter 8), were based almost entirely on technical and financial considerations. Today, however, it is realised that such premises have caused destruction of the environment and, as a result, a lowering of living standards.

A balance must be made between the 'ideal technical design' of a communications system and the ensuing economic advantages, and the effects on the quality of life. Thus, in the analysis of any system, economic gains (both short and long term) must be related to social and environmental considerations. Take, for example, the closing of an uneconomic railway which may seriously inconvenience the local population. To make good these closures, additional roads requiring additional land may be necessary, using up further 'natural' resources.

On an altogether larger scale, the inquiry into the siting of the Third London Airport (7.1) (which has since been abandoned for reasons of national economy and pressure from local environmental organisations) is an excellent example of the complexities and conflicts involved in planning an integrated system and terminal. Major political, socio-economic and environmental considerations conflicted, and a Royal Commission was convened to reconcile these conflicts. By an overwhelming majority decision, based on predominantly economic considerations, the Commission recommended an inland site. However, a minority report by one member of the Commission, Professor Sir Colin Buchanan, recommended an off-shore site at Foulness as the least detrimental to the total environment. The minority report was accepted by the British Government and this, indeed, was an historic decision of great international significance. The quality of life had at last triumphed over purely material considerations.

### 4. Environmental Impacts

It is self-evident that the environmental impacts of the development of a communications system are very closely linked with land use and landscape considerations. However, before dealing with these considerations in more detail in relation to different systems, it is instructive to look at the broader implications.

As already suggested, in recent years environmental questions have had a profound influence on the siting and type of system used, but much damage has already been done. For instance, the last century saw the introduction of a comprehensive network of railways in many countries. These were constructed to similar engineering standards as are modern motorways, i.e. flat gradients and wide horizontal curves. The routeing took little cognisance of the environment and cut through cities and towns and often followed easy coastline routes, cutting foreshore and beaches from the adjoining towns. The Italian Government in the 1930s aligned motorways at rooftop level over cities, over-riding any environmental considerations for the sake of political and military prestige. In the United States the elevated railways have blighted a number of cities. Now, however, an increasing number of nations are establishing minimum environmental standards as far as visual interference and noise levels are concerned.

A country's communications system sterilises a large part of its most valuable resource, land, and the conservation of land is of supreme importance, whether the country be agrarian or industrial. Thus, the need to plan for an integrated communications and transportation network which is designed in relation to the environment (a full account being taken of the conservation of land and betterment of the quality of life) cannot be overstated.

Turning to the land use and landscape factors involved in the planning, design and development of communications systems, first interchanges and terminals are discussed and then individual forms of transportation, while transmission lines and pipelines are considered in Chapter 8.

# Transport System Terminals and Interchanges

Any transport and communication system is dependent on its accessibility and this means well-sited, co-ordinated and well-designed terminals and interchanges.

Planning individual transportation systems without proper interrelationship invariably causes chaos, and is wasteful of land and capital. Frequently, the problem is one of unco-ordinated facilities for the transfer of people or freight from one system to another. The multi-purpose terminal will ensure rapid and convenient transfer and should be high on the priority list in urban and rural planning.

The location of terminals should be such that as many transportation systems as possible are brought together, where possible linking air, underground and surface railway, sea and road transport; it is desirable to combine both public and private transport. This will maximise capacities and minimise land take, and also avoid duplication of many facilities which would be required if separate terminals were provided.

The movement of freight is no less important than passenger transportation, and it is in this field that one of the greatest advances has been made, with the almost universal adoption of container systems. Containers for maritime use are now available up to 2·6 m high by 12 m long. Goods are handled only twice—once when loaded, and once when unloaded—thus giving almost perfect security from theft and damage. One great advantage of containerisation is the speed of handling; for example, it is possible to send a cargo from Italy to Scotland in five days.

Figure 7.1   Southampton container terminal shows the interchange of sea,
road and rail transport for goods. Containerisation solves the problem of the
visual integration of large warehouses in
the dockland scene.

(*Photo by courtesy of Aerofilms Ltd.*)

Figure 7.2   Multi-transport terminals.
Gatwick Airport shows how road, rail
and air transport can interchange under
one roof. Gatwick links domestic and
international air services, a rail link to
London, and a link to the M23
motorway, handling passenger and light
cargo traffic.

(*Photo by courtesy of the British
Airports Authority*)

The earlier problems of one-way journeys to 'consumer' countries have now largely been solved by using end-of-life containers for these journeys; the container is used for other purposes at the 'consuming end', thus cutting out the cost of returning empties.

A coastal location for multi-functional intercommunication terminals is therefore desirable. Such terminals may be sited on low-quality reclaimed land, and the interchange of sea, river, air, road and rail transport may be fully integrated. Dredging will not be required to bring large container ships up river, and there should be many other waterway benefits, particularly for hovercraft and hydrofoils. Further advantages would, of course, be possible with the linking of the terminals to the canal system.

It is not possible to examine in detail all the future prospects of co-ordinating transportation, but many interesting projects appear to be under development. These include passenger container capsules lifted by helicopter between multi-system terminals and the development of the vertical and short take-off aircraft enabling planes to operate from city centres and eliminating the often congested city-airport road link, provided noise problems can be overcome. Whatever form terminal developments may take, they present splendid opportunities for imaginative architectural and landscape treatment.

## Transportation Systems

The form of communication which has the greatest impact on landscape planning is the transportation system of a region. Roads, railways and canals have a considerable effect on the landscape, not only visually, but because they alter the ecology, settlement pattern and land use of the surrounding landscape. Therefore the national and regional transport policies are a matter of concern and involvement for the landscape planner.

In 1976, the British Government published a consultative document on Transport Policy (7.2) in which the main aims of a national transport policy are summarised as follows:

*Efficiency*: to maintain a safe and efficient transport system which provides good transport facilities at the lowest cost in terms of the resources used;

*Social*: to give high priority to the social welfare aspects of transport, and in particular to the public transport needs of those without access to a car;

*Environmental*: to protect and relieve the community from the unwarranted impact of transport on the environment;

*Resources*: to secure the efficient use of scarce resources, notably energy;

*Choice and local democracy*: to leave as much freedom of choice as possible both to users and to democratic decision;

*The interests of transport workers*: to ensure that the changes ahead are accomplished in the context of full trade union involvement;

*Public expenditure*: to recognise the need to restrain public expenditure and in particular to confine subsidy to the area of greatest need.

'Government must thus develop a controlled and managed market in transport, rejecting both the market philosophy of a free-for-all and, at the other extreme, the approach of those who would rigidly allocate transport between different modes by administrative direction. The aim should be to set a framework for transport policy which reflects all economic, social and environmental objectives, making use of the various instruments available to the Government.'

## Highway Networks

During the last few years there have been significant changes in British Government policy towards the location of highways in the environment. Fundamental rethinking by Government and planners, together with increasing public pressure, has led to a situation where monetary considerations are no longer the overriding issues, and environmental factors are assuming greater importance. Perhaps in Britain, with its small-scale landscape and exceptionally high densities, this is understandable, but even countries with an abundance of land can benefit from the lessons which the British Government has learned.

In 1976, the Jefferson Report, *Route Location with regard to Environmental Issues* (7.3), highlighted many environmental problems and tried to quantify many of these. This report was followed in 1977 by the Leitch Report on Trunk Road Assessment (7.4), whose Committee's terms of reference were broadly:

1. To comment on, and recommend any changes in, the Department of the Environment's method of appraising trunk road schemes and their application, taking account of both economic and environmental factors...
2. To review the Department of the Environment's method of traffic forecasting, its application of the forecasts and to comment on the sensitivity of the forecasts to possible policy changes.

The Leitch Report recommended a major shift in official policy; namely that monetary considerations must no longer be the overriding determinant in major trunk road evaluation, but that environmental considerations must in future predominate. This, and all other major recommendations of the report, were endorsed by Government in the White Paper, *Policy for Roads: England 1978* (7.5).

The following extracts from the Leitch Report set out clearly the recommendations of the Committee on the new approach to highway routeing and design.

## Recommendations of the Leitch Report

### TRAFFIC FORECASTING

1. The Department should indicate the likely range of uncertainties involved in the forecasts and demonstrate the consequences of selecting different values within that likely range. It should never put itself in the position of appearing to defend a single figure as if it was uniquely correct.

2. The Department should as soon as is practicable move away from the extrapolatory form of model currently used towards basing its forecasts on causal models. The car ownership forecasting model which forms part of the RHTM* package might form the basis of the approach we recommend.

3. There should be further study of the relationship between kilometres travelled per car and the price of fuel (including tax), income and different journey purposes for different sections of the population.

4. More attention should be paid to the forecasting of commercial vehicle traffic.

### BEFORE AND AFTER STUDIES

5. Procedures should be established for the execution of before and after studies and a programme of such studies should be drawn up and implemented.

### A FRAMEWORK FOR THE ASSESSMENT OF TRUNK ROAD SCHEMES

6. The Department should adopt a framework for the assessment of trunk road schemes along the lines of the one we illustrate in Chapter 20.

7. The assessment should take account of the effects of a scheme on five initial incidence groups:

(a) Road users directly affected by the scheme;
(b) Non-road users directly affected by the scheme;
(c) Those concerned with the intrinsic value of the area through which a scheme passes;

(d) Those indirectly affected by the scheme; and
(e) The financing authority.

8. The Departments of the Environment and of Transport should strengthen their research effort into the effects of trunk road construction on land use.

9. The effects of trunk road construction on regional economic development should be included in the assessment only where strong evidence can be adduced to support them.

10. Where individual schemes have significant effects on other modes of transport, those effects should be included within the assessment.

11. The framework should be used to decide between options within a scheme, on a basis of judgement, comprehending all factors whether valued in monetary terms or not.

12. The decision to build a scheme or not should be based on the framework data, again comprehending all factors whether valued in monetary terms or not.

13. Schemes recommended for inclusion in the programme should be given a merit rating. For practical purposes three ratings should be adequate.

14. The time at which a scheme starts should take account not only of its merit rating but also such practical factors as the overall availability of funds and the stage reached in design.

15. There should be the fullest consultation with interested Government Departments, local authorities, national and local interest groups and the general public in the preparation of the framework, and its results should be made publicly available and be fully explained to all concerned.

### THE ECONOMIC COMPONENT OF THE ASSESSMENT

16. The Department should continue to keep the values of working and non-working time it uses under constant review.

17. The Department should consider identifying three types of trip; in work, to and from work and pure leisure, and give appropriate values of time to each.

18. The concept of the 'equity value' of time should be removed and the values attributed should be based on observed incomes of road users.

19. Consideration should be given to allowing the user to vary the standard work: non-work car mix within COBA† to take account of local circumstances.

---

* *RHTM*. In general, traffic modelling identifies and correlates the factors determining traffic generation, attraction and choice of route. The Regional Highway Traffic Model is being developed with the object of improving the quality of traffic forecasting. It is intended to establish a control data bank, to develop forecasting procedures, and to standardise data collection procedures.

† COBA is a computer program for preparing a cost benefit analysis for major road schemes. It includes all environmental factors where these can be evaluated in cash terms, but has been much criticised for the rigidity of its basic cost assumptions and its inability to handle non-quantifiable data.

20. Given the current state of knowledge the Department should continue its practice of aggregating small time savings at a uniform unit value.

21. Attention should be given to updating the police, legal and medical costs used in accident evaluation in the light of more recent evidence that may be available.

22. The value of lost output used in accident evaluation should be based on the average income of the population at risk.

23. The notional allowance for pain, grief and suffering used in accident evaluation should be a matter of further inter-departmental study and of public consultation, and until these processes are complete this component of all accident values currently used by the Department should be increased by 50%.

24. The Department should continue to pursue the research it already has in hand into the attribution of accidents to junctions.

25 The Department should attempt to establish the relationship between speed trend and fuel prices, and the other determinants of speed trend, as accurately as possible.

26. The Department should exercise close supervision over the inputs made at scheme level for time saved through reduced delay at junctions.

27. Traffic counting should be moved from August to April or October (or both) and consideration should be given to devoting more resources to performing more closely specified local traffic surveys.

28. The Department should investigate further whether it is appropriate to apply national average figures to 'holiday areas'.

29. The scrutiny by policy divisions of the way in which COBA is applied to individual schemes should continue.

THE NON-ECONOMIC COMPONENT
OF ASSESSMENT
30. In view of the importance of accident savings the total numbers of casualties divided between fatal, serious and slight should be included within the framework as well as their inclusion in the cost benefit analysis.

31. Driver comfort and convenience should be included within the assessment and the Department should undertake research to determine a method of assessing it in objective terms.

32. Where the effect of a scheme on pedestrians is likely to be significant some form of pedestrian survey should be undertaken to allow time savings to pedestrians to be assessed. These savings should then be evaluated in the same way as time savings to other road users and incorporated in the cost benefit analysis.

33. The Department should consider undertaking further research into the possibility of producing a composite index based on the number of pedestrians, the severity of the effect and, at a later stage, the length of exposure.

34. The number of each type of building which is to be demolished should be identified separately.

35. The Department should cease to set out on a scheme drawing the number of dwellings newly exposed to a noise level of 68 dB(A).

36. Noise contour maps should instead be drawn for appropriate schemes showing the situation with and without the new road and, where night time noise is a problem, for day and night separately.

37. The total number of dwellings by category subject to an increase or decrease in noise levels should be extracted from this map and summated at intervals equivalent to its contours.

38. Visual envelope maps* should be drawn for appropriate schemes and the number of dwellings or other buildings subject to severe, significant or slight visual intrusion listed within the framework.

39. On an experimental basis film using the 'travelling matt'† technique should be prepared for particularly sensitive areas before the line and design of a new road is finalised.

40. Where air pollution is likely to be a problem a special air quality report should be prepared: otherwise it should be excluded from the assessment.

41. Where disruption during construction is likely to be a significant factor in environmental terms it should be explicitly mentioned within the assessment.

42. The direct effects of a scheme on local employment, where they exist, should be included within the assessment.

43. In addition to the market valuation included in COBA the amount of land of each agricultural grade which will be taken by the scheme should be listed.

44. An assessment should be made of the effects of a scheme in severing farm units.

45. In the case of bypass schemes the assessment of severance should be comprehensive, covering all roads affected by the scheme, and should also note the numbers of people affected.

46. The effects of a scheme on the intrinsic value of the area through which it passes, and on environmental and natural assets, should be included in the assessment.

* *Visual Envelope.* Very similar to a zone of visual influence diagram, but shows the locations from which the road will be visible rather than a complete zone.

† *Travelling Matt.* A technique for imposing a road and traffic image onto a film of the landscape along the proposed route line. Expensive and does not cover any aspect except the visual impact on the landscape.

## DESIGN CRITERIA

47. The Department should adopt a more flexible approach to design criteria and standards.

48. The Department should use cost benefit analysis to balance road user benefits against construction costs within a range of permitted limits.

## THE REGIONAL HIGHWAY TRAFFIC MODEL

49. The data provided by the RHTM should at the right time be made available to outside research workers.

50. The project should be opened up to informed debate and, once this has been done, the Department should take careful stock of the aims and objectives of the project as a whole.

51. The Department should intensify its studies of the influence of motoring costs, with particular attention to petrol prices, on vehicle ownership and use.

52. The component parts of the RHTM project should be subject to statistical tests to assess the acceptibility of its hypotheses and the degree of confidence to be attached to the estimates of the explanatory variables.

53. Because of the crucial importance of the calibration of the model the Department should rely on proven conventional techniques for that process.

54. The proposition that motorists always seek to save time, irrespective of the costs of so doing, should be reconciled with the money value the Department places on resource and perceived values of time in other contexts.

55. The development of the commercial vehicle trip end model should be given priority.

56. The Department's training programme for staff in the use of the RHTM should be adequate to ensure that the user has a good overall grasp of the model and of the processes by which the output has been produced.

57. In the implementation of the RHTM the Department's aim should be to ensure that the current degree of central control applied to COBA is generally maintained.

## URBAN TRUNK ROAD EVALUATION

58. The Department should review its implementation of the recommendations of the Urban Motorways Committee in the light of our report.

## COMPARABILITY WITH OTHER MODES OF TRANSPORT

59. Where direct alternatives arise between road and rail schemes the competing solutions should be compared using cost benefit analysis within the broader framework we have discussed in Chapter 20.

60. Strategic or policy studies conducted to compare the rates of return from investment in road and rail should be conducted on the basis of cost benefit analysis, within the framework, rather than financial appraisal.

61. The Department should develop satisfactory methods of assessing accident savings associated with rail schemes consistent with those used for trunk road schemes.

In its conclusions, the Report re-emphasises a number of points contained in the list of recommendations. As shown in the following paragraphs from the conclusions, they reinforce the need for better forecasting techniques, and more particularly the need to give greater cognisance to environmental and social factors which are not susceptible to valuation in money terms.

## TRAFFIC FORECASTING

Uncertainties are fundamental in the forecasting process, arising both from the data used and from the model itself. It is crucial that such uncertainties are acknowledged. The Department's current methods, because they are based on extrapolatory techniques, are generally insensitive to future policy changes. It is therefore preferable to adopt a 'causal' model. The RHTM car ownership model is an example of such an approach.

## A FRAMEWORK FOR THE ASSESSMENT OF TRUNK ROAD SCHEMES

Whilst the current system, based on cost benefit analysis, appears to us generally sound as far as it goes, we believe it to be unbalanced and we suggest a shift of emphasis in the whole approach. It is unsatisfactory that the assessment should be so dominated by those factors which are susceptible to valuation in money terms and we believe it to be inadequate to rely simply on a checklist to comprehend environmental factors.

We believe that the right approach is through a comprehensive framework which embraces all the factors and groups of people involved in scheme assessment. We believe too that such a framework should be employed from the earliest planning stages of a scheme. We also believe that, in the last analysis, the assessment must depend to a considerable degree on judgement. The alternative schemes should be assessed by pairwise comparison. The best option emerging from this comparison should finally be compared with the 'do nothing' alternative, to assess whether on balance the scheme is beneficial to the community.

## THE NON-ECONOMIC COMPONENT OF THE ASSESSMENT

We believe that, although the Department's methods of evaluating environmental factors are still in an experimental stage following the Jefferson Report, they are basically sound for the factors which are included. We do, however, make a number of detailed proposals about how they should be handled and recommend that the indirect effects of a scheme and its effect on the intrinsic value of the area through which it passes should be included within the assessment.

### DESIGN CRITERIA

More use should be made of COBA in making choices at the level of detailed design and we believe that design staff should be encouraged to adopt a greater degree of flexibility in making these choices.

### PUBLIC PRESENTATION

We believe that, since Government has undertaken to consult the public on the decisions it takes about trunk roads, it has a fundamental obligation to ensure that the methods of assessment it adopts are fully comprehensible. We therefore applaud the concept of an annual Roads White Paper. It is also central to the framework approach we have proposed that, at the local level, the entire framework with supporting documents should be made publicly available.

### Comment

It is obvious that the impact of major road proposals on all aspects of national, regional and local planning must be fully assessed. A new road will open up areas hitherto protected from intense use, and the effect on the ecology, water catchment and wildlife must be predicted, analysed and planned for, in order to avoid adverse environmental and social effects.

In nearly all countries in the world, increasing traffic volumes are resulting in large areas being taken every year for new road schemes. For example, the total number of vehicles in Britain in 1950 was 4·4 million, by 1960 it had reached 9·43 million and by 1974, 17·00 million. By 1977, private cars alone totalled over 14 million. The effect of vehicles on the road system depends on the amount of travelling as well as on the actual number of vehicles. The number of vehicle-kilometres travelled annually is a good index of loading on road systems. In the UK in 1976, private cars and taxis travelled $200 \cdot 53 \times 10^9$ vehicle-kilometres, while heavy goods vehicles travelled $20 \cdot 22 \times 10^9$ vehicle-kilometres, and light vans $21 \cdot 36 \times 10^9$ vehicle-kilometres (7.6). On current estimates, by the year 2000 cars and taxis will travel $339 \times 10^9$ vehicle-kilometres, and heavy goods vehicles $28 \cdot 89 \times 10^9$ vehicle-kilometres (7.7). However, as pointed out in the Leitch Report, such estimates are based on extrapolatory techniques and are generally insensitive to future policy changes, therefore the uncertainty of their accuracy must be recognised in assessing the needs for new roads.

Despite such uncertainties, great advances have been made in all areas of transport environment evaluation. However, it is essential to know in what fields these advances have been made and what degree of reliance can be placed on each technique or method.

If an evaluation method claims to be strictly objective, it can only make use of data such as land areas, traffic flows, numbers of buildings and trees, and geological information, as well as measurable environmental factors such as noise, light and pollution. Even cost data are largely subjective, depending on the point of view of the owner or occupier of land or buildings, and the current and potential use of these resources.

In many cases, the values can be reasonably decided by reference to a known threshold of tolerance; for example, that the level of noise and the number of vehicles predicted can only reach a certain limit without causing intolerable conditions. But for other environmental factors, no such straightforward assessment can be made. Even though it is possible to classify and measure elements of landscape and land use, the value that each element carries depends not only on individual perception, but may vary widely according to the regional and local context of the element, and the political, economic and ethnic viewpoint of those involved in the assessment.

One of the most widely used methods of evaluating highway routes is the operational research technique known as *cost benefit analysis* (CBA). CBA puts a money value on those costs and benefits which do not have a direct market price (such as savings in journey time) so that they can be set against items which carry an actual price. In the form of a computer software package called COBA (7.8) it is used extensively for evaluating major road construction and improvement schemes. The purpose of COBA is to calculate the economic return of a road scheme by comparing the costs and benefits incurred in the project. The benefits consist chiefly in savings in journey time, cost of operating vehicles, and the reduction of accident costs; and when all the possible routes for a highway have been assessed in this way, the total benefits for the project can be calculated. In the COBA method the benefits are calculated over a thirty year period and discounted at the test discount rate (Figure 7.3).

COBA is best suited to the analysis of road projects where alternative routes are available, each having different environmental benefits and penalties. It is particularly valuable in route planning close to existing conurbations, or in areas of great landscape value, where the decision as to the preferred route is not easily made. The measurable environmental factors such as noise, pollution, severance, visual intrusion, and land take can be quantified and given an approximate value for each route (7.9). As discussed in the Leitch Report, the COBA package is by no means perfect, but it does at least give a standard method of assessment for comparing alternative routes by reducing the subjective elements to the minimum, and by ensuring that different highway authorities are using a common basis for costing road proposals, thus enabling Government to decide priorities for national roads expenditure.

**COST**

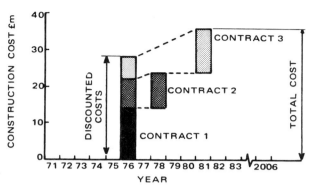

**BENEFITS**

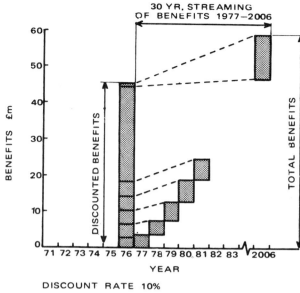

DISCOUNT RATE 10%

NET VALUE 1976 = DISCOUNTED BENEFITS − DISCOUNTED COSTS

| Cost, £m | Discounted Cost, £m | Discounted Benefit, £m | Net Value 1976, £m | Placing in Order of Net Value |
|---|---|---|---|---|
| 35.3 | 32.0 | 47.7 | 15.7 | 1 |
| 45.7 | 42.1 | 40.0 | −2.1 | 16 |
| 51.2 | 47.0 | 38.8 | −8.2 | 26 |
| 38.1 | 34.9 | 40.5 | 5.6 | 5 |
| 38.8 | 35.2 | 44.1 | 8.9 | 2 |
| 47.3 | 43.6 | 44.3 | 0.7 | 12 |
| 44.2 | 40.2 | 42.9 | 2.7 | 7 |
| 52.7 | 48.5 | 43.1 | −5.4 | 21 |
| 39.6 | 36.4 | 44.8 | 8.4 | 3 |

Figure 7.3 These diagrams illustrate discounting techniques. Economic assessment of 45 possible routes using discounted cash flow techniques, discounting costs and benefits of each route to a common base year for the purposes of comparison. Costs including building land and all associated works derived from actual costs of quantities taken from engineering details. Travel benefits attributable to the new routes are represented by the saving in travel costs which are the sum of vehicle operating, travel time and accident costs.

## Planning a New Road

New major roads and motorways may be needed for many different reasons: to complete a national strategic network; to serve new industrial development; to improve access to tourist areas; to relieve intolerable congestion on existing road systems; or to replace an old road too hazardous for modern traffic. Several of these reasons may combine to make the construction of a new road a necessity. But it is important that the new roads do not do more harm than good. Many factors must be measured and considered with great care before the optimum route for the road can be selected. As far as possible, the future effects of the road on the area must be predicted and incorporated in the decision-making procedure.

The factors controlling route selection vary in importance according to the type of area through which the road passes; obviously near towns and villages the factors of noise and

pollution are critical, while in remote rural areas landscape values, particularly visual intrusion, ecological and wildlife conservation will predominate.

Some factors, such as noise levels, traffic flows, and engineering costs, can be measured and predicted with considerable accuracy, while others such as loss of amenity, visual intrusion, and landscape values are less quantifiable. The following sections set out the major factors influencing the choice of the route of a new road:

1. Traffic flows;
2. Engineering constraints;
3. Land use and land take;
4. Landscape values;
5. Visual intrusion;
6. Noise and vibration;
7. Pollution;
8. Community severance;
9. Road safety.

Figure 7.4 (Above)   An excellent example on the M6 motorway of the harmony between motorway and landscape.

(*Photo by courtesy of John Maltby Ltd. and the Civic Trust*)

Figure 7.5 (Left)   Enormous contouring problems on the M62 near Ripponden. Such engineering works require the highest professional skills to rehabilitate the landscape after engineering operations.

(*Photo by courtesy of Aerofilms Ltd.*)

Figure 7.6 (Below)   A good example of aligning a motorway over difficult terrain in Switzerland by allowing the landscape to flow uninterrupted and avoiding large cutting and filling problems.

(*Photo: Derek Lovejoy*)

## 1. Traffic Flows

Future traffic can be estimated from projected changes in physical pattern of the region, population, industry, etc., and the traffic movements determined by origin and destination surveys (7.10). Sophisticated modelling techniques are used to simulate the effects of various estimated traffic flows and densities. Regional Highway Traffic Models for predicting traffic flows are now being developed for the whole of England (see page 197).

It is important to assess not only the actual amount of traffic, but to differentiate between small lightweight vehicles such as private cars, light vans and motorcycles, and heavy commercial trucks and lorries, which ought to be routed away from small towns and villages (see Figure 7.7). Many heavy lorries are larger than the houses in the streets they use, and although the measurable levels of noise, pollution, and hazard may not be excessive, the sensation of intrusion and aggression can be traumatic for local inhabitants.

The origin and destination of traffic are also important; people will tolerate considerable traffic congestion if it is caused by their own community industry or townsmen, and can be seen to be necessary to their economy, but objections will always be raised to 'through' traffic which brings no benefit to the inhabitants. In many instances, the diversion of a proportion of through traffic may be sufficient to satisfy local objections. One of the best examples of this in Britain is the desire of the local people along the A66 to have by-passes for villages and towns on the route—in contrast to the objections from national pressure groups who wish to preserve the landscape.

## 2. Engineering Constraints

There may be special studies needed, for example, in areas where underground mining is extensive and where special precautions must be taken for highways constructed in areas liable to subsidence. Engineering surveys must include the fullest possible study of topography, geology, pedology, water catchment and water table, meteorology and public utilities. Frequently much of this information may be obtained from existing data, but it must be supplemented by further specialist studies.

The meteorological surveys are most important as weather conditions can seriously affect highway safety. Areas with a high incidence of snowfall and fog should be specially avoided in routeing, and the effects of wind carrying most of the snow should be analysed in order to determine where drifting of snow may take place. Frost pockets must, of course, be clearly indicated, as these may cause serious accidents. Very serious accidents involving more than 50 vehicles have occurred on one particular section of Britain's motorways as a result of fog. It is, of course, very difficult to determine where sudden flash mists or fog will occur, but it does illustrate the usefulness of micro-climatological surveys.

The location, elevation and flow of underground services is also important, especially where sections of the proposed highway may interfere with the natural gravity flow of sewage. If these services are interrupted, the capital, running and maintenance costs of diversion by mechanical means must be included in the overall cost of that particular route.

Geological information presents one of the most important engineering factors. Motorways with very easy ver-

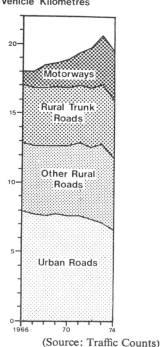

(a)  1966    70    74

(Source: Traffic Counts)

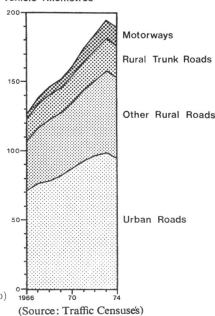

(b)  1966    70    74

(Source: Traffic Censuses)

Figure 7.7 Traffic on British roads. (a) Total lorry traffic and (b) total car and taxi traffic. Not shown on (a) are light vans (goods vehicles under 30 cwt unladen). These account for just over half of the combined light van and lorry traffic overall, and for over 60% on urban roads. Traffic on urban roads from light vans has been increasing slightly, but not enough to balance the drop in lorry traffic.

(*Source:* Transport Policy, *Vol. 2,* HMSO, 1976)

tical and horizontal alignment may necessitate cutting through extensive rock formations or, when sited on marshy ground, may require special construction and drainage solutions, all of which will add considerably to the costs. These problems have been highlighted by an article in *Civil Engineering* (7.11).

'An engineer involved in a route survey whether for a road, railway, transmission or pipeline, would, in any normal event, approach the project in two stages, commencing initially with a feasibility study for route location.

In the United Kingdom this would usually involve taking aerial photography at 1/10,000 scale and subsequently re-compiling existing Ordnance Survey 1/2,500 scale plans into strip form, revising the plans and contouring them at 2 m vertical intervals. This is done over a number of alternative routes, one of which will eventually be chosen for a survey at a larger scale for the engineer's design work.

Photographic mosaics are sometimes requested at this stage of the works in order to give engineers the means of explaining to the public the reasons for the selection of the route in question, especially where public participation has been invited.

The public in many cases cannot understand the complexities of line maps, especially when horizontal alignments are super-imposed on the survey plans. The aerial photograph allows them to identify and relate themselves to the project in question, especially when a certain amount of enhancement of the mosaic is carried out with the major details of the project super-imposed.

Overseas, it is often the photographic mosaic that is used for the initial route location. In particular, this is the case where long distances and difficult terrain are involved. Often the existing topographic maps, if available, are either at the wrong scale, out of date, or do not show features that are of interest to the engineer. Small-scale photography between 1/20,000 and 1/40,000 scale gives the necessary band width to locate alternative routes, and a desk study photo interpretation can be undertaken to establish the extent of drainage patterns, surface geology, existing communications and vegetation.

In under-developed countries where land take is likely to be of little importance and if the project is for a road, the mapping is usually undertaken at 1/2,000 scale with contouring at 1–2 m intervals depending on the terrain likely to be encountered. This information is sufficient to enable the engineer to select his centreline, which is then set out and cross-section data undertaken in most cases by land survey methods.'

## 3. Land Use and Land Take

It is desirable that highways should both minimise permanent land take and avoid highly sensitive areas such as

National Trust land, areas of special scientific interest, areas of outstanding natural beauty and high-grade agricultural land, and that they should also avoid the destruction of good property.

The severance of property, particularly agricultural holdings, is a further important routeing constraint and the fullest possible information on this subject must be made available (see also page 95). Property severance can be divided into three categories (Figure 7.8):

1. Severed;
2. Isolated;
3. Land-locked.

It is not intended here to describe in detail the principles and applications of economics, but obviously land acquisition costs, compensation, accessibility and improvement to affected properties, particularly land-locked tracts, are important factors in comparative evaluation of alternative routes. In the areas of the world where land take is not of great significance, there is greater flexibility of horizontal and vertical alignment, and in the degree to which the road may be harmonised with the landscape. Where there are severe constraints, deeper cuttings and embankments may be required, adding to the designer's problems. Land take is a most important issue at public inquiries and is a valuable lever as far as opposition road lobbies are concerned. It is desirable to utilise land temporarily in order that regrading of the land form may be carried out, to enable it to be returned to agriculture or to its former use.

The fullest information on agricultural land must be obtained from information supplied by Government and other agencies. With the vast expansion of urbanisation and development in the rural areas, it is desirable that highways routeing should avoid land areas which contain the best-quality agricultural land. Also, with the ever-declining

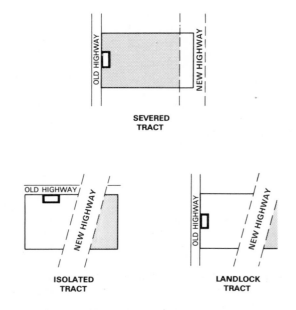

Figure 7.8    Types of damaged land parcel.

(*By courtesy of the State of Ohio, Department of Highways*)

rural and wilderness areas, the conservation of nature reserves becomes imperative, especially on recommendations by Government agencies.

There has for many years been criticism that the British classification of agricultural land is too wide and that the grade 3 group has such a variation of definitions that the grading ceases to have much significance (see page 37). One of the methods suggested for grading agricultural land is that there might be an 'agricultural index', in which land is classified according to its productive capacity in terms of its value to the nation as a food producer. This productivity index could be from 1–20, in which the old grade 3 classification might range between 8 and 13.

The procedures suggested in the Jefferson Report (7.12) for an overall agricultural index as far as roads are concerned are as follows:

1. Calculate the total land take for each alternative alignment;

2. Calculate and list separately:
   (i) non-agricultural land;
   (ii) 'special' land such as national parks, etc.
   In a number of cases, 'special' land would be agricultural and if so its area would be retained in the calculation for the agricultural index.

3. Divide the agricultural land into the five agricultural grades.

4. Multiply each area in hectares by the appropriate Productivity Index.

5. Add the results together and divide by 100 to produce a manageable figure.

6. Repeat for the other alternative alignments.

7. Present the results on a presentational drawing.

ACTUAL EXAMPLE OF CALCULATION WHERE ONLY GRADES 3 AND 4 ARE INVOLVED

Table 7.1. Example of agricultural index calculation

| ROUTE | TOTAL LAND (ha) | AREA IN EACH LAND TYPE | | | |
|---|---|---|---|---|---|
| | | Grade 3 | × 10 | Grade 4 | × 3 | Σ4+6 |
| 1 | 2 | 3 | 4 | 5 | 6 | 7 |
| A | 130 | 38 | 380 | 77 | 231 | 611 |
| B | 130 | 51 | 510 | 69 | 207 | 717 |
| C | 140 | 61 | 610 | 72 | 216 | 826 |

The calculation required to achieve the summation in the final column is simple and needs no further explanation. The example illustrates how an apparent relationship in areal terms only is translated into a rather different picture using the indexing method. In the case in point, the first

relationship is 13:13:14, whereas the second relationship is 12:14:16.

The method of calculation allows easy comparisons to be made between alternative routes for the same scheme. In each case, the gross index, as produced on the table, is related to cost and the constant (multiplier) is applied to produce figures in an approximate range of zero to 100. The formula being used on a provisional basis is:

national agricultural index
= 250 (constant) × cost (£M) divided by gross agricultural index

This method produced a range of values from 1·9 to 92·1, although it is only fair to point out that the higher values (the nearer to 100, the 'better' the situation) arise from schemes in urban areas. If these are ignored, the highest value so far recorded is 17·8, but this still gives a 9:1 ratio in comparing schemes.

## 4. Landscape Values

There has been a great deal of research from a wide range of sources on the classification of landscape quality, and there is far from unanimity as to whether landscape quality can be objectively classified by indices or numerical scores, or whether classification should be based on subjective judgements by professionals or a cross section of the general public.

These questions have been discussed in Chapter 2, and a number of methods are considered in both Chapters 2 and 3. There is no doubt that some methods are better suited to a given situation than others, and it is a matter of selecting the most appropriate in each case. The aim and advantage of a numerical scores method is to quantify that which is quantifiable, and to provide objective and consistent guidance on landscape quality. One thing is certain: while every method will have its 'grey' areas of doubt, such methods do provide partial guidance and information for designers and all those involved in the problems of route location, particularly the decision makers.

It may be interesting and helpful to record the evaluation methods of the Manchester Road Construction Unit (7.13), which the Unit has found particularly useful in classifying landscape quality in the routeing and alignment of highways. (It should be emphasised that the method does not feature the introduction of the road.)

The first version of the method is a structural, subjective appraisal of landscape elements, some of which have a positive contribution, and some a negative contribution to the landscape of the study area.

Positive factors are:
Varied topography;
Pastoral, parkland, or varied farming;
Varied tree and woodland cover;
Extensive views;
Traditional settlements;
Attractive waterscapes.

Negative factors are:

Derelict land;
Industrial development;
Mineral workings;
Overhead power lines.

On the basis of these factors the county planning officer and his colleagues classify the study area into six grades:

Grade 6    Well above average
Grade 5    Above average
Grade 4    Average
Grade 3    Below average
Grade 2    Well below average
Grade 1    Derelict land
           Built-up land

From this classification an amenity index is prepared for each proposed line of road by multiplying each grade of landscape by the length of that grade, adding them all together, and dividing by the length of the road line. Outstanding features can be given an additional weighting.

A second version of the method is to divide the study area into kilometre squares and to analyse them in terms of these elements:

1. *Land Form*    Slope and shape (contours).

2. *Land Use*     Farmland;
                  Woodland;
                  Developed land sub-divided;
                    residential;
                    industrial, other;
                  Parkland;
                  Heathland;
                  Water;
                  Other unused land.

3. *Land Features*  Hedgerows;
                    Hedgerow trees;
                    Watercourses;
                    Roads;
                    Power lines;
                    Railways;
                    Farms;
                    Density of residential development;
                    Listed buildings;
                    Significant features.

The amount of each element is measured from OS maps and field surveys. Each square is then given a subjective score by a number of independent professional observers, and the results correlated to give a visual quality value for each square, which may be modified by its relationship with adjacent squares up to a distance of 5 km. This final value is used in the selection of the optimum road line, and in a large study area values for all squares can be predicted from surveys and evaluations of control squares. While these methods are simple and rapid in use, it should be noted that they do not take into account the effect on the landscape of the proposed road line. (For a further method used in evaluation of highway routeing see page 75).

## 5. Visual Intrusion

It is difficult to assess the exact degree of visual intrusion into an existing landscape that will be caused by new road work, but the impact can be calculated reasonably accurately by measuring the degree of obstruction of a standard angle of view (see also page 35 and page 78). This allows roadworks above and below eyelevel, such as embankments and cuttings, to be taken into account. This method of assessment is most suitable for urban and inter-urban situations where the amount of intrusion is significant, and it has been found to give consistent results among lay viewers, although no method of assessment can completely replace the subjective appraisal of the visual quality of the landscape. Other factors affect the way people feel about visual intrusion; such things as a full view of the carriageway, a contrasting road colour and the disturbance caused by moving vehicles, can raise the viewer's awareness of intrusion; but much more research is needed to determine the relative visual impact of man-made landscape features.

Table 7.2. Intrusion values for cuttings and embankments

| CUTTING (c) or EMBANKMENT (e) (metres) | Distance of residential property from top of cutting or bottom of embankment to produce differing levels of visual intrusion | | |
| --- | --- | --- | --- |
| | LEVEL OF VISUAL INTRUSION | | |
| | High | Medium | Low |
| 2 (c) | 0– 5 | 5– 15 | 15– 30 |
| 1 (c) | 0–10 | 10– 30 | 30– 55 |
| Ground level | 0–15 | 15– 45 | 45– 85 |
| 1 (e) | 0–20 | 20– 60 | 60–110 |
| 2 (e) | 0–25 | 25– 70 | 70–130 |
| 3 (e) | 0–25 | 25– 80 | 80–160 |
| 4 (e) | 0–30 | 30– 95 | 95–190 |
| 5 (e) | 0–35 | 35–110 | 110–220 |
| 6 (e) | 0–40 | 40–125 | 125–250 |
| 7 (e) | 0–45 | 45–140 | 140–280 |
| 8 (e) | 0–50 | 50–150 | 150–300 |
| 9 (e) | 0–55 | 55–160 | 160–320 |
| 10 (e) | 0–60 | 60–170 | 170–350 |

Source: *Route Location with regard to Environmental Issues*

The reactions of viewers vary considerably according to their position; whether they are housebound, in the garden, or moving about the streets; and a detailed study of visual intrusion is really only worth attempting where people are likely to be much concerned with the view, as they are at home, at school, in hospital or at leisure in the open air.

The calculations for embankments and cuttings can be simplified by omitting insignificant intrusion, and by assessing the worst state of intrusion for each case, that is, straight in front of the viewer. Table 7.2 shows intrusion values for cuttings and embankments up to 10 m high; and 3 m extra should be added to each level for large moving vehicles where these are likely to occur frequently.

These methods of measuring visual intrusion will need considerably more testing before they can be accepted as an absolute identification of intrusion values, but they form a useful adjunct to the purely subjective opinions of viewers and professional observers.

### 6. Noise and Vibration

Noise is one of the most important factors in the evaluation of highways. Visual intrusion may be reduced or totally eliminated by good landscape detailing, whereas noise, even when reduced by acoustic banks, fencing or double glazing, penetrates everywhere—into the privacy of homes and disturbing the tranquility of schools, hospitals, public buildings and offices. Being so important, a great deal of information and research material is available. The behaviour of noise is predictable and its characteristics and people's reactions to it are well understood.

Generally, the noise of traffic movement is proportional to the engine power, speed, and highway gradients. There are a number of methods whereby noise may be reduced, but the distance from the source of noise to the receiver or observer is still the most important factor in noise reduction. The space necessary to achieve reductions must be taken into consideration in the assessment of the highway corridor. Noise energy or intensity is measured in terms of the decibel unit on the A scale (dBA). Each increase of 10 dBA approximates to the doubling of loudness.

A noise level of ± 3 dBA is hardly discernible and should be discounted; this figure incidentally represents the doubling or halving of traffic volume. Levels above 3 dBA must be quantified as far as benefits and disadvantages are concerned. Thus, if traffic volumes have been decreased by more than half, due to the existence of a new highway, then the environmental benefit may be assessed. In some situations these figures need to be modified. In other words, it is a basis for presenting noise benefit or disadvantage in terms of building units experiencing not less than a 3 dBA change. The building will be eligible for assessment if the reduction or increase is achieved at the nearest facade to the road.

It should be remembered that distance is a vital attenuating factor and that noise falls by 6 dBA for each doubling of distance from the road. A 74 dBA level at 7·5 m from the side of the motorway will be 68 dBA at 15 m, 62 dBA at 30 m, and 56 dBA at 60 m. If it is not possible to locate the highway clear of residential areas, other means must be adopted to provide satisfactory sound reduction by depressing the highway, or providing acoustic barriers. As a general rule in rural areas it would be desirable to locate major highways some 200 metres from residential buildings. Obviously a different set of standards must be applied for urban highways.

The maximum noise level at the side of a motorway varies between 78 and 92 dBA. To these factors must be added other criteria, for example, the type of traffic, gradients, intersections and speed. The noise of lorries is far greater than that of private vehicles. Some local authorities state that a lorry makes as much noise as five private

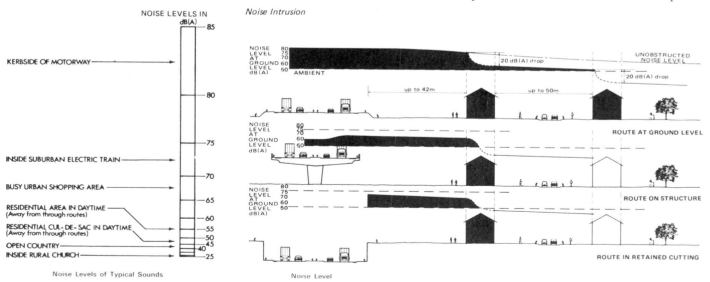

Figure 7.9   Noise levels in various conditions. The noise levels have been correlated, from social surveys, to show the annoyance caused to people.

(By courtesy of R. Travers Morgan and Partners and the Welsh Office)

vehicles, but the Greater London Council has stated a figure ten times that of the private vehicle. In assessing noise growth, therefore, the proportion of lorries to cars must be clearly predicted.

The effect of gradients on noise levels is a most important consideration, especially when these gradients are combined with a high proportion of heavy vehicles. Motorways generally have maximum gradients of 4% and the problems therefore are not so great as other primary roads where the gradients may reach 20%. For each 1% gradient, traffic noise is increased by 1·5 dBA. Therefore, the road with a gradient of 5% will be 7·5 dBA noisier than a level road. There is a further consideration, particularly from heavy vehicles on high-speed motorways—the tyre noise from some 12-wheeled vehicles travelling at speeds in excess of 80 km/h may be 10 dBA noisier than at half the speed. Furthermore, highways may be noisier at points of intersection where acceleration and deceleration are necessary.

The Department of the Environment has published *Calculation of Road Traffic Noise* (7.14), as a guide to the measurement and prediction of noise levels. Conventionally, a level of 68 dBA is regarded as being the threshold of noise intrusion, and it is advisable to note all buildings likely to be affected by this noise level, as they may become eligible for compensation or special treatment.

There are many effective methods of reducing noise emanating from highways. Acoustic barriers may be in the form of masonry walls, fences, or earth embankments. For example, a 3 m masonry wall adjoining the highway will effect an approximate 20-dBA reduction. It should be realised that walls create rather intolerable conditions for motorists travelling on the motorway, as they contain the noise and are visually depressing, increasing safety hazards.

An earth embankment of the same height, and perhaps 9 m wide, will also provide similar sound reductions and will be aesthetically more pleasing. However, the acoustic bank will make more demands on land acquisition. The precise figures are not known for dBA reduction for soft acoustic banks, but there is no doubt that it is considerable and will be even more effective if the banks are seeded, or better still, planted with shrubs.

The effect of trees as a sound barrier has been much exaggerated. A belt of trees 30·5 m wide will provide only 1-to 3-dBA reduction. A single, double or triple line of trees will be completely ineffective from this point of view.

The computer program LTEN is used to calculate 18 hour L10 road traffic noise levels. The calculations are in accordance with the DoE Memorandum 'Calculations of Road Traffic Noise'. The topography of the area is programmed in a three-dimensional co-ordinate form (the O.S. grid reference plus height). The characteristics of the new road are described in terms of road segment data, noise barriers, and sites at each 18 hour L10 noise level (7.15).

The transmission of vibration from moving vehicles to buildings is a combination of tyre pressure, inequalities in road surface, the nature of its subsoil and the structural form of the buildings. With smooth road surfaces, vibration should be barely perceptible at distances of three to four metres from the edge of the road. It has been established that vehicles with a goods weight as high as 44 tonnes need not generate larger dynamic loads or vibrations than that produced by some 32-tonne vehicles (7.16). Unless there are exceptional circumstances, such as the proximity of historic buildings, there is no need to evaluate vibration impact.

## 7. Air Pollution

Air pollution is a significant factor in highway environments, as it affects design—particularly road tunnels—and also causes health hazards and vegetation deterioration. The four vehicle emissions primarily responsible for air pollution are lead, carbon monoxide, oxides of nitrogen, and hydrocarbons, lead being the most dangerous.

### LEAD TETRAETHYL

Lead tetraethyl is a fuel additive for improving combustion characteristics, and the maximum currently permitted concentration in the UK is 0·55 gram/litre. The UK Government intends to reduce the lead content of petrol to 0·4 g/l by 1981, to meet European standards (7.17). 75% of the lead initially present is emitted in the inorganic form from exhausts and it is estimated that 90% of the lead content in the atmosphere comes from this source. The proposed 1978 level in the USA was 0·33g/l, but this is not yet enforced. The land uses alongside the highway may be influenced by concentrations of lead and other emissions, and this must therefore be discussed.

Kerbside levels of lead concentration vary from $1$–$10\,\mu g/m^3$ (micrograms/cubic metre) of air. Acoustic banks or vegetation do not significantly reduce concentration, neither does double glazing stop penetration into dwellings. Lead can be absorbed by the human body by respiration, of which 35% is deposited in the lungs. However, this degree of absorption represents about 25% to 50% of the average daily intake from all sources. Lead deposits can also be left on soils and vegetation, although plants cannot readily absorb the lead and in most crops it can easily be removed by washing. From a land use viewpoint, lead pollution is restricted to approximately 30 metres from the roadside along busy roads. Lead does occur in dust and is potentially dangerous to small children playing close to highways.

The EEC is currently developing draft directives on air quality standards for lead (7.18) and it is being suggested that concentrations of airborne lead at the kerbside on major roads should not exceed $8\,\mu g/m^3$ of air during a four-hour peak traffic flow, and also that the annual mean concentrations of airborne lead should not exceed $2\,\mu g/m^3$ in residential areas more than 50 metres from major roads. The British Government, however, feels that these should be objectives and not standards, as the present research has indicated that the recommended levels cannot be defined with precision.

Research has indicated that an air quality objective of 2 µg lead/m³ would be exceeded (under the assumed conditions) within 5, 20, 50 and 120 metres respectively on roads with traffic flows of 12,000, 24,000, 48,000 and 96,000 vehicles per annual average day (7.19). Methods of achieving the recommended objectives for restricting exposure to airborne lead should include:

1. Maintaining adequate separation between houses, offices, schools, etc., and sources of lead along major roads;
2. Reducing the lead content of petrol;
3. Reducing emissions of lead from the tailpipes of cars by means of special 'lead-trap' silencers;
4. Initiating changes in engine design to promote the use of petrol of a lower octane rating;
5. Initiating changes in engine design to consume less petrol and thus reducing the use of lead.

The United States has carried out much of the recent work in this field, but legislation is far behind the proposals made for reducing pollution.

## CARBON MONOXIDE
Exhaust gases from petrol engines contain up to about 7% carbon monoxide by volume and those from diesel engines rarely contain more than 0·1%. The level of carbon monoxide at distances beyond 50 metres from the centre of a carriageway of a busy road would be below 2 ppm except under abnormally still conditions. Exposure for relatively short periods is unlikely to produce severe symptoms.

## OXIDES OF NITROGEN
Motor vehicles are an important source of these pollutants—about 25% of the levels of these compounds in the air originates from vehicles. However, the total concentration of the nitric oxides and nitrogen dioxides normally lies between 0·1 and 0·3 ppm. Hourly average figures exceeding 0·3 ppm have been recorded on motorways. However, there is no evidence to suggest that existing concentrations present a human hazard.

## HYDROCARBONS
The gaseous hydrocarbon products from vehicle fumes emitted in the exhaust gases comprise a complex mixture of over 100 compounds. Diesel engines contribute a far smaller proportion of hydrocarbons to the total pollutant load in the environment than petrol engines—about 0·01% to 0·04% compared with 0·1% to 1% in petrol engines. The research data produced so far indicate that at distances greater than 50 metres from the carriageways of busy roads, the level of hydrocarbons from vehicles is unlikely to exceed 1·1 ppm (7.20). The motor car is a far less important source of hydrocarbons than of lead; nevertheless, separation between motorways and houses on busy roads is desirable.

As with all gaseous pollutants from vehicles, the concentrations measured at the roadside are determined by traffic density, rate of flow and the meteorological conditions, including the partial enclosure caused by high buildings. There is no doubt that the reduction in pollutants falls very sharply as the distance from the motorway carriageway increases, and this is the main factor influencing land use planning as far as highways are concerned.

## VEHICLE POLLUTION STANDARDS
Both the EEC and the USA are continually revising the permissible levels of pollutant emissions from vehicles, but the benefit of these improvements is being offset by the constant increase in the number of vehicles on the roads and on the land. Pollutant-free fuels are more expensive in use than traditional engine fuels, and there is also a limit to the range of fuel that can be used in the present internal-combustion engine. The best hope of reducing the levels of noxious emissions lies in the development of totally new forms of propulsive power units which do not depend on oil-derived fuels.

## 8. Community Severance
The cutting of secondary roads and pedestrian footpaths, and the isolation of parcels of land are the most obvious forms of severance which occur when a new motorway is constructed, but there are many other, and more far-reaching disruptions which must be taken into account when planning routes. It must be remembered that a busy motorway is more of a barrier than rail or river, which can be crossed by individuals capable of walking or rowing—the major road is intended to be completely impassable by animals or humans.

Any community, whether farm, village or town, builds up innumerable links with neighbouring communities. On the effectiveness of these links depends the supply of goods, the accessibility of services, the choice of jobs and the ties with relations and friends. If they are severed by more or less impassable barriers, the quality of the community's life is certain to suffer until new links with other sources can be formed—a process which can take many years or even decades. Community severance can take place by natural conditions such as changes in river courses, or by man-made barriers such as roads, canals and railways, or in extreme cases, the Berlin Wall. Of the unintentional barriers, express highways represent the most severe obstacles.

The forms of community severance which are most likely to arouse public concern are the economic and social linkages vital to the community's prosperity. Severing a factory from its workers' residential district, cutting off market gardeners and fruit farmers from their local markets, preventing access to shops and commerce from rural villages, and constraining farmers to travel expensive extra mileage for foodstuffs and equipment, are all examples of economic severance.

Social linkages are less quantifiable, but nonetheless important to a busy community. Journeys to school, to welfare clubs, local shopping and postal services, social events, leisure activities and ordinary neighbourly visiting, can be affected by severance of footpaths and minor roads, especially in urban and semi-urban areas, where the cost of bridges or underpasses for every minor road would be prohibitive. Even where these substitutes are provided, it is not always easy for the very old and the very young to negotiate them, and unless heavily used, they tend to become vandalised or gang-haunted.

As already mentioned, it is possible to identify, by means of gravity models and social surveys, the centres to which population groups give their social and economic allegiance and, although it is obviously not feasible to protect every linkage, it may be possible to select new road routes that minimise the cut linkages as far as possible. These routes may not be the obvious ones dictated by land form or land use, but they are likely to meet with less opposition from local inhabitants than routes which sever a community, however superficially attractive these may appear.

There must always be a balance between national considerations and the effect of the development upon the local community. Obviously, every possible step must be taken to ensure that any major transportation development is designed and located with maximum consideration for people living within the influence of such a system. But 'consideration' takes time. The many legal procedures and courts of inquiry, resulting from necessary public participation and dissension, may produce a long protraction from the conception of a route to its implementation.

The severance of parcels of farm land is one of the major problems for the highway designer in rural areas. Farms may be re-grouped to form viable units by rationalising farm boundaries; but where farm buildings are likely to be cut off from their fields, road access, cattle overpasses or cattle creeps must be provided.

In many cases, there may be severe socio-economic consequences for owners, particularly of residential accommodation whose properties adjoin the proposed routes of a highway; such problems of blight are particularly bad in cases of delay.

## 9. Road Safety

Road safety plays an important part in highway design and consequently affects land use. The maximum and average speeds for which any road is designed must be determined by the composition and density of the traffic and the demand for safety and accessibility. Roads of any one class should be of uniform design with respect to the horizontal and vertical alignment, distances between intersections and their design, traffic signs and other equipment.

The principal measure of accident rates used throughout

Figure 7.10   Transportation and road safety. An accident involving more than 60 vehicles on Britain's M1 motorway. Road safety factors are important considerations in motorway design and land take.

(*Photo by courtesy of Aerofilms Ltd.*)

the world is deaths per hundred million vehicle-kilometres of travel. The kilometre death rate varies significantly from country to country, ranging from 3·4 in the United States to over 20 in many developing countries. This wide variation may be due to several phenomena associated with economic considerations working in combination with other factors. These factors include increased urbanisation, higher levels of education, better maintenance of vehicles, standards of driving tests, heavy fines and disqualification for drunken, careless or dangerous driving, and the development of road systems capable of handling many different types of traffic. A similar correlation is found between death rates per 10,000 registered vehicles and motor vehicle ownership rates. In a country with 100 persons per vehicle the death rate per 10,000 is approximately four times the rate in a country with 10 people per vehicle. Raising standards of instruction and driving, together with educating children and the general public, is a significant contribution to road safety.

Due to the increasing size and speed of commercial vehicles, motorway and main road junctions are being constructed with easier bends and gradients, and with long clear sight lines across intervening ground. This open ground, which lies mainly alongside junctions and under sight lines, must be kept clear of all obstructions over 1 m high, or even less in some cases, and this restriction creates constraints for the road landscaper.

Safety considerations prohibit the planting of tall vegetation, or that which is liable to catch fire. In the dry summer of 1976 in Britain, heavy smoke from burning verges caused a severe hazard on some motorways, but the alternative of hard surfacing for verges and banks is aesthetically unacceptable.

As an indication of the economic importance of safety in Britain, about 20 people are killed every day on the roads, and about 200 severely injured. While faults in the design of roads are not a major factor in road accidents, even minor improvements can make a significant impact on an accident bill of £850 million each year (7.21).

Much research has already been undertaken and more remains to be done to examine the relationship between road accidents and traffic environment and its design, and, on the basis of knowledge obtained, to work out principles for the planning of land use and road networks. The traffic environment which has a direct relationship to accidents is:

1. Technical design and character;
2. Traffic equipment and furniture such as lighting, road signs, traffic signals, land markings, etc.;
3. Amenities such as service areas, picnic areas, car parks;
4. Landscape treatment;
5. The traffic itself, i.e. the road user and different classes of vehicle together with their accommodation on the highway system.

The main principles of traffic design are:

1. The location of activities and functions so as to reduce traffic volumes and confusion;
2. Separating different classes of traffic in time and space to eliminate conflict;
3. Differentiation within each road network between function and characteristics to obtain maximum homogeneity of traffic flow;
4. Ensuring a clear view and simplicity and uniformity of design to facilitate decisions and reduce surprise elements.

## Analysis and Presentation of Proposals

Together, the detailed studies described above will present a whole series of environmental, planning and engineering constraints, and the final analysis of each of the routes being assessed may be prepared from overlays of all the survey sheets, or similar means, and should summarise the problems on which design decisions can be based (7.22) (see Figures 7.11–7.13).

Each route must be thoroughly evaluated and studied, and detailed costs of engineering works such as earth movement, bridges, underpasses and public utilities, compared. For each route there must also be a comprehensive cost evaluation related to environmental benefits and disbenefits. The final analysis may suggest perhaps five or six main possible routeing corridors, with a larger number of interconnecting links. (The analysis of Britain's motorways on a typical 20-km section has meant the evaluation of between 40 and 60 possible routes.)

In Britain, a Landscape Advisory Committee, which advises the Minister of Transport on the routeing and alignment of motorways as far as amenity is concerned, then examines the proposals in detail, both in committee and on site, and recommends the most satisfactory route. The site examination is most thorough and every kilometre is evaluated in detail. It is usual that, during the inspection, all the optional routes are clearly defined with luminous markers on the ground, and the suggested alignment viewed from a number of surrounding promontories to determine whether or not the highway will harmonise with the landscape.

It must be emphasised that the local population may have serious objections to the proposed routeing, most objections being to factors personally affecting those objecting. It is therefore necessary to assure the local population that every possible effort has been made to align the highway with the minimum disturbance to the environment and to indicate where, as a result of the highway alignment, beneficial effects may be obtained from the routeing; including the opening up of views, greater accessibility to recreational activities, the clearing of dereliction, and the improvement of the entire landscape values of the scenic corridor.

In calculating the environmental benefits and disadvantages of a major inter-urban highway, the emphasis is usually predominantly on the disadvantages. The 'fringe' benefits tend to be ignored. In a situation where regional traffic is congested, some relief may be obtained from traffic management schemes and a co-ordinated public transportation system, but in spite of such relief measures, the traffic will not disappear. The absence of a free-flow major highway wll force traffic to use the secondary road system through areas which will, as a result, suffer severe environmental problems, where measures for the relief of noise, pollution and vibration are most difficult, if not impossible. These detailed disbenefits are not fully taken into account in the evaluation of a major inter-urban highway, especially its city approaches. Thus there is a weakness in the evaluation system which may tend to falsify the overall assessment.

The uncertainties which occur between the public becoming aware of preliminary highway proposals and the finalisation of the precise routeing, alignment and land take, may cause planning blight. The blight will be alleviated after proposals are confirmed but more problems will arise after the full environmental implications of the highway are known. Owners will find their property values reduced with little hope of compensation, and the costs incurred in moving from their depreciated properties may be considerable. Every effort should be made to inform the public fully of procedures and the period of uncertainty should be reduced to the absolute minimum.

Many highway routes will have been 'protected' under development plans prepared by the local authorities which may have been in existence for a large number of years. Deviations from these 'protected' routes should only be permitted if there are exceptional changes of circumstances. Respecting previous planning proposals gives the public confidence in planning and may help to reduce planning blight. The public must also be assured of the absolute fairness of compensation for loss of amenity within the scenic corridor.

JUNCTION OF A386 WITH A30

A30 EAST OF TOWN

Photographs of traffic hazards on existing roads.

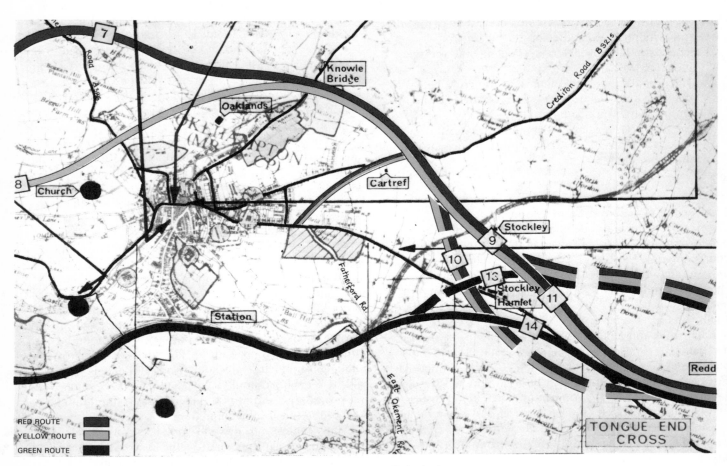

RED ROUTE
YELLOW ROUTE
GREEN ROUTE

Town centre shopping area with attendant pedestrian movement severed by A30 School fronts onto road. 2·2m footways along section of town centre. Proposed school and hospital sites front A30.

Fatherford railway bridge. No footpath or verge. Hazard to pedestrians

11 accesses direct onto A30

13 accidents mainly on steep approach to town

23 accidents, 8 of which involved pedestrians, 7 at junctions.

Map showing alternative routes, with comments on hazards and accident data for existing roads.

Figure 7.11

| YELLOW | The Yellow Route follows the Red Route as far as the junction near Place Cross. A variation passes south of Fowley Cross. From the junction at Place Cross the Yellow Route is on embankment and, passing the Parish Church, it crosses the A386 close to some properties. The route climbs on high embankment across the low-lying land south west of Oaklands and then enters a deep cutting behind the house. The crossing of the river and rest of the route to Willy Farm and Whiddon Down is the same as the Red Route. Variations to the Yellow Route in the area of Stockley Hamlet and Reddaway are the same as those for the Red Route. |
|---|---|

Typical Route description. Each alternative route is described in this way.

| | | | C.O.B.A. | | | | |
|---|---|---|---|---|---|---|---|
| Route Numbers | Length (km) | Cost (£M) May 1975 | Prefe-rence | NPV / PVC | RATE OF RETURN | | |
| | | | | | 1st yr | 3rd yr | 5th yr |
| 1−3−6−8−9−15−17 | 19·1 | 17·79 | 5 | + 0·4067 | 7·1 | 8·9 | 11·0 |
| 1−4−8−9−15−17 | 18·9 | 18·24 | 6 | + 0·3944 | 7·1 | 8·8 | 10·9 |
| 1−3−6−8−9−11−16−17 | 19·1 | 17·46 | 3 | + 0·4341 | 7·2 | 9·0 | 11·2 |
| 1−4−8−9−11−16−17 | 18·9 | 17·91 | 4 | + 0·4208 | 7·2 | 9·0 | 11·1 |
| 1−3−6−8−10−16−17 | 19·3 | 17·86 | 10 | + 0·3595 | 6·7 | 8·5 | 10·5 |
| 1−4−8−10−16−17 | 19·1 | 18·31 | 11 | + 0·3483 | 6·7 | 8·5 | 10·5 |

Cost preference table for alternative routes, using COBA cost analysis

| LAND TAKE | | | | BUILDING UNITS DEMOLISHED | | |
|---|---|---|---|---|---|---|
| LAND AREA (Ha) | | | AGR INDEX | | | |
| Total | Non-Agr | Special | | Domestic | Business | Special |
| 134 | 10 | — | 746 | | | |
| 130 | 10 | — | 706 | | | |
| 134 | 10 | — | 767 | | | |
| 130 | 10 | — | 727 | 0 | 0 | 0 |
| 134 | 10 | — | 765 | | | |
| 130 | 11 | — | 734 | | | |

1. Severance to farm units is more severe on Red and Yellow Routes.
2. The 6 building units demolished by Green Route consists of 2 S/D houses, 1 bungalow and 3 terraced cottages (only 1 occupied).

Estimated land take for alternative routes.

| NOISE | | | | | |
|---|---|---|---|---|---|
| BUILDING UNITS SUBJECT TO ± ≮ 3dB(A) | | | | | |
| Domestic | | Business | | Special | |
| + | − | + | − | + | − |
| 15 | 176 | 0 | 48 | 0 | 2 |

1. Special units are all schools.
2. Noise barrier could protect the 43 units on Green Route. Alternatively about 20 units would qualify for insulation.
3. On Red/Yellow route about 5 units would qualify for insulation.

Noise forecasts.

| POLLUTION | | | | | | REDUCTION IN P.I. ACCIDENTS OVER 15 YEAR DESIGN PERIOD | REDUCTION IN HGV/AVERAGE AUGUST DAY ON A30 IN 1996 |
|---|---|---|---|---|---|---|---|
| BUILDING UNITS SUBJECT TO ± ≮ 2 g/m³ | | | | | | | |
| Domestic | | Business | | Special | | | |
| + | − | + | − | + | − | | |
| 21 | 227 | 0 | 48 | 0 | 3 | 850 | 1400 |

1. Special units are 2 schools and 1 hospital on each alternative route.

Figures are for road network within band of interest.

Figures vary according to traffic volumes.

Figure 7.12

Pollution forecast                                    Accident reduction forecast

| VISUAL INTRUSION | | | | | | | | | | |
|---|---|---|---|---|---|---|---|---|---|---|
| ON LANDSCAPE | | ON BUILDING UNITS | | | | | | | | |
| DESCRIPTION | L.A.C. PREFERENCE | Domestic | | | Business | | | Special | | |
| | | H | M | L | H | M | L | H | M | L |
| Routes cut across the grain of the | | 1 | 13 | 23 | — | — | 7 | — | 1 | — |
| land and would be out of scale with | | 1 | 13 | 22 | — | — | 7 | — | 1 | — |
| the countryside. Route 4 is very | | 1 | 14 | 26 | — | — | 7 | — | 1 | — |
| prominent south of Fowley Cross & | | 1 | 14 | 25 | — | — | 7 | — | 1 | — |
| Route 8 is intrusive through pleasant | 3 | 1 | 15 | 21 | — | — | 7 | — | 1 | — |
| valley near church. | | 1 | 15 | 20 | — | — | 7 | — | 1 | — |

1. The obtrusive effect of the Green Route in the Station area could be reduced by landscaping.
2. Business units on Red/Yellow routes are factories in Knowle Bridge area.
3. Business unit on Green Route is garage at Stockley Hamlet.
4. Special unit on Yellow Route is Parish Church at Upcott.

Levels of visual intrusion for alternative routes.

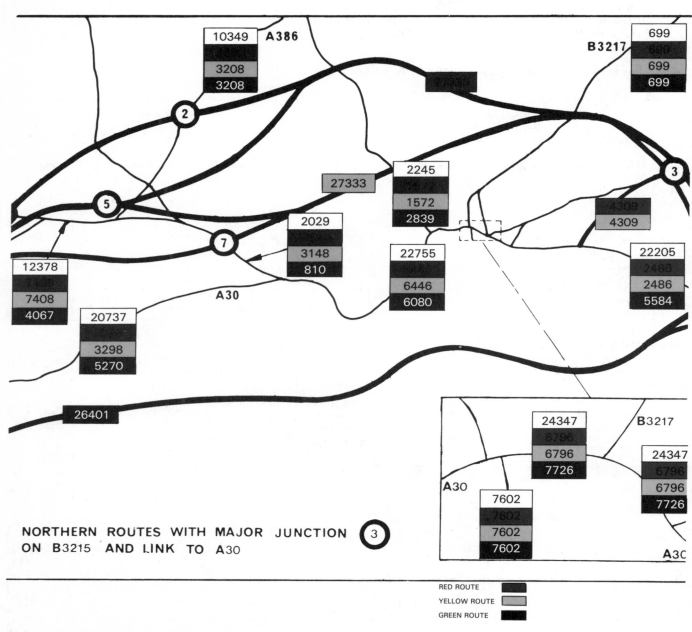

NORTHERN ROUTES WITH MAJOR JUNCTION ③ ON B3215 AND LINK TO A30

RED ROUTE
YELLOW ROUTE
GREEN ROUTE

Figure 7.13  Predicted traffic flows for alternative routes.

Experience has shown that early publication of possible routes has caused blight, and its effect is not limited to a small number of people but often to whole areas and communities. In many cases where there are a vast number of optional routes, the total effect can be extremely serious. The Government has the power to buy, at an unblighted market value, properties on the routes it has published and does so where people would suffer hardship if they could not secure a reasonable price because of the road proposal. The Government is sensitive to the need of keeping blight to the minimum and, of course, must do its utmost to reduce the time taken to investigate alternative proposals.

## Motorway Design Principles and Details

In Britain the high-speed free-flow highway is called a motorway. In other countries, this classification is known by various names such as turnpike, freeway, autobahn and autostrada, but, whatever the name, the basic principles are the same.

The wide horizontal and low vertical alignment of major highways make greater demands on land use than low-speed roads. This is primarily because of increased cuttings and embankments which are necessary. Medium and low-speed roads can follow the natural contours much more closely. However, an enlightened policy of design and land take can reduce permanent land take by regrading steep embankments or cuttings well outside the highway corridor and

returning this land to the original owner for agriculture, etc. It is difficult to reconcile the highway or motorway standards with a small-scale landscape, and it requires great skills on the part of the landscape planner to reduce the impact of a high-speed motorway on a rural environment.

Once the route of the new road has been selected and approved, work begins on the design of the road and its supporting facilities. There are a number of basic principles which must be applied to the design of any motorway, and these may be summarised as follows:

1. The proposed route must satisfy all short and long-term traffic requirements, supplement the existing road network and, at the same time, be co-ordinated with other transportation systems.
2. Each motorway must be subject to satisfactory cost benefit analysis.
3. The motorway must be integrated with the landscape, thus minimising a loss of amenities to surrounding communities.
4. Fullest consideration must be given to environmental standards from the user's point of view.
5. An adequate number of lanes, depending on traffic volume, must be provided to reduce the hazards of slow-moving vehicles. Lane width must be sufficient to ensure satisfactory standards of safety for all classes of vehicle.
6. Dual carriageways should be provided to reduce the possibility of head-on collisions.
7. Free-flow grade-separated intersections must be provided, but at the same time land must be conserved as far as possible.
8. The highway must be of wide horizontal and low vertical alignment to enable heavily loaded vehicles to

Figure 7.14   Junction of the M25 and M23 near Redhill showing the enormous impact of motorways on the rural landscape. Money and professional expertise must be available for its rehabilitation.

(*Photo by courtesy of* The Times)

travel at higher speeds so that the risk of rear-end collisions between fast and slow-moving vehicles may be minimised.

9. Uniform and consistent operating conditions must be provided.

10. There must be specially designed access facilities to enable vehicles to enter and leave with the maximum safety and minimum disturbance to traffic flow. Access elsewhere should be restricted.

11. There must be adequate traffic direction signs in order that drivers may have sufficient time to change direction.

12. Service areas, parking and picnic facilities must be provided in order to allow sufficient rest for drivers, thus reducing the undue strain factor, so important to traffic safety.

13. Pedestrians and non-motorised transport must be excluded.

14. Stable shoulders, to enable vehicles to park in cases of traffic emergency or mechanical failure, must be provided.

Good motorway landscape design demands that some features are considered at the very outset of the design stage, and not merely regarded as a facelift exercise after engineering and economic constraints have been met. These include the design of central reservations, planting, contouring, service areas, and parking.

## Central Reservations

In many countries of the world, regulations exist which determine the precise width of the central reservation. Such inflexible standards inhibit design opportunities and restrict the scope for contouring and planting in harmony with the landscape through which the road passes. As far as land use and land acquisition costs are concerned, varying the reservation width need make no additional demands on land use. A reservation width of 2 metres over half a kilometre distance and 6 metres over the other half, balances out at 4 metres which is the width of the standard British central reservation.

There are four important considerations which may determine the need for minimal widths of reservation: frequency of bridges; land acquisition costs; quality of agricultural land; and engineering considerations.

In Britain and other intensively developed countries with high overall population densities, there are far more bridges per mile than in less intensively developed countries. The cost of over-bridges and under-passes is one of the most important factors when planning highways, and one of the principal disadvantages of routeing carriageways independently of each other, perhaps even one kilometre apart. However, if such a policy is adopted, the reservation areas must be totally accessible for use, whether it be for agriculture or even as common land. While wider central

reservations necessitate longer and consequently more expensive bridges, the extra cost of these may be offset by the lack of necessity for safety barriers and anti-dazzle screens.

Land take must, of course, be reduced to the minimum, particularly in intensively developed urban and rural areas or where land has high acquisition costs. The acquisition of first-class agricultural land for motorways should be kept to the minimum since the acreage of such land, particularly in Britain, is constantly shrinking, and first-class agricultural land is a nation's prime resource. By far the greatest proportion of motorway mileage generally passes through rural areas with medium or low-quality agricultural land and comparatively low land acquisition costs. In these cases, wider central reservations should present few problems.

If wider contoured and planted reservations are to act as effective safety barriers and anti-dazzle screens, the height of the mounds in the central reservation should be sufficient to make it difficult for vehicles to mount and cross the reservation, and the planting sufficiently generous to reduce dazzle. The cost of such contouring and planting should be less than the capital cost and possibly maintenance costs of physical barriers and screens. The additional fill needed for contouring should be included in the basic cut-and-fill calculations of the motorway. The minimum width of reservation to act effectively as a safety barrier and anti-dazzle screen is debatable, but 5 metres may be considered a minimum for contoured or planted reservations.

## Planting

Three basic factors should be considered in the planting of highways—design, ecology and maintenance—and all planting must be related to the entire scenic corridor, and to the surrounding land form and landscape features.

Additional land take is frequently necessary to protect and incorporate natural features in the road environment. The extent of the scenic corridor depends on the local circumstances, but it should extend to the skyline of the nearby hills or a minimum of half a kilometre from the centre line of the motorway.

Not only should trees adjoining the highway corridor be protected during the course of construction, but legislative means should be used in order that owners of adjoining land do not, at some later date, remove existing plantations which assist in harmonising road and landscape. If necessary, some of these plantations and hedgerows could be reinforced by additional planting, in consultation with adjoining land owners, during the landscape treatment of the motorway.

The age, size, species and condition of trees and woodlands in the highway corridor should be surveyed and analysed in order that their importance may be assessed. An outstanding small but established woodland should be conserved rather than obliterated by the motorway.

Figure 7.15 The interchange at Adwalton on the M62 illustrating a vast land-locked area which could be planted.
(*Photo by courtesy of Aerofilms Ltd.*)

The tree cover of most countries is decreasing at an alarming rate and a narrow motorway corridor, with its unproductive embankments and cuttings, could be an ideal location for tree planting, provided that such planting is in character with the surrounding landscape. Such plantations would make no additional demands on land use. In many situations, therefore, it may be preferable to overplant rather than underplant, if only for economic considerations.

When passing through a heavily wooded valley, the motorway could be thickly planted and, if passing through an area of cultural landscape, ornamental species could be introduced in addition to local forest ones. If cuttings on both sides of the motorway occur at frequent intervals, some of these could be planted densely so as to provide contrasts of enclosure and space, and light and shade.

The location of trees in relation to the highway must be carefully considered in order that hazards are not created by restriction of vision or the formation of icy patches due to the cutting out of sunlight. On the other hand, plantations may be used to arrest drifting snow from snow-laden prevailing winds.

Embankments, cuttings and central reservations planted continuously may conceal fine views and introduce monotony in the same way as continuous metal or plastic antidazzle screens. In many cases planting may be totally out of keeping with the surroundings, particularly where the motorway passes through a treeless and open landscape.

The planting of central reservations presents many problems as they are not an ideal habitat for plants. Obviously, the wider the central reservation, the greater the chance of success of the planting. However, pollution from salt, oil, mud and fumes is very considerable, there being a direct relationship between the volume and type of traffic, the number of traffic lanes and the exposure and width of the central reservation. For instance, a three-lane road usually has private cars only on the outside lane and, therefore, the discharge of oil and fumes from heavy vehicles onto the reservation is considerably less than it is on a two-lane road.

Planting is affected in two ways by the application of salt on the road to counteract ice: by salt-water run-off across the reservation, and by spray from moving traffic. Run-off may be overcome by intercepting the water at the edge of the reservation by gulley and also by directing the run-off to the sides of the road. When the reservation is on the lower side of super-elevated sections of motorway, the central reservation will require gulley drainage. Surface-water drainage in West Germany is designed in this manner, whereas in Britain it is generally discharged into an untidy French drain in the central reservation, thus making planting more difficult.

Salt spray is a much more difficult problem and the lower foliage of trees and shrubs is seriously affected. However, central reservations of only 4 metres width have, for many years, been planted in West Germany, and replanting is carried out where plant material has failed.

The density of trees varies widely in many countries. In West Germany the policy is to plant at 450 mm centres, whereas in Britain it is nearer to 2 m. The advantages advanced in respect of the former spacing is that it accelerates maturity, suppresses early weed growth and lowers maintenance costs. Higher capital costs frequently reduce subsequent maintenance costs. Thinning of these plantations is necessary at frequent intervals, possibly quinquennially, and thinnings may be used as transplants for sale or for replanting other sections of the motorway.

The selection of tree species, of course, must receive very careful consideration and must not only respect landscape character, avoiding small flowering trees in forest, rural and exposed areas, but also be ecologically appropriate so far as soils, climate, drainage and exposure are concerned. The planting design should attempt to combine fast and slower-growing species in order to ensure the short and long-term effects of planting.

The Nature Conservancy Council survey (7.23) of the M1 motorway between Hendon and Leeds has shown that 384 species of plants are present, while of 2500 flowering plants in Britain, approximately 800 may be found growing in the motorway corridors, thus providing excellent habitats for wildlife.

So far as grass is concerned, hydraulic seeding with a mixture of fertilisers, mulch and seed is a most economic method of providing a vegetative cover over steep cuttings and embankments, not only from a visual point of view, but also to counteract erosion. The top-soiling of the slopes requires careful supervision in order that the soil does not slip from the subsoil, and terracing is necessary on steep slopes. Compacted subsoil should be ripped before top-soiling. Experiments are now proceeding on seeding direct to subsoil in order to eliminate weed growth.

### Contouring of the Highway Corridor

In many countries, the land take for motorways is restricted for political and economic considerations to the minimum area required for construction. The steepness of embankments or cuttings is frequently as great as the natural angle of repose will allow. Such an inflexible yardstick makes no concessions to the environmental design, particularly with regard to harmonising road and landscape. This limited land take is frequently the result of misguided ideas that the reduced land take will result in lower capital costs. Cuttings and embankments are mostly unproductive and are

there as an engineering necessity and merely seeded or planted to control erosion and for aesthetic considerations.

If the land take is temporarily extended up to, say, 200 metres from the road, extensive regrading can be carried out in order to reduce the steep slopes to acceptable gradients which would be capable of agricultural or afforestation uses. After regrading, the land could be returned to the owners. This would not only reduce the scars on the landscape, but would reduce the permanent land take and make a great contribution to the environment.

### Service Areas

The provision of service areas on motorways is a vital factor in road safety and convenience to the travelling public. Their distribution varies widely in different countries. In Britain the policy has been to space them at approximately 30-km intervals, whereas in Germany they are more than 100 km apart. Their precise location has often been open to question. It has been suggested that they should be located on the periphery of towns, where they may be used not only by those travelling on the motorway but also by the local population, and that their facilities should include not only restaurants, service and fuel facilities, but also hypermarkets, motels and caravan parks.

The siting of service areas in the rural landscape frequently raises serious environmental problems. The large areas of land required for the parking of trucks and private vehicles, and the buildings for restaurants and service facilities often create extensive visual intrusion (see Figure 7.16). Service areas should therefore be sited with extreme care, and where they do not dominate the surrounding landscape. The location should, however, provide a pleasant environment for the buildings and it is essential

Figure 7.16 This service area at Charnock shows the major impact of service areas on the rural landscape. Every effort must be made to avoid visual intrusion in the rural landscape by day and night.

(*Photo by courtesy of Aerofilms Ltd.*)

that the disciplines of architecture and landscape architecture are completely inter-related.

They may be located on twin sites alongside the carriageways linked by pedestrian bridges or underpasses, or on one side of the motorway only with vehicular access by over- or underpass, to give access from both carriageways. The merits of these alternatives depend on such factors as land availability, topography, drainage, visual intrusion, natural features and the presence of land of high agricultural value.

In order to minimise the traffic and engineering problems, the level of the site should not vary greatly in relation to the adjoining motorway. Steep access ramps should, of course, be avoided. Sites below the level of the carriageways may expose the extensive parking to the view of passing motorists and thus require additional land take for contouring and screen planting.

Once the optimum number of service areas for a motorway has been established, detailed investigation must be carried out along the entire route to identify suitable sites. The provision of picnic areas, particularly at points of great scenic value, should be considered during route location, as there is an ever-increasing demand for such facilities. The whole question of service area design and standards has been discussed in the Prior report on Motorway Service Areas (7.24).

Finally, it must be remembered that the artificial lighting of such areas frequently causes severe visual intrusion by night and the intrusion of the lighting columns by day.

### Parking

Almost any form of transport requires parking space as an adjunct to its movement channels. The short-term or long-term storage of motor vehicles—private or commercial—is a serious environmental problem. Acres of hard, shiny, multicoloured objects disfigure the landscape around motorway service stations, airports, railway terminals, tourist attractions, and hypermarkets. The contribution the landscape designer can make to this design problem is immense, and the low standard of design of most car parks is a sad reflection on the low priority given to it.

The car park is, of necessity, visually and acoustically intrusive, but these impacts can be modified by the use of one or more landscape techniques. Parking can be arranged in small units informally set amongst existing mature trees, preferably with loosely defined parking bays paved with gravel or grass-concrete. Hedges and shrubs can be used to break up long lines of vehicles, and to provide windbreaks against dust and rubbish blowing across the area. Parking bays can be grouped on different levels, separated by embankments planted with low cover. Earth banks, with or without hedges and shrubs, can be constructed to cut off the normal pedestrian eye-level view of parked cars and, in a more urban situation, walls of local material can perform the same function. When large-scale interchanges are constructed there is nearly always considerable earth moving to be done, and it is often possible to reduce the impact of large car parks by sinking them or banking them.

# Inland Waterways

Much contemporary interest is being shown in the development and maintenance of the cheapest of all transport—waterways. The inland waterway system includes rivers, lakes and canals, the last being man-made and complementing the natural waterways. The whole system may be international and has great multi-functional advantages.

The British Department of the Environment states that in 1974 15% of the total freight moved in the UK was handled by coastal shipping. The bulk of this freight used to be coal, but nowadays it is 80% tanker cargo, mainly petroleum products. Although sea transport is the most economical of all forms of bulk transport, it is essential that both producer and consumer be located on navigable waterways if the benefits of this cheap transport are to be realised. Sea transport scarcely affects the land use planner, but the place of waterways in the landscape is of great importance.

British Waterways Board waterways fall into three main categories:

> 555 km of 'commercial' waterways
> 1737 km of 'cruising' waterways
> 774 km of 'remainder' waterways

Another 1600 km of cruising waterways are controlled by other authorities (7.25).

The commercial waterways are principally available for the carriage of freight and the cruising waterways are principally available for cruising, fishing and other recreational purposes. The 'remainder waterways' must be maintained by the Board in the most economical manner possible, consistent with the requirements of public health and the preservation of amenity and safety. Local authorities and other bodies are empowered to enter into agreements for their restoration to cruising waterway standards or improvement as a public amenity.

The canal and navigable river system linked to the sea comprises some 560 km of 'commercial' waterways connected to the Mersey, the Bristol Channel, the Thames, and the Humber. Although 95% of waterway freight is carried by private organizations, the waterways are controlled by the British Waterways Board, subsidized by Government finance. Carriage of cargoes by canal, river or sea is competitive in cost to other means of transport, but there is not the same massive national investment in the 'track' as there is for roads and railways, which are more useful for strategic purposes in times of crisis. However, there is a strong opinion that the waterways could be made to carry five times more traffic than their present 5 million tonnes per year, and that as the price of fuels continues to rise, so the advantages of low-energy transport become more obvious. Water-borne transport can handle five times as much cargo as road transport for the same fuel consumption, as can be seen from Table 7.3.

The economic viability of commercial waterways has been increased by the advent of the LASH (Lighter Aboard

Table 7.3. Relative fuel efficiencies of various modes of transport

| MODE | tonne-km/litre | ton-miles per gallon |
|---|---|---|
| Pipe line | 107·91 | 300 |
| Waterway | 89·92 | 250 |
| Rail | 71·94 | 200 |
| Road | 20·86 | 58 |
| Air | 1·33 | 3·7 |

Source: Oak Ridge National Laboratory, USA; *New Scientist* 1972

Figure 7.17    British Waterways Board push-tow barges taking cargo along a Yorkshire canal.

(*Photo by courtesy of the British Waterways Board*)

*SH*ip) ship, ('mother' ship capable of conveying entire barges). There are no dock and handling costs as the loading and unloading of ocean-going shipping is carried out in the estuary. Each LASH barge can carry 435 tonnes whereas the conventional standard container carries only 20 tonnes. The 'portless' ship is a concept which makes little demand on land use and is at present undergoing close scrutiny by many nations who are revolutionizing their transportation systems.

Studies carried out since 1966 have led to the introduction of a push-tow barge system, where a single tug pushes up to three dumb barges of 140 tonnes capacity—basically a waterway version of the articulated lorry providing flexibility of operation and increased efficiency and economy. The development of the push-tow system was further enhanced and widened in scope by the introduction of the Danish barge carrying ship BACAT I (*B*arge *A*board *CAT*amaran) in 1974. This craft now operates between the Humber and Rotterdam and is able to carry ten 140 tonne barges (of the same pattern as the British Waterways Board's push-tow fleet), and three 370 tonne LASH barges. These barges are loaded and unloaded from the stern of the ship and are then pushed to their final inland destination by the Board's tugs. In addition to the aforementioned developments, consideration is also being given to a system of Automatic Remote Control of Locks And Bridges (ARCLAB) on the Commercial Waterways, and experiments are being carried out.

The conclusion that one must reach from this evidence is that there is a great future for canals and inland waterways (and even narrow canals), as an economic method of moving freight. However, the trend in Britain has been an appalling decline and decay of the canal and inland waterway system and erosion of many of the economic and amenity advantages which could have accrued from its development.

In the economic development of canals as transportation systems, the viability of their recreational facilities should not be underestimated. Canals may be used for cruising, angling, canoeing, walking and cycling alongside, and may be the foci of park strip systems with facilities for picnicking, camping, nature study, water-based youth clubs, photography, painting and industrial archaeology.

The use of waterways for recreation and leisure is continually increasing; in 1974 there were 25,000 boats using inland waterways, and about 170,000 anglers fishing the canals (7.26). There are many other ways of enjoying waterways, both at weekends and for holidays and, although these uses cannot be considered as forms of transport, the effect they have in terms of requirements for facilities and the revenue they produce has a considerable influence on waterway policies (see page 170).

The navigable pleasure canals in Britain are generally 10 m to 12 m wide, 1 m to 1·5 m deep with a tow path. Commercial canals can be 30 m wide and 3 m deep, although these do vary. Construction is usually of puddled clay. The canals are ideally located along a single line contour with the aid of embankments and are often in cuttings and tunnels and on embankments, bridges and aqueducts. However, when changes in level are necessary, locks are required to control the water level. The opening and closing of the locks results in water being constantly carried to the lower point of the system, making it self-cleansing. The canal system thus uses a great deal of water and requires its own feeder system from rivers or reservoirs.

There tends to be some conflict of interests between recreational, industrial and other uses, including water supply, flood control and effluent disposal. Co-ordination

**CHARACTER OF PLANTING**
SCULPTURAL FORM OF ARCHITECTURE & LANDSCAPE
IN AREAS OF INDUSTRIAL REDEVELOPMENT FLANKED BY CANAL

Figure 7.18   Sketch showing the rehabilitation of the Rochdale Canal. This outworn canal has been redeveloped as a linear park. (*Sketch by Derek Lovejoy and Partners*)

Figure 7.19   A further example of rehabilitation is the canal at Kingston Row and James Brindley Walk, Birmingham. The photographs show the canal before and after rehabilitation.

(*Photos by courtesy of the Public Works Department, Birmingham and the Civic Trust*)

of all these activities and uses within a national and regional framework may resolve such conflicts. The rehabilitation and maintenance of canals and inland waterways must be integrated, not only within national and regional transportation policies, but also on an international basis because in continental Europe, for example, the canals traverse many countries.

For these reasons, and others, the British Government is now setting up a National Water Authority, which will prepare a national strategy for water services in England and Wales, including the control of inland waterways.

# Railways

The railway systems in most countries have been substantially completed and are not undergoing further development. Their construction absorbed a vast capital expenditure and every effort should be made to encourage their use for freight and passengers by modernisation and possible subsidisation. Mass transportation by existing railways can relieve the pressure of traffic on the highways, and thus perhaps reduce the need for building further major roads, with the massive land take which this involves.

In Britain railway construction started at the beginning of the 19th century and with the assistance of Acts of Parliament development was rapid. Little consideration was given to the impact of the railway on communities adjoining the right of way. Tracks were frequently elevated through towns on arches or columns, resulting in a conglomeration of unsatisfactory uses of the space beneath, and the consequent noise and vibration degraded the environment.

Sidings were constructed where they were convenient to the railway without any consideration of visual and aural disturbance to neighbouring communities caused by the constant movement of freight trains. Railways frequently dissected towns and divorced the coastline from the inland communities. Vast stretches of beautiful coastline were sterilized by such routeing. It must be pointed out, however, that the constraints of railway alignment with wide radii and flat horizontal alignments made routeing extremely difficult through hilly terrain, and often the most satisfactory alignment proved to be along valley bottoms and the coastline. However, if the railways, particularly in Britain, had been constructed with the same care and consideration that is now being given to motorways, many of these previous routeing errors might have been avoided.

At present, the major problem facing the railway system is the need to remain financially viable in the face of rising costs and loss of freight and passengers to road and air transport. Bulk freight, such as iron ore, coal, grain, and petroleum products, is the mainstay of any railway economy; but such freight can only compete against road

Figure 7.20 Leyton in East London. The impact of railways on the urban and rural landscape often involves great damage to amenity. Many land-locked railway junctions could be landscaped with not only economic but visual advantages.

(*Photo by courtesy of Aerofilms Ltd.*)

transport where delivery is from siding to siding without transfer to road vehicles (7.27).

International container services have increased considerably since the introduction of the Freightliner organization in 1968, and the development of rail–road–sea container transport is one of the most promising developments in freight transport. However these services are organised, there will still remain a need for large areas of sidings, depots, and storage yards which not only occupy a great deal of land in themselves, but sterilise an almost equal amount of land between tracks, at junctions and around bridges and cuttings.

Many of these landlocked areas could be used for productive activities including afforestation. These uses would both achieve an economic return and improve the environmental qualities of the railways. Railways, in many respects have been totally neglected as far as landscape treatment is concerned, and almost every conceivable unsatisfactory development is allowed to back onto the railways creating environmental slum corridors. Far more research and determination needs to be given to this matter to make these areas more productive and visually satisfying.

The planting of railway 'waste spaces' is liable to the same constraints of accessibility, fire hazard, and visual obstruction as are the motorway waste spaces, and it is to be hoped that better solutions may be found to the problem of controlling vegetation than the present unsightly burning-off of cuttings and embankments. The advancing electrification of the railways will remove the danger of pollution to vegetation, so that it may be possible to grow feed crops for animals or humans in suitable locations.

The electric overhead system itself creates a landscape presence, with the visual intrusion of pylons and cables, though unless the track is sited on a prominent embankment, this may be reduced to a considerable extent by trackside planting.

Undoubtedly the problem is chiefly one of economics. The railways, subsidised as they are in many countries of the world, are expected to be solvent, and therefore expenditure to improve the environment inevitably comes low on the list of priorities. There should be specific sums set aside, as in the case of highways, for environmental improvement of the railways.

It is encouraging to note that British Rail, conscious of their low environmental image, have now appointed a Director of Environment, backed by an independent Advisory Committee. This is, indeed, a very encouraging step in trying to raise the general environmental standards of British Railways. It is to be hoped that the new Director can encourage local authorities and other bodies to take a greater interest in land use and environmental problems alongside railway tracks.

# Cycle and Moped Routes

The use of these methods of conveyance varies widely and depends largely on national economic circumstances, and social customs, together with the need for a reasonably flat terrain. In Holland, for example, 56% of the population owns cycles compared with 33% in the US, and these percentages are increasing. With ever-increasing costs of petrol and oil, the bicycle, moped and motorcycle are becoming much more popular. Registrations of two-wheeled vehicles in the UK increased by 75% between 1972 and 1975, and there has been a very noticeable increase in the number of people using bicycles for journeys to work.

At present, it is not economic to modify existing traffic systems to make special allowance for two-wheeled traffic, but where new local roads are being designed, some degree of segregation is worth considering. Normal separate provision for cycles is not necessary where the number of cyclists is below 1500 in a 16-hour period. However, the initial provision of cycleways connecting residential, industrial and city centres may encourage a higher percentage of cycle ownership, thus reducing the demands and hazards of other traffic systems.

The main requirement of this system is that it should be separate from busy highways with heavy freight traffic, and only connected to local roads at limited points. Cycle traffic should, in principle, also be separated from the pedestrian system where large volumes of cycle traffic are expected. It may otherwise be integrated with the footpath system, especially where the origins and destinations coincide. Where it is not possible to provide a separate cycle system, provision for cycles can always be made by widening the carriageway of the nearside lane. This cycle lane must be clearly marked, preferably with a different coloured aggregate from that part of the road used by motor vehicles.

With regard to design standards the cycle tracks are normally designed for two-way traffic unless volumes dictate otherwise. The standard width is 2·75 m for two-way traffic with a minimum of 2 m. Cycle tracks should be separated from the carriageway by a verge 2 m wide and from a footway by 1 m. If cycle subways are warranted, they should have a minimum headroom of 2 m and a width of 3 m for one-way working. Maximum ramp gradients should be 1 in 20 upwards and 1 in 15 downwards. The standard of maintenance of the cycle ways must be good, with carefully designed details in the interests of safety and also to avoid damage to grass and planting. It is rare that intersections need be grade-separated.

Traffic at junctions may be controlled by signs or at the last resort by traffic signals. Adequate parking facilities must be provided adjoining residential or industrial areas, schools, shopping centres, etc. The mixing of pedestrian, cycle and moped traffic must, of course, be determined by demand, but it is important that speeds be controlled as moped traffic will not mix with pedestrian traffic without speed controls.

# Design of Pedestrian and Bridle Networks

As with cycling, the extent to which people use their legs as a form of transportation for business and pleasure, depends upon affluence and social customs. Discouragement of the use of the motor vehicle because of its impact on vulnerable landscapes and land resources, and the encouragement, particularly by the medical profession, of healthy exercise has tended to increase the habit of walking in many countries. In Britain alone the Ramblers Association boasts a membership of 25,000, with an annual increase of 15%. Clearly, walking should be encouraged from all points of view and adequate provision made. One of the principal advantages of walking is that as a form of recreation it makes little demand on land use.

Footpaths can follow the hedgerows, woodlands, verges, towpaths, lakes, commons and the uplands. The system should be linked with motor hotels, recreation and equestrian centres and countryside parks, and from these points visitors would be expected to walk on sign-posted paths and fan out into wilder landscapes. Care, however, must be exercised to align the system to minimise damage to agricultural land, particularly avoiding shortcuts through arable land and young plantations. These aspects are developed fully in Chapter 6.

As with roads, there should be a hierarchy of pedestrian networks. Primary footpaths should link urban and rural areas, city centres, residential and industrial area with countryside parks, and secondary footpath networks should connect homes with playgrounds and car parks. Intersections with major roads should be grade-separated and designed with smooth vertical alignments, particularly for the conveyance of invalids and small children. Steps or steep ramps should be discouraged. In order to encourage use of the footpath system, it should pass through an interesting environment, be direct and not unnecessarily circuitous.

# Air Transport

Congestion at airports is now so serious that it is affecting the viability of airlines. Delays and unreliability, particularly on domestic airlines, are forcing passengers to seek other methods of transport and this fact has its repercussions on highways. Air speeds have doubled over the past 20 years but increasing airport delays have eroded these benefits.

Airports make an enormous demand on natural resources in terms of land and materials. It is not merely the land required for runways but land required for car parking and many other ancillary facilities. Los Angeles Airport in the next decade is planning to accommodate 25,000 cars per day.

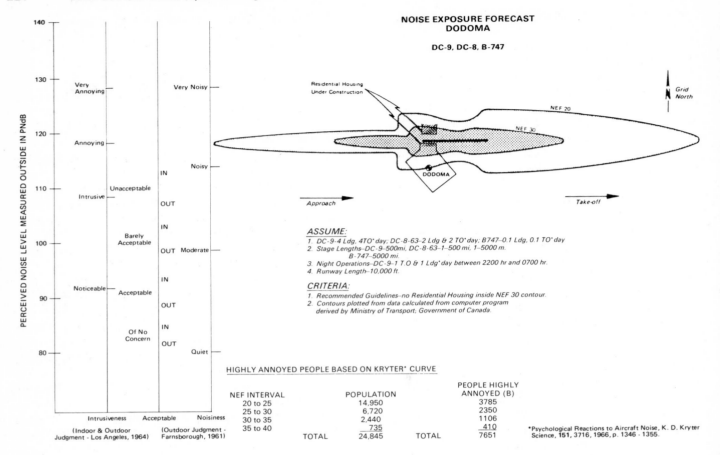

**NOISE EXPOSURE FORECAST DODOMA**

DC-9, DC-8, B-747

*ASSUME:*
1. DC-9-4 Ldg, 4 TO° day; DC-8-63–2 Ldg & 2 TO° day; B747–0.1 Ldg, 0.1 TO° day
2. Stage Lengths—DC-9–500mi, DC-8-63–1–500 mi, 1–5000 m.
   B-747–5000 mi.
3. Night Operations—DC-9–1 T.O & 1 Ldg° day between 2200 hr and 0700 hr.
4. Runway Length–10,000 ft.

*CRITERIA:*
1. Recommended Guidelines—no Residential Housing inside NEF 30 contour.
2. Contours plotted from data calculated from computer program
   derived by Ministry of Transport, Government of Canada.

HIGHLY ANNOYED PEOPLE BASED ON KRYTER* CURVE

| NEF INTERVAL | POPULATION | PEOPLE HIGHLY ANNOYED (B) |
|---|---|---|
| 20 to 25 | 14,950 | 3785 |
| 25 to 30 | 6,720 | 2350 |
| 30 to 35 | 2,440 | 1106 |
| 35 to 40 | 735 | 410 |
| TOTAL | 24,845 | TOTAL 7651 |

*Psychological Reactions to Aircraft Noise, K. D. Kryter Science, 151, 3716, 1966, p. 1346 - 1355.

Figure 7.21   Noise exposure forecasts in the vicinity of Dodoma Airport.

(Source: National Capital Master Plan, Dodoma, Tanzania, Technical Supplement no. 3, Vol. II)

It must be emphasized that as far as land is concerned it is not only the physical dimensions of the airport which is the land-consumer, but the whole area beneath the flight path of an aircraft which partially sterilises an area many times the size of the airport itself. Woodlands, large trees and frequently high ground, must be removed in order to comply with international safety standards. Reference has already been made to the investigations into the Third London Airport where environmental considerations predominated over purely financial and material considerations. The need to link airports to other transportation systems in multi-transportation terminals which are most satisfactorily sited, particularly for environmental considerations, on the coast where they can be linked with sea traffic and cause minimal disturbance to communities has already been discussed.

One of the most critical factors in the design of airports is the environmental impact caused by aircraft noise. Research is concentrating on various techniques for reducing the noise of aircraft engines, but until this succeeds, it is imperative that the effect of noise on the surrounding inhabitants should be considered before deciding on the siting and layout of runways. Figure 7.21 shows the levels of acceptable noise for a normal population and the noise contours for some typical aircraft. The number of people in Dodoma, the national capital of Tanzania, living within the range of 'highly annoying' noise has been calculated, and in a situation like this the alternatives are to move the population, to provide sound insulation to individual buildings, or to provide landscaped sound barriers adjacent to the runway.

# References

7.1  ROSKILL (Chairman), *Report of the Commission on the Third London Airport*, HMSO, London, 1971.

7.2  *Transport Policy*, Vol. 1, HMSO, London, 1976

7.3  DEPARTMENT OF THE ENVIRONMENT, *Route Location with regard to Environmental Issues* (Jefferson Report), HMSO, London, 1976.

7.4  DEPARTMENT OF THE ENVIRONMENT, *Report of the Advisory Committee on Trunk Road Assessment* (Leitch Report), HMSO, London, 1977.

7.5  DEPARTMENT OF TRANSPORT, *Policy for Roads: England 1978*, HMSO, London, 1978.

7.6 DEPARTMENT OF TRANSPORT, *Highway Statistics,* HMSO, London, 1976.

7.7 *Transport Policy,* Vol. 2, HMSO, London, 1976.

7.8 DEPARTMENT OF THE ENVIRONMENT, *Getting the Best Roads for Our Money,* HMSO. London, 1972.

7.9 DEPARTMENT OF THE ENVIRONMENT (1976), *op. cit.*

7.10 DEPARTMENT OF TRANSPORT, *Standard Forecasts of Vehicles and Traffic,* HMSO, London, 1975.

7.11 TAYLOR, J. E., *Civil Engineering,* January 1976, pp. 26–27.

7.12 DEPARTMENT OF THE ENVIRONMENT (1976), *op. cit.*

7.13 *Ibid.*

7.14 DEPARTMENT OF THE ENVIRONMENT, *Calculation of Road Traffic Noise,* HMSO, London, 1975.

7.15 RTM PLANNING PARTNERSHIP, *Traffic Noise Calculations by Computer,* RTM Planning Partnership, East Grinstead, Sussex, 1979.

7.16 LEONARD, D. R. *et al., Loads and Vibrations caused by Eight Commercial Vehicles with Gross Weights exceeding 32 tons,* TRRL Report LR 582, Road Research Laboratory, 1974.

7.17 COMMISSION OF THE EUROPEAN COMMUNITIES, *State of the Environment, First Report,* Commission of the European Communities, Brussels, 1977.

7.18 *Ibid.*

7.19 DEPARTMENT OF THE ENVIRONMENT (1976), *op. cit.*

7.20 *Ibid.*

7.21 *Transport Policy,* Vol. 2, *op. cit.*

7.22 DEPARTMENT OF THE ENVIRONMENT (1976), *op. cit.*

7.23 'Maintenance of motorway verges', *Landscape Design,* 101, February 1973, p. 41.

7.24 PRIOR (Chairman), *Report of the Committee of Inquiry into Motorway Service Areas,* HMSO, London, 1978.

7.25 INLAND WATERWAYS AMENITY ADVISORY COUNCIL, *Priorities for Action,* Inland Waterways Amenity Advisory Council, London, 1975.

7.26 *Ibid.*

7.27 BRITISH RAILWAYS BOARD, *An Opportunity for Change,* British Railways Board, London, 1976.

# Bibliography

ANTONIOU, J., *Environmental Management,* McGraw-Hill, Maidenhead, 1971.

APPLEYARD, D. *et al., The View from the Road,* MIT Press, Cambridge, Mass., 1971.

BLUNDEN, W. R., *The Land Use/Transport System,* Pergamon, Oxford, 1971.

BRITISH ROAD FEDERATION, *Motorways in the Urban Environment,* British Road Federation, London, 1971.

BRUTON, M. J., *Introduction to Transport Planning,* Hutchinson, London, 1970.

DEPARTMENT OF THE ENVIRONMENT, *Getting the Best Roads for Our Money,* HMSO, London, 1972.

DEPARTMENT OF THE ENVIRONMENT, *Calculations of Road Traffic Noise,* HMSO, London, 1975.

DEPARTMENT OF THE ENVIRONMENT, *Route Location with Regard to Environmental Issues,* HMSO, London, 1976.

DEPARTMENT OF THE ENVIRONMENT, *Report of the Advisory Committee on Trunk Road Assessment,* HMSO, London, 1977.

DEPARTMENT OF TRANSPORT, *Policy for Roads: England 1978,* HMSO, London, 1978.

DRAKE, J. *et al., Motorways,* Faber and Faber, London, 1967.

INLAND WATERWAYS AMENITY ADVISORY COUNCIL, *Priorities for Action,* Inland Waterways Advisory Council, London, 1975.

*Layout of Roads in Rural Areas,* HMSO, London, 1968.

PLOWDEN, S., *Towns against Traffic,* Andre Deutsch, London, 1972.

*Transport Policy,* Vols. 1 and 2, HMSO, London, 1976.

RITTER, P., *Planning for Man and Motor,* Pergamon, Oxford, 1964.

CHAPTER EIGHT
# INDUSTRIAL LAND USE AND DERELICTION
Clifford R. V. Tandy

Extension to an industrial complex in Scotland, where the architecture and siting are very sympathetic to their surroundings. Although occupying the majority of the valley floor, the simple horizontal treatment of these buildings offers the minimum conflict to the character of the scenery behind. (see page 202)

*(Photo by courtesy of I.B.M.)*

# INDUSTRIAL LAND USE AND DERELICTION

## Historical Development of Industrial Land Use

Although this book is intended to deal with present-day problems in an international setting, there are good reasons for commencing this chapter with a brief study of the history of the industrial use of land in Great Britain. It was, of course, one of the earliest countries to face industrialisation; it was a small enough country to have felt the effects of industrial expansion throughout, even though the major centres were highly concentrated; it forms a compact 'case study' of the problems arising, and although these have taken place in the past 200 years in Great Britain, they have a decided relevance to newly developing countries today.

'Industry' began much earlier in man's history than is usually assumed. The mining and working of copper and gold, followed by smelting and alloying of bronze, developed from 4000 BC, and recent discoveries of Thracian gold plate give dates some 2000 years earlier. Effects on the landscape of such activities were considerable, though sites were few and widely scattered. These effects were mainly the tipping of quarry and mine waste, the felling and burning of forests for fuel, and the dumping of smelter slag, but there were side effects resulting from the diversion and polluting of local streams.

The extent of landscape damage can be judged by a few examples: By AD 20 large wooded tracts at Laurion near Athens had been laid bare by felling for smelters; in the Roman occupation 80 hectares of the Forest of Dean had been covered by slag tips; one tip in the Weald is believed to have contained 50,000 tons of iron slag (8.1); the Egyptians sank hundreds of shafts of considerable size, on the Red Sea coast, in the search for gem stones; calcining of both copper and iron ores was done in the open air—the sulphurous gas and carbon dioxide fumes must have been a serious form of air pollution even at such an early date.

Until the 17th century Britain was almost entirely agricultural, though early in that century there were industrial complexes in the salt, glass, silk and textile industries, some of which employed up to a thousand workers. There also existed large quarry workings and iron furnaces in the forests, with iron ore mines and hammer ponds. The overall effect upon the landscape was, however, very slight indeed, as most of the quarries, mines and furnaces were isolated and scattered. Textile workers worked in their own homes, and though terraces of weavers' cottages were specially built with large-windowed upper stories, they fitted happily into the village scene.

Three main factors determined the location of industry at this time: the supply of raw material; the source of power; and, for textiles, the local climate. As transport became mechanised, the first of these became less important, for most material could be carried to the factory. It was, of course, an absolute determining factor in the extractive industries which were obliged to work stone and mineral ores where they were found. The second—a source of power—was a strong determinant. The use of water power concentrated groups of industries in river valleys—particularly the geologically 'younger' valleys of the upland areas of the west and north, where a good head of water was to be found. It was this available power supply which led, in the 18th century, to the concentration of workers into

Figure 8.1    Barnard Castle, Teesdale. Early industrial building erected in the centre of a valley, using water as the motive power. In this example, the strong, simple architecture does not offend, even when seen against the historic castle beyond.

*(Photo: Clifford Tandy)*

factories. The need for a humid atmosphere for the production of textiles also attracted these industries to the wetter areas of the north and north-west which coincided, fortunately, with the location of river valleys providing water power.

Water power was clean and created no soot, grime, or smoke. Land at the time was plentiful and building cheap. Consequently, at first the mills, the workers' houses and the owners' houses often formed a pleasant group of stone buildings which were no detriment to the landscape unless the location of the mill blocked off the end of an attractive valley. Soon, however, factories began to rise seven and eight stories high, and workers' houses filled the flat land of the valley bottoms. The mill owners created 'company towns' with schools and sunday schools, and introduced shift working to take advantage of the continuous supply of water power 24 hours a day.

From the middle of the 18th century these isolated industries began to be served by a new network of communications—the canal system. To keep an even water level these had either to follow the contours or to be rerouted through cuttings, tunnels and locks or over viaducts and embankments, and the real engineering assault upon the landscape had begun. Fortunately many of these constructional works were of a high standard of design, and some were a positive asset to a sometimes dull and flat countryside.

The second great phase of the Industrial Revolution was the introducton of steam power in the mid-18th century. Used at first for pumping, the steam engine was later adapted to rotary motion, and so began to operate every kind of mechanical plant—eventually becoming itself mobile, in the form of the railway engine. Fuel supply quickly became the paramount factor: wood burning gave way to coal, and the coal fields of the country became the magnet for the greatest

concentrations of industry. This time it was an invisible component of landscape—the underground coal measures strata—which became the determining factor in industrial location. Their occurrence bore little relation to the topography above. Coal was found under the dull midlands plain, the Yorkshire moors and the beautiful Welsh Valleys.

A new factor in the destruction of landscape now began to appear—the dumping of waste materials. Small amounts of quarry waste had soon been colonised by plants and become invisible, but the vast quantities of mine spoil now appearing, the rate of their tipping, the toxic wastes from glass, chemical and smelting industries meant that they would never be assimilated into the landscape. To industrialists of the 19th century this was all accepted as the inevitable price of progress, and 'muck' was equated with 'money'. Workers lived in tiny back-to-back houses around dark courts and narrow streets in the low-lying badly-drained land alongside the canals, and the word 'slum' (from *slump*: a mire) was born.

The 19th century saw this rate of change increased a hundredfold. Villages of two or three hundred people had populations of 40 and 50 thousand by the middle of the century. Towns grew too. Preston in the 18th century was a fashionable society town. According to Hoskins (8.2) it had six thousand inhabitants before cotton spinning was introduced in 1777. A hundred years later there were 90,000. Railway construction spread tentacles over the whole of the country. Like canals, the early railways needed to be nearly level, so that vast earthworks were undertaken to cross valleys and hills with embankments and cuttings. For economy they needed to be as straight as possible, so they were often cut across the natural topography.

The industries of the period—in fact almost up to the present day—adopted an 'exploit and move-on' policy, which might be called the equivalent of the 'slash and burn' methods of primitive agriculture. The result of such an attitude was the loss of increasing acreages of land to industry and a large legacy of dereliction. The derelict-land aspect of this potted history is continued on page 251.

The late 19th century saw the introduction of new industries, and the expansion of certain older ones, which had a marked impact on the landscape. During the period 1850–1913 the output of coal in Britain rose from 50 million to 287 million tons, with over 3000 pits operating. Mechanical handling, though primitive, speeded up the dumping of millions of tons of shale waste on the surface, which was not only visually disfiguring, but caused water and air pollution. Similar, but on a smaller scale, was the production of iron and steel, giving rise to heaps of iron slag, and the discharge of smoke and fumes.

Extractive industries, which expanded rapidly through mechanisation, were sand and gravel, and brick clay production. Both took flat land in the south and east of the country and created vast shallow voids which could not easily be restored. Many of the sand and gravel pits on low river terraces became water-filled, and partially regenerated themselves, taking on a new ecological form.

# Classes of Industrial Land Use and Their Problems

In order to analyse the effect of industrial land use upon the landscape and to plan for its better incorporation, it is necessary to have a clear idea of the various industrial processes and the factors which influence industrial location, its form, size, successful performance, and the ancillary services required.

It may be convenient to group the types of industrial land use under eight headings:

1. Offices and commercial buildings;
2. Factories in urban situations;
3. Factories in rural situations;
4. Warehousing;
5. Transportation;
6. Ancillary land uses, e.g. cooling ponds, storage land, recreation;
7. Special types of industry, e.g. power stations, water reservoirs;
8. Extractive industries.

### Office and Commercial Building Location

Offices and commercial buildings are usually planned for urban situations, unless perhaps when attached to a factory complex. British planning regulations since the 1947 Act have usually laid down zoning patterns, by which the commercial office centre of a town is segregated from residential and shopping areas. This concept is now going out of favour, as it has led to cities becoming dead at night after office workers have gone home. The type of mixed development which is now acceptable is more human, and more like the organic growth of older cities, and it needs a proportion of 'green' open space to complete it. The problems are those of any intense urban development—problems of density, old boundaries, high land values, car parking, overloaded streets and transport systems.

Among the solutions which have been tried, with varying degrees of success, are: set-backs to daylight angles; plot ratios; height restrictions; central light wells and courtyards; pedestrian precincts; underground car parking, etc. To provide open space in dense urban situations is clearly something which can only be done adequately by the city authority planning or re-planning a whole precinct. Plot owners cannot do a great deal individually, though there are examples of good landscape treatments of pedestrian precincts and courts, open arcaded ground floors, and roof gardens. A common mistake is to try to produce too much 'gardening'. Some green vegetation is restful, but the need for open space in urban situations can often best be met by paved areas, with small amounts of hedges, plants in pots, individual trees, and possibly some water, well maintained. Another common error is to ignore microclimatic considerations, and put planting and pedestrian seating on a bare windswept podium.

### Factory Location in Urban Areas

There is a simple logic in planning factories in urban situations close to other buildings and adjacent to their labour force, rather than on *greenfield* sites. In practice, however, there are difficulties. Of course, 'factories' vary in size from a single-room workshop to a mile-long rolling mill. Cities like Birmingham, Leeds and Glasgow, with a large demand for small workshops, have been able to establish 'flatted factories' in multi-storey buildings, and these are in keeping with the urban scene. Most factories, however, are low sprawling single-storey buildings surrounded by yards, circulation areas and stocking space. These are expensive in land in city centres and do not contribute to urban cohesiveness. They also produce problems of noise, dust, smoke and other effluents as well as traffic problems, both of freight and workpeople.

The solution put forward in the new towns, built in the last 25 years, is to designate an *industrial zone* adjacent to, but separate from, the business and residential areas of the town (Figures 8.2, 8.3 and 8.4). This has many advantages, including the opportunity to handle the design problem of factory buildings and the spaces between at a quite different scale from that in residential and commercial areas. The location must be carefully chosen so that the industrial zone is well served by road and rail transport and by all services, but it must not be so isolated from the town that pedestrian access for workers becomes difficult. Its location must be such that the prevailing winds take smoke, fumes, gases and noise *away* from the town. It must be sited to give space for future expansion either in step with the growth of the town, or, possibly, independently of it. The need for parallel expansion of the different elements of a town has given rise to the more recent concept of a *linear* town in which future growth is planned along a straight, or curved, line of major communications (Figure 8.5). There are several examples of plans for such linear towns, but none has yet been built.

### Factory Location in Rural Areas

It is very tempting for an industrialist to get round many of the problems mentioned by looking at fresh sites in the countryside, particularly today, when motorways have opened up new areas, and given excellent communications to sites previously inaccessible. One should distinguish here between industries which are 'footloose', i.e. can be situated anywhere, provided that certain minimum requirements are met, and those which are obliged to be situated in the countryside because they are winning raw materials 'where found' or have stringent conditions of area, access, or supply, which cannot be met elsewhere.

First thoughts suggest that any industry or factory building is bound to be an unwelcome intrusion into the rural situation. In practice, however, one is obliged to modify such views. There are truly wild areas of the world where a single artifact of any kind would destroy the

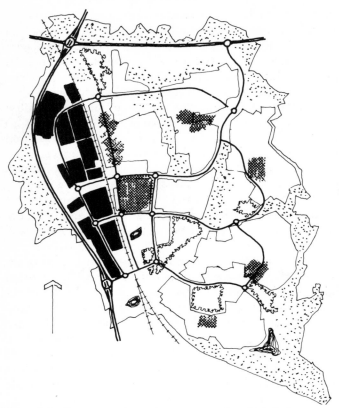

Figure 8.2  Stevenage. An early new town in which industry was confined to a single zone on the 'wrong side of the tracks' and, incidentally, on the windward side of the town.

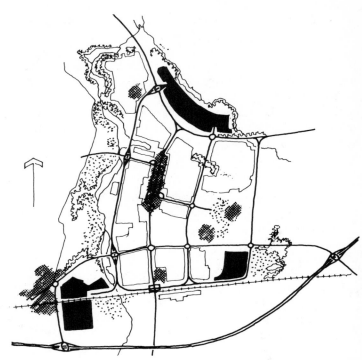

Figure 8.3  The proposed Hook new town which the LCC never built. Here there are three industrial zones around the perimeter.

Figure 8.4  Washington. A later new town with industrial zones distributed through the fabric of the town.

Figure 8.5  Linear town. A hypothetical layout with commerce, residential neighbourhoods, and industry in parallel zones either side of a transport/recreation spine. The linear system offers indefinite expansion in the direction of the spine.

Figure 8.6   Industrial landscaping! An example of failure to appreciate the scale of industrial work. This narrow flowerbed only emphasises the vast size and crudity of the concrete ventilation plant it is supposed to enhance.

*(Photo: Clifford Tandy)*

isolation, but highly populated countries like Britain have virtually no such virgin areas left—every piece of land bears some evidence of man's influence. Even so, magnificent areas of scenery need to be even more strongly protected when they are in short supply, and there is a strong case for keeping national parks wholly free from industry; this argument does not need repeating here. Where intrusion into rural areas is acceptable, the scale and actual size of industrial buildings may very well have a dignity which smaller developments would lack. The precise locating of the factory into the pattern of the land, the concealment of the clutter of small buildings, stores, roads, cars, etc., around its base, and the provision of discreet access roads and services, are an exercise in landscape planning which may produce a satisfying result. Most of the failures which occur, on this level of design, are the result of failing to appreciate the scale of the artifact, and the scale of the landscape treatment needed to cope with it. Small beds of summer flowers around the base of a vast concrete structure, merely emphasise the intrusion, whereas a thick belt of forest trees might make the artifact not only acceptable, but a pleasing contrast.

## Location of Warehousing

Warehousing and distribution centres are becoming a large component of industry today. Production management introduces continuous production and assembly-line processes which result in a flow of materials and products 24 hours a day, which means precise planning of storage and distribution.

Warehousing may be part of the manufacturing process, or it may be divorced from it. There is a tendency today to have warehousing facilities spread around the various

marketing areas, particularly where the industry itself is, by its nature, tied to a location remote from the markets. Warehouses, warehouse estates, and regional distribution centres demand immediate and excellent road access, preferably near motorway intersections. They may also need to be located near to sea ports, airports, inland water and/or railway freight terminals. They are inevitably bulky, large in scale, and need extensive manoeuvring spaces between the buildings. The form is usually simple and straightforward, and can be dull unless sensitively married to the landscape form.

## Transportation

The transportation side of distribution strongly involves landscape considerations. Modern assembly-line techniques mean that, as Estall and Buchanan put it (8.3), 'the manufacturer can treat the highway as virtually part of his conveyor-belt system'. The transport 'industry' uses the same roads, rail, river, and air space as does public transport and private vehicles, so that its particular impact cannot be isolated. There is no distinction in practice between haulage by the transport industry operators, and haulage by manufacturing industries' own vehicles. Furthermore, private cars subsidise the roads, while freight traffic subsidises passenger trains.

Countries vary in the value they place on different forms of transport. Britain and USA have been running down their railway and canal systems, while Germany has been opening hundreds of miles of new ship canals, and Holland has recently built 200 new railway stations. Common sense would indicate that any country would benefit by diversity in its transport networks, but the convenience of door-to-door road transport is causing it to take precedence over all other forms, whether or not they are more economical for heavy freight.

The major landscape impact of the transport industry—apart from general trunk and motorway building as described in chapter 7—is in the increase in the use of heavy road vehicles. The extra-heavy vehicles above 44 tonnes laden are not allowed on public roads, but even 10- to 25-tonne lorries carrying sand, gravel, stone, ores or minerals from a remote quarrying site can completely change the form and pattern of the narrow lanes and small minor roads through which they pass. Widening and straightening may be desirable for safety, but the result may be wholly out of character with the surroundings, and may lead to wider use by other traffic.

## Location of Ancillary Services

Unfortunately, the dramatic factory structure is not the whole of the impact that an industry makes in the countryside. Not only is there the small-scale clutter around the outside of the factory, but a great deal of land is required for service purposes. Transport is discussed in detail in Chapter 7, but one must take note of the wide-ranging effect on the landscape of widening country roads to take lorry traffic. Heavy industry often needs rail access, with the possibility of half-a-mile or more of multi-track sidings, loading bays, etc. Power supply, if the industry is a large one, probably means a special electricity supply line on transmission towers right up to the factory site from the nearest grid line.

Water supply for industry can be taken from the normal mains, but it may be necessary to construct a new reservoir, such as the Cow Green reservoir in Upper Teesdale which destroyed 8 hectares of rare alpine vegetation to provide 20-years supply of industrial water for Imperial Chemical Industries.

Storage of raw materials, fuels, waste materials, and the stockpiling of finished products takes up a great deal of land, and the heaps are usually unsightly. The storage areas separate the factory itself from its surroundings, and make integration so much more difficult.

Considerable disturbance to the landscape can result from building operations during the construction of factories and their associated services. In certain fragile landscapes, success depends upon disturbance of the original surface as little as possible, as any subsequent 'landscaping' would look artificial. This means a great deal of pre-planning, to ensure that contractor's lines of access and working areas coincide with roads, yards or 'introduced landscape' in the final scheme. It also means a strict discipline over the contractor and his workmen during the construction work. This form of discipline is essential in the laying of pipes and underground services. Often an unnecessarily wide and straight swathe is cut, and the line appears as a noticeable scar on the landscape for many years. Although it is possible to hide a pipeline completely under agricultural crops, pasture, grass and lawns, it is extremely difficult to do so on heath or moorland, rocky slopes, and through woodland.

Figure 8.7   Although pipelines can be concealed underground, the 40 ft width of working space allowed to the contractor causes permanent damage when a swathe is cut through woodland.

*(Photo: Clifford Tandy)*

Not all ancillary services are a hindrance, however. The provision of recreational facilities for employees can give the opportunity to plan for large green areas of playing fields, sitting and walking spaces, and even large water areas, which can be a foil to the buildings and working spaces, and can help the assimilation of the whole complex into the countryside.

### Location of Special Types of Industry

We now come to the group of special industries, whose location away from urban areas is determined by certain rigid factors. These include power stations, oil terminals, port installations, Government testing stations, smelters, refineries. The conditions which govern the siting of these forms of plant limit the number of possible sites, but still give a certain degree of choice. The methods of environmental impact analysis and landscape assessment discussed in chapters 2 and 3 enable choice of site to be made with the least damage to the landscape, and this should be the first step. When a location study has been narrowed down to a particular area, the exact siting of the installation can be done either crudely or skilfully, with bad or good effects upon the landscape.

### Reservoir Location

Reservoirs for public water supply are a particular example. Each is a large engineering artifact set inevitably into fairly remote, and often beautiful, cultivated valley landscape. We are not concerned here with the politics of their location, nor the engineering construction, but with the detailed siting and landscape treatment of the dam, the water body, and the ancillary buildings. The dam itself may be concrete or stone-faced (occasionally in the past, brick) curved or straight on plan. Alternatively it may be a low-profile rock-fill or earth dam with clay or concrete core, grass-seeded on its outer slope. While engineering considerations may determine the final form, it is clear that the different shapes suit different landscape forms: the near-vertical curved wall is at home in rugged mountain scenery with rock cliffs on either side; the longer straight wall suits less-dramatic highland scenery, and wide flat valleys; the earth dam—preferably also gently curved on plan, is better for undulating and rolling pastoral scenery.

The form of the valley, and the depth of water needed to give adequate volume, determine the plan form of the water area. This, however, can be adjusted within certain limits, and it is advisable to have an accurate model of the valley made from an air photograph in which various water depths can be tried out. Where the water level cannot be altered to accommodate the perimeter form, the form may itself be adjusted by earth modelling or blasting. It should be remembered that 'draw-down' of water in dry weather is a really serious problem for the reservoir designer. A bare band of different-coloured earth is revealed between upper

Figure 8.8   The Llewyn reservoir dam in Wales showing the water intake tower and drainage trenches on the face of the dam, which is gently curved in keeping with the surrounding countryside.

*(Photo: Clifford Tandy)*

and lower water levels which cannot be planted or given any permanent treatment. This may not matter a great deal where sides are steep and rocky but, where the land profile is gentle, a wide expanse of muddy 'beach' is uncovered. No fully satisfactory solution to concealing or treating this 'draw-down' zone has yet been found, except for 'rip-rap' block or stone pitching, which can probably be afforded on the back of the dam, but not elsewhere. The area of the zone should therefore be kept to the minimum.

A good simple water form and dam shape can be spoiled by a clutter of ancillary buildings. These are no longer built like Scottish baronial castles on top of the dam, but can usually be placed in the valley below the dam and should take simple forms like farm buildings with the minimum of 'frills', either technological or decorative. Having sited the buildings well, it is essential to deal with transport routes for

vehicles and pedestrians, water spillways, by-pass channels, and, sometimes electricity supply cables. As is often mentioned in these pages, attention is only drawn to a particular artifact by the 'spider's web' of communication routes of which it is the centre. If the circumferential lines (usually caused by contractors' men and plant) can be avoided altogether, and the radial lines well planned to fit into the landscape pattern, the whole complex may be not only acceptable, but even pleasing.

**Power Station Location**

Conventional coal and oil-burning power stations are typical of this form of problem. Among the factors to be taken into account in siting are: sheer size of the building; immense weight to be carried by suitable geological strata; large volumes of cooling water and the subsequent discharge of warmed water; discharge of combustion fumes, including sulphur dioxide into the atmosphere; supply and transport of fuel input; easy transmission of power output. Nuclear-powered stations have the further criteria of remoteness for safety reasons, and the safe disposal of radio-active waste.

While the size of the buildings, the mass of the cooling tower complex and the height of the chimney necessary to get the plume above the reach of temperature inversions must be accepted as fixed factors in landscape planning, there is much that can be done to make the artifact acceptable. Everything near to the building must be kept in scale with it. The purity of the simple architectural and engineering statement can be maintained if the surrounding clutter of switchgear, sub-stations, car parks, etc. is enclosed either by the building or by sympathetic shaping of the landscape. Tree planting close to the building will be insignificant, and will probably increase the apparent size. Planning for mass tree planting in the surrounding countryside will, however, help the artifact to be absorbed happily

Figure 8.9   Didcot power station, well sited on an old ordnance depot in the Thames Valley.

*(Architect and landscape consultant: Sir Frederick Gibberd; photo: Clifford Tandy)*

into its surroundings, and, while not hiding it, or even camouflaging it, will reduce the baldness of its impact.

Hydro-electric power stations are a special case so related by necessity to the form of the landscape in which they sit that there are very few sites which are both technically and aesthetically feasible in any country, and each is a unique 'one-off' situation. Because a 'head' of water of several hundred metres is needed, provided either by natural or artificial storage, a location in dramatic highland scenery is inevitable. The planning decision must therefore be based on the need for electricity set against amenity, tourism and aesthetic values, and the landscape treatment will be restricted to siting the details well, softening the hard impact, and conserving the site's present ecology.

### Location of Transmission Lines

In total, probably a far greater landscape planning problem than power stations themselves is the location of transmission lines. Public feeling on this aspect is so strong that great care is taken, but still it would be rare to site a transmission line on aesthetic grounds alone. Technological, sociological, political and financial considerations weigh heavily. While everyone accepts the need for these lines and towers, everyone wishes them somewhere else. Undergrounding is technically possible but the cost is of the order of 12 to 14 times that of overhead lines. Even if the electricity supply authority (and that means, ultimately, the public) were prepared to pay for undergrounding, it is doubtful whether the money could not be spent to the benefit of the landscape in other ways with much better effect. Nan Fairbrother puts it rather well: '... undergrounding is very poor amenity value for money, and at up to £200,000 per pylon we could get rid of far worse eyesores' (8.4).

Accepting then the present necessity for overhead transmission lines, much can be done by careful routeing. The British Central Electricity Generating Board (CEGB) has done some excellent work in this field, and some other countries could do worse than follow its example. There will always be different opinions, of course. Some find every pylon an eyesore. Others can see a certain majestic dignity in a single line of the large 450-kV towers striding across an open landscape. These are a few simple obvious rules: follow natural routes as far as possible and avoid either running along or crossing over high ridges (in other words, follow the 'grain' of the country). Avoid the centre of valleys and route at the bottom of foothills. If following a valley side road, it is better to put the line between the road and the foothills rather than between the road and the open valley. In flat country, the line must be simple, level and straight. In undulating land, the line can wind gently in both the horizontal and the vertical plane. Intersections and junctions are inevitable, but a multiplicity of routes in the same location should be avoided. Sharp right-angles are not only unnatural, but require a very much heavier corner tower. In one or two rare beauty spots a short length of underground line might be justified, but sometimes a pair of very tall, but widely separated, towers, as at the Severn estuary crossing, can be simple and dramatic.

The good things that can be said about the high-voltage grid system do not apply to low-tension wiring. The low height and the frequency of the poles with the cat's cradle of distribution lines, linking and intersecting, make for a much more serious disturbance of the landscape, as can be seen in any country in which overhead distribution is the rule. A far greater contribution would be made by putting low-tension distribution circuits into pavement ducts at much less cost than by seeking to eliminate the main national grid network.

Substations and switching stations have been the subject of much thought by the CEGB in recent years, with considerable improvement in design. At their minimum they are wire cages of rectangular outline containing many 'gallows-like' structures and blocks of switchgear. They are now sometimes contained in buildings made from local materials, and are better sited. This type of industrial structure is an example of the problem where siting is more important than form, because they are very conspicuous when occupying a fenced geometric form cut out from a field or heath, but so much less obvious when placed on an irregular plot which is already part of the landscape pattern. Sinking below ground, enclosing with mounds of earth or tree belts will also help to make the intrusion acceptable. Unfortunately these substations necessarily occur at more-or-less fixed points in a transmission system and are the focus of several converging power lines. No matter how carefully the station itself is located, its position will be proclaimed by the direction of several lines of transmission towers.

### Oil Refinery Location

Oil refineries are a second example of industrial complexes with very stringent siting requirements which demand water-based locations, almost exclusively on or near to the coast. As tanker sizes have increased from 12,000 tons in 1939 to 36,000 tons post war, then to 60,000 tons in the 1960s, so have the number of deep-water berths capable of taking the largest ships reduced the possible locations for refineries. With $\frac{1}{2}$ million-ton tankers now being built, most new sites will require a free-standing terminal in deep water connected to the shore only by a submarine pipeline. This means quite a small shore installation to service the terminal by sea, and the tank farm sited near, but not *on* the coast. The refinery itself may be 30 or 50km away, being connected again by underground pipeline.

Even with this flexibility there are strict requirements for the refinery, including the need for large volumes of cooling water, a site area of something near to 400 ha, heavy loads on the underlying geological strata, and a high chimney to carry off the plume of gaseous effluent. There is also the ancillary construction common to any large industry of roads, construction camps, hostels, overhead power supply, giving rise to noise, dust, new traffic pressures, etc.

A refinery of any size unquestionably gives rise to complaints about smell, even though most companies go well

Figure 8.10    Aerial view of BP's Dalmeny crude oil storage installation, Scotland, showing screening mounds of old colliery shale.

*(Designers: Morris and Steedman; photo: British Petroleum)*

beyond their statutory requirements in constructing deodorising plants and building chimneys in excess of 80 m. Dust and noise emissions are reduced by soil mounding and, to a lesser degree, by tree belts if wide enough, but the growth of trees has not been either rapid or dense in the coastal conditions around most refineries.

The tank 'farm' is an obtrusive element, consisting, as it usually does, of 8 to 20 large cylindrical tanks of considerable bulk. If these can be squat and broad, they take up more area but are less obvious than tall ones. A requirement of the site is that each tank or group of tanks shall be surrounded by an earth 'bund' capable of holding the oil in case of leakage. This earth shaping, particularly if combined with sinking the base below ground level, makes a very significant contribution in bringing the complex down to a simple horizontal element in the landscape. An example of this treatment is the concealment of the British Petroleum tank farm at Dalmeny within mounds of waste shale.

The colour of the tanks is very important. A light colour is essential to avoid heat absorption, but the reflective silver colour of many older installations is not essential in temperate climates. Green should be avoided, but a pale yellow-khaki colour has been successfully used at Llandarcy in Wales. In general very pale blues and greys have been found to be most sympathetic.

Oil, crude or refined, petroleum products and chemicals in fluid form lend themselves readily to transport by pipeline, and local national and international pipelines have long been a feature of these industries. There was a Russian pipeline over 150 km long before the turn of the century. At the lower end of the scale are pipes of a few hundred metres to a few kilometres long feeding refineries from shore terminals or from refinery to storage tanks. These are likely to be 100 mm to 450 mm in diameter and as they are easily curved, they can take an 'easy' path. In the middle of the range are pipelines about 5 to 100 km in length and 250 mm to 500 mm in diameter, used where refineries are inland, where refineries, terminals and storage tank farms are separated by some considerable distance, and also where refinery products may be economically transported to petrochemical industries by pipeline. At the upper end of the scale are the trans-continental and international pipelines 600 mm to more than 1 m in diameter, serving either to deliver the oil from drilling sites to ports of export (possibly direct to refinery) or to distribute the refined products on a national or international pipeline distribution grid. Many of these are over 1500 km long, some over 3000. It is believed that there are now over one million miles of oil and gas pipelines in the world, and it has been estimated that about $2\frac{1}{2}\%$ of the total goods traffic in Britain is carried by pipeline.

It is now possible to pump many different products through the same pipe (the Le Havre–Paris multiple pipeline handles over 40 different products). Many materials which are not fluids in normal form can be pumped, and research is proceeding on the pumping of solid materials within liquid-borne capsules.

In their crudest form, multiple pipelines are carried above ground in straight lines with infrequent bends or junctions, going around or over any obstacles in their path. In remote areas this has been justified on grounds of cheapness, but such pipelines have always been vulnerable to damage, and for security reasons they are now often buried. Smaller pipes, and those passing through populated areas are always put below ground. The usual method of increasing the carrying capacity is not to increase the pipe size, but to duplicate the pipeline.

Burying pipelines does not remove completely the damage to landscape. Grass or crops can be replanted, but in more fragile surfaces such as rock, heather moorland, tundra, the scar may be visible for years. It is not only a width equal to the diameter of the pipe which is affected, but a swathe (usually 13 m) wide enough for working, stacking and transporting the pipe. This can be a very serious gap in a belt of woodland. In general, the damage caused by the construction work is very great compared with the width occupied by the pipe (Figure 8.7).

There is risk of a visible scar when wild slow-growing plants are removed by pipe works and later replaced by a cultivated form of grass or ground cover which will always remain noticeable along the route.

Buried pipes are protected from corrosion by wrapping or by cathodic (electrochemical) protection. Normally, they require little maintenance or attention, but access to them is necessary. There have been particular problems raised regarding possible environmental damage, such as the risk of pollution of the ground over vast areas if a leak should occur, the risk of fire starting from an oil leak, and the ecological (even structural) damage if pipes containing warm oil are buried in layers of permafrost.

Pipelines carrying natural gas have revealed another possible source of landscape damage: small leakages of natural gas may increase the carbon dioxide in the soil to a point where it may kill plant cover.

Landscape treatment of pipelines is largely concerned with advising on the route so that minimum environmental damage will be done—avoiding highly sensitive areas of fragile or rare plant communities, avoiding woodland, and placing working areas where vegetation can be replaced and soil structure renewed by cultivation. New tree planting can be done over working areas, and in the swathe cut for laying, but not over the pipe itself. Obviously, no planting should be done which would emphasise the linear character of the route across the 'grain' of the landscape.

Route selection and construction methods must be designed to avoid any change in the natural drainage pattern, and to counter soil erosion. Wildlife will be protected mainly by avoiding fish breeding grounds and wild bird nesting areas.

This chapter would be over weighted if it continued to describe in detail the landscape planning problems of atomic power installations, smelter plants, petrochemical industries, etc. Of course each of these has individual and specific problems affecting their location and acceptance into the countryside, but it would be unwise to broaden this already generalised résumé, and each new project must be studied for its unique problems and possibilities.

## Location of Extractive Industries

Finally in this look at industrial land use, there are the extractive industries. They are in a special class of their own because they are located in the countryside by no form of choice or decision, but by the location of outcropping seams of the minerals which they produce. Such a statement is, of course, a generalisation, and in practice there probably is some choice, but a choice limited by the scarcity of the mineral, the demand for it, and the economics of various kinds and depths of excavation, from pumping of surface sand to coal mining 3 km out under the sea.

The various extractive industries can be grouped by the ratio of mineral extracted to waste, and by the method of extraction, which will determine both the location and the effect upon the landscape. In world terms the classes of minerals are broadly as shown in Table 8.1.

## Deep Mining

'Deep mining' for coal, lead, salt, tin, copper, gold, etc. by means of shafts sunk down to the vein, with horizontal roads and galleries, usually means a fairly small surface installation, and a degree of flexibility in the location of the shaft. There is, unfortunately, in some of these resources a large proportion of waste rock relative to the amount of ore worked, and therefore there is a large disposal problem. This is seen in the large volumes of shale tipped near the colleries and the tailings* lagoons of tin and copper mines.

## Opencast and Open Pit Mining

Today non-ferrous metal ores are usually mined in an open pit, which is a form of surface working but without the advantage of the coincident backfilling of overburden, which is a characteristic of opencast mining. Such an open pit may be anything up to 100 ha in surface area, and the whole working may occupy a site of about 15 km². 

Before the ore-bearing strata can be reached—possibly 150 m or more below the surface—the overlying rock must be removed and deposited. It may be possible to dispose of this rock for constructional fill, road-making or land reclamation, but transport economics would be critical. If it cannot be disposed of elsewhere, it must be deposited within

*'Tailings' is the name given to waste particles held in a slurry after a wet process for recovering the metaliferous ores from bulk excavated rock.

Table 8.1. Mineral deposits

| | CLASS | EXAMPLES | RELATIVE VALUE | OCCURRENCE AND DISTRIBUTION | RATIO OF PRODUCT MINERAL TO WASTE | WORLD OUTPUT MEASURED IN: | USUAL METHOD OF WORKING | POSSIBLE ENVIRONMENTAL IMPACTS | REMARKS |
|---|---|---|---|---|---|---|---|---|---|
| A | Common rocks | limestone, chalk, granite, sandstone, flint, slate | very low | widespread and abundant | almost all used (a) | tonne × $10^9$ | quarrying on surface or hillside | scenic scars, loss of habitats but interesting when worked out | (a) except for 80% wastage in slate |
| | | sand and gravels | very low | widespread and abundant | 80:20 | tonne × $10^9$ | shallow wet or dry surface pits | voids, flooding, lowered surfaces, bad drainage (b) | (b) sometimes, creating new water habitats and recreation areas |
| | Earths and clays | ball clay, stoneware clay, fuller's earth, brick clay, china clay | low | sporadic but adequate | highly variable, but most used except for over-burden (c) | tonne × $10^8$ | surface working in shallow pits; china clay in large open pits | lowered surface levels, drainage problems, pollution; tips from china clay | (c) except for china clay which has ratio 12:88 |
| | Precious and semi-precious stones | diamond, opal, garnet, ruby, sapphire, emerald, amethyst. | very high to precious | rare and scarce | Precious stones are a minute portion of the rock worked | kg × $10^5$ | open pit (d), underground, and alluvial mining | voids and scenic scars | (d) or found in working other minerals |
| B | Common rock-forming minerals | felspar, mica quartz, fluor-spar | low | widespread and abundant | highly variable | tonne × $10^6$ | surface or hillside quarrying (e) | scenic scars | (e) need selective quarrying |
| | Common minerals | asbestos, talc, alum, gypsum, soapstone | low to medium | widespread and abundant | highly variable | tonne × $10^6$ | mainly quarry-ing or surface workings; some-times under-ground mining | (as rocks above) risk of water pollution | |
| | Less common minerals | vermiculite, wollastonite | low | sporadic | highly variable | tonne × $10^6$ | surface workings and adits into veins and dykes | (as rocks above) risk of water pollution | |
| | Salts | salt, rock salt, borax, lime nitrate, calcite, sodium salts, potassium salts | low | sporadic but abundant | variable 10 to 50% | tonne × $10^6$ | deep mining, surface quarries, alluvial and solution mining | waste heaps, subsidence, saline flashes; pollution | |
| C | Abrasives | corundum, emery, pumice, commercial garnet | medium | limited | | tonne × $10^6$ | surface working of outcrops, and adits into veins (f) | (as rocks above) | (f) also by-products of other minerals |
| D | Common metal ores (ferrous) | magnetite, haematite, limonite | medium | frequent and adequate | average: 3:3:94 | tonne × $10^8$ | deep mining, pillar and stall, longwall, drift mines and opencast | waste tips; hill and vale restoration | |
| | Common metal ores (non-ferrous) | bauxite, zinc blende, galena, pyrites, bornite, nickel ores, cassiterite | medium to high | frequent and adequate | average 30% metal | tonne × $10^6$ | historically by deep mining, now mainly open pit; some alluvial (tin) | voids, waste heaps, tailing dams and lakes, polluted run-off, toxic wastes (e.g. 'red mud') | |
| | Less common metals and refractory metals | vanadium antimony, mercury, wol-fram, titanium | variable | sporadic but adequate | average 8% metal | tonne × $10^3$ | deep mining, mainly by adits, some openpit, some alluvial (g) | toxic wastes | (g) most are only obtained as a by-product |
| | Non-metallic mineral ores | sulphur, carbon, graphite, perlite | medium | widespread and abundant | average 50:50 | tonne × $10^6$ | various, including solution mining | | |
| E | Rare metals and radioactive ores | indium, sodium, caesium, germanium, selenium, tellurium, thorium, cerium, cobalt, uranium, plutonium | high to very high | rare and scarce | 1:100 down to 1:5,000,000 | ore output: tonne × $10^3$ metal output: lb. or oz. × $10^3$ | various (g) | toxic wastes, radiation and similar risks | (g) most are only obtained as a by-product |
| F | 'Noble' metals | gold, silver, platinum, palladium, iridium | very high | rare and scarce | average: ore contains about 0·1% metal | ore output: tonne × $10^3$ metal output: troy oz × $10^6$ | deep mines with shafts and galleries, or drift mines, or alluvial (f) | voids, waste heaps, scenic scars | (f) also by-products of other minerals |
| G | Fossil fuels | coal | low | widespread and abundant | 3:1 (deep mining); 1:15 (opencast) | tonne × $10^9$ | deep mines with shafts and galleries, or drift mines, opencast, strip and auger mining | subsidence, shale tips, scenic damage, air pollution from burning tips, water pollution (h) | (h) and temporary scenic damage from opencast |
| | | petroleum | medium | sporadic but adequate | all used, either in crude, refined or in by-products | tonne × $10^9$ | land or sea wells | oil spillage at sea or from pipelines, spoil heaps from oil shale workings | |
| | | peat | very low | widespread and abundant | all used | tonne × $10^6$ | surface work-ings | lowered land levels, drainage problems; may destroy (or preserve) bog habitats | |

This table has been revised to bring it into accord with the Author's book *Landscape of Industry* (8.5).

*Note: destruction of surface ecology is implicit in most classes.

Figure 8.11   Tailings lagoon and dam of a large open-pit copper mine in Colorado. This is fitted into the floor of a minor valley without causing serious destruction of the main scenery, but it may never be possible to restore the valley floor to any useful purpose.

*(Photo by courtesy of Professor Kitson)*

Figure 8.12   A typical medium-sized opencast coal site in the English Midlands showing three seams being excavated with comparatively small-scale equipment. This site has since been restored and converted to a golf course.

*(Photo: Clifford Tandy)*

a reasonable distance of the site—possibly changing landscape features or creating new ones.

The tailings lagoon is an important element in the mining complex. Because the tailing slurry may never dry out, but remains indefinitely in a porridge-like consistency, it has to be permanently confined in the lagoon, which can form an attractive or offensive element in the new landscape according to the skill of the designer.

A non-ferrous mine may remain open for many years, and it is unlikely that the excavated material can ever be returned to the pit. One must therefore accept two new out-size elements in the landscape—a permanent void and a permanent lagoon.

Strip mining or opencast working for minerals having a fairly large waste to ore ratio, such as coal or iron ore, results in only a comparatively small amount of ore or fossil fuel being removed, the remainder being backfilled into the excavation. The essence of opencast mining is that only a comparatively narrow working face is excavated, and this face travels across the site as large volumes of overburden are 'cast' from front to rear by large draglines. Only the material from the first cut has to be stocked on site, and even this is replaced in the void when the working is finished. The volume of material excavated is largely balanced by the 'bulking' factor, so that a level site is achieved on completion. Occasionally a small void is left which can be used for other waste materials or as a recreation lake.

Similar surface mining methods used to extract the bulky common materials such as sand, gravel, ball clay, stoneware clay, do not go to great depths, but are spread over an area of many hectares. After the soil layers have been stripped and set aside for re-use, almost the whole bulk of the material is removed for use, there being little waste. Pockets of unsaleable material are, however, left unexcavated, so that the site tends to have a rather 'pock-marked' appearance. Reclamation of such a site usually consists of improving the contours by spreading the unworked 'islands' and returning the soil at a lower level, for agricultural use. If the workings

are below water table, the end result will be a lake which can be suitably treated to form a reservoir or recreation lake.

Quarrying for building stone, roadstone, or cement usually means working into the face of a hillside, removing virtually *all* the material, with the expectation that the worked-out quarry will eventually be left as a void with a bare rock face. Fortunately, such quarries appear as a harsh scar only for a few years, for they soon weather and darken and become colonised with vegetation.

The commonest materials—clay, sand and gravel—occur in tertiary and quaternary deposits on flat land in the lowlands of a country (the southeast in Britain) and are sufficiently plentiful to allow a wide choice of sites. This situation may change, however, as the demand for aggregate increases, while more and more of the surface land overlying such deposits is built upon. Stone can only be worked where suitable geological formations occur, and it is usually uneconomic to work them except where they outcrop as hills or scarps. Stone quarries are therefore likely to be locally prominent in the countryside. Most other minerals occur in igneous and metamorphic rocks, or in the older strata, and consequently are likely to be found in mountainous areas of considerable scenic beauty, hence the familiar arguments about prospecting and mining in national parks.

# Industrial Problems in Landscape Planning

### The Ecological Approach
Nan Fairbrother gave sad comment on this subject when she wrote (8.6) '. . . in the last two centuries we have produced a large variety of new land uses which only have one thing in common—they seldom create valid new landscapes. In time industrial use may achieve its own landscape identity, but at

present it is little more than destruction of the old pattern, and is therefore most usefully discussed under the noncommittal name of disturbed landscape'.

It is a purpose of this chapter to bring nearer the time when 'industrial use may achieve its own landscape identity'.

First, we must recognise that the countryside has always been, and presumably will always continue to be, in a constant state of change. It is no more right to attempt to preserve, museum-like, the landscape in its present form than in the form it took at any earlier period of its history, though of course, as has been said earlier, we may elect to *conserve* its highest qualities. It would be absurd to ignore the changes in the English landscape pattern by the enclosure Acts of the 16th, 17th and 18th centuries. This was indeed landscape planning on a vast scale which changed forever the traditional appearance of the country into the one which we now value so highly. It was accomplished on a scale which, as Hackett says, could only be achieved today by some form of co-operative or state ownership (8.7).

While it may never reach the proportions of agricultural change, industry today is big enough in its impact to make seriously significant alterations in the landscape pattern. It is useless to set up an ostrich-like resistance to such changes. It is better to try and ensure that they are made with the full knowledge of ecological implications, and that they are part of an evolving pattern with a different, but still acceptable, character in the future.

There is a grave danger in any form of landscape renewal, but particularly prevalent in industrial projects, that the land owner, the industrial developer, or even public opinion will demand 'instant' maturity. Such an expectation is at variance with the whole ecological basis of landscape planning. Unfortunately technological innovations including such processes as large tree moving, hydro-seeding, and container growing make some form of 'instant' landscape possible. It may however be shortlived, short term in its effects, inappropriate for the locality, or even positively harmful to the ecological balance of a region.

The designer should not start from the position 'as found' after working, or even as existing before working commenced, but should go back into the ecological history of the area and study the trends which had been evolving under broad-scale land use changes during possibly 25 years or more, and should attempt to identify the climax towards which the vegetational pattern was moving. Having identified the potential future climax, any planting programme will be more successful, appropriate, and easier to implement if it tends towards the establishment of that climax.

It is tempting, in this context, to speak of the 'balance of nature' as if it were a finite and absolute state of equilibrium. Such a concept is purely theoretical, and one can only, in practice, speak of trends which lead towards a certain static state, while knowing that the landscape is in constant change and that—for various reasons, including both climatic and human intervention—a static state will never be reached.

It is however reasonable to think in terms of a stable framework able to accept instability within it. Brian Hackett gives an example (8.8). 'An undulating landscape with hill tops under permanent high forest could accept much experimentation in the valleys, and it would be unlikely that an unsuccessful experiment could produce a chain reaction breakdown of the whole landscape; . . . change in a landscape is not necessarily a sign of instability, but can result in a new state of balance.'

A landscape planned on this basis—a broad stable framework related to the main topographical elements could certainly accept within it quite major industrial artifacts such as reservoirs, factory estates, mineral workings, provided that the detailed landscape treatment of the site was sympathetic to the regional character and was not 'gardenesque', exotic or debased in scale.

## Regional Planning and Industrial Development

Before discussing the effect of a single factory on a piece of countryside, it is necessary to consider the effect of industrial development on country towns and villages and on rural areas in general. Since the Scott Committee on Land Utilisation in Rural Areas in 1941 (8.9) successive British governments have been concerned with the spread of 'urban sprawl' and certain, at least, of the proposals in that committee's report have been implemented. These include national parks, long-distance footpaths, amenity forestry, green belts, also the siting of industry in trading estates and small towns and away from villages and the planning control of extractive industries.

Many local authorities have accepted as policy the introduction of new industry into rural areas as a stimulus to growth, but this has not proved to be easy. R. J. Green (8.10) quotes MacKay and Luttrell as saying that a population of not less than 200,000 is necessary to support the viable, economic, self-supporting development of industry. In the rural regions of Britain there is, again according to R. J. Green, only one town of more than 200,000 population, in consequence only the marginal subsidiary elements of industry become established in rural areas.

The Town Development Act of 1952 (8.11) has been used in some cases to support campaigns to attract industrial development to rural areas. It is, of course, much easier to attract it to the larger towns. Thetford, for example, has been very successful. It is less easy for the small towns; very difficult indeed for villages and, even where it *has* succeeded, the employment created has been very largely for female labour. Settlement in the countryside is simply not feasible today without the complete infrastructure of schools, public transport, shopping centres, indoor recreation, etc. Even existing villages dependent upon a defunct industry are not only being allowed to run down, but are being encouraged to disappear, as in Durham and Nottinghamshire. (This policy for the 'D' villages in Durham is still active, even though many of the doomed cottages are becoming 'second homes' or commuter settlements for the car-owning middle class!).

Suggestions in Chapter 4 that an expanding agricultural industry should have priority of first-class land implies that manufacturing, constructional and mining industries, as well as recreational uses should share the poorer lands, As R. J. Green says, however; 'No firm criteria have been established by which to decide the relative merit of, for example, developing on poorer land in poorer locations or developing in better located areas on higher-quality land. Cost benefit techniques are not easily applicable.... On the other hand the supply of land is a fairly fixed commodity ... and the law of diminishing returns must set an upper limit to the extent to which land loss can be offset by increasing the productivity of poorer-quality land'.

Green also quotes the paper given by Geoffrey Clark at the Town Planning Institute Summer School 1957: '...this process of rural industrialisation should be allowed to proceed naturally and steadily, rather than that we should entice industrial units away from their normal settings, and in doing so create pockets of urbanity where they should not be ... the major area of farming England has to puts its own house in order and rely, in general, on its own agricultural industry for long-term prosperity'.

Industrial location in the countryside can vary between isolated and remote sites, country town level, and the rural fringe of conurbations. Differing theories are held regarding the viability of each of these. The Hunt Committee (8.12) believed that small growth points in rural regions would grow of their own accord. The Economic Planning Councils tended to support the growth of the larger towns with the expansion of a few medium growth centres in the middle-size towns. Decisions are limited by economic not physical planning criteria, population support being the critical one—related, of course, to the kind of industry, for only mineral winning, power supply, and similar kinds can exist in areas remote from labour markets.

In Europe, as in UK, urban development is one of the most critical aspects of regional planning, and industrial location is one of the most vital elements of urban development. The great conurbation arc from the English midlands through Denmark, Holland, Belgium, Northern France and the Rhineland produces a vast proportion of the world's steel, coal and manufactured goods. It is littered with power stations, oil terminals and refineries, all of which attract an even greater concentration of industry. Industrial dispersal is a policy of all the Governments of western European countries. France has Regional Planning Commissions (Délégation Général de L'Aménagement du Territoire), Belgium has a National Investment Company which encourages industrial investment through Regional Companies. Germany—particularly the Ruhr area—has been leading the field in landscape planning for industrial growth. It has encouraged growth while maintaining green-belt separation between complexes, and a view of sheep grazing under the shadow of refinery retorts is not an unusual sight in the Ruhr.

In the USA and Canada private enterprise and public utility organisations have had a fairly free hand in selecting the sites they need. Recently they have been under pressure from the environmentalist lobby to avoid sites which are sensitive, i.e. which would result in visual or aural annoyance, which would destroy recreational potential, or which would give rise to pollution or other damage to the environment. At the same time, there has been pressure at state or province level, and incentives from federal funds to persuade industries to move into areas which are depressed from lack of suitable employment or suffering from various forms of social decay.

### Land for Industry

An analysis of urban land uses in England and Wales is made by Best and Coppock (8.13) who reveal the surprisingly small area of urban land in industrial use. Taking all forms of settlement the figure is only slightly over 6%, while even in the northern County Boroughs it is not greatly over 5%. This, they say, is partly due to narrow definitions, by which mainly the manufacturing industries are included while docks, warehouses and railways come under 'commercial' uses. Nevertheless the figures are sufficient to show that the landscape problems of industry are not highly significant in urban situations, though they are serious indeed in the countryside. Unfortunately the statistics are not broken down sufficiently to show the amount of farmland taken for industry alone.

In a paper on Industrial Land (8.14) Max Nicholson refers to the efficiency of industry in managing its resources, its stock of equipment and products, and wonders why land —which is equally a vital and limited natural resource—is not subject to the same kind of stock control. So much land is acquired by corporations, committees and companies who have no idea of how to manage it, and perhaps no immediate or no future use for it. As Nicholson puts it: 'the key to success is to decide at the outset what is to be the after-use of all land which is not permanently required for operations. Such land may, for example, be needed by engineers and contractors for obtaining access or fill, for temporary housing of constructional workers or to safeguard against possible legal claims. Where extractive industry is concerned, it may be needed for strip mining or opencast excavation to remove valuable mineral deposits, after which it becomes of no further interest to the mineral group. In old-fashioned language, this land is 'waste', and as a result, engineers and managers assume that it can be wasted. Not only is a valuable potential asset lost, but grave damage is thereby caused to the image of the responsible corporation'.

### Industrial Location

The location of industry as a planning problem can be looked at in two ways: the physical and economic attractions which draw industry to particular areas; and the constraints and controls imposed by governments which direct industries to depressed areas. Sometimes these two may coincide, more often they are diametrically opposed. While one cannot ignore the second set of factors in planning, they are outside the scope of this book. However, it is important to remember that the very conditions which cause an area to be depressed and therefore unattractive to an industrialist—to his manager and his manager's wife—are often the result of the 'slash and burn' attitudes of early industries.

Quoting Nan Fairbrother again: 'In Britain, industry has got what industrialists would call a bad image...and no wonder...we have treated it like a pariah and not unnaturally it has behaved like one'. 'Industry has developed an attitude of criminally careless squalor and of using the public landscape as a private rubbish dump; old buildings and machines, derelict huts, decrepit fences, battered oil cans, old hard-standings, rotting dumps of building and industrial rubbish—all are simply abandoned when no longer needed and remain to foul the landscape for generations to come' (8.15).

The factors which determine the location of industry, and the ultimate effect of decisions taken on quite narrow evidence, are many and varied, and the permutations of them are legion. One should, of course, attempt to predict the results upon the landscape of any and all decisions, but it becomes increasingly difficult to do so. As an example of the influence of the factors governing industrial location: it was the high cost of transporting crude ironstone which influenced the decision of Stewart and Lloyds to establish a new steel works at Corby, a decision which led eventually to the designation of the new town (8.16). There may even be a cultural consequence. It was the establishment of the Opel-Kadett works at Bochum which was the main factor in setting up a university in the town.

For simplicity, the early pages of this chapter are confined to the identification of the physical constraints of industrial location, and the effects of these constraints upon the physical landscape. Planning and fiscal controls will be mentioned later (see page 264).

The first decision to be made by an industrialist planning to build a new factory is its regional location, preparatory to a site search. The landscape planning consultant brought in at this stage can assist with an analysis of the kind described in Chapter 2. It may be that resource-based analyses have already been done in county planning offices, and that suitable industrial locations have been identified. If not, then a project-oriented study should be carried out. Of course, recommendations based purely on landscape evaluation will not be welcomed unless linked in practical terms to the requirements of the industry itself. A check list of criteria should therefore be prepared, based on a study of the particular industrial process involved.

Any factory location must satisfy basic demands for: supply of raw materials, power supply, labour force, market for products, waste disposal.

The following general check list may serve as a guide:

*Raw materials*
1. 'On the spot' availability if basic, heavy, or extractive industry;
2. Port facilities if materials are imported;
3. Easy road or rail access if materials are transported;
4. 'Fabrication' industries should be near to basic industries supplying their raw materials.

*Power*
1. Availability of electricity grid supply. Power station may be needed for the direct link to high-energy inputs such as smelting;
2. Direct supply (or easy transport) of steam-raising fuels such as coal, gas or oil;
3. Independent source of cheap power, e.g. hydro-electric.

*Labour*
1. Degree of labour-intensiveness of the industry, predominance of heavy (male) or light (female) labour;
2. Nearness of housing for workers—alternatively: adequate public transport or potential sites for workers' housing;
3. Infrastructure of schools, shops, services, etc.;
4. Size of labour pool, i.e. unemployment ratio;
5. Alternative employment for workers' families.

*Market*—(Note: a *local* marketing outlet is rarely important today)
1. Adjacent secondary industries requiring primary products;
2. Easy and rapid access to major transport network, e.g. near to motorway intersection, freightliner terminal, container terminal or railhead;
3. Packaging and loading facilities;
4. Warehousing facilities or stocking grounds.

*Waste disposal*
1. Facilities for disposal of solid wastes: tipping, burying, burning, crushing and/or carting away;
2. Facilities for disposal of liquid wastes: river, sea, sewage system, pumping away;
3. Discharge of smoke, gases, fumes, without damage;
4. Alternatively to the above: internal treatment and recycling plant; local market for waste products, if saleable.

In addition to the above general items, there are specific requirements for some industries, which are of primary importance, such as large volumes of cooling water, precise climatic conditions, traditional skills handed down in families, etc.

## Factors in Planning Industrial Sites

After decisions on general location, there remains the precise placing of the industrial complex upon an actual site. This is where the skill of the landscape designer is strongly tested. He must satisfy the demands of engineering tech-

Figure 8.13 The employees' garden of the Birds' Eye Company at Walton-on-Thames. Here the preservation of an existing mature landscape with the addition of new planting and good maintenance ensures a delightful setting for the building and pleasing surroundings for the employees.

*(Photo: Clifford Tandy)*

nology. economics, and commercial management, while ensuring a harmonious marrying of artifact and countryside. He will not be able to do this well if he does not fully comprehend the industrial process, but neither will he succeed if client and engineer confine him to the role of 'external decorator'. It is not intended to describe the design process here, nor is it possible to do so adequately without relating to an actual site, because each such problem is individual. It may be, however, worth stating some broad principles, and giving some examples.

In recent years industrial building has undergone considerable changes. No longer are smoking chimneys, north light roofs and blackened windowless walls considered inevitable. New industries are increasingly of the 'clean' type, using electricity and gas fuels. While buildings are improving and factories are as well designed as any other form of architecture, it is in the relationships of various buildings to each other, and to the landscape that the greatest skills need to be shown. Good industrial planning must combine orderliness and integration, while keeping options open for maximum future expansion.

It is in America that the highest standard of industrial building design is found—partly due to the 'prestige' value of the design being recognised by the client, partly by public pressures for environmental control, but largely because American architects have got beyond the European Victorian notion that industrial buildings are either mere weather protection for dirty machinery or are 'fringe buildings' hardly worthy of effort.

An industrial plant for a large concern is necessarily both large and long-term, and comprehensive planning of the total complex is essential. This means taking account not only of the process and its enclosure, but of stock yards, fuel dumps, boundary fences, and the subsidiary buildings for staff, first aid, workshops, security, etc. Even more important are the communications—input roads or rail for materials, output roads for products, power lines in, water pipes in, effluent and refuse extracts. Other large elements

may be required such as car parks, cooling lakes, settlement lagoons and waste heaps which will dominate even the largest factory—and of course large areas of land with no immediate use, to be kept for future expansion.

Making allowance for future extension is a very important part of the design programme. Industries which have a linear production process are likely to expand by extension of the direction of the line or by doubling up with a repeat production line parallel to the first. If the correct one of the two alternatives is known, the site can be planned to take care of such expansion by putting in service ducts, power supply, and waste disposal services adequate for any demands on them.

The need for flexibility and rapid obsolescence of manufacturing plant in the USA has led to the design of industrial structures as very large open enclosures in which all parts of the process can be contained in one building, and even future expansion is taken care of. This results in a simple dignified architectural statement but raises the problem of 'scale'.

Any proposed landscape treatment must be in *scale* with the total project. This may mean changing the face of the landscape over a large area—possibly a much greater area than the site itself—in which case permission must be obtained from adjoining owners, by persuading them of overall benefits, and by purchasing way-leaves or offering quid-pro-quo exchanges of land or rights. Electricity generating stations are of exceptional scale, and two examples will illustrate this point.

The first is a CEGB power station at West Burton, Trent Valley (Figure 8.14) for which Derek Lovejoy and Partners were the landscape consultants.

The proposal was described in their report: 'West Burton Power Station is situated in the Trent Valley, Nottinghamshire. In predominantly flat agricultural land comparatively minor vantage points can afford panoramic views. Therefore, rather than attempting to obscure as many views of the station as possible, a more satisfactory answer is to be found in the controlling of views and partial screening to provide stimulating incidents in the landscape. Proposals for the landscape treatment have included recommendations for planting outside the station boundaries.'

The second is a nuclear power station at Oldbury-on-Severn (Figure 8.15). The landscape consultant, Geoffrey Jellicoe, recognised that this vast structure would be seen across a predominantly flat low-lying landscape, and would dwarf the almost domestic scale of small fields and orchards. He therefore proposed using the surplus spoil from the excavations to form a very large 'podium' on which the power station would sit, and which would have a surface pattern similar to that of agricultural crops, but increased in 'field' size to form an intermediate link in scale between the structure and the surrounding landscape.

Very often an engineering structure or large industrial building has a dignity which is acceptable in the landscape, but which is spoilt by the 'clutter' of small buildings, and other objects which surround its base. These can be con-

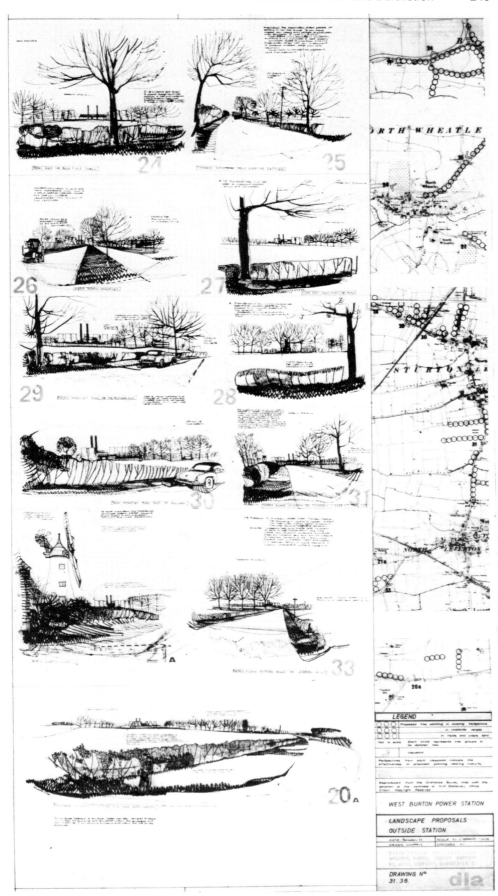

Figure 8.14    West Burton power station. Sketches showing examples of planting proposed outside the power station boundaries. Such planting will not obscure the power station, but will give it a more interesting and satisfying setting.

(*Sketches by courtesy of Derek Lovejoy and Partners*)

Figure 8.15   A design for the landscape treatment of Oldbury-on-Severn power station. The landscape architect, Geoffrey Jellicoe, has employed the device of increasing the scale of the landscape immediately adjoining the power station in order to relate the vast scale of the building to the small-scale domestic landscape of the surrounding field pattern.

*(Photo: Clifford Tandy)*

cealed by tree planting, by ground shaping, or by making use of the existing configurations of the ground. Examples of these are included. The aluminium smelter for Rio-Tinto-Zinc on Anglesey (Figure 8.16) (landscape consultants: Land Use Consultants) is planted with large belts of forest trees which are not designed to hide the building itself, but to allow it to be seen as a dignified statement, free from a foreground of roads, paths, and minor buildings. The electricity switching plant at Lovedean, Sussex (Figure 8.17) (landscape design by CEGB Transmission Design Groups; Landscape Section) has been set within large mounds of soil, strategically placed to fit into the contours of the ground, but to conceal the switchgear, fences, transformers, etc. at ground level, and leave only the lattice towers showing against the skyline and the surrounding trees.

At Trawsfynydd, in the Snowdonia National Park, Sylvia Crowe had the task of moderating the impact of the large

Figure 8.16   The RTZ aluminium plant at Anglesey (landscape designers: Land Use Consultants) which necessitated the relocation of the A5 trunk road and large-scale earth-moving and forestry planting works to enable the vast complex to be assimilated into a flat landscape.

*(Photo by courtesy of RTZ)*

Figure 8.17   An electricity grid switching station at Lovedean in Sussex, where earth-shaping has been used to conceal the smaller engineering elements and to unify the whole.

*(Photo: Clifford Tandy)*

power station upon the landscape. She accepted that the main bulk of the station could not be concealed—even if it were desirable to do so—and that it could still be dominated by the mountains around, if kept to a simple shape. She therefore advised that the siting of the station take advantage of existing ground configuration (and emphasise it by new contours) so that the ancillary equipment is out of sight from public viewpoints. This site is also an excellent example of colour skillfully used to assist engineering artifacts to melt sympathetically into the landscape, without appearing to be 'camouflaged' in a military way.

Landscape design in the more conventional meaning of the term is appropriate to all industrial external spaces, provided that the elements used are themselves in scale with the total complex. This almost certainly means that plant material should be limited to large trees, tall shrubs in large masses, and ground cover plants over large areas. The temptation to make a site more interesting by breaking it up into fussy areas with a variety of different treatments must be resisted. If possible a single simple theme should be used in order to keep unity of the concept. A large expanse of water is an excellent unifying element, and can often have practical value as storage, cooling water, fire tank, etc. The landscape treatment designed for General Motors Detroit by Thomas Church is an example of all these points.

Colour is very important in this context. It may be used to make an engineering artifact acceptable in a landscape. It may even change the scale. It can be used to play down over-obvious elements, and to accent desirable ones. It should *not* be used as camouflage, nor to give an organic appearance to artificial objects.

The planting material used in industrial landscape planning must be carefully chosen, in terms of scale, colour, form and regional character. While the introduction of exotic species is acceptable on a domestic or gardening level, it is highly undesirable in a large industrial estate, where the regional ecology of an area of countryside could be altered by such planting. Where soil, climatic or other conditions have combined to produce a distinctive pattern of plant communities, this should be respected, and any new landscape treatment designed to marry-in with such a pattern (though not slavishly copy it). A factory near Poole, Dorset is built on a sandy heathland, on the fringe of an urban area. In designing the landscape around the factory, Sylvia Crowe has kept the existing pine trees, planting similar species and under-planting with heathers and ericaceous mixtures suited to the locality.

### Industrial Estates and Industrial Parks
There are many advantages to be gained by grouping industries together in a single large complex. In early years this resulted in greater destruction of scenery, amenity and social structure than they could have accomplished separately, but this need not be so. Industrial estates, and the industrial

Figure 8.18   Slough Trading Estate. A typical example of an industrial estate of the 1920s/30s planned entirely for utilitarian purposes.

*(Photo by courtesy of Aerofilms Ltd.)*

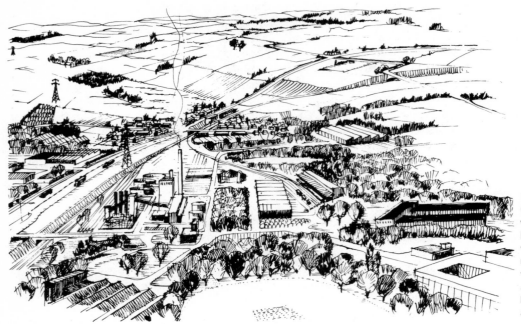

Figure 8.19  A design of Land Use Consultants for an 'industrial park' in which the power unit of a defunct heavy industry is used as the nucleus with communal services, power supply, refuse disposal, packaging and despatch, with the separate industries located to allow green wedges of landscape between them and communal recreation areas.

zones of new towns have shown improved solutions, and the 'garden' factories of Welwyn and Letchworth, though now 'dated' have shown that factory workers can be given tolerable—even enjoyable—environments. The early industrial estates established since the beginning of the century, and often called 'trading estates', have been developed either as early commercial enterprises by joint stock companies (e.g. Trafford Park and Slough); by government investment as a means of giving assistance to declining areas (e.g. Team Valley, Treforest, Hillington); or as conversions from government ordnance factories (e.g. Bridgend, Cwmbran).

While there are many economic and social advantages in this form of development, there are some grave environmental disadvantages which need to be tackled: when unbroken and extensive, the estate becomes too large an urban element to be absorbed into domestic or farming-scale landscape; flat sites are usually chosen, with single-storey buildings, so that a monotonous two-dimensional form results; 'drawing-board' planning or linear growth following roads or railways means lack of any organic growth pattern which would suit landscape form; concentration of industry results in unpleasant atmospheric conditions, polluted air, and lack of contact with natural organisms (grass, trees and water) for refreshment.

Modern versions of such complexes should follow the American development of 'industrial parks', which is a concept combining the technical advantages of trading estates with a wide range of shared facilities, including amenities and recreation facilities for staff, and a high-quality overall environment. There is, of course, in any one country, a limited number of sites where such a complex could succeed. The search-requirements are similar to those for a single industry, but with certain qualifications:

1. A large area is needed—probably rarely less than 40 ha, with three to five times that area available for expansion;
2. Large flat areas must comprise the majority of the site;
3. Communications must be particularly good, with short and direct access to a motorway intersection, and to a rail freight terminal (unless there is a rail connection on the site);
4. An existing, but decaying, heavy industry can often provide a nucleus, including energy source, water supply, workshops, staff and welfare facilities and a potential labour force.

From the planning point of view there are many advantages in a well-designed industrial park. Services of several kinds can be run in ring circuits from a central plant house, with a single tall stack. Wastes and effluents can be collected and disposed of communally—possibly with the advantages of re-cycling or incineration in the power plant. Communal packing and dispatch, security organisation, stockpiling, deliveries, etc. can help to cut down the clutter of small buildings, and improve the layout.

There are many facilities for staff which could be provided on a communal basis, such as medical centre, catering, social clubs, and recreation. The provision of playing fields and other recreational areas is an essential contribution to the concept of an industrial park. Ideally, factory sites should be set in separate flat areas, separated from each other by natural configurations of the ground, belts of woodland or other features. Failing this, they could be separated by new ground-shaping, by shelterbelts of forest trees and also by green wedges, or buffer zones containing playing fields, other sports pitches and possibly water recreation lakes.

There are no completed examples of such industrial parks in Britain, but a sketch shows the possibility of such a development on an actual, but un-named site, using the central plant of a declining heavy industry as its focal centre.

Car parking is a particularly serious problem for industrial sites. The rural situation does not justify expensive urban solutions such as underground or multi-storey parking, yet the numbers involved means large areas set aside for this purpose. Some American sites show a larger area for car parking than for productive use. At least blank squares of hot black asphalt can be avoided if the car parking is integrated into the landscape planning of the whole complex, so that the space is broken up by ground modelling and tree planting.

### Prospecting for Extractive Industries

Once again the extractive industries come into a class of their own, but before looking at solutions for restoration, one must consider the particular problems of *prospecting* for minerals. There is a great fear about the drilling for minerals—in fact there is almost as much public protest about prospecting as there is about working—but surely it is to the benefit of any country to have all possible information about its natural resources.

In 1972 the Zuckerman Commission (8.17) recommended that the first stage of exploratory drilling for minerals should be permitted development for which no planning permission would be needed except in areas, such as AONBs, which have statutory protection. The Commission also recommended that evaluation drilling should need planning permission, under normal planning procedures.

Almost coincidentally with this report, the Department of the Environment took steps to clarify the position (some planning authorities were requiring planning applications for prospecting, others were not) and to encourage the search for mineral resources by making available public funds (of up to £50m) for grant-aiding exploration projects.

Since then (February 1976) the Stevens Committee has published a report (8.18) which included among its recommendations:

1. That exploration (mineral prospecting) should be 'permitted development' and should not require local planning permission—subject to proper notification being given, and certain environmental safeguards observed;
2. That planning permissions should be regularly reviewed and have a maximum life of 60 years;
3. That a special form of planning application should be adopted for mineral applications.

This report was only adopted by the Government in 1978.

### Planning for After-Use Following Extractive Industries

This brings in the next subject—which is a very important part of landscape planning—the after-use of sites which have been worked for minerals.

The extractive industries are no longer tolerated as inevitable destroyers of the countryside in the gaining of mineral wealth. It is now recognised that the operations can be for a limited period, that restoration to agriculture or to new uses is possible, and that the cost of such restoration should be borne by the industry. There is, of course, a danger that an industrial organisation will evade its responsibility for restoration, once its profits have been distributed, or go bankrupt so that no money is available for the work. The most satisfactory solution so far is that, as a condition of planning consent, a proportion of the day-to-day profits of the industry should be placed in a trust fund, the sole purpose of which is to pay for ultimate restoration. This has worked very well in the case of the Ironstone Restoration Fund, and is being applied to china clay working in Cornwall.

It used to be a condition of planning consent that the land be restored to its former condition and use. It is now accepted that it may be possible to restore to a new use, more appropriate to the site, and fulfilling a local need. It is an important part of land use planning to study the site constraints, and local use deficiencies in order to recommend the best form of restoration.

Return to agriculture is an obvious consideration. It may mean a lower grade of land and lower productivity or change from arable to grazing. If, however, the land was originally poor, badly drained, suffering from subsidence or exhaustion, it may be possible to improve it by working and restoring, particularly if a new drainage system, and a five-year programme of intensive cultivation is included in the restoration proposals. There are many examples of well-restored farm land after opencast coal mining; some much more productive than they were before. The opportunity can also be taken to enlarge field sizes, rationalise footpaths and boundaries, plant hedges and shelterbelts, with sufficient standard trees in field corners and boundaries to restore the traditional countryside mosaic, with improved farming efficiency.

Forestry is a safe return on the poorer soils, and in upland districts. It is not even necessary to restore the land to a high standard of surface grading, though it is no longer considered good practice to plant forest transplants directly into the 'hill and vale' tipped overburden. Certainly it is important that drainage should be good, with cut-off drains on boundaries of compartments, that the levels should be adequate to allow proper fencing and rabbit proofing of the perimeters, and that species should be selected to suit the soil and climatic conditions.

Recreation is another obvious use for restored land. The local needs for sports pitches and other recreational uses must be thoroughly investigated, particularly where there is no obvious urban catchment area in the vicinity. The industrialist working the site will not want to be saddled with the upkeep of the land after its restoration to recreational use. Thus it is essential to find an entrepreneur, club, or local authority to take over the site and maintain it on completion. In this, they may be aided by government grants.

Figure 8.20 High-quality restoration to agricultural land after opencast coal mining by the National Coal Board in Nottinghamshire.

*(Photo: Clifford Tandy)*

As an example, golf courses have proved to be a logical use for the undulating topography of former excavations, but the formation of the greens, fairways, tees, club house, car parking and other facilities is expensive, and there is a limit to the number of courses which any area can support. The need for a golf course should therefore be fully proved, and if possible a club or company formed to run the course, before the final decision to restore to such a use.

Particularly appropriate as an ultimate use of mineral excavations is water recreation. Some sand and gravel workings fill with water naturally as the result of high water tables—some are continuously water-filled, and are worked as wet pits. Other forms of quarrying can lend themselves to the creation of lakes, but there is more to be done than mere filling with water. They have to be partly back-filled, to limit the final water depth; the banks need very careful contouring; the bottom may have to be lined with puddled clay to increase its water-holding properties. Again, the site must be handed over to a responsible body, local authority or club for its management and upkeep, but such is the demand for water recreation today that there should be no difficulty in finding users.

There are many good examples of land used for water recreation. The simplest are 'wet-worked' gravel pits which have been taken over, when worked out, by sailing clubs and used with the minimum of treatment. Others, either wet or dry pits have been deliberately planned for recreational use, and the final operations organised to leave a suitable water area. With appropriate detailed landscape treatment, a successful and natural-looking lake has been achieved. Even deep open-cast excavations have been planned to leave a lake area as the final void. Details of construction of such work are included in the section on derelict land restoration, to avoid duplication.

Figure 8.21 Stoke-on-Trent. The area of subsided land due to underground mining which was filled with polluted water and was designated for a boating and swimming lake.

*(Photo: Clifford Tandy)*

Figure 8.22 The same site on a fine day in July showing the lake, now filled with clean water, being intensively used for swimming and boating and for sunbathing on the small artificially-created beach.

*(Photo: Clifford Tandy)*

## Planning and Financial Controls

Governments in many countries have attempted to control the location of industry by planning consents or fiscal measures with varying degrees of success. Usually they combine zoning controls to prevent industry from taking 'greenfield' sites in the countryside with financial or other commercial incentives to encourage expansion into depressed areas.

In Britain such measures were introduced during the inter-war years and have been in existence in some form or other ever since. They include designation of 'Special Areas', tax reliefs and government loans, 'Industrial Development Certificates' and government-built factory estates. Unfortunately their effect on male unemployment has been limited. Parallel with persuasion there has been control, and industry has been largely (but not wholly) prevented from entering areas designated as national parks, areas of outstanding natural beauty, nature reserves, conservation areas and sites of special scientific interest.

The danger in this policy is that areas *not* so designated are regarded automatically as of low landscape value, and so available for exploitation. R. J. Green (8.19) has advocated policies which, if implemented, would ensure studies were made of *all* large landscape changes, with comprehensive district landscape plans, and grants for landscape improvement. This is, of course, strongly related to the position of industry in the countryside, and should include a comprehensive appraisal of the country's natural resources. It might be necessary to set aside reservations for mineral workings, as well as prohibiting mining in sensitive areas and where particular conditions would inhibit successful restoration.

Probably no other country bears direct comparison with Britain in the breadth of its incentives, and the strictness of its planning controls, but many other countries have found similar problems and tackled them by either the 'carrot' or the 'stick' policies. France is divided into twenty-one Regional Planning districts concerned with both physical and economic planning. The Minister of Construction issues building permits, and both grant and tax exemptions are used to stimulate regional development in certain approved growth centres.

In Germany the Government was obliged to stimulate industrial development at village level, and introduced both planning controls and fiscal encouragement to this end. Of particular interest is the system used in the Ruhr, where the planning authority operates a fund which is, in fact a pool for compensation. Any owner or developer who suffers by conforming to the regional plan is compensated out of the fund. This not only operates in a 'negative' sense, but the fund can be used to share the cost of raising the standard of industrial complexes either architecturally or in their landscape treatment.

It seems, however, that in all countries more than persuasion or control is needed to inspire industry to discover a new *rapport* with the landscape, to use its vast technological and financial resources to create new exciting and satisfying landscapes suited to their own needs. In fact it is mainly under the private enterprise regimes of USA, Canada, and Scandinavia that the most imaginative industrial layouts are to be found.

A particular British institution is the amenity clause covering possible damage to the landscape by industrial action from large quasi-government departments. What became known as 'The Amenity Clause' appeared first, according to Bracey (8.20) in the Hydro-Electric Development (Scotland) Act of 1943. By 1957 it had been reproduced and changed several times but appeared in the Electricity Act of 1957 Section 37 as follows:

'Preservation of Amenity: in formulating or considering any proposals relating to the functions of the Generating Board or any of the Area Boards (including any such general programme as is mentioned in sub-section (4) of section 8 of the Act), the Board in question, the Electricity Council and the Minister, having regard to the desirability of preserving natural beauty, of conserving flora, fauna and geological or physiographical features of special interest, and of protecting buildings and other objects of architectural or historic interest shall each take into account any effect which the proposals would have on the natural beauty of the countryside or on any such flora, fauna, features, buildings or objects.' This clause became the stock wording for building amenity protection into any planning permission given to nationalised industry or statutory undertaker and it has influenced development control both in the private sector and in many other countries.

# Industrial Dereliction and its Restoration

## Sources of Dereliction

In his classic paper on exploitation of land entitled 'Devastation' (8.21) Sir John Myers writes: 'In its simplest most diagrammatic form, devastation removes something irreplaceable, and is consequently limited to chemical and physical destruction; all biological destruction being replaceable when natural processes are restored to normal activity. Game is conserved by a close season, deforestation by afforestation, without positive remedial interference of Man. Minerals, on the other hand, whatever their origin, are not replaced in their lodes within any period that can be foreseen. If any of the seam or ore body is left in place, it is not to serve as a root stock or a ferment, but only because its removal is dangerous or unprofitable.... Where exhaustion has been foreseen... the miner's link with the locality has been weak and his economy feckless;... indifference to waste affects also the miner's estimate of his capital expenditure in buildings and means of access; all that is not transferable to another scene of dereliction is written off and left derelict.' Probably the most distressing effects of industry upon landscape are the damage caused by tipping of waste, the dereliction left by industries which have declined, and factories which have gone out of business. The second half of this part of the chapter is therefore devoted to the problems of clearing away the debris of past industrial exploitation. The origins of industry have been briefly touched upon at the beginning of this chapter, but it is necessary to look at the sources of dereliction, and the forms which they take.

Once again, the extractive industries are the worst culprits, but the result varies according to the methods used, and the appearance of the waste material. Abandoned stone quarries can present an attractive weathered face on a hillside if they have not been worked too far into the skyline. They will be less attractive, however, if they were working chalk, which does not easily weather or support plant life, and so presents a hard white scar. Similarly if worked horizontally, as in the portland stone quarries, there is no pleasant scarp face, but merely holes below ground with a tumbled floor of unwanted stone blocks. Deep quarries such as those for Aberdeen granite or Cornish slate have left vast holes some hundreds of feet deep with no obvious future use, and present a serious safety problem. Quarries which have been worked right through a hillside will have left an unpleasant and un-natural looking gap in the skyline on a scale which cannot easily be reshaped. Slate is a stone which, because of its dark colour and hard cleavage planes, leaves behind working faces and waste tips which are particularly depressing, and difficult to reclaim. Stone quarries occur widely in the upland areas of a country, and sometimes on the rare outcrops in the mainly tertiary and quarternary deposits on the flat lowlands. Very few quarries have been fully worked out, because the solid bedrock becomes uneconomical to extract at certain depths and distances. In the worked areas, however, most of the volume will have been removed for sale and only a small proportion of overburden and quarry waste left behind.

In regions which have no bedrock at the surface, but only sedimentary deposits, there has been quarrying for sand and gravel. As mentioned earlier, the methods of working remove most of the material, so that old excavations are usually shallow holes, most of which have backfilled with water. New uses, such as reservoirs, boating and fishing lakes have been found for many of the old sites, but some have been left in such an untidy state that they have remained derelict, the water surface being broken up by hundreds of small 'islands' of poor gravel uneconomical to work.

Quarrying and mining for minerals and ores occurred less frequently, and in selected locations where prospecting had indicated that economic veins existed. The mines were either deep pits or open excavations, but as the proportion of ore or mineral removed was small, there were large tips of waste deposited on the surface. The appearance of the tips will vary according to the geological strata in which the mineral was found, from the shining white of calcite waste from lead

ore mines in Shropshire, to the black shale tips of the coal measures.

Of all the mineral extraction industries, coal mining is the one which has given rise to the greatest amount of dereliction. 20,000 million tons of coal have been mined in Britain in the past 100 years. During this period the annual output had increased from 49 million tons in 1850 to a maximum of 287 million tons in 1913, when the number of pits working was 3267, a figure which has since declined to less than 250. It is not surprising that there are between 1000 and 2000 spoil tips left, each containing from 1 to 18 million tons and together occupying about 8000 hectares of land.

Another large source of dereliction was the winning of brick earths and clays for brick making and clay ware. The end result of such excavations was a worked-out clay pit (or marl hole as it is usually called). These are sometimes dry but usually water-filled because of the impervious nature of the clay. They are steep-sided, deep and dangerous, but lend themselves to filling with waste materials and refuse.

Although potteries are found wherever there are suitable deposits, and usually obtain their fireclay and coal locally, the fine china clay is often transported from a distance. The working of china clay raises particular problems in Britain, because of its intensive operations at only two localities (St. Austell in Cornwall and Lee Moor in Devon). Deep pits are required, and large conical mounds of quartz sand waste are formed next to the void. These are gleaming white and much less depressing than the black tips of slate and coal shales, in fact they have a certain attractive 'moonscape' quality at first sight, but the attraction diminishes if one has to live with them. As the industry is prospering, few if any of the workings have yet been worked out, so there has been little reclamation done to date.

Apart from tips and holes, there is the wasteland left behind by decaying industry. In places (and in times) where land was cheap and in plentiful supply, industry adopted the same nomadic policies as early agriculture and, having despoiled an area, found it easier to move on to new

Figure 8.23    Old workings for china clay in Cornwall. Although the large tips of white quartz sand have a strange, rare and impressive quality, the old pits are sadly derelict.

(*Photo: Clifford Tandy*)

sites. With higher land values and more-stable labour forces, there is slightly more incentive today to rebuild on old sites, but there remains the dereliction from two centuries of old industrial use to be cleared up.

Particularly obnoxious is the damage left behind by certain types of industry such as smelting, mining for metaliferous ores and toxic substances, and chemical processing,which left behind land so contaminated that it will not grow vegetation even after 50 years' weathering. There are now possibilities for reclaiming such land, which will be mentioned later, but they are difficult and expensive.

### Early Efforts at Tackling Dereliction

Reference is made here mainly to British experience, but very few countries tackled the problem much earlier than Britain (though some have been more rapidly successful). Until 1948 the only action was voluntary, as there was no control of industrial waste and tipping. The Aberfan disaster in 1966 brought to light a strange fact that, although there existed a library of books and regulations on mining techniques and safety measures, there were *no* textbooks, regulations, or even recommendations on methods of tipping waste material above ground!

In 1951 a memorandum on the Control of Mineral Workings was published (8.22), which brought together the various Acts and regulations concerning the planning control of mineral workings. The aims were defined in part, as: to ensure that mineral deposits are not sterilised; to make land (or working rights) available for mineral working, but to avoid too great interference with other land uses; to have regard for amenity; and (direct quote) *'to ensure wherever practicable, that land used for mineral working is not abandoned and left derelict when the working is finished but is restored or otherwise treated with a view to bringing it back into some form of beneficial use'*.

The memorandum accepted that waste material could continue to be deposited on land already used for this purpose, and that pits and excavations could be filled with industrial waste (or indeed any waste material) up to normal ground level. Applications for new mineral working sites were required to show proposals for the disposal or deposit of waste materials in tips which are *'shaped to harmonise with the contours of the surrounding landscape'*, as well as proposals for restoring the operations area to its original use or to an alternative use.

### Derelict Land—the Size of the Problem Today

The amount of land lying derelict in Great Britain has been variously estimated at between 37,500 ha and 125,000 ha. The inconsistency of estimates is partly due to lack of accurate data, but in the main is due to differences in the definition of the word 'derelict'. Unfortunately the official British Government definition of derelict land *excludes* any such land which is attached to a working industry. The official area of derelict land in England in 1975 was only 43,273 ha. Although considerable areas of dereliction are being reclaimed each year (2132 ha in England in 1974), there is evidence that the nett area is not decreasing but is still (in the mid-1970s) increasing at a rate of about 1500 ha per year.

It is difficult to obtain figures for other countries, but it seems likely that at least four European countries have a similar-sized problem to that of Britain, and that several American States have an even larger one. Large under-populated countries such as parts of Australia and parts of Africa have dereliction areas which are small in comparison to the size of the country, but may be seriously large in proportion to population and resources.

### UK Grant Methods

The Government of the UK estimated in 1971 that it would be possible to clear the backlog of reclaimable dereliction—which it now estimates on its own narrow definition, as being 33,068 ha—in 10 years, and offered grants to local authorities to pay for this work. The grants are not the same everywhere, but vary according to the prosperity of the area. Local or county authorities have been able to claim a grant (which covers also the cost of professional fees) from 50% to 80% (90% or even 95% if they are already 'rate deficiency' areas). In 1975 the amount of grant for 'development' and 'intermediate' areas was raised to 100%. There are, however, certain limitations: the land must, normally, be in the ownership of the authority before grants can be claimed; the grants cover the cost of reclamation, including earth moving and sufficient drainage work and planting to ensure stability, but they do not cover the various amenities necessary to enable the land to be used as public open space, nor are they payable if the land acquires a future value as housing or industrial sites (though in this case they may be used as a loan).

Furthermore, even at 100% the grants do not seem to be effective in persuading small local authorities to undertake the work. The after-use of the land may be a deterrent. A village situated in the middle of open moorland may be expected to acquire the site of a tip larger than the village itself, which could be reclaimed for no other purpose than unneeded public open space, and thus be saddled with the cost of upkeep of the space thereafter. The fact that so few of the smaller local authorities are taking up these grants is proof that the incentives are not strong enough, and that perhaps the derelict land problem should be accepted as a wholly *national* liability.

### European Methods

European countries have been even slower to recognise the *national* responsibility for clearing dereliction. In some countries it is left wholly to the landowners, developers, or to the conscience of the industry itself. In others it is tackled on a regional basis. In smaller countries—often with a large problem of past dereliction from coal mining—nothing at all is being done, while in eastern European communist countries like Czechoslovakia the work is being done very efficiently by a government reclamation agency.

## US Methods

In the United States, almost half the States have some form of system by which prospective developers have to guarantee the cost of restoration work. This may take the form of a legal bond which is posted by the State and forfeited if restoration work is not carried out. In other cases a levy is imposed which is held in trust and is used to cover the cost of restoration.

## Restoration Problems and Techniques

This section will deal with problems of restoration which occur both in return of land to other uses after the completion of mining, and in the reclamation of derelict land. It is not intended to cover in detail techniques used, but to give an outline appropriate to the type of working and the proposed after-use. Because so many permutations of these factors are possible, they cannot all be covered, and the examples included must be a few typical ones.

In order to avoid repetition in subsequent sections, problems and techniques which are common to all forms of restoration are dealt with first. Typical of these common methods are:

1. Site appraisal;
2. Drainage;
3. Stability;
4. Waste materials, including toxic materials and spontaneous combustion;
5. Soil-forming materials.

### 1. SITE APPRAISAL

The general techniques for site survey and analysis to be used in beginning any landscape planning study are discussed in Chapters 2 and 3. It is not necessary to duplicate any of that material here, but there are special characteristics of derelict land which raise difficult problems of after-use and which need identifying at an early stage. The types of questions that need an answer are best set out in the form of a check list:

### Levels

Are the levels such that the site can be used for (a) building, or (b) recreation grounds, without major earth-moving?

Are the levels such that the site could not be used, even for forestry or public open space without earthmoving?

Are grades so steep that erosion would prevent planting into present surfaces?

Do the levels indicate that the natural drainage pattern of the area has been destroyed?

### Stability

Do the grades of slopes suggest that there is a risk of landslip or rotational shear?

Is the bedrock such that there is a risk of unstable surfaces (e.g. clay, metamorphosed shale, porous rock or highly faulted)?

Do the levels suggest that the site has suffered from slip or subsidence in the past?

### Soil and vegetation

Is there any soil left on the site?

Is there any vegetation on the site of shrub or tree scale?

Is the site colonised by grass or 'weed' invasion?

(If there is no vegetation, one must ascertain whether this is due to lack of soil, or some other reason, such as toxic chemicals left in the ground—laboratory tests may be necessary.)

Is the incidence of vegetative growth affected by other site factors; e.g. aspect, elevation, shade, shelter, sun-facing slopes?

### Previous land use

What is the history of the site?

Was the previous use a form of mining, so that drifts, shafts and subsidence risks exist on the site?

Was the previous use a smelting or chemical process such that toxic substances might be left in the ground (see Soil and vegetation above)?

Is the site still zoned for industrial use?

### Assets

Are any assets left from previous use?

E.g. railway sidings, access and circulation roads, hard standings, power supply, water supply, usable buildings.

### Water and drainage

Is the site well drained at present—naturally or by piped drainage?

Is there a connection to local authority drainage system?

Alternatively, is there standing water on site?

Is this due to impervious surfaces or sub-strates, to subsidence, or to abnormal water-table level?

Is there a natural watercourse entering the site?

Is it clean or polluted?

Is the surface water run-off from the site clean or polluted?

What is the catchment area draining on to the site?

A study of the results of the survey and analysis techniques and the answers to the above questions allow all industrial land to be classified (on an area, county, regional or national basis) according to prospects for reclamation and its likely after-use. This is an essential preliminary to landscape planning.

## 2. DRAINAGE

The next problem common to all kinds of restoration and reclamation is drainage. Even on fertile agricultural land poor drainage can be the cause of complete failure of vegetation cover. How much more important is it therefore that a poor growing medium like shale should have exactly the right drainage conditions to ensure the best possible opportunity for growth. It is not enough to ensure complete drainage of the site. Overdrainage is almost as bad as insufficient drainage, and the average spoil heap of colliery shale or similar material is already experiencing such rapid run-off and such high surface evaporation that insufficient moisture gets below the surface to support plant growth. Another symptom of over-rapid drainage is the gulley erosion which occurs on steep slopes, and which can develop into trenches 2 metres deep or more carrying large volumes of water which scour away the lower slopes and even the soil from the flat land on to which they discharge.

Water falling on to land will find its way inevitably into the water-table, drainage outfall, river or sea, by the quickest route available. If use is to be made of this water for plant growth, then some of it must be slowed down to remain in the topsoil long enough to be available to plant roots; the excess must be removed as quickly as possible without causing erosion as it flows. This is the two-fold nature of drainage planning, and it is a continuous problem, for not only must the present drainage pattern be dealt with, and a final solution proposed for the ultimate use of the land, but some form of drainage system must be kept in operation throughout the whole of the working period, and the subsequent period of upkeep, until the final system can be established. Failure to plan for adequate temporary drainage will result in further erosion, flooding, damage to the soil structure, destruction of new planting and possibly expensive pumping.

Special measures must be introduced to deal with areas of standing water already on site—even if these are temporary such as slurry ponds. They are likely to need draining before earth-shaping commences, and the silty water—possibly mildly toxic—may not be accepted into the public sewers. Furthermore the base of such ponds will have become completely impervious by layers of clay or silt, and will remain as wet patches until re-graded.

## 3. STABILITY

In 1966 the tragedy of Aberfan called attention to the dangers of shale tips becoming unstable in conditions of water and pressure. This situation occurs when coarse open materials (or alternatively, very fine clayey particles) are tipped without compaction, over wet or marshy areas or over a spring line. Movement that commences as a slow rotational slip may develop into a rapid flow slide which can travel many hundreds of metres.

Since 1967, of course, all existing tips in Great Britain have been examined for safety, and many instances of potential instability have been corrected. It is essential in reclamation work to ensure that mounds of material are not put into an unsafe condition, even temporarily, during the workings, and that material is not placed permanently over a water source which could cause trouble in the future. The danger is particularly acute when working with tipped material on top of natural slopes greater than 1 in 10.

Not only can the waste material itself slip, but overloading of ground—particularly sloping ground—by tipping large volumes of material on top of it, may cause the ground to slip or shear away from the underlying strata. After several years of apparent stability, the stress in the ground may be increased further by water pressure, by increased weight through wetness, or by erosion lower down the slope. Excavations and mining operations may also cause increased stresses.

The first indications of a possible slip are either minor movements in the ground or waste heap, or a significant bulge appearing in the lower part of an otherwise even slope. Slips take many forms (Figure 8.24), but the most common are:

1. A shear, parallel to the face, so that the outer layers slide down to a lower level;
2. The 'slump' of a steep face by which the upper part falls away to the bottom and the whole mass adopts a lower angle of repose;
3. A rotational slip in which a curved plane deep in the ground shears and the whole mass 'overturns';
4. A flow slide, this may commence as a simple slip, but the forces acting on the particles turn them briefly into a fluid state so that the whole mass travels down the slope gathering speed.

Detailed methods of stabilization of slopes against

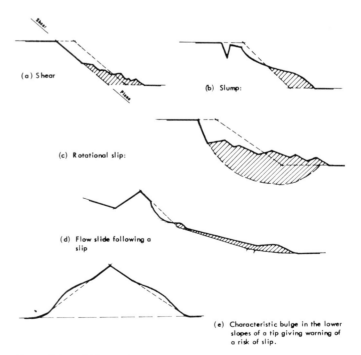

(a) Shear

(b) Slump:

(c) Rotational slip:

(d) Flow slide following a slip

(e) Characteristic bulge in the lower slopes of a tip giving warning of a risk of slip.

Figure 8.24    Different forms of landslip.

possible slip are outside the scope of this book, but they mainly consist of reducing the effective angle of slope by removing material or by some form of terracing.

## 4. WASTE MATERIALS

The type of material has considerable effect on the after-use and methods used to achieve new land forms. It is desirable to have early tests made on the various grades of material on site regarding their chemical composition, pH value, potential fertility, temperature, and possible economic value. Some materials will be worth transporting off the site for resale, others will have greater potential fertility and would be worth setting on one side as a top dressing to improve the surface tilth. (Burnt shale comes into both these categories.) Certain wastes with a high combustible content may, if already hot, be liable to spontaneous combustion when exposed to the air; others are so fused that they cannot be broken down from their present size—which may be boulders a ton or more in weight, Obviously the site formation proposed will have to leave such boulders *in situ*, or bury them in their present locale.

Taking surface samples is not sufficient; a number of deep borings into the heap must be made, and these positions should be carefully surveyed and linked to the survey grid. In addition to providing core samples, the borings will permit a thermocouple to be used to take internal temperatures or—if water pressure is suspected—a piezometer must be inserted and read at regular intervals.

As a result of these tests it can be decided whether the materials are suitable as a fill material, either for use on the site or for sale as an aggregate or hardcore. The tests, if comprehensive, will also reveal what potential the waste has as a soil-forming material. To be decisive on this latter point, fertility tests in a biology laboratory would have to be included.

Particle size, grading, cohesiveness and strength tests will be needed if stability of the material in earthworks is to be checked. Detection of toxic material and gases given off will determine the pollution risk and danger to site operatives, while tests for sulphates will show any possible risk to concrete or brickwork coming in contact with the wastes.

When dealing with coal shale tips it is necessary to determine the amount of combustible material left in the shale. Different methods of testing give different answers to this question. For example, a sample showing $6\%$ free coal by the 'float and sink' test will have about $11\%$ combustible material when tested for calorific value, while a figure of $23\%$ of total combustibles will be found by a 'loss of weight on ignition' test. When specifying the combustible content of colliery shale, it is important to specify the type of test used, the particle sizes and the moisture content. There is a risk of spontaneous combustion only with a particular proportion of particle surface area to air space, and neither large pieces of shale with considerable voids, nor tightly packed and compacted dust-size particles present any risk of ignition. In fact, heavy compaction will eliminate the risk in almost any material.

## 5. SOIL AND SOIL-FORMING MATERIALS

It is obvious that all soil on industrial reclamation sites should be conserved for re-use. Unfortunately little if any top-soil is likely to exist. Soil is not a stable inert permanent material like stone or concrete, but is a living organism kept in a fertile state by regular cultivation, feeding and watering. In the past, agricultural soil was not removed before tipping began, so that in theory there is a layer of soil between the tip and the sub-strata. Of course, due to compaction, heat, and lack of bio-organisms it will no longer be soil.

Soil which is stripped and stacked also deteriorates rapidly. It should be kept for as short a time as possible in a heap which is as low as practicable. Soil which is under a heavy load of other material or equipment—even if temporarily stacked—will be compacted and the soil structure affected or destroyed. As G. P. Doubleday puts it in *Landscape Reclamation* (8.23) 'When [soil] is re-spread it will require special management, and cannot be expected to behave as if it had never been disturbed'.

Most quarry wastes and most organic industrial wastes have *some* potential for supporting plant growth. While deficiences in nutrients can be rectified by adding inorganic fertilisers, the right texture of the growing medium must be produced by mechanical means. Natural weathering will break down most materials in time, so that the outer weathered skin of a tip is probably already fairly fine. Shale is even better reduced by burning, so that it is advisable to keep the red burnt shale and the finely weathered shale on the surface and avoid burying it under the larger plate-like pieces brought up from within the tip.

Texture can be adjusted by mixing: over-coarse material should be mixed with silts and clays; fine tailings need the addition of larger particles such as coarse sands and gravels (but not large unweathered lumps of shale). Both texture and fertility can be improved by the addition of organic wastes, and not enough effort has been made to combine industrial waste materials in this way. The scrap from leather, textile and paper industries, straw, chaff, pulverised domestic rubbish, even the dust and dirt removed by cleaning processes, and many other forms of unwanted waste materials would be excellent components of new soil-forming compounds.

Most waste materials show a highly acid reaction. This may be reduced by weathering of the surface. It may also be worsened in the centre of the stack by long periods under heat, pressure and run-off from industrial processes. Such materials will need heavy application of lime of the order of 1 to 4 tonnes per ha., before they can be grassed or planted.

Britain is fortunate in having a climate which encourages the covering of any bare land by colonising vegetation. Only on unstable slopes, and land made toxic by chemicals, polluted water or sulphurous fumes is there no green covering. In many cases the factors of slope angle, stability, nutrient deficiency, toxicity, water-holding capacity, plant growth and climate are in such a delicate balance that the success of a natural green cover is on a 'knife edge', and only needs a minor change—such as the cessation of sheep grazing or the exposure to public pressures—for the vegetation cover to be lost completely. In other less-temperate climates such natural colonisation would not even begin.

Colonising plants may possibly be attractive in themselves, e.g. alders, birch, willow scrub, but the majority would, in any other situation, be classed as invasive weeds, and are welcomed only because they give a green colour from a distance and require minimum establishment and maintenance. Plants can only come from seed dispersal by wind or birds from the plant communities in the vicinity. In rural areas these may be many, varied and of suitable colonising species. In urban areas, however, very few plant species may occur and most of these of unsuitable cultivated varieties. Nevertheless it is surprising to find so many plant species entering and establishing themselves in urban wasteland.

The fact that there is weed growth on the surface of a tip indicates that the surface is likely to sustain new planting, but does not give any promise that the interior of the heap is equally suitable. The flora of pit heaps follows the usual ecological pattern of pioneer species colonising the 'easy' faces, and gradually spreading over the remainder; an intermediate stage when decaying plant material has improved the soil quality and water-holding capacity so that other species can become established; eventually reaching a mature stage at which a climax vegetation becomes established and probably shades out the early pioneers.

## Wasteland

Wasteland is a general term for derelict land which is neither tips nor holes. It is usually the site of industry which has declined, and which had once supported factory buildings, kilns, mills, engine houses, stocks of raw materials or of finished products, or is possibly land returned to roughly level condition after working of the site has finished.

Planning the redevelopment or restoration of such an area would commence with a survey and analysis by the methods described in Chapter 2 and with the site appraisal check list in the last section of this chapter. Obviously there are special characteristics of wasteland, such as reasonably flat levels, existing hard surfaces, access, possible re-usable drainage systems and services which make it particularly suitable for further industry or for an urban type of after-use.

## Proposals for the Future of Wasteland

Proposals for the future land use of the area must, of course be related to the various land use needs of the locality (as described earlier) and to the development plans of the planning authority. Re-use for industry and possible use for housing should be the first consideration in order to free greenfield sites elsewhere. Next should come possible use for organised recreation, because sport today has become so urban-orientated that it is not necessary to put playing pitches on to good agricultural or pasture land. In fact tennis and netball courts, squash courts, running tracks,

bowling greens and even football and rugby pitches with a large spectator complement, including car parking for spectators, are easier to construct on hard ground, and they certainly do not need a setting of beautiful scenery.

Water recreation is, of course, a special case appropriate only where the ground configuration lends itself to the formation of a water area, and where a sufficiently large catchment area will guarantee the filling and continuous topping up of the lake. Where no other land use needs are obvious, a simple treatment of the site for low-intensity use as public open space or amenity land is probably the best aim, though a return to agriculture, or planting for economic forestry should also be considered.

## Excavations and their Ancillary Elements

The major element of nearly all extractive industries, and the dereliction left behind by those industries, is the void created by the operations. It may be a temporary 'cut' being gradually backfilled as work proceeds; it may be an abandoned hole which was under no form of control at the time, but can now be filled; or it may be a void of enormous size, either working or derelict, which can never be restored within the practical or economic conditions prevailing.

The most straightforward type of void to deal with is that formed recently and temporarily in short-term opencast working to extract a mineral seam. In such work only a part of the site is opened up, and the remainder is excavated by moving successive volumes of soil from the face of the operation to the rear, removing a workable width of the mineral seam, or seams, at each stage. Usually the amount of mineral or ore removed is only 10% or less of the total volume, so that the majority of the overburden is returned to the void. This must be consolidated as much as possible by the heavy machinery used, but bulking causes the soil to take up more space when returned. The final result is probably approximately a 5% deficiency which must be made up by importation of other material, or will mean that the land lies below its original level. Where possible the opportunity can be taken to clear other derelict heaps and put the material into the void. Another alternative is to offer a long-term void for tipping domestic refuse. This is often welcomed by a local authority, and an efficient tip, raised in height by earth banks, with proposals for eventually turning it into a wooded hill is illustrated (Figure 8.26).

Shallow excavations from which the majority of the material is removed such as sand, gravel, fireclay and brickearth workings have little or no overburden to be returned to them, so that they remain permanent depressions in the ground or fill naturally with water up to the normal water table. The latter is a very successful form of after-use, as there seems to be no limit to the demands for water recreation. Dry pits are better filled than left low-lying, but will take unreasonably long to fill with domestic refuse, unless they can take the total output of a large city, such as

Figure 8.25   A typical opencast coal site from the air showing two working faces (one in the centre of the picture, interrupted by the central road, and one to the left of the picture) from which coal is being removed, the overburden being lifted and swung back by large draglines. The overburden is left, at this stage, in hill and vale formation but will subsequently be restored to level ground.

*(Photo by courtesy of the National Coal Board)*

Figure 8.26   A plan for the restoration of an opencast coal site, in which the final void is left open to receive domestic refuse from the local authority. The spoil is mounted up around the hole to give maximum volume and on completion of tipping it will be covered with topsoil and planted to make a small hill.

*(Design: Clifford Tandy)*

Figure 8.27   Sketch of a country park, including a boating lake to be constructed on the site of a large opencast coal excavation after completion of the work. This site was planned so that the main contours of the park could be formed by the large earthmoving machinery in replacing the overburden after the coal had been removed.

the trainloads of London's domestic waste which are taken to the Bedfordshire brickfields. The alternative is to accept industrial waste as fill. Where such waste is delivered by pipeline as a slurry, or is itself semi-liquid, the excavations must be formed into shallow lagoons in which the fluid can stand until its solids settle out and consolidate. One of the common waste products today, which needs treating in this way is pulverised fuel ash from power stations. Several examples of pastureland formed from PFA lagoons have been publicised by the British Central Electricity Generating Board.

### Deep Open-Pit Mine Treatment

Deep voids are a much more difficult problem.* In dealing with an old deep open-pit mine, the main elements requiring broadscale treatment are the main pit, or pits, and the tailings lagoon and dam. These will be dealt with separately, commencing with the pit. The major options for pit treatment are:

1. Leaving it open and 'as worked';
2. Partial back-filling, leaving the remainder open;
3. Turning into a water area;
4. Partial back-filling and then turning into a water area;
5. Re-shaping the void into a new landform.

Taking each of these in turn: The main problem which would have to be dealt with in the case of a dry void is ensuring the stability of its walls. If the public is to have access (permitted or not) it is essential to provide slopes which will not be subject to rock falls. The working benches may be

*This part of the chapter is taken from a draft submitted by the author to the Commission on Mining and the Environment—(Chairman: Lord Zuckerman) in 1972 (8.24).

already stable and safe, but visually undesirable. By advance planning of working angles, aided by the use of explosives after working has finished, it may be possible to break up the benching, allowing it to fall to a natural slope which is both attractive visually, and is safe.

Being almost entirely bare rock, the sides and bottom will not support vegetation unless pockets of topsoil are introduced. There is evidence, following a landslip near Lyme Regis in 1839 that natural re-vegetation does not occur on exposed rock in less than 60 years. However, the type of rock likely to be so exposed in highlands usually darkens naturally to a reasonably pleasant colour.

Putting waste rock back into the void is a possibility very much dependent on cost and, although no methods should be dismissed merely on grounds of cost, it must be realised that *total* backfilling of the void of a deep open-pit mine would involve an order of cost similar to that of the original excavation, and would make almost any ore deposit uneconomic to work. Partial back-filling may, however, be possible where the waste heap is immediately adjacent to the void and where permanent areas for deposit of waste rock are impossible to find.

The decision to turn a pit into a water area is not one that can be taken on aesthetic grounds alone. Unless the climatic and hydrological conditions are right, and the catchment area adequate, there will never be sufficient water to fill and maintain a lake. Conversely if geological and drainage conditions are conducive to water holding, then it will be impossible without pumping, to *prevent* the void from becoming water-filled. All these conditions need to be thoroughly studied in the pre-planning stage in order to predict, with the maximum possible accuracy, whether a water body is possible or even unavoidable. Where a lake is formed, the extent of the pit to be landscaped will be very much less, and so a higher intensity of treatment should be possible—shaping the rock margins into natural-looking features and providing pockets of topsoil for tree planting.

Needless to say, all earthworks must conform to the minimum stability requirements of engineering codes of practice (e.g. British Standards Institution Code of Practice on Earthworks 1959 and any subsequent amendments). Even more stringent are the regulations governing bodies of water held above natural ground level, and if the earth bank holding such water falls within certain defined criteria it is regarded in many countries as a statutory *dam* which must be tested and maintained annually.

There are obviously many intermediate and overlapping alternatives between the main options mentioned. Every mine site is unique and, with imagination, the right solution for each problem will be found. Re-shaping the void to a new landform—possibly incorporating some back-filling and some water area—should be considered. For instance, this might be possible where a mine is situated at a fairly high elevation in mountainous country so that the void could be worked in such a way as to form a new open-end valley on completion, with the minimum of additional earthmoving.

## Tailings Lagoon Treatment

Turning now to the tailings lagoon and dam, the main options open are:

1. Remove the tailings, de-water and use as fill;
2. Leave *in situ* and dry out sufficiently to enable light agricultural restoration of the surface;
3. Leave *in situ* as a water area.

Once again practical considerations will not permit the choice to be made on aesthetic grounds alone. As described above, climatic and hydrological considerations will determine whether the reclamation will be 'dry' or 'wet'.

All experimental work so far done on mine tailings has not revealed any wholly satisfactory method by which they can be de-watered and compressed sufficiently to be used as fill material. Even if drying out is possible in hot climates, it is unlikely to happen in mountain districts. Nevertheless the possibility of technological advances uncovering a use for tailings or a new method of treating them should not be ruled out.* Until such advance is made there seems little advantage in moving the tailings to fill a new site except on the rare occasion when it may be worth pumping the slurry back into the pit to lie at the bottom of a water body.

Even drying out the surface crust to enable it to accept soil-forming materials and be cultivated as grazing land may not be possible in high-rainfall areas. Even if it were possible, the incongruous appearance of flat grazing land in an otherwise sharply undulating mountainous region might be undesirable.

On balance it would appear that the normal end-product of a tailings lagoon in a high-rainfall district—that is a shallow lake—is perhaps the most acceptable choice. The landscape treatment would then be reduced to: design of the water perimeter line; design of the shore, both shallow shore, and steep rock faces; grassing of the dam face, and planting of the dam and lagoon surroundings.

## The Waste Rock Mound

Finally there remains the treatment of the waste rock mound. The successful restoration of the spoil mounds would depend greatly on the possibility of creating a growing medium on the surface. Experience of non-ferrous metal mining suggests that progressive restoration will not be possible, so that some stripped topsoil may not be required for up to 25 years, by which time it may well have deteriorated. In highland zones there is unlikely to be a supply of topsoil adequate to allow its importation in sufficient quantities. As alternatives one must consider:

1. The re-vitalising of old stored topsoil by spreading, fertilising and cultivation—even by introducing a new worm population;

---

*A technique recently adopted in Europe for dealing with mine tailings is to combine them, as they arise, with another waste material such as wood chippings or wood pulp, which absorbs moisture, and creates a new compound material of much higher fertility which supports vegetation easily.

2. The creation of new topsoil from selected soil-forming materials thrown up by the workings;
3. Planting directly into finely ground quarry waste with nutrients added in chemical form.

### The Filling of Voids

Such is the demand for places to dump refuse, that holes are valuable resources today, and can be 'sold' by the cubic yard, as can any other voluminous asset. Unfortunately undesirable holes and unwanted waste do not often coincide in their location, and transport costs are high in proportion to the value of heavy waste materials. Before deciding the future of a derelict void, it should be studied, as any other form of land use, in the light of several factors—its origin, its location, its form (depth related to volume), access, water table, levels, ownership and land use of the surrounding land.

Large and deep holes offer the most intractable problem. The majority of such voids need continuous pumping to keep them free of water. If pumping is stopped and they are allowed to fill with water, they become a permanent danger due to the great water depth. They are also too deep for rubbish tipping and even industrial wastes cannot be merely dumped over the edge, because of the danger of taking vehicles close to the edge, the problem of consolidating, and the need to continue some form of pumping to keep the excavation reasonably dry during tipping. Ideally such voids would provide a place to receive the dumps of mining shale, but the tips are rarely within economical distance of the holes, and so far, the cost of loading, transporting and spreading spoil over a distance of more than a couple of miles has proved an insuperable barrier. The largest holes of this kind in Great Britain are still operating as quarries, so that the problem of restoring them has not yet arisen. What is probably one of the largest of such holes in the world, the Kimberley Diamond Mine has been left open as a tourist attraction!

Not all quarries create holes below ground level; many have a vertical working face going back into a hillside or scarp. Planning control is usually exercised to limit such operations so that they must stop short of the skyline, and do not cut a gap through the hill. Restoration proposals in such a project will consist of softening the harsh, and possibly straight boundaries of the quarry, and assisting it to marry into the adjoining contours. Filling would be inappropriate and probably unnecessary, as the weathered face of an old stone quarry is an attractive feature in the landscape. A certain amount of work may be needed on the floor of the quarry to level it, to bring it up to normal ground level, or to seal it so that it fills as a water area. Forestry scale planting will be the greatest agency for softening the outlines of the excavation.

The closure of deep underground mines presents a particular problem. Even though, by modern methods coal seams are worked out and the void closed by what might be called 'controlled subsidence', there is nevertheless a con-

siderable volume of void still remaining in shafts, roads, haulways and uncollapsed seams. Recent estimates show a difference between the volume of the original underground workings, and the volume of subsidence as of the order of 15%. This must represent the volume of voids still remaining. There are of course many older pits, worked on 'pillar and stall' methods where a considerably greater proportionate volume of voids is left.

It has been said that these cannot be economically backfilled with solid waste materials. However, it is now being found practical to put down wastes in the form of fluids or slurries, which find their way into quite small cavities. As they drain, of course, they solidify, so that there is likely to be a core of waste at the bottom of the shaft which does not spread very far. Each new load tipped tends to liquefy the mass again, so that it spreads a little further.

The demand for disposal space today extends to the need for deep safe places to deposit the many kinds of toxic materials now being produced as waste by-products. Certain mines are suitable for this if they meet certain strict criteria. They must be remote from habitations and urban concentrations; physically isolated from any underground connections with other pits; geologically isolated from any underground connections, faults or porous strata; they must be wholly dry pits, needing no pumping. These strict conditions limit the number of suitable mines, but several which *are* suitable are being considered for stowage of dangerous wastes.

### Reclamation of Tips

Probably the most noticeable features of past industry are the heaps of waste material which are often of monumental size, and situated in what would otherwise be desirable countryside. A few of these are piles of waste or rejected material from manufacturing industries, such as the shraff from potteries. Most of them are products of extractive industries, either directly—as the shale brought to the surface in coal mining, or indirectly—as the rock ores from which the mineral has been extracted, such as iron slag.

In planning the disposal or reclamation of such tips, it is necessary to start by studying their form and character in terms of the type of material, the method used in tipping it, and its location in relation to communications networks, and to possible disposal sites. The first possibility to investigate is whether the tip might contain saleable material, and whether working it for recovery of such material would be economic. Early workings—up to about the 18th century—were narrowly directed to one mineral only, and the heaps of waste thrown out, such as those of the lead mines in Shropshire, contain the ores of many other minerals. Some have already been worked-over two or three times to recover minerals more lately discovered.

Re-working might appear to be the ideal answer to reclamation of tips, but it has certain disadvantages: it disturbs any natural vegetation cover which might have developed spontaneously; it requires a working area larger

Figure 8.28    An old shale tip being worked for the sale of burnt shale. Unfortunately commercial operators destroy any colonising vegetation, take out the most saleable material, and leave the remainder looking, sometimes, worse than before.

*(Photo: Clifford Tandy)*

Figure 8.29    A simple form of restoration after coal working in the remote areas of Ohio, which consists merely of reducing the benching to stable slopes, by bulldozer, and planting with trees.

*(Photo: Clifford Tandy)*

than the tip—it may establish a secondary industry on the site for some years; it often requires large volumes of water and therefore sets up a drainage problem; it leaves behind a smaller, but still considerable, volume of waste material which has to be disposed of, or tipped elsewhere; moreover the final material may be more intractable to deal with than the original; finally the proposal may not be so economically attractive if it has to include the transport and disposal of the remaining waste.

As an alternative to working over the tip for other minerals, the basic material itself may have a value. Almost all hard excavated materials have some value as fill; the critical point is met, however, when the transport costs exceed the hardcore value, and a haul of more than a few miles is likely to tip the balance unfavourably. Some materials are more readily sold than others: red burnt shale is in demand, whereas the black unburnt shale cannot always meet an engineer's specification for filling material.

If a convenient place is available for deposit of the material of the tip, such as an adjacent quarry, worked out marl hole, or opencast excavation, this presents an excellent opportunity, and the critical factor will be haulage distance, together with any intermediate obstacles to be crossed. Ideally the work should be possible by using bulldozers and scrapers within a short range. It is more expensive to load dump trucks; the large 35-cy to 100-cy dumpers would be suitable across country, but they cannot go on to public roads. Road haulage may be impracticable or definitely undesirable. Rail haulage is a more practical proposition provided that room is available for long sidings to make up a large train of wagons, but it is expensive, unless special haulage rates can be negotiated. Pipelines and conveyors may also be considered as a means of transport.

Of course, it is not necessary to remove a tip completely. Tips are undesirable elements in the landscape by reason of their bulk, their height, their hard lines, or their colour. A design for halving the height, reducing the apparent bulk,

softening the shape into more natural looking contours, and planting with green vegetation finds ready acceptance. A tip may even be a welcome landmark on flat or dull land. A public relations exercise at Stoke-on-Trent revealed a desire on the part of all those who took the trouble to reply, to keep the large familiar Sneyd tip as a landmark, while improving its appearance on the lines described, in preference to totally removing it.

A tip may, of course, be objectionable because of its location: if situated on a mountain skyline, on steeply sloping valley sides, or blocking the bottom of a narrow valley; but there are exceptions to all rules, and the tip which is probably at the highest elevation in South Wales—the National Colliery tip above Tylorstown in the Rhondda was a magnificent red peak which could be seen from Somerset in clear weather. That tip, if any, deserved to be kept as a monumental landmark to the coal industry of South Wales.

Generally speaking, however, while geometric and man-made forms can be visually exciting in certain contexts, the cones of waste tips—particularly of coal shales and similar wastes tipped by aerial ropeways—are too regular, and too familiar as a reminder of past social degradation to be kept. Their re-shaping should not be a deliberate camouflage operation but they can easily approximate to one of many natural forms so that they are a prominent but acceptable part of the landscape.

Design for reshaping must commence with a study of the present shape, and this will have resulted from the way in which the heap was originally formed. Some of the forms created by different tipping methods are illustrated (Figure 8.30). These forms are common for many industries, but in addition there are the forms left by heavy excavating machinery such as 'walking draglines' which deposit small bucket-sized cones (but buckets are up to 300-ton capacity) along a ridge, leaving the site in what is known as 'hill and vale' formation.

The height of a tip is much more noticeable than its bulk,

Halving the height of a tip by removing only one-eighth of its volume

Tip material spread behind a 'military' crest

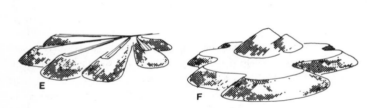

Figure 8.30    Tip shapes. A to F show tip shapes formed by different methods of tipping.

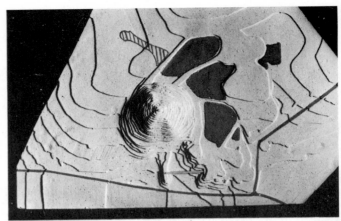

Figure 8.31    Polystyrene working models. *Above:* a model of a large conical tip with disturbed foreground and slurry lagoons behind—as existing. *Below:* a model of the same tip, reshaped to resemble a natural feature, with the foreground tidied up and the main bulk of the tip reduced to half its height and drawn back to wrap around the lagoons as would a natural hill. The sculptural form of this was designed in clay before being transferred to polystyrene sheets, from which a contour drawing could be made.

*(Photos: Clifford Tandy)*

and perhaps the first effort in re-shaping should be to reduce the height. This can be by removal of all or part of the tip but this will be expensive unless a market or dump for the material is available almost immediately adjacent to the site. The actual amount of material moved need not be great, and can probably be absorbed on the site itself, unless it is a very confined urban location. As the illustration shows, only one-eighth the volume of a conical tip needs to be removed in order to reduce its height by half, and this material does not greatly increase the dimensions of the remaining bulk.

Ideally one should have additional room for spreading equal to the area of the tip. (This is not always possible—the seven tips at Aberfan covered 22 ha; the material removed, spread in low terraces took up 32 ha of land!) This additional land should preferably be mainly to one side of the tip to allow an asymmetrical re-shaping, but there should be some space all around the tip to give working manoeuvrability. A practical example (Figure 8.31) illustrates the before and after contours of the 'Steer Pit' tip in South Wales. The design (by Land Use Consultants) takes a fairly regular and steep cone, and reduces its height by half, by dragging the bulk of the material back in the form of a comma (,) with one long flattish slope, and one steeper face—having an affinity with the 'crag and tail' formation resulting from glacial action.

Angles of slope are, of course, critical in all landform design. Existing slopes may be standing at 1 : 2; 1 : 1½ or, in extreme cases 1 : 1. The grades to which they must be lowered will depend upon the use to which the land is to be put. For example: playing pitches should be over 1 in 150 otherwise they will not drain properly, and must not be steeper than 1 in 50 cross fall. Arable crops should be kept below 1 in 10, cattle meadows preferably 1 in 40 to 1 in 20, but steeper slopes are acceptable on small areas. Sheep will graze anything up to 1 in 5. Casual walking is pleasant up to about 1 in 8, but people tend to take a winding route to ease the slope on anything steeper than 1 in 10. Slopes will fit naturally into the topography up to about 1 in 4, but at this angle the top and bottom curves should be eased off. In all this, it should be borne in mind that run-off begins to reach a state which will start erosion at about 1 in 30, unless precautions are taken to prevent it.

Another factor is the type of material being tipped. Fine rounded particles will adopt a low angle-of-repose. Large flat or angular lumps will remain at a steeper angle, while some materials which are tipped hot, such as iron furnace slag, set on cooling to quite steep smooth slopes, or fuse into large lumps highly resistant to weathering.

Other changes take place during weathering—either directly to the form of the heap or to the composition of the material—which then indirectly affects the form of the heap. Some materials are broken down by weathering to much finer particles; others manifest chemical changes; while some form a protective skin by oxidation, and become highly resistant to further weathering. Another form of change is that brought about by spontaneous combustion of coal shales. Burnt shale has quite a different character from black shale—is potentially more fertile, and also has more economic value as a saleable commodity.

Drainage is a critical factor in designing land form. It must be remembered that natural land forms are dictated entirely by the valleys formed by water run-off and the ridges left between them. A complete pattern forming continuity of gentle downhill flows is essential to a reasonably stable landscape. In all new work therefore the same continuity of drainage pattern must be achieved with slopes gentle enough to balance run-off and absorption, without gulleying (bearing in mind that newly cultivated slopes, before seeding or planting is established, are much more vulnerable to erosion and gulley formation).

Land forms should also be designed to allow straight-forward air drainage on the site and not restrict natural air flow, for any restriction would result in frost pockets. Mass tree planting, and shelterbelt planting can also cause frost pockets by holding up air drainage, and the lines of possible planting should be kept in mind when designing land form to prevent this.

### Cultivation and Planting Methods

Because of the limitations in the capacity of shales and waste materials to support growth, the methods used to establish plant growth on derelict industrial sites must differ somewhat from normal horticultural methods. It would be inappropriate to go into great detail here, but some idea of the main principles is essential to the landscape planning of this type of land.

If the waste material has been re-shaped by heavy machinery it is bound to have become compacted and will need scarifying, sub-soiling or ripping with heavy tines to break it up—but preferably without bringing large pieces to the surface. It will be an advantage to spread finely weathered or burnt material as a top layer.

Discing and tine-harrowing are needed to produce as good a tilth as possible, and lime, basic slag and superphosphate can be incorporated while discing and harrowing, but of course lime and manures must be put on at different times.

Seeding may be by conventional fiddle, barrow or mechanical spinner. A light harrowing will cover the seed if

Figure 8.32    Example from South Africa showing reed windbreaks being laid out prior to planting a shaped mine sand dump on a future motorway route.

*(Photo by courtesy of Johannesburg Chamber of Commerce)*

the ground can stand the weight of the tractor, but rolling should not normally be done. As this work is usually undertaken under the strictist economy, such niceties as pre-seeding and pre-germination dressings can rarely be afforded, and the contract is usually put out for the simplest agricultural rates.

The use of hydroseeding methods may well be considered. These have some advantages, such as the ability to reach difficult places without direct access, and the capacity to enclose the seed in a fertilised mulch which protects and sustains it for the first few weeks. They also have some disadvantages, including the compaction and gulleying caused by the weight of the vehicle or sled used, and the cost—which is almost certain to be higher than conventional agricultural methods.

Shrubs are best planted by conventional methods—into a prepared hole with room for root spread, with manure forked in below the roots, and some soil added to the back-fill. Certain shrubs which do not transplant easily or grow from cuttings will need to be pot-grown, and this can be an expensive item. As an alternative some shrubs normally pot-grown such as gorse, may be sown as seed, but a high rate of sowing to allow for failures would be needed, and the method is wasteful of seeds which are in short supply.

Forestry methods are the usual economic way of mass tree planting, but the poor conditions and high failure rate on shale and wastes mean that the common way of putting 1 + 1 year transplants into a mattock slit, is unsuitable. Some form of simple pit planting is essential—possibly only a spade-sized hole, but, if possible, with fertiliser and some

Figure 8.33 Hanley Forest Park, Stoke-on-Trent, at an early stage of planting. This park will occupy an area of nearly 200 acres in the centre of an urban complex which used to be five towns and is now one city of Stoke-on-Trent. The form of a forest park was selected by the designers, Land Use Consultants, as large enough to knit together the areas of the town separated by industrial dereliction and it involves reclamation of coal shale tips, marl pits, old brickworks, and other industrial dereliction. It is linked to the other reclaimed open spaces in the town by pedestrian greenways using the routes of derelict railway lines.

(*Photo: Clifford Tandy*)

added soil. Plants with a couple of years' growth will succeed better than young transplants, but they need to be vigorous specimens and not spindly drawn whips. If the trees are too tall, wind-rocking will loosen the roots. It is worth obtaining short sturdy stock and getting it quickly from the nursery to its final position to minimise drying out.

There are benefits in getting both grass and trees established in the early stages even though the grass is only expected to be temporary. However, the young trees must be protected from competition, and it is usually considered that an area of half a square metre around each tree should be stripped of weeds and grass. It has been found, however, that on shale, the drying out of the surface is more serious than the competition, and long grass may be left as a 'shade-mulch'.

Single tree planting (as distinct from mass forestry) can also be undertaken with the same methods (but perhaps a little heavier stock and a little more individual care), but it is not advisable to attempt to use nursery standards, extra large nursery stock, nor semi-mature trees except when land has been brought to near-level grades, and the growing medium improved and cultivated to a quality approximate to that of normal soil. Large pits should be dug and trees planted, preferably with balled roots, and backfilled with a 50-50 mixture of the medium and good soil. (Note: planting in 100% imported good soil would mean that the tree would get a setback when its roots grew out of the pit and into the shale.)

Failures of grass seeding have occurred on even mildly toxic wastes, particularly those derived from metalliferous ores. Work on this subject by Professor Bradshaw of the Department of Botany, Liverpool University has shown that grasses which have managed to colonise such ores in small patches, have developed an immunity. His Department has commenced propagation of seed collected from such grasses with the expectation of producing commercially a resistant strain of some grass species.

## Planning Trends and Planning Legislation for Industry

In the UK much of the planning policy for industry is still that of the 1950's—that each town should have an area zoned for industry—preferably on the lee-side to reduce air pollution problems and on the 'wrong side of the railway tracks'. This has been modified somewhat in that the need of light industries for female workers has led to the establishment of small 'light' industrial establishments with areas zoned for housing. The latest new town plan—that for Milton Keynes—shows a form of grid plan in which industrial/commercial employment areas are fairly evenly distributed throughout the town so that they are shared among all the 'neighbourhoods'.

Another trend which can be seen developing is the increasing importance of communications over all other factors. Sites near motorway intersections, and sites within 3 miles of motorway entry points are becoming increasingly attractive for industry—so much so that one sees large warehouse type complexes sitting in rural surroundings within reach of motorway junctions, but apparently without any nearby labour force or urban infrastructure. Similar attractions hold for railway freight-terminals—particularly container terminals—but as these are already situated in urban areas the grouping of industries around them is not so obvious.

As always, the extractive industries are in a special category, and are in direct competition for land not only with agriculture but with housing and with other industries. A strong distinction must be drawn between minerals in relatively plentiful supply, such as roadstone, sand and gravel, etc., and those which are rare. Mineral extractors have often got a bad name for the state of their operations and poor restorations, but they are not vandals. They perform a valuable function in a nation's economy and, having invested considerable capital in their organisation, they are entitled to a reasonable continuity of work. Rural planning must therefore include a programme of possible extraction areas for common minerals with priorities and built-in safeguards. Rare minerals must be balanced against other land uses (including amenity) and compared with imported materials and substitute materials. Where there is a conflict of uses, e.g. fluorspar in a national park, the decision to work it or not, must be a national one.

As urbanisation increases, the demands on public utilities increase and become more concentrated. Large conurbations make demands on land for water catchment areas, sewage disposal plants, and power station sites in rural areas, possibly hundreds of miles from the conurbation itself. As the demands for electric power have been doubling every 10 years and that for water supply doubling in 30 years, an increasingly important aspect of landscape planning is the location and treatment of sites for reservoirs, coastal barrages and power stations.

The system used for the past 25 years in Great Britain for implementing planning policies has been the production and use of development plans. Planning for industry comes into the system at several levels: structure plans for county or county borough areas are designed to include both survey data and proposals for Employment, Resources, Industry and Commerce, Utility Services.

*Employment* covers industry only in terms of factory location; *Resources* deals with land, water, gravel and similar raw materials, and existing industrial sites as a resource; *Utility Services* is the section concerned with the existing installations for gas, electricity, water, sewage and refuse, and estimates of future requirements, including pipelines and overhead cables. The section specifically dealing with *Industry and Commerce* requires survey of existing industries and ancillary services, estimates of changes in response to observed trends, i.e. expansion or contraction, land requirements, technological developments, locality and market changes. It is also expected to cover policy proposals related to industrial expansion, new industries, heavy transport for industry, provision of storage areas, small factory sites, industrial estates, drainage and services to industry, and the effects upon the community of noise, fumes and other forms of pollution.

These records and proposals are, where appropriate, expounded on a larger scale in local plans, district plans and action area plans, but there is also provision for special 'subject' plans, and these are particularly appropriate for dealing with mineral extraction and derelict land reclamation, particularly in areas of the country where there is a larger proportion of these in the locality. Many of the planning techniques described earlier can be indicated on these subject plans, but in addition the local planning authority can expound on its policies for relating working to demand; for keeping certain mineral reserves; for conserving areas of landscape against working; for controlling noise, dust and other nuisances; for visual screening of

working sites; for planned reclamation and restoration after working; for relating the whole to a time-scale and a programme of priorities.

**Planning Legislation**

Certain aspects of planning legislation are directed to landscape planning, though they are never defined as such, except in parts of Germany where there is specific control of *Landschaft-Planung*. Because of the large-scale effects which can result, much of such legislation is concerned with industrial land use. The significant aspects are worthy of mention in this chapter.

Considerable changes in attitude have taken place since about 1940. Before that date emphasis was largely on industrial growth and expansion, with legislation directed mainly to making working conditions more humane. Since such milestones as the Scott, Uthwatt and Barlow Reports (8.25) planning legislation has taken a protective attitude towards the countryside—often against industrial intrusion—and towards the *quality of life*, defending it against deterioration through noise, pollution and landscape damage.

Britain has probably some of the strongest legislation controlling the *location* of industry, in national parks, areas of good landscape, and nature reserves. Some adopt persuasions or grants to attract industry to suitable locations; others, like USA adopt zoning procedures.

Pollution is a growing subject for legislation (see also chapter 7). The emission of industrial fumes has been under supervision in Britain through the Alkali Works Regulations Act of 1906, since when there have been several Acts concerned with public health and clean air. Other countries have been slower to act, but some have now even stricter regulations. Water pollution control has been fairly primitive even in developed countries until quite recently, and only in the 1970's were rigid standards of water quality introduced. Tipping of solid wastes on to land has been accepted as normal, with only broad rules of guidance in most countries, such as the Public Health Acts. Only with the spate of dangerous chemical wastes being dumped in the last few years has the problem of land pollution been properly recognised. A Royal Commission (8.26) has considered the subject and in 1974 the Control of Pollution Act was passed, which replaced a number of earlier measures and gave local planning authorities stronger powers over the pollution of land by dumping of wastes; over the pollution of water by noxious effluents; and powers to exercise control over noise.

In many parts of the world extractive industries are given a free hand to exploit national resources, with encouragement rather than hindrance, though this attitude is gradually changing. In Britain there has been specific legislation, such as the Mineral Workings Act 1951, (8.27); the Mines and Quarries Act 1954, (8.28); and Opencast Coal Act 1958 (8.29). Since the Aberfan disaster in 1966 a new

Act, the Mines and Quarries (Tips) Act 1969 (8.30) has come into force to control tipping. Only in very recent years have American States begun to introduce bills to control strip mining and to demand some form of restoration. Most of those that have taken action have introduced a form of levy or bond to guarantee restoration being done.

As far back as 1949 the National Parks Act gave British local authorities powers to get reclamation work done on derelict land. Later, the Industrial Development Act of 1966 and the Local Government Act 1966 made grants available for this work, and higher grants in so-called 'Development Areas'. These grants have gradually been increased from 50% to 75% up to 85% in rate-deficiency areas, and in 1978 stand at 100%. No other country, apparently, has comparable aid, from central government, for the reclamation of dereliction.

Recently there has been a wave of concern for the environment, expressed in legislation. Much of it has been related to *conservation*; other parts to preventing industrial technology from becoming too destructive through pollution, noise, energy usage, waste and scenic damage. There has been far less legislation on the positive aspects of planning for good industrial development which makes the minimum impact on the environment.

Conservation measures include the almost total exclusion of new industries from national parks, national nature reserves, national trust land, and severe restrictions on industry in areas of outstanding natural beauty, areas of high landscape value, and green belts. Britain has not only controls, but also gives *grants* to encourage industry to move to areas considered suitable. Even on non-controversial sites in rural areas, planning controls cover such matters as screening, landscape treatment and pollution control. The initial requirement may be rigidly enforced, but it is much more difficult to ensure that the measures are properly maintained in the succeeding years.

The Town and Country Amenities Act of 1974 was almost wholly limited to conservation areas in its environmental controls, leaving *industrial* development still governed by the consolidated Town and Country Planning Act of 1971. Some exceptions were, however, made by the General Development Order of 1973 in respect of numerous classes of work, including agricultural and forestry buildings, minor industrial extensions, mining underground and the continuation of working at existing (pre-1948) quarries.

The same order required plans for reinstatement to be included in applications for mineral extraction—particularly mentioning opencast coal mining. It also permits planning authorities to require plans for the landscaping of a site after development, to be included in the application for planning permission.

The most interesting recent development in planning control is the use of environmental impact statements (EISs), which are obligatory in the USA, Australia, and a few other countries, but still only a recommended procedure for certain large and controversial industrial projects in Britain. The details of this procedure are covered in Chapter 3. Since their introduction in the 1960s, these have become an important part of planning policies and programmes in the USA where the method has been adopted so thoroughly that the collected material on thousands of projects has become an indigestible obstruction in the planning machinery. Germany is in the process of adopting an 'environmental compatibility procedure'; in France the Quality of Life Ministry has so far failed to introduce legislation requiring authorisation for projects which cause environment risks; some Australian states have already adopted an environmental impact study procedure for inquiries into major developments; the Netherlands are seriously considering the introduction of such a procedure.

Although Britain has probably the most stringent planning system in the world, many other countries are rapidly catching up, and, particularly in regard to environmental aspects, may already be ahead of British practice.

Germany, Denmark, Sweden and Japan are adopting quite stringent measures on conservation. Some of the German legislation—for air and water pollution—is recent, but in landscape planning for industry, Germany has been a pioneer since 1910.

American practice is somewhat inhibited by independent 'State' legislation, and until recently, planning control on industry was mainly through broad *zoning* regulations. However, Federal Acts on Clean Air, Water Pollution and Noise have been introduced in the last 10 years. Several States have, themselves, begun to introduce much more stringent regulations on such subjects as strip and contour mining, with a compulsory levy to build up a trust fund for eventual restoration of mining damage.

The future use of land for industry depends upon several factors—some of which can be extrapolated from present conditions—others can only be guessed at. Two of the most critical are at present subject to much speculation. Will world population growth continue on its present exponential curve, and will a stable state replace economic growth in highly developed countries.

Without an answer to these two questions, as described in chapter 1, other considerations are minimal in their impact. It is certain that most of the Third World countries will not even consider adopting theories of zero growth while they are so far behind the material affluence of older nations. It is also certain that the presently known natural resources of the planet will not be adequate to permit more than a few countries to reach the consumption of a country like the United States.

Until better solutions are forthcoming one must base hopes on such attainable prospects as technological advances in new substitute resources and power sources; agreements to leave large reserves of scarce resources untapped; modest reductions in population growth rate; and the recycling of waste.

In the majority of urbanised countries, *land* is one of the scarce resources which must be both husbanded and recycled. Industrial growth is still expanding nearly everywhere, but there is a trend towards less heavy industries and less waste land. Technological advances often mean higher productivity with less power, less labour, and less space, so that the 'take' of land for industry is already at a lower rate than industrial growth itself. To be sure of survival in the future we must ensure that less land is damaged, destroyed or sterilized by waste deposits, and that land left waste after the close of an industry is re-used in preference to taking new green-field sites.

# References

8.1  CLEERE, H. F., 'Roman ironworks in Britain', *British Steel*, March 1969.

8.2  HOSKINS, W. G., *The Making of the English Landscape*, Hodder and Stoughton, London, 1955.

8.3  ESTALL, R. C. and BUCHANAN, R. D., *Industrial Activity and Economic Geography*, 2nd ed., Hutchinson, London, 1966.

8.4  FAIRBROTHER, N., *New Lives, New Landscapes*, Architectural Press, London, 1970.

8.5  TANDY, C. R. V., *Landscape of Industry*, Leonard Hill, London, 1975.

8.6  FAIRBROTHER, N., *op. cit.*

8.7  HACKETT, B., *Landscape Planning*, Oriel Press, Newcastle, 1971.

8.8  HACKETT, B., *op. cit.*

8.9  Ministry of Works and Planning, *Land Utilisation in Rural Areas*, (The Scott Report) Cmd. 6378, HMSO, London, 1942.

8.10  GREEN, R.J., *Country Planning*, Manchester University Press, Manchester, 1971.

8.11  Town Development Act 1952, HMSO, London, 1952.

8.12  Hunt Committee Report, *The Intermediate Areas*, Cmnd. 3998, HMSO, London, 1969.

8.13  BEST, R. H. and COPPOCK, J. T., *The Changing Use of Land in Britain*, Faber and Faber, London, 1962.

8.14  NICHOLSON, E. M., 'Industrial land—a question of stock control', *Modern Government*, June/July, 1972.

8.15  FAIRBROTHER, N., *op. cit.*

8.16  GREEN, R. J., *op. cit.*

8.17  ZUCKERMAN, SIR SOLLY, (Chairman), *Report of the Commission on Mining and the Environment*, Land Use Consultants, London, 1972.

8.18  STEVENS, SIR ROGER, (Chairman), *Planning Control over Mineral Working: Report of the Committee on Planning Control over Mineral Working*, HMSO, London, 1976.

8.19  GREEN, R. J., *op. cit.*

8.20  BRACEY, H. E., *Industry and the Countryside*, Report of an Inquiry for the Royal Society of Arts Action Society Trust, Faber and Faber, London, 1963.

8.21  MYERS, J. L., 'Devastation', *Nature*, **158**, 1946, p. 605.

8.22  MINISTRY OF HOUSING AND LOCAL GOVERNMENT, *The Control of Mineral Working*, (revised), HMSO, London, 1960.

8.23  NEWCASTLE UNIVERSITY, *Landscape Reclamation*, Vol. 1, IPC Science and Technology Press, Guildford, 1971, chapter 8.

8.24  ZUCKERMAN, S., *op. cit.*

8.25  MINISTRY OF WORKS AND PLANNING, *Land Utilisation in Rural Areas, op. cit.*
MINISTRY OF WORKS AND PLANNING, *Compensation and Betterment*, (The Uthwatt Report) Cmd. 6386, HMSO, London, 1942.
MINISTRY OF WORKS AND PLANNING, *Distribution of Industrial Population*, (The Barlow Report) Cmd. HMSO, London, 1940.

8.26  ASHBY, E. (Chairman), *Royal Commission on Environmental Pollution*, 2nd Report, Cmnd. 4894, HMSO, London, 1972.

8.27  MINISTRY OF HOUSING AND LOCAL GOVERNMENT, *The Control of Mineral Working, op. cit.*

8.28  Mines and Quarries Act 1954, HMSO, London, 1954.

8.29  Opencast Coal Act 1958, HMSO, London, 1958, chapter 69.

8.30  Mines and Quarries (Tips) Act 1969, HMSO, London, 1969, chapter 10.

# Bibliography

ARVILLE, R., *Man and Environment*, Pelican Original, Penguin Books, 4th edn., 1977.

ASHBY, E., (Chairman), *Second Report, Royal Commission on Environmental Pollution*, Cmnd 4894, HMSO, London, 1972.

BARR, J., *Derelict Britain*, Pelican Original, Penguin Books, Harmondsworth, 1969.

BEAVER, S. H., 'Minerals and Planning', *Royal Geographical Society Journal*, **CIV**, 5, 6, Nov./Dec. 1944.

BEAVER, S. H. and WOOLRIDGE, S. W., 'The Working of Sand and Gravel in Britain', *Royal Geographical Society Journal*, **CXV**, 1, 3, March 1950.

BLUNDEN, J., *The Mineral Resources of Britain: A Study in Exploration and Planning*, Hutchinson, London, 1975.

CASSON, J., 'The Landscape of Industry: The Extractive Industries, Paper in *Institute of Landscape Architects Journal*, London, February, 1961.

CIVIC TRUST, *Reclamation of Derelict Land*, Report of Conference, Stoke-on-Trent, 1970.

COSSONS, N., *The BP Book of Industrial Archaeology*, David and Charles, Newton Abbot, 1975.

COUNTRYSIDE IN 1970:

C-1970 Secretariat, *Technology in Conservation*, Report of Study Group No. 3, Countryside in 1970, 2nd Conference, London, 1965.

C-1970 Secretariat, *Reclamation and Clearance of Derelict Land,* Report of Study Group No. 12, Countryside in 1970, 2nd Conference, London, 1965.

C-1970 Secretariat, Report on Damage to the Countryside by Industry by Sub-group of Advisory Committee on Industry and the Countryside, Countryside in 1970, London, 1967.

C-1970 Secretariat, *Working with Industry* by Advisory Committee on Industry and the Countryside, Countryside in 1970, Final Conference, London, 1970.

DEPARTMENT OF THE ENVIRONMENT, *Survey of Derelict and Despoiled Land in England 1974,* DOE, London, May, 1975.

DEPARTMENT OF THE ENVIRONMENT, (Originally Ministry of Housing and Local Government) annual returns of derelict land in counties and country boroughs of Britain; available on request.

DERRY, T. K. and WILLIAMS, T. I., *A Short History of Technology,* Oxford University Press, Oxford, 1960.

DOWNING, M., (ed.), *Planning Outlook* special issue on Ecology and Landscape planning. New Series. Vol. IV, 1968, University of Newcastle-upon-Tyne Town and Country Planning Dept., Oriel Press, 1968.

EVANS, W. DAVID, 'The Opencast Mining of Ironstone and Coal', *Royal Geographical Society Journal,* **CIV**, 3, 4, London, Sept./Oct., 1944.

GOODMAN, G. T., (ed.), Sub-committee survey of the Nature of Technical Advice required when Treating Land Affected by Industry, British Ecological Society Papers, Blackwell, London, 1968.

HARTWRIGHT, T. M., *The Sand and Gravel Industry* in Landscape Research Group Symposium, University of Reading, 1971.

HAYWOOD, S., *Quarries and the Landscape,* The British Quarrying and Slag Federation Ltd, London, 1974.

HILTON, K. J., (ed.), *The Lower Swansea Valley Project,* Longman, Harlow, 1967.

IUCN, Papers of 10th Technical Meeting, published as New Technical Series No. 8, IUCN, Switzerland, 1967.

JONES, G. A., PENMAN, A. N. D., and TANDY, C. R. V., *Industrial Spoil Tips,* Report on the Conference—Civil Engineering Problems of the South Wales Valleys, Cardiff, April, 1969, Institute of Civil Engineers, London, 1970.

JONES, W. R., *Minerals in Industry,* Pelican Original, Penguin Books, Harmondsworth, 1963.

KEEBLE, D. E., 'Industrial Movement and Regional Development in the U.K.', *Town Planning Review,* **43**, 1, 1972.

KNOLLES, A. S. and COOK, T. L., *Reclamation for Recreation,* National Playing Fields Association, London, 1972.

LEE, D., *Regional Planning and Location of Industry,* Heinemann, London, 1969.

MOHLG, *New Life for Dead Lands,* HMSO, London, 1963.

NATIONAL COAL BOARD, *Opencast Coal—A Tool for Landscape Renewal,* NCB, London, 1967.

NORTH, F. J., *Mining for Metal in Wales,* Amgueddfa Genedlaethol Cymru, Cardiff, 1962.

OXENHAM, J. R., *Reclaiming Derelict Land,* Faber and Faber, London, 1966.

RANWELL, D. S., (ed.). Sub-Committee Report on Landscape Improvement Advice and Research, British Ecological Society Papers, Blackwell, London, 1967.

SAGA, *Pit and Quarry Textbook,* Sand and Gravel Association of G. B. MacDonald, London, 1967.

SENIOR, D. (ed.), *Derelict Land,* Civic Trust, London.

SHOLTO DOUGLAS, J., 'Rehabilitation of Mined Areas', *Mining Magazine,* **120**, 2, 1969.

SINCLAIR, J., *Quarrying, Opencast and Alluvial Mining,* Elsevier, Oxford, 1969.

SUMMER, J. (Chairman), Report of the working party on Refuse Disposal, DOE, HMSO, London 1971.

TREVELYAN, G. M., *Illustrated English Society History,* Longmans, Harlow, 1949 and Penguin Books, Harmondworth, 1964.

VYLE, C. J., *Reclamation of Industrial Waste—A Landscape Plan,* MS submitted to Science and Life, Czechoslovakia, 1971.

WALLWORK, K. L., *Derelict Land,* David and Charles, Newton Abbot, 1974.

WARREN, K., *Mineral Resources,* David and Charles, Newton Abbot, 1973.

WEDDLE, A. E., Industrial Landscape, reprinted paper given at Conference on Industrial Landscape, Belfast, 1966.

WHITE, R. O. and SISAM, J. W. R., *The Establishment of Vegetation on Industrial Waste Land,* Commonwealth Agricultural Bureaux, Joint Publication No. 14, Aberystwyth, 1949.

WHITTAKER, C., BROWN, P., and MONAHAN, *Handbook of Environment Powers,* Architectural Press, London, 1977.

WISE, J. MICHAEL, 'The Midland Reafforesting Association 1903–1924 and the reclamation of derelict land in the Black Country', *Institute of Landscape Architects Journal,* 57, February 1962.

CASE HISTORY ONE

# MERGELLAND: THE IMPACT OF LIMESTONE QUARRYING ON A SCENIC RURAL AREA

Klaas Kerkstra, Peter Vrijlandt and Meto J. Vroom

Anyone familiar with the geography of the Netherlands will be aware that limestone hills are an unusual feature in the Dutch landscape. They are found only in the extreme south-east of the country, in the province of Limburg. Here an area of some 500 square kilometres is characterised by high plateaus, valleys, steep slopes and edges, that are the product of geologic processes terminating in a series of successive erosion periods of Tertiary formations by the river Meuse and its tributaries.

The area is considered to be of high value not only for its topography and, for the Netherlands, rather unusual scenery, but also because of its ecology: some of the most diverse and highly developed vegetation types in the Netherlands are found on its calcareous slopes. The land use is predominantly agricultural, although limestone quarrying has been an important activity throughout the area for a long time. There are a number of quarries of varying size. Limestone is used for the production of fertilizer, but is mainly processed into cement.

Near Maastricht (St. Pietersberg) the Netherlands Cement Industry ENCI operates a large quarry, which produces nearly all the limestone required by the Dutch market: 3,000,000 m³ per annum. In 1991, this quarry will be exhausted, and ENCI has started preparing plans for a new location in the area. In view of the necessary capital investment, the opening of a new quarry can only be justified if a quantity of limestone can be produced warranting 40 years of uninterrupted production.

In 1976 ENCI formally requested Government permission for the exploitation of a new limestone quarry, covering an area of 433 hectares, to be located near the village of Margraten. If this permission is granted, an area of about 2 km by 2 km will be excavated to a depth of 35 metres.

When some time ago the possibility of the request was rumoured in the regional and national press, it at once became apparent that one of the most controversial issues in regional planning was being born. Environmental action groups, nature conservation societies and Government agencies are in strong opposition to any activity that may destroy or even change historic ecological and scenic values, especially here. Indeed, the area had already been included in nationwide studies concerning landscape conservation, and it had been put forward as one of the new Dutch national parks or protected areas.

In 1975 ENCI invited the Department of Landscape Architecture of the Wageningen Agricultural University to assist in drawing up plans for the site near Margraten. After some consultation, the assignment was changed to a study of the ecological and visual impact of large-scale quarrying in several alternative locations in the region, and the objectives of the study were to provide both industry and local government authorities with some sort of instrument for weighing possible alternative solutions.

The question of whether or not limestone quarrying should be allowed in this region was not considered within the scope of the landscape study. It was quite evident that large-scale mining or quarrying operations in the area would result in drastic changes in the landscape, whatever measures were taken to prevent, or compensate for, the damage done. It was also evident that this activity would create jobs and produce a much-needed commodity. The balance between socio-economic and environmental arguments is hard to find and landscape research of itself cannot give such answers.

During an initial survey of the area it became clear that the impact of quarrying operations would not be the same throughout the region and that a search for alternative sites would be advisable. The research effort therefore focused on the question of where and under what sort of conditions, variable types of impact could be predicted.

# Theoretical Framework

In view of the existence of various definitions and concepts of 'landscape' and landscape values (see Chapters 2 and 3), the research team decided to formulate a theoretical framework before delving into an analysis of the region. It was considered important to give this background information with the report in order to make clear what approach to the problem was used.

Landscape is taken here as an expanse, a territory in which numerous elements are visible, both of natural origin and man-made; hills, valleys, copses, tree belts, farms, settlements, etc. This collection of elements is not a haphazard one—between all elements, which together result in 'landscape', a complex set of relations exists in time and space. This set of relations is specific in its composition in each locality.

One may distinguish three sets of factors which together constitute the system called 'landscape' (Figures 1 and 2). These are:

> Physical factors (rocks, soil, water);
> Biological factors (plants, wildlife);
> Human factors (land use).

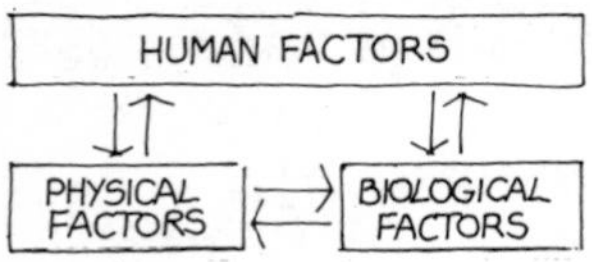

Figure 1.

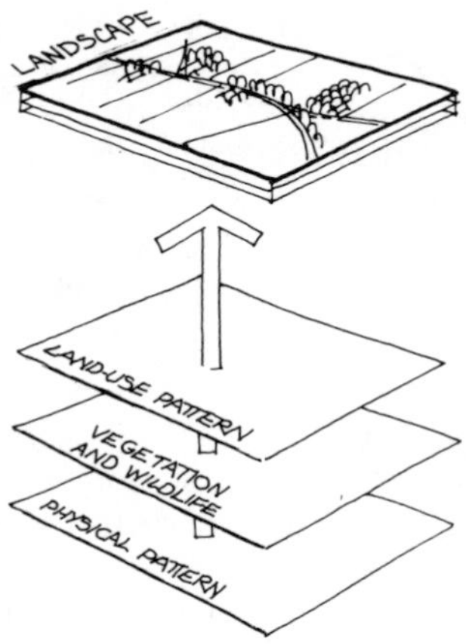

Figure 2.

Variations in interaction between these three factors result in one place differing from another; this we term *spatial variety*.

Changes in the nature of these factors or rather in the degree of interaction are called *landscape processes*. Some of these processes result in *temporal variety*. Some of these processes result in rapid change, such as developments in land use. Other processes are so slow that no change is apparent to the human eye; for example, some geological processes. Viewed over a long time-span, the whole set of forces constituting landscape is in constant change. The actual outward appearance of the landscape in any given area is but a momentary glimpse of a continuous process. Landscape, therefore, must not only be viewed as the result of the processes that gave shape to it in the past; it is also a framework from which future developments germinate and develop, whether they be consciously planned or not (Figure 3).

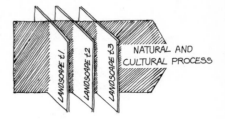

Figure 3.

Man occupies a very special position within the process of change in landscape; he is able to look at landscape consciously and see it as his own living environment. He is also capable of implementing (drastic) change. He changes landscape in order to adapt the environment to his changing needs. Man and environment interact continuously (Figure 4). His interaction in his environment can only have a lasting positive effect if he understands what he is doing, and is capable of predicting the direct and indirect impact of his actions.

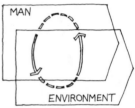

Figure 4.

He must also be aware and have knowledge of the *meaning* of the landscape to him. Meaning, value or significance of landscape to man is primarily based on functional relations, such as the dependence on ecological stability in the environment. Meaning of landscape is also derived from the fact that landscape serves as a source of (visual) information. Value is not a property; a characteristic of landscape. The human mind always serves as an intermediary between the source of information and the response to that information. As part of a learning process, man discovers new values all the time, that is, he attaches different meanings to landscape at different moments. Thus his appreciation of landscape changes with time—as landscape itself changes under the influence of processes described above.

Thus if landscape research is to contribute to environmantal planning, it cannot limit its attention to the assessment of landscape values. Since both the existing landscape and its significance to man are in the process of continuous change, it is necessary to investigate the basic conditions underlying existing quality and at the same time to search for opportunities for future development. This means combining a descriptive analysis and a creative design approach.

## Procedure Followed

In order to be able to predict and describe the impact of limestone quarrying in the study area, the team split up the problem into three parts:

1. The development of (so-called) landscape criteria on the basis of which alternative locations could be checked against different quarrying techniques and methods.

The criteria are derived from:

A description and analysis of the area;

A conceptual framework based on ecological and physiological theory.

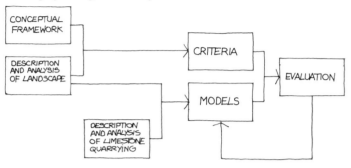

Figure 5.

The concept may be put succinctly as:

Bio-ecological regulatory processes (implying resistance to diseases and stability of microclimate) depend on the existence of spatial variety and on structural consistency.

Likewise the amount of visual information available and, to use Kevin Lynch's terminology, the legibility of the environment depend on the same set of conditions. Variety tells us only about the difference between places.

'Structure' refers to:

*In a horizontal sense*: the specific way in which differences are ordered within the area, the spatial sequences, the hierarchy of spaces, etc;

*In a vertical sense*: the conditions underlying variety, visible through the occurrence of superimposed patterns such as forest being limited to steep slopes in the area.

2. The development of a number of alternative possibilities (models), or techniques of limestone quarrying.

These models are needed in order to check the specific quarrying techniques and variations in techniques against site conditions.

3. The comparison and checking of different techniques on various locations within the study area.

How and in what way are conditions for spatial diversity and structure affected by specific ways of limestone quarrying?

## The Landscape in the Study Area

An initial survey of the landscape of the area shows that spatial diversity is largely determined by topographical conditions (Figure 7). Differences in level and natural land forms dominate to such a degree that patterns of soils and vegetation, as well as land use patterns, conform to these. The reason for this apparent hierarchical relation—the dominance of one set of factors—is the presence of an unusual amount of geomorphological and geological variety in the area. In the Netherlands, in particular, this is an unusual phenomenon.

The area is part of a region renowned for its attraction to tourists. Particularly during the summer holiday season it is crowded with visitors and there are many summer hotels, lodges and camp sites. Not only the visual variety, but also the existence of historical buildings and town centres contribute to the scenery (Figure 11). The presence of a number of highly valued nature areas boasting rare species of flora and fauna, and the existence of nature trails and guided tours add to the attraction. Plans are being studied to give parts of the whole of the area the status of a national park.

For visitors, the contrasts between plateaus, valleys and the steep slopes joining the two are the most striking landscape features. Each of these has its own functional and spatial character. The total drainage pattern is interesting in that it shows a fine drawn pattern and a hierarchical sequence, which is the basis of the structural quality of the area (Figure 6).

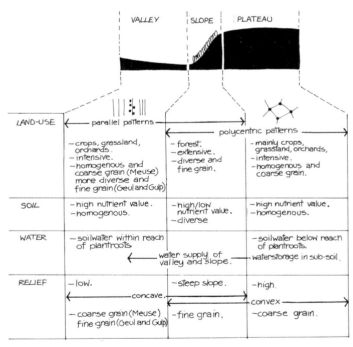

Figure 6.    Functional pattern of the study area.

### The Plateaus

The plateaus can be described as large, somewhat spherical geomorphological units. Soils here are predominantly rich in nutrient and of a homogeneous character. The soil water is below the reach of plant roots, and plants are thus dependent on capillary water. Agricultural land use is intensive; crops alternate with grassland.

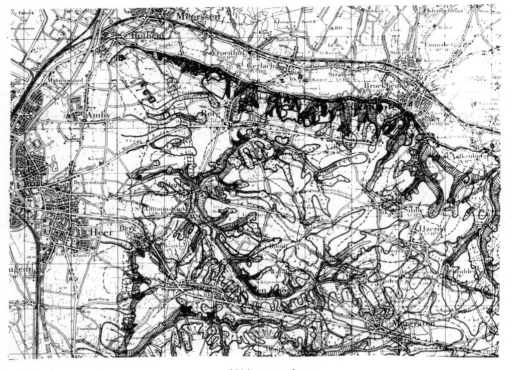

1 higher terrace forms
2 lower terrace forms
3 fanshaped slope
B escarpment <10m
C escarpment >10m
D very steep slope  30%
E steep slope (15°-30°)
F shelving slope (2°-15°)
G slope discontinuity ⌒convex ⌣concave
H shallow long-drawn depression
I niche form
J flat valley bottom
K valley watershed
L1 first order watershed
L2 second order watershed
M peculiar form

KM

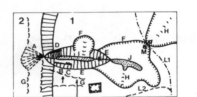

Figure 7.  Geomorphology of the study area.

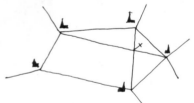

Polycentric pattern on the plateau.

Figure 8.  Topography of the study area.

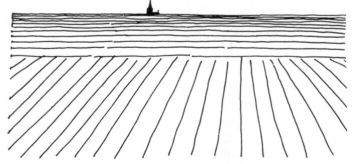

Figure 10.  Large-scale open views of the plateaus.

Figure 9.  The spherical form of the Margraten plateau.

In general, the plateaus offer large-scale open views. Variety is in a polycentric pattern, formed by roads and settlements at road junctions (Figure 8), and a sequence of different types of agricultural land use radiates from each settlement. On the plateaus, with their fairly uniform soil pattern, the distance in relation to farm buildings affects the intensity of land use. Starting from the built-up areas, where all farm buildings are concentrated, a sequence of types of land use with decreasing intensity of production is found (Figure 13).

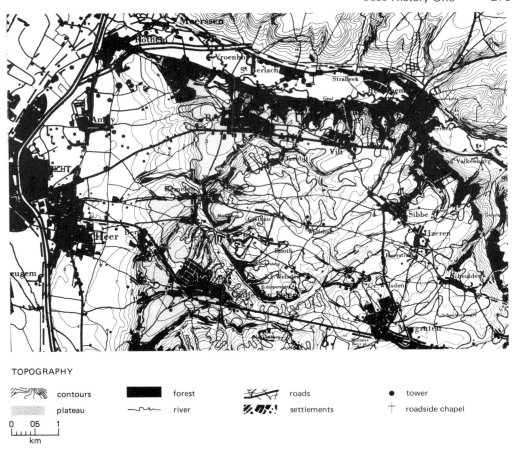

TOPOGRAPHY

| | | | |
|---|---|---|---|
| ~~~ contours | ▓ forest | ✕ roads | ● tower |
| ░░ plateau | ~∿~ river | settlements | + roadside chapel |

0  05  1
km

Figure 11.

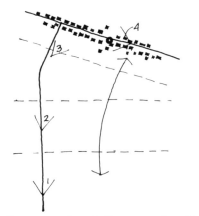

A settlement
B grassland, orchard
C crops
D forest

| | crops | less intensive | coarse grain |
|---|---|---|---|
| ▦ | grassland/orchard | intensive | fine grain |
| | Built-up road | | |
| | grassland/orchard | | |
| | crops | less intensive | coarse grain |

Sequence inside the polycentric pattern on the plateau.

Figure 12.

Figure 13. Sequence of activities around settlements on the plateaus.

Figures 14, 15, 16 and 17. Examples of the sequence of activities on the plateaus corresponding to 1, 2, 3, 4 on Figure 13.

Figure 15.

Figure 16.

Figure 17.

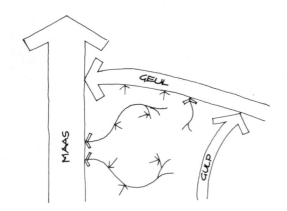

Figure 18.   The valleys. A sequence from large to small.

Figure 19.   View of the Meuse valley from Rasberg showing the large dimensions of the valley.

Figure 20.

## The Valleys

Valleys are characterised by a low position in relation to the plateaus, a hollow cross section, and a linear shape. Valleys in the study area can be classified according to their size and form: wide or narrow; symmetrical or asymmetrical; steep or gentle slopes; flat or hollow bottoms, etc.

There is a certain degree of order in this variety of forms and there is a sequence from large to small:

1. Water-carrying valleys of the rivers Meuse, Geul, Gulp;
2. Dry vales;
3. Eroded roads and gulleys.

## 1. THE WATER-CARRYING (RIVER) VALLEYS

In the water-carrying valleys, the geological and soil patterns show little diversity and are generally coarse 'grain'. This is especially the case in the larger valleys such as the valley of the Meuse and the lower stretches of the river Geul. The upper reaches of the Geul and Gulp are more diverse and show a finer grain. Soils are in direct contact with subterranean water, and the valleys are mainly in intensive use.

Their linear character is reinforced by the sequence of different land uses which run lengthwise along their bottoms, slopes and upper edges (Figures 21 and 22). They are

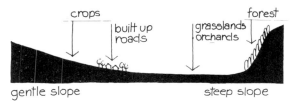

crops
built up
roads
forest
grasslands
orchards

gentle slope          steep slope

Cross-section of watercarrying valley.

Figure 21.

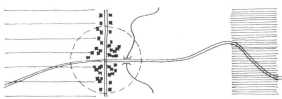

View of a-symmetrical valley (Gulp).

Figure 22.

The valleys are subdivided by more or less built-up cores sitting at the junction of intersecting roads and river.

Figure 23.

subdivided by more or less built-up cores situated at the intersections of road and river (Valkenburg, Wijlre, Gulpen).

## 2. DRY VALES

The course of the dry vales, from their upper reaches on top of the plateaus to their exits into a river, demonstrates a sequence of changes in size and shape. They originate from the upper plateaus where they are wide and fairly flat. The spatial pattern in the stretch above is highly diverse and fine grained as a result of the existence of different branches of eroded roads and gulleys, and of the type of land use adapted to this situation. Lower down they

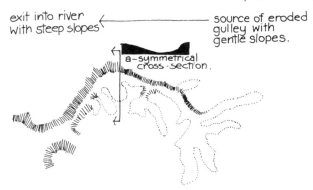

exit into river with steep slopes          source of eroded gulley with gentle slopes.

a-symmetrical cross-section.

Dry vales. Sequences of size and shape.

Figure 24.

Figure 25.     The upper reaches of a dry vale.

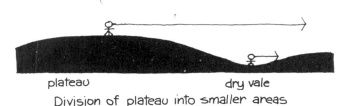

plateau          dry vale

Division of plateau into smaller areas

Figure 27.

acquire a more linear shape and become asymmetrical in cross section. Where they emerge into a river, the slopes are steep and the spatial pattern is fairly coarse.

The Margraten plateau is divided into smaller areas by the dry vales. As a result of this the area, which looks uniform from a high viewpoint, contains a great deal of visual variety. This variety may be seen by an observer crossing the plateau.

Figure 26.     Dry vale lower down. Typical asymmetrical cross-section.

## 3. ERODED ROADS AND GULLEYS

Eroded roads and gulleys are the smallest of the valleys. They were formed by erosive action of melting glaciers, and more recently by their use as footpaths and tracks.

These valleys belong to the lowest level in the hierarchy of the drainage pattern, but their hollow and linear shape is quite defined. The mostly symmetrical shape is reinforced by symmetry in land use patterns.

Figure 28.    Eroded road at the edge of a plateau.

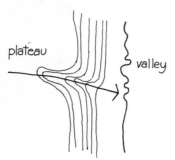

Gulley used as path.
Figure 29.

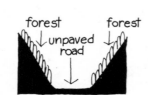

Figure 30.    Symmetrical cross-section reinforced by land use.

### Edges or Slopes

The edge between plateaus and water-carrying valleys consists of slopes of varying steepness. Soil patterns in these areas are diverse and show a fine grain; extremes in nutrient value, in wetness and dryness, are spread out in complex patterns.

Land use on the slopes is of an extensive character, predominantly forest, because of the susceptibility to erosion, and forest-covered slopes are visible in the landscape as continuous edges of the valleys. This is important in the characterisation of the area. From the few locations where forest cover is absent one has a wide panoramic view over the valleys and can see the existing variety and its context.

Figure 31.    Forest cover on steep slopes. View from the top of a plateau.

### The Hydrological Regime

The pattern of valleys, edges and plateaus is not the only determinant of spatial coherence of the area. An example of functional interdependence, related to the existing differences between high and low areas, is the hydrological regime.

The water supply of the valleys, and locally of the slopes, is partly dependent on the capacity of the soils and the geological formation under the plateaus to function as an aquifer, that is to store, filter and release water. At the same time run-off from the plateaus to rivers ensures periodical water supply for the slopes. Thus, changes in the hydrological regime may result in effects on the landscape over fairly large distances.

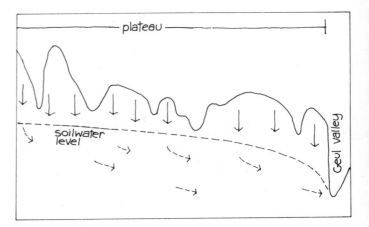

The hydrological system.
Figure 32.

## Limestone Quarrying and its Impact

Existing quarries in the region illustrate the different ways in which limestone may be excavated. These quarries differ in size from 3 to 50 hectares and may vary in depth between 10 and perhaps 50 metres.

In this context it is important to bear in mind that the new quarry to be developed by ENCI will be almost 10 times the size of the largest existing quarry. This does not mean that all of the 430 hectares will be worked at the same time. Only 100 hectares are expected to be in production at any given moment, and once the limestone is removed the site is to be restored in such a manner as to meet conditions to be set by the Government.

Damage to the surrounding area as a result of transportation of large quantities of limestone is to be avoided by installing an underground conveyor-belt system which will carry the material from the quarry to the existing processing plant on the west bank of the river Meuse.

The research team investigated the possible variations in location and shape, and the conclusion arrived at was that, in principle, two different methods of approach can be followed.

Excavation along the edge of a plateau.

Figure 33.

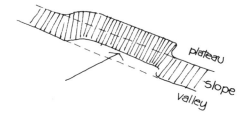

Figure 34.

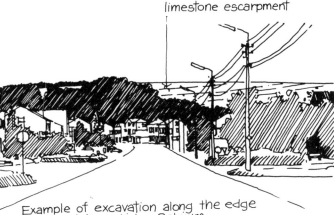

limestone escarpment

Example of excavation along the edge of the plateau, Lixhe, Belgium.

Figure 35.

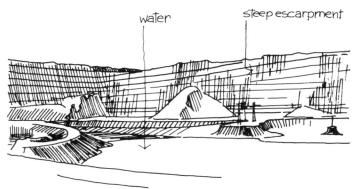

water          steep escarpment

Close-up of existing quarry near Lixhe.

Figure 36.

1. Excavation along the edge of a plateau starting from the bottom of a river valley (Figures 33 and 34).

An, example of this method is found near Lixhe in Belgium. A considerable stretch of the western slope of the Meuse river valley is being excavated from the bottom upwards, leaving a steep escarpment which is visible from a long distance. The yellowish colour of the limestone makes this escarpment stand out even more.

2. Excavation of a hole starting from the upper level of a plateau and digging down (Figures 37 and 38). This hole may or may not be connected to a narrow outlet into the river valley. The natural slopes along the river valleys are for the most part left untouched. From the bottom of the valleys little if anything can be seen of the quarrying activities. (Examples of this kind are found near the villages of Rooth and Bergh.)

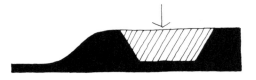

Excavation of a hole starting from the upper level of a plateau.

Figure 37.

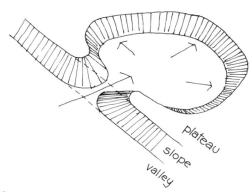

Figure 38.

In deciding on the alternative sites for the new ENCI location, the research team based its choice on the opportunity presented to compare these two means of excavation. Other considerations affecting the choice of locations were:

1. In the case of excavation along the edges of plateaus, slopes covered by highly developed natural systems should be left untouched. Most of the forest-covered steeper slopes belong to this category. In some places, however, less-steep slopes have been in agricultural cultivation for a long time and represent lower ecological values. This is particularly the case along the western rim of the plateau, bordering on the valley of the river Meuse.

2. There should be sufficient quantities of 'high grade' limestone available to warrant production equivalent to needs.

3. Locations should be within a maximum distance of 10 km from the existing processing plant south of Maastricht (Figure 40). This is in order to meet technical requirements such as the maximum possible length of (underground) conveyor-belts to be installed.

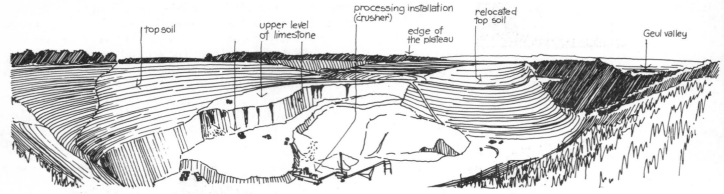

Figure 39.

Example of excavation on top of plateau near Bergh close to proposed ENCI excavation.

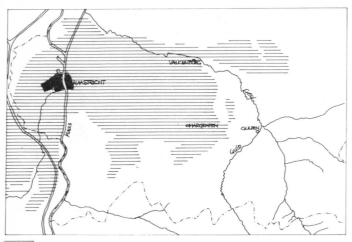

Location of Maastricht limestone.          source: W.H. Felder.

Figure 40.

On the basis of these criteria the number of available sites proved to be limited to two, and these sites were subjected to further study.

One location was fairly similar to the one previously selected by ENCI, that is a large excavation on top of the plateau near Margraten (Figure 41). The other one was sited on the western rim of the plateau. In this location, called Rasberg, the excavation could start from the bottom of the Meuse valley upwards on to the plateau (Figure 42).

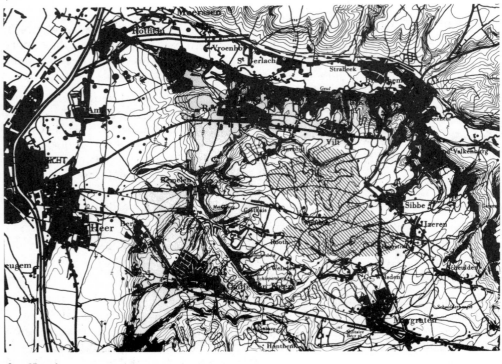

0   05   1
km

Location of quarry on Margraten plateau.

Figure 41.

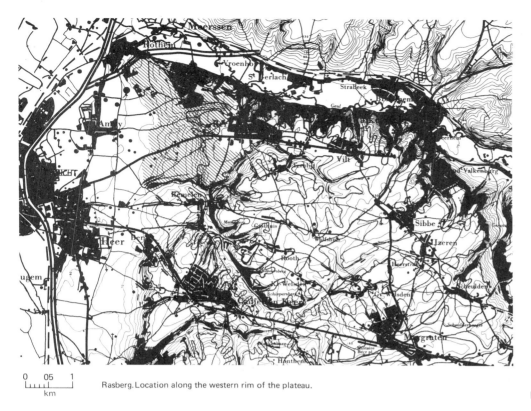

0    05    1
km

Rasberg. Location along the western rim of the plateau.

Figure 42.

## A Comparison of the Sites at Margraten and Rasberg

One can safely say that large-scale quarries as described here, however they are located, designed and operated, will always result in drastic change in an area.

However, large-scale quarrying would not necessarily result in a decrease in the relief of the area or in a less varied topography, which might affect its attraction for tourists. It would be possible to design the finished quarry in such a way that relief is intensified, enhanced locally. New slopes and escarpments could stand out, and be made accessible for recreational activities, or perhaps be used to stimulate new growth of natural vegetation.

Further, there would not be a permanent loss of a large area of *agricultural land*. On the bottom of the excavated area the land could be restored and recultivated. But individual farmers would be temporarily cut off from their land, and they would suffer a severe set-back.

However, severe and permanent damage can be predicted as a result of the disruption of the existing coherent system of plateaus and valleys, which has been described above. Ecological values and spatial quality are based on the existence of spatial variety and structural consistency.

Water flow, its direction, quantity and quality, is a critical factor. Not only run-off along the surface but also percolation through subterranean layers and the permanent buffering capacity of soils under the plateaus are regulating factors. The impact of limestone quarrying on this system varies according to location, shape and size of quarries.

The consequences for the hydrological balance remain an uncertain factor in view of the complex geological situation.

### Rasberg Location

In the case of excavation along the edge of the plateau, the sequence plateau–slope–valley remains essentially intact. A slice of the plateau is removed and a new slope is formed. This slope can be designed to blend into the existing topography, or used to emphasise differences more markedly than under the present conditions.

It is assumed that the hydrological regime will remain more or less the same in character.

Problems will arise as soon as the quarry is enlarged and cuts into the subtle gradients of existing dry vales adjoining

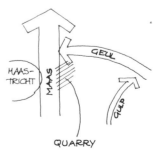

location Rasburg
Quarry connected with the Meuse valley which is the largest in the sequence of water carrying valleys.

Figure 43.

exit into river
steep slopes and coarse grain.    ←————————    upper reaches of dry vales
gentle slopes and fine grain.

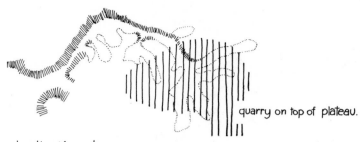

quarry on top of plateau.

location Margraten
Situation of quarry relative to sequence of dry to wet valleys.    Figure 44.

the site on the east side, as it is connected with the Meuse valley which is the largest in the sequence of water-carrying valleys.

### Margraten Location

Excavation on top of the plateau will result in the inversion of land form: a convex land form will turn into a concave one. The diversity in levels, and the typical sequences from high to low will be disturbed or interrupted. Water flow along the surface will be reversed or stopped altogether. Excavation below ground-water level will diminish the the amount of water retained and reduce percolation to the slopes and into the valleys.

The upper reaches of a number of dry vales will be cut off, sequences in scale and form and the existing fine-drawn pattern will be destroyed.

## Conclusion

Regarding the consequences of the two chosen variants (and their sub-variants not shown here) the scale of operations is so large that the establishment of a relation between future quarries and existing land form seems to be very difficult if not impossible to achieve.

However, a comparison between the two locations shows that the situation on the edge of the plateau promises a

better chance for future quality than the other one.

The industry has stuck to its choice of the Margraten location. Important arguments were:

> More limestone available in this area;
> Less top soil has to be removed;
> Precious natural vegetation types are absent here; in consequence less opposition on the part of nature conservation interests is expected;
> The quarry will be invisible from main roads and neighbouring towns; the population in the area will hardly be aware of the activities (excepting a number of farmers).

The last two arguments are an example of pragmatic thinking which ignores the long-term impact on the whole system, but attempts to circumvent immediate drawbacks.

At the time of publication of this condensed version of the report, no official Government reaction is known. The final decision will involve weighing more factors than the environmental impact; for example, the existing local socio-economic system, the employment situation, and the availability of alternative sources of limestone across the national frontiers must be considered.

## Reference

1. LYNCH, K., *The Image of the City,* Harvard University Press, Cambridge, Mass., 1960.

CASE HISTORY TWO
# THE MUSKINGUM WATERSHED CONSERVANCY DISTRICT
## A STUDY IN INTEGRATED LAND USE AND RESOURCE CONSERVATION

John Foster

Situated in the eastern part of the State of Ohio, the watershed of the Muskingum River extends from the edge of Columbus, the state capital, eastwards to within 30 km of the Ohio River which marks the boundary with Pennsylvania. The northernmost limit of the watershed is at Akron, extending south for 160 km to Marietta where the Muskingum River flows into the Ohio. In all, the watershed takes in over 20,700 km², a fifth of the State of Ohio, and is situated within 18 counties.

In many respects the Muskingum Valley is the cradle of Ohio. The Ohio River was the great waterway leading westwards and the Muskingum was the gateway to the territory of Ohio. Its character of hill and valley offered shelter and agricultural opportunity for early settlers. Initially farming was confined to the better lands but, as the valleys became heavily settled, later arrivals were forced up into the higher lands, which they soon discovered produced good crops when cleared. By 1880, less than 20% of the original hardwood forests remained.

The changes from woodland to farmland over more than a century of settlement increased the rate of run-off dramatically, and removed the fertile topsoil which had produced such good yields for the early upland farmers. It has been estimated that during the period of agricultural use an average of 13 cm of topsoil has been removed from the farmlands on the watershed, representing one-half of the soil resources of the basin.

By the turn of the century erosion was making it necessary to convert a large proportion of the cropland to pasture, but this had a low carrying capacity and consequently many farms became unprofitable and had to be abandoned. For those who hung on, farming became an increasingly hard and chancy business, with floods in the spring and drought in the summer regular occurrences.

The severe depression of the local agricultural economy hastened the movement from countryside to city, from farming to industry and commerce, which characterised much of the United States in the early part of the present century. The countryside of the Muskingum watershed had long been sprinkled with small settlements keyed to the farming economy of the area and, as these increased in size, both land and water problems increased. The flood plains became more densely populated and flood losses increased in scale and frequency. More and more industrial and downstream waste was added to streams and rivers already clogged with silt, and pollution became a serious hazard.

A major flood disaster in 1913 cost Ohio the loss of nearly 500 lives and $300 million in damage to property and resulting economic values. Although by no means the only one of its kind experienced in the State, this disaster set in motion the chain of circumstances which eventually, two decades later, established the Muskingum Watershed Conservancy District and allowed it to begin its major task of rehabilitation and development, which today makes the watershed one of the best examples of integrated land use and resource conservation in the United States.

This study describes how the machinery for organising the Muskingum Watershed Conservancy District was set up, how the policies for rehabilitation were worked out, how these policies were translated into action on the ground and how the Muskingum watershed is managed today.

## Enabling Legislation and Early Activity

The first action occurred in the year following the 1913 disaster when the General Assembly of the State of Ohio passed the Conservancy Act, which had the basic purpose of enabling the citizens of a threatened area to work together in planning, financing and managing a flood control project. The Act provided powers enabling a watershed area to be organised into a conservancy district, with the status of a public corporation and power to plan, build and run flood control and conservation projects, issue bonds, levy assessments, raise taxes and enter into contracts with the state and federal governments for any necessary work.

Dayton, in south-west Ohio, the principal city of the Miami Valley, had suffered the greatest loss in lives and property in the 1913 flood and was the first community to make use of the new legislation. By the time the Conservancy Act was passed, the community had already raised $2 million to employ specialists in engineering and law to carry out extensive studies into how future disasters might be avoided. The Conservancy Act enabled the community to organise itself as the Miami Conservancy District. Its flood control project was completed within 10 years and, although in retrospect fairly limited in concept, it was a pioneer enterprise which provided a useful example for similar activities elsewhere and which encouraged interest at federal level in the subject of positive flood control.

## Establishment of the Muskingum Watershed Conservancy District

The people of Muskingum were slower in recovery from the 1913 flood than those of the Miami Valley, for their watershed was much larger and the cost of any control project seemed to them so great as to be impracticable of achievement. This cost difficulty was borne out in 1928 by the results of a local flood control study carried out by the Zanesville Chamber of Commerce. Fortunately, the studies were nevertheless continued and one of the consultants pressed that the flood control project should be broadened to include soil erosion control and water conservation. A drought within the next year emphasised the urgency of the need to take water conservation into account. A new association covering the whole of the Muskingum watershed was organised and, with modest private and state funds, set in train a major study covering the water problems of the whole watershed.

Out of this the Muskingum Watershed Conservancy District was officially established in 1933, under the Conservancy Act of 1914, by a special common pleas court which included a judge from each of the 18 counties within the District. The court appointed a three-member board of directors who established at an early stage four basic heads of policy which have since been followed. These were: (1) that payment of the regular tax on all land acquired should continue; (2) that the raising of income by tax should be kept to a minimum; (3) that duplication of the work of other agencies should be avoided; and (4) that the project should be developed so as to provide the maximum public benefit.

The funding of the project developed on three levels— local, state and federal. First, at local level, the District levied an assessment against 7500 property owners in the watershed who stood to benefit directly from the elimination of flood risk. This assessment came to $12 million, to be payable in half-yearly instalments by the property owners concerned. The District collected the first instalment—a modest $46,000, but enough to get the project started. Remarkably, no further payments have ever been collected; the District always waives them on the grounds that current income is adequate for operational purposes.

The State element of funding derived from the advantages to the State of being free from flood damage to roads and bridges, and to other public lands and utilities. This advantage not only applies within the watershed, but also downriver from it, and it was seen that if there were flooding on the Ohio river and the Mississippi, the Muskingum river system would cease to be a contributing factor to it. The State of Ohio put this interest at $6½ million and contributed accordingly.

The establishment of the Muskingum Conservancy District in 1933 coincided with the announcement by President Roosevelt of his proposed emergency Public Works Programme. The District sought federal support for its project and within a few months the Public Works Administration approved an initial grant of $22½ million for construction operations. Further federal grants were made later to meet the remaining cost elements of the project. The total cost of land acquisition, construction of the 14 dams and accommodation works was $47 million.

Federal interest in the Muskingum project derived from two aspects. First, it was seen as an experiment which might have value in its application to similar problems elsewhere in the U.S. At that time the general practice in flood control was to impound one large lake on the biggest river in the watershed, whereas the earlier studies of Muskingum had favoured a series of small lakes on the headwater rivers. If the Muskingum solution was successful, federal interests reasoned that there would be useful lessons to be learnt to pass on to others.

Secondly, the National Park Service saw in the headwater lakes which would be formed a potential recreational value for the growing communities in the vicinity. The Park Service had learnt from general experience that such communities seldom had the foresight to set aside land at an early enough stage for future recreational needs, and later acquisition was usually very expensive. They were able to put some kind of price-tag on the recreational value of the lakes and this was incorporated in the federal contribution to the overall project.

## Design and Construction of the Project

In the early stages of activity by the Zanesville Chamber of Commerce some years before the Conservancy District was established, the Army Engineers had proposed a single large dam on the main channel of the Muskingum River. However, this would have created a lake some 22 km long, flooding out much of the most valuable land remaining on the watershed. This solution was not seen by those advising the local community as a satisfactory answer to the problem, nor one which would do anything towards stabilising soil erosion. Control in flood situations was considered as becoming progressively more difficult as one moved down from the headwater streams towards the larger rivers, in this case the Muskingum and the Ohio itself.

The engineering advice in favour of a series of small dams on the headwater streams prevailed, and the system was designed on that basis. This solution had the cost advantage of using land in narrow winding valleys which was of little commercial or agricultural value. Fourteen dam sites were selected and further study showed that, in ten of them, by raising the height of the earth dam high enough, they could impound permanent lakes and still have enough storage capacity to be effective for their primary flood control function. By storing the excess water in these 10 lakes and allowing it to flow out gradually, a stable rate of flow downstream was possible, thus assuring a dependable water supply for public and industrial use to the communities within the watershed. In this way, it was argued, the functions of flood control and water conservation could be combined.

Land acquisition for the project amounted to 26,500 ha, with a further 15,500 ha covered by easements to secure an efficient flow system. Of the area acquired, 6500 ha were covered by the 10 permanent lakes, which range in size from 170 to 1400 ha, the other four dam sites being designed to impound water only in times of flood. Over 225 km of highway were rebuilt outside the lake areas, farms and small communities were moved to higher ground, and major public utilities were relocated in the course of executing the project. During the work the Conservancy District—a local authority—successfully supervised the operations of a variety of federal and state agencies—something at that time unusual in the history of major work programmes in the United States.

While construction was going on, the Ohio Conservancy Act was amended to allow recreational facilities to be included in the project. The District had already recognised the opportunities for recreation which the new permanent lakes would provide, and had started to acquire substantial margins of land round each of them where this land was not already within their ownership.

The US Soil Conservation Service assisted with land use studies of the 20,000 ha of land outside the 10 permanent lakes. Most of this land which is generally hilly, was found to be badly eroded. All of it had originally been covered by trees and about 6000 ha still remained in low-grade woodlands. With other advice from the US Forest Service, in order to reduce erosion run-off into the new lakes, it was decided to reforest as much as possible of the adjoining land, comprising the 6000 ha still carrying trees and a fur-

ther 8000 ha of former farmland.

By the time the Muskingum project was officially dedicated in mid-1938, the major engineering works had been completed and the broad lines of policy worked out for the development and management of all the District-owned land. In the following year Congress authorised the US Corps of Army Engineers to take over responsibility for the flood control aspect of management, the Corps having been the construction agency in the first instance. Apart from the dam sites, the District retained full title to all the lands within the project area and responsibility for the recreational development and conservation programme. This co-operative arrangement between the Corps and District has since worked satisfactorily, both in terms of economy of operation and provision of facilities of public benefit.

## Land Use: Forestry

A significant part of the proposed forest planting has been completed with $12\frac{1}{2}$ million trees planted on approximately 5000 ha, and early planting is already yielding a timber crop in addition to the sale of Christmas trees, which has gone on continuously from the outset of the development. The 6000 ha of then existing woodland, much of which has since been improved, comprised mainly deciduous trees and there was public pressure for the new forest areas also to be planted wholly with hardwoods. A start was made on these lines, but hardwoods would not grow on the hot bare hillsides and first planting was therefore undertaken with softwoods, mainly red, white and pitch pine. Now that the ground has become enriched by this planting, hardwoods are pushing back in and are also being introduced wherever practicable to improve variety.

In order to secure as quickly as possible an adequate woodland protection round the lakes to reduce the risk of silting, new methods of planting were developed using a special plough which forms contour ridges, or 'work benches', each about 2 m apart. This ploughing is undertaken up to a year in advance of planting to allow time for the ridges to settle and for water capillaries to become reestablished. A tree-planting machine was also developed which has an average planting rate of around 1300 seedlings an hour when set up for a run.

The District employs its own forestry officer and a small team of foresters, these being augmented by temporary field teams taken on during especially busy times arising from either planting or cropping. For over 20 years the District has run its own sawmill. All costs of forest planting and improvement programmes are met out of sales from felling operations.

## Land Use: Farming

Farming activity on the watershed generally has increased significantly since the completion of the project, not only in the extent of land in productive agriculture, but also in the

Figure 1. Early agricultural improvement of the catchment land around the lakes used contour ploughing methods new to farming in this part of Ohio.

level of economic return consequential on freedom from flood risk, better yields and a real opportunity to plan ahead.

Although much of this farmland has remained in private ownership, the District inevitably took over a considerable area in its acquisition of the 26,500 ha required at the outset for the project. On the advice of the Soil Conservation Service, as already has been said, substantial parts of this District-owned land has been afforested as its most effective and productive use. Nevertheless, over 5000 ha have remained as open farmland, with further usable land in the beds of the four damsites designed to impound water only in flood conditions.

The 400 farm units which existed when the District took over the land have now been reduced to 150. These are widely scattered over the watershed and, from an initial policy of improvement and thereafter management by the District, there has been a change to tenant-holding and, where it does not interfere with efficiency of watershed operations, some transfer back into private ownership. In particular, most of the croplands in the dry reservoirs have been sold, subject to appropriate flood-water storage easements.

It was seen as particularly important, from the outset of farming operations within the District ownership, to undertake a careful consolidation of the individual areas of farmland into economically viable units and to secure the earliest possible improvement of the quality of the soil for better crop yields. Thereafter, tenancy and sometimes outright sale, with suitable safeguards for watershed interests, has been seen as making overall management sense, at the same time contributing usefully to the income of the district. An advisory service, covering farm methods to avoid the recurrence of soil erosion and to improve cropping potential, is available to farm tenants and others, from the District's farm management staff.

## Land Use: Recreation

The recreational element of the Muskingum project was built into its design after work had started on the basic

provision for flood control and soil and water conservation. Today recreation is seen by the public as one of the greatest and most obvious benefits from the whole development. At the time that the National Park Service first estimated the recreational value of the project as a factor to be taken into account in the amount of federal support for its construction, the figure arrived at was $807,000 a year. Today the annual value is many times this amount, with the probability that recreational benefits will increase at an ever more rapid rate than those deriving from flood control. District-owned recreational facilities receive over 8 million visitors a year, mainly from among the 15 million people who live within $2\frac{1}{2}$ hours' drive of them.

The early acquisition of the land around all of the 10 permanent lakes has ensured that development has been adequately controlled, and has made possible the dedication of a strip of shoreline 30 m wide for public use for all time. The policy of the District has been to limit commercial recreational provision to 20% of the 585 km of lakeshore, and to keep one of the lakes free from development by surrounding it completely with woodlands. Along the shores of the other nine lakes there are pleasant wooded parks, with bathing beaches, playgrounds and picnic areas, all served by informal car parks, generally situated among trees well back from the shoreline. There are 53 holiday cottages available to rent at a number of locations, and camp sites are liberally provided for use by permit. There is also a 100-bed holiday lodge, two golf courses and a lighted ski slope with snow-making equipment.

Boating and fishing are popular pastimes on the lakes. The marina concessionnaires have boats for hire, and visitors bringing their own craft pay a licence fee and can use the launching facilities provided. The problem of noise is recognised, and for those who choose a motor rather than sail there is a 10-horse-power maximum on six of the lakes, with a varying maximum on three others up to 165 horse-power. On the tenth lake—Pleasant Hill—there

Figure 2. (Opposite) Of the ten lakes within the Muskingum Conservancy District, six are located in the eastern part of the watershed, well placed to serve the recreational needs of the substantial population resident in the vicinity.

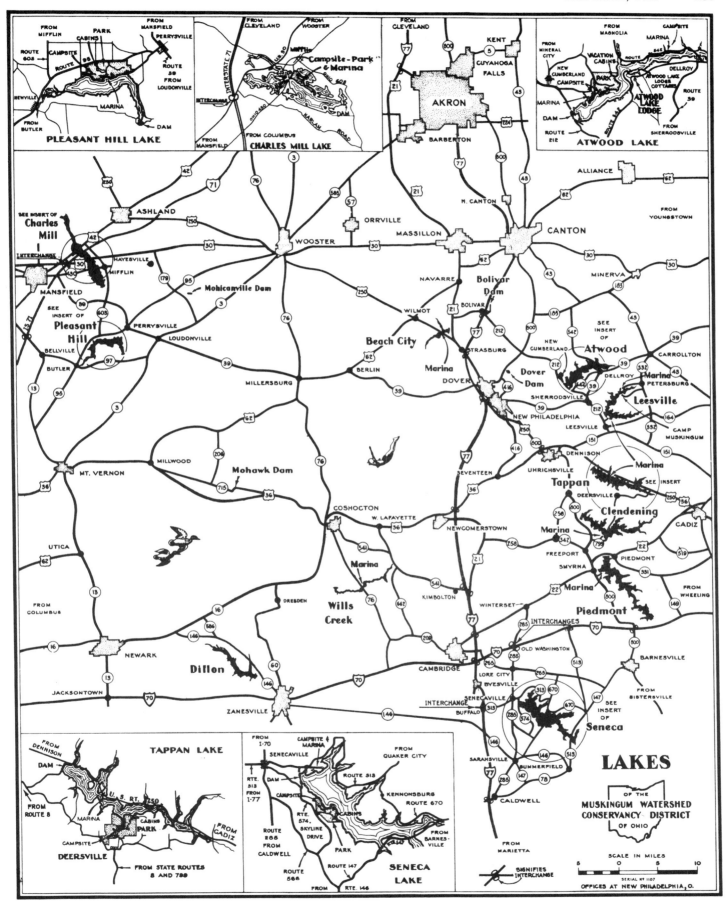

### PLEASANT HILL LAKE
FROM MIFFLIN
PARK CABINS
FROM MANSFIELD
PERRYSVILLE
ROUTE 603
CAMPSITE
ROUTE 95
ROUTE 39 FROM LOUDONVILLE
NEWVILLE
FROM BUTLER
MARINA
DAM

### CHARLES MILL LAKE
FROM CLEVELAND
FROM WOOSTER
INTERSTATE 71
MIFFLIN
US 30
Campsite-Park & Marina
OHIO 603
OHIO 430
INTERCHANGE
MARLIN ROAD
DAM
FROM MANSFIELD
FROM COLUMBUS

FROM CLEVELAND
800
KENT
5
77
CUYAHOGA FALLS
21
43
AKRON
224
BARBERTON

### ATWOOD LAKE
FROM MAGNOLIA
CAMPSITE
MARINA
FROM MINERAL CITY
VACATION CABINS
ROUTE 542
NEW CUMBERLAND
PARK
DELLROY
ATWOOD LAKE LODGE COTTAGES
CAMPSITE
ATWOOD LAKE LODGE
ROUTE 39
MARINA
DAM
ROUTE 212
FROM SHERRODSVILLE

### LAKES
OF THE
MUSKINGUM WATERSHED
CONSERVANCY DISTRICT
OF OHIO

### TAPPAN LAKE
FROM DENNISON
DAM
FROM ROUTE 8
U.S. RT. 250
MARINA
PARK
CABINS
CAMPSITE
DEERSVILLE
FROM CADIZ
FROM STATE ROUTES 8 AND 788

### SENECA LAKE
FROM I-70
SENECAVILLE
Campsite & Marina
FROM QUAKER CITY
RTE. 313 FROM I-77
DAM
ROUTE 313
CAMPSITE
KENNONSBURG ROUTE 670
RTE. 574 SKYLINE DRIVE
ROUTE 285 FROM CALDWELL
PARK
CABINS
FROM BARNESVILLE
ROUTE 147
ROUTE 568
FROM RTE. 146

SIGNIFIES INTERCHANGE

SCALE IN MILES
5    0    5    10

SERIAL NY 1107
OFFICES AT NEW PHILADELPHIA, O.

Figure 3.    Holiday cottages owned by the Conservancy District at four of the lakes are well situated among trees with good access to the water for recreation.

Figure 4.    Fishing is one of the most popular pastimes on the lakes and catches are substantial both in number and size.

is no horse-power limit, but a speed limit of 10 km/h operates on a portion of it. A number of private sailing clubs have facilities for which they pay a rent to the District.

Of all the attractions offered, fishing is probably the greatest. The lakes are so well populated with fish that there is no official close season. Nevertheless, to keep up quantity and quality, a corrective stocking programme is operated by the District on the advice of the Ohio Division of Wildlife. Hunting is also popular, with geese, duck, squirrel, fox, grouse and pheasant as the main attractions for sportsmen.

The District has followed a policy of making recreation self-supporting across the board, recognising that some

elements, such as playgrounds, cannot pay their way, while others can and do produce substantial revenues in relation to their capital and running costs. The total capital investment in recreational facilities so far is of the order of $8·5 million.

### Off-Site Benefits

The benefits within the watershed are by no means limited to District lands. Reference has already been made to the general improvement in the local farming economy, both in terms of much improved crop yields and capital investment in forestry on the less fertile areas. Some farmers, and landowners too, have gone in for a crop of another kind, either selling off some of their land in plots for holiday cottages or building these themselves for sale or to rent.

The communities in the vicinity of the lakes, some of them relocated as part of the construction operations, are prospering in providing services for the many visitors who pass through them during the year. Retail businesses have expanded greatly, with new shops selling recreational equipment for sailing, fishing and hunting, while motels, restaurants and cafes provide accommodation and refreshment. In these communities too, and in others more remote from the lakes, but still enjoying the benefits of flood control and water conservation within the watershed, new industries have become established over the years. These have not only held the population which was drifting away to less flood-prone areas in the 1920s and 1930s, but have brought in new population to settle and revitalise long-established villages.

## The Policies Reviewed

In describing earlier the setting-up of the District and its board of directors, reference was made to four heads of policy which were established at the outset. These have been operated consistently now for over 40 years, and have been an important element in the success of the project, both in terms of its financial stability and its public acceptability.

The first of these four policies concerned the payment of taxes. Until 1959 the District continued to pay the regular real estate tax on all the land within its ownership. A State tax amendment of two years earlier allowed this tax to be reduced, something which was considered to be justified by the substantial increase in tax valuations which by then had flowed from the District's programme for flood control and soil and water conservation. To date, however, despite this reduction in its liabilities, the District has paid over $1 million in taxes.

The second policy was that the raising of income by tax should be kept to a minimum. Apart from the one modest

claims to be the only governmental agency in the US that both pays taxes and operates without the benefit of any tax revenues.

The third policy which the District has observed throughout its programme has been concerned with avoiding duplication of its work with the activities of other agencies. It is this policy, carefully followed, which has been mainly responsible for the financial success of the project. Rather than set up new specialised development and management organisations to undertake particular aspects of the project, the District has brought in already existing agencies for specific tasks. During the main construction period in the depression years of the 1930s, as many as 20 different government agencies were helping the District. At federal level, expertise and development resources were brought in from such agencies as the Corps of Engineers and the Geological Survey, while at state level supporting agencies included the Department of Highways and the Divisions of Wildlife, Forestry and Watercraft.

The last of the four policies is in some respects the most remarkable and is one in which the District has in particular been a pioneer body. The initial concept of developing its facilities to provide the maximum public benefit first produced the idea of designing the reservoirs to provide for water conservation as well as flood control. This was followed by a programme for their development for recreational purposes and at the time of completion the reservoirs increased the State of Ohio's inland lake area by 50%. Not only has this concern with recreational provision improved the natural environment of the reservoirs more than might otherwise have been the case, but the income from the facilities, combined with that from forestry and farming activities, makes a valuable and continuing contribution to the District's operational costs.

# Conclusion

Based on studies done by the Corps of Engineers, the flood control benefits afforded by the Muskingum project were valued at $327 million by 1976, of which almost 80% were allocated to the Ohio and Mississippi valleys completely outside the Muskingum watershed. This, it will be remembered, was the justification—in anticipation of the event—for Federal and State levels of Government making contributions towards the initial capital costs of constructing the reservoirs.

It may be argued that there is little in the Muskingum project which could be said to have been new in engineering terms at the time of its design, except perhaps the principle of damming the headwater valleys rather than the main river. Nevertheless, the project was a remarkable demonstration of self-help by a relatively small group of communities sharing a common watershed and, in retrospect, points up both the value of undertaking thorough studies before starting work on the ground and the wisdom of establishing sound policy objectives at the outset and keeping strictly to them thereafter.

In terms of size, Muskingum is one of about 200 smaller watersheds in the US. Some of these have drawn direct benefit from following the Muskingum experience in designing and carrying out their own flood control and soil and water conservation schemes. Perhaps, in retrospect, it is in this aspect of providing for use by others a proven formula for combining national resources with local control, that the Muskingum Watershed Conservancy District has made its greatest contribution in the field of resource conservation and the integration of land use.

# LANDSCAPE PLANNING IN THE RHINELAND BROWN COAL AREA

G. Olschowy

The encroachments of opencast mining have a deep impact upon the landscape, its natural balance and its visual features. In the Federal Republic of Germany, limestone, iron ore, and brown coal are mined in opencast mines. The size and number of mines in the Lower Rhine makes this area a focus of interest, especially for environmental protection and landscape management. Legal control of land use zoning and landscape planning during and after mining are vital to reclamation and restoration of agricultural landscape. Planning has to start at an early stage in order that the mining plan and the landscape plan can be coordinated.

The division of the landscape plan into an assessment part and a development part has proved successful in the Rhineland Brown Coal Area. The basic part includes the survey of natural resources, the effects of excavation on individual landscape factors and the results of ecological studies. From analysis of these studies possibilities and restraints in reconstructing the landscape are distinguished. Finally the development part of the landscape plan contains the necessary measures for the protection, management, and development of the landscape.

## Introduction

The brown coal deposits in the Lower Rhine area are the most important in the Federal Republic and the largest coherent brown coal area in Europe. The area is about 2500 km$^2$ extending from the area Brühl–Bonn–Euskirchen in the south-east to the Dutch border via Mönchengladbach–Rheydt in the north-west. The southern border fringes the Eifel, and the eastern border the Rhine.

The coal seams in the Rhine district, up to about 100 m thick (averaging 40 m), were disturbed by numerous dislocations. The seams originated in the Mid-Tertiary, 12 to 20 million years ago, at the transition between the Oligocene and the Miocene and during the Miocene. The *Sequoia* played a major role in the formation of the coal. The virgin forest also included *Nyssa, Tsuga,* and *Taxociaca.* Because the seams were not exposed to such intense pressures and temperatures as those developed during the formation of mountains in other areas, the coal in the Rhineland area is only in the brown coal stage. The total supplies of brown coal have been estimated at $55 \times 10^{12}$ metric tons, of which $10 \times 10^{12}$ metric tons are exploitable by present-day techniques in opencast mining.

According to natural land classifications, the brown coal area belongs to the Lower Rhine Bay. The Bay forms a triangle between the Eifel mountains and Bergische Land mountains, and extends to the south-east into the Rheinische Schiefergebirge. Through a tectonic incision, a settling plain evolved which, since the end of the Tertiary, has been filled with Pliocene shingle and major terrace shingle, sands and clay of the primeval Rhine, the primeval Maas, Erft and Ruhr. In addition, in the northern part of the brown coal area there are loess covers of different thicknesses originating from aeolian deposits on the major and middle terraces. The extensive loess loam layers are called *Börde* because of their exclusive use for agriculture. Later occurring tectonic movements and deep cracks displaced and tilted the deposited layers. From this, three major layers evolved. The most important layer is the Ville layer which clearly stands out morphologically as foothills. The 'Ville' is a long narrow range of about 40 km, at a height of 160 m above sea level in the north. Its width varies from approximately 2·5 to 8 km. The Ville extends in a south-east to north-west direction between the Rhine and Erft valleys.

In this area the coal seam was so close to the surface that it was easily excavated over a thin layer of Rhine shingle, sands, and clay.

When exploitation started in the southern part of the Brown Coal Area, the depth of overburden was 10 to 20 m. The proportion of waste material to coal was 0·3 to 1. The situation changed when operations expanded to the north. At the present time, opencast mines in the Inden area are over 100 m and in the northern area 250 m deep. In the near future the depth of overburden removed will reach 400 m and the ratio of overburden to coal will be between 4:1 and 6:1.

## Effects of Opencast Mining Upon the Landscape

The large-scale and intensive exploitation of brown coal in opencast mines results in deep encroachments upon the landscape and its natural balance. This is particularly true of the *water balance* of the area, making extensive hydrological measures necessary; but the subject of this case study does not permit an in-depth discussion of the hydrological problems. It only needs to be said that in an area of 2700 km² the damage through water deficiencies for the population, agriculture, and industry must be avoided or adjusted if possible, the outfall of waterways regulated, and the sewage problem solved.

In order to keep the groundwater away from the mining area, a series of wells are installed around the excavations. Through drainage, the water table is lowered to pit level.

Figure 1.   View into a large-scale brown coal opencast mine. It can be seen how the coal layers were dislocated by tectonic forces, and how the thickness of overburden varies.

*(Photo: Professor Olschowy)*

The pumped groundwater flows via the Erft and a specially built canal into the Rhine. The pumps discharge about 30 m³ of water per second. On the average, 13,000 litres of groundwater must be pumped before a ton of brown coal is mined.

Since opencast mining involves the removal of overburden, the entire cultivated landscape is used and the *relief of the landscape* is completely altered. The overburden is used, as much as possible, to refill the coal excavation sites. However the excess material is deposited in large tips which reach a height of 100 m and a volume of 270 million m³.

The incorporation of such tips into the agricultural and forest landscape creates particularly difficult landscape planning problems. In addition, difficulties arise from the relocation of farms, villages, roads, water courses, and railways. The loess obtained by mining operations—a welcome present of nature—must be utilised. These considerations show how closely large-scale opencast mining must be related to landscape ecology and design. Hardly anywhere else do the different interests conflict so much as in the Rhineland Brown Coal Area. Agriculture is endangered because it has to give up its best loess areas. The counties ceased to be agrarian some time ago and are already, to a great extent, industrialised. The population, especially from the nearby large city of Cologne, requires adequate recreational areas with manifold facilities. It is by planning and organisation that these problems can be solved. It is obvious that the cultivated landscape, which must be reconstructed after the termination of the large opencast mines, must be formed differently from in the past. The Rhineland Brown Coal Area offers the opportunity to design a landscape for the future which can be realised using the latest scientific data, years of practical experience and progressive development trends.

## Legal Foundations

Securing organised planning in the Rhineland Brown Coal Area necessitates a special legal foundation. On 25 April 1950 the 'Act for Comprehensive Planning in the Rhineland Brown Coal Area' (Gesetz für die Gesamtplanung im Rheinischen Braunkohlengebiet) was passed by the State Parliament of the Nordrhein-Westfalen Länder. Under this law, a master plan for the Area must be drawn up within the framework of the North Rhine-Westphalia State Planning Law. The planning area which includes the counties contained within the Brown Coal Area, is 1500 km². The master plan, which can be drawn up in sections, contains:

1. Determination of areas in which mining and other industrial operations can be located, and of the areas which are reserved for agricultural and forestry use;

2. Determination of towns, sections of towns, or single buildings which in the interest of mining need to be terminated, and their relocation sites;

3. Determination of areas in which roads, railway lines, and power and water lines can be located, re-located, or terminated;

4. Planning of waterways;

5. Agriculture and forest reclamation;

6. Agriculture and forestry and general landscape and nature management.

The amendment of the General Mining Act, which was also passed on 25 April 1950, determines that the mining authority also supervises the 'securing and zoning of land use and landscape planning during and after the mining operation'.

Also, on the date stated, an Act concerning the establishment of a community chest was enacted. This Act ensures community liability for reclamation measures in the Rhineland Brown Coal Area. Contributions to this 'chest' are mandatory; one German penny per ton of raw coal excavated. In this way, recultivation is financially secured in the event that the mining company is unable to pay upon termination of the mining project.

Under the General Mining Act only general reclamation responsibility is regulated. The Act was made more concrete by an agreement between the 'Rheinische Braunkohlenwerke AG' and the North Rhine-Westphalia State Government on 7 March 1961 and amended on 13 June 1966. It regulates the fill of loess overburden for reclaiming agricultural areas.

## Scientific Studies

Ecological and resource research, as a basis for all planning and especially landscape planning, is particularly difficult in an opencast mining area. Difficulties originate because the sites, for example the tips, have not been studied although landscape planning has been undertaken. Here the issue is to analyse the used overburden material, especially the soil to be used as fill—its water balance, nutritional and calcareous contents and its erosion vulnerability. The result of agro-meteorological studies on similar sites must be evaluated. If necessary, model tips must be built and their reactions to wind in a wind tunnel determined. Also, in comparison with related sites and older tips, it can be determined what potential natural vegetation will develop on reclaimed areas and what natural factors in the use and design of the planning area must be considered.

In the past years, with the support of the State of North Rhine-Westphalia and the 'Rheinische Braunkohlenwerke

AG', a series of valuable scientific studies was completed. These studies include: pedological research and loess studies of the Geological State Council in Krefeld, North Rhine-Westphalia, and the State Institute for Pollution and Soil-Use Protection in Essen; studies on slurry areas carried out at the Institute of Plant Cultivation, Bonn University; the ecological and ornithological studies in the old southern part of the mining area by the Regional Institution for Nature Conservation and Landscape Management in Aachen; the agro-meteorological measurements on tips by the German Meteorological Service; the wind tunnel experiments by the Technical University, Hannover; mapping of vegetation in the Erft valley and studies of vegetational succession carried out by the Federal Research Centre for Nature Conservation and Landscape Ecology in Bonn-Bad Godesberg. The elaborate landscape planning expert reports were based on the results of these studies.

The Federal Research Centre for Nature Conservation and Landscape Ecology undertook the establishment of a permanent vegetation plot on a newly deposited tip inside an excavation from which the brown coal had been removed. This experimental plot serves as a study area for the natural succession and development of vegetation on such an artificial site. Continuous observations from the first settlement of pioneer flora and fauna on raw soil via several stages to the forest stage have, until now, been unavailable when disregarding short-term observations. Within the first year of observation, 42 species of phanerogamic plants invaded the virgin soil.

## Master Plan—Operating Plan—Landscape Plan

The *master plan* for reclamation, which is legally required in the Brown Coal Mining Act, must be drawn up by the Rhineland Brown Coal Area Planning Committee, a special council of the Rhineland State Planning Association. The State Minister of North Rhine-Westphalia, as the State Planning Authority, declares the reclamation plan binding.

The General Mining Act only allows mining operations to function according to an *operating plan* which is approved by the Mining Authority. In the Rhineland Brown Coal Area the operating plans must additionally be co-ordinated with the master plan. These operating plans present details of the future design of the area including: relief design; water drainage; water storage; road access; agricultural and forest use; farm locations, etc.

The content of the operating plan is closely related to the landscape plan and landscape development. Therefore the 'Rheinische Braunkohlenwerke AG' requires that a *landscape plan* must be drawn up for every opencast mine that will be reclaimed. The landscape plan becomes binding

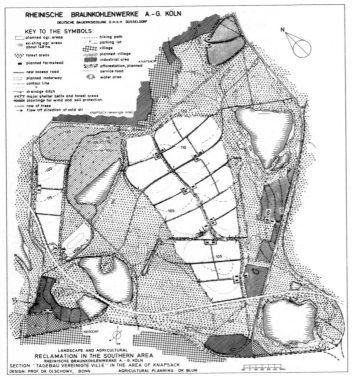

Figures 2 and 3.   Examples of landscape and agricultural reclamation plans.

through integration into the operating plan or as a detail plan of the operating plan. The measures of the operating plan are detailed in the landscape plan, for example, the design of the area's surface to prevent soil erosion by surface water.

Since the recreation factor is playing an important part in the Rhineland Brown Coal Area the planning and development of recreation areas must be incorporated in the landscape plan. For the establishment of recreation areas, sufficient natural resources such as forests, meadows, open valleys, alternating relief, and water areas must be available. The value of a recreation area is not measured by the size of its forest but by the border areas between forest and field, and water and land. These are the areas which people are looking for and which can be used as a scale for the recreation value of the landscape. The natural potential of the area must then be supplemented by suitable recreation facilities. Large-scale recreation areas are normally equipped with a sufficient number of parking lots at their periphery, circular walks for car drivers who have to return to their cars, paths for people who want to venture farther into the landscape and forests and who want to discover nature by foot, bicycle, and horseback riding paths. Access roads to natural and historical monuments as focal points have to be built as well as viewpoints, huts, sanitary installations, and hostels. It is also very important that beaches are pro-

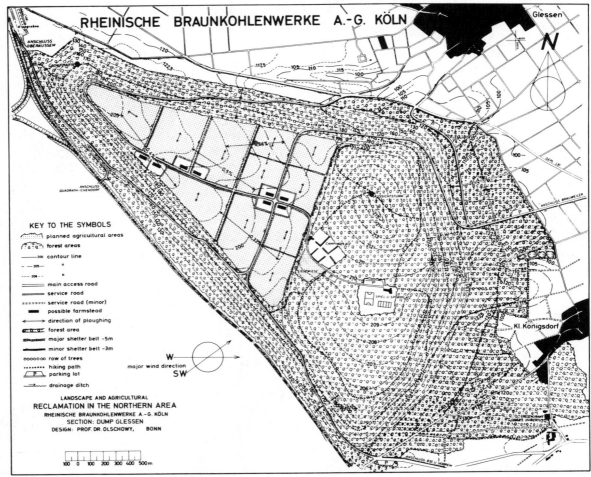

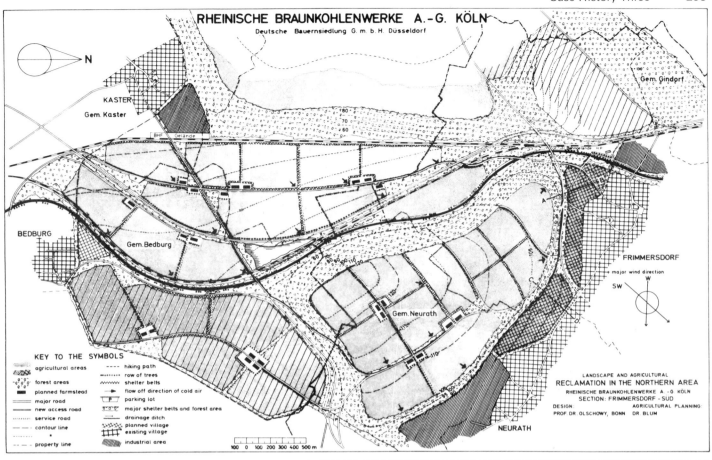

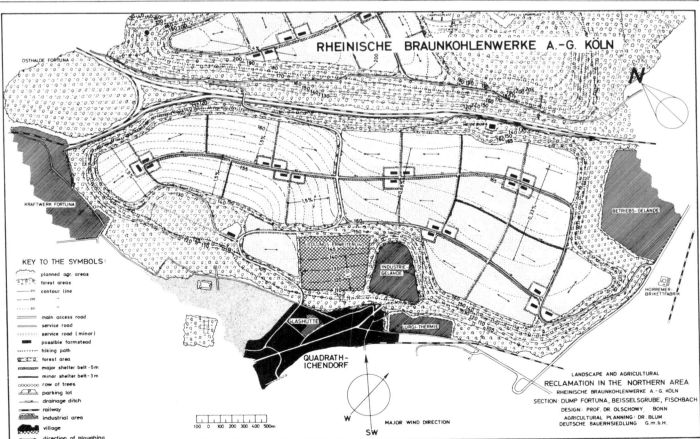

Figures 4 and 5.  Examples of landscape and agricultural reclamation plans.

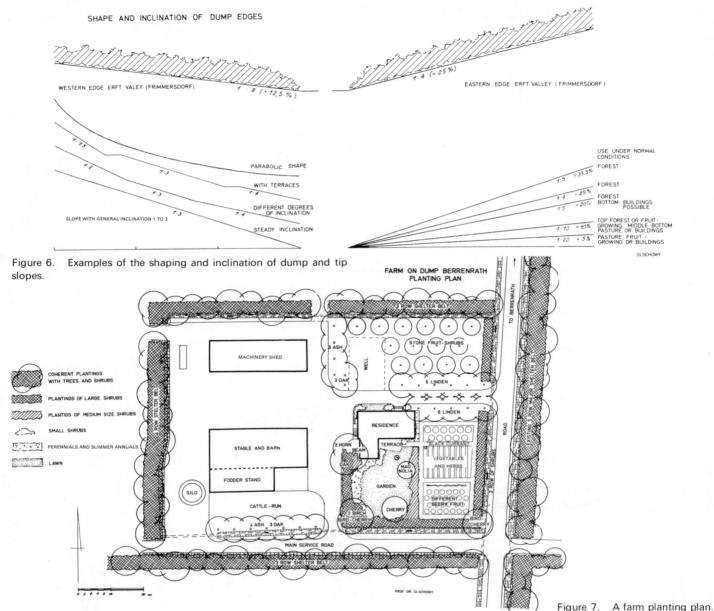

Figure 6.    Examples of the shaping and inclination of dump and tip slopes.

Figure 7.    A farm planting plan.

vided at the lakes that remain after opencast mining. The separate detail plans of the landscape plan contain specifications about the moulding of dump and pit slopes, the design of the banks of water areas, the establishment of shelter belts and forest border areas, and the planting of farms and hamlets.

## Measures for Reclamation and Landscape Development

*Relocation* of single farms into villages is the most difficult task involved with opencast mining. Up to the end of 1976 23,600 individuals and 4300 residences, including property, had been relocated in the Rhineland Brown Coal Area and

further relocation is planned. Most of the new residences will be attached to already existing villages in order to meet the tendency for intensification of housing areas and to make better use of existing infrastructure. The development plans for the new sites are drawn up in cooperation with a qualified city planner.

For the relocation of farms, it was intended, at first, that the farmsteads be placed adjacent to the consolidated farmland. It was later recognised that it was better that the farmsteads be consolidated as hamlets or small villages. This type of consolidation makes access easier, allows for better adjustments to changes in agricultural structure, and promotes cooperation. In order to receive constructive suggestions for the relocation of farms, the Minister of Food, Agriculture and Forestry for the State North Rhine-Westphalia, set up in 1966 a European idea competition for a 830-ha reclaimed area having the theme 'The New

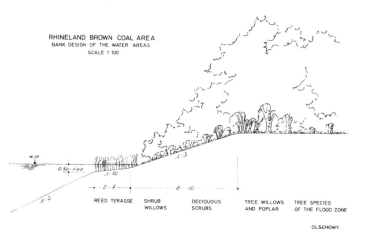

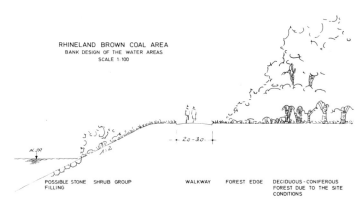

Figure 8.    Design of banks of water areas.

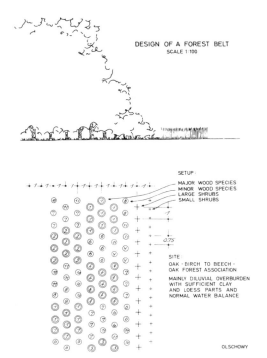

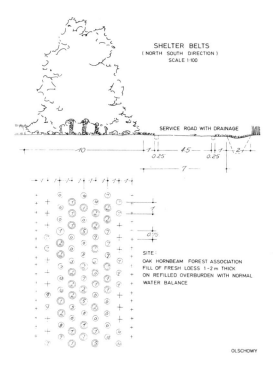

Figure 9.    Design of forest and shelterbelts.

Agrarian Community in Reclaimed Economic Areas'. The proposals received ranged from the conservative single farmsteads to complete integration of farmsteads to business and land-use cooperatives. The jury for the competition decided in favour of a plan having three focal settlements, which also emphasised the concentration of businesses.

The new farms are surrounded by shelterbelts as a result of planting plans and are connected to the afforestation which surrounds the cultivated areas.

*Agricultural reclamation measures* are determined to a great extent by the available loess material in the north and west of the area. The layers reach a thickness of up to 20 m. It is mainly young fresh loess, very calcareous, with relatively little clay and much fine sand. In a natural profile, the above-mentioned loess is overlain by its weathered product, the loess loam, which develops into a soil containing a high percentage of adhesive material. The value of the loess soil for agriculture lies in the high calcerous content and in its average pore volume of almost 50%, which results in a good air and water balance. On the other hand, experience and studies have shown that, when the loess is excavated and then deposited in another area, it will soon develop a poor water balance and will become very vulnerable to erosion caused by water run-off. Due to this vulnerability to erosion, newly created arable lands should have a slope less than 1·5%. This is especially necessary when shaping the dumps for agricultural purposes.

Depending upon the distance from the origin of the loess material, the new areas destined for agricultural use are covered with loess layers of 1 to 2 m. A loess covering of this thickness results in optimum yields. Of the different methods of placing loess on the restored lands, two types have proved to be most effective: (1) spreading with large machines, and (2) flooding with loess slurry (wet procedure). In exceptional cases, filling is done by trains, trucks or conveyor belts. In the so-called 'wet procedure', loess and water are mixed in a 1 to 1·5 ratio. The mixture is poured on the tip area into previously established polders of 3 ha. Studies of the value of the slurry soil for agricultural use show that one year after cultivation the loess placed on the lands by this method has a higher pore volume than the loess remaining on its natural sites. Original loess areas cultivated in the normal manner show a pore volume of about 46%. Loess layers put on the reclaimed lands by the 'dry procedure' show figures between 43 and 45%. But loess layers put on the lands by the 'wet procedure' reach a pore volume of 48 to 50% after 12 months of cultivation. The impressive figures primarily originate from the high calcareous content of the loess. In addition the figures are influenced by the desiccation of the loess following the swelling of the soil particles when they were in contact with water. By this desiccation, hollow spaces which fill up with air are created.

It is notable that the slurry procedure creates completely flat areas and it is possible to organise the sloped tip areas into horizontal polders, which are advantageous to soil protection, especially erosion. In order to prepare the loess

Figure 10.    Loess water slurry in a ratio of 1 to 1.5 is pumped into established polders of 3 ha. The areas are later used for agriculture.

(*Photo by courtesy of Rheinische Braunkohlenwerke AG*)

slurry area for agricultural use, deep-rooted crops must be cultivated; alfalfa and a special variety of clover (Steinklee) are especially suitable. Both crops produce, to a great extent, organic substances which enrich the soil with nitrogen. Alfalfa with its 7–8 m roots also supplies the deep areas.

By the end of 1976 the reclaimed agricultural areas in the Rhineland Brown Coal Area amounted to 4565 ha, 1151 ha since 1970.

There is long experience in forest reclamation. By the end of 1976, 5400 ha were reclaimed with forest. In 1968–1976, on the average about 160 ha (2·1 million plants) were afforested each year by the forest department of the Rheinische Braunkohlenwerke AG. The oldest plantations were founded nearly 50 years ago.

The afforestations, initiated in the 1920s, contain an extremely high variety of tree species. During the first systematic afforestations, which were orientated towards the securing and planting of the pit slopes, tree species with intensive roots were preferred such as locust (*Robinia pseudoacacia*), common alder (*Alnus glutinosa*), and grey alder (*Alnus incana*). During and after World War II there was a lack of cultivation. Since 1950, the lack has been compensated with huge poplar plantations.

At the end of the 1950s, the poplar and alder plantations, which can be called pre-forests, were replaced with indigenous deciduous species. The latter were mixed with poplar which served as an umbrella. In these plantations the beech tree dominated, followed by different varieties of oak, maple, elm, linden and cherry trees, and other indigenous species of the natural forest. Plantation of the mentioned species without first planting the pioneer forest is possible through the use of forest gravel. Forest gravel is a diluvial mixture of gravel, sand, and shingle from the first section of the opencast mine. Since 1960, this mixture, judged best by soil scientists, is used for forest recultivations in a thickness of 3–5 m. The nutritional supply and the physical structure allow the roots to go deep. Despite the low water table and the relatively small water capacity, the mixture has a good water balance.

In determining forest reclamation areas two measures are used. Agriculture areas must be separated and protected from industrial and residential areas by wide forest strips. In addition, the wide edges of the tips which originate from their integration into the landscape are planted with indigenous forest associations.

The tips create a number of severe problems for good landscape *design*, but they can be used to provide a dynamic and varied scenery. Moulding of the tip edges proves to be a most important factor for blending into the surrounding landscape. The shape must be designed so that there will be no abrupt changes from the tips to their surroundings and wind currents will be led upwards without causing undesirable effects. To acheive these two aims, the slope of the edges has to show a ratio of inclination not steeper than 1 to 3. Broad steps or terraces must be constructed to prevent erosion, and afforestation should be the principal method of revegetation.

As enough material to fill all the excavations is not available, ground water runs into the depressions and turns them into artificial lakes. The 39 lakes and ponds cover a total area of 472 ha. The lakes and ponds in the older southern portion of the mining area determine the character of the landscape. In the plans of the area, the use of the different lakes is determined. The Heider Bergsee and the Liblarsee in the southern portion as well as the Echtzer See

Figure 12.    The Obersee near Liblar in the southern part of the Rhineland Brown Coal Area is a reclaimed water area which serves as a bird reserve as well as for pisciculture.

(*Photo by courtesy of Rheinische Braunkohlenwerke AG*)

and the Dürener See in the western portion will mainly serve as recreation areas. Public beaches with sand beaches, boat rentals and camping areas, as well as water-skiing areas and sailing areas, will be established. The 'Kierdorfer Teiche' and many smaller ponds with their surroundings in the southern portion which are not in the close vicinity of roads are designed as habitats for wildlife, especially birds, certain game species, and fish populations. This area will serve as a reserve and be kept separate from mass tourism. The value for recreation or as an ecological asset must be judged by how well the lakeshores have been designed and constructed. They should be kept nearly flat, with an inclination not steeper than 1 in 3, and without any sharp incisions at the foot or the upper end of the slope, so that the transition to adjacent levels is smooth. Lakesides to be used for bathing must be levelled to a slope of 1 in 10. Lakes to be used for fishing must have some steep banks to serve as shelter for the fish; also, flatter portions should be set aside for spawning. Such lakesides should be designed to fit into the surroundings through the use of the indigenous vegetation. Through these measures, the environment will be created for water fauna as well as for birds. Permanent protection of the lakeshore has to be achieved and biological self-purification of the water must be promoted.

The oldest artificial lakes in the southern portion are in the meantime so well integrated into the landscape that their flora and fauna do not differ from those of natural lakes. In the lake areas, wildlife is especially rich in birds.

The northern and western portion of the Rhineland Brown Coal Area is mainly reclaimed for agricultural use while the central portion is increasingly afforested. In the southern portion reforestation measures are already dominant. Because of the large water areas, the southern part of the mining area offers good *recreation facilities* for the

Figure 11.    The Heider Bergsee in the southern part of the Rhineland Brown Coal area is designated for recreational use. The lake is used for bathing and sailing. In the surrounding area many recreational facilities are installed such as camping grounds, boat rentals, beaches, parking lots, and restaurants.

(*Photo by courtesy of Rheinbraun/Kramp*)

Figure 13.    The Villenhofener Maar is one of the older lakes in the southern part of the Rhineland Brown Coal Area. Due to its flat banks a natural vegetation has developed so that the artificial lake cannot be differentiated from a natural water area.

*(Photo by courtesy of Rheinische Braunkohlenwerke AG)*

inhabitants of the city of Cologne and the North Rhine-Westphalia industrial district. Already some larger areas have been opened to the public, for example, a hilly forest area totalling 644 ha in the area of Fortuna, Glessen, Horrem, and Quadrath-Ichendorf, and a forest lake area of about 2000 ha in the southern portion near the cities of Brühl and Liblar. Here there is a beautiful and impressive scenery of lakes, forests, and hills which is to a great extent protected as a 'landscape reserve' (Landschaftsschutzgebiet). The 'landscape reserve' was included in the 'Naturpark Kottenforst'.

Some ecologically very valuable sections, especially landscapes along water courses, have been proposed as 'nature reserves' (Naturschutzgebiet) which means that no alterations in the areas are allowed without the permission of the nature conservation authority. Access was provided through paths, shelters were built and a deer park including red deer and fallow deer was set up. Motor vehicles are prohibited in the recreation area. The association 'Erholungspark Ville e.V.' was founded for the development and maintenance of the recreation area. The increasing recreation traffic has to be constantly considered in the landscape plan of the reclaimed area. This can be achieved by the right composition of forests, forest strips, hedge plantings, and shelter belts. Hiking paths must connect forests, lakes, and also farm areas which are made attractive by the above-mentioned hedge plantings and shelter belts. The recreational use of forests has to be considered in the reafforestation and restructuring of the forest areas in the southern portion. Attempts must be made to achieve a synthesis between the timber yield on the one hand and recreational use of the forest on the other hand. In order to reach an almost natural forest, lumbering is only allowed in single cuts.

## Final Remarks

By order of the Federal Ministry of City Planning and Housing Development, a federal competition was conducted under the theme 'Industry and Landscape'. Sixty-four industries and businesses of all sizes throughout the Federal Republic of Germany participated in the competition. Among the participants were members of the metal, chemical, and mining industries. In the competition the following criteria were used for judging: correct choice of sites in co-ordination with regional and land use planning; integration into the surrounding landscape with good city planning, organisation, and building design, as well as measures for environmental protection.

In this first competition, which was decided in 1969, the 'Rheinische Braunkohlenwerke AG' in Cologne was awarded the gold medal. Its problems in connection with country management and environmental design have been described in this case study.

The technical director of 'Rheinische Braunkohlenwerke AG', Dr.-Ing. E. Gärtner, was awarded the 'European Prize for Country Management 1970' in Strasbourg through the FVS Foundation in Hamburg. He received the prize for his reclamation work in the Rhineland Brown Coal Area. His suggestions concerning the construction of the Erft basin as a surface and subsurface large-scale water reservoir deserve recognition. At the termination of excavation at the Garsdorf opencast mine, a hole of 700 million m³ will be left; and at the termination of excavation at the Hambach opencast mine, the hole will be 2500 million m³. The area will be used as a reservoir which will have a larger capacity than all reservoirs together in the Federal Republic of Germany. Through the conversion of part of the water needs from ground to surface water, increasing water needs could be balanced out. Therefore, neighbouring industries and cities could be supplied with enough water. Dr. Gärtner believes that the project can be realised. It is not only technically possible but it also incorporates many advantages. After termination of brown coal mining in the Rhineland a large lake would have favourable influences on the water utilisation, landscape ecology, and landscape management of the area.

## Bibliography

ANONYM, 'Braunkohle—Chance für die Raumordnung', *Industriekurier* (Sonderausgabe), Düsseldorf, 14, 1966.
BEKUHRS, J., Rekultivierung im rheinischen Braunkohlenrevier. Paper presented in Pfaffendorf on 3rd March 1971, MS, Information Rheinbraun, Köln, 1971.
BUNDESANSTALT FÜR VEGETATIONSKUNDE, NATURSCHUTZ UND LANDSCHAFTSPFLEGE, 'Industrie und Landschaft—

Bundeswettbewerb 1968', *Natur und Landschaft,* 12, 1969.

DALLDORF, H., 'Umsiedlung ist, Raumordnung', DAI, *Deutsche Architekten- und Ingenieur-Zeitschrift,* **9**, 5, 92–95, 1971.

DARMER, G., and BAUER, H. J., 'Landschaft und Tagebau', *Neue Landschaft,* Berlin/Hannover, 11 and 12, 1969.

DEUTSCHER RAT FÜR LANDESPFLEGE, 'Landespflege und Braunkohlentagebau', *Schr.-Reihe d. Dt. Rates für Landespflege,* 2, 1964.

DILLA, L., 'Landschaftsgestaltung im rheinischen Braunkohlenrevier unter besonderer Berücksichtigung der forstlichen Rekultivierung und Anlage von Erholungsgebieten'. *Der Forst und Holzwirt,* **21**, 17, 1966.

DILLA, L., 'Wälder, Höhen und Seen, forstliche Rekultivierung im rheinischen Braunkohlenrevier'. In brochure: Wo neue Wälder wachsen, Edit., Information Rheinbraun der Rheinische Braunkohlenwerke AG., Köln, 1970/71.

GÄRTNER, E., Ansprache anäßlich der Verleihung des Europapreises 1970 am 20. Oktober 1970 in Straßburg. Schr.-Reihe der Stiftung FVS zu Hamburg, 1970.

GÄRTNER, E., 'Die Ausbildung des Erftbeckens als over- undunterirdischer Großwasserspeicher zur zukünftigen Wasserversorgung'. *Braunkohle, Wärme und Energie,* 37–43, 1968.

MINISTERIUM FÜR ERNÄHRUNG, LANDWIRTSCHAFT UND FORSTEN DES LANDES NORDRHEIN-WESTFALEN, Europäischer Ideenwettbewerb 'Die neue Agrargemeinde im rekultivierten Wirtschaftsraum', Düsseldorf, 1967.

OLSCHOWY, G., *Belastete Landschaft—Gefährdete Umwelt,* W. Goldmann, München, 1971.

OLSCHOWY, G. 'Bergbau und Landschaft', in G. Olschowy (editor), *Natur- und Umweltschutz in der Bundesrepublik Deutschland,* Verlag Paul Parey, Hamburg, 1978.

OLSCHOWY, G., 'Casestudy Industry and Landscape— using the Rhineland Brown Coal Ash as an example', Fallstudie aus Anlaß der UN-Umwelt-Konferenz, Stockholm, 1972.

OLSCHOWY, G., 'Das Rheinische Braunkohlenrevier-Abbau und Wiederaufbau von Kulturlandschaften'. In *Der Mensch und die Biosphäre,* pp. 202–214, Verlag Dokumentation, München, 1974.

OLSCHOWY, G., 'Landschaftliche Gestaltung von Abfalldeponien', in *Der Landkreis,* 8 and 9, 1977, pp. 337–341.

OLSCHOWY, G., 'Landschaftspflegerische Rekultivierung des Abbaugebietes Frimmersdorf-Süd (Erfttal) im Rheinischen Braunkohlengebiet', *Natur und Landschaft,* 3, 1963.

OLSCHOWY, G., *Landschaft und Technik,* Patzer, Berlin/Hannover, 1970.

OLSCHOWY, G., *Natur- und Unweltschutz in fünf Kontinenten,* Verlag Paul Parey, Hamburg, 1976.

OLSCHOWY, G., 'Rekultivierungsmaßnahmen im Braunkohlenbergbau am Beispiel des Kippraumes Berrenrath im Rheinischen Braunkohlengebiet', *Informationen des Instituts für Raumforschung,* Bonn-Bad Godesberg, 20, 1961.

PETZOLD, E., 'Bessere Existenzstruktur durch neues Ackerland im Braunkohlenrevier'. In brochure: Neues Ackerland folgt dem Tagebau, Edit. Information Rheinbraun der Rheinische Braunkohlenwerke AG., Köln, 1970.

PETZOLD, E., 'Landwirtschaftliche Rekultivierung im rheinischen Braunkohlenrevier', *Z. Deutsche Geologische Gesellschaft,* **118**, 135–143, 1966.

RHEINISCHE BRAUNKOHLENWERKE AG, 'Neues Ackerland folgt dem Tagebau'. *Landwirtschaftliche Rekultivierung im rheinischen Revier,* 6, Rheinische Braunkohlenwerke AG, Köln, 1975.

RHEINISCHE BRAUNKOHLENWERKE, *Wo neue Wälder wachsen,* Rheinische Braunkohlenwerke AG, Köln, 1974.

# FLOTTA OIL HANDLING TERMINAL
W. J. Cairns

## A Terminal—Initial Concepts

Following the discovery, in 1973, of the Piper Oilfield 150 km east of Wick, Scotland, in the British sector of the North Sea, the Occidental North Sea Consortium* began the search for a suitable site for an oil handling terminal on the Scottish mainland or in the Northern Isles. A shore terminal was favoured for the initial processing, storage and onward shipping of the oil and liquid petroleum gases (LPG). Other groups operating in the area opted for off-shore processing and storage on large production platforms with direct tanker loading—a system vulnerable to interruptions resulting from the North Sea's often treacherous weather conditions.

The Occidental Group preferred the higher initial investment and construction challenge of a pipeline to shore, and so nine possible locations for the terminal were short-listed and each scrutinised to assess environmental impact, cost implications, and accommodation for tanker operations.

After detailed studies and consultations with Orkney Islands Council, the Scottish Development Department, and the Highlands and Islands Development Board, Flotta emerged as the chosen location.

Occidental engaged an environmental planning consultancy, W. J. Cairns and Partners, and the Institute of Offshore Engineering of Heriot-Watt University, Edinburgh to conduct detailed surveys and studies of the terrestrial marine environment. The local planning authority for their part contracted their own planning and biological monitoring consultants and carried out economic and employment studies as part of their structure plan preparation.

* The Occidental Consortium, formed in 1971, consists of Occidental Petroleum, 36·5%; Getty Oil (Britain) Limited, 23·5%; Allied Chemical (North Sea) Limited, 20%; and Thomson, 20%.

## Development Philosophy

The Occidental design team and their advisers identified potentially significant environmental effects of the proposed undertaking, and incorporated practical measures in their development plans to protect adjacent land and marine environments, and to monitor any changes so that corrective action could be initiated. Their aim was to resolve conflicts between the social, visual, ecological and engineering requirements during all stages of the terminal's life, including construction, operation and the restoration phase which would follow the cessation of operations.

It was appreciated that some local social problems would appear during the construction phase because of the influx of a large labour force to the area, and a temporary construction work camp was arranged for the site. Site management was required to maintain an open and sympathetic dialogue with local people, and a system of *ad hoc* settlements evolved whereby construction-related damage to property was dealt with quickly.

Occidental's policy has been to provide priority of employment opportunities to Orcadians and about 65% of the 250 permanent staff are Orcadians.

## Engineering Design Proposals

The initial engineering proposals assumed a maximum daily throughput of 250,000 barrels (bbl) of oil, and outlined the terminal plant that would be required to handle this amount of oil.

The proposals included five floating roof tanks each of 500,000 barrels capacity, process facilities including two gas/oil separation trains; two single point moorings (SPMs) in Scapa Flow designed for tankers up to 200,000 DWT; and an LPG loading jetty capable of taking 30,000 DWT

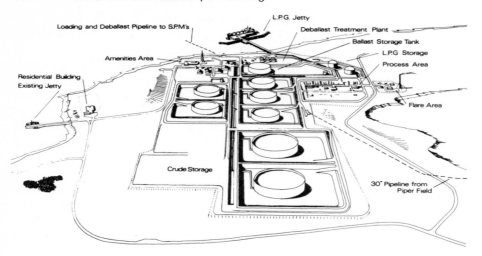

Figure 1. Layout of the Flotta oil terminal.

tankers. In addition, a suitable landfall for the 215-km 30-inch crude pipeline from the Piper Field (and subsequently the Claymore Field) had to be decided, and consideration given to the routeing of the two 48-inch crude loading lines to the single point moorings to shore and the 36-inch effluent outfall line from the ballast treatment plant.

Construction of a further expansion of the terminal has recently been completed to handle input from the Claymore Field. Claymore production is transported to the terminal via the same 30-inch pipeline. The terminal now includes two additional process trains, two 920,000-bbl crude storage tanks, and an expansion of the terminal support systems.

Figure 1 shows the overall layout of the terminal.

## Construction

The terminal is situated on Flotta island located on the south side of Scapa Flow in Orkney. Flotta, an island of 930 hectares, has a maximum elevation of 60 m; vegetation is principally grass and heather. The terminal site comprises an area of 135 hectares on the north shore of the island.

The construction of the terminal presented a number of challenging problems, the first of which is wind. Wind direction and strength are highly variable, with winds of over 65 km/h occurring on at least 130 days per year. Design 3-second gust velocity is 210 km/h with an expected frequency of 1 in 50 years. Other weather elements are not extreme, average annual rainfall being 90 cm, and poor visibility due to fog occurring only occasionally.

The island, although low-lying and accessible, has a surface soil layer of peat, resulting in major earthmoving works being required for foundation construction. At the terminal site the thickness of the peat layer varied from 0·3 to 1·5 m. The area available for peat stockpiles was limited, but advantage was taken to incorporate the peat in the construction of landforms required as part of the landscape proposals for integration of the terminal buildings.

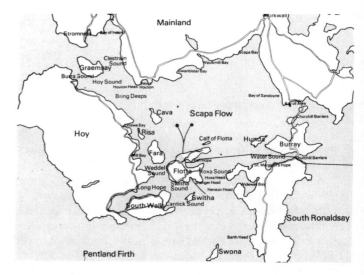

Figure 2. Map showing the location of Flotta.

Soft sandstones underlie the peat, and provided an adequate foundation. A strong blue-grey siltstone seam was located on the south-east part of the island, and a quarry was developed there to provide suitable road and foundation materials for the terminal construction. Similar siltstones outcrop on the shorelines of Flotta and these required blasting along the pipeline approaches.

The remote island site presented logistical problems for construction. A materials receiving base was established at Peterhead on the Scottish mainland, and all materials destined for Flotta were consigned there, with shipment of materials and equipment to Flotta being handled by coasters and roll-on roll-off ferries. Where possible, process area equipment and piping were skid-mounted off-site and shipped to the site for erection on their foundations, and subsequent tie-in of inter-skid piping and instrumentation.

A 650-man construction camp was established on Flotta and this was supplemented by camps and housing on other Orkney islands with personnel transported daily to Flotta by personnel launches.

## Process Area

The incoming crude oil from the Piper Field passes through a double train process unit, each consisting of electrostatic desalters, separators and stabilisers. The associated gas separated from the crude is progressively fractioned in a single train LPG system consisting of a de-ethaniser, de-methaniser and a de-propaniser. The $C_1$ and $C_2$ streams are used for plant fuel while the $C_3$ stream is dehydrated and refrigerated before being passed to storage for ultimate shipment. All process heat requirements are provided by three direct-fired heaters, each rated at 54 million BTU/h (approximately 16 million watts); process heat transfer is accomplished by using a circulating hot-oil system.

## Marine Loading System

Scapa Flow is ideally suited for a marine loading terminal in that it provides deep and sheltered water for mooring areas, a deep water access to the open sea, and being largely land-locked is protected from ocean swell. Although subject to frequent strong winds, wave conditions are tolerable by service craft in all but the most extreme weather conditions. In addition, Scapa Flow does not serve a large urban area as a port and, with the decreased use of the area for defence purposes, it is rarely congested with shipping. Currents are not severe except in a few narrow channels during tidal peaks.

Two major types of crude berth were considered for Scapa Flow: jetty and single point moorings (SPM). The SPM system was chosen because of the higher utilisation factor expected in the extremely variable wind conditions of the area, and the cheaper and faster construction that can be achieved by this type of berth.

The locations of the two SPMs were chosen in close co-operation with the Orkney Islands Council. Initially the locations selected satisfied Occidental's design criteria for water depth, spacing, minimum length of loading and deballast pipelines, and possible future terminal expansion,

requiring an additional SPM berth. However, discussions with the Orkney authorities indicated that the sites chosen could limit the development of marine berths on an adjacent island; accordingly the Flotta berth locations were moved, adding cost to the development, and limiting the area available for future expansion by SPM-type berths for Flotta.

In view of the need that oil pollution be minimised to the greatest practicable extent, investigations were made of the various types of SPMs available and their susceptibility to pollution. It has been Occidental's experience in operating other SPM berths that a large proportion of operating difficulties, and consequent pollution, results from problems experienced with underwater hoses on SPM systems. A technical review of proven SPM systems and analysis of quotations for the Flotta berths resulted in a tower type SPM being selected for Flotta. Figure 3 shows the major components of the SPM chosen.

During the early years of terminal operation it is expected that crude oil from Flotta will be shipped mainly to UK and Northern European ports. Therefore tankers using the terminal in these early years are not expected to be of the VLCC class, but more typically 60,000–70,000 DWT with up to a maximum of about 100,000 DWT. However, the berths are designed to handle tankers up to a maximum of 200,000 DWT.

## Ballast Water Treatment

It is expected that all tankers arriving at the Flotta terminal for crude and LPG loading will be in ballast. Ballast water will then be pumped from the tanker to the onshore deballast storage tanks simultaneously with crude loading.

The purpose of the ballast water treatment system is to remove oil from the ballast water. Other contaminants will not be removed. The treatment system is designed to reduce the total oil content of the plant effluent to a maximum of 25 ppm. The plant is of the aeration type where small bubbles of air are forced through the water, picking and taking up oil and solid particles to the surface where they are removed by skimmers and pumped to crude tankage. The aeration system removes free and partly emulsified oil only. In the event that finely emulsified or dissolved oils are present, flocculation will be employed. Alum was chosen as the coagulant, being a chemical which will add to the effluent only minimal quantities of constituents which could have environmental side effects. It is expected that the alum treatment will be only rarely required.

The oil content of the effluent will be continuously monitored by an ultra-violet oil-in-water analysis system. When oil content exceeds 25 ppm an alarm will alert the operator who will recycle the effluent until the oil-in-water content falls below 25 ppm.

The effluent is discharged through a 36-inch pipeline into the Pentland Firth to the South of Flotta. A multiport diffuser discharges the effluent into an area where currents

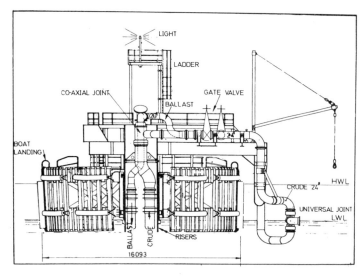

Figure 3.    Diagram of a single point mooring.

regularly exceed 3 knots. Surveys of currents were carried out to determine an acceptable outfall location. These were planned and the results analysed jointly with the Orkney Islands Council's environmental consultants, and the outfall location chosen is in an area where the effluent will be readily dispersed in the Pentland Firth by the prevailing strong currents.

### Submarine Pipelines
The submarine pipelines serving the terminal were installed by lay barges, which proved a reasonably economical technique in this instance because the barges were on charter to Occidental for the installation of the 215-km 30-inch main line from the Piper Field to Flotta.

Approaches for the pipelines through the rocky foreshores were prepared by carpet blasting and clamshelling. The loading and deballast pipelines, and the incoming oil line across Scapa Flow were pulled from a lay barge by a shore-based winch, and in the case of the effluent line pulled from the lay barge by a barge winch.

As with other facets of the project, pipeline shore approach work and pipeline installation were closely coordinated with the Orkney Islands Council and the local residents, all above-water areas being restored to their original state after completion of construction.

## Planning and Environment

In the events which led to the granting of outline planning permission for the construction of the Flotta Terminal in January 1974, it is an indication of the cooperation between Occidental and the Orkney Islands Council that Occidental placed their initial application before the Council only six months prior to this date. The proposed terminal site was on lands zoned for agriculture in the County Development Plan. Thus a direction from the Secretary of State for Scotland was required for the necessary changes of land use to be achieved. Such zoning change has to be advertised for a minimum period of six weeks, during which time representations and objections to the proposed change in land use are considered by the Secretary of State who has the power to call for a public inquiry.

It was felt that the most effective approach to the planning issues was by means of an environmental impact assessment procedure.

### Environmental Impact Procedure
The Occidental Environmental Impact Procedure was designed to enable the issues to be investigated jointly with the local planning authority and the other consent or licensing agencies. The aim was to achieve an integrated

assessment of the likely environmental impacts resulting from the construction and operation of the Flotta terminal. It was considered essential to incorporate environmental criteria at the conceptual and design stages of the development in order that the layout and future operation of the terminal would be influenced by relevant environmental considerations, rather than have these imposed later in a remedial context.

The following objectives guided the procedure:

1. To identify and evaluate all potentially significant environmental effects of the proposed undertaking at the outset in order that alternative solutions, including remedial measures, are taken into consideration at the design and decision-making stage.
2. To take all practicable measures to protect the environment of both land and sea, maintaining the health of natural systems by measuring and monitoring change in order to take corrective action when this is necessary.
3. To resolve conflicts that may occur between the social, visual, ecological and engineering requirements during all stages of development, including the period of construction and operation, as well as restoration of the land following cessation of operations.

The overriding concern expressed to the Occidental Group by the objectors and the several official 'consent' and 'referral' agencies were in two main areas:

1. *Impacts of scale and extent.* How would the proposed development affect its surroundings, what effects would it have beyond the boundaries of its own site, and how would it appear to the eye of a beholder in the immediate or more distant setting or when viewed from the air? Would such a development fit into the rural landscape of Flotta?
2. *Impact on plant and animal life and on habitats and ecosystems.* What controls would be set up to safeguard the health of ecosystems? What measures would be taken to prevent accidental oil spillages? What procedures would be adopted for surveillance, detection and clean up of oil in the environment? Who would monitor these controls and be responsible for the effective management of the oil port? What restorative measures would be taken to re-instate the land following construction and following the closure of the terminal at some future and distant date?

The third sector of impact assessment, dealing with the possible effects the development might have on people's lives (the socio-economic and infrastructural aspect) was examined in general by Occidental and in more detail by the Orkney Islands Council. It is obvious, however, that the greatest impact of a development of this kind is during construction, when considerable stress is placed upon community facilities. The procedure followed five stages.

Figure 4. Typical Flotta landscape showing the flat, lowlying terrain.

STAGE 1. PROJECT PROPOSAL ASSESSMENT

1. Study of terminal engineering proposals, siting and layout requirements.
2. Assessment of engineering parameters including process and operational requirements.
3. Study of future expansion and of areas where this would be feasible.
4. Study of the linkage points between land-based and marine facilities.

The above assessments were made on the basis of the Occidental Report on the Development of an Oil Handling Terminal on the Island of Flotta and on the report on Marine Facilities Design and Operations Outline, Volumes 1 and 2.

STAGE 2. ENVIRONMENTAL ASSESSMENT

Survey to determine the key environmental factors which would affect or be affected by the project proposals, including: solid and drift geology; climate; drainage; soils; vegetation; wildlife and marine ecology; settlement; demography; employment; infrastructure including housing community facilities, roads and services; and land use, particularly agriculture, fishing and landscape character.

The purpose of the assessment was to establish a secure factual basis from which to consider the impact of the development proposals relative to environmental considerations. From this broadly based study, selection was made of those areas which would require further in-depth analysis and appraisal.

The findings of this study were published in the first of three environmental planning reports prepared by Occidental for submission to the Orkney Islands Council.

From the study and discussions with the Orkney Islands Council, Government and other agencies, the two most relevant issues for the project proposals were, first, to secure the effective visual integration of the terminal into the landscape and, secondly, to secure comprehensive measures for protecting the marine environment of Scapa Flow. This gave effect to two parallel impact studies: first, the visual environment; and secondly, the marine environment. These formed, as in-depth studies, the next two stages of the procedure.

STAGE 3. VISUAL IMPACT ASSESSMENT AND LANDSCAPE

This study examined the engineering proposals, and the visual and landscape characteristics of Flotta, Scapa Flow and established the areas and points from where the terminal would be visible from different points. The object was to minimise the visual impact of the terminal within engineering and site constraints. A series of location studies to fix the orientation and siting of individual components of the terminal were carried out by both project engineers and landscape architects. The visual criteria used in the siting study were the following:

*Profile.* The defining edges of an artifact; their similarity or dissimilarity to natural flowing forms;
*Bulk.* The size of individual elements; the visual area they present, in particular their height; the disposition of the elements in the scene; compaction; dispersion;
*Edge.* The sharpness of edges as perceived against background, particularly the skyline silhouette;
*Overlap.* The individual definition of objects in relationship to each other in a field of vision;
*Depth.* The placing of all objects in relation to the foreground and background;
*Colour.* The hue (colour quality); chroma (colour intensity); and tone (lightness/darkness) of changing natural scene;

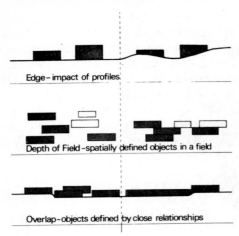

Figure 5.    Techniques for reducing the visual definition of forms.

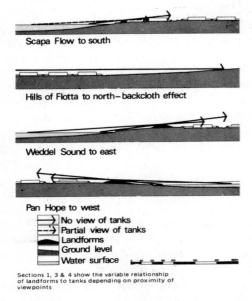

Figure 6.    Sections showing views from sea level indicating the role of landforms and high ground backcloth.

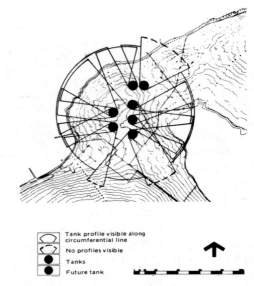

Figure 7.    Visual profile—final scheme without landforms.

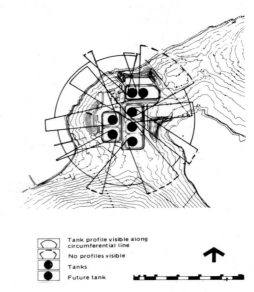

Figure 8.    Visual profile—final scheme plus landforms.

*Texture.*    The reflectivity of components;
*Shadow.*    The effect of shadow on the relief of elements.

The siting of the components of the terminal and the land modelling of the area affected by construction, including landforms for screening, were undertaken as a composite exercise with the project engineers (see Figures 5–8).

The revegetation of the site is to be carried out largely using seed mixtures selected from indigenous species. For example, the natural cover over a substantial part of the site is heather (*Calluna vulgaris*). Trials were undertaken to establish the feasibility of re-establishing a heather cover by seed harvested from Flotta. So far, trials indicate that favourable results may be expected.

Tree cover is virtually absent from the Orkney landscape because of severe climatic conditions; thus an important component in the reduction of visual impact is not naturally available on Flotta. A study is being carried out to determine the feasibility of establishing, in wind-protected areas, dense thicket planting to provide textural change to the ground and secure to some extent the amelioration of scale of the facilities.

Colour studies have been carried out to determine whether a single basic colour or colour differentiation should be applied in the paint rendering of the terminal components. The decision to blend the terminal rather than accentuate it is obvious since the objective is to reduce visual impact. Colour selection was examined relative to vegetation cover, light quality (reflected and direct sunlight), azimuth, and weather under as many prevailing conditions as possible.

The assessment of visual impact and landscape proposals forms the second of the Occidental Environmental Reports.

## STAGE 4. MARINE ENVIRONMENT IMPACT ANALYSIS AND PROTECTION

Studies which analysed the potential impact of the terminal on marine ecosystems resulted in the incorporation in the design of a system of protecting the marine environment from oil pollution.

The studies were primarily concerned with researching the likely effects of oil pollution in the environment of Scapa Flow; measuring winds, tides and currents; advising on the location and design of treated ballast water outfalls; the establishment and management of pollution monitoring systems; and methods of dealing with minor and major oil spills.

Extensive tidal surveys in and around Scapa Flow led to the treated ballast water outfall pipe being located outside the Flow, and an effluent water treatment monitoring system being installed. If the quality of treated water deteriorates below a set standard, re-treatment of the effluent water is initiated automatically.

An independent pollution monitoring programme set up by the Department of Biological Science of the University of Dundee on behalf of the Orkney Islands Council in 1974 established some 50 sampling sites in the Flow to provide base line data for interpretation and comparison with samples taken now the terminal is operational.

Close attention was given to eliminating chances of oil spillage, with the installation of advanced fail-safe systems into the terminal and tanker loading facilities, and the enforcement of strict operating disciplines for all oil transfer operations. Both Occidental and the Harbour Authority have invested in such facilities, which include purpose-built pollution control vessels equipped with skimmers, low-toxicity oil dispersants and fire fighting equipment. The emphasis is on containment and removal, on occurrence, before winds and current drive the oil ashore, which would be a potentially greater hazard to the environment. Should oil reach shore, a pre-planned set of mechanical and, if necessary, low-toxicity chemical clean-up procedures are ready to be committed for land rehabilitation.

Occidental's marine impact studies have been published in two consultative reports, which were submitted to the local planning authority and the licensing agencies.

## STAGE 5. TERMINAL OPERATIONS AND CONTINGENCY PLANNING

Unlike many other forms of development, regulations governing the design and construction of oil storage and processing facilities rigorously govern operational procedures throughout the life-span of a plant. Provision is built into these procedures for continuous environmental and safety surveillance. Fourteen separate Acts of Parliament and ten separate administering agencies govern construction and operation of the Flotta Terminal.

The fifth stage was concerned with extending the principles regulating design and construction into the operational phase. This is mainly done through the provision of operator manuals prepared for each of the separate components of the facilities, in addition to contingency plans in the event of breakdown or accident. As a result of continuous feed-back, design modification and contingency plan development is an on-going process. Guidelines for limited expansion of the existing plant, including visual and locational criteria, are built into the operator's manual for landscape, obviating the tendency for initially established guiding principles to be lost sight of on completion of the construction phase.

# Conclusion

In planning the Flotta Terminal, it was appreciated that engineering requirements had to be considered in relation to environmental factors. As a result of team working, the initial layout proposals for the terminal were radically changed, resulting in the overall compaction of layout and reorientation of storage tanks to reduce visual impact.

It was decided to follow an environmental assessment procedure, involving co-operation with the local planning authority, meeting objectors, recognising their views and considering with them development intentions.

The environmental assessment procedure, following a preliminary analysis of a broad spectrum of possible impacts, selected the two most significant areas of impact for detailed study and evaluation, namely visual impact of terminal facilities on the landscape and impact upon the marine environment. The assessment of the economic and social impacts of the development was considered by the Orkney Islands Council. Occidental established a Community Relations Office to assist local interests.

An environmental baseline of the marine ecosystems involving some 50 sites has been established through population counts of selected organisms sensitive to oil. Semi-annual monitoring of the organisms will reveal both dramatic or gradual changes in population. Chemical monitoring will determine hydrocarbon levels, and correlations will determine impacts attributable to any increase of oil at given monitoring stations.

Because of the speed of the initial construction programme and the incremental process through which detailed engineering design is developed in such projects, it was essential to develop and secure acceptance of broad principles for landscape design, thus allowing detailed design proposals to evolve in line with engineering. This has required the continuous involvement of landscape design expertise as the project has progressed.

There are some interesting summary lessons to be drawn both from the principles involved and the application of these principles to real world problems. For example, visual analysis, impact assessment and proposals should be developed early in the project; cost savings in terms of engineering and time are both potentially real. Furthermore, the constraints imposed and objectives held by

Figure 9. The terminal facilities showing the effective use of a 'blend and blur' policy in integrating man-made forms into a rural landscape.

engineering and landscape professionals are invariably complementary, and can be of mutual benefit. Another lesson is that while one cannot quantify aesthetic judgement one can use hard-edged representative techniques to great effect in assessing the impact of alternative development strategies. Finally, neither image making nor camouflage are likely to be appropriate in large-scale industrial development in rural areas; a policy of 'blend and blur', encouraging definition loss of the man-made forms, is the most sensitive policy, and has been the approach followed in this case.

# Bibliography

BETCHELL INTERNATIONAL LTD (in consultation with Occidental of Britain Inc.), *Piper Field Development; Flotta Terminal, Orkney. Marine Facilities Design and Operations Outline*, Vols. 1 and 2, October 1974.

W. J. CAIRNS AND PARTNERS (in consultation with Bechtel International Ltd., for Occidental of Britain Inc.), *Flotta Orkney, Oil Handling Terminal. Environment Report No. 1, Environmental Assessment*, December 1973.

W. J. CAIRNS AND PARTNERS (in consultation with Bechtel International Ltd., for Occidental of Britain Inc.), *Flotta Orkney, Oil Handling Terminal. Environmental Report No. 2, Visual Impact Appraisal and Landscape Proposals*, June 1974.

W. J. CAIRNS AND PARTNERS (in consultation with Bechtel International Ltd and the Institute of Offshore Engineering, Heriot-Watt University, for Occidental of Britain Inc.), *Flotta Orkney, Oil Handling Terminal. Environmental Report No. 3, Marine Environment Protection*, May 1975.

HALLIWELL *et al*. Institute of Offshore Engineering, Heriot-Watt University (for Bechtel International Ltd., on behalf of Occidental of Britain Inc.), *The Effect on the Marine Environment of Discharges into the Sea from the Flotta Project*, Orkney, October 1974.

JOHNSTON, C. S. and HALLIWELL, A. R., *Environmental Considerations in the Design of Ballast Water Outfalls*, OTC 2466, 1976.

MACKAY, G. A., *Prospects for the Orkney Economy*, University of Aberdeen, Occasional Paper 8, 1976.

OCCIDENTAL OF BRITAIN INC. (in consultation with Bechtel International Ltd.), *A Proposal for Development of an Oil Handling Terminal on the Island of Flotta*, July 1973.

APPENDIX ONE
# AERIAL PHOTOGRAPHY IN LAND USE PLANNING
Maurice A. Keech

In the study of land, its uses and its development, the need to get a better view of what there is on the ground has had many solutions. The most ancient, and the one still most frequently used, is to climb a hill—as Moses did to see the Promised Land or as tourists now go to the top of the Post Office Tower to see London. These examples reveal one human deficiency—man is not tall enough to see the land around him in such a way that he can relate one thing to another.

Maps have partly overcome this problem. Surveyors, by defining what is to be identified and then surveying those features on the ground, can show on a map the positional relationship in a horizontal plane, and with the techniques of cartography it is possible to illustrate the vertical relationships to some degree as well. However, maps give only a limited picture. The facts are expressed according to the ability of the cartographer, and their interpretation, however skilled, is bounded by the limits of cartography.

One has only to study an area on a map and then on an aerial photograph to realise how much more detail is recorded on the latter. Just how much more information can be obtained depends on the nature of the photography, the ability of the interpreter, and the sophistication of the interpreting equipment. In its simplest form the aerial photograph gives a bird's eye view of the country with an infinite amount of detail. It does show what is over the other side of the hedge, wood or hill without the necessity to go there. It can reveal the shape and distribution of features in the approximately correct position, and the use of the stereoscopic image can show land form in three dimensions.

Aerial photography has been developed over the last century and the techniques of fact evaluation from photography have now become very highly developed. Aerial photography was first introduced by Tournachon in 1858 when he used a camera carried in a balloon to photograph Petit Bicestre near Paris. This technique was developed further in the American Civil War, when the Union troops used balloon-mounted cameras to record Confederate positions near Richmond in 1862. In the field of natural sciences, foresters in Germany were photographing forest areas as early as 1888, and using the information to plot maps relating to the forest stands.

Within a very short time of the Wright brothers' first flight, planes were being used to carry cameras, and by 1914 Zeppelins were equipped to take aerial photographs. The First World War produced very rapid development of all aspects of aerial photography. This development and constant improvement in camera and film efficiency continued and, between the wars, the use of aerial photography to record natural resources expanded rapidly.

Further development was stimulated during the Second World War and the momentum continued with the space research programme. Greatly improved camera equipment, the introduction of other sensing devices which recorded information not only about Earth, but other planets, and major advances in film types and sensitivities have greatly increased the sophistication of aerial photography in all fields of application, not least in its usefulness to the land use planner.

## Techniques of Aerial Photography

The first film material produced was sensitive to the blue end of the spectrum only, but by combining a filter to cut out blue light and treatment with chemicals, the sensitivity of film has been extended throughout the visible light range and into the invisible infrared band. The panchromatic film used today records, in black and white, nearly the entire visible light spectrum. Combining layers of emulsion sensitised to different wavelengths of light, and using emulsion filters gave the foundation for the production of colour film. Further treatment of this type of film produced an emulsion combination sensitive to infrared light.

In the case of infrared photography, what is photographed is invisible to the human eye, which is not sensitive to this range of the spectrum. However, infrared film converts this invisible information into a visible form. The pictures produced are of a completely unfamiliar form in that all green living matter is shown in red; the greener the grass, the redder it is on the film. Originally produced to detect camouflaged objects, this form of photography provides valuable information about the surface mantle and has extensive applications in natural resource analysis.

## Scale of Aerial Photography

By the geometry of aerial photography, the scale of the photograph is derived from the ratio of the flying height above the ground and the focal length of the lens on the camera. An almost infinite variety of scales exists: ultra-small scale lies between 1:80,000 and 1:1,000,000; small scale between 1:30,000 and 1:80,000; medium scale between 1:8000 and 1:30,000; and large scale is greater than 1:8000.

Ultra-small-scale photography gives a good synoptic view of an area, allows the observer to establish positional relationships, and to observe changes in the form of the landscape easily. With increasing scales it becomes more difficult to establish spatial relationships without putting

together two, three or more photographs to make a photo-laydown or mosaic. The larger scales permit more detail to be seen with increasing definition—at 1:125,000 one can see the woods; at 1:1250 one can see the twigs on the trees! In all photographic studies, the detail revealed is of great value and it is possible, within the limits imposed by photographic distortion, to carry out measurements, to count and to establish objective statistical relationships based on photoanalysis.

Figures 1, 2 and 3.    Examples of different scales of aerial photography. Left: 1:50,000, top: 1:26,000, above: 1:1200. These photographs show the variation in range of detail which may be obtained.

*(Photos by courtesy of the National College of Agricultural Engineering and Hunting Surveys Ltd.)*

## Height Determinations

To those accustomed to using maps to establish height relationships and who have adequate maps available, the potential to measure height differences using aerial photographs will be of little importance. However, in many parts of the world maps are still very simple and frequently lack details of the relative heights of the terrain. In such cases, photogrammetric techniques are of great value. Based on the principle of parallax (that the parts of objects near to a point of vision are apparently displaced more than parts farther away, in relation to some fixed point) a mathematical formula is derived which uses this apparent displacement to calculate the height of an object. The author used this technique with success in the Amazon Basin to measure the height of hills in an inaccessible part of the Amazon forest.

There are limitations on height determination because of photographic distortions caused by variations in flying height and aircraft tilt. Height differences can only be assessed between points close together when simple equipment is used. More complex optical equipment can be used to allow the operator to eliminate these errors over the whole viewed area of the photograph. Such equipment is now used for map preparation in many parts of the world.

## The Stereoscopic Image

Normal human vision is in three dimensions—length, breadth and depth. However, those with only one eye see images as flat; they perceive depth by shadow, by perspective and by experience. The reason that one can appreciate depth with two eyes is that each eye sees an object from a different angle, and the brain is able to interpret these different images in terms of depth perception.

It is possible to simulate the three-dimensional image using photographs in the horizontal and the vertical plane. Aerial photography for stereoscopic use has a minimum overlap of 50% between photographs along the line of flight so as to ensure that the same object on the ground is recorded on two photographs and is then seen from two different viewpoints. Thus human vision is imitated on a large scale with the camera in the position of the eyes. The stereoscope allows the left eye to see one photograph and the right eye to see the other, and the brain integrates the two images to produce the three-dimensional image with which we are familiar.

# Use of Aerial Photography in the Planning Process

As is evident from the foregoing chapters of this book, in land use planning, whether large or small scale and whether territorial or problem-solving (see chapter 2), the need for accurate and objective survey information as a basis for

evaluation and as part of on-going land management is considerable. Aerial photography provides a valuable tool in this respect. It may be used in two ways: first to record information which is directly observable. Map correction is a classic example of this type of use. Secondly, it may be used in conjunction with ground work to obtain information that can only be inferred from evidence which can be seen directly. For example, the number of houses in an area can be counted on aerial photographs, but the number of dwelling units within a block of flats can only be estimated. Thus, field work must be used in conjunction with air photoanalysis to establish factors which, when multiplied by the air photo counts, give a high level of accuracy in the estimation of facts of this nature. Such a method was successfully used by the author and others to establish the population of an agricultural area in Rhodesia in the early 1960s. Collins and others conducted an experiment in Leeds to carry out a population census using air photoanalysis and field work with some success.

Land use maps may be readily prepared from aerial photography, with the added advantage that further photography at later dates may be used to monitor change without the necessity for further extensive ground work. However, it must be emphasised that the greater the detail of land use required, the larger the scale of photographs and the greater the amount of field work needed to produce the degree of accuracy.

## Forestry

As may be expected, the use of aerial photography for identifying and measuring the land use and land use potential has been established for a long time. The first applications, as mentioned earlier, were in forestry, and between the two World Wars a tremendous amount of survey work of this kind was undertaken in all parts of the world, and is continuing today. It has been possible to separate conifers from deciduous stands rapidly and precisely, and considerable advances have been made in species identification of the conifers by integrating ecological and photographic information. Deciduous species have proved a little more difficult to identify, because their form changes during the year, and many of the main species demonstrate a similar appearance on panchromatic photography. False colour photography, perhaps more than ordinary colour photography, has been a great aid in this identification process. It also has a great advantage in identifying disease in vegetation. Any stress on a plant, because of disease or other cause, reduces the infrared reflectance, and the resulting change is easily identified using false colour photography.

Experience has shown that for species identification large scales are required. Vegetation complexes can, however, be located on much smaller-scale photographs, whether they be tropical forests or temperate forests of higher latitudes.

In Canada, the assessment of timber volumes in a particular stand of timber has been studied by Sayn-Wittgenstein (1961) and others, and considerable success has been achieved in volume calculations. With stand boundaries, species identification and volume calculations available, and with a clear expression of the land form, forest management can be based very soundly on relatively simple air photo interpretation techniques.

### Agriculture

In the field of agricultural development, the use of aerial photography for planning purposes has been firmly established for the last 40 or 50 years. The problems of erosion in the United States in the mid-thirties stimulated the use of aerial photography, and stereoscopic techniques were used for laying out water courses and other erosion control measures making the best use of the natural form of the land. Much of this work was done by the Agricultural Stabilisation and Conservation Services of the US Department of Agriculture.

The Soil Conservation Service subsequently developed a system of land classification which was based on aerial photography analysis combined with field work. Eight classes of land were defined: class I was land considered to have no hazards and no limitations to use in relation to a basal hazard of erosion. Three other arable classes were defined in which the erosion hazard increased, and therefore the management input to control it had to be increased. The other classes had less potential for agricultural development, and it was possible to make suggestions for alternative uses. It must be emphasised at this point that several of these classes could be identified directly from air photos.

## Landscape Classification

The concept of land classification, based partly on air photo interpretation, and the use of aerial photography as a tool in the work of developing land in many parts of the world has been accepted as a sound basis for planning. The Soil Survey of England and Wales has recently published a system of soil survey based on aerial photography (1976).

In many cases, air photo interpretation has replaced field surveys for route planning into undeveloped land and for the purpose of land evaluation. The necessary field work is now subsequent to the air survey photoanalysis, and is made considerably more effective by this preliminary photo-analysis. The importance of the three-dimensional image in demonstrating clearly the variable terrain features and allowing a fact-grouping procedure to be effectively applied, cannot be overstressed.

Since the Second World War, the terrain analysis type of approach has been made more sophisticated and has been used by military research organisations to classify land for military purposes. The technique has been successfully applied in major road development schemes in many parts of the world, including the United Kingdom, where motorway planners have made extensive use of aerial photography in planning the routes of motorways, and in measuring the effect of the motorway on the landscape.

### Landscape Factors

It is suggested that 'landscape' can be analysed in terms of two groups or factors which can be identified and classified in a mathematical form. The groups are *land form*, which is essentially geomorphological, and *surface cover*. As already described, aerial photo interpretation allows both these groups to be identified and quantified much more accurately than with the use of maps alone.

LAND FORM

The factors considered important in describing land form are *relative elevation* and *length of slope break*. Relative elevation is quoted in terms of units of elevation per unit area. The data can be obtained from topographical maps or from height measurements on aerial photographs. In the United Kingdom it can be the difference between the highest and lowest points in a 5 km × 5 km National Grid square, or some other defined unit of area. With these data it is possible to prepare frequency distribution curves. These may be normal in the statistical sense or skewed. The relative elevation distribution for one evaluation carried out in Wales was positively skewed; it was insensitive to the flatter areas and too sensitive to the highland areas in terms of grouping procedures. By applying a mathematically approved procedure of taking the square root of the individual readings, it was possible to normalise the curve, increase the sensitivity at the lower end of the scale and decrease it at the upper end. When this was done it became possible to calculate the mean figure and the standard deviation. Grouping of the factors was then carried out in the manner illustrated in Figure 4.

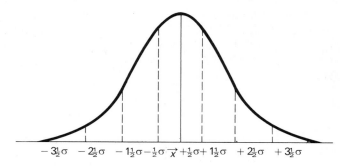

$-3\frac{1}{2}\sigma \quad -2\frac{1}{2}\sigma \quad -1\frac{1}{2}\sigma -\frac{1}{2}\sigma \ \overline{x} \ +\frac{1}{2}\sigma + 1\frac{1}{2}\sigma \quad +2\frac{1}{2}\sigma \quad +3\frac{1}{2}\sigma$

Figure 4.   Grouping of landform factors.

This system of analysis was applied to the factor of relative elevation first, but subsequently was applied to all the factors analysed.

The vertical aerial photograph was used to supplement the map in obtaining relative elevation. In stereoscopic format, it was the only possible way of obtaining the length of slope break. This is defined, on the stereo model, as the position where there is a distinct change of slope. Usually such a change limits the field of view, and it is measured in terms of length of slope break per unit area. Where the result is a high number, the areas of vision are small; conversely, where the number is low, the fields of vision are more extensive and the country generally more rolling. Aerial photography reveals clearly the scarp slopes which have such a powerful effect on landscape. Again the process of grouping is based on a simple statistical procedure.

### SURFACE COVER

Surface cover can be defined in terms of *field density*, *trees*, *woodlands, forests* and the *nature of land use*. All, except the last, can be analysed and grouped in a similar manner to that already described.

Field numbers can be recorded from maps or aerial photographs directly. Figures obtained from the former can be checked for change by using the latter, which may show differences arising from the process of consolidation.

Individual trees, which can exert a dominant influence on landscape, can be identified on aerial photographs and their distribution quantified by counting and relating the count to a unit area. Other analyses can be carried out if required. Crown diameter and tree height measurements using aerial photoanalysis are standard practice among foresters in some parts of the world. Tree distribution patterns can be transferred from photographs to maps, and this process can reveal relationships with other factors which might not be apparent at the first examination.

Woodland areas are usually well demarcated on maps and can be seen on aerial photographs—which can confirm their existence at a particular time. The treatment for evaluation processes is the same as for the other factors.

Forests tend to dominate the landscape because of the large areas they cover. Under forest, all surface features are eliminated as visible landscape features for a considerable period of time. However, a comparison between the mapped areas of forests in Wales and the same area on aerial photography shows considerable differences in appearance. These stem entirely from the different stages of development of the forests as a result of management procedures. While unique, the forest landscape is always changing, and this change is clearly revealed by aerial photography.

Moorland and the different types of moorland vegetation can be identified with ease on aerial photographs after initial field work has been done. With this information, moorland landscapes can be more easily described and boundaries demarcated from air photo interpretation. The correct photographic scale to suit the needs of the survey has to be available, but the result is always more reliable than any field work unsupported by aerial photographs.

Much land use information can be obtained from agricultural statistics for districts or regions, but aerial photography reveals this land use picture in a dynamic form. For example, in Wales it is possible to separate the temporary pasture areas from the permanent pasture or rough grazing areas precisely using aerial photography; the synoptic view that it gives is so much clearer than that from any map or sheet of statistics.

Opencast mining and other landscape artefacts produced by mineral extraction can be seen clearly. Colour photography can be particularly effective in this respect; for example, peat cutting in East Fife shows up remarkably clearly on 1977 colour photography. Derelict land is also revealed on false colour film. The variations in the strength of spectral reflectance in the green band of the spectrum is emphasised by the different shades of red which are recorded on the false colour film. Normal managed agricultural land has a uniform tonal appearance, while derelict land, because of the growth of shrubs and weeds, and the dying out of some patches, leads to a very uneven tone.

The data obtained from such aerial surveys can be analysed statistically and the different factors combined, thus enabling the objective comparison of one area with another. With an understanding of the meaning of the classification, it becomes possible to create a mental image of the landscape and to consider the aesthetic aspects.

It is certain that landscape evaluation will use aerial photography increasingly and will apply the more sophisticated photo-interpretative techniques already used by other land resource planners.

Since 1972, satellite imagery has been available to land resource planners. Each image covers an area of 185 km × 185 km, and this synoptic view enables many different regions to be seen in their correct relationship to one another.

It seems highly probable that in the near future machine analysis of the magnetic tapes from which images are obtained will make possible the definition of different landscape types with a high level of precision.

## Applications in Urban Regions

Today, the acquisition and analysis of information upon which development policy can be based is one of the major tasks of all levels of government. In many parts of the world systematic aerial photography is organised by central government. In Britain, many counties organised aerial surveys of their respective areas to coincide with the 1971 Census, and an extensive area of South Eastern England was photographed to provide information for the Greater London Council Strategy Planning.

With aerial photography, new development can be modelled and it becomes possible to anticipate the effect that it might have on the urban landscape. By studying the three-dimensional image, the zone of influence of a high-rise building can be established and a sequence of aerial photographs taken over a period of time can demonstrate the change that has taken place, because the three-dimensional image does allow the re-creation, at least in part, of the building which used to exist in an area.

Aerial photography has been used extensively in the United States and to a lesser degree in Europe in transport surveys, to record the flow of traffic and the causes of bottlenecks. Sequential photography at rush hours has shown points of congestion and alternative routes used to avoid them.

# Bibliography

BECKETT, P. H. T. and WEBSTER, B., 'A classification system for terrain,' MEXE Reports 872 and 873 MEXE, Christchurch, 1965.

CLOUSTON, J. B., 'Techniques of landscape analysis and inventory of landscape factors,' Paper delivered to ILA Conference, Stirling, 1971.

CLWYD COUNTY COUNCIL, *Clwyd Study on Evaluation of the Landscape Quality of Clwyd C.C.*, 1974.

COLLINS, W. G., and EL BECK, A. H. A., 'Population census with the aid of aerial photography. An experiment in the city of Leeds', *Photogrammetric Record*, 7, 37, 1971, pp. 16–26.

FINES, K. D., 'Landscape evaluation. A research project in East Sussex', *Regional Studies*, 2, 1, 1968.

KEECH, M. A., 'The application of aerial photography to the planning of agricultural development overseas', *Photogrammetric Record*, 8, 43, 1974, pp. 19–26.

KEECH, M. A., and DISPERATI, A. A., 'Use of satellite images in development management of forests', (in Portuguese) *Floresta* 7, 2, Federal University of Parana, Brazil, 1976.

KEECH, M. A., 'An assessment of ERTS 1 imagery as a base map for natural resource surveys in developing countries', in Barrett and Curtis (eds.), *Environmental Remote Sensing II.* Edward Arnold, London, 1977.

LAND USE CONSULTANTS, *A Planning Classification of Scottish Landscape Resources,* Countryside Commission for Scotland, Perth, 1972.

MINISTRY OF AGRICULTURE, FISHERIES AND FOOD, *Agricultural Land Classification,* Tech. Report No. 11, Agric. Land Service, HMSO London, 1966.

SAYN-WITTGENSTEIN, L., 'Recognition of tree species on air photographs by crown characteristics', *Photogrammetric Engineering,* 27, 5, 1961, pp. 792–809.

SOIL SURVEY OF ENGLAND AND WALES, *Land Use Capability Classification.*

SOIL SURVEY OF ENGLAND AND WALES, *Air Photo-interpretation for Soil Mapping,* Rothamsted, 1976.

UNIVERSITY OF MANCHESTER, *Landscape Evaluation,* Landscape Evaluation Research Project 1970–1975, Manchester, 1975.

WARWICKSHIRE COUNTY PLANNING DEPARTMENT, *Coventry, Solihull, Warwickshire: A strategy for the Sub-region,* County Planning Department, Warwick, 1971.

# COMPUTERS IN LAND USE PLANNING
Charles E. Chulvick and Thomas C. Waugh

## Introduction

Traditionally landscape planning has been seen as a delicate net dependent on the creative skills of the individual, and there are many who would scorn any use of mechanical contrivances, particularly that *enfant terrible* of modern technology—the computer. However, the landscape planner has always used a variety of tools to overcome technical difficulties and, as the technical difficulties become ever more numerous and complicated, the landscape planner has need of more sophisticated tools in order to maintain the highest professional standard. The computer is just such a tool and, like all other tools, when used with an understanding of its capabilities and limitations, it can be a help, but used incorrectly it can be useless, or even a hindrance.

Two myths should be dispelled at the outset. First, the computer is not a mechanical Frankenstein, which with one flick of a button will overwhelm the user with its superior force. It can only perform the functions for which it is programmed, and the output depends directly on the input. Secondly, in spite of its complexity, the user does not have to master computer technology to use it to his advantage; he need only know its capabilities, and the operating procedures needed to achieve the required result.

In some areas, such as mapping, computer techniques are already being applied directly to landscape planning. Indirectly, through their relations with regional and transportation planners, architects, engineers, geologists, and others, landscape planners are becoming increasingly aware of the applications of computer technology to land use planning. As the problems set for the landscape planner are often influenced by the developments in these allied fields, it is essential that his understanding and expertise be commensurate with the standards of these professions. In land use planning, computers are used regularly for statistical analysis, creation of simulation models, and the compilation and analysis of data.

Certainly there is nothing the computer can do for the landscape planner which he could not do for himself. However, the computer can complete many tasks quickly and efficiently, thus allowing the landscape planner to use his time and intellect to solve those problems which are not suited to analysis by machine.

The job of the landscape planner is to make the caprices of nature compatible with the built environment, and the caprices of man to harmonise with nature. Any tool, such as the computer, which can make this job less laborious and more successful is well worth consideration.

## Introduction to the Computer

A computer is essentially an electronic device which receives input, processes it and generates output. In many ways it can be considered similar to a television receiver which receives input signals from the aerial (and thus from the transmitter), and the controls (i.e. the viewer), processes them, and generates output which is, of course, the picture on the screen. The range of input and output devices available to a digital computer are many and varied, and the processing capability covers wide-ranging applications.

The user of a computer system can provide input to a computer in numerous ways, using various devices. The most common input devices are keyboards which will produce a computer-readable medium such as a punched card or punched paper tape. Becoming more common is the use of terminals which allow direct input from the keyboard to the computer. Keyboards, however, can only input text, and the data sources available to landscape planners often

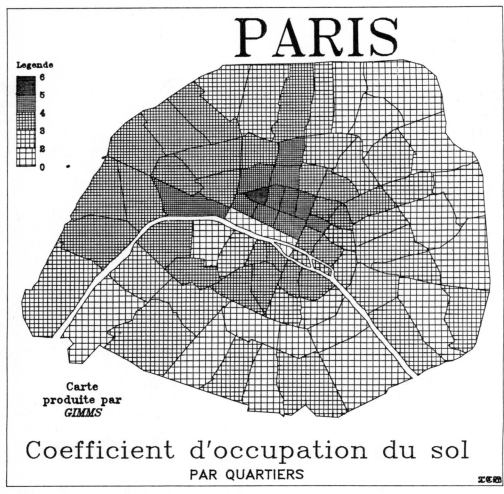

Figure 1. Example of graphic output from a computer showing relative population densities in Paris.

include graphic information. These data can be entered into the computer using various forms of graphic input devices, such as digitisers, scanners, graphic tablets, etc.

Output from a computer generally comes in one of two forms, text output or graphic output. The most common device to produce text output is the line printer which produces lines of text across standard computer paper. A line printer is generally fast, producing typically between 300 and 1200 lines of print per minute. Graphic output from a computer is generally produced by some form of graph plotter (see Figure 1) but graphic results can also be produced by the line printer (see Figure 2) although the quality is not as good.

In addition to the devices already mentioned, there is a large, and growing, class of devices which can both input to the computer and receive output from the computer. These display terminals are often in direct communication with the computer, and more advanced terminals have graphic as well as text capability. Thus the user can see graphic results on a screen almost immediately without needing to wait for the output from a graph plotter.

The physical devices form the 'hardware' of a computer system, and the other major component of a working computer system is the 'software' which comprises the instructions to the computer to enable it to function correctly. At the lowest level the instructions to the computer are very simple, but various languages are provided which can be translated into machine instructions. Good systems allow the user to specify actions in a form appropriate to the analysis required. For example, a command 'MAP LAND USE' could be a valid user command.

A major feature of computers is the large amount of data that can be stored and processed. In fact the primary impetus to most planners to use the computer in data analysis is the vast amounts of data that may be used and the repetitive nature of the tasks involved. It is the repetition of even fairly simple tasks on large numbers of data values which has made the computer an intrinsic part of our everyday life. But, the results of computer analysis are only as good as the data and the methods employed. A planner using a computer should therefore assure himself that the data used are appropriate, and the analysis methods meaningful.

## Applications

The use of computer applications by planners, engineers, and other professionals has escalated dramatically over the

1.75

2.25

3.00

3.75

0    50    Kms    100    150

Figure 2.    Example of line printer output from a computer showing scales of remoteness in Scotland.

past 15 years. The writing of special 'one off' programs was superseded by the creation of a stable suite of programs—'packages'—in the early sixties (MIADS, SYMAP, *et al.*). There are now several such packages widely available throughout the world. These technical advancements have been complemented by the growth of data sources resulting from improvements in aerial photography and the use of satellite imagery to provide more land use data to supplement the ground surveys, maps and site plans traditionally used by planners. Large surveys concerned with socio-economic data (e.g. census of population) are widely available for automatic processing and often include a locational reference to allow for better interaction with land use data. These developments are now culminating in the establishment of information systems which aim to provide a large bank of data which can be accessed by users and analysed by using various packages and programs.

## Statistics and Data Analysis

Survey analysis is now carried out by using one or more of the many statistical packages designed to do 'number crunching' painlessly and easily. Packages such as SPSS, DATATEXT, OSIRIS, GENSTAT and CLUSTAN all provide the user with a wide range of statistical techniques, and provide not only numerical output but also tables, graphs, and histograms. These packages allow non-computer-oriented people to carry out analysis without the aid of programming support. Indeed, a package such as SPSS makes it very easy for a user to carry out rather sophisticated statistical techniques such as multiple regression, Guttman scaling, and factor analysis. Unfortunately the interpretation of the results must still be carried out by the user, and the danger of overstretching oneself statistically must not be overlooked.

Possibly of more importance to the landscape planner is the continuing progress in the development of modelling, evaluation, and simulation techniques. Forecasting techniques (population projections, network analysis) have been in use for some time, as have some of the more simplistic models used to associate land use data and socio-economic data (gravity models—Lowry model, potential surface techniques). However, more recent developments have been made in the area of simulation, which allow the user to construct scene analyses by using software such as VIEWIT and programs developed at the Department of Landscape Architecture, Harvard. Allocation techniques and automatic design techniques further complement the range of modelling and evaluation techniques available to the landscape planner. However, evaluation is still the area where further developments will be necessary, with greater monitoring of land use changes and the continuing development of analytical techniques providing a strong basis for achieving this end.

## Automated Cartography

The use of automated cartography or computer mapping techniques has often been perceived as a logical extension to statistical analysis and a vehicle for presenting data in an alternative format to tables and graphs. This is obviously a useful exercise but the value of computer mapping as a research tool in its own right should not be overlooked. The analytic value of mapping techniques which employ point-in-polygon or polygon overlay routines, and radial or path searches, allow the user to understand and manipulate spatial data by viewing a map or drawing either on paper or on a visual display unit.

A wide range of programs is now available in the field of automated cartography and a basic classification should differentiate between mapping techniques using either the line printer, graph plotter, or visual display unit (VDU) to produce output and the three-dimensional graphics packages, which use plotters or VDUs to produce output.

Line printer mapping programs have been in existence for some time and are both numerous and easily available. SYMAP, developed at Harvard University, may have a strong claim to be the first such package, and probably is best known. However, there are many others which should also be considered: MIADs, from the US Forestry Commission; GRIDS, developed by the US Bureau of the Census; and GRID, which was also developed by Harvard. In addition to these US products, many similar packages have been developed in the UK: TRIP, CMS and CAMAP, all developed at the University of Edinburgh; and LINMAP, which is now operated by the Department of the Environment. The multiplicity of programs prohibits a detailed description of each to be presented here since each has unique features and requirements. However, the user should be aware that most of these programs relate to data organised on a co-ordinated grid such as the Ordnance Survey national grid, but a few like SYMAP require that the user define areas or points in a digital format and then associate his data to these areas or points. Despite these differences the types of maps produced by any of these programs (see Figure 2) are similar in appearance. Alpha/numeric characters are printed by the line printer using different characters and combinations of characters to differentiate between areas and/or different data values. This type of map is often criticised for being crude and of a low quality, since the characters on a normal line printer are not square, and hence there is some distortion. However, line printers can be modified by adding special square character sets, which allow special symbols to be produced, thus eliminating some of the distortion. It is also common for printing techniques to be used to enhance the quality of the finished maps by adding colour or outsized text. One important point in favour of maps produced by line printer is the speed and low cost of production; this can be an important consideration when large numbers of different maps are required for a particular study.

Graph plotter mapping programs are not as numerous as the line printer programs but their numbers are continuing to increase. GIMMS, another product of the University of Edinburgh, CALFORM from Harvard, and NIMMS, developed in Sweden, are only some of the programs which can be used to produce graph plotter or line drawn maps (see Figure 1). As with line printer programs each of these programs has unique features and requirements, but generally requires the user to define areas or points by digital co-ordinates. The map produced is of a similar appearance to those produced by manual methods, and the cartographic quality and accuracy is usually dependent upon the type of hardware available to the user. While the map is of a higher standard than line printer maps, the user will have to pay for this higher quality in higher operating costs. It should also be noted that the use of graphic visual display units allows the user not only to view maps but also to edit them by use of graphic cursors and other equipment.

Three-dimensional graphics are also available to the landscape planner or architect using automated cartographic techniques. These programs (SYMVU, VIEWIT *et al.*) allow the user to operate in three dimensions rather than two, and produce drawings (see Figure 3) which can be useful for assessing land form, elevation, relief, or for particular design criteria. The Computer Aided Design Centre at Cambridge has made great advances in this field, and the availability of programs of this type is increasing. Output from these programs can be directed either to a plotter or to a graphic display screen to allow for editing. Further advances in this field should prove to be of great importance for those involved in landscape design.

### Systems

Over the last 10 years, various systems have been developed for land use data and processing. Some of these are general purpose in that they can be used for any geographic area

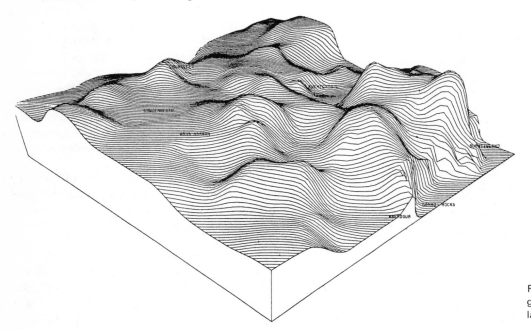

Figure 3.    Example of three-dimensional graphics which may be used in assessing land form.

and with a wide range of types of data. Systems such as NIMMS (Stockholm), IMGRID (Harvard) and GIMMS (Edinburgh) find general use in analysis and display of geographic data and the analysis functions of NIMMS in particular can be a powerful tool for analysing land use data.

There has been a tendency for agencies (or groups of agencies) to sponsor systems which can provide them with land use data and, in many cases, the creation of the system involved the creation of large bodies of data to go with the system. One of the first systems of this kind is the Canadian Geographic Information System (CGIS, formerly the Canada Land Inventory) which contains data relating to agriculture, forestry, land use, census, watersheds, and other subjects. In the UK, the TRIP system has recorded data of the same kind for Scotland.

## Current and Future Developments

There are many current developments which are of interest to the land use planner and which might radically change methods of areal analysis. Foremost in these is the expansion of remote sensing procedures to encompass aerial photography at large and medium scales, and satellite imagery (e.g. from LANDSAT) at small scales. The resolution of remote imagery is always on the increase, and computer processing of the imagery is becoming increasingly more sophisticated. The sophistication of these new procedures allows detailed and almost continuous analysis of land use patterns, with the effect that new developments can be easily recognised.

At a much more detailed level, many topographic mapping agencies are already producing (or are planning to produce) digital data banks of their basic map series. The Ordnance Survey of the UK is well advanced in this kind of project, and the data bank produced should prove to be of great value to land use planners in conjunction with other types of data.

In parallel to these data collection projects, there are movements in the design of computer hardware and software which will benefit the practising planner. Examples of the former are the spread of interactive systems allowing 'hands-on' access to data banks, and array processors which have the potential of doing sophisticated land use analysis on remote imagery very quickly. Examples of the latter are the increasing sophistication of systems for geographical analysis and the move towards making it easier for non-computer people to use the systems.

The use of computer techniques by landscape planners and allied professionals is constantly increasing. The landscape planner can no longer claim that his needs are not considered by computer scientists. Indeed planners and other similar professionals are now regarded as major clients by both hardware and software manufacturers. The landscape planner must now further articulate his particular needs in order to assure that he will be provided with the up-to-date technology he needs to attain the level of precision and refinement that his profession demands.

## Bibliography

BAXTER, R. S., *Computer and Statistical Techniques for Planners*, Methuen, London, 1976.

BICKMORE, D., *Automatic Cartography and Planning*, Architectural Press, London, 1971.

GARDINER-HILL, R. C., The Development of Digital Maps, Ordnance Survey Professional Paper 23.

RHIND, D. W., The state of the art in geographic data processing—a UK view, Proceedings of Seminar on Geographic Data Processing, IBM UK Scientific Centre.

# Index